P9-BXW-070

THE BEST
HOME
BUSINESSES
for the 21st Century

Other Books by Paul and Sarah Edwards

Finding Your Perfect Work

Getting Business to Come to You,
2nd Revised Edition
(with Laura Clampitt Douglas)

Home Businesses You Can Buy
(with Walter Zooi)

Secrets of Self-Employment

Teaming Up
(with Rick Benzel)

Working from Home,
5th Edition, Revised and Expanded

Making Money with Your Computer at Home,
Expanded 2nd Edition

Making Money in Cyberspace
(with Linda Rohrbough)

Cool Careers for Dummies
(with Marty Nemko)

THE BEST HOME BUSINESSES

for the 21st Century

*The Inside Information
You Need to Know to Select a
Home-Based Business
That's Right for You*

3RD EDITION

Paul and Sarah Edwards

JEREMY P. TARCHER/PUTNAM
a member of Penguin Putnam Inc.
New York

Most Tarcher/Putnam books are available at special quantity discounts
for bulk purchase for sales promotions, premiums, fund-raising,
and educational needs. Special books or book excerpts also can be created
to fit specific needs. For details, write Putnam Special Markets,
375 Hudson Street, New York, NY 10014.

Jeremy P. Tarcher/Putnam
A member of
Penguin Putnam Inc.
375 Hudson Street
New York, NY 10014
www.penguinputnam.com

Copyright © 1999 by Paul and Sarah Edwards

All rights reserved. This book, or parts thereof, may not
be reproduced in any form without permission.
Published simultaneously in Canada

Library of Congress Cataloging-in-Publication Data

Edwards, Paul, date.
The best home businesses for the 21st century : the inside
information you need to know to select a home-based business that's
right for you / Paul and Sarah Edwards.
p.   cm.
"3rd ed."—P.   .
Rev. ed. of: The best home businesses for the 90s / Paul and Sarah
Edwards. 2nd ed., rev. and expanded. c1994.
ISBN 0-87477-973-1
1. Home-based businesses.   2. Home-based businesses—Management.
I. Edwards, Sarah (Sarah A.)   II. Edwards, Paul, date.   Best home
businesses for the 90s.   III. Title.
HD2333.E34   1999   99-28186 CIP
658′.041—dc21

Printed in the United States of America

10   9   8

Book design by Lee Fukui

ACKNOWLEDGMENTS

Books are supposed to be easier in successive editions, but this third edition has taken as much or more time and effort than went into either of the first two editions. First, there's been an explosion in information. Second, virtually every business has changed, many in fundamental ways. A significant number of businesses were added and a significant number dropped.

We especially acknowledge the patience of the team of people who guide and produce our books in New York, including Joel Fotinos, our ever-supportive publisher; Mitch Horowitz, our wise editor; and Lily Chin, the assistant editor. Kristen Georgio, Ken Siman, and Maria Liu support our efforts to spread the know-how we present to you. No book gets made without the people in production including copy editor Chris Fortunato, Coral Tysliava, and Claire Vaccaro.

We could not have done the job we have with this book without our assistant, Joyce Acosta. She lined up the hundreds of interviews for us with the deftness of an angel and the efficiency of quartermaster and has done the support work that makes a book like this possible. We especially appreciate Donna Gould, who from her home office is a source of special wisdom and encouragement.

Most important, we acknowledge the now thousands of people we have interviewed for more than ten years about their businesses whose experience helps provide the backbone for this book. Without their openness and honesty to share their experiences, we could not have made this book as sensible and exciting as we hope you find it.

As we look at what the future holds for home businesses, we see more change that in large part will be brought about by increases in bandwidth that will make what we as home businesses get and send over the Internet more personal and more demanding of us in many ways. We'll endeavor to keep you updated on such charges and their effects on our Web site, *www.paulandsarah.com.*

CONTENTS

PART II
THE REST OF THE BEST

*Note: Italics refer to related businesses.

INTRODUCTION

Finding the Best Business for You

Our purpose in writing this book is to point you toward the most viable options for joining the millions of people earning their livings from their homes so you can enjoy the freedom of being your own boss. Whether you're looking for new ideas or already have some idea of what you'd like to do, this book is designed to help you narrow down the many possibilities and find a business that's right both for you and for the economic climate of the new century.

There are literally hundreds of possible home-based businesses. You'll find many books filled with interesting, ingenious ideas about businesses you could start. But haven't you ever wondered if many people are really making money in those businesses? We certainly have. The fact that something is a clever idea that could be done at home doesn't mean people can make money doing it.

In fact, people want to know which businesses are truly viable. They've heard about work-at-home scams; they've heard stories about businesses that fail. So they want to know:

- which businesses are actually succeeding

- who can succeed in these businesses

- how much it costs to start them

- how much money you can actually make from them

- will there be a market for this business in the future

1

We wanted to be able to answer these questions with confidence, so we set out to identify what we consider to be the best home-based businesses to start, given the realities of this decade. Before we introduce you to the businesses we have identified and outline what's involved in operating them, we would like you to know how we went about picking them.

When we began research on this book, we felt somewhat humbled by the task of selecting what we think will be the best home businesses for the new century, especially in providing specific information about their viability. We decided, however, to set specific criteria and make sure the businesses we chose would live up to their reputations.

First, we drew on our own experience. We have been working from home ourselves since 1974, and ever since we began writing our book *Working from Home* in 1980, we have been tracking which businesses people have been running successfully from home. Through the thousands of interviews we have conducted on our radio and television shows, the questions we receive for our columns, the various forums and Web sites we participate in online, the seminars we teach, the multiple newspapers and magazines we read, and, of course, the hundreds of interviews we conduct for each edition of this book, we have developed a sense for which businesses are doing well. We have also been hearing back from readers from past editions of *Best Home Businesses*.

To project what people will be doing successfully is a somewhat different task, however, from describing what people have been doing and are doing now. Fortunately, we have always been future oriented. We began reading the World Future Society's *Futurist* magazine in 1970, and forecasts from pundits like John Naisbitt, Alvin Toffler, and Faith Popcorn have stimulated us to think about what their projections mean for home businesses.

To screen our selections, we also went to the Bureau of Labor Statistics in Washington, DC, where we examined the job projections this government office develops and interviewed the experts who synthesize the information that forms the basis for the bureau's projections. Although these projections focus on outside jobs, we find that their work is relevant to home businesses as well. For example, growth in certain job categories may signal other business opportunities, and sometimes the shrinkage of jobs in a category is compensated for by the emergence of small businesses that can be operated from home.

Once we identified businesses that seemed to have a good future, we had to address the issue of what qualifies a business as the best. Income potential was certainly one criterion. We also considered other factors like lifestyle considerations, since today people want more than money from their work. In sum, to be one of our best, a business had to meet the following criteria:

Real Businesses with a Successful At-Home Track Record

Too many people fall prey to an endless stream of business opportunities touted as "work-only-a-few-hours-a-week-and-make-thousands-immediately," requiring no specialized background or experience. Unfortunately, offers that look too good to be true are too good to be true.

You will even see testimonials from "real" people on television. We have seen how this worked. A representative of one of the companies that ran TV infomercials came onto the Working From Home forum on CompuServe and posted a message offering a free cruise to people who would appear on an upcoming infomercial. Why did the company recruit people outside the ranks of those who had bought its mix-and-stir business packages for its infomercial?

If such just-add-water packages were what they are claimed to be, wouldn't everyone be doing them? Wouldn't you meet lots of people who have become wealthy in such businesses? In fact, if these so-called opportunities were real, wouldn't most people on your block be self-employed, working just a few hours a week, and wouldn't everyone be driving a Mercedes? When you think about it, have you ever met anyone who is making good money from one of these come-on's? After all the years we have been in this field, we haven't met a single person who is making a lot of money from a get-rich-quick scheme. To be sure, we have talked with people doing well with packaged business opportunities but when they tell us how much they work, we find they work as hard as people who start businesses from scratch. If a packaged business appeals to you, our book *Home Businesses You Can Buy*, written with Walter Zooi, will help you identify and select such a business. This book covers franchises, multi-level or network marketing, as well as business opportunities.

Be assured that we have met thousands of people who are working from home successfully year after year, earning a living by using their own capabilities, wits, and experience. The businesses we have selected for this book are the types of businesses these successful people are running. However, not just anybody can start many of the businesses we have identified. Truly profitable businesses are not like unskilled jobs on an assembly line. They require a combination of interests, skills, aptitudes, background, knowledge, and contacts that relate to the needs of real people. But everyone has some interests, talents, skills, aptitudes, and background. Therefore, in describing each business, we have attempted to portray honestly what's required and what you can expect, so you can objectively and realistically match your own strengths to a truly successful home business.

Good Income Potential

We have selected only businesses that can and are producing a sufficient income for people to support themselves in a reasonable lifestyle. Living at the poverty line is not our idea of a good life, so missing from our book are businesses like making geneology charts, handicrafts, and pet breeding, from which it's difficult for most people to make more than a part-time income. We have included a business only if it has the potential to produce a steady, full-time income.

We recognize that what constitutes a good income is highly subjective. What for some would be ample would for others be insufficient, so we have been as specific as we can be about potential earnings.

To make sure that people are in fact making money in the businesses we have selected, we conducted interviews with professional and trade-association executives from each field whenever possible. We also did in-depth interviews with owners of the businesses that were likely candidates for our list. In addition to determining whether people are making an adequate living from these businesses, we also wanted to know what they are able to charge and how they go about getting business.

We drop businesses from previous editions when we find that markets, legal requirements, or technology change unfavorably for a business. Gone are businesses like 900 numbers, bill auditing, calendar services, collection agencies, paralegal services, and temporary help services.

We considered dropping several other businesses such as medical billing, because so many vendors are selling it as a business-in-the-box and some markets are saturated, and the gift basket business, because many people find it hard to make enough income from it. But we got enough positive feedback on these businesses, and we find the underlying trends still support them, so we continue to include them.

We also have upgraded three businesses (fitness training, travel services, and pet services) from the *Rest of the Best* in the last edition to the *Best of the Best* in this edition. In doing this, we added more detailed information about them. We demoted indoor environmental tester; it's still good but the market has been slower than anticipated. Some businesses morph like mail order into Web merchant. In addition, we have identified and profiled as either a *Best of the Best* or a *Rest of the Best* business thirteen new businesses (elder services, financial planner, medical coding, pet services, photography, translation service, Web designer, Webmaster, alternative energy installer, aromatherapist, astrologer, doula service, computer-aided design/drafter, Feng Shui consultant, fund-raiser, handwriting analyst, personal historian, red tape expediter, and relocation expert). As we did in the first edition, we bundled kindred businesses under one category, such as editing, indexing, and proofreading under editorial services. Similarly we have grouped related businesses under elder services, financial counseling and planning, hands-on healing, pet services, and travel services.

Although all the businesses we describe can provide what many people find to be adequate full-time incomes, we still suggest that, in selecting the best business for you, you carefully consider how much income you need and want and the demand in your own community or market.

Reasonable Ease of Entry

While we have found that many professionals such as accountants, software engineers, and psychotherapists are doing well working on their own from home, we have excluded any business that requires a specific college degree. We consider this important because as corporations continue to reduce their staffs and as jobs go out of existence, many people need to do something other than what they were originally trained to do or have had previous experience in. Few people have the time and resources to go back to school full-time to prepare for a new profession, although in today's world education is not a one-time event. However, some people can qualify for government funds to help them make this transition. If you have been injured to the point of not being able to earn your livelihood from your occupation, you may be able to get vocational rehabilitation money to pay for the training to learn a new field. If you qualify as a dislocated, unemployed, or underemployed worker under the Job Training Partnership Act and are willing to accept employment prior to going out on your own, which is a good way to get experience, you may be able to get the cost of learning a new field financed under this legislation. Contact the agency responsible for Job Training Partnership funds in your community.

Some of the businesses we have chosen can be operated with any general background. Your existing skills, aptitudes, and experience may ideally qualify you for many of them. Some businesses, however, require certain skills and experience that you may need to pick up by taking some course work or working for a period of time in a particular field. Should you not have the required background for the businesses that interest you the most, you will find specific steps outlined for how you can gain whatever background you need.

While some of the businesses you'll find most appealing may require that you take time to gain certain skills or experience, keep in mind that the best investment you can make is an investment in yourself. An investment in building experience, education, and training is never wasted. Even if preparing yourself for your chosen home business would take a year or more, that period of time will most certainly pass whether you pursue the needed preparation or not. So if you start now, you'll be ready to succeed that much sooner.

In fact, a classic Canadian study of entrepreneurs showed that those who succeed are the ones who have prepared themselves prior to starting their business so that they have the necessary skills and expertise to make it. The successful ones begin with realistic expectations for how much they can earn and then do their homework for at least six to nine months, taking courses and calling on experts, for example.

What we can assure you is that the businesses described in this book do not require that you be without a job while you prepare yourself for them. In fact, for some of the best businesses, like being a private detective, the ideal way to learn is to first take a job working for someone else in that business. While you may have to take a pay cut at first in order to do this, you can think of it as a way to get paid for on-the-job training.

Also keep in mind that even if a business requires no prior experience, if it is in a field you know well, getting started will be much easier. You will be able to use contacts you already have, and your reputation in the field could be valuable in qualifying you. The greater your experience in a field, the shorter and less challenging your learning curve will be once you get out on your own.

Low or Modest Start-up Costs

We have also selected businesses that do not require tens of thousands of dollars to get under way. Some businesses, like cleaning services, can be started for as little as a few hundred dollars, while others, like a desktop video business, require sophisticated computer technology and an initial investment of over $10,000.

In calculating start-up costs, we are assuming that you will be starting your business in a home office space other than on the kitchen table. People have started successful businesses from kitchen tables, but by setting up a specific desk and office area devoted to your business, not only will you avoid unnecessary backaches and eyestrain, but you'll be able to work more productively, and you and your customers, family, and friends will also be more likely to take your new business seriously.

The fact that you will be working from your home without the overhead of office or storefront rent means you will be able to start most of the businesses we have selected for this book on a part-time basis while you still have a job. We think starting out while you have the security and cash flow of a job is the safest way to finance a home-business start-up and to carry you through the months it takes to launch a business.

In addition, as soon as you start your own business, whether full- or part-time, you can convert some of your costs of living into tax-deductible business expenses (which as a salaried employee you're not eligible for) thereby reducing your annual federal and state income taxes. By starting your business while you still have a job, you can actually use the federal tax system to help fund your start-up costs. Doing this involves changing the number of allowances you claim on your W-4 so that you have several hundred additional dollars each month in take-home pay. Before doing that, however, we recommend seeing a tax consultant to make sure that you set up your home office so that such expenses are deductible.

Ability to Operate from Home

Not all businesses can be run from home profitably. In fact, we found that upon close scrutiny several businesses that you might think would be good home-based candidates are really not best suited to be operated from home. Auto brokering, with its state licensing requirements, was one such business. Similarly specialized temporary help services cannot practically be done at home because of federal requirements that identification documents of workers be personally inspected. This requires an ongoing flow of complete strangers coming to your home, raising security concerns, and triggering zoning or homeowner association violations in many communities.

All the businesses in this book can be operated successfully from home without employees. Most of them, however, can also be expanded by hiring employees or using subcontractors who may either work on your premises or from their own homes. We have found that expanding by teaming up with others has become such a trend that with Rick Benzel, we wrote a book, *Teaming Up*, describing the possibilities and methods for expanding. Such expansion is not necessary, however, in order to earn a decent living.

In fact, we have talked with many people who expanded their home businesses only to find that while adding employees increased their gross revenues, once they paid for salaries, fringe benefits, and insurance, they decreased their net income. What's more, some people who expanded by adding personnel also found that they had to work longer hours and contend with more aggravation. By cutting back to what they could handle themselves, they ended up netting more income with greater satisfaction. For each of these businesses, growth is an option, not a prerequisite to success.

Variety: Something for Everyone

The businesses we selected are varied enough that virtually everyone can find something to do from home. Whether you prefer to be outdoors or at a desk, work with people or manipulate information, use your hands or your head, be alone or with others, get involved with computers or stay away from technology altogether, whatever your interests, hobbies, talents, experience, and preferences, you should be able to find a business in this book that's suited to you.

Sometimes when we talk about these businesses, someone will say, "Who would ever want to do that?" But we have learned that there is someone who can find satisfaction in doing virtually any task imaginable. There are people whose brain endorphins start to flow when they're busy cleaning things, and they're perfectly happy running a cleaning service or an auto-detailing business. For others who are turned on by doing highly detailed work, a business like bookkeeping or medical transcription is enjoyable.

Still others enjoy the thrill and challenge of standing in front of an audience, even though most people list public speaking as their greatest or second-greatest fear. For them, employee training may be a perfect match. Someone who loves helping people solve problems might relish running a collection business. Should nurturing others be your passion, doing hands-on-healing or becoming a facialist could meet your needs. Ultimately, enjoyable work is in the brain of the beholder!

What the Business Profiles Will Tell You (and What They Won't)

In describing the businesses we have selected, our objective is to give you the best possible information we could obtain so that you can make a true comparison and a well-informed choice among the businesses we believe offer the best potential as many people nervously anticipate the new century. The first sixty-eight businesses are what we consider to be the *Best of the Best*. These businesses have an established track record of success and a strong continuing demand.

The *Rest of the Best*, which follow, are businesses that are sometimes less well known and at this time less common. They are being done successfully, though, and are well suited to grow and flourish in this decade. Some of the *Rest of the Best* are so new that it was difficult to find as much about them as we needed for a full profile.

Each *Best of the Best* profile begins with a general description of the business, the types of customers and clients it serves, and what makes it a good business. We then go on to address the following issues.

Knowledge and Skills You Need to Have

This section lists what you need to know and be able to do in order to operate this business, as well as any special training or licenses you may need. Here we also highlight the aptitudes, preferences, talents, and tolerances each business demands, as identified by people we have interviewed who have enjoyed and succeeded at doing it, as well as people who have not done well or enjoyed the business.

In short, this section of the profile gives you the opportunity to determine whether you already have or would be willing to acquire the needed capabilities and competencies the business requires. Sometimes the businesses of most interest to you will be a perfect match. You'll say, "Hey, I could do that right now!" At other times, however, you'll find that you have some of what it takes but need to develop additional skills and talents. For example, you might be able to start a business doing professional-practice management for chiropractors by taking on a relative as your first client, but you may need to develop your knowledge of billing procedures. Or you may have the expertise but not the interest or the contacts.

Not only can reviewing these profiles help you make sure you are qualified to start a given business, it can also help you avoid the mistake of focusing only on the potential opportunities a business provides. One person who came to one of our seminars learned this lesson the hard way. He decided to start a medical-transcription business because he knew there was a high demand for it and it paid well. And indeed, when we met him he was making $60,000 a year. But, not being someone who enjoys sitting still, he said the work was driving him crazy. So he was attending our seminar to find a business he would enjoy more.

The special training some of the businesses require may be acquired through community colleges, trade schools, and professional associations, or by working for/apprenticing with an existing business in the field.

Reputable trade schools will readily provide information on attrition and graduation rates as well as references. Some industries provide on-the-job apprentice programs through trade and professional associations.

We are increasingly convinced of the value of apprenticing and specifically recommend it in a number of profiles as a First Step. Apprenticing may mean working as an employee for the type of business you wish to enter, or it may mean literally following in the footsteps of someone in the business and assisting them for a week or several weeks. Doing this can be so worthwhile; it may even be worth paying for the privilege of assisting. You are not just reading about theory when you're out with someone actually calling on their customers, seeing and hearing how they handle problems, and enjoying the rewards of the business. Even in businesses where we do not specifically mention it, finding an apprenticing situation is worth considering.

Internships are another possible way to gain needed experience. *Internships 1999*, available through Peterson's (Princeton, NJ; 800-338-3282), lists 40,000 internship opportunities and provides guidance about how to apply for and get these coveted experiences, both paid and unpaid.

Where there are specific training programs available for a particular business well suited to people wanting to learn at home, we have listed these resources in the section titled "Where to Turn for Information and Help."

Start-up Costs

This section indicates what someone starting each business can expect to spend in order to get the business under way. Each item will usually have a low and high figure. The low figure is for what we consider to be a minimally equipped office; the high figure is for the optimally equipped office. Prices are as of Fall, 1998.

To be competitive today, most businesses require an adequate investment in office furniture—business cards, letterhead, and envelopes—and a computer of some kind. While these start-up expenses add up to a minimum of around $2,000, do not let this amount deter you. You may have some of the needed items already. You may be able to delay some purchases until your business produces the income to buy them. You can buy used equipment and furniture. You may be able to lease items, although leasing is more expensive than buying, even if you finance your purchases.

You may notice that some of our start-up costs appear somewhat higher than those you might read about in other publications. The reason for this is that while we heartily recommend that people bootstrap their business, we do not recommend trying to limp by with less than a minimally professional setup. So although you might be able to forego some of the items we recommend initially, these are the expenditures you should anticipate and plan for.

Others may consider our numbers optimistic. Consider that the Small Business Administration has found that two out of every three U.S. businesses begin with less than $5,000.

Office Furniture   Unless the business requires something special, we have calculated standard office furniture to run around $600 at the low end and $800 at the high. This range is based on the following: a standard four-drawer filing cabinet at $150, a desk at $200 (with $200 you can buy a new economical steel desk, a used wooden desk, or a hollow-framed door placed upon two two-drawer filing cabinets), a basic ergonomically designed chair at between $200 to $400 (to keep your costs at the low end of that range, name-brand chairs can be purchased used), a printer table or stand for $100, and $50 for office supplies and accessories.

Computer Hardware and Software   Unless a business requires a higher-performance computer, our estimates for computer costs are based on your buying a Windows-compatible computer costing around $1,000, including monitor. Since software is usually included with a computer, and people who already have a computer probably have the basic word processing and money management software to get a business underway, we are not stating a separate price for software in this edition unless special software is required. Software prices are based on discounts widely available by mail or in stores that heavily discount software. Printer prices vary from $200 for an ink-jet printer to $1,500 for a laser printer. A low-budget solution for obtaining word-processing software is to use an integrated program, such as Microsoft Works, Lotus Works, or Claris Works, that includes basic spreadsheet, database, and communications functions as well. Suites of the best full-powered programs (word processing, spreadsheet, database, and presentation graphics) are also now available for about $250 from Microsoft, Lotus, and Corel.

Initial Marketing Costs   Included in the estimated initial marketing budget are printed materials, such as business cards, stationery, and envelopes, dues for local organizations and networking groups, and the cost of attending meetings. Because making business contacts through formal

The Five Basic Skills Required for All Businesses

There are five basic skills we believe anyone must have to run any kind of business. Although they are required for all the businesses in this book, we do not repeat them in each business profile. And while we do not discuss these skills in the book, the other books in our series of *Working from Home* guides do. If you are lacking in any of these vital areas of expertise, you can turn for help to the other books in our series, which we have indicated throughout this chapter.

1. Basic money-management skills. While you don't need to have a lot of money to start a business successfully, you do need the ability to make the most of the money you have. Being able to focus on the bottom line and pay attention to the numbers is as essential as the ability to price your products and services, manage your cash flow, and make sure you collect payment for the work you do. If you are lacking in these skills you can get training in business courses, books, and so forth.

2. A marketing mindset. You aren't truly in business until you have business. No matter how much your product or service is in demand or how great a job you do, if people don't know about you, you won't have much business. You must be able to make your business visible to the people who need it, and this means understanding marketing.

3. Self-management skills. To make it on your own, you must become a goal-directed and self-motivated individual. You must be able to get yourself started each day, stick to business, and close the door on work at the day's end.

4. Time-management skills. In your home business, you will need to wear many hats, from chief executive officer to janitor. You'll have to do the business, get the business, and run the business. This means you'll need to manage your time effectively to make sure the most important and urgent things get done in a timely fashion.

5. Basic office organization. Since one of the roles you will probably play is that of your own office administrator, you will need to be able to organize, equip, and manage your office space so that you can work effectively in it, having a place for everything and keeping everything in its place so that you can find it easily when you need it. Today, this also includes the ability to use a computer to at least produce correspondence, invoices, price quotes, and proposals.

For more information on mastering these five basic skills, refer to the other books in our series: *Working from Home, Getting Business to Come to You* (with Laura Clampitt Douglas), *Secrets of Self-Employment, Making Money with Your Computer at Home, Teaming Up* (with Rick Benzel), and *Making Money in Cyberspace* (with Linda Rohrbough).

or informal networking is one of the most effective methods for home businesses to get business and because feeling a sense of isolation from one's peers is one concern people have about leaving the traditional office setting, we recommend selectively joining and participating in organizations. But unless you participate, the money spent on dues can better be spent on other marketing activities.

We don't recommend investing in elaborate brochures when starting out for two reasons. First, you are apt to find they don't express the way in which your business evolves over the first year. You may specialize in an unexpected way in response to business you get that establishes you with a niche. Second, you can save yourself investing in hundreds or thousands of brochures that may be irrelevant to the prospective customer or become rapidly obsolete.

In fact, business consultant Alan Gregerman, president of Venture Works, in Silver Spring, Maryland, recommends that many businesses use what he calls a customized brochure. Using your computer with word-processing or desktop publishing software and an ink-jet or laser printer, you can create a basic format for your brochure and then tailor the content for each person or company to whom you send it. In such cases your brochure becomes a custom-made proposal at a fraction of the cost of a standard printed brochure. Gregerman finds that such a brochure has great impact.

Since you're apt to have invested in a computer, and most newer (and inexpensive) printers are capable of printing good quality, you can use attractive preprinted papers from companies like Paper Direct. To make this easier, you can get software templates designed to match the specific papers. Then you can experiment with and test the look you want for your business, how you describe it, and even your company name. The cost of doing this is mere pennies per item instead of hundreds of dollars for comparable offset printing. For example, you can create five hundred brochures for about $100. With this same capability you can also individualize your message to particular prospective customers or clients. You can also customize letterhead. We still recommend getting business cards printed in the traditional way because the card stock that will go through printers is relatively thin and thus less impressive to the touch than business cards printed on heavier stock.

Special Expenses   Beyond the basic costs listed above, we have also included any expenses that are particular to a business. Some businesses, for example, demand specialized equipment, more sophisticated computer technology, or specific software.

In some cases, you'll be able to postpone buying more costly equipment by leasing it or by contracting out for services. Desktop publishers, for example, can use service bureaus when they need to provide a higher level of clarity than their printers are capable of producing. Buying used equipment can also cut down on your initial costs. The lower cost of new technology has forced down the cost of everything produced before it.

Costs Not Included   Our start-up estimates do not include the costs of an answering machine, telephone equipment, or telephone service because many people already have these items covered and there are a constantly expanding range of options. However, we recommend a separate business telephone line and either an answering machine, an answering service, or voice mail for taking calls when you are not in your office. These costs should be added to the start-up estimates you'll find in this book.

Ongoing marketing expenses for a Web site, advertising, and direct mail are reflected in overhead estimates and not in the initial marketing budget. Overhead estimates expressed as a percentage is contained in the section titled "Potential Earnings."

Most important, our estimates of start-up expenses do not include what you will need to cover your living expenses. If you have a job or your spouse has a job, you may be able to cover your ongoing expenses with those earnings until your business begins to generate income sufficient to support your lifestyle. Otherwise you should have some other plan to cover your living expenses and overhead for at least three, and preferably six to nine months while you get your business on the way to producing your income.

Later in this chapter, you will find a list of the five most common plans used to finance home-business start-ups.

Advantages and Disadvantages of Each Business

Selecting a business is always a matter of balancing the best aspects with those that are least desirable. Every business has its pros and cons. These two entries will help you identify businesses that may be especially appealing to you as well as those with characteristics that you would find disagreeable. They are intended to help you avoid businesses that won't be of interest to you and businesses you would only abandon later.

If you hate to work under the pressure of deadlines, for example, you won't want to consider technical writing or book indexing. But if you want to be in a business that holds the potential for establishing a steady stream of repeat business, being a facialist or running a mailing-list service could fill the bill.

Pricing

This section in the profiles answers one of the most common questions people starting a home-based business ask. In most cases, we give a range of fees or prices. These ranges are based on several variables.

First, unless otherwise indicated, the prices stated are typical for urban areas. Also local prices can vary substantially from one part of the country to another and competition in a given community may push prices downward or drive the rate higher. For example, we found desktop publishing to be a particularly competitive business. The hourly desktop-publishing prices ranged from $20 to $25 an hour when offered by a word-processing firm, but as high as $100 by a desktop-publishing firm. We believe, however, that the more typical rate is around $40 an hour.

The prices you can charge are also affected by your particular background, skills, and contacts and by the type of clients you decide to serve. For example, nonprofit organizations typically operate on tighter budgets than marketing departments for large corporations. They therefore are likely to hire people who will charge less for the same service a corporation might be paying more for. Student and educational markets also pay a lower range of fees.

In setting your own prices, you should make calls to comparable businesses in your area to find out what the going rate is for the business you are considering. If you charge too much, you're apt to wait a long time for that first customer; but if you charge too little, colleagues and prospective customers may very well question your capability. So do check local prices before setting yours, and remember that what other people charge should be only one factor in determining your prices. In *Working from Home*, Chapter 22 discusses various pricing strategies and the procedures for setting your prices.

Potential Earnings

The figures stated in this section are based on estimates of what you can earn from operating the business full-time without employees. By working full-time, we mean spending forty hours a week or more doing work for which you are paid, as well as marketing and administering your business. For many of the businesses, the income estimates are based on being able to bill twenty hours per week (1,000 billable hours per year). Some occupations such as bookkeeping and word processing, however, can bill out closer to the standard forty hours per week. In still other businesses, like corporate training and wedding planning, we presume you are billing a certain number of days or events each week.

Typical annual gross revenue for a programmer, for example, is $50,000. This figure is based on billing twenty hours per week, fifty weeks a year (1,000 hours a year), at $50 an hour. Many programmers, however, are able to bill in excess of forty hours a week and earn up to $100,000 per year.

We have attempted to be conservative in our income estimates, as research has shown that having realistic expectations of what you can earn is an important criterion for business success. Our figures do presume, however, that the business owner is successful in effectively marketing the business and therefore has ample business coming in.

For most of these businesses, you can exceed our projections by hiring an employee or using subcontractors. This is especially true when the business involves selling your time as the only or the principal source of revenue, as is the case with word processing or transcribing court reporters' notes. There are only 174 hours in each week, and producing revenue in more than 25 to 30 of these hours is difficult when you must not only do the business but also get the business and run the business.

Overhead In calculating overhead, which covers the basic costs of being in business (like marketing, telephone, business taxes, insurance, postage, printing, supplies, subscriptions, and so forth), we indicate whether the overhead for this business is high, moderate, or low. These estimates are based on information gathered directly from successful business owners and, whenever possible, from reports by national trade associations such as the Professional Association of Innkeepers International and the American Society for Training and Development.

We consider low operating expenses to be 20 percent or less of your gross income, moderate to be over 20 percent but less than 40 percent, and high to be more than 40 percent. We have used these estimated ranges for two reasons.

First, we find that most home-based business owners do not know exactly what it costs them to operate, beyond the calculations they do for income-tax purposes. But the tax system is designed to collect taxes, not to serve as an information system for financial planning. While how much you can deduct from your taxes does reflect your business expenses, the amount you deduct depends on how disciplined you are in keeping records of things like automobile usage for business purposes and how well you engineer social engagements to make them tax deductible. Therefore, actual expenses and deducted expenses can often vary. In our estimate of overhead, no allowance is made for using your home or automobile unless this is a significant part of operating your business (for example, a bed-and-breakfast inn or an errand service).

Second, many home businesses have wide latitude in what they must spend for overhead. Furniture used in the home office may be a $500 Steelcase chair, or it may be an "early relative" dining-room captain's chair that costs nothing.

Best Home Businesses Estimate of Market Potential

We've also included some usually brief comments about the forces affecting the potential for each business. Keep in mind, however, that someone in a growing community like Austin, Las Vegas, Orlando, Tucson, Provo, or Salt Lake City is apt to find more demand than in the older cities. A businessperson in Boise, Idaho, for example, told us that someone starting any one of the businesses we profiled in the first edition could be making a profit within six months. He attributed this to the numbers of people moving in from the coasts who expect big-city services that were not available. But will a county that is growing because of its attractiveness for recreation or retirement necessarily support a business that is needed in a big city? Maybe. Maybe not.

Keep in mind that while most rural counties are growing, reversing a long period of declining populations, living in the country or a small town may not be for you. Most people who move to small-town and rural "paradises" discover they don't like it as much as they thought they would or find their new neighbors unwelcoming. One study found that 50 percent of people moving to a small city or town moved elsewhere after two years; the figure was 90 percent after five years. So consider well before heading off to unfamiliar locales. Many small towns don't readily welcome strangers; in some places, anyone who hasn't lived in a town for three generations is considered a stranger. So you see that picking a best business to start in a new community is more than a matter of the seeming demand.

Best Ways to Get Business

When we ask operators of successful home businesses to tell us the best way to get business, over and over again they tell us the same thing:

The best source of business is referrals from satisfied customers. In fact, they tell us that once a home business is established, most business comes from word of mouth. For example, Steve Burt, a résumé writer in Gainesville, Florida, put it this way: "If you do a good job for someone, take a little extra time to talk with them, or give a client something extra, I guarantee you'll get referral business."

But, of course, you can't get referral business until you have business. To avoid the proverbial chicken-or-the-egg dilemma we have limited our list of best ways to get business to those that can help you get your initial clients and customers. In this category, you'll find the most likely and cost-effective ways to market each business based on our interviews with people who have successfully established these businesses. We've included this information for two reasons. First, you're probably not psychologically in business until you have business, so it's crucial in selecting a business to know that there are identifiable methods others have used and found reliable for getting business. Second, in your own business you may spend up to 40 percent of your time marketing, so it's important to select a business for which the most reliable marketing methods are ones that you feel comfortable doing. Therefore, in reviewing the businesses, we suggest considering this section as another important way to judge which businesses are best suited to you.

In general, we have usually not listed advertising because, for a home business being started with limited capital, it can be costly. In the process of writing our book *Getting Business to Come to You* with marketing expert Laura Clampitt Douglas, we interviewed over one hundred successful home-based businesses earning over $60,000 a year and discovered that the most successful marketing methods for home-based business are often the least expensive ones. The most successful home-business owners use their time and energy, not their money, to market themselves.

Finding the best marketing method is always an experiment, so you can use our list as a starting point to test various methods until you find the ones that will actually be the most effective in your community with your prospective clients and customers. The fact that a method does not appear on our list does not mean it will not work for you. What's most important is whether you're comfortable with using a method and whether it is effective in reaching the people you need to reach.

For step-by-step information about how to use these methods, refer to our book *Getting Business to Come to You*. It also includes recommendations for how to name your business to achieve maximum marketing effectiveness, proven start-up strategies, instant business-getting techniques, and methods for getting repeat business.

Ann McIndoo, a million-dollar-a-year computer tutor whose business, Computer Training Systems, is located in her home in southern California, offers this marketing suggestion for whatever business you are in: Build a client and prospect database of everyone whom you could work with, and then whenever you aren't busy, make unbillable moments productive by giving them a call. She finds it always generates work.

Related Businesses

This section provides the names of other businesses that are related in terms of the type of work done, skills required, or markets served.

Franchises

We have included names and addresses of franchises that are available for starting some of the business being profiled. Buying a franchise instead of starting a business from scratch has advantages in that a proven franchise provides a tested formula for starting a business that has worked for others. It can save you from making costly errors, shorten your learning curve, and help you make a profit more quickly. There are trade-offs in buying franchises, however: start-up costs are often higher, and franchising organizations require that you follow their procedures instead of doing it your own way. We describe many more franchises you can operate from home in our book, *Home Businesses You Can Buy*. Updates to this book and all our books can be found on our Web site, *www.paulandsarah.com*.

First Steps

If you decide you would like to pursue a given business, this section provides suggestions on how to obtain the knowledge and skills you will need, as well as ideas for getting your business under way. To gather this information we asked people who are in the field what advice they would give to someone wanting to start this business.

Where to Turn for Information and Help

Here we list books, trade associations and professional organizations, special training programs, and magazines and newsletters recommended by people in the field that can be of value to someone starting out in each business. Where training and courses are listed, in the spirit of working at home, we sought to limit these to home-study or correspondence programs.

How to Choose a Business That's Right for You

Selecting a business from among the many that are viable requires finding a match between two things: (1) your particular interests and capabilities, and (2) what people will pay for in your community. Finding this match is vital to your success, and this book is designed to help you find the best possible match. As you read through the businesses we have profiled, you can begin by making a list of those that hold the greatest appeal to you and in which you believe you could do well.

Finding Something You Want to Do That You Do Well

Being able to do a good job is a must in any business. A poor or even mediocre job usually guarantees that you won't have return customers, but that's not all. Sometimes clients and customers will refuse to pay for inferior work, and worse yet, an unhappy client usually tells at least seven other people what poor service he or she received. So first and foremost, you must be confident that you will be able to do a satisfactory if not superior job in whatever business you select.

Obviously, having a background in the business and a track record of success would therefore be ideal. For example, if you have worked as an employee for a florist doing gift baskets and have received rave reviews on your work, you're in a position to feel confident about your ability to do a good job in your own gift-basket business. Or if you've been doing book-keeping on a salary for several years and your clients respect you and refer others to you, you're certainly well positioned to start a bookkeeping service.

But what if you don't like what you've been doing? What if you're looking for a change or if what you've been doing can't be done from home? You still have many options. You can look for a business in another field that utilizes skills similar to those you've acquired. For example, if you're good at bookkeeping but want to do something different, you could look for businesses that involve financial management, attention to detail, or record keeping.

If you are seeking a complete change, you can turn to hobbies or other interests and talents you have. When work repairing televisions dried up for Ted Laux, for example, his wife pointed out that he had years of experience cataloguing and indexing his extensive record collection and therefore might enjoy starting a book-indexing business. She was right. That's exactly what he did.

In fact, while being good at your business is essential, our research shows it's not sufficient. You also need to enjoy it. We think it's profoundly sad that so many people feel they're squandering the precious moments of their lives doing work they dislike. We also believe that a hefty percentage of business failures, physical illnesses, and addictions of mankind can be traced to choosing the wrong job or business.

And most important, succeeding as your own boss is almost always a matter of taking the initiative and going the extra mile despite the stresses that accompany any business. Picking a business you like and that likes you is essential to staying motivated through the ups and downs of being on your own. It could even mean your business or personal survival. Besides, it feels good to wake up in the morning eager to get to work because you like your work so much. We believe one's work should be stimulating, exciting, enjoyable, interesting, and fulfilling. And since your work is likely to be one of the primary ways you express what you have to contribute to life, your work should also be a platform through which you can give the best you have.

Therefore, in selecting a business, use your interests, talents, and likes and dislikes as a filter through which to examine the businesses we have profiled. If you are not fully confident about your ability to do a particularly appealing business, you can take the time to build your skills through practice, attending courses, or even apprenticing for a while before going out on your own.

What follows is a series of worksheets designed to help you identify what you are most interested in doing. If you already have a good idea of what type of business you want to do, you may wish to skip these next few pages. Before you do so, however, consider that it could be useful to compare your intended choice with other possibilities before you fully commit to it.

Determining If There's a Need

Once you've identified two or three businesses you think you would enjoy and do well at, we suggest that you invest a few weeks, even a few months, to test out whether you are likely to find ample customers for these businesses in your local community.

The fact that a business appears in this book means that people are succeeding at running this business from home. Clients and customers in many parts of the country are willing to pay for what these businesses offer. The market looks good for others to succeed in this business. But as we said before, the demand for a business varies from community to community. A community can become oversaturated with a particular business or otherwise not have much need for it.

In fact, we found that while many people were succeeding in these businesses, in all cases there were others who were not. Therefore, before you invest time and money in starting a particular business, it is crucial that you determine if you will be able to find enough people who are willing to pay you when you open such a business in your community. Here are several ways you can go about checking out the actual need for a business in your community.

1. Look in the Yellow Pages, do searches using Web search engines, look in directories where such businesses might be listed and see if there are other such businesses. Be sure to check the Web sites of trade associations because some of them list their members by locale. Check all the sources you can since only a minority of home-based businesses list in the yellow pages and virtually no trade association has 100 percent of its possible membership as actual members, whether they're home-based or not. How many individuals or firms are listed? If there are a number of similar businesses, this is a good sign that there's a strong market for the business, but you will need to determine whether they are doing well and whether the market can support yet another one. Should the market be oversaturated, only the best are going to survive.

If you discover there are no such businesses in your area, this could mean that there's an unmet need and the community is ripe for such a business or it could mean that there is not enough need to support such a business. You'll need to investigate further.

2. Call or contact your competition. Find out what services they actually offer and whom they serve. You might be able to specialize in some aspect of the work that they do not provide, or you might offer your services to a market they are not serving. Let them know you are thinking of starting a similar business and ask if they ever need to refer out overload or if there is a type of clientele they cannot or don't wish to serve and therefore are turning away. Also, find out how long they've been in business. This will give you an idea of how persistent a need there is for this business.

In a good market, while there may always be one or two people who fear competition, the majority of competitors will tend to be forthcoming with information and even glad that 40 others are joining the field. Some will even offer to help you. But if you find that all or most of the people you talk to are consistently closed-mouthed or are complaining about business, this could mean there's not enough business to go around.

3. Read business, trade, and professional journals and visit Web sites, particularly ones with message boards, related to your field. These resources, especially local ones, can provide a wealth of information about the demand for a business. Sometimes business publications list new businesses and bankruptcies, track sales volumes, cover booms and busts by region or area, and feature success and comeback stories. Also read the trade journals your potential clients read to see what their concerns are and to follow emerging trends.

4. Attend local business, trade, and professional meetings. Follow the topics addressed at these meetings and listen to the table talk. Are people singing the blues or whistling "Dixie"?

5. Talk directly to potential customers. Locate and contact potential clients to find out how they are currently being served and if they are happy. Listen to what they complain about. See if you can identify how you could provide faster, cheaper, or better service. You can do this online as well making contacts on forums, on message boards, and in newsgroups. Keep in mind that e-mail can be both more and less informative.

6. Talk with the chamber of commerce and local government planning agencies about the size of your market and community developments that will affect your business potential.

7. Analyze the marketing literature of your competitors to see how they are addressing the market and what they are and are not offering.

Checking Your Zoning

Zoning regulations vary from community to community, so another important step in determining which business is best suited to you is to determine what restrictions, if any, have been placed on the type of work you can do from home.

Zoning regulations typically divide communities into residential, commercial, industrial, and agricultural zones, with subdivisions within these categories. Even in residential areas, many zoning regulations allow so-called home occupations. But some communities prohibit working from home altogether in residential zones, or allow certain activities but not others. In some locales, for example, you can't have clients coming to your home. In others, you can't have employees, use your address in advertising, or sell retail.

Therefore, it's important to find out specifically how your home is zoned and what business activities can and cannot be legally carried out on your premises. To determine if your home can be used for business purposes, you will need to check the zoning ordinances at either your city hall or your county courthouse. To know whether you need to check with the city or the county, a general rule of thumb is that if you would call the police for an emergency, you are governed by city zoning; if you would phone the sheriff's office, you deal with the county.

For more information about zoning and specifically what you can do if you are not zoned to do the types of businesses you wish to do from home, refer to Chapter 9 of *Working from Home*.

Choosing One and Only One

Once you've gathered the needed information and weighed what you've discovered, we urge you to settle upon one single business to pursue. We think it's an error to diffuse your efforts by trying to start up several businesses at once. Instead, we urge you to focus your energy on one undertaking. This will greatly maximize your chances for success.

Focusing on only one business will enable you to be sure that the message you deliver to other people about what you do in your business is clear. We know too well the glazed look that comes across people's faces when they hear someone go into describing three or more things he or she can do for them.

People want to trust their business to experts; they want to do business with people who are specialists. And few people will believe that you can be an expert in multiple fields. There is rarely enough time to do all that needs to be done in one business, let alone in multiple businesses. So select the one business you want to pursue and develop a plan for how you will proceed.

Tailoring a Business to Get the Right Fit

If you don't immediately find a business profiled in this book that suits your needs and those of your community, don't despair. Having read about the types of businesses that are doing well and the kind of skills and background you need to do them, you can use this information to create a unique business tailored to you and your community. Many of the most successful home businesses we discovered came about in just that way. Another of our books, *Finding Your Perfect Work,* can help you create a customized business. Its appendix provides characteristics of over 1,500 different self-employment careers. And, if after exploring self-employment, you want to reconsider the job world, a book we did with noted San Francisco career consultant Marty Nemko covers a fresh approach to getting a job. It's called *Cool Careers for Dummies,* which, of course, is not really for dummies.

Preparing a Business Plan

The profiles in this book should not be confused with a business plan. This book is intended to stimulate your thinking and provide information to help you choose the best business. If you've done the things we suggested above, however, you will be well along the way to gathering the information you'll need to prepare a solid plan.

A business plan is simply a road map. It sets out your goals. It outlines where you're going with your business and how you plan to get there. As a home-based business you will probably not be seeking investors or getting a loan to start your business, so preparing a business plan is not for someone else's benefit. It's for you so you'll know what you're doing and how you're doing at each step along the way. Having such an operating plan to guide your daily activities can prevent you from making costly mistakes.

There are three key parts to such a business plan:

1. *Three descriptions of your business.* Three brief statements, one of 25 words, one of 65 words, and one of 125 words, that describe what your business is, whom you serve, and what benefits you provide will help you know precisely what you intend to do and will enable you to talk successfully about it with business contacts, potential customers, and clients.

You can use the 25-word description as part of your standard introduction of yourself and who you are. The 65-word description is the answer you can give to the question, "What do you do?" or your reply to the statement, "Tell me more about your business." The 125-word description can be used as the basis for writing proposals and advertising and brochure copy describing your business.

2. *A plan for how you intend to market your business.* Identifying as thoroughly as possible the people who need what your business has to offer and how you will let them know about your business can help you select the best marketing methods to make sure you have enough business. In this portion of your plan you should:

- define exactly who your customers or clients are

- identify who your competition is

- clarify what advantages you have over your competition in terms of price, service, quality, variety, ease of use, and so forth

- determine how big your market is and if there are enough buyers for you to reach the level of income you desire or need

- identify how you will let the people who need your product or service know about what you have to offer

3. *Financial projections.* Identifying how much you need to earn in order to survive and thrive and then checking out the going prices in your community can help you know what you will need to charge and how many clients or customers you will need to have each month to reach your income goals. You should also identify which start-up expenses you will have and identify how long you will need to supplement your income before your business can support you. Keep in mind that a business can take anywhere from three months to over a year to turn a profit. You should have a plan for how you will cover your living and operating expenses during that period. Some people advise that to be on the safe side you should double the time you think it will take to break even. With careful planning, however, most home businesspeople are basically able to finance their start-ups themselves.

Opening Your Business

Once you know what you want to do and have a solid business plan, there are a number of important details you must take care of to actually set yourself up in business. These include selecting which form of business you wish to operate, getting the necessary licenses and permits, setting up and equipping your office, opening your business bank account, setting up an easy-to-follow record-keeping system, and having your letterhead and stationery printed. In this country, however, taking care of these details is the easiest part of starting a business. Let's go through them one by one.

Dealing with Legalities

In operating on your own, you must choose one of three forms of business. Your business can become a sole proprietorship, a partnership, or a corporation. We recommend beginning as a sole proprietorship unless your business faces the danger of being sued for damages, needs to establish independent contractor status with companies that require it, or you will be working with a partner, in which case you will probably want to incorporate. You should consult an attorney and an accountant, however, in selecting the best form for your business.

Selecting the name for your business is one of the most important decisions you will make, so once you've decided on your name, you will need to register and protect it.

If you are a sole proprietor and use a name for your business other than your own, you will need to register the fictitious business name with your county clerk or secretary of state. Specific requirements vary by state. If your business is a corporation, you will need to reserve the name with the secretary of state.

You may wish to trademark your name to protect it from use by others. You do this through your state; if you meet the qualifications, you may also register it with the U.S. Patent Office in Washington, DC. Federal registration takes about one year to eighteen months and currently costs several hundred dollars.

Because state, county, and local regulations vary from place to place, you will need to determine whether your business requires any of several licenses and permits. These could include a city or county license, a state sales permit if you need to charge sales tax, a federal employer's identification number, and any other special licenses.

Setting up Your Financial System

When you open your business you should set up a separate business checking account. We recommend selecting a bank where your business will be noticed and valued. If you're happy with your existing bank, you may want to open your business account there because they already know you. Find out what the bank's policy is on holding checks deposited for collection, however. Some banks won't credit your account for checks over a certain amount until the checks have cleared. This could cause cash-flow problems for you, so accept only immediate access to your funds.

Cash flow is the lifeblood of being self-employed. Making sure you collect what you are owed is like making sure you get your paycheck. The best strategy for having ample cash on hand, of course, is to make sure you have plenty of business. But you also have to make sure you get the money you're owed in a timely fashion. To keep your cash flowing, get money up front, take deposits, get retainers, and require partial or progress payments. Request payment in cash at the time of sale or delivery of your service. Take bank cards instead of extending credit. Experts claim that offering MasterCard or Visa can increase your business 10 to 50 percent. Unfortunately, most banks will not offer MasterCard or Visa merchant accounts to home-based businesses. On our Web site, you will find a list of sources through which you can obtain merchant status.

If you must bill your clients or customers, always bill promptly instead of waiting until the end of the month. Also offer discounts of 2 to 5 percent if payment is made within ten days from the date of the invoice. And be sure to act promptly on any overdue account.

One of the best ways to make the most of your money is to keep careful track of it, so set up a reliable bookkeeping and accounting system right from the beginning. The purpose of keeping good records is to enable you to know how your business is doing. With good records, you'll know where you're making a profit and where you aren't. You'll know what your costs have been, where you can cut expenses, and in which ways you'll need to modify your plans and projections. Good records also will enable you to take the greatest advantage of allowable tax deductions and will protect you should you be audited.

Today the easiest way to keep simple, accurate records is to use a computer with software like *Quicken* or *QuickBooks*. Such programs keep your bank balance for you and can quickly print out income and expense reports.

To help make sure you get the basic insurance you need to protect your home office and your business, refer to Chapter 11 in *Working from Home* in which we discuss which types of insurance you might need and under what circumstances you need it.

Setting up Your Home Office

Where you locate your home office and how you set it up are two of the most important factors in determining whether you'll be able to run a business successfully at home. Many people are concerned about interruptions from family or distractions from household activity; others worry that they'll feel compelled to work morning, noon, and night, because their work is always there. Where you put your office and how you set it up can protect you from these potential problems. For a full treatment of this topic (including claiming your tax benefits) see Chapters 8, 10, 17, and 19 in *Working from Home*.

Developing Your Business Identity

Selecting the right name for your business may be one of the most important business decisions you make. If your name is memorable, distinctive, pronounceable, and understandable, it can be a valuable sales tool. On the other hand, if your name is hard to pronounce, confusing, and difficult to spell, it can actually cost you business.

In our book *Getting Business to Come to You*, you'll find a list of rules for naming your business and the pros and cons of the five most common strategies for choosing a business name. We suggest that you follow these guidelines to select several possible names for your business. Then list your top choices on a sheet of paper and ask several potential customers which company they would be most inclined to contact and why.

Once you've selected your name, you need to create a graphic image for your business cards and stationery. Now that you're in business, your cards and stationery are more than paper you use for correspondence. You should think of them as miniature billboards for your business. They create a first impression for people with whom you don't have face-to-face

---

Questionnaire 1
Questions to Ask Yourself in Choosing a Business

1. Based on your education, your current or past jobs, and any special interests and hobbies, what three things do you know the most about? This expertise could be the basis for a business.

2. What other experiences in your background could you draw upon for a business?

3. What do people tell you that you do well? Think about the times you've heard someone say, "You know, you really ought to start a such-and-such, you're so good at that." Maybe they're right. And maybe they would be your first customer. What things do you like doing most? Think, for example, about these questions:
   - What do you like to do on your day off?
   - What kinds of things do you leap out of bed for?
   - What magazines, newsletters, and books do you enjoy reading?
   - What headlines catch your eye?
   - What things did you love doing most when you were a child?
   - What is it you've always said you were going to do someday?
   - If this were the last day of your life, as you looked back on your life what would you say you wished you had done?

4. How much do you want to be involved with people? All the time? Sometimes? From a distance? Not at all? The answers can help you rule in or out businesses that have a lot of or very little people contact.

5. How many hours a week are you willing to invest in your business? Do you want a full-time or a part-time business? Be realistic about this. The amount of time you're willing to invest is what separates full-time from part-time and profits from losses.

6. How much money do you need to make? How much money do you want to make? Each week? Each month? Each year? You'll notice that some of the businesses can charge considerably more than others, so choose a business that will produce the income you want and need.

7. What resources do you have available to you in terms of property, equipment, and know-how? These resources could become the basis of a business. If you look around your home, you may have many untapped resources right under your nose, such as a personal computer, a van, a

spare room, an automobile, a camcorder, your kitchen stove, vacuum sweeper, backyard, or mailbox.

8. Do you want to start a business from scratch, or would you prefer a franchise or direct-selling organization such as Amway or Avon that will train you in what to do?

Questionnaire 2
What Do You Like and Do Best?

Circle the work activities on this list that you like to do, and use the list to help stimulate your thinking as you complete Questionnaire 3.

Information-Oriented Work	People-Oriented Work	Thing-Oriented Work
Working with words	Advising	Cleaning
Working with numbers	Caring	Making
Analyzing	Communicating	Organizing
Compiling	Helping	Repairing
Creating	Informing	Working with animals
Evaluating	Organizing	Working with food
Finding	Negotiating	Working with plants
Keyboarding	Performing	Working with tools
Organizing	Persuading	
Synthesizing	Planning events	
	Teaching	

---

contact. Some of the people you do business with may know you only through your stationery. So think about your graphic image as part of your promotion and sales effort. Design your logo, cards, and stationery to make a statement about your business. Make sure they convey the image you want to create. For example, if you are a computer consultant, you might want to project a modern, high-tech look, so you could use a paper, type style, and design that convey a clean, sleek, and forward-looking image. On the other hand, if you are an errand service, you might want to convey a warmth and friendliness, in which case you may choose a paper, type style, and design that are rounded, warm, soft, and reminiscent of the

---

Questionnaire 3
Business Selection Worksheet

Your Long List

List your six best or strongest skills, talents, abilities, capabilities, or aptitudes.

1. _____
2. _____
3. _____
4. _____
5. _____
6. _____

List the six subjects or fields you know the most about, are the most competent in, or have the most experience and expertise in.

1. _____
2. _____
3. _____
4. _____
5. _____
6. _____

---

familiar past. Don't leave these important decisions up to the standard format at your print shop.

Establishing Your Work Schedule

Even though as your own boss you are free to work when and if you want to, we urge you to set up a work schedule. A schedule not only will help you organize your work, but will also help your family and friends know when they can and cannot interrupt you. Business contacts will know when they can best reach you. A schedule will even help you to avoid having your work take over your life, because it will tell you not only when it's time to start working, but also when it's time to stop.

If you are operating a part-time business, we suggest that you make a commitment to work at least eight hours a week in your business. And

Your Short List

Now narrow the long list down to the three skills and subjects that you like most, in rank order.

Skills	Subjects
1. _____	1. _____
2. _____	2. _____
3. _____	3. _____

With this short list in mind, you can look through the profiles for the businesses that best correspond to what you know about, what you're good at, and what you enjoy.

Some people also find it useful to make a list of the things they dislike doing, because a negative filter can prevent you from entering into a business that has a fatal flaw for you. If a business is otherwise appealing to you, however, consider the possibilities of working with someone else who would do those aspects that for you are disagreeable. That person might be a partner, a subcontractor, or an employee. For example, a desktop publisher who isn't an especially fast typist can subcontract with a word-processing service to do text entry. Many partnerships form because one person is good at being the inside person, handling production and administration, while the other is the outside person, handling sales and customer contact.

don't plan to squeeze all eight hours in on Saturday. Spread the eight hours throughout the week, so that you'll be sure to get some work done even when things you want to do come up on the weekends. In Part II of *Secrets of Self-Employment,* we provide guidelines for managing your time so you can balance the three principal aspects of being your own boss: getting the business, doing the business, and running the business.

Having completed these basic start-up steps, not only will you be in business, but you will be in position to make sure that you have business.

Using the Resources in This Book

At the end of each profile, we have listed resources that can be useful to you in learning about or actually operating each business. This information is intended as a starting point. Most of the resources are not specifically about how to start such a business.

Questionnaire 4
Other Criteria for Selecting the Right Business

Circle the answer that best describes the business you want.

Income Potential
How much money you think you need to:

- Survive? How much do you need to get by?
  Under $25,000 $25,000 to $50,000   Over $50,000

- Thrive? What do you need to meet or exceed the standard of living afforded by your job?
  Under $25,000 $25,000 to $50,000   Over $50,000

- Get rich? How much money would you really like to make?
  Under $25,000 $25,000 to $50,000   Over $50,000

Where You Want to Work
Work at home   Work from home

Amount of People Contact
Mostly working   Some work   Not working
with people   with people   with people

What's Required
A business I'm already prepared to enter.
Something that will require me to learn new talents and skills.

Start-up Money Needed
Low: Under $2,500   Moderate: $2,500-$7,500   High: Over $7,500

So, unless otherwise indicated, *do not* phone these resources, especially the associations and organizations, expecting that they will help you get started in a business. Some may provide you with general information and others may be useful for networking, but unless indicated, none are in the franchising business or offer actual business plans to get you started.

PART ONE

THE BEST
OF THE
BEST

Abstracting Service

If you like to read and have a special expertise or affinity for technical subjects, an abstracting business may appeal to you. The main job of an abstracting service is to read content of all kinds, such as articles from journals and magazines, and distill it into a brief synopsis of ten to fifteen sentences for database storage and retrieval. In some cases, the articles are indexed instead of, or in addition to, being condensed. Indexing means that the abstractor creates a list of key words based on the article or selects terms from a controlled vocabulary list so that a computer can locate an article quickly. Abstracters may also create abridgements of larger works into shorter ones.

Ten thousand databases from over 300 producers (such as Chemical Abstracts Service, Information Access Company, and Dow Jones) provide a continuing supply of work to freelance abstracting and indexing workers. According to Richard Kaser, Executive Director of the National Federation of Abstracting and Information Services, with the movement away from proprietary hardware and software to producing abstracts in Microsoft Word, more work can be outsourced by the database producers. Many database producers specialize in areas such as law, medicine, engineering, science, and other technical fields.

In addition to such database applications, abstracting and indexing services also may work for corporations, creating summaries of books and articles of interest to the company's executives, technical people, or clients. Some large corporations make extensive use of abstracting and indexing to stay up-to-date and competitive in today's world of rapidly changing information.

Knowledge and Skills You Need to Have:

- You need to be a quick reader. Producing two to three abstracts an hour requires speed.

- You need to have sufficient knowledge of the subject areas in which you are abstracting or indexing or a broad-enough general knowledge and interest to be able to ferret out central ideas and relevant information on a wide range of topics. Subject specialists, however, are generally more valuable and successful abstracters are keenly interested in their subject and care about information.

- You must have the ability to synthesize and consolidate information. This requires learning how to read an article or book differently than you normally would. You need to be able to skim through and pick out key points, condense the points into the required number of lines, and pick out key words that someone would use to search for that information.

- You need excellent writing skills and the ability to communicate the material you're abstracting clearly and concisely.

Start-up Costs	Low	High
Computer	$ 1,500	$ 3,000
Printer	$ 300	$ 800
or		
Multi-function printer/fax/scanner/copier	$ 150	$ 600
Cell phone	$ 75	$ 200
Office furniture, especially an ergonomic chair	$ 400	$ 1,000
Initial marketing budget	$ 1,000	$ 2,000
Reference books and dictionaries	$ 200	$ 600
Total	$ 3,625	$ 8,200

Advantages

- The work can be interesting and intellectually stimulating.

- You learn constantly about a variety of subjects and can keep abreast of significant changes in many fields.

- You may have a great amount of flexibility in choosing your working hours: days, evenings, weekends, etc.

- The kind of writing you do for abstracting in which you focus and summarize in a clear and concise manner is valuable for doing other kinds of writing.

- The business is a good add-on to an editorial service, indexing service, or technical writing service.

Disadvantages

- In some cases, you may have tight deadlines and turnaround times; so stress is a factor.

- The work is highly detailed and requires intense concentration, precision, and careful organization.

Pricing

$5 to $15 per article for doing a full abstract with index. Specialists, particularly those in scientific disciplines, particularly chemistry, earn top money.

Potential Earnings

Typical Annual Gross Revenues: $45,000 based on billing thirty hours per week, fifty weeks per year, averaging $30 per hour.

Overhead: low (20 percent or less).

Best Home Businesses Estimate of Market Potential

While artificial intelligence and search engines help people find relevant information, the role of human intelligence in summarizing and evaluating content will grow as more and more information is available. Therefore, we anticipate the market for abstracters to grow. The number of firms for whom work can be done may grow as well as more types of organizations, such as libraries and publishing companies, are producing abstracts and indexes for the Web.

Best Ways to Get Business

- Directly solicit database publishers by sending samples you have written along with your résumé emphasizing any relevant background you may have.

- Since many types of database producers hire local freelancers, in order to find database publishers in your area, decide which type of database you want to work with and search a directory like Ebsco Index and Abstract Directory or Gale Directory of Online Databases to identify publishers in that field by address. You can find these directories in many large public and academic libraries.

- To get corporate work, contact corporate librarians and the department responsible for technical writing.

- Have your own Web site with meta tags and links that will direct people to your site.

- Responding to online and occasional newspaper classified want ads.

First Steps

- Identify a specialty.

- Find out what producer companies want and establish relationships by setting up appointments to discuss their needs and your qualifications to work for them.

- Create a portfolio of samples to show prospective clients. Then call several database publishers in your local area for an appointment to show your work.

Where to Turn for Information and Help

ORGANIZATIONS

AMERICAN SOCIETY OF INDEXERS. P.O. Box 39366, Phoenix, AZ 85304; (623) 979-5514; fax (602) 530-4088. While primarily for back-of-book indexers, this is the closest organization for individual providers. The Society publishes and distributes to publishers without charge the *Indexer Services Directory,* a directory of freelance indexers, listing its freelance members in terms of their specific subject expertise or background. Web site: *www.asindexing.org*

NATIONAL FEDERATION OF ABSTRACTING AND INFORMATION SERVICES (NFAIS), 1518 Walnut Street, Suite 307, Philadelphia, PA 19102; (215) 893-1561, fax (215) 893-1564. This organization, whose members are 60 of the largest database producers, offers information, conferences/workshops, a monthly newsletter, and a variety of books on topics of interest to abstractors and information professionals. The organization's Web site, *www.nfais.org,* has an employment section with links to members who post ads on their individual Web sites. Newsgroup: sci.finance.abstracting

BOOKS

Careers in Electronic Information: An Insider's Guide to the Information Job Market, Wendy K. Wicks, National Federation of Abstracting and Information Services. See address above.

Guide to Careers in Abstracting and Indexing, Ann Marie Cunningham and Wendy Wicks, is another NFAIS publication.

The Information Broker's Handbook, Sue Rugge and Alfred Glossbrenner, New York: Computing McGraw-Hill, 1997. ISBN: 0070578710. An overview of abstracting, databases, and the electronic information industry.

 Advertising Agency

By the year 2003, advertisers will be spending $1,203 per person each year to get their message to the nation. That's more than the per capita income in many countries. They'll be reaching their audiences through the newspapers, television, magazines, and the radio, but the largest increase in spending will be for online advertising. An online advertiser can communicate interactively with the exact individuals they wish to reach. Creating ads for microniches lends itself to small, boutique advertising agencies and experts.

This, of course, has been the direction the advertising industry has been moving in during the 90's. Large companies that once dominated the market have lost clients to smaller, upstart agencies and have had to divide into smaller components in order to compete with the little guys. The very center of gravity of the business has shifted from New York and Los Angeles to San Francisco, Minneapolis, Boston, Portland, Oregon, and Richmond, Virginia.

In short, the industry is more competitive than ever, which means new opportunities for the creative advertising professional who may be home based. While home-based ad agencies aren't likely to wrest the million-dollar corporate accounts from the major firms, there are a lot of different ways to split the $138 billion U.S. advertising pie. Using a computer, some specialized software, and a high-resolution printer, someone with experience in the business who has the necessary skills can make a good living running an ad agency from home. After all, bright ideas can germinate and flourish anywhere. You can choose to specialize in one particular type of product or service, or in one specific medium (TV, radio, print, America Online . . .).

Steve Shoe runs a home-based advertising agency in Denver, Colorado, called Railroad Promotions. After many years in the business, Shoe finally realized that the overhead on his office was draining his resources, so he decided to take a few of his steady clients and move his office into his house. A model railroad hobbyist, Shoe was approached by a local rail line to do ads for them. He agreed to represent the company "if it didn't ruin my hobby." That was ten years ago, and he's still going strong. In fact, he now has an employee who works with him in his home. Shoe's decision to specialize helped him establish a name for himself. It built his reputation as someone with expertise in the field and also gave him easy access to potential clients in professional and amateur groups. Some of his current clients include the Colorado Railroad Museum, the Model Railroad Association, and Craig Thorpe, an artist who photographs and paints trains (he did a calendar for Amtrak). He has also pitched his services to a construction company that manufactures nothing but railroads.

"Are we making a fortune? Living high on the hog? No," says Shoe. "But we're doing something we feel good about, something we like, and making all the bills."

Shoe recommends a similar course of action for someone who is just starting out. "Pick something you like, a hobby." Possible clients include a local hobby shop, a magazine dealing with the topic, a specialty bookstore, and other things related to the hobby. Shoe says for ethical reasons it's best not to solicit businesses that are in direct competition with each other, such as two model railroad shops in the same city. He points out a benefit of focusing on one of your hobbies: you already know what the people you'll be dealing with are like, because you're one of them. Chances are that you also have some ideas about which advertising approaches would appeal to hobbyists, have contacts in the field, read the literature, and know when and where the trade shows and conferences are held.

Small firms can specialize by audience, industry, and medium. Industry and audience are more typical ways of niching than specializing by medium, according to Christine Hilferty, Director of Marketing of the American Advertising Federation. However, the Internet—a medium—is a rapidly growing specialty. Still another kind of specialization is to function as an advertising planner, responsible for strategy, creative direction, and budgeting. Research may be done by the planning firm or supplied by the client. Execution is done in-house by the client or by another firm. Increasingly, small firms emphasizing their skills as planners call themselves marketing agencies. In this case, they may handle all or some aspects of executing the plans they develop.

Knowledge and Skills You Need to Have

- Advertising can be very technical, which means having at least an understanding of the "little picture." At the same time it requires a "big picture" understanding of advertising as an industry within the context of a total marketing perspective.

- You need to know basic principles of design, layout, and typography.

- You must be good at writing copy that conveys your client's message in a catchy, appealing, and memorable way.

- You should have a portfolio of your best work in order to get new business.

- There is no substitute for experience in this field.

Start-up Costs	Low	High
Computer	$ 1,000	$ 3,000
High resolution printer	$ 1,000	$ 2,500
High resolution scanner	$ 600	$ 800
Photo editing, presentation and other software	$ 500	$ 1,000
Fax	$ 150	$ 600
Digital camera	$ 600	$ 2,500
Initial marketing budget	$ 1,000	$ 3,000
Organizational dues	$ 250	$ 500
Office furniture	$ 400	$ 1,000
Total	$ 6,500	$ 14,900

Advantages

- Advertising is a creative endeavor. You get to use both your verbal skills and your artistic talents.

- You can specialize in a field you enjoy, which means you get paid to do the things you like best.

- You get to meet a lot of interesting, colorful, and knowledgeable people.

- Loyal clients will give you repeat business and referrals.

Disadvantages

- Deadlines are often tight.

- Heavily competitive in part because many people who lose jobs at major agencies go out on their own.

- The broad range of things you must know, understand and at least know where to go to find other people who will dependably do those things for a reasonable price.

Pricing

Few advertising agencies are now paid with the fixed 15 percent commission, which covered most services provided by the agency. Instead a myriad of ways have been substituted, including sliding scale commissions, volume rebates, cost-plus-profit, minimum guarantees, fixed fees, and flat fees plus hourly charges. Most small firms charge by the hour or by the project. Hourly rates vary according to the kind of work done. Tasks generating higher rates include art direction, digital photo manipulation, illustration, and layout and design at $50 to $85 an hour. Account management and production art rates are generally in the $40 to $65 an hour range. Projects may range from creating designs for Web sites in the hundreds of dollars to creating advertisements for print media in the thousands. Rates will vary depending on region of the country, whether you are in a major metropolitan area, the type of client you're servicing, and the medium in which you're working.

Potential Earnings:

Typical Annual Gross Revenues: $40,000 to $85,000, based on billing 20 hours a week at $40 to $85 an hour, 50 weeks a year.

Overhead: moderate (20 to 40 percent).

Best Home Businesses Estimate of Market Potential

The trend toward boutique advertising agencies favors home-based work and independent contractors, particularly for smaller local and regional businesses and Web-based enterprises located anywhere.

Best Ways to Get Business

- Networking with other people in the advertising field, going to ad club meetings.

- Networking with your contacts in clubs and hobby groups.

- Networking in online forums.

- Immediately becoming aware of research that benefits clients and leads you to new business.

- Advertising in a trade publication where professionals who might need your services will see your ad.

- Teaching at a community college or adult school, which can also produce income.

- Have your own Web site, which can serve as an example of your capability.

First Steps

- Before going out on your own, get some experience in an agency or company. This may be by apprenticing with a boutique agency.

- Read extensively, which includes both paper and online literacy.

Where to Turn for Information and Help

ORGANIZATIONS

THE ADVERTISING COUNCIL, 261 Madison Ave., New York, NY 10016; (212) 922-1500. The Council creates public-service messages of nationwide interest. The Ad Council operating revenue is funded by donations, and the creative work is done by top ad agencies pro bono. Web site: *www.adcouncil.org*

AMERICAN ADVERTISING FEDERATION, 1101 Vermont Avenue, N.W., Suite 500, Washington, DC 20005; (202) 898-0089; fax (202) 898-0159. Parent organization of 50,000 members for many local ad clubs or ad federations, which interestingly do not require being in the advertising business as a requirement for membership. Look in your telephone directory for your local affiliate; sponsors meetings, workshops, and competitions. Publishes *American Advertising* magazine as a member benefit. Web site: *www.aaf.org*

INTERNATIONAL ASSOCIATION OF BUSINESS COMMUNICATORS, 1 Hallidie Plaza, Suite 600, San Francisco, CA 94102; (415) 433-3400. Web site: *www.iabc.com*

BOOKS

Enterprise One to One: Tools for Competing in the Interactive Age, Don Peppers, Martha Rogers, Currency/Doubleday, 1997. ISBN: 0385482051.

How to Open and Operate a Home-Based Communications Business, Louann Nagy, Werksma, Globe Pequot Press, 1995. ISBN: 1564406318.

How to Start and Run Your Own Advertising Agency, Allan Krieff, New York: McGraw-Hill, 1993. ISBN: 0070352194.

CLASSICS BY AL RIES AND JACK TROUT:

Bottom-Up Marketing, Plume, 1990. ISBN: 0452264189.

Positioning: The Battle for Your Mind, Warner Books, 1993. ISBN: 0446347949.

Marketing Warfare, New American Library, 1986. ISBN: 0452258618.

The Twenty-Two Immutable Laws of Marketing, Harper Business, 1994. ISBN: 0887306667.

CLASSICS BY JACK TROUT AND STEVE RIVKIN:

The New Positioning: The Latest on the World's #1 Business Strategy, McGraw-Hill, 1997. ISBN: 0070653283.

NEWSLETTERS

Creative Business, 275 Newbury Street, Boston, MA 02116; (617) 424-1368. Published ten times per year, this newsletter is directed at copywriters, designers, art directors, and principals of creative businesses. Subscribers also receive free unlimited telephone consultation. It was founded by Cameron Foote, who also gives Creative Business Workshops around the country for people in creative businesses. Web site: *www.creativebusiness.com*

DIRECTORIES

Standard Directory of Advertising Agencies, Published annually by The National Register Publishing, 121 Chanlon Rd., New Providence, NJ 07974; (908) 464-6800. Web site: *www.adweb.com*

MAGAZINES

Advertising Age, Crain Communications, 220 E. 42nd Street, New York, NY 10017; (212) 210-0170; subscriber service (800) 678-9595; 740 N. Rush, Chicago, IL 60611-2590; (312) 649-5200. Web site: *www.adage.com*

Adweek, 1515 Broadway, New York, NY 10036; (212) 536-5336; (800) 722-6658. Web site: *www.adweek.com*

Folio, Cowles Business Media, P.O. Box 4949, Stamford, CT 06907-0949. Targeted to magazine publishing. Web site: *www.drmag.com/ magazines/Folio.htm*

Promo magazine—promotional marketing, including media cause-related promotions, couponing direct marketing, entertainment and sports promotion, fulfillment games, contests, sweepstakes, in-store marketing, interactive promotions, licensing tie-ins, newspaper inserts, point-of-purchase advertising, premium incentives, promotion research, redemption, sampling, special events, specialty printing, television, and radio tie-in promotions. 71 Riverbend Drive South, P.O. Box 4225, Stamford, CT 06907; (203) 358-9900. Web site: *www.promomagazine.com*

Target Marketing magazine, North American Publishing Company, 401 N. Broad Street, Philadelphia, PA 19108. Covers direct marketing, telemarketing, use of catalogues, etc. Web site: *www.napco.com/tm/ tmcover.html* or *www2/targetonline.com/tm/tmcover.html*

Association Management Service

Organizations of all types from nonprofits with a local mission to professional and trade groups and even the chambers of commerce are contracting out their management functions. Since many organizations have grown beyond the size that volunteer officers can effectively manage, but are not large enough to justify renting office space and hiring employees, they turn instead to the services of association managers, people who make a living administering professional and trade associations on a contractual basis.

The association manager provides a cost-effective solution to staff an organization. He or she also enables the organization's volunteer leadership to concentrate on program and policy issues rather than administrative tasks and provides the organization with continuity during leadership changes.

Association management services, also called executive director services, have existed for over one hundred years. What association managers specifically do depends on which functions their clients want them to handle. However, to serve clients well, they need to be prepared to do just about everything an organization needs to have done. They may keep membership lists, write and publish the association's newsletter, answer phone calls, handle incoming mail, send out information about the organization, keep the financial records, collect dues, pay bills, make arrangements and take reservations for membership meetings and events, help raise funds, and book speakers for meetings as well as national conventions. They may also get involved in membership development, professional education, lobbying, and marketing. With today's office technology, all the tasks involved, however, can be done from someone's home.

There are literally thousands of associations from which your clients can come, and new ones form every year. Some associations are national trade associations for manufacturers such as the Model Railroad Trade Association, managed by Steve Shoe (who got into the position from an advertising background), and the Windsurfing Association, managed by Scott Sea (formerly a Wall Street broker who decided to leave his high-pressure job to enjoy working full time with his hobby). Other associations may be state and local professional associations or hobbyist organizations like the Lake Amphibian Flyers Club, a group of 400 individuals worldwide who pilot Amphibian aircraft on lakes. One association manager, Bill Goddard, also finds churches to be in the market for executive director services, because they often have many administrative needs but not the budget to hire full-time staff. Emerging fields are fertile grounds for forming an association. Mary Jo Ginty and Brad Bangerter formed the Managed Care Consultants Association in southern California. When we began writing about working from home, *managed care* was a term most people did not even know.

Many people get into this business by first working for an association as a volunteer. Other people find their first clients through a want ad in a newspaper or magazine and convince the association to let them work from home. Some people manage just one association; others work with two or more at a time.

Another alternative is simply to start your own association. For example, consider starting one based on your own profession, hobby, or special interest. While it's best to start an association around something you know and care about, there are many businesses that lack an association, and this provides opportunities. For example, in researching the current edition of this book, we could find no associations for a number of the businesses profiled. We can't predict whether these would be viable as organizations, but the possibility is there.

Starting your own association can be doubly profitable, since you can obtain a fee for managing the association as well as take a profit on your annual convention or any advertising you can get for your association's newsletter. Associations may be organized as nonprofit or for-profit ventures, although arguably it is easier to market an association as a "not-for-profit" entity.

Knowledge and Skills You Need to Have

- You need to be good at organizing paper, information, and people. You'll be handling lots of details and administrative work. You must make sure that everything runs smoothly and that everyone is taken care of.

- You need to be able to manage an office at a secretarial level or higher.

- You need to manage either a Web site or hire and manage a Webmaster.

- You need good people skills to deal with members, and if you manage associations with a boards of directors, then their constantly changing members and officers with changing goals and priorities. It helps to have a modicum of political savvy to handle personality and ego conflicts that arise within associations.

- You may need to be a good writer, because you may compose press releases, newsletters, and correspondence on behalf of your organizations.

- You'll need sensitivity to motivate and guide volunteers, most of whom are involved with the association as a labor of love or for personal development, and who generally respond better to persuasion than to commands.

- You should have marketing skills in order to bring in new members.

Start-up Costs*	Low	High
Computer	$ 1,500	$ 3,000
Printer	$ 300	$ 800
or		
Multi-function printer/fax/scanner/copier	$ 150	$ 600
Cell phone	$ 75	$ 200
Office furniture, especially an ergonomic chair	$ 400	$ 1,000
Initial marketing budget	$ 1,000	$ 5,000
Bond covering your management of funds.	$ 200	$ 400
Total	$ 3,625	$ 11,000

*In some cases, your client organizations may pay for your equipment and supplies.

Advantages

- Association work offers ample variety to keep almost anyone from being bored.

- You get to attend and possibly travel to many interesting meetings and conventions, with the costs paid for by your clients. Some of your other travel can be tax-deductible.

- This business provides a lot of visibility. You can meet many interesting people, often some who are leaders in their industry.

- When you do your job well, your efforts will be greatly appreciated.

- Some people can build their business extensively, taking on more and more associations and hiring employees to handle the clerical work.

Disadvantages

- Navigating organizational politics can be tricky. You must watch out not to insult an important member of the association or to step on anyone's toes in the line of your work. Your job could suddenly end if a new officer decides to hire someone else.

- You're on call. You need to be available when your clients need you. Sometimes you will be extremely busy.

- Organizational meetings are often held in the evenings or on weekends.

- Except for associations organized around hobbies and avocations, which typically don't operate on rigid time lines, you're apt to find that there will always be some big event or project in the works, so your vacations and time off will be pretty much confined to December and August.

Pricing

Professional association managers usually operate on a monthly or yearly retainer. The amount of the retainer depends on what functions you perform for the association and the amount of time you spend on the job. You therefore need to estimate how much of your time the tasks will take each month and negotiate a fixed monthly fee. Average monthly rates range from $2,000 to $4,000, plus office costs. Another way of pricing used by association expert Stuart Sandow is for members to establish a deposit account. As they have questions answerable by association experts, they call and at the rate of a dollar a minute pay the association personnel for the time they use.

Potential Earnings

Typical Annual Gross Revenues: For managing associations: $24,000 to $48,000, based on a monthly retainer of $2,000 to $4,000. One person can manage several associations. For running your own association: $20,000 to $40,000, based on an organization with 400 members, each of whom pays $35 to $100 a year for dues. Conference fees can greatly increase your income.

Overhead: low (20 percent or less without employees).

Best Home Businesses Estimate of Market Potential

Occupational and business specialties are growing and with them grow associations suited to management by home-based association management firms. Another contributing factor to the growth of association management as a home-based business is an effect of corporate mergers in reducing the number of companies that belong to trade associations. This causes the remaining members of the trade associations to downsize and contract the operation of the associations out to self-employed association managers.

Best Ways to Get Business

For engaging existing associations as your clients:

- Contact the presidents of professional and trade associations directly. Refer to the *Encyclopedia of Associations*, published by Gale Research, which is available in most libraries.

- Identify state associations that are not represented by lobbyists in your state capitol and propose to represent them.

- Respond to the occasional classified ads in newspapers for associations seeking managers.

- Network with professional, trade, or industry groups to learn about potential openings.

- Volunteer to do seminars on administration and management for association leadership teams.

- Have your own Web site with meta tags and links that will direct people to your site.

For starting your own organization:

- Identify affinity groups without an association; it's better if you have some background or relationship to an unformed group. Incorporate or otherwise declare as the association for the heretofore unformed group.

- Mail a brochure to a list of potential new members.

- Establish a Web site for the group.

- Get publicity for your organization or advertise in the publications your audience likely reads.

- Get a board of directors for your association and ask them to network to find members.

First Steps

If you don't have any administrative experience, you might volunteer to administer a group to which you belong or another association that needs help. Or you could get elected to an office in an organization to gain the experience of running an organization.

If you already have business administrative experience, find a niche you could serve, such as medical associations or professional organizations. Survey the officers of such potential clientele regarding their likes and dislikes in administering their organizations, and see if you can locate one that would need your services.

In either case, join ASAE (see below) or network with other independent association managers to learn more about their work.

Where to Turn for Information and Help

ORGANIZATIONS

AMERICAN SOCIETY OF ASSOCIATION EXECUTIVES, 1575 I Street, N.W., Washington, DC 20005; (202) 626-2723. Fax on Demand: (800) 622-ASAE; International (402) 271-9293. The principal organization in this field, ASAE has local chapters and offers certification. The Web site has a career headquarters. Web site: *www.asaenet.org*

INTERNATIONAL ASSOCIATION OF ASSOCIATION MANAGEMENT COMPANIES, 414 Plaza Drive, Suite 209, Westmont, IL 60559; (630) 655-1669. The association for association management companies. The Web site has a listing of member companies. Web site: *www.iaamc.org*

THE SOCIETY FOR NONPROFIT ORGANIZATIONS, 6314 Odana Road, Suite 1, Madison, WI 53719; (800) 424-7367 or (608) 274-9777; fax (608) 274-9978. A resource center for nonprofit organizations of all types, including associations, throughout the country. Web Site: *www.danenet.wicip.org*

Many states also have regional organizations of independent association executives. Check your Yellow Pages.

BOOKS

Encyclopedia of Associations: Regional, State, and Local Organizations, Detroit: Gale Research describes over 50,000 trade associations, professional societies, labor organizations, fraternal, sporting, patriotic, and charitable organizations. Published annually and costing over $500, it's available as a reference in libraries.

Legal Risk Management for Associations: A Legal Compliance Guide for Volunteers and Employees of Trade and Professional Associations, Jerald A. Jacobs, David W. Ogden, American Psychological Association, 1997. ISBN: 1557983046.

Managing Your Future As an Association: Thinking About Trends and Working With Their Consequences, 1993–2020, Jennifer Jarratt (Editor), Joseph F. Coates, American Society of Association Executives, 1994. ISBN: 0880340843.

Principles of Association Management, Henry Ernstthal and Vivian Jefferson, Washington, DC: American Society of Association Executives, 1988. ISBN: 0880340088.

Bed-and-Breakfast Inn

In the past when homeowners had more house than they needed, they took in boarders. Today's version of this is the bed-and-breakfast (B&B) inn, which offers travelers the comfort of a home environment often at a cost less than what a hotel would charge for a comparable room. The idea of bed-and-breakfast inns developed in the 1980s. Although they represent less than 1 percent of the hotel industry, they are a well-established lodging choice, with some B&B inns even rated by auto clubs. From only 400 bed-and-breakfast inns in the United States in 1975, today there are more than 20,000, half of which are in private homes.

This is an ideal business for someone who loves to have houseguests, decorate, and keep a beautiful home. Pat Hardy, co-author of the book. *So You Want to Be an Innkeeper* and co-director of the Professional Association of Innkeepers International, points out that with their emphasis on service, bed-and-breakfast inns have influenced the traditional hotel industry to introduce more services to their guests, such as concierge floors and complimentary breakfasts. She emphasizes that the key to being competitive is to offer even more services customized to your guests.

Though B&B guests are usually leisure travelers, staying typically for two nights a trip, this business encompasses every type of proprietor and establishment. Keep in mind, however, that location of a bed-and-breakfast inn is of critical importance. The most successful inns are commonly located in areas that attract tourists or business travelers. We've seen some beautiful homes that have been turned into inns that are starving for guests because they're off the beaten path or in a locale that otherwise offers little to attract visitors. To do well in this business, you need to live in a desirable area that draws travelers who want a more private and personal overnight stay.

You can make innkeeping your full-time occupation and run a fully licensed inn or manage a B&B as a part-time venture, occasionally renting out three or fewer rooms for extra income. Pat Hardy points out that 60 percent of innkeepers depend primarily on some outside source of income. "Don't expect to grow rich operating a bed and breakfast inn," she warns. "Operating an inn is a lifestyle choice."

If you hope to make a good profit, the more rooms you have available to convert into guest rooms the better. Profitability with fewer than six guest rooms is difficult according to a national study by the Professional Association of Innkeepers International (PAII). Smaller inns with a higher occupancy rate can make money, as can those located in the West, where the weather is more suitable for year-round travel.

Operating a B&B provides some additional financial perks. Expenses such as interest on your home mortgage, the cost of operating your car, your insurance, eating out, magazines, cleaning supplies, and even travel may be tax deductible. But the IRS can be rigid with B&Bs about deducting expenses like gardening, an outside sign, and exterior painting.

Start-up Costs

Acquisition cost. If you are converting your existing home, you will not have any acquisition costs; however, if you're buying a functioning inn, you can expect to pay $35,000 to $150,000 per guest room, depending on the area.

Renovation cost. If you are converting your existing home into a fully licensed inn, you can expect to spend $15,000 to $50,000 per guest room, depending on the locale and your taste.

Working capital. To open an inn in your home you should allow for $10,000 per room up-front to cover the costs of utilities, insurance, marketing, maintenance, supplies (towels and linens), and so forth. New businesses need additional capital in the initial years. Expect a minimum of three years for break-even in most cases.

Knowledge and Skills You Need to Have

Though almost any life experience, from housework to knowledge of a local sport, can be effectively applied to operating an inn, you need to have or develop business planning and marketing skills. Being a good host may be more of a matter of personality than skill, but it's a necessary part of building a successful B&B.

Advantages

- You can live in a desirable location in the country or city.

- You meet a wide diversity of people and may learn about other countries and their customs.

- Operating an inn provides an increased opportunity to enjoy family life. This business can be an opportunity for couples to work together. Also, this is a business in which your teenagers can easily get involved working for you. (Having young children around is more difficult.)

- Being an innkeeper is a way to earn an income while your property appreciates in value.

Disadvantages

- Your income is limited to the number of rooms you have and today's travelers are more demanding of space.

- As an innkeeper, you need to be at home most of the time, and you're often tied to the telephone.

- With small properties in particular, you are on the job seven days a week. You have few weekends off.

- Even small inns are subject to food, health, fire, and building codes. Bed and breakfast inns are now inspected more than other forms of lodging, according to PAII. Expect that regulation will be part of your life.

- You need special insurance. Regular homeowners' insurance does not apply.

- Because of their popularity, the inn business is becoming more competitive.

- Operating an inn is hard work.

Pricing
Rates per Room

Type	Range	Average
Basic with shared bath	$45–110	$ 70
Room with whirlpool or spa	$75–250	$ 142

Potential Earnings
Average Nationwide Occupancy Rates

Year	Percent Occupancy
1992	50%
1995	52%
1996	53%

Average Gross Income

1–4 bedrooms	$ 38,000
5–8 bedrooms	$ 98,000
9–12 bedrooms	$ 136,000

Operating Expenses and Net Income

1–4 bedrooms	82%	$ 6,987
9–12 bedrooms	55%	$ 80,561

Data from the Professional Association of Innkeepers International's *1996 Country Inn Study.*

Best Home Businesses Estimate of Market Potential

The popularity of inns will continue with more and more people finding inns primarily through the Web. This makes having a Web site essential.

Best Ways to Get Business

- Getting your inn listed in travel and guidebooks, including auto-club guides. Travelers increasingly want to know if an inn is inspected by someone. So having approval from someone is important.

- Have as much presence on the Web as you can. This means having your own Web site with photos of your rooms so travelers can choose their room as well as being listed in guides found on the Web. By 1998, many B&Bs attributed one-third of their guests to the Web.

- Having a niche, such as serving birders or members of ethnic groups.

- Offering special services like having Jacuzzis in the rooms, accommodating meetings, providing sensational food, meals in addition to breakfast (such as box lunches and dinner).

- Providing extra services related to the recreational activities people come to your area for, such as hiking, skiing, and fishing.

- Happy guests will generate referrals, so one of the best business-getting strategies is to provide a good-quality room, spectacular breakfasts, and some other distinguishing service.

- Travel sections of newspapers and magazines, even TV news and talk shows, sometimes run feature stories on unique, charming, and colorful inns, so sending out news releases can lead to valuable visibility.

- To get repeat business, do regular mailings to your former guests announcing special services, offering special discounts, and informing them of upcoming events or activities in your community.

- Cooperative marketing through your state or regional inn association, chamber of commerce, or state division of tourism.

- Reservation services in your community or region can refer business to you for a percentage of the fee you receive, usually between 10 and 35 percent. You can find reservation agents in your local Yellow Pages or through the national association for such agencies, listed below.

First Steps

- Check your zoning to determine if B&B's are allowed and, if not, the feasibility of getting it changed. Later you will need to get fire department and, if you serve food, health department approval.

- Be a guest at a bed-and-breakfast inn yourself, particularly ones listed in directories and books, both in print and on the Web. Read critiques to see what's recommended and what's not.

- Obtain information from the associations listed below and attend any workshops offered in your area.

- To gain experience, consider taking work as an inn sitter for vacationing inn owners. There's now a national association of inn sitters.

Where to Turn for Information and Help

ORGANIZATIONS

THE INN & LODGING FORUM ON COMPUSERVE (GO INNS) has a message board and library for those in the inn business. Topics range from the merits of software for operating an inn to a recipe exchange.

PROFESSIONAL ASSOCIATION OF INNKEEPERS INTERNATIONAL (PAII, pronounced "pie"), Box 90710, Santa Barbara, CA 93190; (805) 569-1853; fax (805) 682-1016. Offers a free kit for people interested in running an inn, called the *Aspirers Intro Package,* which includes a catalogue of books and research reports, a list of workshops scheduled around the United States. It also contains lists of consultants and realtors who specialize in the inn business. The Association's web site, *www.paii.org,* has discussion groups, including one for aspiring innkeepers.

BOOKS

Bed and Breakfast/Country Inn Industry Study of Marketing, Operation and Finance. Published every two years. Available from PAII, listed above. The Association also publishes *The Marketing Handbook for Bed and Breakfast/Country Innkeepers.*

IRS Audit Protection and Survival Guide: Bed and Breakfasts, Gerald F. Bernard and D. J. Baran, New York: John Wiley & Sons, 1996. ISBN: 0471166340.

Open Your Own Bed and Breakfast, Barbara Notarius and Gail Sforza Breuer, New York: John Wiley & Sons, 1996. ISBN: 0471130443.

Opening Your Own Bed and Breakfast, Jan Stankus, Old Saybrook, CT, Globe Pequot Press, 1997. ISBN: 0-7627-0063-7.

The Romance of Country Inns: A Decorating Book for Your Home: Rooms, Gardens, Crafts, Recipes, Restoration, Gail Greco, Rutledge Hill, 1993. ISBN: 1558531750.

So You Want to Be an Innkeeper, Mary E. Davies, Pat Hardy, JoAnn M. Bell, and Susan Brown, Chronicle Books, 1996. ISBN: 081181226X.

NEWSLETTERS

innkeeping, Box 90710, Santa Barbara, CA 93190; (805) 569-1853; fax (805) 682-1016.

Yellow Brick Road, P.O. Box 1600, Julian, CA 92036.

CYBERSPACE

BED AND BREAKFAST CHANNEL—*www.bbchannel.com*—lists over 20,000 B&Bs

BED AND BREAKFAST INNS ONLINE—*www.bbonline.com*—online guidebook

FODOR'S B&B FINDER—*www.fodors.com*—the renowned guidebook's database of B&Bs

INNROADS—*www.inns.com*—reviews B&Bs

INNSTAR—*www.innstar.com*—online guidebook

YAHOO DIRECTORY OF B&Bs—*http://dir.yahoo.com*

Bodywork and Massage Therapy

Bodywork has been called the coffee break of the millennium. You see massage therapists' chairs and tables at airports, art shows, doctors' offices, gyms, health clubs, health food stores, resorts, salons, shopping malls, spas, sporting events, work places, in hospices, hospitals, locker rooms, nurseries, storefronts, and on cruise ships and movie sets.

Bodywork in its many forms is booming. Americans are spending an estimated $2 to $4 billion dollars a year having their aches, pains, and anxieties massaged away. Membership in professional associations of massage therapists nationwide has more than doubled to over 40,000, and the number of schools and training programs has also doubled. Beginning with a revival in the 60's, the old image of a "massage parlor" is largely gone.

Why is bodywork and massage growing?

- Relieving stress is one reason. Nine out of ten adults from executives to overworked supermoms say they experience "high levels" of stress. Thus it's not surprising that primary-care physicians report that 75 percent of office visits involve stress-related problems. Forty percent of worker turnover is stress-related, and one way that businesses are combating this is by allowing massage therapists to come work on their employees during working hours.

- Another impetus is that massage is now an integral part of many physical rehabilitation regimens and may be covered by insurance if prescribed by a physician or chiropractor. Some health plans cover massage now too because it seems to produce highly therapeutic results. Chronically ill patients who receive massage need less pain medication. Immune systems rebound in HIV patients, and blood pressure stabilizes in post-operative patients receiving touch therapy. Daily massage has helped teenagers with emotional problems. Premature babies who are massaged have gained 47 percent more weight and have been discharged six days earlier than other pre-emies. Colicky infants are reportedly less irritable and the elderly more alert. Some studies even show improved student math scores.

- The heavy use of keyboards and mice in computing has resulted in large numbers of people developing repetitive stress injuries. This has prompted recognition that people in many other occupations, from chicken pluckers to violin players, suffer from repetitive stress injuries as well.

While Swedish Massage is the most common form of bodywork, there are many variations. Few fields have so many names—massage, massage therapy, therapeutic massage, touch therapy, somatic therapy, myomassage, myotherapy. Some practitioners describe themselves in terms of one of the approximate 150 massage and bodywork modalities they use—acupressure, cranial sacral therapy, energy healing, Feldenkrais, Hellerwork, lymphatic drainage, polarity therapy, Reflexology, Reiki, Rolfing, Shiatsu, sports massage, Trager, and trigger-point or neuromuscular therapy, to name a few. Each modality has one or more treatment aims, ranging from relaxation to dealing with specific maladies.

Most practitioners employ multiple techniques in seeking to provide their clients with maximum benefits, but specialization is also common. Some specialize based on the particular technique they use. Others specialize based on the type of clients they work with. Gabrielle Greenberg of New York City, for example, teaches baby massage to parents in parenting centers. Sports massage therapist Kate Montgomery of Nashville, Tennessee, has developed a 12-step touch program for people suffering from carpal-tunnel pain. Tiffany Field, who is known as the "Jane Goodall of massage," works with newborns. Carol Koncan specializes in a particular form of facial massage targeted at rejuvenating and restoring facial tissue

Other massage therapists are working with autistic children, asthma suffers, diabetics, people with chronic migraines, and post-mastectomy patients. Still others specialize in working with dancers, musicians, office workers, the elderly, hospice dwellers, bone-marrow transplant recipients, and drug and alcohol rehabilitation patients.

Some specialize in working with particular problems, such as easing aches and pains, lessening injuries, balancing and restoring energy, promoting healing, re-educating movement because of disabilities, and reducing stress.

Touch therapy is growing in the animal world as well. As a professional horse trainer, for example, Linda Tellington-Jones saw many examples of the emotional and physical suffering in animals. Determined to help, she studied bodywork techniques such as the Feldenkrais Method and developed her own unique brand of animal bodywork called Tellington Touch or T-Touch.

Many bodyworkers like Michelle Weitzman of Venice, California, provide relaxing hour-long massages to clients in their own homes on a portable massage table. Increasingly popular, however, are chair massages like those offered by Jodi Leavy of New York–based Healing Hands and Holden Zalmac of Culver City, California. Zalmac takes his chair into an office, sets it up in a corner and employee after employee takes turns in his chair. He charges one dollar a minute and often has eight to fifteen employees in a row for 10 to 20 minute massages. Some companies pay part of the bill to keep their employees happy, relaxed, and productive.

Bodyworkers and touch therapists can work either from home or at home. Michelle Weitzman, for example, has her own home-based salon although she also travels to see clients at their homes. But others like Jodi Leavy work strictly at her client's site. Some, working independently operate in rented office space, at health clinics, salons, spas, or hospitals.

Our pick for an emerging niche is providing massage for menopausal and peri-menopausal women who often suffer from severely tight neck and shoulder muscles, general tension, and anxiety.

Knowledge and Skills You Need to Have

- A thorough knowledge of anatomy, physiology, pathology, and kinesiology.

- Manual dexterity.

- Effective communication skills to create empathy with clients.

- Sensitivity to others' needs.

- Problem solving ability, what Rolfer Ben Shields of Los Angeles calls "being a detective." He says the issue is not just seeing the evidence of what's troubling a client, but interpreting the evidence.

- Ability to abide by ethical standards.

Advantages

- The personal and professional satisfaction of helping people.

- Personal contact in a way you can get to know people.

- Personal growth seems to result from becoming proficient.

- Challenging for those who are interested in research and studying people.

- Elliot Greene, who practices in the Washington, DC, area, says, "If someone is good at this work and has any people skills at all, they will become successful."

Disadvantages

- Patience and effort is required to build a private practice. Expect it to take a year.

- Physically demanding work requiring you to be in shape.

- Some negative perception because of the history of massage, resulting, if you advertise, in getting harassed by some individuals who seek more than massage.

- Females need to be sensitive to possibly difficult clients, though they're rare.

Start-up Costs*	Low	High
Table and/or chair for seated massage	$ 350	$ 2,000
Portable accessories such as a face rest and carrying case	$ 85	$ 200
Consumables: Linen and oils	$ 100	$ 300
Training	$ 4,500	$ 6,000
Answering service, cell phone, or pager	$ 75	$ 200
Office furniture, especially an ergonomic chair	$ 400	$ 1,000
Text books	$ 150	$ 250
Initial marketing budget	$ 1,000	$ 3,000
Professional liability insurance	$ 1,000	$ 1,500
Total	$ 7,660	$ 14,450

* If you use your own home, the cost of decorating and furnishing it for clients.

Pricing

$25 to $125 an hour depending on locale and specialization. Some offer a reduced hourly rate as a package price for buying ten massages.

Potential Earnings

Typical Annual Gross Revenues: $60,000, based on four clients a day, five days a week for fifty weeks, at $60 per session. About thirty client hours a week is about as many as a massage therapist can physically handle.

Overhead: low (approximately 20 percent).

Estimate of What the Market Will Be

The conditions that have caused the rapid increase in bodywork show no signs of going away. Additional factors, such as the desire of people to maintain and improve their health, the shortcomings of traditional medicine and the willingness of people to turn to alternative forms of health care; research on the effectiveness of massage therapy that creates acceptance in the medical community leading to referrals; and a better educated public will spur continuing growth.

Best Ways to Get Business

- Because of the highly personal nature of this business, getting and retaining clients is based on personal contact.

- Demonstrate your work at shows and fairs doing seated massage.

- Volunteer at charity events, health fairs, and other events.

- Make presentations that include demonstrations.

- Develop relationships with other health care practitioners, hotels, and other sources of referrals. Sometimes these can be accomplished with mutual referral agreements; at other times, fee splitting is required.

- Encourage satisfied clients to refer others.

- Referral organization, both formal and informal.

- Affiliate with one or more national organizations that refer people who are seeking massage therapy.

- Yellow Pages listing if the Yellow Page publisher screens out adult entertainment ads.

- Introduce your services at corporations for no or a reduced fee.

- Have your own Web site. Without a Web site, you will not get as many leads from database directories or locator services maintained by organizations that help consumers find a professional. Most online directories provide the ability to link the consumer directly to your page.

First Steps

- Check into whether licensing is required in your state. Each state sets its own criteria. Some states take the position that any touching relationship be licensed or registered. Twenty-seven states so far have licensed massage, and bills are pending in most of the other states. Some counties and cities also regulate massage. So you must check both state and local requirements.

- Get training from one of the approximately 70 schools accredited by the Commission on Massage Therapy Accreditation. These require a minimum of 500 in-class hours of instruction.

- Obtain national certification through The National Certification Board of Therapeutic Massage and Bodywork. Most states that license have adopted this examination as a requirement. In other states, it's a recognized credential.

- Decide how you are going to focus your practice or specialize and get the additional training, credentials, and experience you need.

- Decide whether you will establish a practice in your home, by going to your clients' workplaces and homes, or whether you will affiliate with a spa, health club, or doctors' offices.

Where to Turn for Information and Help

ORGANIZATIONS

AMERICAN MASSAGE THERAPY ASSOCIATION, 820 Davis Street, Evanston, IL 60201; (847) 864-0123. Offers a locator service; publishes *Massage Therapy Journal*. Web site: *www.amtamassage.org*

ASSOCIATED BODYWORK & MASSAGE PROFESSIONALS, 28677 Buffalo Park Road, Evergreen, CO 80439; (800) 458-ABMP (2267). Publishes *Massage and Bodywork Magazine*. Web site: *www.abmp.com*

THE NATIONAL CERTIFICATION BOARD OF THERAPEUTIC MASSAGE AND BODYWORK, 8201 Greensboro, Suite 300, McLean, VA 22102; (800) 296-0664; (703) 610-9015. Operates the credentialing program recognized in at least 16 states. Web site: *www.ncbtmb.com*

COURSES AND TRAINING

For the names of accredited or approved schools, contact the National Certification Board or see its Web page.

BOOKS

Bodywork Shiatsu: Bringing the Art of Finger Pressure to the Massage Table, Carl Dubitsky, Deane Juhan, Inner Traditions International Ltd; 1997. ISBN: 0892815264.

Business Mastery: A Guide for Creating a Fulfilling, Thriving Business and Keeping It Successful, Cherie Sohnen-Moe, Sohnen-Moe Assoc., 1997. ISBN: 0962126543.

Massage: A Career at Your Fingertips (Enterprise Publishing), Martin Ashley. Independent Publishers Group; 1995. ISBN: 0964466201.

Massage Therapy: Career Guide for Hands on Success, Steve Capellini, Milady Publishing Corporation; 1998. ISBN: 1562533827.

Mosby's Fundamentals of Therapeutic Massage, Sandy Fritz, Sandra Fritz, Mosby-Year Book; 1995. ISBN: 0815132514.

The Professional's Guide to Reflexology, Shelley Marleen Hess, Annette D. Danaber, Milady Publishing Corporation; 1996. ISBN: 1562533347.

Save Your Hands! Injury Prevention for Massage Therapists, Lauriann Greene, Robert A. Greene, Infinity Press; 1995. ISBN: 1883195039.

MAGAZINES AND NEWSLETTERS

Massage Therapy Journal published by the American Massage Therapy Association. See above.

Massage Magazine, 1315 West Mallon Avenue, Spokane, WA 99201; (800) 533-4263.

Pulse, International Spa and Fitness Association, 546 East Main Street, Lexington, KY 40508; (888) 651-4772.

Bookkeeping Service

The mushrooming number of small businesses is good news for bookkeeping services. Entrepreneurs and growing businesses often need assistance in understanding the ins and outs of financial record keeping, yet can't afford to hire full-time personnel with this needed expertise. As Chellie Campbell, of Campbell Consulting of Los Angeles, points out, "While doing business is getting more complex, people are not getting better at handling their money. Today, virtually everybody needs some professional guidance."

Despite the availability of easy-to-use accounting software, many small-business owners have neither the time nor the inclination to use the software themselves. Wise businesspeople also realize that their time can better be spent in marketing and doing the income-producing work of their business. As a result, bookkeeping can be a good business year in and year out. Bookkeeping assistance is needed even during difficult economic downturns because businesses realize that if they aren't careful about their money, they soon won't be in business. However, "In downtimes, you may have more competition, because some accountants not able to keep busy will seek to pick up bookkeeping business," says Adrian Seaford, who operates a New Orleans bookkeeping service.

Clients range from one-person home businesses to companies with up to 100 employees. Some bookkeeping services specialize in particular types of businesses, like medical or legal practices, or they may serve a variety of clients. Often clients will do some aspects of their own bookkeeping. As a bookkeeping service, what you can do for your clients depends on what services they need and will pay to have done, and, of course, on what you can do for them. This may extend from minimal record keeping to virtually all the tasks up to preparation of financial statements, which a few bookkeepers also prepare. Bookkeeping tasks range from making deposits, reconciling bank statements, and recording transactions to doing payroll, billing, managing accounts receivable and payable, and preparing financial reports for tax or accounting purposes.

Accounting, which is not in the purview of the bookkeeper, involves interpreting the financial statements (income statement, balance sheet, profit and loss) and determining how best to use that information in business and tax planning. Sometimes people confuse bookkeeping with accounting, especially since software manufacturers refer to their products as accounting software when in fact this software simply helps keep track of information and doesn't interpret it. Bookkeepers keep the records; accountants audit and analyze them.

A bookkeeping service is a business you can start with a personal computer. Although computer experience is not necessary, using the computer and an accounting software package are absolute necessities for a bookkeeping service today. Fortunately some software programs are easy to learn.

Bookkeeping services can be conducted from your home office, although you may have to go to your clients' offices periodically. Using remote bookkeeping, however, made possible with software like *PC Anywhere* and *Laplink*, means you can serve clients anywhere. Mobile bookkeeping services have also become popular. A mobile bookkeeper can travel to an office with a notebook computer and software or use a van equipped with computer, printer, and electrical generator as a traveling office. However, Adrian Seaford cautions, "If you work in someone's office, you don't have control over working conditions. It can be too noisy, too hot, too cold; you may have to work at a conference room table that has your computer in your face."

Knowledge and Skills You Need to Have

- You must know how to do bookkeeping accurately and reliably. This includes knowing basic principles of bookkeeping and what types of information must be kept in what form for legal and tax purposes.

- You must feel comfortable using a computer, since most of your work will require the use of accounting and sometimes spreadsheet software.

- You need a clear, logical mind and enough real-world experience that you recognize whether your client's numbers make sense when they're tallied.

- You need to be thorough, dependable, and accurate.

- You need to enjoy paying attention to details.

- You need excellent communication skills and the ability to recognize whether your client wants detailed information or just to know how much money is in the bank. This includes being able to handle people who become emotional about money matters.

- You need honesty and integrity. If you would go along with a client who asks you not to report or to hide income, it's in your interest to find a business that is less apt to compromise your integrity and get you in trouble. Also, a client who will ask you to use questionable practices may have no compunction about not paying your bill.

Start-up Costs*

Surprising as it may seem to some, as of 1997, 65 percent of small businesses still did their books manually. Of course, this number is declining, but it will be possible for some time to be a bookkeeper without a computer. Of course, you will need to know more about accounting because accounting software does a lot of things for you.

	Low	High
Computer	$ 1,500	$ 3,000
Accounting software	$ 50	$ 350
Printer	$ 300	$ 800
or		
Multi-function printer/fax/scanner/copier	$ 150	$ 600
Printing calculator	$ 50	$ 150
Paper shredder	$ 50	$ 200
Office furniture, especially an ergonomic chair	$ 400	$ 1,000
Initial marketing budget	$ 1,000	$ 5,000
Errors and omissions insurance AIPB offers	$ 150	$ 300
Total	$ 3,650	$ 11,400

* Add $8,000 to $12,000 to buy a used van if you want to be a mobile bookkeeping service.

Advantages

- Bookkeeping is an essential, not discretionary, business activity; therefore it is generally recession resistant.

- Bookkeeping is not hard to sell with established businesses, but new businesses often do not recognize the central role of bookkeeping to their business.

- This career allows you to learn a lot about business in general and about many specific kinds of businesses.

- If you like numbers, the work is challenging and fun like solving puzzles.

Disadvantages

- Bookkeeping is very technical and demands careful attention to detail. Mistakes can result in your clients' facing substantial interest assessments on late payments or penalties from the government.

- People get very emotional if there is a penalty for filing something late. "They forget they were late in providing a check or the needed information when the penalty is assessed three months later," says Adrian Seaford. So you need to document when clients provide you with what you need and personally supervise the mailing of vital documents. It's a good idea to go to the post office and see items hand stamped.

- Collections can be a problem unless you are on retainer and refuse to work when clients get behind.

- You need to keep current about tax-law changes relative to payroll and record keeping.

- Using accounting software, many businesses that might have outsourced their bookkeeping in the past are doing it themselves. However, because mistakes and errors inevitably are made, opportunities arise and even specialized practices can be built around straightening out messes companies have made of their books.

Pricing

Hourly rates range from $10 to $60 an hour, according to a 1997 survey of self-employed freelancers by the The American Institute of Professional Bookkeepers. Locale influences rates, but generally higher fees are obtainable for preparing a company's financial statements (balance sheet, income statement, profit and loss), analyzing the balance sheet, and tax preparation, particularly corporate tax returns. Some bookkeepers can also charge for travel time to clients' offices.

Some bookkeeping services charge a flat fee per month rather than an hourly fee. The fees range from $150 to $600 for small businesses, depending on the complexity of their accounts and the number of checks they write per month.

Potential Earnings

Typical Annual Gross Revenues: $48,000, based on working 1,500 hours a year (or 30 billable hours a week) at $32 an hour, the average rate for full-time self-employed bookkeepers in 1997. Some bookkeepers are able to bill more hours per week if they have steady clients.

Overhead: low (20 percent or less).

Best Home Businesses Estimate of Market Potential

Growing at the rate of several new businesses every minute, the demand for bookkeeping services is fed by nearly thirty million small businesses of fewer than one hundred employees. In addition, not-for-profit organizations add to this demand.

Best Ways to Get Business

- Networking with business and trade organizations such as the chamber of commerce.

- Focused advertising and promotional efforts to retail stores and services within a twenty- to thirty-minute drive from your home.

- Your own personal contacts with small businesses in your community.

- Advertising in the Yellow Pages.

- Have your own Web site with meta tags and links that will direct people to your site.

- Obtaining overload or referral business from CPA firms, other bookkeeping firms, and financial planners.

- Making speeches and offering workshops on financial topics.

Related Business

Bill-Paying Service

Many people need or want help taking care of their finances. That's what a bill-paying service provides. You create a budget for each client and then pay bills, balance the checkbook, handle filing and may also help with medical claims. Bill-paying services may be an add-on service to another business, such as bookkeeping, medical claims assistance or professional organizing. This field has grown to have its own association, which is listed under Organizations below. A business opportunity is available from SBS, 2700 Braselton Highway, Suite 10293, Dacula, GA 30019; (770) 995-9740.

First Steps

If you have no prior background in bookkeeping, you can learn this skill from community-college courses, books, or on-the-job experience. If you have a bookkeeping background already, your need is to develop clients. If you have no business experience, you can consider purchasing a franchise from companies such as ABS Systems, Comprehensive Business Services, General Business Services and Padgett Business Services. However, such franchises are expensive, and people in the field question whether a franchise is necessary to get started as a bookkeeper.

Where to Turn for Information and Help

ORGANIZATIONS

AMERICAN ASSOCIATION OF DAILY MONEY MANAGERS, INC., P.O. Box 8857, Gaithersburg, MD 20898; (301) 593-5462. Web site: *www.aadmm.com*

THE AMERICAN INSTITUTE OF PROFESSIONAL BOOKKEEPERS, 6001 Montrose Road, Suite 207, Rockville, MD 20852; (800) 622-0121; fax (800) 541-0066. Current membership includes 40,000 employed, part-time, and independent bookkeepers. Membership is currently $39 per year. Benefits include reports and *The General Ledger*, a monthly newsletter containing updates about tax laws and other key information, a toll-free telephone hotline to get expert answers to questions, free federal and state tax forms, and discounts on Airborne Express delivery. The Web site, *www.aipb.com*, will offer links to tax offices and past issues of journals.

BOOKS

Bookkeeping on Your Home-Based PC, Linda Stern, New York: Windcrest/McGraw-Hill, 1993. (Out-of-print, but worthwhile if you can obtain it.)

The Encyclopedia of Journal Entries. Published by the American Institute of Professional Bookkeepers. All entries conform to FASB, APB, and other GAAP standards. $77.

Keeping the Books: Basic Record Keeping and Accounting for the Small Business, Linda Pinson and Jerry Jinnett, Dover, NH: Upstart Press, 1998. ISBN: 1574101072.

Small Business Accounting Handbook, Small Business Association Publications, Box 15434, Fort Worth, TX 76119. The SBA also has many other free or low-cost publications, such as *Keeping Records for Small Business* and *A Handbook of Small Business Finance*. Check its Web site (*www.sbaonline.sba.gov*) or write for a list of publications.

MAGAZINES AND NEWSLETTERS

Journal of Accounting, Taxation, and Finance for Business. The American Institute of Professional Bookkeepers, 6001 Montrose Road, Suite 207, Rockville, MD 20852; (800) 622-0121. Four quarterly issues of approximately ninety pages each. $69 a year.

Practical Accountant. Faulkner & Gray, 11 Penn Plaza, 17th Floor, New York, NY 10001; (212) 967-7000.

GOVERNMENT RESOURCES

THE INTERNAL REVENUE SERVICE offers seminars on federal taxes. State and municipal tax offices are a source for information about rules for sales taxes and local income taxes.

COURSES

THE AMERICAN INSTITUTE OF PROFESSIONAL BOOKKEEPERS offers self-teaching courses on basic bookkeeping, payroll, adjusting entries, depreciation, inventory, financial-statement analysis, completing the four basic business tax returns, and more. (800) 622-0121. Web site: *www.aipb.com*

McGRAW-HILL'S NRI SCHOOLS offer a course in bookkeeping and accounting. McGraw-Hill Continuing Education Center, 4401 Connecticut Avenue, N.W., Washington, DC 20008; (202) 244-1600. Web site: *www.mhccc.com*

UNITED STATES DEPARTMENT OF AGRICULTURE GRADUATE SCHOOL offers reasonably priced correspondence courses in accounting. Write for a catalogue: Correspondence Programs, Graduate School, USDA AG 14th and Independence S.W., Room 1112S, Washington, DC 20250; (888) 744-GRAD. Or call to speak with a counselor at (202) 314-3670. Web site: *http://grad.usda.gov*

Business Broker

Business brokers bring together a client who wants to sell a business with someone who wants to buy a business. They generally focus on businesses with a price of under $1,000,000, exclusive of any real estate the business owns. Business brokers function much like real estate brokers; in fact, in over twenty states, business brokers are required to have a real estate license; some states require a business broker's license as well.

Business brokerage is a growing home-based business. According to the International Business Brokers' Association, 40 percent of its 700 members in the U.S. are one-person businesses and 200 out of the 700 are specializing in merger and acquisition work. The U.S. Department of Commerce estimates that there are sixteen to eighteen million businesses in this country and that 20 percent change hands every year.

Fortunately, 70 percent of these are priced under $500,000, so there are plenty of opportunities for business brokers. One reason for the high turnover of businesses, according to *Inc.* magazine, is that more people prefer to buy an ongoing business because failure rates for businesses that are bought are lower than those for businesses started from scratch or even franchises.

Because they often operate under real estate laws, brokers must represent one side or the other. Ninety-nine percent of business brokers choose to represent those who are selling a business. The most successful home-based brokers specialize in selling a particular size or type of business, such as restaurants, bowling centers, medical practices, or businesses in a particular geographic area.

Home-based business brokers can make a profit with a relatively small number of sales per year. Whereas a small two-to-three-person brokerage might need to make twenty sales annually in order to stay afloat, a home-based solo broker probably can manage quite well with between ten and twenty sales per year because of lower operating expenses. However, Julie Johnson, Vice President of Venture Resource, Business Brokers, states, "Making good money as a general business brokerage is a matter of numbers, meaning lots of listings. This is because only 25 to 30 percent of listings will actually sell."

Finding people who want to buy a business is not difficult. Brokers tell us that advertising in the business-opportunities sections of newspapers draws six to twelve inquiries per ad. Nine out of ten people who buy businesses are first-time buyers. Tom West, owner of the Business Brokerage Press, says business brokers spend about 40 percent of their business time out of the office calling on sellers to get listings; 40 percent dealing with buyers; 10 percent working with outside professionals such as attorneys and bankers; and 10 percent doing analysis.

A growing niche in business brokering comprises those specializing in mergers and acquisitions (M&A). In fact, Julie Johnson states, "Someone doing mergers and acquisitions can more easily make it as a sole practitioner than general business brokers because of the volume of listings needed."

Knowledge and Skills You Need to Have

- Because of the complexity of brokerage transactions and the significant assets at stake, it is essential for a business broker to have a solid business and legal grounding. Brokers need to have the ability to read and evaluate financial reports such as profit-and-loss statements to be able to represent their clients honestly and effectively. You also need to be familiar with the legal aspects of selling a business.

- This business requires considerable perseverance and patience to get listings and to find the right match between buyers and sellers. While some sales happen quickly, most take several months or even a year between getting the listing and closing a sale.

- Brokers must have good sales skills. First you must convince an owner to sell and have you represent him or her. Then you must sell buyers on the merits of the businesses you represent.

- A broker needs to have good communication and interpersonal skills to build a strong relationship with both buyers and sellers.

You must be able to listen and empathize in order to structure deals that are satisfactory to both parties. And you must be able to negotiate successfully with buyers, attorneys, accountants, and sellers.

- You should have a conference area or separate office space in your home for meeting with people who are interested in the businesses you represent.

- A real estate broker's license is currently required to sell a business (or to get paid for selling one) in the following states: Alaska, Arizona, California, Colorado, Florida, Georgia, Idaho, Iowa, Kentucky, Michigan, Minnesota, Nebraska, Nevada, Oregon, South Carolina, South Dakota, Texas, Utah, Washington, and Wisconsin. However, there is always change, so you should check with your state's real estate commission and with other brokers in your area.

- Someone specializing in M&A must be more sophisticated in business financial transactions and be able to hold one's own in dealing with attorneys, accountants, and sophisticated sellers. However, two or three transactions a year will provide $600,000 to a million a year.

Start-up Costs	Low	High
Computer	$ 1,000	$ 3,000
Accounting software and software for evaluating businesses	$ 50	$ 350
High resolution printer	$ 1,000	$ 2,500
High resolution scanner	$ 600	$ 800
Fax or multi-functional	$ 150	$ 600
Digital camera	$ 600	$ 2,500
Telephone system with two lines with "hold" and "trip" features to handle many calls. A good answering service is necessary. You need to have a live person answering your phone. To get premium service, voluntarily pay the answering service $50 more a month.	$ 1,200	$ 2,500
Initial marketing budget	$ 1,000	$ 5,000
Total	$ 5,600	$ 17,250

Advantages

- Being able to serve your clients well is easy because buyers will come to you. Brokers fail only if they don't get listings.

- The costs of starting this business are minimal and expenses are low.

- You are like a matchmaker. When you do your job well, everyone is happy.

- Fees are high; overhead is low.

- There's little to lose if this business isn't right for you; you should know this within six months. Says Julie Johnson, "While an easy entry business, it's an easy exit business."

Disadvantages

- Getting listings is just plain hard work.

- You don't make any money until the sale is complete.

- It takes three to six months to make your first sale requiring patience and persistence.

Pricing

Ten to twelve percent of a business's selling price, with a $10,000 minimum, is a standard fee.

Potential Earnings

Typical Annual Gross Revenues: $100,000, based on one sale a month for ten months of the year at a minimum fee of $10,000 each. Some brokers earn much, much more. As Tom West says, "With a $10,000 minimum, it's all up to you."

Overhead: low (20 percent or less).

Best Home Businesses Estimate of Market Potential

The growing numbers of small businesses should translate into a demand for business brokers, though the Internet is playing an increasing role in enabling buyers and sellers to find one another without the assistance of a broker.

Best Ways to Get Business

- Getting to know people by personally going up and down the street introducing yourself and talking with business owners. This is a lower-key approach than soliciting listings by phone or mail.

- Networking in organizations of business owners or, if you're specializing in an industry, participating in a trade association.

- Contacting business owners directly by phone—telemarketing.

- Using direct mail. You can rent lists through mailing-list brokers or obtain them directly on the Web.

- Getting referrals from lawyers, accountants, and bankers.

- Renting lists of names of franchises and private companies for sale all over the country.

- Have your own Web site with meta tags and links that will direct people to your site.

First Steps

- If a real estate broker license is required in your state, contact the state agency responsible for licensing realtors for the procedures necessary to become licensed.

- To gain experience in this business, you might begin by working for an established broker, but be aware if you do this you may be required to sign a noncompete agreement.

- If you have no experience with analyzing financial statements, take a class in basic business finance through a community-college class or one of the courses offered by one of the associations in this field.

- Talk with other business brokers. Decide whether you are going to specialize. To succeed in a large metropolitan area, you will probably need to specialize in a type of business, such as bowling alleys, car dealerships, restaurants, printing companies, or restaurants.

Where to Turn for Information and Help

ORGANIZATIONS

INSTITUTE OF CERTIFIED BUSINESS COUNSELORS, 3485 West First Avenue, Eugene, OR 97402; (541) 345-8064. The Web site (*www.nvst.com*) has a Business Valuation Forum.

INTERNATIONAL BUSINESS BROKERS ASSOCIATION, 11250 Roger Bacon Drive, Suite 8, Reston, VA 20190; (703) 437-7464; fax: (703) 435-4390. It offers a certification program and two conferences a year with educational courses including a track for beginners in the field. Web site: *www.ibba.org*. Lists members in a database with links to their sites and lists local and regional organizations. A related site endorsed by the association is *www.bizquest.com*.

BOOKS

A Basic Guide for Valuing a Company, Wilbur M. Yegge, John Wiley & Sons, 1996. ISBN: 0471149454

Business Reference Guide, updated annually. Contains court cases, rent guidelines, price comparisons, pricing rules, and other valuable information. Business Brokerage Press. Box 247, Concord, MA 01742; (978) 369-5254; Web site: *www.businessbrokeragepress.com*

Business Brokerage: Managing for Profit, Tom West. John Wiley. Business Brokerage Press.

Handbook of Business Valuation, Thomas L. West and Jeffrey D. Jones, John Wiley & Sons, 1992. ISBN: 0471537551.

Mergers and Acquistions Handbook of Small & Mid-Sized Companies, Thomas L. West and Jeffrey D. Jones, John Wiley & Sons, 1997. ISBN: 0471133302.

The Small Business Valuation Book, Lawrence W. Tuller, Bob Adams, Inc., 1994. ISBN: 1558503552.

Valuing a Business: The Analysis and Appraisal of Closely Held Companies, Shannon P. Pratt, Robert F. Reilly, Robert P. Schweihs, Irwin Professional Publications, 1995. ISBN: 1556239718.

OTHER PUBLICATIONS

The Business Brokerage Press offers many marketing materials for those in the business brokerage field:

Today's Business Scene. Newsletter for distribution in broker's name.

The Professionals Information Package for Sellers

The Professionals Information Package for Buyers

NEWSLETTERS

The Business Broker (monthly)

M&A Today (monthly)

MANUALS

Tom West's Complete Guide to Business Brokerage

VIDEO AND AUDIO PROGRAMS

The Dynamics of Business Brokerage (video)

Taped conversations with successful business brokers (audio)

SOFTWARE

BBPricer for 1998. Available from Business Brokerage Press.

Wiley-ValuSource, 7222 Commerce Center Drive, Suite 210, Colorado Springs, CO 80919; (800) 825-8763. Offers a variety of accounting and taxation software products including *Value Express* for businesses under $300,000 and *ValuSource Pro* for larger businesses. Web site: *www.wiley.com*

REFERRAL SERVICES FOR FINDING BUYERS AND SELLERS

FRANCHISE BROKER NETWORK, 3617A Silverside Road, Wilmington, DE 19810; (302) 478-0200.

NATION-LIST, INC., 5310 DTC Parkway, Suite H, Greenwood Village, CO 80111; (800) 525-9559; (303) 741-9680. Web site: *www.nationlist.com*

Business Network Organizer

A business network organizer solves two of the most common problems small-business owners have. First is their need to get business. Seventy per cent of small business owners say getting enough customers is their #1 challenge. Second is finding time to exchange information with other small-business owners in their community. A network organizer sets up groups of small-business owners to meet regularly, usually weekly, in order to give one another business referrals and to help one another get business. Each group or club has only one person from any particular business or profession, so there's no competition among the members of the group. Such networking organizations are a structured way for professionals and business owners to refer clients and customers to one another.

Also called word-of-mouth marketing, getting business through referrals from other people has always been a common practice. Traditional service and fraternal organizations such as Rotary, Eagles, Elks, Lions, and Moose have long served as indirect and informal ways of obtaining referrals. Many of today's small-business owners, however, are seeking a more focused approach to getting referrals by joining what are referred to as leads clubs or networking groups. The sole purpose of these groups is to enable members to give and get referrals.

That's where the business network organizer steps in. Rather than people joining loose networking groups that often turn into coffee klatches and social gatherings, the networking organizer helps business owners form a more formal group that follows specific procedures to get business from one another and from outside the group. Members pay a fee to the organizer who conducts their meetings, establishes procedures, and ensures that the group is networking smoothly.

There are two ways to become a network organizer: start one or more groups yourself or purchase a franchise from one of the companies already established that teaches you how to run your business. For example, one franchise organization, Business Network Intl., founded in 1985 by Ivan Misner, Ph.D., offers a two-hundred-page manual for network organizers to learn the business along with a solid training program and direct experience.

While some critics believe that networking is a fad, Misner says, "Networking has proven to be as much of a fad as having a sale." In fact, Tom

Peters, coauthor of *In Search of Excellence* and *Thriving on Chaos,* advises small businesses to devote 75 percent of their marketing time and money to developing a structured word-of-mouth network. Networking is, as it always has been, the most reliable and cost-effective way for a small business to make sure that it has business.

Knowledge and Skills You Need to Have

- You need to have an outgoing personality.

- You need to be comfortable speaking in front of groups and able to speak well extemporaneously.

- You must be able to motivate, lead, and educate people in the skill of networking.

- You have to be able to set up and run an organization.

Advantages

- The market for networking organizations is expanding.

- Running a networking group provides an excellent opportunity to market another business or profession you may have.

- You may make valuable contacts and friends throughout the business community.

Disadvantages

- Unless you run multiple chapters, a networking organization will not provide a full-time income. But it can be a route to expanding another business.

- Networking means constantly attending early-morning meetings.

- Members who don't use what the organization teaches about effective networking techniques may blame you or the organization for not providing them with enough business leads.

Start-up Costs*	Low	High
Computer with software	$ 1,500	$ 3,000
Printer	$ 300	$ 800
or		
Multi-function printer/fax/scanner/copier	$ 150	$ 800
Cell phone	$ 75	$ 200
Office furniture	$ 400	$ 1,000
Initial marketing budget	$ 1,000	$ 5,000
Total	$ 3,425	$ 10,800

*The above figures are for starting your own business; add franchise fees if you decide to purchase a franchise.

Pricing

Members pay from $200 to $1,500 per year to be in your groups.

Potential Earnings

Most new organizers run only a few groups in their first one or two years as they build up their own network of clients. Projected earnings for four groups with 20 members in each who pay $250 per year are $16,000.

With experience and time, a leader can run 10 to 20 groups, each with 25 or more members. Projected earnings for a leader running 20 groups, each with 25 members paying $250 per year, are $125,000.

Overhead: high (over 40 percent: includes room rentals, promotional materials, and mailings).

Best Home Businesses Estimate of Market Potential

As trend forecaster John Naisbitt predicted, we have seen a relationship between the growth of high tech and high touch. Business networking has grown dramatically right along with the dramatic use of technology in business. As the use of technology continues to expand, we expect to see a continuing growth in the role of business networking.

The Best Ways to Get Business

- Personal contacts (your own word of mouth, of course).

- Referrals from current group members.

- Attending and exhibiting at local trade shows.

- Using direct-mail advertising to small businesses and professionals.

- Have your own Web site with meta tags and links that will direct people to your site.

FRANCHISES

Business Network International (BNI). 199 South Monte Vista Avenue, Suite 6, San Dimas, CA 91773; (800) 825-8286 (for southern California, call 909-305-1818); Web site: *www.bni.com*. In business since 1985, Business Network Intl. has over 300 chapters in twenty-five states at the time of this writing. To become a franchisee, you must begin as a regional director for six months, which is a paid position giving you the chance to learn the ropes and see if you enjoy the business. The franchise fee includes several days of on-site training and a two-hundred-page operating manual. If your chapter does well and the relationship is mutually satisfactory, there is an opportunity to franchise. The fee is $5,000.

First Steps

If you've had experience networking and getting business through word of-mouth marketing, develop procedures for running your network. Then begin recruiting a membership. Don't start a networking group until you have at least twenty paid members. To recruit members, invite people to free meetings at which you describe the organization and demonstrate the process; then follow up by phone with those who are seriously interested. Don't begin a second chapter until your first one is thriving.

If you have had no experience with networking, your first step should be to join a network or two and become familiar with what works and what doesn't. You may wish to consider one of the franchise opportunities listed above that can accelerate getting your business off the ground.

Where to Turn for Information and Help

BOOKS

How to Work a Room, Susan Rowane, Warner Books, 1989. ISBN: 0446390658.

Power Schmoozing: The New Etiquette for Social and Business Success, Terry Mandell, McGraw-Hill, 1996. ISBN: 0070398879.

The World's Best Known Marketing Secret: Building Your Business with Word-of-Mouth Marketing, Ivan Misner, Austin, Texas: Bard Productions. Available from BNI Products; (800) 688-9394.

NATIONAL REFERRAL ORGANIZATIONS

BUSINESS NETWORK INTERNATIONAL, described above under Franchises, updates nationwide referral groups you can join. (800) 825-8286; s. Calif. (909) 305-1818. Web site: *www.bni.com*

LEADS, P.O. Box 279, Carlsbad, CA 92018; (800) 783-3761; (760) 434-3761. Web site: *www.leadsclub.com*

LeTip INTERNATIONAL, INC., P.O. Box 178130, San Diego, CA 92117; (800) 255-3847; fax: (619) 490-2744. Web site: *www.letip.com*

THE NATIONAL ASSOCIATION OF WOMEN BUSINESS OWNERS, 1100 Wayne Ave., Suite 83D, Silver Spring, MD 20910; (301) 608-2590. Web site: *www.nawbo.org*

EXPANDING REGIONAL ORGANIZATIONS

CONSUMER BUSINESS NETWORK, 4320 Campus, Suite 160, Newport Beach, CA 92660, (714) 550-4785. Web site: *cbni.org*

LET'S TALK BUSINESS NETWORK, 54 West 39th, 12th Floor, New York, NY 10018; (212)742-1553. Web site: *www.ltbn.com*

WOMEN'S REFERRAL SERVICE AND WOMEN'S YELLOW PAGES, 13601 Ventura Boulevard #221, Sherman Oaks, CA 91423; (818) 995-6646. Web site: *www.wypwrs.com*

Business Plan Writer

Prevailing wisdom is that anyone who's starting a business should write a business plan. In reality, however, unless a business needs outside financing, most new business owners don't have a written business plan despite the fact research shows that those with a good business plan increase their likelihood of success. The primary reason most people don't develop a formal business plan is simple; they don't know how to write one. But once the business grows to the point of seeking loans, attracting investors, getting acquired, or franchising, a business plan becomes a must. At that point the business can't grow further without a plan, so that's when an owner will most likely turn to a business plan writer. Thus, best locales for business plan writers are those that have lots of businesses starting up or expanding.

Business plan writers function in one of two ways. Some are like Linda Elkins of Maryland who works mostly with start-ups and businesses seeking second-round financing and told us, "You are basically a translator. You listen to your client's ideas, review their financial data and the other information they have gathered, and then put this information into the clearest, most direct format possible."

Others like Jane Deuser, who specializes in working with companies seeking venture capital, find that many investors require that management itself put together the business plan. So Jane helps her clients develop their business plans as a group exercise in the context of team-building. This gives managers a sense of ownership of the plan and creates a tighter working team in the process.

Sometimes the business plan writer's job is also to point out additional information the client needs to gather in order to formulate a good plan. Software programs make writing business plans easier and quicker, and gives them a more professional appearance. Such programs also make it easy to examine and present alternative scenarios for a business, using spreadsheets and what-if scenarios. But as Marcia Layton, a business plan writer in Rochester, New York, states, "Owning the software does not make you a business plan writer; if it were that easy, businesses wouldn't need you either." You also need to have a good sense of business and finance and be able to work with your clients to help them gather information on markets, sales potential, and income projections. "All in all," says Marcia, "it's an exciting field" that nevertheless demands a combination of writing skill, business expertise, and creativity.

Knowledge and Skills You Need to Have

- You need to have a general business background (accounting, bookkeeping, and marketing) and familiarity with financial statements, business jargon, and your local business community. While not needing to be an accountant, you need to be able to assess the financial viability of an enterprise.

- You should have already written a few business plans so you know how to put one together and what issues are most important to owners and/or financing sources. Jane Deuser of Deuser Clarkson Business Development recommends that you should have those plans critiqued by persons such as bank lending officers or merchant bankers.

- You need to have the ability to see a business situation from the viewpoint both of the owners and of potential funding sources.

- Good business-writing, grammar, and organizational skills are required.

- You need the ability to present yourself professionally and credibly as an expert who can be relied upon.

- You need the ability to motivate and inspire cooperation from your clients.

Start-up Costs	Low	High
Computer (notebook preferred)	$ 2,000	$ 4,000
Printer (can be portable)	$ 300	$ 800
Fax or multi-functional machine	$ 150	$ 600
Office furniture, especially an ergonomic chair	$ 400	$ 1,000
Initial marketing budget	$ 2,000	$ 5,000
Cost of incorporating or forming a limited liability company*	$ 500	$ 2,000
Total	$ 5,350	$ 13,400

* Because liability is possible for misrepresentations in a plan, it's best to form a legal entity that will protect you personally. In a similar vein, it's wise not to list yourself as the author of a business plan.

Advantages

- The work is challenging and varied. Each business situation is different.

- You have the opportunity to learn about new people and new business ideas.

- It can be highly rewarding to assist others in achieving success.

- If you take an equity interest in a client's business as part of your fee, you have the potential to strike it rich.

Disadvantages

- Business start-ups and expansions are sensitive to economic cycles, so your client base may fluctuate, and you may be subject to feast-or-famine cycles.

- Because you are often working with new or changing businesses, you may encounter clients who have collection or legal problems.

- You must continuously market your services to find new clients; once you work with a company to write their plan, it does not usually generate repeat business for several years.

Pricing

Fees range from $2,500 to $5,000 for each business plan, depending on the time it takes to write it (generally two to four weeks) and the amount of research you may need to obtain financial data, analyze the competition, and develop sample marketing plans.

Proven consultants can charge as much as $25,000 working on a major plan for a corporation seeking new financing. Many writers charge a flat fee such as $5,000 to work with a company until the client is satisfied.

Business plan writers can also get business editing and rewriting business plans already developed by a client. Fees for this kind of work may be based on an hourly rate such as $100 per hour or a flat fee such as $500 to review and edit a business plan.

Potential Earnings

Typical Annual Gross Revenues: $20,000 to $100,000. An example is a writer who creates ten plans per year at an average of $5,000 each, plus edits ten plans at $500 each, generating $55,000 in gross revenues.

Overhead: low (20 percent or less).

Best Home Businesses Estimate of Market Potential

Many of the well over 500,000 new small businesses that form each year will expand. As they do, they require business plans for obtaining loans and capital. While business-plan software is fully able to help someone develop a business plan for his or her own use, experience suggests that sophisticated investors and lenders expect business plans that are more individualized. Increasingly, investors want to be assured that the plan is actually developed by the entrepreneurs being funded. In situations like this, the role of the professional business plan writer is to train and coach his or her clients.

Best Ways to Get Business

- Teaching courses at local colleges and extension schools in writing business plans and small-business development. Your students are likely to be entrepreneurs who may hire you to help them write their plans.

- Networking through personal contacts at organizations such as trade shows and business associations for those industries or fields in which you have experience. You should join at least two organizations and become active in both.

- Making contacts with bankers, lawyers, venture capitalists, and other gatekeepers at universities or organizations such as Small Business Development Centers that might run new-business incubator workshops, offer mentor programs, or have an entrepreneurship center.

- Writing articles in the local press about the value of business plans. Advertising in local business newsletters and getting publicity about your work in the business media in your area.

- Having your own Web site with useful information that falls short of giving away your outline.

- Specialize in one or a few industries where you will have in-depth knowledge and contacts.

- Get listed on sites such as *www.brs-inc.com* that list business-planning consultants.

First Steps

If you have some business background, begin by doing a few plans without fee to gain experience and develop a portfolio of work to show to prospective clients.

- Read and study business-planning guides and learn to use business-planning and spreadsheet software. Caveat: Buying a business-planning software package with prewritten templates does not automatically transform you into a business-plan writer. You need to custom-tailor each plan you write to your clients and not produce a "plan in a can."

- Even with your first paying jobs, get agreements in writing that cover rewriting caused by changed orders and amendments.

Where to Turn for Information and Help

BOOKS

Business Plans for Dummies, Paul Tiffany, Steven Peterson, IDG Books, 1997. ISBN: 1568848684.

The Complete Book of Business Plans: Simple Steps to Writing a Powerful Business Plan, Joseph A. Covello, Brian J. Hazelgren, Sourcebooks, Inc., 1995. ISBN: 0942061411.

Model Business Plans for Product Businesses, New York: John Wiley & Sons, 1995. ISBN: 0471030287.

Model Business Plans for Service Businesses, William A. Cohen, Ph.D., New York: John Wiley, 1995. ISBN: 0471030376.

The One Page Business Plan, Jim Horan, Rent.aCFO℠, 5917 Kipling Drive, El Sobrante, CA 94803; (510) 222-0805. Web site: *www.rentacfo.com*

The Successful Business Plan: Secrets & Strategies, Rhonda M. Abrams, Oasis Press, 1993. ISBN: 1555711944.

COURSES

Many colleges, universities, and extension schools offer courses in writing business plans. These are targeted to entrepreneurs starting a business but are equally useful to the person starting a business-plan-writing business. Other courses include:

AMERICAN WOMAN'S ECONOMIC DEVELOPMENT CORPORATION offers a course for women on how to put together a successful business plan; 71 Vanderbilt Avenue, Suite 320, New York, NY 10169; (212) 692-9100.

GOVERNMENT RESOURCES

Small Business Development Centers are located throughout the United States. They are affiliated with educational institutions and sometimes chambers of commerce. The centers tend to specialize in particular types or sizes of small business. Contact the nearest office of the Small Business Administration for the Small Business Development Centers in your area.

SOFTWARE

Software such as the following packages can take you and your clients step-by-step through developing a business plan.

BizPlan Builder, Jian Tools for Sales, 1975 West El Camino Real, Suite 301, Mountainview, CA 94040; (800) 346-5426; (415) 941-9191. Web site: *www.jian.com*

Business Plan, Ronstadt's Financials for Windows is part of a family of software by Lord Publishing that's available for making financial projections. It comes in a professional as well as a standard version. The series includes *Venture Feasibility Plan* and *Database of Venture Capital and Funding Sources* for locating funding. There's a downloadable demo on the Lord Web site: *www.lordpublishing.com.* Or contact Lord Publishing at 32325 Pacific Coast Highway, Laguna Beach, CA 92677; (800) 525-5673; fax: (949) 499-4580.

Business Plan Pro, Palo Alto Software, 144 East 14th Avenue, Eugene, OR 97401; (800) 229-7526. Palo Alto also publishes *Marketing Plus* software for developing a marketing plan and *Hurdle: The Book on Business Planning,* by Tim Berry. Web site: *www.palo-alto.com*

PlanWrite, Business Resource Software, Inc., 2013 Wells Branch Pkwy #305, Austin, Texas 78728; (800) 423-1228. Web site: *www.brs-inc.com*

 Caterer

What's a party or any important event without good food? Everyone loves good food and eating is central to most social occasions. That's what makes catering such an attractive career. Also, becoming a caterer doesn't require years of training, and you can begin in this business without a large capital investment. What it takes to be successful, though is a combination of cooking knowledge, business sense, and people skills.

Another appeal of catering, particularly if you cater social events, is that you can launch your business in your spare time, since most special events take place in the evenings or on weekends. Starting the business on a part-time basis gives you considerable flexibility and lets you "test-market" your product with a minimum of risk. Meanwhile you can earn profits ranging generally between 10 and 20 percent of the price of the event.

Most catering services begin at home. Because food safety is such a growing consumer concern, however, in many cities caterers must meet a variety of stringent governmental requirements that have been instituted to regulate food preparation. Contending with these regulations make operating a catering service from home more difficult. Therefore, many home-based individuals who want to be in the food-service business but can't meet stiff facility requirements are gravitating to a new specialty, the personal chef. This growing field is described in greater detail as a related business later this profile.

Another increasingly popular aspect of the catering industry is food delivery, especially delivering lunches to offices and corporations. This trend can be attributed to two factors. First, changes in the economy have exerted pressure on workers to spend more hours on the job, so instead of going out for lunch, they're eating at their desks. Second, the tax law creates an incentive for businesses to feed clients and employees in-house (fully tax deductible), instead of dining out (only partially deductible).

Another niche market for caterers is delivering prepared food to people who are homebound. Relatives of senior citizens are likely to be the source of payment for this service. As the number of seniors increases and outpaces government and nonprofit programs, this kind of service is likely to grow.

Yet another market for delivering specially prepared food is people who aren't homebound but want meals prepared according to the guidelines of specific diets (such as macrobiotic, the Zone, blood-type, or that of a particular ethnic cuisine) that may not be available in conveniently located restaurants. Also, food made from all organically grown ingredients appeals to health-conscious individuals even if it is not prepared pursuant to a specific dietary regimen.

While many home-based caterers begin by simply whipping up confections in their own kitchens, it's illegal in most states to sell food to the public that has been prepared in a home kitchen. Therefore in calculating your start-up costs, you will need to figure in the cost of renting a commercial kitchen. Renting a kitchen in a church, fire station, 4-H camp, or state park kitchens is an inexpensive way to start, and some states provide incubator kitchens for start-up food businesses. You can cut costs by sharing kitchen rental expenses with other caterers, a practice that is becoming increasingly common. Another alternative, though one that is relatively expensive, is to install a commercial kitchen in your home. This, however, requires zoning that would allow you to have a commercial kitchen as part of your home and the kitchen must pass state and local health code inspection.

Besides social catering and office and home delivery, there are a number of other catering opportunities for home-based entrepreneurs. According to Denise Vivaldo, owner of a food styling and consulting firm and author of *How to Open and Operate a Home-Based Catering Business: An Unabridged Guide,* the possibilities include:

- Preparing private banquets at hotels.

- Furnishing meals to airlines.

- Cooking for parties aboard chartered yachts.

- Supervising supermarket takeout counters.

- Catering for department stores.

- Serving as an executive chef in a company dining room or in someone's home.

Caterers are also in demand on movie and TV sets and at events such as art auctions and charity fund-raisers. Vivaldo suggests getting a foot in the door by offering fancy gourmet specialty cookies or muffins to an established supplier and then building on your reputation. Suzan Schatz of Tulsa specializes in gourmet wedding cakes in the commercial kitchen she created adjacent to her home, and her customers include other caterers. Arlene Breskin in Westchester County, New York, caters from the commercial kitchen she had built in her basement, producing "cookie bouquets." Dinnerworks in Ottawa, Canada, shops for and prepares two weeks of meals for clients in their kitchens.

Since caterers must scrupulously observe health, safety, zoning, product liability, labor, workers' compensation, and other laws and regulations, it makes sense to hire a good attorney at the outset to help you comply with all pertinent government codes. Violations can be more than merely costly; they can put you out of business. You also need to keep detailed records of your income and expenses as well as your inventory of food, equipment, and supplies; your employees; your clients; your jobs; and the like. There are several inexpensive computer programs available that can simplify much of this record keeping, although some caterers prefer to hire a bookkeeper.

Knowledge and Skills You Need to Have

- Although you don't necessarily have to be a gourmet cook, you should have experience cooking for groups and enjoy experimenting with new recipes, preparing food, and planning menus. And it goes without saying that you should find entertaining pleasurable.

- You must be a people person, someone who can get along well with clients, staff, suppliers, bureaucrats, and others and keep them all happy. You need to be pleasant, courteous, and tactful, even when problems develop.

- You should have a manager's mentality, meaning that you are well organized, because catering involves attending to lots of details and costs. Without controlling these, you cannot make a profit or be successful. You also need to know how to write up a good contract for your jobs.

- You need to be assertive enough to market your services actively. It is a competitive business in which getting a regular client is hard and keeping one is tough.

- You must be knowledgeable about sanitation, safe and proper food preparation, and storage techniques. In addition, you need to develop many contacts among suppliers so that you can find top-quality ingredients at good prices.

Start-up Costs	Low	High
Equipment (pots, pans, etc.)*	$ 500	$ 1,000
Portable warmers for keeping food warm	$ 200	$ 500
Insurance	$ 1,000	$ 2,000
Legal and professional fees	$ 1,000	$ 3,000
Kitchen rental†	$ 8,000	$ 12,000
Initial marketing budget	$ 1,000	$ 5,000
Computer	$ 1,000	$ 1,500
Multi-function printer/fax/scanner/copier	$ 150	$ 600
Total‡	**$12,850**	**$ 25,600**

* Dishes can be disposable-ware or rented
† Based on $100 to $150 per day, 2 days per week, 40 weeks per year. Price reflects average rental rates for a major city in mid-1994. Denise Vivaldo recommends that people starting catering businesses cut costs by sharing the rental of a commercial kitchen and using it on different days.
‡ An additional cost may be a van or delivery vehicle.

Advantages

- Cooking is one of the most natural and pleasant experiences for people who enjoy food. You get to do something creative that also makes people happy.

- You can work as much or as little as you like. How much you earn depends in part on how much you choose to work,

- Demand is high and growing. And, as Denise Vivaldo points out, you'll never starve or be unwanted in the kitchen at parties.

Disadvantages

- Successful catering takes a tremendous amount of work and careful long-range planning. Success doesn't come quickly, and competition has been increasing over the past ten years. Hospitals, schools, and churches have gotten into this business. The highest rate of failure among new businesses is among people involved in restaurants and other food businesses.

- Many jobs require that you spend time meeting with clients to learn about their needs, and then you must prepare a competitive bid or proposal, without a guarantee that you will get the contract.

- Social catering involves working evenings and weekends, which takes away from personal/family time. Some markets for catering are seasonal, such as parties, which occur mostly in November and December. However, weddings have become less seasonal.

- Besides the menu planning and cooking, you also have to do serving and cleanup, unless you hire people to do those things for you, which means you need to find excellent help. The success of your events depends in large part on other people, including your staff such as servers or bartenders.

- Health department requirements, licenses, certification and standards for such things as dishwashing and transportation of food have become more stringent as a result of concern over food-born illness.

Pricing

Caterers try to price events so that food costs run between 28 percent and 35 percent of the total fee. In other words, as a general rule, you should charge about three to four times what you pay for food to cover your time and profit. For example, a sandwich costing you $1.50 is priced at $5.25; a dinner costing $8 is priced at $28 per person.

But every job is different. Preparation time, the number of guests, the elaborateness of the menu and the decor all should figure into your pricing calculations. Remember, too, that there are other costs that you may or may not want to charge separately for: china, silver, linens, glasses, tables, chairs, serving staff. Some caterers add a built-in gratuity. The goal is to factor in all your costs for food, labor (including your own), overhead, incidentals, and leave yourself some profit. When you are just starting out, it is helpful to find out what your competition charges so you don't stray too far from the norm.

Potential Earnings

Typical Annual Gross Revenues: $30,000 to $50,000 for a home-based caterer averaging $500 to $1,000 per week. Energetic caterers with extensive networks of contacts can make up to $70,000 to $80,000, but they have a reputation and steady list of clients, which takes years to develop.

Overhead: High, greater than 30 or 40 percent.

Best Home Businesses Estimate of Market Potential

Catering, though subject to fluctuations of the economy, will grow particularly in parts of the U.S. experiencing substantial population and economic growth. Because of regulation, however, a better bet for people with a love for preparing food may be personal chefing.

Best Ways to Get Business

- Networking among wedding planners, bakeries, bridal shops, florists, cooking stores, and others who might be willing to refer clients to you.

- Contact business associations and your local chamber of commerce to get a list of professional associations in your community with whom you can make contact to discuss your services.

- Leave business cards and sample menus at churches, synagogues, reception halls, and country clubs.

- Send press kits to newspapers and radio and television stations.

- Write articles for the food sections of local papers or give speeches to civic and business groups.

- Send out menu postcards, preferably once a month, to previous and prospective clients.

- Volunteer your catering services to a charity to develop some word-of-mouth business.

- Have your own Web site, which can be your company brochure.

First Steps

- If you don't have experience in the field, Chicago caterer Larry Osborn recommends getting a part-time job even as a waiter or waitress with a caterer to learn the business. When you're ready to step out on your own, begin by volunteering to do a couple of parties to get exposure and to see if you like the business and are any good at it. You might organize an event for your child's school, a local scouting group, a sports team, or for friends or neighbors.

- Network within your community to learn about the potential need for your services. Do "informational" interviews with your own colleagues, businesses, and companies to see if they are interested in a new catering service. And network through professional organizations (see below).

- Because there may be a wealth of other caterers in your area, you'll need to identify what distinguishes your service from others right from the start. Consider such factors as type of menu items, cost, plate presentation, linens, appetizing appearance, and special garnishes. Be prepared to send a compelling proposal to each prospective client and then follow-up quickly. Always ask for feedback.

Related Business

Personal Chef

Twelve years ago Susan Titcomb was a burned-out restaurant chef in San Diego. To humor her friends she began cooking dinners for them in their kitchens. One year later she and her husband David MacKay opened the first personal chef service, Personally Yours®. It was wildly successful and led the way to an entirely new industry. Today chefs, cooks, caterers and others with a background in the food service world are plying their skills in people's home as personal chefs. This rapidly growing segment of the home meal replacement market generates over $50 million in revenues each year and is projected to reach over $100 million by the year 2000.

The United States Personal Chef Association, founded by Titcomb and MacKay in 1991, has grown to over 1,800 members including 250 Certified Personal Chefs. Experiencing less stress than working in a restaurant kitchen, the personal chef provides the following services:

- Customized menus, including personalized menus.

- Complete grocery shopping.

- Meal preparation in the customer's home.

- A wide variety of choices for fresh and healthy meals.

To become successful as a personal chef, Titcomb and MacKay recommend having a business plan, reviewing and testing many recipes, finding out about local food service regulations, and developing a sound marketing plan that will attract long-term customers. The USPCA helps over 400 new personal chef services get established every year. They offer a comprehensive training manual for becoming a personal chef. It includes recipes, a marketing plan, and step-by-step guidelines for being up and running in 30 days (see resources, below). Income projections: $200 a day for 6 to 8 hours of work.

Where to Turn for Information and Help

ORGANIZATIONS

AMERICAN CULINARY FEDERATION, 10 San Bartola Drive, St. Augustine, FL 32086; (904) 824-4468. Offers accreditation to experienced chefs.

AMERICAN INSTITUTE OF WINE AND FOOD, 1550 Bryant Street, 7th Floor, San Francisco, CA 94103; (800) 274-AIWF; (415) 255-3000. A national nonprofit organization founded by Julia Child, Robert Mondavi, and others. Holds monthly meetings and periodic fund-raisers. Local chapters in many cities. Web site: *www.aiwf.org*

INTERNATIONAL ASSOCIATION OF CULINARY PROFESSIONALS, 304 W. Liberty Street, Suite 201, Louisville, KY 40202; (502) 583-3783. Organization of teachers, cooking-school owners, caterers, food writers, chefs, radio and television cooking personalities, food writers, cookbook authors and editors, publishers, restaurateurs, and food stylists. Web site: *http://iacp-online.org*

NATIONAL ASSOCIATION OF CATERING EXECUTIVES (NACE). Funds the Catering Research Institute, which helps caterers develop menus and themes. 60 Revere Drive, Suite 500, Northbrook, IL 60062; (847) 480-9080. Web site: *www.nace.net*

THE NATIONAL RESTAURANT ASSOCIATION, 1200 Seventeenth Street, N.W., Washington, DC 20036-3097; (800) 424-5156; (202) 331-

5900. Keeps members updated on relevant national and state legislation and maintains a library for members. The group's Educational Foundation cosponsors restaurant shows around the country.

THE UNITED STATES PERSONAL CHEF ASSOCIATION (USPCA). Provides training and on-going services to professional personal chefs, including chapters, Internet advertising, referrals, conferences, networking, insurance, certification, a magazine and continuing education. 3615 Highway 528, Suite 107, Albuquerque, NM 87114; (800) 995-2138. Web site: *www.uspca.com* or *www.hireachef.com*

BOOKS

The Guide to Cooking Schools 1999 (Annual), Dorlene V. Kaplan, ShawGuides. ISBN: 094583425X.

How to Open and Operate a Home-Based Catering Business: An Unabridged Guide, Denise Vivaldo, Old Saybrook, CT: Globe Pequot Press, 1996. ISBN: 1564409856.

How to Become a Caterer: Everything You Need to Know from Finding Clients to the Final Bill, Susan Wright, Citadel Press, 1996. ISBN: 0806518278.

Start Your Own Catering Business, Kathleen Deming, Prentice-Hall Trade, 1997. ISBN: 0136033091.

Successful Catering, Bernard Splaver, William N. Reynolds, Michael Roman, John Wiley & Sons, 1997. ISBN: 0471289256.

BOOKSTORES FOR COOKS

THE COOK'S LIBRARY, 8373 W. Third Street, Los Angeles, CA 90048; (213) 655-3141.

KITCHEN ARTS AND LETTERS, 1435 Lexington Avenue, New York, NY 10128; (212) 876-5550.

MAGAZINES

Bon Appetit, Knapp Communications Corporation, 6300 Wilshire Blvd., Los Angeles, CA 90018-5202; (213) 965-3600. Web site: *www.epicurious. com/b_ba/b00_home/ba.html*

Food & Wine, American Express Publishing Corp., 1120 Avenue of the Americas, New York, NY 10036; (212) 382-5618. Web site: *www.pathfinder.com/FoodWine/* or *www.amexpub.com*

Food Arts: The Magazine for Professionals, Food Arts Publishing, Inc., M. Shanken, Publishers, 387 Park Avenue South, New York, NY 10016; (212) 684-4224. For restaurateurs and caterers.

Special Events Magazine, Miramar Publishing, P.O. Box 8987, Malibu, CA 90265; (800) 543-4116. Covers party trends and offers tips for making parties extra-special. Web site: *www.specialevents.com*

SOFTWARE

CaterMate, 100 Franklin Avenue, Nutley, NJ 07110; (973) 284-0052. The company has the same name as their event-planning software. It can be used in conjunction with *Food Track* from System Concepts, Inc., 6560 N. Scottsdale Rd., Building H, 2nd Floor, Scottsdale, AZ 85253; (602) 951-8011 or (800) 553-2438. This is sophisticated software for managing food and beverages and is priced accordingly.

Cleaning Services

Survey after survey tells us that most people report having less free time. The harried pace of daily life leaves too little time to do the things we'd like to do, so the tasks we don't like doing become low priorities in our tightly squeezed precious free time. For two out of every three people, cleaning is one of those things they don't like doing. Housecleaning ranks as American's most disliked daily task, even more unpopular than grocery shopping, cooking, and going to work.

In a survey by *Family Circle* magazine of 35,000 working women and homemakers, 42 percent say they end up ignoring household chores. The combination of not liking to clean and not having enough time in the day makes cleaning one of the first things we drop from our "to do" lists. But a *Good Housekeeping* survey shows that two-thirds of women are unhappy with the way they keep house because they can't keep up with the standards by which they were raised. The result, according to Roper Starch Worldwide, is that 17 percent of American households pay someone to do their housecleaning sometimes or often.

But some people like to clean. Their brain endorphins start flowing when they start cleaning. If that describes you, the cleaning industry provides many business opportunities. Cleaning services of all kinds are one of the fastest-growing segments of the economy. The number of residential and commercial cleaning services more than doubled in the last five years. The Bureau of Labor Statistics says there will be more than half a million people cleaning things for others by the year 2000. Even if cleaning is not high on your list of favorite things, as someone in the cleaning business said, "It may not smell good to you but it smells like money to me."

Growing concern about indoor air quality in both businesses and homes is also propelling the growth of the cleaning field. Respiratory illness is linked to air pollution and molds in air ducts and air filters. "Sick" buildings and homes have become a common term. As a result, more and more people want to live in a clean environment not just for the sake of appearance but for their health. People with allergies and multi-chemical sensitivities need to live free of toxic chemicals that harm them, and many other people want to protect the environment from harmful chemicals as well. As a cleaning service, you can cater to this market by using non-toxic or green products and vacuums with HEPA filters.

While home cleaning is a $100-million-a-year segment of the cleaning-services market, commercial cleaning of office and government buildings as well as industrial plants and retail establishments is an even larger segment. Commercial cleaning contracts can become a steady, reliable source of business. However, residential cleaning has two advantages over commercial accounts. First, commercial cleaning is more competitive, and the profit margin is usually lower. Second, cash flow is better for residential cleaning. You collect immediately after finishing your work, and extending credit is not expected or good practice. Bills for commercial cleaning are typically not paid for 30 to 60 days, but as an employer, you will have to pay employees during that time.

A cleaning service is one of the easiest businesses to start profitably from home. You do the work on the customers' premises. Your equipment may be minimal if customers who have their own cleaning equipment allow you to use theirs. This will also save you the chore of hauling and maintaining your own equipment. You can do the work by yourself, with your family, or, if you choose, you can hire employees to do the actual cleaning, while you market and manage the business.

Nonspecific cleaning or janitorial services are the most common, serving residential or commercial clients or both. But there are also specialization possibilities galore in this field. Specializing is usually the most profitable way to operate as a cleaning service, though in a smaller community you may need to offer a combination of services in order to make a good living throughout the year. Here is a list of possible specializations followed by a description of some of the major specialties:

- air-duct cleaning
- apartment and rental property turnover
- auto detailing
- carpet cleaning
- ceiling cleaning
- chimney cleaning
- concrete floor cleaning
- construction cleanup
- crime scene cleanup
- decontaminating "clean rooms" in high-tech manufacturing plants
- disaster cleanup
- drain cleaning
- drapery cleaning
- floor cleaning
- furniture cleaning
- high pressure or power washing
- large commercial space (such as airports and arenas, schools and supermarkets)
- metal cleaning
- parking lot sweeping
- pool cleaning
- snow removal
- stone and masonry cleaning
- upholstery cleaning
- venetian-blind cleaning
- window cleaning
- yard and lawn maintenance

Air-Duct Cleaning

Cleaning heating and air-conditioning ducts involves using vacuums and other equipment to remove dust and debris from the ducts in commercial or residential buildings. This is actually an environmentally oriented business, because inefficient heating systems can waste 50 percent of the energy they generate, and clogged air-conditioning systems waste electricity. This is a year-round business: air-conditioning in the summer, heating in the winter.

Auto Detailing

Home-based auto detailing goes beyond what a car wash can do to make an automobile look and feel like new. Auto detailers work on their client's premises where they polish and clean a car inside and out, right down to the finest detail. It takes about three hours to detail a car thoroughly. So if you work quickly, you can do two to three cars a day. In addition to working for individuals, you can also work for used-car dealers or companies with fleets of cars that routinely need to be detailed.

Carpet Cleaning

Carpet-cleaning services can serve both residential and commercial clients and can be easily started on a part-time basis. Wall-to-wall carpeting is commonplace in both homes and offices, but since cleaning carpets requires special equipment, most people hire someone instead of trying to do it themselves. Carpet-cleaning methods today include steam, dry extraction, and carbonation. Some carpet cleaners also clean draperies and upholstery.

Ceiling Cleaning

Although most commercial facilities need to have acoustical ceilings cleaned, most cleaning services don't provide this, so there's a need for this service. You can buy one of the many chemical cleaning packages available from ceiling-cleaning distributors, who will instruct you in how to use them.

Chimney Cleaning

Did you know there are 25 million fireplaces in the United States, and sooner or later they all need cleaning? In fact, failing to clean a chimney that's being used regularly can cause a serious fire hazard, and in some states there are now laws about the level of pollutants emerging from chimneys. So if you live in a climate and community where people burn wood in their fireplaces regularly, you can earn up to $400 a day as a chimney sweep. This is a low-overhead business. All the equipment you need fits easily into a car. In addition to a specialized vacuum and a set of tools, you need a ladder and the knowledge of how to do the work.

Floor Cleaning and Refinishing

In his book *Cleaning Up for a Living,* Don Aslett says there are few good floor-care professionals, and yet stripping, waxing, sanding, and refinishing hardwood floors is certainly a service needed by homeowners and business establishments like restaurants, galleries, and boutiques. The necessary equipment can be purchased from a wholesale janitorial service for less than $2,000. And you can charge considerably more per hour than a general housecleaning service.

Mobile Power Washing

Mobile power washers go where large things need cleaning. You use a truck equipped with a tank that holds hundreds of gallons of hot water that is propelled through high-pressure hoses. You clean construction sites; aluminum siding; old brick, cement, and marble on buildings being restored; farm, industrial, and construction equipment; garbage trucks, airplanes, and boats; parking lots; restaurant freezers and vent hoods; awnings and signs; air-conditioning units, phone booths, shopping carts, and hotel dumpsters. You also travel to residences to clean driveways, patios, kitchen floors, siding, basements, pool decks, and mobile homes.

Pool Cleaning

If you live in a community where many homes have year-round swimming pools, a pool cleaning service can be a way to earn a steady, regular income working out-of-doors. As anyone who has a swimming pool knows, pools have to be cleaned properly and on schedule or you've got trouble. Therefore, most pool owners turn this task over to someone they can rely on to make sure it gets done right.

You need to learn how to do this business, because it involves using various hazardous chemicals, which must be used in the proper ways. If you don't have any experience, chemical manufacturers provide some training, as do stores that sell spa and swimming-pool equipment. The best route, however, would be to work for a time as an assistant to someone in the business.

Franchises

The large number of franchises, licensing arrangements and training programs available in the cleaning field are evidence of just how good an opportunity cleaning services can be. But do you need a franchise? Don Aslett, who's known as the "King of Clean," and Mark Browning, authors of *Cleaning Up for a Living,* point out that "For a fee, maybe $10,000 or $15,000, the franchise gives you a name, some forms, a few gallons of cleaner, some advertising info, and some secrets of success. In three months, with a little hustle, a sharp operator can accomplish the same thing independently." He points out that seminars are going on all the time for people in the cleaning field, many of them free. Bill Griffin, author and owner of Cleaning Consultant Services, Inc., says, "People don't need franchises as much as they once did because the software is commercially available and information is, too."

However, if the structure and support of a franchise or business opportunity is appealing to you, you can find the names of franchises that enable you to operate from home on our Web site (*www.paulandsarah.com*) and more detail on selecting a franchise or business opportunity in our book, *Home Businesses You Can Buy.*

Knowledge and Skills

One of the greatest advantages of starting a cleaning service is that there is very little formal knowledge or experience needed. Even most specialties can be learned quickly. You simply need:

- the appropriate equipment and supplies, including "green" products

- knowledge of how to use them

- the willingness to work hard and produce superior results

- a growing awareness of health and safety

Start-up Costs*	Low	High
Supplies and basic equipment[†]	$ 1,000	$ 2,000
Cell phone	$ 75	$ 200
Initial marketing budget	$ 500	$ 2,500
Insurance and bonding[‡]	$ 500	$ 1,000
Total	$ 2,075	$ 4,700

* In addition to the items listed here, you will need a vehicle, which, depending on the equipment you need to transport, may be a car or a van.

† Equipment can often be rented. However, if you are going to perform janitorial services regularly, you will want to invest in such items as floor buffers and commercial vacuums. Equipment for specialized services generally ranges from $3,000 to $5,000.

‡ You will need to show proof of insurance, usually $1,000,000 in general liability coverage, to larger commercial customers, and if you have employees, you will want insurance to cover breakage or theft of customer property.

Advantages

- "You meet people and get exercise," says Don Aslett.

- Generally start-up costs and overhead for all types of cleaning services are low.

- The business can easily be started as a part-time or sideline business.

- You can operate a cleaning service virtually anywhere.

- You can get free technical expertise from janitorial supply houses and product manufacturers.

- Usually there are ample customers who need cleaning work.

- By adding crews of workers, your business can grow very large and still be home based.

- You can build a base of regular clients who will use your services repeatedly.

- Some types of cleaning services, such as auto detailing, allow you to work outdoors.

Disadvantages

- Cleaning is hard, dirty work. You'll have to be willing to roll up your sleeves and get your hands and clothes dirty or hire employees. Some types of tasks are dangerous.

- In general, most types of cleaning businesses have a low-status image, which must be overcome by creating a very clean, neat, and professional identity. Don Aslett points out that teachers are warning kids they'll grow up and be a cleaner. Parents punish children by making them clean, creating a negative association for many.

- Cleaning is a highly competitive industry because of the low entry requirements.

- Some cleaning is seasonal or periodic in nature or subject to weather conditions.

- Unless you hire employees, your income is limited by the number of hours you can work in a day. And when you hire crews, you will need to bill, which can lead to collection problems.

- Hiring employees and handling both their problems and the customer relations problems they create can be extremely stressful. You will need insurance and bonding and will be wise to organize your business as a limited liability company or corporation. You will need to pay fringe benefits or risk penalties if IRS or state tax agencies classify your personnel as employees and not independent contractors, which they are likely to do. You should also check criminal background before hiring employees.

Pricing

Housecleaning services today are getting $12 to $35 an hour. Environmental or green cleaning services can be priced at the high end of the range. Prices include time and cleaning materials. Specialized work is usually priced by the square foot or by the item. Although you make quotes or bid a fixed price, the way you calculate pricing is still based on time. Commercial jobs can generate about $20 an hour. Don Aslett and Mark Browning in their book *Cleaning Up for a Living* have pages of charts with pricing for different kinds of jobs at varying degrees of difficulty translated into how much cleaning can be done per hour and the proportion supplies will represent of cost. They also have sample bid worksheets. What you figure your hourly rate at is subject to local conditions. Phoning services in the area and checking Web sites that post rates will help you determine current prices.

Earnings

Working on your own, you can earn between $20,000 and $50,000 a year. You can increase this by specializing or getting enough jobs that enable you to take on employees. However, in many areas, finding good employees can be your #1 problem. Overhead: Low if you work without employees.

Best Home Businesses Estimate of Market Potential

Growing since the eighties, cleaning will continue to be an expanding industry. Turning to enterprises that do cleaning and janitorial work of all kinds is part of the continuing change in the way we manage our lives and businesses. Businesses and governments make cleaning and janitorial services high on their list of activities to convert from employee-done to work done by outside contractors who offer a variety of specialized services. The health implications of clean air and a clean environment favor the development of specialties, and specializing translates into higher earnings.

Best Ways to Get Business

- Don Aslett maintains that a cleaner who satisfies customers will get all the business they want. Referrals come naturally.

- Taking out classified ads in weekly community newspapers. This is one home business for which advertising works very well. Find the local paper that produces the best results and advertise there indefinitely.

- Have your own Web site. Affluent customers are apt to look to the Web before the Yellow Pages.

- Listing in the Yellow Pages. You also will be findable as a business in the Internet telephone directories. What you name your business can be a way to distinguish your service from others.

- Distributing flyers in neighborhoods or business districts.

- Calling directly on businesses that could use your services.

- If you operate as a *green* cleaning service, letting doctors, particularly allergists, know about you.

- Offering some type of introductory discount with a direct mail solicitation and then turning each customer you get into a regular weekly or monthly account.

- For more periodic types of services, keeping names of past clients in a computer database and calling them periodically.

First Steps

- Take advantage of free training and expertise from janitorial supply houses.

- Wait until you see what character your service takes before you invest in significant amounts of supplies and equipment.

- If you do commercial cleaning, you can start as a sideline business because you are usually working evenings and weekends. In contrast, residential customers expect cleaning to be done during weekday hours.

- Residential cleaning costs less to start because commercial services are often required to have a bond, and the equipment needed is larger and more expensive.

- For equipment you use infrequently, rent rather than buy.

- Offer to help out other services on days you don't have business. You can learn from them and they can help you in return when you get busy.

- Carry a pager or cellular phone or use an answering service to make sure you don't miss calls while you are working.

Where to Turn for Information and Help

ORGANIZATIONS

BUILDING SERVICE CONTRACTORS ASSOCIATION INTERNATIONAL, 10201 Lee Highway, Suite 225, Fairfax, VA 22030; (800) 368-3414; (703) 359-7090; fax: (703) 352-0493. The trade association of the building service contracting industry offers seminars, publications, video-training programs, and networking. Web site: *www.bscai.org*

CONTACT CLEANING CONSULTANTS, INC., 3693 East Marginal Way South, Seattle, WA 98134; (800) 622-4221; (206) 682-9748. Publishers of dozens of books, videos, software and consulting on cleaning and restoration services listed in their annual *Cleaning Industry Training Materials Catalog*. Examples of specialized titles they publish are: *Comprehensive Rug and Carpet Cleaning; Fire Restoration and Insurance Work; Food Service: Health Sanitation and Safety; Infection Control for Lodging and Food Service Establishments;* and *Restorative Drying: A Complete Guide to Water Damage Restoration*. Their Web site lists forums and chat rooms for the cleaning industry. Web site: *www.cleaningconsultants.com*

THE INTERNATIONAL WINDOW CLEANING ASSOCIATION, 7801 Suffolk, Alexandria, VA 22315; (703) 971-7771. Web site: *www.iwca.org*

MAGAZINES AND NEWSLETTERS

American Window Cleaner, 27 Oak Creek Road, El Sobrante, CA 94803; (510) 222-7080. "The voice of the professional window cleaner." Web site: *www.awcmag.com*

Cleaning Business Magazine, Published by Cleaning Consultant Services, listed under Organizations.

Cleaner Times Magazine, Advantage Publishing, 4600 W. Markham, Little Rock, AR 72205; (800) 443-3433; (501) 280-9111. Web site: *www.adpub.com/ctimes*

Professional Carwashing & Detailing, Cleaning Management Institute (a subsidiary of National Trade Publications), 13 Century Hill Drive, Latham, NY 12110; (518) 783-1281. This company also publishes *Cleaning & Maintenance Management* magazine and offers training. Web site: *www.facility-maintenance.com* or *www.carwash.com*

BOOKS

Cleaning Up for a Living, Don Aslett and Mark Brown, Betterway, 1994. ISBN: 1558702067.

Entrepreneur magazine publishes three $59 start-up guides: *Janitorial Service, Maid Service, Lawn Care Business.* Web site: *www. entrepreneurmag.com*

How to Sell and Price Contract Cleaning, William R. Griffin, John G. Davis, Cleaning Consultant Service, 1988. ISBN: 0944352030.

How to Start a Window Cleaning Business: A Guide to Sales Procedures and Operations, Judy Suvall, Cleaning Consultant Service, 1997. ISBN: 0944352057.

Opportunities in Cleaning Services Careers, Adrian A. Paradis, Vgm Career Horizons, 1992. ISBN: 0844240176.

WEB SITES

ALLERGY CLEAN ENVIRONMENT. Lists and describes products and equipment to improve indoor air quality for asthma and allergy sufferers with prices and ordering information. Web site: *www.w2.com/allergy.html*

GLOBAL CLEANING SERVICES RESOURCE CENTER. Lists thousands of housekeeping, janitorial, maid, butler, other domestic services and products by country, state, and city. Has discussion groups and chat rooms. Web site: *www.housekeeping.com*

IDS GLOBAL. A member-owned national distribution network for janitorial supplies and packaging products. Web site: *www.idsglobal.com*

Thomas Register of American Manufacturers. Thomas lists millions of products and services. Use the Web site at *www.thomasregister.com* or the bound volumes in your library's reference section. Product sources can also be discovered by going to trade shows and local cleaning supply stores and by asking others in your business as well as customers.

Coaching

If you believe most people have the capability to change and improve their lives without plumbing the depths of their psyches and you'd like to help others fulfill their potential, personal coaching may be the field for you. Timothy Gallwey, author *of The Inner Game of Tennis,* defined coaching as "unlocking a person's potential . . . helping them to learn rather than teaching them." Most of the time you work one-to-one and over the telephone, meaning you can work from anywhere.

Coaching crystallized as a distinct field in 1992 when Thomas Leonard, a financial planner, created public awareness of coaching in founding Coach U. People had been doing coaching prior to that time but calling it consulting, counseling, or something else. Coaching is a way of transforming and distilling the core knowledge of many fields to improve the human condition by working one-on-one with individuals. Coaches migrate to this work from many fields: psychotherapy, accounting, law, career counseling, human resource development (this term sounds multiple stories away from contact with people), management consulting, training, professional speaking, theatre, financial planning, or, as Thomas Leonard did, from engineering and sales.

Some people would question whether coaching is a new field or just a consolidation or refinement of older ones. Regardless of its originality, it's a growing phenomenon that has come about from the dissolution of the concept that big organizations, private or public, will reward loyalty and hard work with lifetime employment. People have a sense now that they're on their own, more like their ancestors before the Industrial Revolution who tilled the land as their own bosses. Of course, people at that time had neighbors they knew who would help them out in times of need. Today, coaches are like neighbors-for-hire, counselors-on-call providing relationship and structure for people on their way up the career ladder as well as for those who need support to hold on to positions they've worked so hard to achieve. Keeping up wherever you are in your career is often a matter of gaining new skills; sometimes companies invest in their employees by hiring coaches to help them develop. Usually employees simply hire their own coaches.

Actually, coaches help people with all kinds of issues because it's becoming generally recognized that the lines between work life and personal life blend, with one influencing the other. In fact, emotions, particularly anger leading to interpersonal conflicts—formerly expected to be hung on the coat rack—have prompted companies to pay for coaches to work with volatile but otherwise valuable employees.

Despite the business therapy aspects of coaching, Rich Fettke of the Coaches Training Institute reflects the underlying belief held by most coaches when he describes coaching as "a partnership between two equals." Cheryl Richardson, author of *Take Time for Your Life: A Personal Coach's Seven-Step Program for Creating the Life You Want* (Broadway Books, 1998), says, "Clients are smart, capable people who want support in several ways from being asked provocative questions to getting direct advice or help with focus as well as a structure for ongoing support." Cheryl calls coaching "acting as a steward for the life they most want." Not surprisingly, many people compare this late-twentieth-century coaching to the role athletic coaches play in developing their charges.

Coaches emphasize that what they do differs from consulting, mentoring, and therapy. Career coaching is also distinct from career counseling or consulting. Coaches mostly listen, then ask questions, offer strategic advice, give clients a *nudge*, and sometimes give direct feedback, such as "Your business is on the road to failure." Conversation is the basic mode of coaching, but coaches will also engage in role-playing, use assessment tools that clients complete, and assign clients books to read.

While some coaches specialize in working with particular clienteles (writers, speakers, executives, self-employed, people diagnosed as ADD) and particular subjects (life purpose, executive, dating, etiquette, witness, parenting, shyness, time management), many coaches do not specialize. Laura Berman Fortgang, author of *Take Yourself to the Top* (Warner Books, 1998), who began coaching at 28, says that terms like *personal, career,* and *business* are "names you put before what it is the client is looking for."

Coaches address a wide range of needs that can only be expected to grow in the years to come.

Knowledge, Skills, and Personal Qualities You Need to Have

- Life experience with ability to distill wisdom from it.

- Insatiable curiosity about people combined with sensitivity and a nonjudgmental attitude so you can be "really open."

- Communication skills but not as much "a command of language as a command of truth" according to Jeff Raim of Cheyenne, Wyoming. Thomas Leonard is attributed as saying, "The less you say on the call, the more successful you're being."

- Ability to ask provocative questions.

- A high level of integrity and courage because clients pay to tell them the truth.

Advantages

- Low overhead.

- Work from anywhere because most coaching is done on the phone. Cyber coaches working by e-mail are emerging.

- Coaching by telephone, appointments can be clustered so that a coach can earn a full-time income working two days a week.

- Once established, a steady, predictable income.

- Personal fulfillment that comes from working with people you choose to work with and helping them.

Disadvantages

- Tendency to become isolated.

- No passive income.

Start-up Costs*	Low	High
Training costs	$ 500	$ 2,500
Computer	$ 1,500	$ 3,000

Printer	$	300	$	800
or				
Multi-function printer/fax/scanner/copier	$	150	$	600
Office furniture, especially an ergonomic chair	$	400	$	1,000
Initial marketing budget	$	200	$	2,000
Total	$ 3,050		$ 9,900	

* If you wish to serve a national clientele, you will need to provide a toll-free number for out-of-town clients.

Pricing

Fees range from $200 to $1,000 a month for half-hour weekly phone sessions. Phone sessions are the most common, but face-to-face meetings at the client's place of work or at the coach's office are common. Monthly retainer arrangements are also common. Some coaches require a minimum commitment of three months. Some coaches will work on a project or short-term basis at an hourly rate, typically $50 to $200 an hour; however, coaches working with corporations may command fees of $500 or more a session. Some clients will work with a coach for years. Another type of service is group coaching using phone bridges.

Potential Earnings

Full-time coaches conduct 25 to 80 coaching sessions a week. These are typically 30 minute sessions. At 30 sessions a week, $50 a session, coaches working 48 weeks a year will gross $72,000; at $75 a session, $108,000.

Overhead: low (under 20 percent).

Estimate of What the Market Will Be

Coaching is growing rapidly and the reasons for its growth should continue to propel it. Attempts to license coaching, spurred by licensed professionals in other fields, may or may not be successful.

Best Ways to Get Business

- Offering sample (free) 30-minute consultations.
- Speaking before groups.

- Having your own Web site with electronic brochure, information about coaching, and self-quizzes. Without a Web site, you will not get as many leads from database directories maintained by organizations that consumers use to find a coach. Most directories provide the ability to link the consumer directly to your page.

- Getting media attention.

- Writing articles about coaching.

- Networking in organizations.

- Newsletter that may be mailed, faxed and/or posted on your Web site.

- Holding monthly gatherings for clients, encouraging them to bring guests. At the gathering, do live coaching on the spot to demonstrate what you do.

- Producing and using products that support your coaching, such as audio cassettes and introductory booklets.

First Steps

- Obtain training. As part of your training program, obtain coaching for yourself.

- Identify a market you will serve.

- Work without charge with selected individuals for 90 days.

Where to Turn for Information and Help

ORGANIZATIONS

THE INTERNATIONAL COACH FEDERATION (ICF), P.O. Box 1393, Angel Fire, NM 87710; (888) 423-3131. ICF has chapters in almost every state and over 10 countries; accredits training programs. Members can get referrals from the referral service operated on its Web site. Web site: *www.coachfederation.org*

TRAINING PROGRAMS

COACH UNIVERSITY, P.O. Box 881595, Steamboat Springs, CO 80488; (800) 48COACH. Offers a two-year program leading to certification. Web site: *www.coachu.com*

COACHES TRAINING INSTITUTE, 1879 Second Street, San Rafael, CA 94901; (800) 691-6008. Offers both initial and advanced training. Web site: *www.thecoaches.com*

COACH FOR LIFE, 5275 Joan Court, San Diego, CA 92115, (888) COACHING; (619) 287-1186. Web site: *www.coachforlife.com*

CORPORATE COACH UNIVERSITY INTERNATIONAL, P.O. Box 881595, Steamboat Springs, CO 80488; (888) 391-2740. Web site: *ww.ccui.com/about.htm*

LIFE PURPOSE INSTITUTE, 8775 Aero Dr., #233, San Diego, CA 92123; (619) 573-0888.

BOOKS

Coach: Creating Partnerships for a Competitive Edge, Steven J. Stowell, Matt M. Starcevich, Center for Management Organization; 1987. Eight-step process on "how-to" be a business coach. ISBN: 0916095398.

Coaching for Performance, John Whitmore, Nicholas Brealey, 1996. ISBN: 1857881702.

Developing High Performance People: The Art of Coaching, Oscar G. Mink, Barbara P. Mink, and Keith Owen, Perseus Press, 1993. ISBN: 0201563134.

The Dos & Don'ts of Work Team Coaching: A Comprehensive Study of the Worker/Coach Interpersonal Relationship, Randy Glasbergen and Steve Herbelin, Herbelin Publishing, 1998. ISBN: 0966131940.

Masterful Coaching, Robert Hargvove, Pfeiffer & Co, 1995. ISBN: 0893842818.

Personal Coaching for Results: How to Mentor and Inspire Others to Amazing Growth, Louis E. Tice, Joyce Quick, Lou Tice, Thomas Nelson, 1997. ISBN: 0785273557.

The Portable Coach: 28 Surefire Strategies for Business and Personal Success, Thomas J. Leonard, Byron Laursen, Scribner, 1998. ISBN: 0684850419.

Win-Win Partnerships: Be on the Leading Edge With Synergistic Coaching, Steven J. Stowell, Matt M. Starcevich, Center for Marine Conservation, 1997. ISBN: 0965272907.

Computer Consultant

Although some programmers call themselves computer consultants, there is a distinction between what a computer consultant does and what a programmer does. Whereas programmers are valued for their specialized know-how and are paid to write code, computer consultants take a broader view of an organization and its computer needs in an effort to help solve information-management problems of all kinds. In a sense, a computer consultant is actually a combination of hardware and software expert, programmer, technical writer, and business adviser.

The consultant asks people what they want to achieve and explores possibilities for how a computer can help them accomplish it. Whereas programmers work on fixed, objective targets, consultants deal more with broader, moving targets. According to consultant Nigel Dyson-Hudson, "The programmer is like the chief scientist sitting atop a triangle of ever more highly specialized knowledge. Consultants, on the other hand, work on an inverted triangle; the more skilled they get, the broader their knowledge must become."

In general, consultants may perform many types of work. In fact, consultant coach Bill Mooney has identified 14 different types of work that computer consultants might do:

- Business requirements analysis

- Preliminary system design

- Preliminary cost/benefit analysis

- Software analysis

- Hardware selection

- Hardware acquisition and installation

- Documentation

- Implementation

- Validation

- Training

- Technical support

- Management of the system

- Maintenance of the system

- Periodic evaluations/audits

As Mooney points out, some computer consultants do only one of these, some do two or three, some do even more. In Mooney's view, each of these tasks can be an entire field to be mined by the savvy computer consultant; alternatively, a consultant can contract for the whole enchilada, and subcontract out the work to others such as programmers, maintenance people, and technical writers. In short, there is a wide range of ways to conduct a computer consulting practice. Debbie Handler, past president of Independent Computer Consultants' Association, finds, however, that to be a successful consultant, one needs to be highly technical and highly specialized. She specializes in a very tiny niche, working with a product (*Paradox* for DOS) that "died in the retail market, but clients swear by it and it serves as the backbone of their businesses."

For all computer consultants, having a customer service orientation is a key to getting business. One rule of thumb, according to consultant expert Alan Simon, is that computer consultants must have four nontechnical traits to get along with and keep their clients:

- They must understand the client's business needs and what they are trying to do.

- They must speak the language of the client, without using technical jargon or discussing the software.

- They must propose solutions that make sense or are at least convincing to the client.

- They must appear to be professional.

For additional information on consulting as a self-employment career, also read the profiles for Management Consultant, Computer Programmer, and Specialty Consultant.

Knowledge and Skills You Need to Have

- Technical knowledge of hardware and software is a must. You need to be an expert in several technical or functional areas (databases, intranets, legal software, medical software, and so forth).

- In order to market yourself as a consultant, you need to have a specialty, but you must also have an overview of everything in the field so you can provide the entire solution. Once you have a client, you don't want to have to refer him or her to someone else. But you do need to know when to bring in a subcontractor and whom to choose.

- You need to be able to inspire trust in your client. You need to have the ability to communicate on the client's level and know how much information he or she really wants to have. You need to be able to convey with confidence that you understand a client's situation and can take care of it. Without this, even high-level technical skills and knowledge can go unused.

- You need to be good at splitting your time among your clients, your work, any team members you work with, and keeping up with the industry. This can be difficult with multiple clients who expect quick response and turnaround time. You need to be able to make decisions about your time based on criteria other than who screams the loudest. Some in-demand consultants take the position "If you want to be first on my list, then you have to pay for it." Expect to spend a significant proportion of your time interacting with clients.

Start-up Costs	Low	High
Computer*	$ 1,500	$ 3,000
Printer or	$ 300	$ 800
Multi-function printer/fax/scanner/copier	$ 150	$ 600
Additional software (contact management, presentation software, clipart, desktop publishing, etc.) to do your own presentations, brochures, newsletters, and to remotely access your clients' computers	$ 500	$ 1,500
Office furniture, especially an ergonomic chair	$ 400	$ 1,000
Initial marketing budget	$ 1,000	$ 5,000
Total	$ 3,850	$ 8,900

*You need to have access to computers that are as advanced as the computer systems of your clients.

Advantages

- As a computer consultant, problems are opportunities. The Y2K (Year 2000) problem, which will stretch out for years, both in terms of programming needs and lawsuits, is an example of this. Essentially, as a consultant, you're in the business of solving problems.

- People are grateful when you help them. You can make or break a business through your skills.

- You can often work any time of the day or night you wish as long as the job is done on time.

- If you're good at landing clients and instilling confidence, you can do this work from anywhere using programs such as *PC Anywhere*, *Laplink*, and *Desklink*. (At the time we interviewed Debbie Handler, she was signing a fourth year-long contract and had not seen her clients in two years.)

- You perform varied activities, and there is seldom boredom or repetition.

- The demand is high. If you're good, you don't have to be concerned about competition.

- Some contracts can last for many months or even a year, guaranteeing you steady income.

- While you still experience the pressure to perform that you would as an employee, you can go home at the end of the day, and when a job is over, it's over.

Disadvantages

- At least part of the time, you may have to work under time pressures due to client deadlines.

- You must devote considerable time to keeping current in the ever-changing computer field. To stay current, computer consultants typically read 10 to 20 hours a week.

- If you must work on fixed bids you have to be skillful at estimating, as project costs can easily exceed estimates.

- Cash flow can be difficult to control; you have to stay on top of your billings with clients and be sure they pay you periodically for your work.

- It can be hard to survive unless you have a few big clients or are willing to work for an agency (although agencies can provide you with a few good jobs, which can become leads to your own contracts down the road).

- Computer consulting at one time became saturated with "closet consultants," that is, people who called themselves consultants but lacked skill and won projects by underbidding. This hurt the market for more professional consultants.

Pricing

Computer consulting rates range from $40 to $125 per hour with $75 the most typical rate. Factors that influence rates include:

- Demand: Y2K needs are creating a terrific environment for many consultants.

- Specialization: Rates vary depending on which industries you serve and which hardware and software you work with.

- Which of the fourteen types of work you are performing for the client: Design and analysis pay the highest, but you can also make good money at the maintenance or training level.

- Community size: Rates are higher in metropolitan markets and not as relevant if you are highly specialized.

- Client size: Rates are higher for large corporations.

- Length of project: Some consultants discount for long projects, but there's a case to made for charging a premium since one is committing over a period of time in which conditions may change to the disadvantage of the consultant.

- Whether you work through a broker who finds the jobs for you: Brokers who refer you to or place you with clients typically take 20 to 30 percent of your hourly rate.

- Bidding a fixed price per job is risky for an inexperienced consultant. A high bid that protects the consultant may scare off a potential client; a low bid can cause heavy losses for the consultant if the project costs exceed estimates.

Potential Earnings

Typical Annual Gross Revenues: $60,000 based on billing 16 hours per week, 50 weeks a year (800 hours per year) at $75 an hour; however, many consultants earn over $100,000 a year.

Overhead: moderate (20 to 40 percent).

Best Home Businesses Estimate of Market Potential

The market for consulting services will continue to grow over the next five years, driven by Y2K, intranets, the Internet, e-commerce, and companies upgrading their systems, but this is a competitive market.

Best Ways to Get Business

- Getting certified by a vendor or software publisher as a developer or trainer using their system. Customers call publishers for referrals to consultants.

- Joining and participating in organizations, such as trade and professional associations, particularly in industries or fields in which you have experience, and letting people know what you do.

- Answering questions and participating in forums, newsgroups, and message boards that are apt to have potential clients in your market.

- Having your own Web site and generating traffic to it through an active linking effort.

- Coming into contact with potential customers at meetings and in the course of your daily life. The best place is at computer stores, especially at stores where the salespeople are salaried versus commissioned.

- Performing market research to identify a range of clients who can use your services, based on your knowledge, expertise, and background.

- Speaking to civic, trade, and professional organizations.

- Writing articles to help you develop a reputation for your expertise.

- Participating in selective voluntary activities to get your name around, such as helping people at computer and software user-group meetings and special-interest groups, without expectation of compensation.

- Joining or forming a business referral group. Women's organizations can be particularly helpful.

- Going to computer shows and other places where new products are demonstrated.

- Referrals and repeat business from former clients are the best on-going sources of business. Keeping in contact is vital. One way of accomplishing this is sending newsletters to gatekeepers and former and prospective clients.

- Getting work through brokers and job shops, but you risk your self-employment status.

First Steps

1. Work as an internal consultant for a large company for a limited period of time, or offer yourself as a subcontractor to another consultant to help build your name and reputation.

2. Start with a contract in hand that is large enough to cover your overhead and living expenses to the extent that you do not have reserves, a spouse's income, or a cash reserve to cover you for 18 months.

3, Identify a niche or specialty. Ask yourself, "What kinds of problems can I solve, for whom can I solve them, and what platform can I work in (hardware, software, system, function)?"

4. Join the Independent Computer Consultants' Association, especially a local chapter. Through contacts there, you may be able to get subcontracts or referrals if you have a specialty.

Where to Turn for Information and Help

In addition to the resources shown below, see also the resources for Computer Programmer, Computer Repair, and Consulting to Business.

ORGANIZATIONS: NATIONAL

INDEPENDENT COMPUTER CONSULTANT'S ASSOCIATION (ICCA), 1131 South Towne Square, Suite F, St. Louis, MO 63123; (800) 774-4222. The Independent Computer Consultants' Association has over 1,500 members with specialties more or less evenly divided among the major subfields. ICCA has about twenty local chapters. Web site: *www.icca.org*

INSTITUTE FOR CERTIFICATION OF COMPUTER PROFESSIONALS (ICCP), 2200 East Devon Avenue, Suite 247; Des Plaines, IL 60018; (847) 299-4227.

SOFTWARE & INFORMATION INDUSTRY ASSOCIATION (SIIA), 1730 M Street, N.W., #700, Washington, DC 20036-4510; (202) 452-1600.

LOCAL

In addition to user groups locatable through these organizations, consider participating in the associations relevant to the fields in which you work (legal, medical, banking, etc.) and in user organizations formed around the vendor products with which you work.

ASSOCIATION OF PERSONAL COMPUTER USER GROUPS (APCUG); (914) 876-6678.

USER GROUP CONNECTION, 221 Arnold Avenue, Ben Lomond, CA 95005; (831) 336-4508. Web site: *www.ugconnection.com*. To locate a nearby MAC users' group, call (800) 538-9696, # 5.

BOOKS

The Computer Consultant's Guide: Real Life Strategies for Building a Successful Consulting Career, Janet Ruhl, New York: John Wiley & Sons, 1997. ISBN: 0471176494.

The Computer Consultant's Workbook, Janet Ruhl, Technion Books, 1996. P.O. Box 171, Leverett, MA 01054. ISBN: 0964711605.

Contract and Fee Setting Guide for Consultants and Professionals, Howard Shenson, New York: John Wiley & Sons, 1989. ISBN: 0471515388.

Exploring Requirements: Quality Before Design, Donald Gause and Gerald M. Weinberg, New York: Dorset House, 1989. ISBN: 0932633137.

Get Certified and Get Ahead, Anne Martinez, McGraw-Hill, 1999. ISBN: 007134781X.

Handbook of Walkthroughs, Inspections, and Technical Reviews, Daniel P. Freedman and Gerald M. Weinberg, New York: Dorset House, 1990. ISBN: 0932633196.

How to Be a Successful Computer Consultant, Alan R. Simon, New York: McGraw-Hill, 1998. ISBN: 0070580294.

How to Be a Successful Internet Consultant, Jessica Keyes, New York: Computing McGraw-Hill, 1996. ISBN: 0070345317.

Janet Ruhl's Answers for Computer Contractors: How to Get the Highest Rates and the Fairest Deals from Consulting Firms, Agencies, and Clients, Technion Books, 1998. ISBN: 0964711621.

Peopleware: Productive Projects and Teams, Tom DeMarco and Tim Lister, New York: Dorset House, 1987. ISBN: 0932633056.

Software Inspection, Tom Gilb, Dorothy Graham, Susannah Finzi, Addison-Wesley Publishing Co., 1993. ISBN: 0201631814.

SEMINARS

How to Start and Build a Profitable Full-time or Part-time Computer Consulting Business, one-day seminar offered around the country by the Center for Consulting and Professional Practices, Division of William Mooney Associates, 19401 South Vermont Avenue, Suite K100, P.O. Box 6159, Torrance, CA 90504; (310) 324-2386. Mooney also provides one-on-one coaching to help independent consultants attract more and better clients. E-mail: coachconsult@earthlink.net

WEB SITES

COMPUTER CONSULTANTS FORUM sponsored by the Independent Computer Consultants' Association (ICCA) on CompuServe.

GOVCOM: *www.govcom.com* publishes the content of the *Commerce Business Daily* without charge to users, the Federal Acquisition Regulation (FAR), Cost Accounting Standards, teaming and employment opportunities.

JANET RUHL'S COMPUTER CONSULTANT'S RESOURCE PAGE: *www.realrates.com*

Computer Programmer

Demand for programmers has been strong since the 1970's. Despite occasional cycles, "There has never been a time when you could not make a living as a programmer if you kept your skills current," says Janet Ruhl, who conducts an ongoing survey of the earnings of people in this field. Programmers earn their livelihoods preparing the step-by-step instructions that a computer follows to perform tasks. The type of work they do can be divided into two categories:

1. Systems programmers who write programs that tell the computer how to carry out its own internal instructions.

2. Applications programmers who write programs that solve problems and carry out the daily activities of businesses and people, like record keeping and e-commerce (databases), word processing, billing, invoicing, flow charting, and a wealth of other tasks. Of course, the Internet and intranets are focuses for many programmers' work. Web site design crosses over into graphic design.

A substantial amount of the work in this field is done by contract or freelance programmers for several reasons.

- Rapidly changing technology dictates using people with the most up-to-date skills; it's difficult and impractical to hire and keep such people as full-time permanent staff.

- Continual corporate downsizing in good times as well as bad. Meeting needs "just in time" has become a way of adding staff as well as obtaining materials for factories.

- Small to mid-size companies often use contract programmers to help them gear up quickly to handle upsurges in their business.

- Software to make things easier has resulted in more work for programmers adapting commercial packages around the specific ways their customers' businesses work. Users have not replaced programmers.

- Clients need customized programs.

A programmer will begin working with a client much as a computer consultant does, assessing the client's needs and getting an understanding of the tasks that the client wants the computer to perform. Once the programmer has a full understanding of what has to be done, he or she may have to design, write original code for, or modify an existing program to do the job desired. Intranets replacing older networks are requiring more sophistication on behalf of the programmer.

After writing a program and loading it into the client's system, the programmer must also test and implement the program. Programs seldom work the first time, and it can often take hours of trials and analysis to figure out how to make them work without any bugs. In fact, David Lake of Boulder, Colorado, who has been an independent programmer for the past fifteen years, says, "I spend two hours of my time testing for every hour of programming. I hire people to try to break my programs. If they do, I fix it."

Many programmers have created utility programs, games, and even full-scale business software in their spare bedrooms, often offering it as shareware (which we discussed in earlier editions of this book). Janet Ruhl points out, however, that there have been "very few shareware success stories in the last five years. Shareware was a function of the late 80's." The small percentage of people who actually paid for what they downloaded and the increasingly low prices of most commercial software has made shareware no longer a bargain.

As the Y2K problems illustrate, computerization of every aspect of our society has become a de facto standard. Each day brings a new wave of products, devices, and concepts that use computers, and each must be controlled by some kind of program. Dave Bennett, a San Diego programmer, has written dozens of applications over the past few years. He says of this field, "The work is growing more challenging and complex."

Knowledge and Skills You Need to Have

- You need to be able to do computer programming. How much knowledge you need depends on whether you will work with clients who have problems for which you must design solutions or clients who already have solutions in mind and want you to program their solutions. Some routine applications programming can be performed by workers with a high-school education. However, most companies expect applications programmers, particularly independents, to have some college training or vocational school background. Systems programmers usually have a college degree and a strong knowledge of the computers they work with.

- Working as an independent programmer requires more expertise than you will be able to develop by simply taking a community college course on programming. You need to be able to do more than write code. Most programmers find they must be familiar with the operations of a wide range of hardware and software.

- In addition, Glenn Casteran of Laguna Vista Systems in Newport Beach, California, points out that it helps to have a background in databases, accounting, and general business because so much of a programmer's potential business will revolve around one of these fields. Your business knowledge should also cover the fields in which you are working (medical, legal, industrial, and so forth). You must know the procedures of that business and speak the "lingo" so that clients will feel that you understand their needs.

- Ideally you should have two to five years of programming experience so that you know how long it takes to complete jobs and thus tell clients with confidence what you will charge for a finished project.

- Working as an independent programmer requires that you have excellent communication skills and customer service skills. Programmers may be very good, but unless they can speak to their clients in ordinary language, they will not be hired or rehired. You must also know how to treat the client with respect. As Casteran says, "Don't argue with the client."

- You must be willing to sell yourself and do regular marketing skills that are sometimes lacking in a computer programmer.

- Finally, you must learn quickly and be ready to keep learning because the computer industry changes very quickly and new technologies (hardware and software) are constantly emerging that you need to understand.

Start-up Costs	Low	High
Three-node network of computers	$ 8,000	$ 15,000
Compiler and miscellaneous software	$ 1,700	$ 2,500
Printer	$ 300	$ 800
or		
Multi-function printer/fax/scanner/copier	$ 150	$ 600
Vendor training courses	$ 2,000	$ 6,000

Office furniture, especially an ergonomic chair	$	400	$	1,000
Initial marketing budget	$	1,000	$	3,000
Errors and omissions insurance	$	200	$	500
Total		**$13,750**		**$ 29,400**

Advantages

- Programming for personal computers is one of the fastest-growing occupations.

- Programmers are in demand and are respected as experts.

- You can work your own hours, choose your own projects, and work in a wide variety of fields.

- Programming is a challenge, and it can be very satisfying to develop a program that makes an entire business work.

Disadvantages

- You are often under pressure. As software becomes more powerful, the inherent difficulty of directing computers shifts to programmers, not the user.

- As a home-based programmer, you need constantly to update your skills through courses and books as well as by purchasing new hardware and software products. Your biggest cost is hardware and upgrading it.

- Although it's necessary to specialize in a particular platform (the hardware or operating system that computers run on), uncertainty as to which platforms will be in future demand heightens the risk of your skills becoming obsolete.

- Sometimes the more interesting projects are not the most profitable ones.

- The IRS often regards independent programmers who work on large projects that take months or years to be employees rather than independent contractors. The IRS position has grave tax repercussions for both you and the company that hires you unless you fulfill all requirements to be considered an independent.

- As the price of commercial software has come down, many clients experience sticker shock at the cost of custom programming, so charging what you are worth can cause arguments.

- Some clients will keep changing their minds about how they want the software to work, so you must make sure your contracts are specific about the design and payments for work. It is best to get "milestone" payments so that a client does not end up owing you thousands of dollars at the end of the project (and not paying it if he or she doesn't like your work).

- You need to market continuously to keep projects coming into your shop.

Pricing

Rates range from below $30 to $75 an hour; but they can be as high as $125 an hour in some cases. Variables are determined by which platform you are working on, the type of work you are doing, and your location.

Potential Earnings

Typical Annual Gross Revenues: $48,000 based on billing 800 hours (sixteen hours per week times fifty weeks per year) at $60 an hour, the median rate for contract programmers according to Janet Ruhl's survey of computer consulting rates. Many programmers are able to bill forty or more hours a week and thus their incomes exceed $100,000 a year.

Overhead: moderate (20 to 40 percent).

Best Home Businesses Estimate of Market Potential

The Bureau of Labor Statistics identifies programming as one of the fastest-growing occupations. The keen demand for programmers is evidenced by the outsourcing of programming work all over the world (India, Mexico, Russia at $10 an hour) and the continuing effort by industry to get Congress to expand the number of foreign high-tech worker visas granted each year. While these evidences of demand may provide some downward pressure on hourly rates, being able to speak English fluently and have "face time" with clients translates into work.

Still clouding the lives of some programmers are federal and state efforts to classify programmers and other technical personnel as common-law employees instead of independent contractors because of Section 1706 of the Tax Reform Act of 1986. This section denies high-tech contractors the same "safe haven" from harsh tax rules granted to similar professionals in other industries. Repeal of Section 1706 will improve the ease of marketing for and earnings of independent programmers.

Best Ways to Get Business

- Turning your former employer, ex-managers, ex-coworkers into clients.

- Assisting people at computer and software user-group meetings and special-interest group sessions. Answering questions online in areas that cater to your area of specialization.

- Have your own Web page that presents you professionally and has meta tags and links that will direct people to your site.

- Making personal contacts in trade and business associations and other organizations, particularly in industries in which you have experience.

- Joining or forming a business referral group of others who can cross-refer business to one another.

- Getting referrals from other professional contacts such as business consultants and accountants.

- Teaching classes on programming for businesspeople.

- Getting listed as a consultant with companies with whose software you work.

- Writing articles or columns about how a computer can make a business more productive.

- Contacting computer stores, particularly smaller independent stores, about what you do. Retail computer stores can be a source of business. A customer who has taken the initiative to go to a computer retailer is already sold on using a computer but may need custom software or software.

- Getting work through brokers and job shops but you risk your self-employment status.

First Steps

- Programming courses are available at most universities, community colleges, and commercial trade schools. Many small business applications are written using the macro programming languages of Visual Basic and Access (technically a database) with some Foxpro and Delta; larger corporation work is usually done in C++ and COBOL; for Web development, HTML and Java.

- To develop your skills you might consider doing temporary work through technical job shops until you feel you can take on clients on your own. The best training is to get a job working as an employee.

- To develop the social skills you need and to market yourself, Dave Bennett suggests you "learn to play golf and then get out on the course with businessmen and -women."

Where to Turn for Information and Help

In addition to the resources below, see also those listed under Computer Consultant and Computer Repair.

ORGANIZATIONS

ASSOCIATION OF INFORMATION TECHNOLOGY PROFESSIONALS, 315 South Northwest Highway, Suite 200, Park Ridge, IL 60068-4278; (847) 825-8124. They have many chapters, most of which are tied to educational institutions. Web site: *www.aitp.org*

ASSOCIATION FOR COMPUTING MACHINERY, One Astor Plaza, 1515 Broadway, New York, NY 10036; (212) 869-7440; (212) 302-5826. The world's largest educational and scientific computing society offers local chapters and a large number of special interest groups. Web site: *www.acm.org*

THE INSTITUTE OF ELECTRICAL AND ELECTRONICS ENGINEERS (IEEE) COMPUTER SOCIETY, 1730 Massachusetts Ave NW, Washington, DC 20036; (202) 371-0101. Part of IEEE, the world's largest technical professional organization, the Society has local chapters and a listing of educational resources on the Internet at its Web site: *www.ieee.org*

SOCIETY OF INFORMATION MANAGEMENT, P.O. Box 2212, Chicago, IL 60690; (312) 372-6540. Approximately 2,700 executives and managers of information technology (IT) organizations, academicians, and consultants. Web site: *www.simnet.org*

INDEPENDENT COMPUTER CONSULTANTS ASSOCIATION (ICCA), 11131 South Towne Square, Suite F, St. Louis, MO 63123; (800) 734-4222; (314) 892-1675. ICCA has about twenty local chapters. Web site: *www.icca.org*

INSTITUTE FOR CERTIFICATION OF COMPUTING PROFESSIONALS, 2200 East Devon Avenue, Suite 247, Des Plaines, IL 60018; (800) U-GET-CCP; (847) 299-4227. Offers professional certification, which entitles you to use the ICCP designation after your name on a resume or business card. Web site: *www.iccp.org*

COURSES AND TRAINING

McGRAW-HILL's NRI SCHOOLS offer a home-study course in computer programming. McGraw-Hill Continuing Education Center, 4401 Connecticut Avenue, N.W., Washington, DC 20008; (202) 244-1600. Web site: *www.mhcec.com*

VATTEROTT COLLEGE, a private technical college, offers an accredited associate degree in computer programming and network management entirely via the Internet. 3925 Industrial Drive, St. Ann, MO 63074-1807; (314) 428-5900. Web site: *www.vatterottglobal.com*

For vendor training courses, see the training resources in the Computer Repair profile.

WEB SITES

JANET RUHL's COMPUTER CONSULTANT's RESOURCE PAGE has a survey of rates. Web page: *www.realrates.com*

JOB BOARD OF THE THE NATIONAL ASSOCIATION OF COMPUTER CONSULTANT. Independent programmers and other computer consultants can post their résumés. Web site: *www.isjobbak.com*

BROKERS AND JOBSHOPS

DAY & ZIMMERMAN, INC., 1818 Market Street, Philadelphia, PA 19103; (215) 299-8000.

TAD RESOURCES INTERNATIONAL, 100 Redwood Shores Pkwy, Redwood City, CA 94065; (650) 610-1000.

VOLT INFORMATION SCIENCES, INC., 1221 Ave. of the Americas, 47th Floor, New York, NY 10020; (212) 704-2400.

BOOKS

Applied Software Measurement: Assuring Productivity and Quality, Capers Jones, T. Capers Jones, McGraw-Hill Text, 1996. ISBN: 0070328269.

Estimating Software Costs, T. Capers Jones, McGraw-Hill Text, 1998. ISBN: 0079130941.

How I Sold a Million Copies of My Software . . . and How You Can, Too!, Herbert R. Kraft, Adams Publishing, 1997. ISBN: 1558507248.

Janet Ruhl's Answers for Computer Contractors: How to Get the Highest Rates and the Fairest Deals from Consulting Firms, Agencies, and Clients, Technion Books, 1998. ISBN: 0964711621. See other books useful to programmers by Janet Ruhl in the resources for the Computer Consultant profile.

A number of publishers specialize in technical books for programmers. Among these are:

CORIOLIS GROUP, 7721 East Gray Road #204, Scottsdale, AZ 85260; (800) 410-0192; (602) 483-0192. Web site: *www.coriolis.com*

HOWARD W. SAMS, HOWARD W. SAMS & CO., 2647 Waterfront Parkway East Dr., Indianapolis, IN 46214-2060; (317) 298-5400. Web site: *www.hwsams.com*

O REILLY, 101 Morris Street, Sebastopol, CA 95472; (800) 998-9938. Web site: *www.oreilly.com*

QUE, 201 West 103rd Street, Indianapolis, IN 46290; (800) 428-5331. Web site: *www.mcp.com/que*

SYBEX, 1151 Marina Village Pkwy, Alameda, CA 94501-1013; (510) 523-8233. Web site: *www.sybex.com*

MAGAZINES AND NEWSLETTERS

Advisor Publications publishes a group of magazines such as *Access-Office-VB Advisor, E-Business Advisor, File Maker Pro Advisor, Foxpro Advisor, Lotus Notes & Domino Advisor,* and *Security Advisor.* From its Web site, it offers Microsoft certification and other online classes. 5675 Ruffin Rd., San Diego, CA 92123-5675; (619) 483-6400. Web site: *www.advisor.com*

Software Success, weekly newsletter for small and mid-sized software companies whose average transaction is worth at least $1,000. P.O.

Box 9105, Dedham, MA 02027; (888) 479-6663; (617) 320-9460 ext. 540. Web site: *www.softwaresuccess.com/newsletter*

Visual C+++ Developer Magazine. Portions of the print magazine are published online as *The Visual C++ Developers Journal* (VCDJ), at its Web site: *www.vcdj.com*

Fusion Interactive, a division of TPD Publishing, Inc., 1600 Fairview Avenue East, Suite 300, Seattle, WA 98102; (206) 336-3045.

Computer Repair

The over 100 million computers installed in businesses and homes across the United States and Canada have something in common: At some point in each of their lives, they will probably need repairing. The problem might be with the main board, a hard drive, controllers, a fan, a network card, peripheral cards, the monitor, or printers. Whether each breakdown becomes a crisis or is only an inconvenience, chances are the owner will need help, and that's the role of the on-the-spot computer repair technician. A computer repair specialist is the computer equivalent of the paramedic arriving in an ambulance with the problem-solving skills and abilities to troubleshoot and fix whatever is wrong.

Linda Rohrbough, co-author of *Start Your Own PC Repair Business,* found computer repair is a good business for a number of reasons:

- Many computer owners, particularly small businesses, find it cheaper to repair an older computer than to lose business due to the downtime involved in converting to a new computer. Even Bill Gates says he only changes computers every two and one-half years.

- Many businesses keep older computers in service because they continue to serve their needs. For example, telemarketing firms often continue to use 286's and 386's; Internet hosting services keep 486's in operation.

- Computer makers like Dell, Gateway, and Micron that offer on-site warranty service need help in outlying areas.

- Repairs are usually in response to a crisis, and most repairs do involve an upgrade.

- Some maintenance contracts don't allow for upgrading a component that needs replacing with a newer and better one; it must be the same.

- Some organizations, like school districts, have budgets for repair but not for replacement of equipment.

Many repairs simply require swapping boards. While this is not difficult, requiring few tools (screwdrivers, cloths, air sprays, and disk drive cleaning disks), a computer repair service will also find itself involved in:

- Data recovery.

- Disaster recovery (fire, floods, hurricanes, lightning strikes, power surges, smoke damage, shipment damage, thunderstorms, tornadoes).

- Checking back-up systems and performing backups.

- Installing software.

- Removing viruses.

- Rendering second diagnostic opinions.

- Repairing network problems.

- Repairing notebook computers.

- Troubleshooting modem and communications problems.

A number of these tasks require training. Certification, expected by corporate and other sophisticated customers, also requires training. Fortunately, there are many sources of training—community colleges and trade schools, correspondence courses in print and on CD, and online education—that lead to certification. There are many types of certification in addition to A+, the basic certification for computer repair technicians. There is certification for hardware (Compaq and IBM); operating systems (Windows, Unix, AS/400); network hardware (Cisco, Bay Networks, Xylan); network operating systems (Banyan VINES, Windows NT Server, Novell NetWare); software applications (Corel, Lotus, Microsoft); databases (Oracle, Informix, Sybase); Internet (Microsoft, Novell, USWeb). Certification goes along with specialization and leads to being able to charge higher rates.

While repairing computers is the focus of this business, some firms offer scheduled maintenance and tune-ups. Rohrbough points out that maintenance is a "harder sell." Just as people don't call the fire department until they see flames, they don't summon a computer repair service until something's not working. Nevertheless it's in the customers' interest to have their computers maintained, which means cleaning them once or twice a year, and sometimes more often if they are located in dusty or high-traffic environments.

In some businesses, an unmaintained computer can crash after a year or two often due to overheating from a fan brought to a halt by collected dust. Regular cleaning can enable the computer to keep on ticking for five years or more. Getting scheduled maintenance work provides a predictable source of income and is best done as an adjunct to a computer repair or back-up service you can offer after you're already in the door. Each satisfied customer will likely refer others to you as well.

Knowledge and Skills

- Being comfortable with the insides of computers, their quirks and their connections and interfaces with other computers and with the telephone system.

- Knowing how to solder.

- Knowing how to get components.

- Knowing operating systems from DOS to Windows NT.

- Being diplomatic and sympathetic with computer users in the face of irrationality is necessary and keeps people calling.

Start-up Costs*	Low	High
Computer	$ 1,500	$ 3,000
Printer	$ 300	$ 800
or		
Multi-function printer/fax/scanner/copier	$ 150	$ 600
Training and certification	$ 1,000	$ 2,500
Reference books	$ 100	$ 500
Tools, cleaning supplies, diagnostic software	$ 500	$ 2,000
Spare parts	$ 500	$ 1,000
Initial marketing budget	$ 1,000	$ 5,000
Cell phone	$ 75	$ 200
Total	$ 5,125	$ 15,600

*You will need a van or truck for hardware.

Advantages

- As the amount of office technology in offices and homes grows, so does the need for its repair.

- Not a desk job; you make money while you're on the go.

- Many problems are solved by swapping boards, so that if you have any aptitude for technical work, you will become proficient quickly.

Disadvantages

- You may feel pressure because people are apt to communicate a sense of emergency or panic when their systems are down. On the other hand, maintenance can be done at your own pace.

- You need to have access to older equipment and keep up with the new. This means you have a constant learning curve.

Pricing

Hourly rates range from as low as $25 for beginners and those in smaller communities to several hundred dollars, but most rates are between $40 and $85 an hour. Network repair rates, however, can be in the $140 to $160 an hour range. Some repair services charge for travel time; others do not. Those who charge for travel or drive time either charge their hourly rate "port to port" or a flat fee for a service call, such as the equivalent of two hours. With experience in knowing how long a repair will take, it's possible to charge by the job, which is favored by many customers. Typical flat rates run from $75 for a dot matrix printer to $200 for a large monitor.

Potential Earnings

Typical Annual Gross Revenues: $90,000 based on billing twenty-four hours per week, fifty weeks per year, averaging $75 per hour.

Overhead: moderate (25 percent or less).

Best Home Businesses Estimate of Market Potential

Personal computers are outselling TV sets, in part because of decreasing cost. This might suggest that people will start discarding their computers when they break down and replacing them with new ones as they do with TV sets and telephones. But this is not likely to be the case. Indeed, there's evidence people are keeping, not discarding, their old personal computers. Printers and monitors may be another matter, but because of the time involved in installing software and configuring networks and printers, the question with a broken computer is more likely to be "How soon can we get this fixed?" On-site repair of customer equipment offers the advantages of timely service and convenience not available when taking or mailing a product in for service. As long as there's a cost advantage over buying and installing a new computer, the outlook for computer repair is good.

Best Ways to Get Business

- To get your first customers, print up plenty of business cards and leave them in office buildings, computer stores, and other locations where businesspeople may see them.

- Have your own Web page listing your services, prices, and certifications.

- Take out Yellow Page advertising. Research shows that people needing computer repair frequently turn to the Yellow Pages.

- Have car magnets made up or a sign painted on your vehicle with an easy-to-remember phone number and Web site.

- Teach computer classes and seminars, even if for free, to enable people to become aware of your expertise. Adult-education programs, however, will usually pay you.

First Steps

- Obtain certification and the training it requires.

- Gain experience maintaining computers. Once you feel comfortable and know what you are doing, you are ready to set up your business.

- Determine if you need a state license. Perhaps if you do, during the course of qualifying for a license, you can farm out business you generate to a licensed repair shop with whom you have an arrangement to share in the fees or work under its license.

Where to Turn for Information and Help

In addition to the resources below, see also those listed under Computer Consultant and Computer Repair.

BOOKS

Computer Monitor Troubleshooting & Repair, Joseph Desposito, Kevin Garabedian, Prompt Publications, 1997. ISBN: 0790611007.

The Component Identifier & Source Book: The Ultimate Cross Reference for the Electronics Industry, Victor Meeldijk, Prompt Publications, 1996. ISBN: 0790610884.

The Computer and Network Professional's Certification Guide, J. Scott Christianson and Ava Lee Fajen, Sybex, 1998. ISBN 0782122604. The authors offer updates and links on their Web site. The page on which they provide links to certification programs is *www.certification-update.com/certlinks.html*

Get Certified and Get Ahead, Anne Martinez, McGraw-Hill. ISBN: 007134781X.

Start Your Own Computer Repair Business, Book and Disk, Linda Rohrbough, Michael F. Hordeski, McGraw-Hill, 1995. ISBN: 0079119018.

Upgrade Your Own PC, Linda Rohrbough, Foster City, CA: IDG, 1998. ISBN: 0764532154.

Upgrading and Repairing PCs Quick Reference, Scott Mueller, Carmel, IN: Que Education & Training, 1998. ISBN: 0789716690.

Troubleshooting and Repairing Computer Printers, Stephen J. Bigelow, New York: McGraw-Hill, 1996. ISBN: 007005732X.

Troubleshooting and Repairing Computer Monitors, Stephen J. Bigelow, New York: Computing McGraw-Hill, 1996. ISBN: 0070057346.

PERIODICALS

The Computer Shopper, 1 Park Avenue, 11th Floor, New York, NY 10016; (800) 274-6384; (212) 503-3800. Filled with information on prices of computers and their components, this is a large-format publication widely available on newsstands. Web site: *www.computershopper.com*

Computer Hotline, Printers Hotline and Telecoms Gear, 15400 Knoll Trail Drive, Suite 500, Dallas, TX 75248; (800) 866-3241. Traderlike publications for finding used supplies and equipment.

TRAINING

As stated earlier, training in computer repair is widely available. For a list of links to training sources on the web, go to *www.certification-update.com/certtraining.html.* Some prominent providers of training are:

CBT Systems, a major developer of self-paced computer-based training has a number of subsidiaries offering pertinent courses, including:

- **FOREFRONT DIRECT,** 25400 U.S. Highway, 19N. #285, Clearwater, FL 33763; (800) 475-5831. Web site: *www.ffg.com.* Courseware for PC/network technicians.

- **SCHOLARS.COM,** 125 Hanwell Road, Fredericton, NB, E3B 2P9, Canada; (506) 457 1285. Web site: *www.scholars.com.* Offers subjects ranging from Microsoft certification to general knowledge courses.

McGraw-Hill, NRI Schools offers a home-study course in PC servicing in preparation for A+ Certification. Course covers electronics, data recovery, hardware interactions, RAM troubleshooting, CD-ROM repairs, Windows, and the Internet. It includes computer and diagnostic hardware and software. McGraw-Hill Continuing Education Center, 4401 Connecticut Avenue, N.W., Washington, DC 20008; (202) 244-1600. Web site: *www.mhcec.com*

TOOLS, SUPPLIES AND TECHNICAL INFORMATION

JENSEN TOOLS, 7815 South 46th Street, Phoenix, AZ 85044; (800) 426-1194 or (602) 968-6231; fax: (800) 366-9662 or (602) 438-1690. Major supplier of tool kits, tools, test instruments, and specialized and hard-to-find items, some of which are exclusive. Web site: *www.jensentools.com*

MICRO HOUSE, 4900 Pearl East Circle, Suite 101, Boulder, CO 80301; (800) 222-5916; (303) 443-3388. Subscription service providing instant access to tens of thousands of pages of technical information on over 15,000 hardware and operating system topics, including jumper settings, diagrams, and configuration details. Web site: *www. microhouse.com*

Consulting to Businesses and Other Organizations

Consulting remains among one of the fastest-growing segments of our information society. There are over a half-million consultants of all kinds in North America, split among hundreds of specialties ranging from affirmative action to automation, from agriculture production to utility-rate analysis, from cash management to competitive analysis, from forms design to turnaround management, from geochemical to graphological, from managed care to order processing, from parenting to purchasing, from packaging appearance to political risk, from telecommunications to traffic, from wage and salary administration to warehouse arrangement, and the possibilities go on. The Institute of Management Consulting breaks its membership into 279 different specialties.

What is consulting? According to Bill Mooney, who has made a business of introducing people to the world of consulting, "Consulting is the business of solving problems for people in organizations." In this profile we focus on consultants who deal with organizations (for profit, nonprofit, and governmental). Consulting fields such as wedding planners and image consultants, whose clients are primarily individual consumers, are treated as separate profiles in this book. Also profiled separately are fields of consulting where the work is sufficiently distinguishable that we feel obligated to describe them individually. These are computer consultants, public relations specialists, and security consultants.

Management and marketing consultants are the most populated specialties while the fastest growing are engineering and technical consultants. Other fast-growing specialties are environmental compliance, diversity in the workplace, and retirement planning.

Consulting fields can be viewed primarily as "hard side" and "soft side."

- Hard side consulting develops out of the physical and mathematical services and covers consulting in mechanical engineering, chemical engineering, physical sciences, space sciences, medical areas, television and radio electronics, and the many other mathematical/scientific fields.

- Soft side develops out of the humanities and psychology and covers technologies developing from them in human resources, health administration, education, law, government, and business.

American companies tend to rely on the use of consultants more than companies in other countries. The principal reasons for the growing use of consultants are:

- As corporations scale back experienced personnel (as they have been rampantly doing for more than a decade whether the economy is up or down), consultants are increasingly being paid to implement projects as well as provide guidance and expertise.

- More and more companies need to solve problems to be in compliance with dozens of government agencies (federal, state, city, or county) or quasi-governmental agencies such as the Air Quality Management Department.

- Companies constantly need to introduce and integrate new technologies from either the hard side or the soft side.

- Because of the ever-changing economy and the increase in global competition, problems must be solved in an efficient, cost-effective manner, which means engaging outside consultants to save on the costs of hiring the expertise in-house. Outside consultants also provide a company with a wider breadth of experience and a wider variety of contacts than its in-house employees have.

- Smaller companies are increasingly contracting out whole functions, such as human resources and purchasing, to people who function as consultants. Renting a CFO (chief financial officer) who perhaps comes in one day a week or a chemist to run a lab has become a trend. Some consultants are growing significant businesses by setting up separate divisions of their consulting practices to take over full functions, such as Electronic Data Interchange (EDI), from companies or nonprofit organizations. Companies need an EDI system for incoming and outgoing transactions that must be handled electronically. Companies that do not want to make the capital investment for EDI or to have the headaches of having it in-house are happy to find reliable consultants to do this for them. Such an arrangement operates somewhat like a service bureau in which paper from the company is converted to data that is then sent to its destination (like a Wal-Mart), and then information is received and passed along to the client.

Paul Franklin, former publisher of *The Professional Consultant*, believes that change itself has become a driving force behind the increasing use of consultants. Companies now may either use a consultant to help plan new strategies and then do the work inside or use their internal managers to strategize and implement a new business plan, but use a consultant to validate the work.

We add to these factors the fact that consulting provides a lifestyle people want. People at the level of skills needed by consultants want more control over their work. They want greater variety, more challenge, and more respect. They want to be their own boss without a significant capital investment, and consulting fills this bill. Management consulting is thus an excellent home-based business if you can fulfill the qualifications listed below and are able to develop a reputation for helping companies large or small become more successful and profitable.

Knowledge and Skills You Need to Have

- "Consultants are the high priests of the information revolution," observed the late Howard Shenson. "They possess the knowledge that drives our economic system." Knowledge is therefore first on the list of prerequisites for being a consultant. Bill Mooney points out that technical knowledge is not sufficient to succeed. Beyond that, they must have expertise and experience. Expertise covers both a consultant's knowledge base and technique base. Experience is the track record of using expertise to solve problems of people in organizations, adding value and conferring benefits in the process. Your clients will always ask you who else you have helped to solve problems like theirs. As Mooney points out, it is best to be seen as an authority; and if you can't do that, you should be an expert; and if you can't do that, you should be a specialist rather than a generalist.

- You must know what you are talking about at all times. There is no room for equivocation as a consultant. Clients expect that you will deliver on what you promise.

- Consultants need to have people skills in order to understand client needs and problems and to articulate what they understand. Not everyone has the counseling skills that must supplement technical expertise.

- You need excellent communication skills, written and oral, as you will be dealing with the CEOs, senior executives, and managers of companies. You will likely write many reports and speak in front of groups of executives.

- You must have skills similar to those of a psychologist in order to understand your clients, their goals, the kind of help they need, and the best way to help them. As an outsider, it can take time to figure out the politics of the organizations you work with, and what is really happening to explain why they brought you in. Often what the owners or on-staff marketing people tell you is what they think you want to hear or what they need to say to protect their own jobs. You must be able to roll up your sleeves and figure out how to solve problems as if it were your own company, which requires good management sense.

- You need to be research-and-development oriented. This means you have to know how to use questions to get significant information. Beyond that, you must also know how to analyze the answers you get and apply them to the benefit of both your business and your clients.

- You have to use strategic planning to get a competitive edge. This means you must be able to identify needs and directions that your clients may not have even thought about yet. You must have the ability to see future trends and directions for the industries you are working in.

- You have to be willing to take risks.

- Bill Mooney stresses that a continuous improvement program to update your knowledge, technique, and skills is imperative. You stay aware of the latest developments affecting the industry in which you work and in the consulting business. You have to learn how to analyze your own problem-solving record, to identify what you can specialize in and when to specialize, to evaluate the market for your type of work, and to position yourself against the competition.

Start-up Costs	Low	High
Computer	$ 1,500	$ 3,000
Printer	$ 300	$ 800
or		
Multi-function printer/fax/scanner/copier	$ 150	$ 600
Cell phone	$ 75	$ 200
Specialized software such as for project management and contact management	$ 250	$ 1,000

Office furniture, especially an ergonomic chair	$ 400	$ 1,000
Initial marketing budget including dues for professional and trade associations	$ 2,000	$ 5,000
Professional liability insurance	$ 900	$ 1,200
Professional development seminars, reference books and continuing education	$ 500	$ 1,000
Total	$ 5,775	$ 13,800

Advantages

- You receive maximum pay for what you know and can do.

- Consulting stimulates your creativity. Most consultants are problem solvers. They have a different way of looking at situations than their clients and can therefore respond with innovative solutions.

- The work offers variety and challenge. You can work with many different companies and be involved in a wide assortment of problems and solutions. Your work is seldom done. In the past many people would try consulting, but if a job opened up, they would take it. Now, once they become consultants, they more often stick with it and make it their permanent occupation.

- It can be satisfying for you to see your ideas and strategies implemented and to get positive feedback when they are working.

- New laws and regulations at the federal, state, and sometimes local level create demand for people who are able quickly to learn more than anyone else and who are able to consult. Newly introduced technology can afford such a window as well. A well-known name in desktop video was a cook when he heard about a new technology that interested him.

Disadvantages

- Consultants want to sell their knowledge and advice; clients want to buy added value that can be quantified. To market successfully, you need to demonstrate to the client that he or she is going to see tangible results as a result of your work. This is the consultant's Catch-22.

- Depending on the size of the client, your impact on the bottom line can be highly visible, and all eyes stay on you. You are held accountable for the success or failure of the entire company, even when market forces beyond your control or a bad product cause its demise. In other situations, the result of your work may not be known until far into the future when the company succeeds or fails.

- The solitary portions of the work can be lonely.

- Depending on your location and specialization, you may have clients all over the continent or world who require you to travel frequently or for long periods of time.

- Some clients can obsess you to death.

- Cash flow can be a problem. It can take a long time to close a deal. You must get clear written contracts with milestones indicating when you will be paid and follow through on paperwork and if payments are late. Large corporations can be the worst at paying bills late.

- The failure rate is high, in part because many people make a less-than-required commitment to consulting while wishing for new opportunities for employment.

Pricing

Most consultants charge an hourly or daily rate for their time; however, consultants fare better when they bill on a project basis. A project fee may be a flat fee for the job, as for a workshop or speech, which means the consultant needs to predict safely the amount of time that will be spent. A project fee may also be a contingent fee based on the results achieved or value added, such as an increase in sales, an appreciation in value, or a decrease in costs for the client. Some consultants bill by unit of work, such as per person interviewed.

Many consultants work out retainer arrangements for three, six, or twelve months, which provides them with regular, ongoing payments in return for being available to the client for an agreed upon number of hours a month for a defined scope of work. A retainer typically will result in the client getting a discount if they use the consultant for the number of hours they are entitled to use. However, some consultants do not limit hours but tightly define the scope of work covered. In this way, the client can be comfortable about getting all the help they will need to solve the agreed-upon problem.

A 1997 survey by Carey Associates, Inc. showed that hourly rates range from under $50 to over $350 an hour, with a median rate of $150. Rates depend on experience, reputation, success rate in the industry in which you work, the complexity of the assignment, the nature and size of the client (consultants serving the public and nonprofit sectors generally earn less; larger corporations generally pay higher fees), location of the client, and the urgency with which the client needs the work.

Time-billing is usually done against an estimate. Sometimes consultants agree to an absolute limit on their total fee. The survey further showed that most consultants bill about 1,000 hours a year.

Consultants can test the waters in face-to-face situations by quoting a top price for a broad scope of work and seeing if the client blinks. It's considered even better practice to provide choices to most clients, which may go beyond the scope of work the client may have defined. Using the blink test, if the client reacts adversely, negotiate a lower fee for a reduced scope of work so that the fee has some reasonable relationship to what you stated your original fee to be.

Expect former employers, who may have reduced their workforce to the point where they can no longer get the work out, to pay you a premium rate, for instance, a multiple of your prior salary plus fringe benefits.

Potential Earnings

Typical Annual Gross Revenues: $150,000 based on $150 an hour for 1,000 hours a year. However, it is apt to take two or more years to reach this rate and level of billable hours.

Overhead: moderate to high (20 to 60 percent).

Best Home Businesses Estimate of Market Potential

The more change there is for corporations in their structure, size, operations, and markets, the greater the demand for consultants for both their expertise and their labor.

Best Ways to Get Business

- Referrals are the number-one way consultants get business. You must nurture repeat and referral business consistently and continually. It's estimated that it costs a consultant five times more to land a new client than to get a contract with a former client. Have an ongoing program for staying in contact with former clients and colleagues and people who have work to give out. To stay "top of the mind" requires a combination of phone calls (with something interesting or useful to say), sending articles of interest (by mail, e-mail, or fax), having your name seen in credible venues—in print on conference programs, and online. Invaluable to a top-of-the-mind marketing program is contact management software such as *Act!, Ecco Pro, Goldmine, Maximizer, Outlook,* and *Telemagic.* It's worth checking out the special capabilities of each program so you will find a fit between your needs and the strengths of each particular program. The more you can automate, the more energy you can have to be creative; and generally the more creative one's marketing, the better.

- "Informational inquiries" are the second most productive way to get clients, according to Bill Mooney. This is done by calling companies to ask some general questions about a business or management problem you are studying or for which you would like to write an article. Such inquires give you an opportunity to get to know a company and to begin building a relationship with their key people. It may be that one of your questions rings true with someone at the company, and they then hire you to find the answers for them.

- Develop and present proposals. A marketing consultant sent out 200 résumés cold and got zero responses. After reflection, he decided to try the following tactic. He identified ten companies and developed a proposal that outlined what he could do that would add value to their organizations. He sent out his proposals and got two responses, out of which he got one contract offer, which turned into a major moneymaker for him.

- Build relationships with clients. Consultants are not only selling expertise, but themselves as problem solvers. Once a client is convinced a consultant has a track record, the client will check if the consultant has the breadth and depth to handle other assignments. Increasingly, consulting is coming to mean implementing, not just advising.

- Develop an informational brochure featuring the key information your prospects need to know about what you do. This brochure can be on your Web site or advertised as a free brochure in classified ads and mentioned in the articles you write with the offer you will send one to anyone who requests it.

- Join and participate in multiple trade associations and professional organizations. To find associations of value, ask experienced consultants, check business calendar listings in your area, and search the Web.

- Speak and present. Giving speeches, seminars, and workshops can be an effective way to establish your expertise. Choose issues of current importance and give them compelling titles. If you have speaking experience and wish to make presenting a significant part of your revenue, consider joining the National Speakers' Association.

- Write. This ranges from letters to the editors of newspapers and business journals (this can lead to appearing on business talk shows and being used as a source by journalists), to articles for newsletters or your own promotional newsletter, to writing a business book.

- Create audio tapes, videotapes, and other educational/informational tools with which prospective clients can get to know you. While these may be sold, they can also be used as "calling cards."

- Get listed in print and online directories used by prospective customers.

- If you work in several industries or have several consulting products, develop separate print collaterals and Web sites for each.

First Steps

- You need first to "position" yourself as a consultant so people will be able to identify and find you. Ask yourself: (1) what kinds of problems you can solve, (2) what kinds of clients need those problems solved, and (3) what kinds of problems do you have experience solving? Use these answers to develop a sense of your technical know-how, expertise, and experience. Research the industry and disciplines and trends within your industry, as well as consultants already serving that industry. Figure out a way to differentiate yourself from competitors, either by defining a specialty for yourself or by creative pricing, that is, making an offer they can't refuse. Remember you can't be all things to all people. Develop a business plan, including your marketing plan for the first year. You can use a software program or actually write out your plan. The 47 questions and the structure for answering them in our book *Making Money with Your Computer at Home* can guide you.

- Join both organizations for consultants and trade organizations in the field in which you want to work.

- Make a list of everyone in your area whom you know personally who would make a good prospective client or who is in a position to refer clients to you. Don't stop until you have at least twenty contacts. Send a letter to each of these people saying that you've gone into business for yourself as a consultant and want to take him or her to lunch. Let the person know in the letter that you would like to ask several questions about his or her most pressing issues. Then call to set up a time. Most will accept the invitation for lunch. Start small with a few clients on projects that have a finite beginning and ending, so that you have some specific results to point to when at full speed in marketing your services. Your first project or two may need to be done without a fee in order to get the experience.

- Proceed with marketing by researching the companies or organizations you can work with, determining their probable needs. Present proposals identifying exactly what you can do. If you have zero clients, invest 100 percent of your time in marketing.

- Make a commitment to be successful. If you are successful in other areas of life, you can be successful in consulting with a full commitment. Imagine yourself as being on the top and believe in your own abilities to succeed.

Where to Turn for Information and Help

SEMINARS

HOW TO BUILD & MAINTAIN A PROFITABLE CONSULTING PRACTICE, one-day seminar offered around the country by the Center for Consulting and Professional Practices, a division of William Mooney Associates, 19401 South Vermont Avenue, Suite K100, P.O. Box 6159, Torrance, CA 90504; (310) 324-2386. E-mail: coachconsult@earthlink.net. Mooney also provides one-on-one coaching to help independent consultants attract more and better clients.

ORGANIZATIONS

THE ALLIANCE OF THE INSTITUTE OF ELECTRICAL AND ELECTRONICS ENGINEERS (IEEE) CONSULTANTS' NETWORKS COORDINATING COMMITTEE supports self-employed IEEE members through local IEEE Consultants' Networks, a yearly national conference. They help members generate business by offering a National Electrotechnology Consultants Directory from their Web site with links to information about each consultant listed. IEEE is located at 1730 Massachusetts Ave NW, Washington, DC 20036; (202) 371-0101. Web site: *www.ieee.org./consultants*

AMERICAN ASSOCIATION OF PROFESSIONAL CONSULTANTS (AAPC) AND NATIONAL BUREAU OF CERTIFIED CONSULTANTS (NBCC). AAPC is for consultants with less than five years experience. The National Bureau (NBCC) offers certification, which requires five years of full-time consulting or ten years of part-time consulting. AAPC offers the long distance learning course, *The Complete Consulting Success System,* that leads to a certificate. 2728 Fifth Avenue, San Diego, CA 92103; (800) 543-1114; (619) 297-2207. Web site: *www.national-bureau.com*

INSTITUTE OF CERTIFIED BUSINESS COUNSELORS, PO Box 70326, Eugene, OR 97401; (541) 345-8064. Offers a certification program. Web site: *www.nvst.com./cbc*

INSTITUTE OF MANAGEMENT CONSULTANTS, 1200 19th Street N.W., Suite 300, Washington, DC 20036; (800) 221-2557; (202) 857-5334. Membership of more than 2,000 consulting firms, including sole practitioners. Offers a certification program for consultants with more than five years' experience. Web site has back issues of the Institute's publication, *Management Consulting Times.* Web site: *www.imcusa.org*

WEB SITES

EXPERT MARKETPLACE lists consulting contract opportunities, listing service, and resources; (800) 983-9737; (303) 790-7474. Web site: *www.expertmarketplace.com*

NATIONAL CONSULTANT REFERRALS, INC. offers an online referral service, downloadable articles, an electronic newsletter and resources. (800) 221-3104. Web site: *www.referrals.com*

BOOKS

Are Your Lights On?: How to Figure Out What the Problem Really Is, Donald C. Gause, Gerald M. Weinberg, Dorset House, 1990. ISBN: 0932633161.

The Business Plan Guide for Independent Consultants, Herman Holtz, New York: John Wiley & Sons, 1994. ISBN: 047159735X. Holtz has also produced *The Consultant's Guide to Proposal Writing* (ISBN: 0471515698), *The Independent Consultant's Brochure and Letter Handbook* (ISBN: 0471597333), *How to Succeed as an Independent Consultant* (ISBN: 047157581X), and *Databased Marketing* (ISBN: 0471551872), also from John Wiley & Sons.

The Complete Guide to Consulting Success, Ted Nicholas, Paul Franklin, Howard L. Shenson, Upstart Publishing, 1997. ISBN: 1574100556.

The Complete Guide to Consulting Contracts, Herman R. Holtz, Dearborn Trade, Upstart Publishing, 1997. ISBN: 157410070X.

Consultant & Independent Contractor Agreements, Stephen Fishman, Nolo Press, 1998. ISBN: 0873374576.

Consultants & Consulting Organizations Directory, Gale Research, 27500 Drake Road, Farmington Hills, MI 48331; (248) 699-4253. ISBN/ISSN: 078762084X. The directory accepts free listings and is available at reference libraries in print and on CD-ROM. Web site: *www.gale.com*

The Consultative Approach: Partnering for Results!, Virginia LaGrossa, Suzanne Saxe, Pfeiffer & Co, 1998. ISBN: 0787911003.

Consulting for Dummies, Bob Nelson and Peter Economy, IDG Books Worldwide, 1997. ISBN: 0764550349.

How to Become a Successful Consultant in Your Own Field, Hubert Bermont, Prima Publishing, 1997. ISBN: 0761511008.

Inside the Technical Consulting Business, Harvey Kaye, New York: John Wiley & Sons, 1997. ISBN: 0471183415.

Marketing Your Consulting and Professional Services, Dick Connor, Jeff Davidson, Richard A. Connor, Jeffrey P. Davidson, New York: John Wiley & Sons, 1997. ISBN: 0471133922.

Million Dollar Consulting, Alan Weiss, Ph.D., New York: McGraw-Hill, 1994. ISBN: 0070691789.

The Performance Consultant's Fieldbook: Tools and Techniques for Improving Organizations and People, Judith A. Hale, Jossey-Bass Publishers, 1998. ISBN: 0787940194.

The Secrets of Consulting: A Guide to Giving and Getting Advice Successfully, Gerald M. Weinberg, New York: Dorset House, 1986. ISBN: 0932633013.

Shenson on Consulting, Howard L. Shenson, New York: John Wiley & Sons, 1994. ISBN: 0471009253. Other classic books from the late Howard Shenson are *The Contract and Fee-Setting Guide for Consultants and Professionals* (ISBN: 0471515388) and *138 Quick Ideas to Get More Clients* (ISBN: 0471589519), also from Wiley.

The Six-Figure Consultant, Robert W. Bly, Upstart Publishing Company, 1998. ISBN: 157410120X.

MAGAZINES & NEWSLETTERS

Consultants need to read widely. Successful practitioners read at least six if not a dozen magazines in many different fields to increase their awareness of business, government, and the fields in which you work. Read any and all magazines in your field of specialization. Keep up-to-date with the names, companies, and technologies of your industry. Also read business publications, particularly what your clients and prospective clients read, such as *Business Week, Forbes, Fortune, Inc.,* and *The Wall Street Journal*. Each of these publications is read by more than 50 percent of senior corporate executives. A majority of affluent small-business owners read *The Wall Street Journal*, according to a study by Payment Systems, Inc. Most corporate executives and business owners read the business section of their local newspaper. Listed below are periodicals of special note to consultants:

Consultants News, Kennedy Publications, Templeton Road, Fitzwilliam, NH 03447; (800) 531-0007; (603) 585-6544. Web site: *www.kennedypub. com*. Kennedy also publishes *What's Working in Consulting*, aimed at solo practitioner, written by Giles Goodhead. Kennedy Publications is a major publisher of consultant information, including the newsletters, a directory of consulting firms in North America (*Directory of Management Consultants*), and a catalogue of 100 titles and special reports on marketing, client-consultant relationships, inspiration, and practice improvement (*Catalog of Management Consulting Books*).

Consulting Opportunities Journal, New Ventures Publishing Group, 123 World Trade Center, Suite 327, P.O. Box 420726, Dallas, TX 75342; (972) 227-5326; Published since 1981. Web site: *www.bizhowto.com*

Knowledge Management Magazine. Covers information technology. Published by Learned Information Europe Ltd. Web site has content including case studies and you can order a free sample issue from the Web site: *www.knowledge-management.co.uk/kbase*

Marketing Conferences and Seminars, Learning Resources Network Inc., 1550 Hayes Drive, Manhattan, KS 66502; (800) 678-5376, (785) 539-5376. Web site: *www.lern.org*

Copywriter

Every human organization, private and public, represents itself to the world with words. But their words don't always get the desired results. Crafting words that produce the desired effects is the work of professional copywriters. The copy in advertising, on Web sites, direct mail pieces, and brochures not only needs to be clearly and concisely written, it must also capture attention, impress, inspire trust, and motivate the reader to buy or to make contact. Small and medium-size businesses and agencies often lack the time, talent, or know-how to describe themselves, what they do, and what they are selling well enough. So they turn to independent copywriters.

Copywriters create copy for a vast variety of materials.

- ads
- brochures
- newsletters
- instruction manuals
- grant proposals
- press releases
- company names and slogans
- consumer information booklets
- captions for photographs
- product literature
- company annual reports
- product names

- media kits
- feature stories
- ghostwritten magazine articles
- direct mail pieces
- Web sites content
- TV and radio spots
- print and Web catalogues

- packaging labels
- marketing communication plans
- restaurant menus
- speeches
- telemarketing scripts
- video scripts
- storyboards

Clients include major corporations, doctors and lawyers, small manufacturers, automotive dealers, retail stores, hotels, restaurants, banks, health clubs, consumer electronics firms, and direct-mail catalogues.

Bob Bly, a prolific copywriter based in New Jersey, writes many things, from ads to brochures to direct-mail copy. He enjoys the writing, likes having a flexible work schedule, and earns a good living. In fact, he says he makes more money than he could make in a staff job. But he feels pressure trying to meet deadlines, which are shorter today than ever, and working on multiple projects at once. Bly, whose numerous publications include several books, reports, and monographs targeted to other writers, gets most of his business as a direct result of his books. He also does some advertising and other forms of promotion and gives seminars.

Versatility can be a real plus as a copywriter, but increasingly copywriters are developing niches for themselves. Don Hauptman, for example, a New York-based freelance copywriter, specializes in writing sales copy for financial newsletters with subscription rates in the hundreds of dollars. Stephanie Gallagher, who regularly hired top copywriters as a newsletter publisher and is the author of *Bargains of the Rich and Lazy,* advocates specializing from the beginning of your career. She says, "Take a field you are knowledgeable about—the law, baseball, mutual funds, flowers, tools, cooking—that's where you will probably produce the best copy because you are a consumer of that."

The earnings of top copywriters can be breathtaking. The top one percent make between $10,000 and $25,000 for a direct-mail package, though they sometimes accept a lower flat fee in exchange for a royalty of one cent per piece mailed. What does it take to write top copy? Gallagher says, "You can be clever and creative if it works and boring if that's what it takes. You need to be the kind of person who can get inside someone else's shoes and understand them. If you can do that, you can make a good copywriter."

Knowledge and Skills You Need to Have

- A strong background in communications and English or in whichever language you will be working in.

- A logical, organized mind that can assimilate information, synthesize it, and integrate it into a theme or message.

- Curiosity about how something works and a sense of what makes it appealing, beneficial, better, interesting, and unique.

- The ability to write clear, interesting, arresting, and compelling copy.

- Creativity and, in particular, the imagination to say something in a way that hasn't been said before.

- The self-discipline to overcome writer's block and to see a project through even when ideas don't flow readily.

- The ability to visualize the layout of a printed page and work closely with graphic designers.

Start-up Costs	Low	High
Computer	$ 1,500	$ 3,000
Printer	$ 300	$ 800
or		
Multi-function printer/fax/scanner/copier	$ 150	$ 600
Office furniture, especially an ergonomic chair	$ 400	$ 1,000
Dictionaries, word books, CD-ROMs	$ 100	$ 500
Initial marketing budget	$ 1,000	$ 5,000
Total	$ 3,450	$ 10,900

Advantages

- No fixed schedule means you can work anytime you want, with the exception of meetings, which are on clients' schedules.

- Copywriting is creative work taking plain, even dull, information and producing something original through your writing and creative talents.

- You have the opportunity to try out your ideas and discover how your work influences people.

- This work is concrete and finite. When you finish a project, you have something in your hands that didn't exist before.

Disadvantages

- Frequently you will need to work under the pressure of tight deadlines.

- Pricing your service appropriately is sometimes difficult. Nonwriters don't appreciate how long it takes to write.

- To be successful, you have to work on and juggle several projects at once, which can be stressful.

- The actual copywriting is something you must do alone.

- You may come up against a wall because the subject is difficult to write about, or you cannot find a new idea to fit into your campaign.

Pricing

You can charge by the hour, by the day, or by the job. Keep in mind that pricing for copywriting can vary regionally.

By the hour: Fees can range from $10 an hour for a novice to over $150 an hour for speechwriters. For professionals with some experience, on average, fees run from $40 to $75 an hour with $50 being the most typical rate.

By the day: Fees for consulting on a direct-mail project range from $1,500 to $2,000 a day.

By the job: Fees generally range from $2,000 to $7,000 for a single direct-mail package or a series of renewal mailers for a magazine; $2,000 to $4,000 for a sales letter; $1,000 to $2,000 for a radio script. When you bid by the job, you estimate the total time you will spend. Therefore, you need to keep accurate records of the hours you spend on projects so that you will know how much time a job will take and can price it accordingly.

Potential Earnings

Robert W. Bly, the author of *The Copywriter's Handbook,* has surveyed attendees at his workshops in cities across the country. He has found that people who approach copywriting as a business typically earn:

- $20,000 to $40,000 a year during their first two years, which he calls phase I

- $40,000 to $80,000 a year during what he calls phase II

- $80,000 to $175,000 a year when they become real pros during phase III, which often occurs in three to five years.

Overhead: low (20 percent or less).

Best Home Businesses Estimate of Market Potential

The need to communicate only increases as society grows more complex with technology. New media spawns new markets for copywriters. The Web has provided lots of work, but the pay has not been as good for writers in general.

Best Ways to Get Business

- Talking to former clients or employers and businesspeople you know or meeting and showing them samples of your work. Send samples to them and let them know what you really do at a level they understand.

- Networking in organizations, such as trade and business associations, particularly in industries or fields in which you have experience.

- Developing affiliations with related professionals such as marketing consultants, graphic designers, desktop publishers, newsletter publishers, photographers, and printers who can refer business to you.

- At the conclusion of a successful project, ask for a reference letter you can use in talking with prospective clients.

- Go to conventions of the industry or trade. Be proactive about making contact.

- Make speeches and conduct workshops to develop a reputation that you know what you are talking about. Get lists of attendees to use as a mailing list.

- Dropping off samples of your work at the offices of other businesses in your clients' office buildings or business centers, indicating that you work for their neighbor and would like them to see a sample of what you do.

- For direct mail, Stephanie Gallagher says, "Be bold, get outside the box by creating a direct-mail package for the prospective client. A sales letter with some samples of your work gets tossed." You want your sales letter to produce reactions such as "Who wrote that?" or "I want to meet the person who wrote this."

- Having your own Web site and getting listed in directories of freelance writers. Without a Web site, you will not get as many leads from the online database directories where consumers go to find a writer. Most online directories provide the ability to link the consumer directly to your page.

First Steps

- Take courses offered by local writers' groups, extension programs, colleges, and universities.

- Join special-interest sections of writers' groups that meet to read their material to one another and compare notes.

- Develop a look for your own business card and letterhead that is an advertisement of what you can do for others.

- Create a portfolio of at least five samples to show clients.

- Join an organization of people who can refer you to clients; for example, printers, graphic designers, photographers, or marketing consultants. Also join associations in the fields you might typically be working in.

- Read books and go to writers' workshops. Never assume you're done learning.

Where To Turn For Information And Help

ORGANIZATIONS

AMERICAN ADVERTISING FEDERATION, 1101 Vermont Avenue, N.W., Suite 500, Washington, DC 20005; (800) 999-2231; (202) 898-0089; fax (202) 898-0159. Association that brings together corporate advertisers, agencies, media companies, suppliers and academia and is the parent organization for many local ad clubs or ad federations. Look in your telephone directory for your local affiliate or use the Web site *www.aaf.org,* which has a list of local federations with links to them.

AMERICAN MARKETING ASSOCIATION, 311 South Wacker Drive, Suite 5800, Chicago, IL 60606; (312) 648-0536. Comprehensive professional society of marketers with 500 chapters in North America. Web site: *www.ama.org*

DIRECT MARKETING ASSOCIATION, 11 West 42d Street, 25th Floor, New York, NY 10036; (212) 768-7277. Web site: *www.the-dma.org*

EDITORIAL FREELANCERS' ASSOCIATION, 71 West 23d Street, Suite 1504, New York, NY 10010; (212) 929-5400. Membership includes copywriters. Web site: *www.the-efa.org*

BOOKS

Catch Phrases, Cliches and Idioms: A Dictionary of Familiar Expressions, Doris Craig, McFarland & Company, 1990. ISBN: 0899504671.

The Copywriter's Handbook, Robert W. Bly, Henry Holt and Company, 1990. ISBN: 0805011943.

Cybertalk That Sells, Herschell Gordon Lewis, Jamie Murphy, NTC/Contemporary Publishing, 1998. ISBN: 0809229234.

Phrases That Sell: Ultimate Phrase Finder to Help You Promote Your Products, Services, and Ideas, Sally Germain, Edward W. Werz, NTC/Contemporary Publishing, 1998. ISBN: 0809229773.

Persuading on Paper: The Complete Guide to Writing Copy That Pulls in Business, Marcia Yudkin, 1996.

Positioning: The Battle for Your Mind, Al Reis and Jack Trout, Warner Books, 1993. ISBN: 0446347949. A classic.

Scientific Advertising and My Life in Advertising, Claude Hopkins, National Textbook Co., 1986. ISBN: 0844231010. A classic.

Secrets of a Freelance Writer: How to Make Eighty-five Thousand Dollars a Year, Robert W. Bly, Henry Holt and Company, 1997. ISBN: 0805047603.

Tested Advertising Methods, John Caples, Prentice-Hall, 1998. ISBN: 0130957011.

Words That Sell, Richard Bayan, NTC/Contemporary Publishing, Reprint Edition. ISBN: 0809247992. A classic.

Writer's Profit Catalogue, 22 East Quackenbush Avenue, 3d Floor, Dumont, NJ 07628; (201) 385-1220. This catalogue is a listing of dozens of books, pamphlets, and audio tapes produced by noted copywriter Bob Bly.

MAGAZINES AND NEWSLETTERS

Creative Business, 275 Newbury Street, Boston, MA 02116; (617) 424-1368. This newsletter is directed at copywriters, designers, art directors, and principals of creative businesses. Subscribers also receive free unlimited telephone consultation. Founded by Cameron Foote.

The Direct Response Specialist, Stilson and Stilson, Box 1075, Tarpon Springs, FL 34688; (727) 786-1411. Newsletter focused on selling by direct-mail and direct-response advertising.

Writer's Digest Magazine, 1507 Dana Avenue, Cincinnati, OH 45207; (513) 531-2222. Web site: *www.writersdigest.com*

SOFTWARE

Ideafisher and Writer's Edge, 2222 Martin Street, Suite 260, Irvine, CA 92612; (949) 225-1100. Web site has links to other creativity products. Web site: *www.ideafisher.com*

Writer's Dreamtools, Slippery Disks, Box 1126, Los Angeles, CA 90069. Lists by day and date thousands of birthdays and historical events, the feast days of every saint, and holidays around the world; there's also space for users to add their own information.

Zillion Kajillion Cliches, Eccentric Software, P.O. Box 2777, Seattle, WA 98111; (800) 436-6758; (206) 760-9547. Contains over 10,000 figures of speech—cliche, catch phrase, and idiom thesaurus.

WEB SITES

FREELANCE ONLINE: Jobs, message boards, a searchable directory of over 700 freelancers. Web site: *www.freelanceonline.com*

PHRASE FINDER: The site is a thesaurus of phrases. *www.shu.ac.uk/web-admin/phrases*

RESOURCE CENTRAL: Links and resources for writing. *www.resourcehelp.com*

USEIT.COM: Tips and resources for writing for the Web. *www.useit.com*

THE WRITE MARKETS REPORT: Print and electronic magazine featuring new and updated markets for freelance writers and journalists. Articles and columns focus on selling the written word. *www.writersmarkets.com*

THE ZUZU'S PETALS LITERARY RESOURCE: *www.zuzu.com*

Desktop Publishing

Desktop publishing, growing out of enhancements to word-processing software, exemplifies the quick speed of change brought about by personal computers. As an occupation, the Department of Labor predicts desktop publisher to be one of the fastest growing vocations, expecting it to leap 74 percent by the year 2006.

Today, desktop publishers are apt to be preparing documents for electronic use rather than for print, but the ability to publish for print still remains the key to being identified as a desktop publisher. Of course, desktop publishing eliminates many steps in the process of preparing printed materials, replacing the services once provided by a layout artist, typesetting service, color separator, and sometimes it eliminates the printer. Also, print shops no longer have cameras, so all images must be scanned into documents, creating one more role for the desktop publisher.

Even sophisticated word-processing programs with desktop publishing capabilities are limited in their ability to develop complex designs, and they don't have a full range of typographic controls. This is another advantage offered by desktop publishing services.

The market for desktop publishing both print and electronic is extensive, including large companies, nonprofit organizations, government agencies, and other small businesses. Organizations of all kinds need material for both their internal and their external communications, from memos and papers, to training manuals, annual reports, quarterly journals, and sales/promotional brochures and ads. Since the arrival of desktop publishing in 1985, crudely typed and photocopied price lists, contracts, newsletters, or bulletins are no longer acceptable. Now proposals, flyers, forms, newsletters, reports, and presentation materials of all types are expected to look professionally done and be produced quickly for both print and Web use.

But changes in technology not only provide more desktop publishing opportunities; they've also affected what it takes to succeed in desktop publishing today. Norman Paddock, founder of the Association of Desktop Publishers, says, "The day of the general desktop publisher is diminishing. Now you must find a specialty and market the blazes out of it." Self-employed desktop publishers not only need to know more than their clients but they also must have better technology and sharper skills. Because many people have the ability to produce desktop published materials with their own software, a professional desktop publisher must offer something special. This includes understanding and being able to manage the mechanics of what's going to happen to material once it's designed, whether it will be in electronic or print form.

Aysha Griffin, owner of Studio A in Colorado Springs, works with businesses and nonprofits in producing their marketing materials. Because she is a writer and former business editor, she recognizes the business challenges of her clients and develops writing and consulting assignments to assist them. While some desktop publishers still take on any work that comes their way, the trend is to focus on specific industries, sizes or types of clients, or selected types of documents. You can specialize in newsletters or catalogues, but you can specialize still further by doing only newsletters for law firms or catalogues for mail-order craft companies. The possibilities are limited only by your imagination. The trend is to distance oneself from being considered an ordinary desktop publisher. "Remember if you can't do better than the clients can do themselves, they won't give you the business," says Norman Paddock.

Desktop publishing work can be done at home, but someone skilled in desktop publishing may also work on-site for client companies. Some desktop publishers have begun calling themselves Web-page designers because while there has been pressure toward lower hourly rates for desktop publishing, Web-page design rates run higher—as much as double.

Knowledge and Skills You Need to Have

- You need to learn to use desktop publishing software in depth, have good computer skills and knowledge of scanner technology.

- You need a feel for design and typography, plus an ability to edit other people's writing and to write. Lawrence Miller, a designer who operates Daddy Desktop, points out that "too many desktop publishers can't write. They mistake typing for writing. They also can't design. They mistake technology for the ability. It is possible, and desirable, to learn to design and write well, but you won't learn it in a software manual. It's a process of being aware of what you want to do, studying, doing, taking more courses and doing some more." Norman Paddock says the more you can work with copy, by creating it or polishing it, the more valuable you are.

- You need to be able to read standard editing symbols, because clients may use them in marking up copy for changes and corrections.

- Good communications skills are a must, both to get business and to draw out of clients what their objectives are. You must help your clients as visual concepts are often difficult to articulate clearly.

- You should know or be willing to learn about typesetting, layout, and printing practices and procedures. This enables you to estimate the time it will take you to design and lay out desired material when you bid on projects.

- Finally, you also need patience because clients often change their minds once they see what they thought they wanted in print or on the computer screen.

Start-up Costs

	Low	High
Macintosh or Wintel (Windows-Intel) computer with a large hard disk and full-page monitor with removable hard drives, Zip, Syquest, Jax, Recordable CD	$ 4,000	$ 8,000
Color laser printer (high-resolution)	$ 2,500	$ 12,000
Software for desktop publishing, Web-page design, page layout, graphics and photo editor, digitial camera, word-processing, drawing, fonts, and clip art	$ 2,000	$ 3,500

Color scanner	$ 400	$ 800
Fax	$ 300	$ 800
Office furniture, especially an ergonomic chair	$ 400	$ 1,000
Initial marketing budget	$ 1,000	$ 5,000
Total	$10,600	$ 31,100

Advantages

- The work is interesting and creative. People who dreamed of doing design work can now do it with desktop publishing.

- Desktop publishing is a rapidly changing field, and if you market aggressively, you can earn a good living.

- There is ample opportunity to develop new skills including Web-page design, copywriting, and providing advertising-agency, marketing-consulting, and multimedia services.

Disadvantages

- The field is increasingly competitive with a resulting downward pressure on prices. In order to stay profitable, you need to find a way to distinguish yourself from your competition and market your services energetically, which can be time-consuming.

- You are often working under the pressure of deadlines, and sometimes you'll have to work nights and weekends.

- There is a constant demand to keep current with the latest advances in software.

- Unless you take necessary precautions, you risk developing repetitive-motion injuries as a result of constant keyboarding.

- Clients are expecting faster and faster turnaround—"instant gratification" was how one desktop publisher expressed it. You may find yourself answering the phone or the front door during personal time if you haven't responded to e-mail promptly or even if you have. One downside to a home-based desktop publishing business is that people are becoming less respectful of your business hours, expecting you to answer the phone or come to the front door yourself anytime day or night.

Pricing

Desktop publishers may charge by the hour, by the page, or by the job.

By the hour: Typical hourly prices range between $25 and $65. Heidi Waldman of St. Paul, points out that "in a metropolitan area, a desktop publishing business is not going to survive charging under $40 an hour." Scanning may need to be billed separately at $25 to $30 an hour or by the scan (approximately $5) but cleanup of graphic images can be billed at or near the rate for desktop publishing.

By the page: Typical prices range between $25 and $50.

By the job: Pricing by the job involves estimating how many hours the job will take and allowing a fudge factor for corrections and changes. This method of pricing is popular, because many clients prefer to pay a fixed price.

Potential Earnings

Typical Annual Gross Revenues: $40,000 based on four billable hours a day (1,000 hours a year) at $40 per hour. While the key to getting earnings up is to work more billable hours a day, earnings may be increased by offering additional services, such as pickup and delivery, extra-fast turnaround time, high-quality printing, a wider variety of font types.

Overhead: moderate (20 to 40 percent).

Best Home Businesses Estimate of Market Potential

Though desktop publishing is past its period of rapid expansion, professional quality work still needs to be done and someone's going to do it. We project future growth in specialty areas and in parts of the country where people are relocating from urban areas.

Best Ways to Get Business

- Person-to-person networking with "end users" in business organizations, trade shows, chambers of commerce, visitors bureaus.

- Directly soliciting print shops, small service and retail businesses, professional practices, and nonprofit organizations with a portfolio of your work.

- Networking in publishing and desktop publishing organizations. Contact mail list services, too, as they may have clients who do mailings and need help with producing effective flyers and brochures.

- Having a Web site that shows your capability and displays samples of your work in the form of an electronic catalog.

- Using direct mail in the form of a letter, a sales flyer, or an introductory brochure sent to a specific market in larger cities or, in smaller communities, to businesses that advertise in the Yellow Pages and in newspapers.

- Following up these mailings with a personal phone call in which you ask for an appointment, to which you bring samples, perhaps customized for the prospective customer's business.

- Phoning and then writing companies that have placed help-wanted ads seeking graphic-arts personnel to do their backup or overflow work.

- Advertising in the Yellow Pages.

- Placing three- to five-line ads in local publications, particularly computer publications, in which you provide specific information about your operation such as the software you use, the output you can offer, and so forth.

- Offering a discount with the first job, for instance, one hour free with a minimum two-hour job.

First Steps

- If you have no experience in the graphic design field, you need to take several courses in design or engage in self-study. Courses and teaching materials are widely available.

- Learn to use desktop publishing software and related drawing, photo editing and Web-page design programs.

- Become facile at using the Internet and knowledgeable about working with printers. You must enable customers to print economically.

- Identify one or more specialty markets not being served and do this before you acquire the expensive software and equipment needed for desktop publishing.

Where to Turn for Information and Help

ORGANIZATIONS

ASSOCIATION OF BUSINESS SUPPORT SERVICES, INTERNATIONAL, 22875 Savi Ranch Parkway, Suite H, Yorba Linda, CA 92887; (714) 282-9398. Web site: *www.abssi.org*

GRAPHIC ARTISTS GUILD, 90 John Street, Suite 403, New York, NY 10038; (212) 791-3400. Web site: *www.gag.org*

NEWSGROUP: comp.text.desktop

BOOKS

The Desktop Publisher's Idea Book: One-Of-A-Kind Projects, Expert Tips, and Hard-To-Find Sources, Chuck Green, Random House Reference, 1997. ISBN: 0679780068.

Design Principles for Desktop Publishers, Tom Lichty, Wadsworth Pub. Co., 1994. ISBN: 0534230822.

Desktop Publishing & Design for Dummies, Roger C. Parker, IDG Books Worldwide, 1995. ISBN: 1568842341.

Graphic Artists Guild Handbook: Pricing & Ethical Guidelines, Graphic Artists Guild, 1997. ISBN: 0932102093.

How to Open and Operate a Home-Based Desktop Publishing Business, Louise Kursmark, Old Saybrook, CT: Globe Pequot Press, 1996. ISBN: 1564408582.

Looking Good in Print, Roger C. Parker, The Coriolis Group, 1998. ISBN: 1566048567.

Redesigning Print for the Web, Mario R. Garcia, Hayden Books, 1997. ISBN: 1568303432.

For pricing manuals, see "Books and Manuals" in the Secretarial and Office Support Services profile.

MAGAZINES AND NEWSLETTERS

Adobe Magazine, Adobe Systems Incorporated, 345 Park Avenue, San Jose, CA 95110. Web site: *www.adobe.com*

Before & After-Pagelab, 1830 Sierra Gardens Dr #30, Roseville, CA 95661; (916) 784-3880. Desktop publishing design.

Desktop Publishers Journal, 462 Boston Street, Topsfield, MA 01983; (978) 887-7900. Web site: *www.dtpjournal.com*

How Magazine, F&W Publications, 1507 Dana Avenue, Cincinnati, OH 45207; (513) 531-2222; fax: (513) 531-1843. Emphasizes business aspects of graphic design. Web site: *www.howdesign.com*

Publish! Magazine, Integrated Media Inc., 501 Second Street, San Francisco, CA 94107; (800) 656-7495. Web site: *www.publish.com*

Step-By-Step Electronic Design®, *Step-By-Step Graphics*® and *Dynamic Graphics Magazine*™, Dynamic Graphics, Inc., 6000 North Forest Park Drive, Peoria, IL 61614; (800) 255-8800; (309) 688-8800. Three separate publications. Web site: *www.dgusa.com*

COURSES

Low-cost courses are available in virtually all communities offered by community colleges, computer schools, and continuing education programs such as The Learning Annex. Instructional material is also available on video and CD-ROM. Art schools are another source of training.

McGraw-Hill's NRI Schools offer a home-study course in Desktop Publishing. McGraw-Hill Continuing Education Center, 4401 Connecticut Avenue, N.W., Washington, DC 20008; (202) 244-1600. Web site: *www.mhcec.com*

ONLINE

Digital Forte. While this web site is primarily devoted to desktop video, it has an active desktop publishing forum. Web site: *www.digitalforte.com*

The Publishing Forums on CompuServe consist of the Desktop Publishing Forum, the Professional Publishing Forum, the Quark Online Users Forum, and two vendor forums.

Desktop Video

People are commemorating all manner of life experience on video from birth to death and everything in between. Enabling this is the fact that 30 percent of U.S. households had camcorders by 1998. But contrary to what you might think, "the proliferation of camcorders has helped us," says Stuart Dizak of Video Data Service. Dizak explains that this is because people want some of their videos professionally edited and with more camcorders out there, there are more videos to edit.

That's where desktop video comes in. Desktop video, often called DTV, uses computer technology to produce professionally edited videos at a lower cost than can be done with traditional editing. While the focus is on producing video, like with other forms of new media, it can integrate animation, photos, music, sound, and other finishing touches into video footage. (See the separate profile on New Media.)

With such a large number of camcorders in use, it's not surprising that consumer versions of video-editing software are available, but most people won't be editing their own videos. Even most small businesspeople aren't using financial software to pay their bills. According to a survey of small business owners by Mindscape Research for NEBS, only 35 percent are using their computers for this comparatively easy task. As you can imagine, they're not chomping at the bit to start editing their own promotional videos.

A desktop video business can offer several services:

- Desktop editing. DTV services use computers to cut, paste, and edit footage in the right sequence, add sound, and perform many sophisticated editing tasks such as fades, wipes, animation overlays, and titles.

- Duplicating videos and converting video from one format to another, as well as transferring from one medium to another, such as print or film to video and video to CD or DVD.

- Desktop authoring, which involves using a software authoring system to create an interactive presentation that combines video with sound, animation, photos, and other images. (Authoring is close to new media, but the final product is video footage, though the resulting video can be transferred to CD and DVD.)

- Desktop animation, in which a DTV service uses the power of computers (rather than dozens of costly animators) to create animated footage using special software products that allow you to create graphics, draw your own artwork, "morph" photos (making an image turn into another image), and utilize many more techniques.

Each of these services can be a distinct business, but one or more may also be utilized to serve one or more markets to produce such things as:

• *Advertising agency prelims:* Most large advertising agencies spend millions of dollars creating proposals for alternative campaigns they can present to their clients to give them a choice of themes or concepts. In the past, showing the client these ideas required intensive storyboarding using illustrators and graphic artists. DTV is now used by many advertising agencies to create a higher-quality first draft of the commercial so that a company can visualize more clearly what their ad campaign may look like.

• *Business proposals:* Videos or animations are used to show how a company proposes to do a project under bid.

• *Cable television commercials:* DTV brings the cost of producing television commercials down so far that even small businesses can afford to buy a commercial to air on cable television.

• *Family tributes and memorial videos created for living individuals:* Tribute videos are sometimes called "through the years" videos and personal history videos. Some cemeteries are beginning to allow videos to perform the function of gravestones. Typically such videos are several dozen photos transferred to video or video clips from the person's life.

• *Education and training:* Tutorials and other instructional materials are widely used by companies, businesses, and schools. Changing technologies and a TV-oriented workforce creates continuing demand.

• *Entertainment and special interest videos:* Particularly strong is the adult market. Special interests include underwater, skydiving, and travel videos.

• *Home sales:* Many real estate agencies are using DTV to preview homes for prospective buyers. DTV thus saves them travel time and money.

- **How-to videos:** Many DTV services focus on producing commercial products that teach people how to perform a task or a sport. Such products can be marketed by direct mail or by classified ads, or they can be sold in video stores.

- **Legal video depositions:** Nearly all lawsuits and criminal cases require lawyers to interview witnesses and defendants. In the past, their statements were recorded by a court reporter, but increasing numbers of lawyers are using videotape to document testimony more fully, because showing exactly how a witness appears can often help a jury decide if the person is telling the truth. In addition, videos are being used to show how accidents happened and what a day-in-the-life of an injured plaintiff is like. Such videos are used both for negotiations as well as in trial proceedings. Note that in some states, doing legal videos requires state certification.

- **Medical/surgery videos:** May be used by doctors and dentists to educate patients or to document surgery and procedures.

- **Sales and marketing videos:** Many companies from computer and car manufacturers to carpet companies and sports equipment vendors use videos to sell their products. You have probably received sales videos in the mail. With DTV, companies of any size can afford to produce a product demo that can be mailed out to prospective clients inexpensively or used for in-store and tradeshow demos. Some catalogs also lend themselves to video.

- **Promotional videos:** Bands, professional speakers, actors, singers, comedians, and others who need to showcase their talent are now often expected to send videos to prospective clients and employers.

- **Seminar videos:** Some seminars are sold to attendees and/or to an after-market. Some are conducted specifically for the purpose of creating a video for later sale with attendees participating without a fee.

- **Video yearbooks for high schools and colleges:** Video yearbooks consist of stills of students recorded onto video with musical background from school and class songs. They also include opening and closing titles and may also include footage from the homecoming game, prom, and graduation ceremony. Yearbooks are sold to students and parents.

- **Wedding and event videography:** Most desktop video firms and videographers get the majority of their business serving this market. They produce videos for such events as weddings, school sporting events, re-unions, business meetings, dance and other recitals, and for some families now, funerals.

These are just some of the applications of DTV; there are many more. The variety illustrates the point that many home businesses can now compete in this field, which was once the restricted territory of large video production houses. Kevin McFarland, whose home-based company is called Desktop Video and Graphics, saves his clients two-thirds of what it would cost them to produce presentations at a studio. He points out, "There are ten million presentations made every week in the United States, and most of them use slides and flip charts. I feel like I'm on the crest of a wave." So if you are visually oriented and believe there is a George Lucas or Steven Spielberg lurking inside you, the world of DTV beckons.

Knowledge and Skills You Need to Have

- You need to understand images and how they fit together. This ability can be acquired by studying film or video in or out of college. However, learning video production requires more studying. It demands hands-on experience that can be acquired by doing an apprenticeship, working for an established professional, or working for a cable television station that has local programs. Virtually every local cable system offers such training. A background in animation, graphic design, or cartooning is also helpful.

- You need to be technically and mechanically inclined. Robert Goodman, a Philadelphia film and video producer, says that to be good at desktop video a person needs to be "an artist with a technical side or a technician with a good visual sense."

- Because this is an art form, you need to be sufficiently right-brained that you can work without using logic for every decision, according to Jim Mack, who runs a video- and film-editing service in Michigan.

Start-up Costs

The start-up costs for a desktop video business depend on which platform (Wintel or Macintosh) you will use. For each platform, there is also a wide range of levels of sophistication that you can choose from in terms of how much equipment to buy, the quality of the equipment, and the range of services you need to offer. If you work on more than one platform, you also need additional equipment to import and translate images from one format to another. Because this equipment is relatively expensive, firms using desktop video are constantly upgrading, making their near-new good quality equipment available in the second-hand market, so you should consider buying your first equipment used.

Start-up Costs Common to Desktop Authoring and Editing	Low	High
Computer with 9 gigabyte* hard disk	$ 2,500	$ 4,000
Printer	$ 300	$ 800
or		
Multi-function printer/fax/scanner/copier	$ 150	$ 600
Backup drive	$ 150	$ 600
Nonlinear digital editing card for editing and special effects	$ 3,000	$ 6,000
Scanner	$ 50	$ 400
Office furniture, especially an ergonomic chair	$ 400	$ 1,000
Initial marketing budget	$ 1,000	$ 5,000
Subtotal	**$ 7,550**	**$ 18,400**

* Five minutes of video requires a gigabyte.

Desktop Authoring

	Low	High
Authorware or desktop presentation software	$ 400	$ 3,000
Writable CD-ROM and software	$ 500	$ 1,200
Total for desktop authoring	**$ 8,450**	**$ 22,600**

Desktop Editing

	Low	High
Dedicated editing suite such as an Avid Express, Casablanca, Frame Factory, Media 100, Trinity instead of using a personal computer with card	$ 4,000	$ 12,000

Digital camera	$ 3,500	$ 6,000
Two color monitors	$ 400	$ 1,200
One to three high-quality video recorders	$ 3,500	$ 22,000
Total for editing	$18,950	$ 40,400

Advantages

- DTV provides many opportunities for work. Other than print, video is the most accepted medium today.

- The work is creative and challenging. The people you deal with are creative, and work is done in an informal manner.

- The variety of projects provides interesting problems. Most aspects of the work are not routine.

Disadvantages

- There is a learning curve for getting into this field unless you already have a background in video or new media.

- You can spend hours on a single minute of video if you work as part of a team and people disagree about what to do or how to handle an edit.

- Video production is a highly competitive field; it helps to specialize.

Pricing

Video editing is generally billed by the hour with different rates for VHS, VHS-S and nonlinear editing. Nonlinear editing rates range from $95 to $175 an hour; VHS and VHS-S rates are approximately one-third and one-half the rate for nonlinear editing. Other services have different prices, such as on-site videotaping, $75 to $125 an hour; project proposal writing, $350 a day; scriptwriting, $50 per minute of video time; digitizing video, $50 an hour; music scoring, $50 per minute of video time; special effects at $250 to $750 per special effect. Videotape stock and travel mileage or time charges are additional charges. It is common to charge for a minimum amount of time, with minimums ranging from half an hour to two hours.

People doing desktop video often find that the amount of time spent on a particular project is not always in proportion to how much they earn. Thus, if required to bid or make a proposal or binding quote, keep in mind that most jobs take more time than you anticipate, so it's best to include a fudge factor. If using a contract or proposal, add a clause that enables you to bill for requested work not listed or agreed to in the initial written document.

Potential Earnings

Typical Annual Gross Revenues: $60,000 to $120,000 a year, based on billing 800 hours during the year at an average rate of $75 to $150 an hour.

Overhead: moderate (20 to 40 percent).

Best Home Businesses Estimate of Market Potential

While CDs and DVDs and other new media may eventually replace video, video will be with us for years. People who have the necessary skill to be effective at video editing and authoring will be able to use these skills with other media as well.

Best Ways to Get Business

- Research industries or business areas in which you might get clients based on your skills, background, and interests. Identify some clients who would benefit from a product demo or training tape.

- Network and develop cross-referral relationships with wedding coordinators and meeting and event planners.

- Participate in organizations such as trade or business associations.

- Network with videographers. There are so many ways to specialize. Video professionals do not need to compete; they can refer specialty and overflow work to one another. To introduce yourself, show a sample of your work.

- Yellow Page advertising featuring specialities you offer that others do not. If you do videography, this might mean listing types of events you do or indicating that you offer multi-camera services.

- Take contract work from videographers who need editing services or production services you can supply.

- Send a direct-mail piece to ad agencies, video services, studios, and product designers.

- Teach classes on video production and editing.

- If you are producing your own videos, begin by identifying a film idea or educational product that has not yet come to market because it would have been too costly using traditional video methods. For example, one DTV service contacted a psychologist who had a sex-education program for couples; the service agreed to share the risk with the psychologist, and together they produced a tape to be marketed to other professional therapists as a training tape.

First Steps

Take classes in video production. Read as much as you can about the field both in print and online. Join forums, newsgroups, and discussion lists.

- Apprentice at a local cable television station to learn the technical aspects of video production. If you are not technically oriented, take courses in design at community colleges or art schools.

- Work as a volunteer to develop a reputation, or apprentice through a service bureau.

- Create a few demo products of your own work to show to potential clients.

- Start small; take a small job at low pay just to get some work under your belt and have a finished tape to show to larger clients.

Where to Turn for Information and Help

ASSOCIATIONS

AMERICAN GUILD OF COURT VIDEOGRAPHERS. The Office of the Administrator, c/o Marquette Associates, 1628 East 3rd St., Casper, WY 82601.

BOOKS

Digital Nonlinear Editing: Editing Film and Video on the Desktop, Focal Press, 1998. ISBN: 024080225X.

Nonlinear: A Guide to Digital Film and Video Editing, Michael Rubin, Triad Publishing Company, 1995. ISBN: 0937404845.

Nonlinear Editing Basics: Electronic Film and Video Editing, Steven E. Browne, Focal Press, 1998. ISBN: 0240802829.

TRAINING

FIRST LIGHT VIDEO PRODUCTIONS, 2321 Abbot Kinney Blvd., Venice, CA 90921; (800) 777-1576. First Light has a thirty-two-page catalogue filled with videotape-based training courses about all aspects of video production. Web site: *www.tmwmedia.com*

VIDEO UNIVERSITY offers a series of "Desktop Video Handbooks" at its Web site: *www.videouniversity.com/dtv1.htm*

FRANCHISES

VIDEO DATA SERVICE, 3136 Winton Road South #304, Rochester, NY 14623; (800) 836-9461. A videography franchise. The fee of $22,500 includes equipment and training. Video Data Service franchisees primarily tape weddings, make film-to-tape transfers, tape legal depositions, and duplicate and edit videotapes. Web site: *www.vdsvideo.com*

MAGAZINES (PRINT AND ELECTRONIC ONLY)

AV Video & Multimedia Producer Magazine, Knowledge Industry Publications, Inc., 701 Westchester Avenue, White Plains, NY 10604; (800) 800-5474; (914) 328-9157. Web site: *www.avvideo. com*

DCC (Digital Content Creation), 201 E. Sandpointe Avenue, Suite 600, Santa Ana, CA 92707; (714) 513-8400. Web site: *www. digitalstudiomag.com*

Digital Producer Magazine. Web site: *www.digitalproducer.com*

Digital Video Magazine, P.O. Box 1212, Skokie, IL 60076; (888) 776-7002. Current issue and back issues are available in their entirety. The magazine operates the DV Live Forum. Web site: *www.dv.com*.

eMediaweekly. An online magazine for Macintosh electronic publishers from the publishers of *MacWeek*. Web site: *www.emediaweekly.com*

Videography for Video Production Professionals magazine, 600 Harrison Street, San Francisco, CA 94107-1370; (415) 905-2200. Web site: *www.vidy.com*

Videomaker Magazine, P.O. Box 4591, Chico, CA 95927; (530) 891-8410. Web site: *www.videomaker.com*

ONLINE

As would only be expected in a high-tech field, people in desktop video use the online universe extensively. Newsgroups, such as rec.video.desktop and rec.video.production, and listservers like Adobe Premiere and DV-L abound. Below are some of the leading web sites:

DIGITAL FORTE is a comprehensive site: *www.digitalforte.com*

DIGITAL VIDEOMAKING FORUM operated by the Digital Institute of Video Arts, 1630 N. Main Street, Suite 132, Walnut Creek, CA 94596; (800) 537-3050; (510) 932-2282. The company seeks high-quality instructional videos on computer and consumer topics which it will market for you. Web site: *www.dvarts.com*

ELITE VIDEO. This company, which sells products, provides a number of newsletters on the site; (800) 468-1996. Web site: *www.elitevideo.com*

LOW BUDGET SPECIAL EFFECTS DISCUSSION. Web site: *www.likeastory.com/boards/fxdex1.html*

THE VIDEOGRAPHER'S FORUM. Has a marketing discussion group with archived messages. Web site: *http://206.210.79.196/default.htm*

THE VIDEOGUYS. Through their Web site, *The Electronic Mailbox*, they sell video editing equipment and accessories. At the site, they offer the online version of The Desk Top Video Handbook containing primers on video capture cards, nonlinear editing, video storage, and digital video; (800) 323-2325. Web site: *www.videoguys.com*

WEDDING VIDEO FORUM. Web site: *www.videouniversity.com/wwwboard/ wedding/*

Editorial Services

Every book that's written gets edited, and increasingly the more than 20,000 book publishers in the United States are outsourcing their editorial work. Even though more books are being published than ever, the number of employed publishing professionals in New York declined by 16 percent during the 90's. This is a clear sign that more editorial work is being contracted out by the major publishing houses.

Most publishers, however, are small and count on outside editors, proofreaders, and indexers as a matter of course. Authors themselves are also hiring independent editors, as understaffed publishers give them less editorial attention. Those wishing to become authors often hire editors too, hoping to give their manuscripts enough polish to land an agent or a publisher. *The New York Times* reported that authors are paying independent editors fees ranging from $1,000 to $25,000.

In addition to book publishers, other markets for editorial work on books, journals, reports, research papers, documents for clients, and contracts include:

- Book packagers
- Businesses of all kinds, particularly high-tech manufacturing firms
- Government agencies
- Law firms
- Newspapers and magazines
- Nonprofit organizations
- Professional and trade associations that publish journals
- Professional training companies
- Smaller printers

The Web is opening up new editorial opportunities as well for those willing to learn its ways. Manufacturers are putting software and equipment documentation online that requires editorial work, for example. One only need spend a few hours on the Web to know there's a need for editing and proofreading. Companies and other entities concerned with their professional image need and will pay for editorial help. In short, there's a growing market for self-employed editors.

While some editorial service providers perform all three editorial tasks—editing, proofreading, and indexing—each type of work has distinct responsibilities and requires different skills and can be stand alone businesses in themselves. So it's worthwhile to examine them separately.

Editing

Editing involves a broad range of manuscript wordsmithing and picture-editing activities. Developmental editors work with authors to develop or rework initial concepts into a logical, well-organized manuscript. These editors may help a writer plan the sequence of chapters or sections, develop ideas, do research, shape and polish their words, and even rewrite portions. When the manuscript is complete and being prepared for typesetting, copyeditors check for proper grammar and clarity, make corrections and style improvements, and double-check the content and consistency. Line editors rewrite and change manuscripts to the point of restructuring them. While most editors work with words, some work with pictures and this is a specialty unto itself.

Proofreading

Depending on your skills and experience, one of two types of proofreading services may suit you. Content proofreaders read word-for-word, comparing the typeset proofs against the original manuscript to check for typos, misspellings, and so forth. Design proofreaders, in addition to proofing content, check the proof for adherence to design specifications, typographical correctness, kerning, improper or excessive hyphenation, and so on, once copy has been typeset.

Indexing

Indexes are created for nonfiction books, professional books, and reference materials to help readers find information quickly. While indexers traditionally work with book publishers constructing a key-word index for the back of a book, the area of greatest opportunity is creating indexes for the Web and documentation. Indexers must be highly detail-oriented and have keen reading and analytic skills as well. The best indexers have a feel for how people will seek out material and will create user-friendly indexes. Indexing documentation requires familiarity with the documentation process, the software or technology product itself and its class of technology. Indexing for the Web also requires the ability to work with HTML. Indexing is the most specialized and detailed skill of the three services and may not appeal to all people.

Some editorial services specialize in an industry or type of work, such as business, medicine, law, software documentation, and various fields of science, especially environmental science. Because of specialization, referrals among those providing editorial services are common. However, with the exception of indexers, most providers of editorial service don't stick to providing just one service. Often this is because customers who think they need a proofreader may actually be needing a copyeditor and so forth.

The New York metropolitan area accounts for about half the freelance editorial work available, according to Sheila Buff, Co-Executive Director of the Editorial Freelancers Association. Yet other areas offer opportunities and specialization that go hand-in-hand with the type of publishing work available in that locale. Unless a company's policy requires it, however, there's no reason an editorial service must be located nearby. Editing services can work with companies virtually anywhere in the world.

Knowledge and Skills You Need to Have

- You need to have an excellent knowledge of grammar and punctuation. You also need to know the standard markings and procedures followed in copyediting and proofreading by publishers and typesetters.

- Good communication skills are a must; you will be working with authors and other editors, and your notes and comments to them must be clear and written in good English.

- You need to be detail-oriented and meticulous. Editing, proofreading, and indexing all require a high level of attention to detail.

- You should be highly organized. Most editorial services work on more than one project at a time, often under pressure to complete the work by a deadline that cannot be missed.

- It helps to be visually oriented, able to imagine how the printed word will look on the page in a designed piece.

Start-up Costs	Low	High
Computer	$ 1,500	$ 3,000
Printer	$ 300	$ 800
or		
Multi-function printer/fax/scanner/copier	$ 150	$ 600
Cell phone	$ 75	$ 200
Office furniture, especially an ergonomic chair	$ 400	$ 1,000
Initial marketing budget	$ 1,000	$ 5,000
Reference books (dictionaries, etc.)	$ 300	$ 500
Total	$ 3,725	$ 11,100

Advantages

- Editorial work and publishing are usually interesting, creative, and intellectually stimulating. You have a chance to read a variety of books and articles before their publication.

- You can often choose your own hours in which to work: day or night.

- Editorial work can sometimes help you develop your own ideas for books and make the contacts needed to get your own writing contracts.

- This is a portable business. You do it from anywhere via telephone, fax, modem connections, and overnight package delivery services.

Disadvantages

- Some editing and proofreading can be tedious and repetitive.

- The publishing cycle is speeding up, making long nights and lost weekends common in order to meet fast turnaround requirements. Some editorial services specialize in overnight jobs. One has the motto, "In by nine, out by five." That means 9 P.M. and 5 A.M.

- Unless you take precautions to prevent it, you can develop a repetitive-motion disorder from keyboarding.

- Editorial work is usually done alone, and so you may have little socialization with other people on a regular daily basis.

Pricing

Developmental editors average about $30 an hour with some earning as much as $75 an hour. Some charge by the manuscript, with charges generally ranging from $2,000 to $4,000 to review and comment on a 400-page manuscript.

Copyeditors typically charge $25 or $30 an hour with some earning as much as $75 an hour. Rates depend on the complexity of the work and the turnaround time. The highest rates go to people in medical specialties, doing work such as proofreading the warnings in prescriptions.

Indexers usually charge from $3 to $5 per printed book page they read to produce the index, or from $20 to $50 per hour. A service that uses computer software for indexing can receive the higher fees. Documentation and Web-site indexing get the higher hourly rate.

Proofreaders typically get from $15 to $30 an hour with some specialists getting as much as $55 depending on the field and locale.

Picture editors average between $30 and $40 an hour.

Potential Earnings

Typical Annual Gross Revenues: According to the *Rates and Business Practices Survey* done by the Editorial Freelancers Association in 1995, 29 percent of its full-time members earned less than $20,000, 25 percent earned $20,000 to $30,000, 23 percent earned $30,000 to $40,000, and 23 percent earned over $40,000. The average income was $35,758. Those who establish themselves with a specialty tend to be the high earners. Enterprising indexers, according to the American Society of Indexers, can earn $40,000 or more a year.

Overhead: low (20 percent or less).

Best Home Businesses Estimate of Market Potential

The structural changes occurring in the publishing industry and the dynamic growth of the Web provide a large market for people providing independent editorial services. Feeding this demand is the consolidation in the publishing industry. This has the following consequences favoring outsourcing editorial services: (1) loss of in-house staff, (2) the speeding up of the production process, (3) the increase in the number of small publishers producing information in multiple media, and (4) the increasing number of books and documents being published both in print and electronically.

Best Ways to Get Business

- Personal contacts are the best marketing tool for editorial services. Get to know in-house editors at publishing companies, magazines, journals, and newsletters who are responsible for hiring out. Take them out to lunch to find out what kind of work they usually have available, how they decide whom to pick, and how much they typically pay. Leave your business card and stay in touch on a regular basis so that you remain foremost in their minds. If you specialize in corporate work, get to know copywriters who may be getting contracts for business brochures, annual reports, and other business documents.

- Participate in organizations related to your work; people frequently share leads for work at meetings.

- Indexers can get referrals by participating in a chapter of the American Society of Indexers. The Society has chapters in major cities and its annual conference draws publishers with whom attendees can connect for work.

- Proofreaders need to target their marketing efforts to production or managing editors.

- Refer to *Writer's Market* or *Literary Market Place* to locate names and addresses of publishers to whom you can send a résumé and samples of your work.

- Check Web sites that post work for freelancers.

- Check the ads for freelance work that appear in two trade magazines, *Publishers Weekly* and *Library Journal,* both of which are available in many public libraries. Look also in specific trade magazines for advertisements for writers and editors who know how a specific industry works. These are sometimes under "part-time." However, only a fraction of the available work gets advertised.

- Have your own Web site. Without a Web site, you will not get as many leads from database directories maintained by organizations that consumers use. Most online directories provide the ability to link the consumer directly to your page.

First Steps

- Book indexers need samples to send production managers in publishing houses. Some people even prepare samples of a book from the publisher's house to show how they can enhance an index.

- You must be skilled before you begin work as a freelance proofreader. Working for temp agencies can help develop skills, and some temp firms offer training.

- To get developmental and line editing work, you need several years of editorial experience or be a published author yourself. Editors usually come from the ranks of a publishing house or magazine. Copyediting is more available, however, if you have good writing skills and an excellent command of English. Copyeditors should be prepared to pass a test.

Where to Turn for Information and Help

ORGANIZATIONS

THE AMERICAN COPY EDITORS SOCIETY. Professional membership is open to employed copy editors; freelance editors qualify only for associate membership. Web site: *www.copydesk.org*

AMERICAN SOCIETY OF INDEXERS, 7308-C East Independence Boulevard, Charlotte, NC 28227; (704) 531-0021. The roster currently includes about 1,100 members, about one-third of whom are home based. The society publishes numerous books and informational materials on a career in indexing, has local chapters, and conducts professional development workshops. A list of publications is available on the Web site, as well as tips on getting started along with links to publishers. Web site: *www.asindexing.org*

EDITORIAL FREELANCERS ASSOCIATION, 71 West 23rd Street, Suite 1910, New York, NY 10010; (212) 929-5400; fax: (212) 929-5439. Provides a job phone service updated twice a week that is available to members only. The association has affinity groups in some areas, publishes a newsletter, *The Freelancer*, and topical publications like a *Rates and Business Practices Survey*, and offers health insurance. Past newsletters are archived on the Web site. Web site: *www.the-efa.org*

FREELANCE EDITORIAL ASSOCIATION, P.O. Box 380835, Cambridge, MA 02238; (617) 576-8797. Primarily a regional organization. Web site: *www.tiac.net/users/freelanc*

SPECIALTY ASSOCIATIONS

ASSOCIATION FOR DOCUMENTARY EDITING, P.O. Box 1600, Lexington, VA 24450; (540) 463-7103; fax: (540) 464-5229.

ASSOCIATION OF EARTH SCIENCE EDITORS, 554 Chess Street, Pittsburgh, PA 15205-3212; (412) 622-3287; fax: (412) 622-8837.

BOARD OF EDITORS IN THE LIFE SCIENCES, P.O. Box 8133, Radnor, PA 19087-8133.

COUNCIL OF BIOLOGY EDITORS, 11250 Roger Bacon Drive, Suite 8, Reston, VA 20190; (703) 437-4377. Web site: *www.sdsc.edu/cbe/*

NATIONAL ASSOCIATION OF REAL ESTATE EDITORS, 1003 N.W. 6th Terrace, Boca Raton, FL 33486; fax: (407) 391-0099.

LOCAL ASSOCIATIONS

Many regional and local organizations serve writers and editors. Check links on Web sites for writers and editorial services for contact information.

COURSES

The United States Department of Agriculture offers a course in indexing. For more information, contact Correspondence Study Program, Graduate

School USDA, Room 1112S, 14th and Independence Avenue, Washington, DC 20250; (888) 744-GRAD, (202) 314-3670. Web site: *http://grad. usda.gov*

University continuing education programs offer courses in editorial skills and journalism departments in community colleges.

BOOKS

The American Society of Indexers at the address above offers a series of publications that include:

Directory of Indexing and Abstracting Courses and Seminars, 1998. A directory created for people interested in indexing as a career, which helps them find courses or seminars in their region.

ASI Recommended Indexing Agreement.

Starting an Indexing Business, 1995.

Running Your Indexing Business, 1995.

Managing Large Indexing Projects, 1994.

Marketing Your Indexing Services, 1998.

Guide to Indexing Software, Linda Fetters, 1995.

An Indexer's Guide to the Internet, Lori Lathrop, 1995.

Indexing Specialties: History, 1998.

The Complete Idiot's Guide to Making Money in Freelancing, Laurie Rozakis, Macmillan: 1998. ISBN: 0028621190.

Indexing Books, Nancy Mulvaney, University of Chicago Press, 1994. ISBN: 0226550141.

Literary Market Place, Bowker's. Updated yearly and priced just under $200. Available in most public libraries. ISBN: 0835240533.

Writer's Market, Writer's Digest Books, 1507 Dana Ave., Cincinnati, OH 45207; (800) 289-0863; (513) 531-8250. ISBN: 0898798507. Updated yearly. Writer's Digest also publishes *Children's Writer* and *Illustrator's Market, Guide to Literary Agents & Art/Photo Reps,* and other specialized market directories.

MAGAZINES AND NEWSLETTERS

Copy Editor: Language News for the Publishing Profession, P.O. Box 604, Ansonia Station, New York, NY 10023; (212) 995-0112. Focuses on changes in the English language. It covers courses available for freelancers. Its Web site has a sample issue of the newsletter. Web site: *www.copyeditor.com*

Editor & Publisher, 11 W 19th St., 10th Floor, New York, NY 10011-4209; (212) 675-4380.

Editorial Eye, Editorial Experts, 66 Canal Center Plaza, Suite 200, Alexandria, VA 22314; (800) 683-5859, fax (703) 683-4915.

Editors Only, 275 Batterson Drive, New Britain, CT 06053; (860) 827-8896. Web site: *www.tiac.net/users/wid/eo.html.*

Freelance Writer's Report, P.O. Box A, North Stratford, NH 03590; (800) 351-9278; (603) 922-8338. Web site: *www.writersandeditors.com.* Of interest to writers and editors alike.

Freelance Success, a marketing newsletter for nonfiction writers, is published by the Freelance Success Institute, which also offers correspondence courses with all the course work done by e-mail. Web site: *www.freelancesuccess.com*

Library Journal, 833 W. South Boulder Road, Lewisville, CO 80027; (800) 677-6694.

Publishers Weekly, 249 W. 17th Street, New York, NY 10011; (800) 278-2991.

Writer's Digest, Subscriber Service Department, P.O. Box 2124, Harlan, IA 51593-2313.

WEB SITES

FREELANCE ONLINE. Jobs, message boards, a searchable directory of over 700 freelancers. *www.freelanceonline.com*

THE SLOT. Has resources for copyeditors including *The Curmudgeon's Stylebook. www.theslot.com*

Elder Services

Like a migration of continental proportions, the population of the Western world is aging. In the U.S., one in every six people will be over age 65 by the year 2020. In 1970, that number was less than one in ten. By 2020, nearly seven million will be over 85 years old. That's five times as many people who lived that long in 1970.

Regardless of age, what the elder population wants is to remain independent. A survey by the American Association of Retired Persons (AARP) found that 85 percent of seniors want to stay in their own homes. It's no surprise that most elderly people are not in nursing homes; in fact, the number of seniors over 85 years living in nursing homes has decreased 10 percent between 1985 and 1995.

But in order to live independently, seniors need help—a lot of help, so much so that one in every three adults between the ages of 35 and 54 has provided hands-on help for family members or friends needing long-term care. But because most adults this age work, sometimes hundreds or thousands of miles away, business services are evolving to play the role families used to play in helping older people.

Of course, government is providing funding for many types of services and large corporations are securing immense contracts to render these services. Still, there are avenues for small, independent businesspeople to develop businesses that serve the growing senior population. Here we present you with a number of possibilities that have emerged as of this writing that someone without a special academic degree can pursue as a business.

Elder Relocation Service

Often an elderly person will need help in downsizing her or his home. Many older folks need to trade their now too-large home for a smaller place, but the hassles and complexities of moving can be intimidating. In addition to the physically daunting tasks of moving, leaving one's home and parting with possessions is usually emotionally painful and involves a myriad of difficult decisions. People like Dawn Provan and Mercedes Gunderson have recognized this need and began providing "elder mover services."

Provan, a licensed realtor in Rochester, New York, for 15 years, created New Dawnings, a company that assists seniors with selling the family home and moving into an apartment, condo, or retirement community. In 1987, Gunderson was involved in helping her mother move from her lifelong home in Wisconsin to Minneapolis and decided to turn what she learned from this experience into a business. She calls it Gentle Transitions. Seven years later, her son Greg was ready to leave his corporate career and opened another branch of Gentle Transitions in Manhattan Beach, California.

The Gundersons specialize in the gentle art of helping the elderly sift and sort through a lifetime of household possessions. They help sort and label what will be sold and what will be moved to the new home. When needed, they call specialists to stage estate sales. The Gundersons also handle utilities, phone service, and the moving companies. They pack and unpack everything. When their senior clients walk into their new homes at the end of the moving day, everything is in its place—toothbrush, knicknacks, television remote control, and slippers by the correct side of the easy chair.

Knowledge and Skills You Need to Have

- Good communication skills for counseling people
- Patience
- Compassion
- Organizational abilities
- Packing know-how

Advantages

- Low entry cost
- Low overhead
- Prospective clients are identifiable and accessible through retirement homes whose applicants often need help in order to relocate.

Disadvantages

- Finding personnel with the combination of caretaking, counseling, planning, logistical, packing, and handyman skills to orchestrate the moving process.
- Easy for competitors to enter the field.

- The need to protect yourself from potential litigation and liability with your form of legal organization and liability insurance.

Start-up Costs	Low	High
Computer	$ 1,500	$ 3,000
Printer	$ 300	$ 800
or		
Multi-function printer/fax/scanner/copier	$ 150	$ 600
Cell phone	$ 75	$ 200
Incorporating or forming limited liability company	$ 1,000	$ 3,500
Initial marketing budget	$ 2,000	$ 5,000
Liability insurance	$ 500	$ 1000
Bond	$ 200	$ 500
Packing supplies	$ 400	$ 600
Total	$ 6,125	$ 15,200

Pricing

The hourly fee ranges from $30 to $40, with the total price of moves ranging between $300 and $6,000. The average move costs between $1,500 and $2,000.

Potential Earnings

Typical Annual Gross Revenues: One person can accomplish two to three moves a week or ten a month. This requires planning in advance, then packing on one day, followed by moving on the next. Based on ten moves a month at $1,750 a move, you can gross $210,000.

Overhead: low (under 20%).

Best Home Businesses Estimate of Market Potential

An array of social trends converge to favor this type of service. The numbers needing the service will escalate even more dramatically as baby boomers move into their elderly years.

Best Ways to Get Business

The elderly themselves are less likely to hire services like this than either their children or their childrens' employers. Children often find themselves unable to care for their elderly loved ones because of distance or other family and career demands. The 49 percent of children who can provide care themselves often arrive late to work, leave early, and take time off both during the day and for whole days. In 1997, Metropolitan Life Insurance Company did a survey of lost employee productivity related to elder care needs, which it "conservatively estimated" to be at $11.4 billion a year. The best ways to reach those needing this service include:

- Developing relationships with the intake personnel at retirement homes, hospital discharge planners, and realtors. "Referrals are key to this business," says Greg Gunderson.

- Bundle information in with retirement home marketing packages.

- Post flyers on senior centers' bulletin boards.

- Place brochures on tables containing information for seniors.

- Advertise in senior directories and senior publications.

- Have your own Web site with meta tags and links that will direct people to your site.

First Steps

1. Learn packing techniques by reading guides from moving companies and watching the professionals do it.

2. Put together marketing materials.

3. Volunteer to assist a friend, acquaintance, or relative with one or more moves to gain experience with handling the tasks and timing involved. Work up and test out your routines and provide references and examples about which you can refer when talking to prospective customers.

Elder Companion

Often the elderly living on their own need someone to help with housekeeping, cooking, grocery shopping, bill paying, grooming or just some conversation. The Administration on Aging estimates that nearly one in five need help performing *activities of daily living* (ADL). This need has created the role of eldercare companions. At least two companies, Home Instead Senior Care in Omaha, Nebraska, and Special Care in Erdenheim, Pennsylvania, are franchising nonmedical home care.

Elder companions fill a niche not met by the traditional home healthcare agencies, which provide trained and licensed medical personal to administer medications, monitor vital signs, and even lift and bath elderly patients in their homes. The elder companion provides nonmedical care exclusively. Although elder companions do not have to be medically trained, they do need to be bonded and have liability insurance.

Elder companions need to be able to:

- Engage seniors in conversation and to inform family members about the condition and needs of the senior.

- Cook.

- Do light housekeeping.

- Provide transportation.

Pricing

Elder companion services bill at $10 to $15 an hour with the higher rates involving transporting seniors.

FRANCHISES

HOME INSTEAD SENIOR CARE, 1104 S 76th Ave #A, Omaha, NE 68124; (402) 498-4466. Web site: *www.homeinstead.com*

SPECIAL CARE, 717 Bethlehem Pike, Erdenheim, PA 19038; (215) 402-0200.

Other Elder Services

The elderly are target customers for other businesses profiled in this book, including errand services, medical claims assistance, and bill paying (an offshoot of bookkeeping). Keep in mind that these services need to be marketed to the children and families of seniors, even though seniors are the recipients of these services.

Geriatric care management, which requires a professional degree such as nursing, social work, psychology, or gerontology, is also a fast growing field. Geriatric care managers may work independently of an agency. They assess the needs of frail older people and arrange and coordinate a wide range of services so they can remain at home. Geriatric care managers may be called upon to intervene in crises, and they may need to make financial arrangements. They handle the many difficult and time-consuming tasks of negotiating services from a complex array of public and nonprofit agencies, many of which have waiting lists. They are paid well for their effort with fees ranging from $70 to $150 an hour.

Where to Turn for Information and Help

Moving companies provide a wealth of material on techniques for moving effectively and efficiently, so contacting several companies and requesting their literature is a good place to start learning about the mechanics of moving.

ORGANIZATIONS

NATIONAL ALLIANCE FOR CAREGIVING, 4720 Montgomery Lane, Suite 642, Bethesda, MD 20814. Web site: *http://caregiving.org*

NATIONAL ASSOCIATION OF AREA AGENCIES ON AGING ELDERCARE LOCATOR. Toll free line providing eldercare resources: (800) 677-1116.

THE NATIONAL ASSOCIATION OF PROFESSIONAL GERIATRIC CARE MANAGERS, 1604 North Country Road, Tucson, AZ 85716; (520) 881-8008, publishes a book entitled *The Business of Becoming a Professional Geriatric Care Manager*. Web site: *www.caremanager.org*

NATIONAL ELDERCARE REFERRAL SYSTEM is a service that links families with geriatric care managers and other eldercare professionals; (800) 571-1918.

NATIONAL FAMILY CAREGIVERS ASSOCIATION, 10605 Concord St., Suite 501, Kensington, MD 20895; (800) 896-3650. Provides newsletters, networking and resources for family caregivers.

BOOK

Caring for Your Aging Parents: A Planning and Action Guide, Donna Cohen and Carl Einsdorfer, Putnam, 1993.

NEWSLETTER

Caregiving, P.O. Box 224, Park Ridge, IL 60068. Covers emotional issues, hiring home health help, purchasing medical supplies.

WEB SITES

ADMINISTRATION ON AGING provides projections on the aging population and many reports. Web site: *www.aoa.dhhs.gov*

AMERICAN ASSOCATION OF RETIRED PERSONS' AARP WEBPLACE. Web site: *www.aarp.org/caregive/1-care.htm*

TRANSITIONS, INC., a Minneapolis eldercare consulting firm offers a variety of assessment tools and forms, as well as a good deal more at its Web site: *www.asktransitions.com/testimon.html*

Errand Service

Compared to 1969, we're spending the equivalent of an extra month a year working and commuting, says the Economic Policy Institute. Other studies show that leisure time has decreased by over ten hours a week. Now that two-career couples outnumber single-income families, most households have little time for running errands and taking care of odds and ends. Exercise and fitness regimens, once considered to be leisure pursuits, have now become must-do activities for many, further compressing our tight daily schedules and cutting into discretionary time.

As people face the limits of how much they can squeeze into a 24-hour day, the demand for errand services is growing. More people are willing to pay others to handle time-consuming errands and other forms of *necessitrivia*. According to a recent survey, 36 percent of people will pay to have groceries delivered to their door, for example. Many errand services that specialize in transporting children to doctors' and dentists' offices and after-school activities are so busy they're turning away business.

Businesses, too, have many tasks that must be done. The costs, difficulties, and risks involved in employing someone to work full-time as a "gofer" are making the regular use of errand services attractive to small businesses.

Errand services do just about whatever their clients need to have done, such as:

- Chauffeuring children

- Finding a dress for a special occasion

- Getting chilled medicines from a doctor's office

- Grocery shopping

- Hand delivering important documents

- Picking out a last-minute gift

- Picking up and delivering dry cleaning and laundry

- Picking up theatre and sports tickets

- Running to the post office or UPS

- Standing in line for registrations, license renewals and applications

- Taking a vehicle in for servicing or repair

- Taking pets to the to the vet or caring for them in a clutch

- Taking shoes in to be repaired

Customers range from those who spend money extravagantly to those who are frugal with it. Errands may be matters of convenience or matters of urgency. They may involve waiting in line for coveted concert tickets or driving through rush-hour traffic to hand deliver a last-minute payment on an outstanding bill. The best customers are regular ones who use the services several times a week. Such clients might include:

- Small retail companies such as dry cleaners, pharmacies, and restaurants that don't have their own delivery person on staff.

- Auto dealerships needing to file DMV registrations. (Some states like New York require a special license to do courier work with documents for the Department of Motor Vehicles.)

- Nursing homes.

- Lawyers or tax professionals with documents to be hand delivered or filed in court.

- Senior citizens needing help with shopping.

- Busy two-income couples.

- Single working women with children.

- High-income individuals who can afford to hire someone to meet such special needs as driving to every button shop in town to find a certain kind of button.

Though some errands services call themselves *concierge* services, this term is also used by private firms specializing in services to travelers, companies supplying audiovisual equipment, videography, and training to corporations, and firms providing short-term services to conventions, trade shows, office buildings, apartments and hotels.

While the scope of what errand services do is broad, they do draw limits. As one errand service operator told us, "As long as it's legal, we do it. However, we don't transport people and we don't pick up children. But we do take items back to stores to be returned or exchanged. We buy gifts. We take gifts to be wrapped. We make pickups and deliveries and do grocery shopping for small or new companies. We deliver wedding cakes for a bakery, for example. Hiring us is cheaper than hiring a driver and leasing a truck."

Knowledge and Skills You Need to Have

- A customer-service orientation is critical. You need to like doing things for others. You must have patience for standing in lines, driving in traffic, and waiting for people, and you must believe in your heart that the customer is always right.

- Stamina is necessary. You need to have ample energy for a full day of tiring activities like running in and out of stores, hopping in and out of the car, climbing stairs, and lugging groceries.

- Organizational skills are needed to plan a route for your errands. Effective routes can save you two hours a day.

- You have to be assertive so you can get assistance quickly. You need to be able to ask questions like where to find the return counter in a store and know how to cut through red tape to get to the right person.

- You need to know how to get around in your city and be able to read a map so you can get from place to place quickly and efficiently.

- And, of course, you need to like driving because you will be doing a lot of it.

Start-up Costs

Start-up Costs	Low	High
Late-model car or van	$ 4,000	$ 20,000
Cell phone or pager	$ 50	$ 200
Initial marketing budget	$ 500	$ 5,000
Insurance, bonding, licenses	$ 1,000	$ 3,000
Total	$ 5,550	$ 28,200

Advantages

- The satisfaction of knowing you're making people's lives easier.

- Not being confined to an office or desk; you're outdoors, moving around and doing lots of different things.

- You're apt to have interesting experiences because of the variety of errands you do and the people you meet.

Disadvantages

- Errand services will not work in all communities. They work best in places where life seems hectic and complicated. They won't work, for example, where there is a mom-and-pop store handy on every corner or where parking is so limited that you'll spend your earnings on parking fees.

- Errand services are susceptible to the ups and downs of the economy. In order to keep busy, you need several steady clients; having one major client who consistently uses you provides you a core income, but having only one makes you vulnerable if you lose that customer's business.

- It takes six or more months to build up business.

- Because you personally can run only a limited number of errands in a day, the key to earning a significant income is in having others working for you.

- Unless you can afford to hire staff, you have to handle all tasks yourself, from answering the phones to billing, banking, and running the errands. If you do have employees, however, it means you'll have to bill clients, instead of collecting at the time you provide service. This can cause cash-flow problems, so you will have to stagger your billing in order to have money coming in every day.

- Because employees get paid on a per-job basis, rather than by the hour, you may experience high staff turnover when business is light. You are competing against hourly-wage workers who are willing to do the same type of work for less money.

- The work can be wearing day after day, both on you and on your motor vehicle.

Pricing

Errand services charge for their services in a variety of ways. Most services charge by the hour. Rates range from $15 to $25 per hour, though some will discount their rate for long-term customers; some for next-day service. Some services require a one- or two-hour minimum to account for driving time to and from where they start and where they finish; having even a lot of fifteen- to thirty-minute jobs doesn't add up to enough to make a decent living. Some errand services have a schedule of flat rates between communities in a metropolitan area that build in the minimum. Other services charge by the errand or by the stop, with fees ranging from $12 to $75 each. One online grocery shopping service charges a $5 to $7 annual membership fee plus $5 plus 5 percent of the grocery bill for each delivery.

Potential Earnings

Typical Annual Gross Revenues: Working by yourself: $30,000, based on working six hours a day, five days a week, fifty weeks a year, at $20 an hour. With two employees who pay all their own expenses and receive 50 percent of the revenue: $60,000.

Overhead: moderate (20 to 40 percent).

Best Home Businesses Estimate of Market Potential

Gone are the days when people went for drives in the park; now many people don't have time to wait in lines, pick things up, and do other chores. Yet they need to be done. The rapid growth of the senior population increases the demand for errand services, too. Both their physical limitations and fear of crime prompt senior citizens who can afford it to hire others to do their errands for them; sometimes their relatives pay the bill.

Best Ways to Get Business

- Directly soliciting work from firms that have the potential of becoming regular customers like small bakeries, gift-wrapping services, auto dealerships, and independent pizza parlors.

- Yellow Pages advertising under Delivery Service, Messenger Service, and/or Shopping Service.

- Having a Web site in which you post the information prospective customers want to know about you. Increasing numbers of people turn to the Web before the Yellow Pages.

- Taking out advertising in the program booklets of charity events to attract the interest of well-to-do patrons; then follow up with direct mail, such as an attractive postcard. Get mailing lists from charity rosters or membership directories.

- Delivering flyers to homes in select neighborhoods.

- Placing classified advertising in local and community newspapers.

- Networking with business and special interest groups who have members who could use your service.

- Getting publicity about your business in newspapers and magazines.

- Requesting establishments (dry cleaners, shoe shops, and so forth) you go to because these are where you go when you're running errands to allow you to post a flyer in their shops or have your cards on their counter.

- Offer a free gift-reminder service to regular customers, which may stimulate their using you to select, shop for, and deliver the gifts.

Related Businesses

- **Messenger Service** (regulated by state utility commissions in some states)

- **Firewood Delivery Service**

- **Publicity Escort Service** for authors, celebrities, and corporate spokespeople

- **Hauling Service** (see separate entry under Rest of Best)

First Steps

- Check into what licenses may be required for the types of errands you plan to run or specialize in.

- Pick a catchy name for your business.

- The key to getting established is finding a major long-term client to keep you busy several days a week while you are building a clientele.

Where to Turn for Help and Information

BOOKS

Get Paid to Shop: Be A Personal Shopper for Corporate America, Emily S. Limpkin, Forté Publishing, 1999. ISBN: 0966635108.

How To Start And Operate an Errand Service, Rob Spina, Legacy Marketing, 1996. ISBN: 096570310X.

Ultimate Service: The Complete Handbook to the World of the Concierge, Holly Stiel, Delta Collins, Prentice-Hall, 1994. ISBN: 0131753576. Though written as a training manual for hotel concierges, its material on handling both routine and unusual requests as well as irate customers is applicable to errand services.

ORGANIZATION

NATIONAL CONCIERGE ASSOCIATION; (612) 376-8013. Membership is open to people managing or owning a concierge service or company. Web site: *www.conciergeassoc.org*

SEMINAR

CAPITOL CONCIERGE, 1400 Eye Street, NW, Suite 750, Washington, DC 20005; (202) 223-4765. Capitol Conciege teaches a one-day seminar in how to start a concierge service. Web site: *www.capitolconcierge.com*

Executive Search

The practice of matchmaking people with employers can be traced back to the fourteenth century in Germany. Such matchmaking is now referred to as the executive search business or *headhunting* and its practitioners are variously called recruiters and, not surprisingly, head-hunters. Paul Hawkinson, publisher of the *Fordyce Letter*, a newsletter for the recruitment industry, says of this field: "Our business is unique. I know of no other business where the players start with nothing to sell and no one to sell it to, and wind up at the end with a five-figure fee for doing it."

Companies turn to executive search firms to find top-notch personnel for management, professional, and technical positions. Unlike employment agencies, which usually collect their fees from the people they place, executive recruiters are paid by employers. Also unlike employment agencies, which are heavily regulated by state laws, recruiters are free of licensing requirements.

Because the overwhelming amount of work is not done face-to-face, executive searchers can work from anywhere. Of the 26,000 recruitment firms, estimates are that 15 to 35 percent operate from home. In fact, Paul Hawkinson found he was more successful after he moved his executive-search firm to his home. He says, "I was running a forty-employee operation from two floors of office space. Our billings were excellent, but my accountant told me that everyone was making money except me. I fired everyone, closed the offices, and moved the business to my house. My blood pressure went down, my happiness quotient soared, and I finally started putting some money into my pocket."

Some states prohibit recruiters from meeting with clients or candidates in their home offices, but since most of the work is done by phone, e-mail, or at trade shows, where one's office is located becomes increasingly less relevant. This is what Tom and Renae McAnally determined. They started JobLine, Inc., a registry serving the manufactured-building and building-component industry in Orange County, California, but found they could serve this niche market just as effectively from a locale they would find more suitable for raising their children. Now they happily operate their firm in remote Seeley Lake, Montana.

Anthony Byrne, a consultant and trainer in the executive-search industry, says the opportunities in the search field are excellent because it's one of the fastest-growing service industries in the world. The executive-search industry is going in two directions: toward companies with six- to fifteen-person offices, which make heavy use of technology, and toward small firms with a specialized niche. Successful home-based recruiters are therefore often highly specialized or doubly niched by industry (such as biotechnology, construction, or restaurants) and by the type of personnel they place in that industry (such as CEOs, CFOs, CIOs, or chefs).

Bill Vick of Plano, Texas, developed such a highly successful recruiting firm in his home that we was able to sell it. He exemplifies how someone in this field must keep up with the times. In the 80's he created a search firm specializing in the software industry. As he began using computers in his business, he recognized the need for specialized software that would help manage the recruiting process, so he developed a program called *Solo*™. Vick also learned early that he could make use of the Internet to do joint sales or splits with other recruiters (i.e., one recruiter matches his or her client with another recruiter's candidate). Vick says that recruiters really have three different "customers": the client (the company seeking an executive), the candidate (the potential hire), and other recruiters with their own pool of clients and candidates. Using this approach led him to develop several online enterprises including Recruiters Online Network and the Internet Business Network, used by 10,000 recruiters worldwide.

Vick says, "My business is in my mind, in the information and knowledge I have and my ability to apply what I know. My office has only electronic walls. I can conduct business from anywhere and anyplace, at any time."

About this business, Vick observes, "Finding people to fill the jobs is the easiest thing, but finding the clients is the most important thing. By this measure recruiters should be paid for finding clients, not people. But the opposite is true." Although Vick thinks the field is "grossly misunderstood" even by practitioners, it is a $11-billion-a-year business with excellent potential for skilled, knowledgeable recruiters.

While the Internet and the telephone are indispensable tools, recruiters continue to make face-to-face contacts, particularly at trade shows. Building personal relationships can be critical.

Knowledge and Skills You Need to Have

- Knowledge of the kind of people needed in a specialized field and realism about the marketplace of available candidates and their worth.

- The "people" skills of establishing rapport, developing relationships, judging character, assessing what people need, and developing trust.

- You need to be at ease with selling. Most successful recruiters have a sales personality. Paul Hawkinson calls what recruiters do most "smiling and dialing."

- Patient yet tenacious. You must have high self-esteem and strong self-confidence to deal effectively with rejection. You'll hear twenty no's for every yes when looking for clients.

- Self-motivation. Home-based recruiters don't have the camaraderie of working with other recruiters to keep them motivated to work hard without a guaranteed return; therefore they must be self-motivated to keep themselves going.

- The ability and desire to read and synthesize large amounts of diverse information. For example, some advise reading three to five magazines a day to keep up with trends and changes in the field you're working in.

Start-up Costs	Low	High
Computer with software	$ 1,500	$ 3,000
Printer	$ 300	$ 800
or		
Multi-function printer/fax/scanner/copier	$ 150	$ 800
Telephone headset	$ 40	$ 100
Office furniture, especially an ergonomic chair	$ 400	$ 1,000
Initial marketing budget	$ 1,000	$ 5,000
Total	$ 3,050	$ 10,700

Advantages

- Start-up costs are low.

- Bringing a candidate and an employer together can be satisfying. With a good placement, the future of both parties is enhanced from the match. A company can turn around because of a placement you've made.

- The income can be high, as fees are usually substantial.

- This business provides a great deal of flexibility. Your office can be totally portable. You can take a month to travel in Europe, and your business doesn't have to stop.

Disadvantages

- Recruiting is risky because most recruiters work on a contingency-fee basis. In other words, they get paid only when they locate a suitable candidate. If you miss out on finding someone, you have no income.

- The competition is stiff.

- For its earning potential, the work has a relative lack of prestige.

- The business is stressful; there are big wins and big losses.

- Most of the work consists of making phone calls, and only highly motivated people can keep at it without colleagues and coworkers around for support.

Pricing

- Recruiters charge 25 to 30 percent of the first year's earnings of someone they place in a position, with 30 percent the norm for the industry. However, according to Hawkinson, most home-based recruiters charge 25 percent, thereby competing in terms of price with larger office-based competitors, which have higher overhead.

- Although the trend is toward contingent searches, some recruiters work on a retainer. With a retainer, a recruiter receives 30 percent of the fee upon accepting the search; 30 percent at thirty days; and 30 percent at sixty days. The closure rate on such searches is about half.

Potential Earnings

Typical Annual Gross Revenues: $200,678 (the industry average in 1997, according to a survey of 2,545 consultants conducted by the *Fordyce Letter*). Hawkinson estimates that 25 percent of those surveyed were solo practitioners and half of the solo practitioners were home-based. He adds, "Most home-based, self-employed recruiters complete fifteen searches a year and earn a higher gross for lower fees with higher net earnings." Bill Vick estimates 40 percent of recruiters using the Internet ("Internauts") are solo practitioners and 30 to 45 percent are home-based.

Overhead: low (20 percent or less), with expenses basically telephone and computers.

Best Home Businesses Estimate of Market Potential

The number of searches continues to grow. This is an industry that is made up of small firms. The ten largest firms in the field have only 11 percent of the market. At the same time, some companies, particularly those in the high-tech sector, are using the Web to fill positions, eliminating or reducing the role of the search firm. Such searches are limited, however, because desirable people not seeking to change jobs don't read want ads or upload their résumés; they must be sought out.

Chunking, outsourcing, or brokering ingredients of searches, particularly tasks such as developing lists of potential candidates, are all increasing and can be expected to continue to grow. As videoconferencing becomes more commonplace, the Web's role in the search industry will grow in importance.

Best Ways to Get Business

- Calling companies that have repeatedly advertised for a particular position in trade and professional publications. Carefully script your telephone calls, and use the same script over and over.

- Going to trade shows to make and renew contacts.

- Having your own Web site can help you attract candidates and sometimes clients. Without a Web site, you will not get as many leads from online database directories where companies go to find personnel. Most online directories provide the ability to link the consumer directly to your page.

- Providing an electronic or print newsletter to prospective and existing clients.

- Speaking about recruitment issues to professional and trade associations.

- Mailing postcards advertising your business to companies that are prospective clients.

- Participating in recruiter organizations that facilitate joint sales.

Related Business

Registry Service

A variant of executive search is a registry service. Like executive search, with a registry the fee for the service of matching an individual with an employer is paid by the employer, but the fee is a flat rate that is paid only when a candidate has been hired. This is the type of company Tom and Renae McAnally operate in Montana.

First Steps

Don't start out cold in this business. Go to work for an existing search firm, where you can be trained in the industry, and decide whether this is a business you will enjoy and succeed at. Spend a year or two learning the ropes. Despite the potential rewards, the turnover rate in the industry is high. Only two in ten stay with it after the first year, one in ten after two years.

Where to Turn for Information and Help

ORGANIZATIONS

THE INTERNET BUSINESS NETWORK, 346 Starling Road, Mill Valley, CA 94941; (415) 380-8244. Offers a free daily electronic newspaper, the *Electronic Recruiting News*. Web site: *www.interbiznet.com*

NATIONAL ASSOCIATION OF PERSONNEL SERVICES, 3133 Mount Vernon Avenue, Alexandria, VA 22305; (703) 684-0180; fax: (703) 684-0071.

Certifies Personnel Consultants (CPC). Publishes an *Owners Manual* and an *Operation Analysis Survey* containing operating ratios enabling comparison with others in the field. Web site: *www.napsweb.org*

RECRUITERS ONLINE NETWORK, 3325 Landershire Lane, Suite 1001, Plano, TX 75023; (888) 821-2490; fax-on-demand: (888) 810-0110. Association of over 7,000 registered recruiters, executive search firms, employment agencies, and employment professionals. This site provides a job broadcaster or publisher (if a recruiter has a job search they are doing, they publish it on their site and (600 other sites and newsgroups), a résumé database, and a means of splitting fees. Individuals seeking a job submit résumés to a database accessible only to recruiter members. Web site: *www.recruitersonline.com*

BOOKS

Billing Power! The Recruiter's Guide to Peak Performance, Bill Radin and Betsy Smith, Innovative Consulting, 1995. ISBN: 0962614742.

The Placement Strategy Handbook, 1988, Paul Hawkinson and Jeff Allen, The Kimberly Organization, Box 31011, St. Louis, MO 63131; (314) 965-3883.

Placement Management, 1990, Paul Hawkinson and Jeff Allen, The Kimberly Organization, same as above.

Recruiting: How to Do It, Ian Maitland, Cassell Academic, 1997. ISBN: 0304333158.

Shut Up & Make More Money: The Recruiter's Guide To Talking Less and Billing More, Bill Radin and Betsy Smith, Innovative Consulting, 1995. ISBN: 0962614734.

Take This Job and Sell It!: The Recruiter's Handbook, Richard Mackie, Q E D Press, 1994. ISBN: 0936609303.

DIRECTORY

The Directory of Executive Recruiters, Kennedy Publications, Templeton Road, Fitzwilliam, NH 03447; (800) 531-0007; (603) 585-6544; fax: (603) 585-9555. Lists over 2,500 search professionals in North America indexed by specialities, geography, industries, and contact persons. Also available in an electronic version called *Search Select.* Web site: *www.kennedypub.com*

NEWSLETTTERS

Executive Recruiter News, Kennedy Publications, see above. Trends and statistics, with emphasis on retained recruiters.

The Fordyce Letter, Box 31011, St. Louis, MO 63131; (314) 965-3883. Web site: *www.fordyceletter.com*

SOFTWARE

Solo™ (for Macintosh) and *Identidy*™ (for Windows) available from Identidy Software, Inc., 4010 Oleander Drive, Suite 2, Wilmington, NC 28403; (910) 350-0000. Web site: *www.identidysoftware.com*

Expert Referral Service/Brokerage

In a constantly changing world economy, most companies lack the in-house personnel to deal with the complexities of all the financial, marketing, political, and technical issues and challenges they face. The result is a demand for help and advice from consultants and experts who can step in to address special needs as they arise, but the expert with the right combination of know-how, availability, and cost may not be readily obvious. Hence the rise of expert referral or broker services that will match the specific needs of clients with the right consultants, specialists, and experts.

If, for example, a company has a problem that requires the expertise of a chemical engineer but the company doesn't have one on staff, management can turn to an expert referral service to find the chemical engineer they need who can step in and solve the problem. A client may need the expert advice of an Internet marketing specialist, a toxic-waste manager, or a human-resources expert with experience in downsizing. The assignment or work may be for a one-shot consultation or to serve as short-term staff on a specific project or for a limited period of time.

Clients may also call on the service broker to provide them with trainers who can teach specific skills to their employees. A company might turn to a referral service, for example, to find someone to teach their staff how to set up, use, repair, and sell new technology. Laurel Garrett became a service broker when she discovered that small-business owners often need help but don't know exactly what they need or where to find it. She says, "My business is to find the most efficient, economical way of getting a job done that is beyond the range of my client's capabilities."

Attorneys in need of locating expert witnesses are frequent users of expert referral services. Other referral service specializations include helping help clients locate experts in aviation, insurance, maritime, and even party planning.

Carl Kline, founder of National Consultant Referrals (*www.referrals. com*), points out that expert referral services are not employment agencies because they don't find the expert a permanent job. They are not temporary agencies because they don't actually employ the expert after getting a job listing. And most services are not actually brokers in the technical sense of the term because true brokers sign the client as their own and then subcontract out the work. "Working with someone like me is like working with a matchmaker," Carl Kline says. "When a company needs an expert, they don't want to spend hours reading the Yellow Pages or scouring the Web, picking out names, and calling some unknowns. They want to find someone quickly, so I can provide them with a résumé and description very quickly, and they can see who the candidate is and whether or not there's a match."

Knowledge and Skills You Need to Have

- You need to be proactive and aggressive to find both assignments for your list of experts and suitable experts for your clients. You need to be expert at finding experts. This means going to lots of meetings, making phone calls, and keeping your name in front of the business community in your area. The saying that "Success lies not in what you know but who you know" is literally true in this business.

- You need to know something about consulting or have been a consultant. This allows you to be familiar with the nature of the consulting business and to understand better the expectations that a client has.

- You must know what makes a good consultant. The experts you provide are the key to your success. If the experts you refer are not up to par, your clients will not call upon you again. So you must be able to locate, recognize, and recruit top talent.

- You need to be a good listener. An expert service broker needs to be able to listen carefully to clients and help them identify precisely what they need. Often what they need may not be exactly what they say at first, so you must have good communication skills to help people articulate their needs.

- Objectivity and a desire to serve are essential. You can't just be intent upon finding work for yourself or your friends. You aren't an agent; you are an "honest broker." So if your friend is not the best one for the job, you have to be able to say no.

Start-up Costs	Low	High
Computer	$ 1,500	$ 3,000
Printer	$ 300	$ 800
or		
Multi-function printer/fax/scanner/copier	$ 150	$ 600
Contact management or database software	$ 100	$ 1,000
Telephone headset	$ 40	$ 400
Office furniture, especially an ergonomic chair	$ 400	$ 1,000
Initial marketing budget	$ 3,000	$ 5,000
Total	$ 5,853	$ 11,800

Advantages

- Because companies are undergoing change so rapidly and are finding it more difficult to keep in-house experts, this is a business that is responsive to a fundamental change in the economy.

- You get to meet a lot of interesting people and keep up-to-date about new technologies.

- You are providing a win/win service. When you make a good match, everyone is happy.

- The work offers a lot of variety and is intellectually stimulating because you can work with a wide range of clients and experts who are involved in solving a wide range of problems.

- This is a business that can be done from anywhere.

Disadvantages

- To make money, you must spend a lot of time on the phone selling. This is a five-day-a-week job, says Kline, and that means you cannot leave the phones for very long or hire an answering service to take messages. When clients call, they usually want to talk now.

- You feel time pressures from clients who often wait until the last moment to seek help and then need it immediately.

- You can be deluged with people who may or may not be qualified, wanting you to find them work. You also need to keep tabs on how much your consultants are charging, because their rates must be competitive but not excessive. Companies won't continue using you if your consultants charge too much.

- It can take a year or more to develop and build your business.

- As a referral service, you don't get paid until your expert gets paid; if you operate as a brokerage, the opposite is true. You get paid directly by the client once the service is rendered and then you pay the expert. To keep experts, you will need to pay before you get paid.

Pricing

- Referral services receive 20 to 35 percent of the fee paid by the client to the expert. An agreement to this effect needs to be in writing. The agreement also needs to provide that if the expert is rehired by the same firm within the next twelve months, the expert will pay the referral service its commission.

- For services operating like brokers, bill clients directly and then pay the consultant a daily rate. For example, if a broker gets a training contract for $700 a day, the broker pays the trainer $400 to $500 per day and keeps the difference.

Potential Earnings

Typical Gross Revenues: An active broker who matches one to five consultants per week can gross $50,000 to $150,000 per year, based on commissions of $500 to $2,000 per match.

Overhead: moderate (20 to 40 percent) but decreasing because of e-mail, the Web, and the decreasing cost of long distance telephone service.

Best Home Businesses Estimate of Market Potential

The demand for referral services should remain strong for several reasons. First, downsizing of corporations rolls on in good times and bad so companies are relying more heavily on project-by-project consultants to fill their needs. Second, the increasing global nature of business makes the need for experts a worldwide one. The Internet is playing an increasing role in marketing this service.

Best Ways to Get Business

- Attending business meetings, associations, trial lawyers' association meetings, and all other professional meetings as frequently as possible to meet potential clients and potential consultants

- Phoning likely clients to identify their needs.

- Having a Web site with links and meta tags that contain the phrases your potential customers would use to describe their field and its problems.

- Yellow Pages advertising under the categories of Expert Referral Services or Consultants.

- Direct mail to firms in your specialty area.

- Advertising in trade journals.

- Offer experts a commission (25 percent of your fee) on work they refer that you are then able to send to other consultants.

First Steps

- Identify a specialty; your choice should be influenced by the kind of experience and contacts you have. Your own contacts are a key resource to start this business, so your own Rolodex or database is your key asset. Carl Kline advises beginning on a regional basis or being highly specialized because of the advertising and marketing expenses. In this way, you can develop more depth of experts and specialists than the broad-based referral services on the Web that primarily list consulting firms.

- Learn as much about consulting as you can. Attend seminars, participate in online forums, and read business and trend books and publications.

- Start signing up qualified experts. This means finding people independent enough to take an assignment on short notice. Corporations will work with you only if you have some names of good people and the type of consultants they need. Qualified consultants are interested in being part of your database only if you have contacts with corporations who need them.

- Contact and develop relationships with firms that are likely to need expertise in your industry. Volunteer to help them analyze what needs they have.

Where to Turn for Information and Help

BOOKS

How to Start and Manage a Personnel Referral Service Business, Lewis & Renn Associates, 1996. ISBN: 1887005447.

Also see the books listed in the resources in the Consulting to Businesses and Computer Consultant profiles.

WEB SITES

NATIONAL CONSULTANT REFERRALS, INC., offers a database of articles and resources: *www.referrals.com* and *www.4expertise.com*

Export Agent

"Products from the United States overall are more in demand than products from anywhere else," John Jagoe, Director of the Export Institute reports. "American goods have overcome their past reputation for quality problems and now have the best warranties and customer service in the world." From chemicals and adhesives, to manufacturing equipment and plastics, to electronics and consumer products, most countries in the world are wide open to American products.

While the cost of American goods is subject to the relative value of the dollar, the United States has become a relatively low-cost place to manufacture goods. Wishing to expand their markets, many American firms look overseas for new customers. The Internet has also spurred the growth of international commerce. Taken together these two trends mean that exporting will continue to grow into the next century.

Many if not most foreign customers prefer to work through intermediaries, however, and foreign companies don't have the time to scour the U.S. for products even though the Internet has made doing research and conducting business internationally cheaper and easier. Companies simply don't have the expertise or time to find international customers and arrange to sell their goods overseas. Many smaller manufacturers in particular need someone who can oversee export sales and establish relationships with foreign import agents who have the necessary business and political contacts. Thus there's a continuing role for export agents.

As an export agent, you work with American manufacturers as an independent agent to sell their products overseas. Getting into exporting can be exciting and lucrative, but according to John Jagoe, "The secret to your success as an export sales agent will depend on the quality of your preparation. You've got to do your homework." You also need to have a supportive family support-system because you'll be operating in as many as twenty-four time zones and telephone calls can come at all hours.

Knowledge and Skills You Need to Have

- You must have proficient verbal and written communication skills to be good at developing empathy. You need to be able to explain the exporting process to manufacturers and sell to people from other cultures. Plus you must have the ability to maintain your composure, not being easily rattled by hassles, in dealing with language barriers, different cultural habits, and red tape.

- The ability to develop a systematic marketing plan is important along with having persistence to implement and the patience to deal with the various steps in the exporting process.

- You must be knowledgeable about government regulations, such as when an export license is required, means of financing exports, methods of assuring payment, insurance, customs, and shipping terms. Since many countries have distribution methods and pricing structures different from those in the U.S., you need to learn about those.

- You need the ability and willingness to do research and communicate on the Internet, which has become the key medium for conducting international business.

- The know-how to price correctly for export is also vital as is the ability to negotiate for a price that will make your clients' goods competitive.

Start-up Costs	Low	High
Computer	$ 1,500	$ 3,000
Printer	$ 300	$ 800
or		
Multi-function printer/fax/scanner/copier	$ 150	$ 600
Cell phone	$ 75	$ 200
Telephone headset	$ 40	$ 400
Office furniture, especially an ergonomic chair	$ 400	$ 1,000
Initial marketing budget	$ 1,000	$ 5,000
Reference books and publications	$ 200	$ 500
Trade association dues	$ 200	$ 500
Total	$ 3,715	$ 12,000

Advantages

- Growing international commerce is a long-term trend.

- Opportunities for international travel.

- Long-term relationships with businesspeople in other countries based on providing good service can lead to other opportunities.

Disadvantages

- To be truly successful, exporting requires knowledge of foreign countries and usually either the ability to speak a foreign language or the necessity to hire people who do.

- Because international business transactions take longer, one's patience is tried. It can take months before deals are finalized.

- Because of the complicated nature of international transactions, Murphy's Law (anything that can go wrong will go wrong) often applies.

- Differences in time zones may stretch your normal working day.

- Exporting is subject to economic cycles.

Pricing

Commissions range from 2 to 3 percent for high-volume consumer items such as sports apparel to 5 to 15 percent for costly proprietary items such as software.

With experience and a track record of success, it becomes possible to obtain retainers. To encourage getting a retainer, offer to deduct up to 50 percent of the retainer from your initial commission.

Potential Earnings

Typical Annual Gross Revenues: $60,000 to $100,000 within three years from start-up.

Overhead: high (more than 40 percent). Overhead is high because of international communication costs, translation expenses, secretarial services for major projects, and travel. A twenty-four-hour answering service is preferable to an answering machine because calls must be taken at all hours of the day and night. Travel costs are high, but you should get your suppliers to share in the travel costs. Seminars to keep up on the field and to network can run $50 a month or more; entertainment, $100 a month and up.

Best Home Businesses Estimate of Market Potential

With 50 percent of U.S. exports coming from companies with fewer than 19 employees, there are many potential customers for export agents. The soft spots for exporting are fluctuations in economies around the world and the strength or weakness of the dollar.

Best Ways to Get Business

- Making direct contacts with U.S. manufacturers by phone and fax to find out which are seeking to export their products; you also should make contact with importers and manufacturers in other countries to find out what they are seeking. This is a market-driven business.

- Speaking and offering seminars at meetings, trade shows, and conferences.

- Contact foreign embassies, consulates, and trade offices in Washington, DC, and major cities. Ask their commercial officers for leads. (The State Department publishes a Diplomatic List annually, listing all foreign embassies in Washington.)

- Write to the commercial sections of U.S. embassies overseas and U.S. consulates telling them what you are looking for. Many will reply with a list of prospects.

- Read the *Journal of Commerce,* an international newspaper that lists leads for exporting obtained from the U.S. Department of Commerce's Trade Opportunity Program in which dealers and distributors worldwide contact American embassies seeking U.S. sources. Call (800) 221-3777.

- Having a Web site with links and meta tags that contain the phrases potential customers for your specialty use to describe their industry and its products.

First Steps

- Read about and attend seminars on export procedures. The federal government has many useful services and a wealth of information is available on the Web, a good deal of it free. See the resources below.

- Identify businesses and/or industries on which you wish to concentrate and learn about the countries where such products would be well received.

- Make use of the free advice offered by experts with state and federal governments.

- Start contacting U.S. companies you'd like to represent. It is wise to begin this step in your local area so you can keep communication and travel expenses down at first.

Where to Turn for Information and Help

ORGANIZATIONS

CHAMBERS OF COMMERCE WORLDWIDE, P.O. Box 455, Loveland, CO 80537. Offers a directory of overseas chambers of commerce. Web site: *www.uitc.com/chambers*

FEDERATION OF INTERNATIONAL TRADE ASSOCIATIONS, 11800 Sunrise Valley Drive, Suite 210, Reston, VA 20191; (800) 969-FITA (3482) or (703) 620-1588. The federation's Web site has links to hundreds of Web sites with searchable listings to thousands of trade leads. Web site: *www.fita.org*

INTERNATIONAL UNION OF COMMERCIAL AGENTS AND BROKERS, Office I.U.C.A.B. De Lairessestraat 158, 1075 HM Amsterdam, Holland; (31 20 470 01 77); fax: 31 20 671 09 74. Has information on contracts and the laws of the land for many countries. Web site: *www.iucab.nl/index.htm*

MANUFACTURERS AGENTS NATIONAL ASSOCIATION (MANA), P.O. Box 3467, Laguna Hills, CA 92654-3467; (949) 859-4040. MANA is the national association for independent sales agents, including agents interested in export. They are also a member of the International Union of Commercial Agents and Brokers above. Web site: *www.manaonline.org*

BOOKS AND MANUALS

Export/Import Procedures and Documentation, Thomas E. Johnson, AMACOM, 1997. ISBN: 0814403506.

Export Sales and Marketing Manual, Export Institute, 6901 West 84th Street, Suite 157, P.O. Box 385883, Minneapolis, MN 55438; (800) 943-3171. ISBN: 0943677114. Provides step-by-step plans for starting an export business; includes sample correspondence, contracts, pricing and budgeting worksheets, and shipping documents. $309.95. Quarterly updates, $175 a year. Mention this book to receive a 20 percent discount. Web site: *www.exportinstitute.com*

The Big Ten: The Big Emerging Markets and How They Will Change Our Lives, Jeffrey E. Garte, New York: Basic Books, 1998. ISBN: 0465006868.

Going Global: Four Entrepreneurs Map the New World Marketplace, William C. Taylor, Alan M. Webber, New York: Penguin USA, 1997. ISBN: 0140248994.

Multinational Direct Marketing: The Methods and the Markets, Richard N. Miller, New York: McGraw-Hill, 1995. ISBN: 0070423563.

Selling to Newly Emerging Markets, Russell R. Miller, Quorum Books, 1998. ISBN: 1567200443.

Multinational Distribution: Channel, Tax and Legal Strategies, R. Duane Hall, Ralph J. Gilbert, Praeger Publishing, 1985. ISBN: 0275901157.

REFERENCE MATERIALS

Dun and Bradstreet Information Services Global File provides marketing and sales information for pinpointing prospects, locating partners, and finding selling opportunities on more than 4 million businesses in 200 countries. Available in print or on CD-ROM, priced from $5.95 to $4,995; (800) 624-5669. Web site: *www.dbn.com*

Thomas Register of Manufacturers, Thomas Publishing Company, 5 Penn Plaza, 9th Floor, New York, NY 10119; (800) 222-7900, ext. 200. Available both in print in libraries and as an online database. Provides the names and addresses of manufacturers and can be used as a prospect list. Web site: *www.thomasregister.com*

Tradeshow Week publications, P.O. Box 6340, Torrance, CA 90504; fax: (310) 978-6901. Publications such as the *Data Book,* a comprehensive directory of trade shows and consumer expos and *Tradeshow Week.* Web site: *www.tradeshowweek.com*

FEDERAL GOVERNMENT RESOURCES

THE U.S. DEPARTMENT OF COMMERCE'S TRADE INFORMATION CENTER describes itself as "the first stop for information about all federal export assistance programs, as well as country and regional market information." You can contact this office for personal export assistance from a trade specialist. You can obtain a basic information packet including the publication, *Export Programs: A Business Guide to Federal Export*

Programs by calling (800) USA-TRADE (800-872-8723). Web site: *http://infoserv2.ita.doc.gov/tic.nsf.* In major cities, agencies such as the International Trade Administration and the U.S. and Foreign Commercial Service office are located together in "export assistance centers" to make obtaining information about exporting as centralized as possible. A list of the export assistance centers can be found on this Web site at *www.ita.doc.gov/uscs*

SMALL BUSINESS ADMINISTRATION RESOURCE CENTERS. From this Web site, you can gain access to all types of resources the SBA supports. The SBA offers personal assistance and free advice through its Small Business Development Centers and Service Core of Retired Executives (SCORE) located throughout the country. In addition, the SBA has an Office of International Trade Assistance, Office of Procurement Assistance, and Office of Minority Business Opportunities, 1129 20th Street, N.W., Washington, DC 20036. Web site: *www.sba.gov/services/resource.html*

STATE GOVERNMENT RESOURCES

Most state governments have international trade offices to help companies within their states become successful exporters. Find the list of state offices at the U.S. Department of Commerce's Trade Information Center Web site or at the address cited above.

WEB SITES

COBLE INTERNATIONAL, 1420 Steeple Chase Drive, Dover, PA 17315; (702) 912-1765. Coble offers an international search engine, the ability to post offers to buy and sell, free reports, and other resources. Web site: *www.cobleintl.com*

THE IMPORT-EXPORT BULLETIN BOARD, an affiliate of the United Nations, is a source of trade leads. Web site: *www.iebb.com*

I-TRADE has both free and fee-based services, lists of links that will enable you to develop a business plan. Web site: *www.i-trade.com*

THE EXPORT INSTITUTE operates *www.exportagent.com,* which also may be reached as *www.exportinstitute.com.* Among the resources available on the site is a free twenty-page booklet entitled *How to Be a Successful Export Agent.*

THE EXPORT LEGAL ASSISTANCE NETWORK (ELAN) sponsored by the Small Business Administration is a nationwide group of attorneys with experience in international trade who provide free initial consultations to small businesses on export-related matters; (202) 778-3080. Web site: *www. tradecompass.com/library/books/terms/ExportLegalAssistanceNetwork. html*

EXPORT TODAY ONLINE is operated by Trade Communications, 733 15th Street, N.W., Washington, DC 20005; (202) 737-1060. Offers a free magazine subscription and enables you to create your own online listing on the site. Web site: *www.exporttoday.com*

Facialist/Aesthetician

The beauty business is a perennial one. People want to look and feel their best all year long, in good economic times as well as bad. This is especially true now that the baby-boom generation is aging. By the year 2000, over half the population will be over 35 years of age. As people age, they spend more money more frequently on skin care. In fact, throughout the 90's, it is estimated that revenues from skin-care products have been growing at the rate of better than 7 percent a year and will continue to do so.

Facialists help men and women take care of their skin. They work to slow down the visual aging process of the skin, avert wrinkles and skin problems, and keep the face looking as young and healthy as possible. Using electricity, chemistry, and pressure the facialist has an increasingly exotic array of services and treatments to offer such as peels, waxing, collagen, seaweed, mud, oxygenating and lifting masks, lash and brow tinting, drainage massages, and freeze-dried treatments.

Care of the skin is an ongoing process, so satisfied clients can become regular customers. And because skin needs ongoing care, facialists usually sell their clients an array of skin-care products as well.

Facialists draw their best clients from occupations that emphasize visual appearance where looking your best is important to success. Executives, performers, service personnel, professional speakers, and airline attendants are just a few of the groups for whom appearance is a particularly important element. Facialists can provide each client with an array of treatments from basic care to deep pore cleansing, rejuvenating and hydrating.

Lori Tabak, a Los Angeles facialist, often puts clients on anti-aging regimens that involve weekly treatment over a period of six to eight weeks followed up with ongoing monthly sessions. Treatments may include applying oxygen to the skin and electric facial toning. Many clients continue their monthly follow-up treatments indefinitely.

When Gloria Martell had an assistant working with her, she was able to see between five and ten clients a day, but she emphasizes that facialists who work alone are seldom able to schedule that many clients a day without affecting the quality of the service. It takes time for clients to disrobe and dress again, and you need to spend time counseling each client on proper follow-up care and to demonstrate and sell skin-care products that can both boost the facialist's income and better serve their clients.

Knowledge and Skills You Need to Have

- You need to have a nurturing personality and genuinely enjoy pampering people.

- You should feel completely comfortable touching and having close physical contact with your clients.

- You need to understand and implement good hygiene and sanitation because of the potential for contracting or spreading communicable diseases.

- If your business also involves product sales, an outgoing personality is helpful.

Start-up Costs*	Low	High
Training	$ 2,000	$ 3,000
Products, towels	$ 500	$ 1,000
Table for clients	$ 600	$ 2,500
Steamer	$ 1,000	$ 2,000
Sterilizer	$ 600	$ 700
Specialized equipment that enables add-on services and additional income	$ 2,000	$ 4,000
Initial marketing budget	$ 500	$ 5,000
Professional liability insurance	$ 1,000	$ 1,500
Total	$ 8,700	$ 19,700

*Not included are remodeling or decorating costs for transforming a room in your home into a treatment area.

Advantages

- The market will continue to expand as the population ages and more people, including numbers of men (both older and younger) want to stay youthful.

- The work is less stressful than many other kinds of work.

- Your income potential is good if you market correctly or are perceived as an expert.

- You can see clients at the hours of your choosing.

- You can build a steady, repeat clientele.

Disadvantages

- This business requires having a separate room in your home, which must be decorated, equipped, and dedicated to use as a salon.

- Clients will be coming through your home unless you have a separate entrance to your treatment room.

- Zoning may be an issue because many zoning codes do not permit a continual stream of clients and customers coming to a home business.

- You put yourself in contact with many different people and there is the possibility of contracting an illness or disease. Rubber gloves are sometimes used to avoid direct contact.

Pricing

Facialists charge by time or service and operate on an appointment basis. A basic facial runs from about $50 up. Additional services and products can increase the basic facial from 20 percent to 100 percent. A regular customer will come monthly, yielding a yearly income from each regular customer of $600 or more.

Potential Earnings

Typical Annual Gross Revenues: $40,000, based on four clients a day, four days a week for fifty weeks, at $50 per session. About six appointments a day is the maximum unless you have an assistant because appointments often take more than an hour. Earnings may be increased by selling products and teaching classes and seminars.

Overhead: low (approximately 20 percent).

Best Home Businesses Estimate of Market Potential

A baby boomer turns 50 every eight seconds, but it's usually long before the age of 50 that people become interested in professional skin care to maintain a youthful appearance. This growing market is fed by new skin-care technologies and products for cleansing, hydrating, exfoliating, and toning the skin. More technology and products means more complexity and roles for professionals.

Best Ways to Get Business

- Providing complimentary initial sessions.

- Making personal contacts and doing informal networking among friends, social organizations, and at your health club.

- Networking in professional organizations, such as "leads" clubs.

- Passing out catalogues through friends.

- Creating a newsletter to send to past and prospective clients.

- Doing direct mail featuring special prices or offering complimentary facials.

- Giving your clients complimentary gift certificates to give to their friends.

- Holding an open house at which you provide information about your services.

- Having a Yellow Page listing under Beauty or Aesthetics (sometimes spelled *Esthetics*).

- Work with a hair salon that will require you to work on their premises although you remain independent and split the fees you receive with the salon.

First Steps

- Becoming a facialist requires training as a cosmetologist, cosmetician, aesthetican or beauty therapist. You can find training at private cosmetology schools and community colleges. Cosmetology schools are listed in the Yellow Pages, though they may be found under Beauty or Aesthetics. Training usually takes about six months, though community college training may take longer. Training leads to certification, which may be a requirement for licensing.

- You can't touch a person's skin unless you're licensed as a cosmetologist, cosmetician or aesthetician. (Aestheticians usually can treat other parts of the body, such as the back.) Some states provide for student licenses. To find out about your state, check your state's site on the Web or look in the telephone book for the agency in your state that handles professional and occupational licenses. Facialists who also perform electrolysis need an additional license.

- Decide on a specialty. Says Debbie Purvis, education columnist for *Cosmetics* magazine, "You can't be everything to everybody because so many people are doing this kind of work. So develop an area of expertise for which you are known."

- Check the zoning in your community to be sure you can set up this type of business in your home and then set up a private, separate room in your home for your salon.

- Begin marketing your service. What can be an effective marketing technique is to give complimentary sessions to 100 people in a position to pay for it. If they are happy, some will become repeat customers and even more will tell others about you. In the initial sessions, educate individuals about their skin using a mirror to show them what you see, relating what you find to the benefit of regular professional facials for them.

Where to Turn for Information and Help

ORGANIZATIONS

Aesthetics' International Association, 2611 Beltline Suite #140, Sunnyvale, TX 75182; (972) 203-8530. Web site: *www.beautyworks. com*

CANADIAN COSMETICS CAREER ASSOCIATION, 309 Main Street, Unionville, ON, Canada, L3R 6AS; (416) 410-9175. Offers a cosmetics correspondence course. Web site: *www.cosmeticscareers.net*

NATIONAL COSMETOLOGY ASSOCIATION, 3510 Olive Street Road, St. Louis, MO 63103; (800) 527-1683. Web site: *www.nca-now.com*

BOOKS

The Business of Beauty, Debbie Purvis, Wall & Emerson, 1994; (905) 426-4823. E-mail: odyssey7@idirect.com

A Consumer's Dictionary of Cosmetic Ingredients, Ruth Winter, Crown Publishing, 1999. ISBN: 0609803670.

Clinical Cosmetology: A Medical Approach to Esthetics Procedures, Victoria Rayner, Milady Publishing, 1993. ISBN: 1562530569.

Milady's Standard Textbook of Cosmetology, Milady Publishing Company, 1995. ISBN: 1562532065. Milady is the world's largest publisher of cosmetology education and professional reference materials. The firm also operates a Career Institute that offers two-day courses in many locations. Milady is located at 3 Columbia Circle, Albany, NY 12212; (800) 347-7707. Web site: *www.milady.com/catalog/index.html*

MAGAZINES

Cosmetics, 777 Bay Street, Suite 405, Toronto, Ontario, Canada M5W 1A7. Canada's business magazine for the cosmetics, fragrance, toiletry and personal-care industry. Web site: *www.mhbizlink.com/cosmetics*

Dermascope, 2611 Beltline, Suite #140, Sunnyvale, TX 75182; (972) 226-2309. Published in both English and Spanish. Web site: *www. dermascope.com*

WEB SITE

BEAUTYWORKS is sponsored by *Skin, Inc. Magazine,* the Aesthetics' International Association, the International Guild of Professional Electrologists, and the American Society of Esthetic Medicine, Inc. The site has resources directories, including ones on facial massage and skin care, which you can apply to be included in. Web site: *www.beautyworks.com*

Family Child-Care Provider

The era of Ozzie and Harriet is just a memory, part of our national nostalgia to be memorialized on *Biography* shows. Women no longer work only until they have babies. Today, more than 70 percent of married women with children under 6 work outside the home, and a majority of divorced women with preschool-age children work. So who takes care of the infants, toddlers, and preschoolers while Mommy and Daddy are at work? Child care is the solution for nearly a third of full-time working mothers.

The Bureau of Labor Statistics reports that parents spend over $20 million on child care each year, and that figure continues to grow. Not only do two-career households need child care, but millions of working single parents are becoming a large market as well. Even women working at home often need to use child-care services. According to a study by Dr. Kathleen Christenson of the New School for Social Research, 50 percent of women who work at home use some form of child-care help, at least part-time.

A large proportion of commercial child care is provided in people's homes in what is called *family* child care. These home-based programs contrast with child care that's provided by larger centers serving an average of 60 children that are located in commercial buildings, schools, churches, and temples.

Many factors are contributing to the growth of family child care. First is the growing need for child care overall. Second, rising operating costs from increased regulation have caused commercial centers to consolidate, causing overcrowding in the surviving centers.

Studies indicate that many communities simply don't have enough child-care resources particularly for infants and toddlers. Now many businesses are seeking to include child-care services as part of their employee benefit programs, further increasing the demand. Small companies in particular that can't afford on-site child-care centers have become potential new customers for home-based family child-care providers.

More important, quality family child care is at a premium. According to a five-year study by the Families and Work Institute, just 9 percent of family child-care providers in a sample survey were rated "good," while 56 percent were ranked only "adequate." This leaves a lot of room for new home child-care providers who are committed to providing a safe, intellectually and socially stimulating environment for young children.

All these factors bode well for someone interested in turning a love for caring, teaching and playing with children into a career. Opening your own family child-care business is relatively easy. Most states require a license or registration with a government agency if you intend to have more than three children. The licensing process usually requires an inspection of your home for space, cleanliness, and safety, and some states also require that you have taken a training course in CPR, emergency care, and perhaps child development.

One other regulation to keep in mind is that you'll most likely need approval from your zoning board to operate a home-based child-care business. Your home may be located in an area that isn't zoned to allow family child care or that limits the number of children to no more than three or six. Due to concerns about the additional noise and traffic home child-care generates, some zoning ordinances allow such care businesses only if all abutting neighbors consent to it.

The procedures for passing the proper zoning and licensing vary greatly by state and city, but there are strong incentives for taking these required steps. First, the unzoned, unlicensed child-care operator risks being ordered to close down. Second, licensed child-care providers are eligible for food subsidies from the U.S. Department of Agriculture to help pay for costs of breakfasts, lunches, and snacks you give to your children. Licensing is also needed for liability insurance, which anyone involved in providing care needs to have to protect his or her business and personal assets in the event of an accident. Finally, being fully licensed opens up the opportunity to become accredited by the National Association for Family Child Care and being accredited will help you gain the trust and confidence parents need to be attracted to your service.

The mark of high-quality family child care, according to the Families and Work Institute, is a purposeful commitment to create home environments in which children can be both nurtured and taught. This means that you should have ample toys for children to play with both indoors and out that are suitable to their developmental level. Also you must take every precaution to remove dangerous chemicals, cleaning fluids, and other things that could be harmful to children. In addition, child-care homes need to stimulate children's mental, physical, and social development by providing them with a variety of learning experiences.

Child care has traditionally been a low-paying career and although it may have less income potential than most businesses described in this book, it provides a wealth of psychic rewards for someone who wants to earn an income at home and loves working with children.

Knowledge and Skills You Need to Have

- To enjoy this business, you must like taking care of and parenting other people's children and giving them the warmth and attention they seek.

- You need patience and understanding because you are, in effect, a professional parent dealing with temper tantrums, tears, and fights. You must have an upbeat personality and not get angry quickly because children will test your patience regularly.

- A knowledge of child development and how to handle various behaviors at different ages is especially useful.

- Getting along with parents requires tact and tolerance.

- You need to be able to schedule, organize, and manage four or five things at the same time.

- Making time for the various types of developmental tasks the children need to do each day requires organizational skills.

- You need to be able to give first aid.

- You need to enjoy children's games and stories or at least be able to enjoy the children's enjoyment.

Start-up Costs for Accommodating Six Children

	Low	High
Licenses, fees and inspections	$ 100	$ 250
Liability insurance	$ 400	$ 600
Toys, books, tapes, activity supplies and outdoor equipment	$ 250	$ 2,000
Beds and cribs or playpen for children under two	$ 350	$ 500
Fire extinguisher(s); smoke detector(s); special locks	$ 75	$ 175
Children's table(s) and chairs	$ 75	$ 150
Cordless telephone	$ 40	$ 125
Training, professional books, dues	$ 100	$ 200
Initial marketing budget	$ 200	$ 750
Total	**$ 1,590**	**$ 4,750**

Advantages

- If you love taking care of children, this business means you can make money doing what you love.

- You can earn a living and stay home with your own children, who become part of your career.

- Providing home child-care makes you eligible for important tax deductions. You can take deductions for the rooms you use for child care even if those rooms are used at other times for non-business purposes.

Disadvantages

- You are essentially confined to your home and yard every weekday. You can't run out somewhere for lunch or for errands.

- Unless you have an assistant, you can't take a day off unexpectedly to go to the doctor or dentist or just to relax.

- You can't go to your own children's school events during daytime hours unless you make special arrangements for someone to relieve you.

- For ten hours a day your conversation is limited to talking with small children.

- Ordinary auto insurance doesn't cover transporting children you are paid to care for, so unless you get a commercial policy or special coverage, you may have to call an ambulance if a parent can't come to get a child in the event of illness or injury. Check with individual insurance carriers for their requirements.

Pricing

Pricing varies considerably with age of child, hours of care, parents' income, and location. In the Northeast, parents on average will pay more than $600 a month for suburban daycare, but in small communities in the Midwest, the rates may be under $400 a month or less, and in the South, under $300. Therefore it is essential to call other child-care providers in your area to learn what they are charging. It's best to talk with as many other providers as you can. In assessing what they are charging and actually determining what you will charge, take into account the number of children you intend to care for, whether or not you will employ staff, the cost of living in your area, and the quality of the environment.

Potential Earnings

Although family child-care homes work best both financially and psychologically when two adults are present, the calculation below is based on a one-person operation.

Typical Annual Gross Revenues: $20,000 to $45,000, plus additional revenues you can get in reimbursements from the Child Care Food Program. These figures are based on charging an average of $100 to $150 per child for six children, fifty weeks per year.

Some states will license home child care for up to twelve children; however, you must hire an assistant if you have more than six children, which means paying someone else to assist you, and this may also cause a zoning problem.

Overhead: moderate (about 30 percent).

Best Home Businesses Estimate of Market Potential

While the number of families in the 25 to 34 age bracket, who are the heaviest users of child care of all types, is declining about 1 percent a year, the overall shortage of child-care facilities, coupled with the consolidation of larger commercial child-care centers, means a bright future for family day care.

Best Ways to Get Business

- If your business is new, get a listing with a referral agency. Child Care Resource and Referral Agencies provide free services; they are funded with government grants. They may also provide loans for toys and other equipment.

- Networking with other family child-care providers and receiving their overflow.

- Putting notices on bulletin boards in supermarkets, laundries, and other retail locations.

- Advertising in local parenting newspapers and magazines.

- Make up T-shirts and sweatshirts with the name and logo for you and the children.

- Have your own Web page.

- Contacting small businesses to locate companies that might be interested in contracting directly with you to supply child care for children of employees.

- Once your business starts, encourage referrals from your current families.

Ways to Specialize

Ann Mead, who trains family child-care providers, identified niches emerging in home child care: serving special ed or medically-frail children or having part-day pre-school programs and before-and-after school programs. In addition to training, Ann operates a before-and-after school program herself.

FRANCHISES

MONDAY MORNING AMERICA. Family day care management service. 276 White Oak Ridge Road, Bridgewater, NJ 08807; (800) 335-4MOM; (908) 685-0060. Web site: *www.mondayam.com*

SITTERS UNLIMITED. In-home child care. 23015 Del Lago, Laguna Hills, CA 92653; (800) 328-1191.

WEE WATCH PRIVATE HOME DAY CARE. Supervised private child-care agencies. 105 Main St., Unionville, ONT L3R 2G1 Canada; (905) 479-4274.

First Steps

- Call the government agency in your state that licenses or registers home child care. There is no uniform name for this agency. In some states, child care is regulated by state health departments; other states have children's departments; others have different names.

From the agency, you will learn of the requirements in your state, about training programs, and how to get other useful information.

- Check your zoning to see if you can offer child care in your home. However, local zoning ordinances may be superseded in some states by state law that will allow you to provide home child care. It's a good idea to talk over your plans with neighbors to avoid their opposition, even if you don't have zoning problems.

- Contact a child-care information agency in your area (these agencies are listed in the Yellow Pages under Child Care) or the local family child-care association to learn about the demand for child care in your area, licensing requirements, and sources for training, such as the Red Cross and community colleges. Elementary schools are another source of information about the need for child care in your area.

- Apply for a license or registration according to the requirements of your state.

- Take classes in first aid emergency preparation (for example, earthquakes, hurricanes, tornadoes) and operating a child-care business in your home, if available.

- Learn about the needs and behavior related to the developmental stages of the ages of children you will be caring for.

- Establish your rates and written policies, including hours of operation, deposits you require, late fees if children are picked up late, medical issues, holidays, notice of termination, and payment. To avoid collection problems, have parents pay on Friday prior to the next week. Never let unpaid bills go for more than one week.

- Obtain equipment and childproof your home. You may be able to buy used equipment and toys (wood is more durable than plastic) at garage sales and secondhand stores. You can even borrow books and sound recordings from your library.

Where to Turn for Information and Help

ORGANIZATIONS

CHILDREN'S DEFENSE FUND, 25 E Street, N.W., Washington, DC 20001; (202) 628-8787. Publishes a study of child care in the U.S. Web site: *www.childrensdefense.org*

NATIONAL ASSOCIATION FOR THE EDUCATION OF YOUNG CHILDREN, 1509 16th Street, N.W., Washington, DC 20036; (800) 424-2460 or (202) 232-8777. Web site: *www.naeyc.com*

NATIONAL ASSOCIATION OF CHILD CARE RESOURCE & REFERRAL AGENCIES, NACCRRA Field Office, 1319 F St. NW, Suite 180, Washington, DC 20004. Call Child Care Aware at (800) 424-2246. This association refers parents to local referral agencies that help them locate child care. Those local agencies also provide information and assistance to people interested in starting a family child-care home business. Web site: *www.naccrra.net*

NATIONAL ASSOCIATION FOR FAMILY CHILD CARE, 525 SW 5th St., Suite A, Des Moines, IA 50309; (800) 359-3817; (800) 359-3817; or (515) 282-8192. Web site: *www.nafcc.org;* has listings of meetings and training. The association offers accreditation to child-care providers who meet their states' requirements and have been providing care in their home for 18 months. It annually publishes the National Directory of Family Child Care Provider Associations, listing almost 2,000 local support groups of child-care providers. Materials for starting your own child-care home.

QUALITY CARE FOR CHILDREN, 1447 Peachtree Street, N.E., Suite 700, Atlanta, GA 30309; (404) 479-4200. The center annually presents a national family-care conference. It publishes a variety of materials. Call or write to be added to the conference mailing list and/or receive a list of publications. Web site: *www.qualitycareforchildren.org*

WEB SITE

CHILD CARE CERTIFICATION SERVICES, 4502 Jonlow Circle, Richmond, VA 23234; (804) 275-4086 certifies child care providers. Certification includes a listing in a database, discounts on insurance and food items, as well as marketing services. *www.cccs1.qpg.com*

BOOKS

Basic Guide to Family Child Care Record Keeping, Tom Copeland, Redleaf Press, 1997. ISBN: 188483406X.

How to Start a Home-Based Day-Care Business, Shari Steelsmith, Globe Pequot, 1997. ISBN 076270067X.

How to Start and Run a Home Day-Care Business, Carolyn Argyle, Citadel Press, 1997. ISBN: 0806518529.

Profitable Child Care: How to Start and Run a Successful Business, Nan Lee Howkins, Heldi Kane Rosenholtz, New York: Facts on File, 1993. ISBN: 0816022364.

Start Your Own Childcare Business, Dawn Kilgore, Prentice-Hall Trade, 1996. ISBN: 0136033253.

Setting Up for Infant/Toddler Care: Guidelines for Centers and Family Child Care Homes, Annabelle Godwin, Lorraine Schrag, San Fern, National Association for Education, 1996. ISBN: 0935989757.

Start Your Own At-Home Child Care Business, Patricia Gallagher, Mosby-Year Book, 1994. ISBN: 0943135087.

Your One-Year-Old: The Fun-Loving, Fussy 12-To-24-Month-Old, a series by Louise Bates Ames, Frances L. Ilg, and Carol Chase Haber, New York: Doubleday, 1995. ISBN: 0440506727.

Your Two-Year-Old: Terrible or Tender, Delacorte Press, 1993. ISBN: 0440506387.

Your Three-Year-Old: Friend or Enemy, Delacorte Press, 1993. ISBN: 0440506492.

Your Four-Year-Old: Wild and Wonderful, DTP, 1989. ISBN: 0440506751.

Your Five-Year-Old: Sunny and Serene, Delacorte Press, 1995. ISBN: 0440506735.

TRAINING COURSES

An increasing number of states will provide you with the names of approved training programs offered within the state. To tap into this information, contact your state's licensing agency.

AT-HOME PROFESSIONS, 2001 Lowe St., Ft. Collins, CO 80525; (800) 359-3455 or (970) 225-6300. Offers a training course in home child care.

NEWSLETTER

Family Child Caring, Redleaf Press, 450 North Syndicate, Suite 5, St. Paul, MN 55104; (800) 423-8309 or (651) 641-0305.

SOFTWARE

Private Advantage, Mount Taylor Programs, 716 College Ave., #B, Santa Rosa, CA 95404; (800) 238-7015; (707) 542-1230; fax: (707) 542-1521. Web site: *www.privateadv.com*

Financial Advisor

Will I have enough money?" This is the number one question asked by those who call the International Association for Financial Planning financial hot line. Callers ranged from millionaires to financially pressed and stressed baby boomers who are struggling to support both their children in college and their elderly parents.

Their concern, financial planners believe, is justified. Baby boomers, they report, are saving only a third of what they will need to retire comfortably. This is primarily because people are living longer and the demands on their money are greater. Demographers estimate that by the year 2030 half a million Americans will live to at least 100. One in every 26 baby boomers, or 3 million people born from 1946 to 1964, are expected to live that long.

When it comes to money, "Baby boomers are asking for advice," says Paula Hogan of Milwaukee, a Certified Financial Planner (CFP). "This generation has lived through the growth of the financial industry in which credit cards and mutual funds came of age. Before credit cards, you had to live within your income and before mutual funds, investment choices were limited."

There has been a shift in retirement funding from the defined benefits of traditional pension plans to defined contributions of 401(k) plans in which the employees themselves are largely responsible for protecting their portfolio and making it grow. People must make these decisions on their own now in a state of continual change because Congress is constantly rewriting the tax laws that affect retirement planning. Added to this conundrum are looming changes in Social Security, the net result of which analysts say is that one generation is going to pay twice—once for itself and once for the preceding generation.

Contributing still further to rising financial concerns is the fact that most Americans are living beyond their incomes. America's credit debt is almost half a billion dollars. At the end of 1997, credit-card balances stood at a record high, over $1,600 for every man, woman, and child in the USA!

All of these factors add up to a pressing need for knowledgeable and objective professional financial advice. Thus, there are now many ways to earn a living serving this need.

Financial Planner

Once a service primarily for the wealthy, financial planning has taken off as a burgeoning field. Since the1970's and 80's so many varieties of investment products have come on the market that people need help in deciding what to do with their money. Usually someone engages the services of a financial planner during a time of some major change like a marriage, promotion, or a death in the family.

The role of the advisor varies depending on the needs of the client and the specialty of the advisor. You may serve primarily as someone who analyzes and strategizes with your clients on their overall financial situation and prepares a written plan for how they can protect and get the assets they're seeking. In this case, clients implement their own plans. Alternatively, you may take a more active role in working with your clients and purchase or manage products for them. Depending on your specialty, you may advise your clients on investing, retirement planning, estate planning, taxes, insurance, and more.

Over 200,000 men and women call themselves financial planners including stockbrokers, insurance agents, accountants, real estate agents, and attorneys. Some use this term to help them market the financial products they sell without taking the specific training and series of examinations required to become registered or certified as a financial planner or investment advisor and thereby entitled to use the initials that indicate this professional designation. Most states do not have statutes that regulate financial planners as *financial planners,* so in most places people can legally use this term to describe themselves without completing formal certification.

However, all the states (except for Colorado, Iowa, Ohio and Wyoming) and the federal government do regulate what financial planners do—providing investment advice, selling securities or insurance. Even in those states that don't require registration, individual investment advisors must register with the SEC.

If you wish to pursue financial planning as a new career, whether you will sell financial products or not, you need to choose how you'll be licensed and how many professional designations you want to acquire. Some credentials for financial planners are available only to people with certain educational backgrounds. Others are relevant to specific services or financial products. Some organizations publicize and market the credential they issue more than others which can result in their members getting clients more readily. Some credentials may carry more weight among the people who will be potential referral sources for you. So we recommend researching your alternatives for credentialing carefully. Following are the major organizations that issue financial-planning credentials and how you can contact and learn more about them.

Accredited Estate Planner (AEP)

Persons with this designation belong to the National Association of Estate Planners and Councils. Most members are accountants, financial planners, insurance agents, lawyers and trust bankers and have passed an examination. 270 S. Bryn Mawr Avenue, P.O. Box 46, Bryn Mawr, PA 19010-2196; (610) 526-1389. Web site: *http://naepc.org*

Certified Financial Planner (CFP)

Persons with this designation belong to the Institute of Certified Financial Planners. Members have passed a ten-hour examination administered by the Certified Financial Planner Board of Standards. The Institute publishes a journal; it makes referrals to members. 3801 East Florida Avenue, Suite 708, Denver, CO 80210; (800) 322-4237, (303)759-4900; Web site: *www.icfp.org.* The College for Financial Planning offers an educational curriculum leading to taking the CFP examination. 6161 South Syracuse Way, Greenwood Village, CO 80111; (303) 220-1200. Web site: *www.fp.edu.*

Certified Investment Management Consultant (CIMC)

Persons certified by the Institute for Investment Management Consultants specialize in fee-based asset management. 1101 17th Street

NW, Suite 703, Washington, DC 20036; (800) 449-4462; (202) 452-8670. Web site: *www.theiimc.org*

Chartered Financial Analyst (CFA)

Persons with this designation are securities analysts, money managers and investment advisers who analyze investments and the securities of companies and industry groups. Many actively manage client investments. The CFA designation requires passing an examination administered by the Association for Investment Management and Research, P.O. Box 3668, 5 Boar's Head Lane, Charlottesville, VA 22903-0668; (800) 247-8132; (804) 980-3668. Web site: *www.aimr.org*

Chartered Financial Consultant (ChFC)

Persons with this designation belong to the American Society of Certified Life Underwriters & Chartered Financial Consultants. Most members have an insurance background and must pass examinations administered by the American College. The Society publishes a journal and makes referrals to members. 270 South Bryn Mawr Avenue, Bryn Mawr, PA 19010; (888) ChFC-CLU; (610) 526-2500. Web site: *www.financialpro.org*

The following organizations do not credential in the same sense as those above, but they are noteworthy for their size and what they offer.

International Association for Financial Planning (IAFP)

The association is "open to anyone who is active in the financial-services industry." It offers training, books, and other materials and makes referrals to members. While the association draws from all areas of the financial-services industry, many of its members also have the CFP designation. 5775 Glenridge Drive N.E., Suite B-300, Atlanta, GA 30328; (888) 806-PLAN; (404) 845-0011. Web site: *www.iafp.org*

National Association of Personal Financial Advisors (NAPFA)

Members are fee-only financial planners, many of whom also have the CFP credential. Offers educational conferences and seminars; makes referrals to members. 355 West Dundee Road, Suite 200, Buffalo Grove, IL 60089; (888) FEE-ONLY; (847) 537-7722. Web site: *www.napfa.org*

Credit Counselor / Consultant

Because so many Americans are living on credit with debt piling up, people like Bill Jabs of Rochester, New York, are stepping in to help. Jabs teaches "Freedom from Debt," a course that shows people how to get out of debt.

His course covers such things as which bills to pay first, how much to pay off over what period of time, how to change buying habits and so forth. Following his program, a person can normally be debt free within five to seven years. One of his students, however, has paid off nine of her ten credit cards in only six months.

Jab's mission in life is a debt-free America, and his plans include getting the citizens of entire communities out of debt.

Resources. **National Institute for Consumer Education,** 559 Gary M. Owen Building, 300 W. Michigan Avenue, Eastern Michigan University, Ypsilanti, MI 48197; (734) 487-2292. Web site: *www.nice.emich.edu.* Provides a teaching guide and is affiliated with the Institute for Personal Finance, 3900 Camelback Road, Phoenix, AZ 85018; (614) 485-9650. The Institute offers an examination to become an Accredited Financial Counselor (AFC). Web site: *www.emich.edu/public/coe/nice/afcpe.html*

Financial Educator

Polls show that 32 percent of Americans say they're always worried about money and making ends meet. That's up from 20 percent in 1995, according to a survey by Marist College Institute for Public Opinion. Money matters are among the top of everyday stressors. In fact, other studies report more family arguments about money than virtually any other subject.

Hence, people like Chellie Campbell of Los Angeles, California, are creating courses to help people learn new attitudes about money and new money habits. Campbell offers several Financial Stress Reduction courses every week and they're always full.

While operating a bookkeeping service for several years, Campbell noticed how stressed her clients were by the financial aspects of their lives.

"Financial Stress Reduction" became her company motto, and clients needing help repeatedly urged her to offer a stress reduction course. She now provides these seminars full time. Most of her business comes from word-of-mouth as students tell others about how they're taking the financial stress out of their lives.

Start-up Costs*	Low	High
Computer	$ 1,500	$ 3,000
Printer	$ 300	$ 800
or		
Multi-function printer/fax/scanner/copier	$ 150	$ 600
Contact management software	$ 100	$ 1,000
Office furniture, especially an ergonomic chair	$ 400	$ 1,000
Initial marketing budget	$ 1,000	$ 5,000
Credentialing and annual dues and licensing	$ 1,000	$ 2,000
Furnishings unless you see clients at their places. Increasingly people have offices as it makes clients feel more comfotable with you.	$ 0	$ 7,500
Errors and Omissions insurance	$ 700	$ 900
Total	$ 5,150	$ 21,800

* If you plan to have clients who will come to your home office, it will need to look like the office of a prosperous professional. This may require relocating or redecorating your residence.

Knowledge and Skills You Need to Have

- Good listening skills are a must.

- You need technical expertise and to keep up with a changing field.

- The ability to establish and maintain long-term relationships is essential.

- You must be someone who is trustworthy and be able to communicate this quality to your clients.

Advantages

- Financial planners are held in relatively high regard by the public. A 1995 survey by the Certified Board of Financial Planners Board of Standards found that when prospective clients were asked which professional they would most likely consult when seeking financial advice, 25 percent would choose a financial planner, 22 percent would choose a stock or investment broker, and 13 percent a CPA/accountant.

- Financial planning is a field in which age adds to credibility, not like some careers in which age is a liability.

- People enter financial planning from other fields and are able to utilize their past experience.

- Most advisors believe they are making people's lives better and therefore feel satisfaction with what they do.

- You see people at their best, unlike doctors, who often see people at their worst.

Disadvantages

- Financial planners are responsible for absorbing and understanding a great deal of information.

- Every day you need to do your best.

- You need to be a junkie for information because you must keep up.

- You need to be a trend spotter. To help people plan for the future you need to know what's coming.

- The potential for liability dictates having professional liability insurance.

- Many people believe the most objective advice comes from sources that are not both making financial recommendations and benefiting from those recommendations in the form of commissions. So some people say they are fee-only planners but have been found to be collecting commissions resulting from recommendations they make. This stains the field.

Pricing

For purposes of compensation, there are three types of financial planners.

- Fee-only planners, who charge either by the hour, on a project or retainer basis, or they charge based on the value of the assets they manage. Hourly rates range from $50 to $150. Annual surveys by the College for Financial Planning show a median hourly rate of $100 during the 90's. Some planners, however, charge as much as $350 an hour. Some charge based on the client's net worth. One percent is typical but it can go as high as 3 percent. The charge for managing assets is typically .5 percent.

- Commission-only planners, who do not charge for their time but receive commissions on the investment products they sell. Commissions depend on the products they are selling.

- Fee-and-commission planners, who charge hourly fees for their advice and get a commission on the products they sell.

Potential Earnings

Typical Annual Gross Revenues: $90,000 based on billing $100 an hour, eighteen hours a week, fifty weeks a year.

Overhead: moderate (33 percent based on surveys by the College for Financial Planning).

Best Home Businesses Estimate of Market Potential

Some believe the financial-advice industry will consolidate, but for people who want a professional to review their entire financial situation and who demand service tailored to their personality and needs, financial planners will continue as individual practitioners for those who can pay their fees.

Best Ways to Get Business

- Make presentations at employee workplaces, particularly at companies with 401(k) plans. Offering free refreshments helps get attendance.

- Teach courses at local colleges, extension programs, and schools without walls.

- Write a column or articles in publications that reach your market.

- Develop mutual referral and other relationships with attorneys, particularly those specializing in estate and divorce law, accountants, and insurance agents.

- Speak to local organizations.

- Have your own Web site. Without a Web site, you will not get as many leads from database directories maintained by national organizations that consumers use to find a professional. Most online directories provide the ability to link the consumer directly to your page.

- Send out newsletters to stay top-of-mind with existing clients.

First Steps

- Decide how you will function as a financial advisor and get the appropriate certification and license. If you will be managing funds and it will be less than $25 million in funds, you need a state license as an investment advisor; if over $25 million, you are regulated by the Securities and Exchange Commission (SEC). Licenses in some states are difficult to get; some are easy. Regardless, you need to get licensed in order to advise clients.

- Choose how you will seek to be compensated. Will you be fee-only, commissioned or a combination of fee and commission?

- Identify the kind of clients you will target. For example, a woman might target divorced or widowed women; a retired dentist might target dentists; a retired executive might specialize in working with people from his or her former industry. A growing specialty is comprehensive family planners.

- After working with a number of clients, decide if your practice and specialization is satisfying or needs refocusing.

Where to Turn for Information and Help

COURSES AND TRAINING

See the organizations listed earlier under Resources.

BOOKS

Best Practices for Financial Advisors, Mary Rowland, Michael R. Bloomberg, Bloomberg Press, 1997. ISBN: 1576600068.

Essentials of Investments, Zvi Bodie, Alex Kane, Alan J. Marcus, Richard D. Irwin, 1998. ISBN: 0256164592.

The Financial Advisor's Analytical Toolbox: Using Technology to Optimize Client Solutions, Ed McCarthy, New York: McGraw-Hill, 1997. ISBN: 0786310529.

How to Become a Successful Financial Consultant: How to Make a Living Investing Other People's Money, Jim H. Ainsworth, New York: John Wiley & Sons, 1997. ISBN: 0471155616.

The Management of Investment Decisions, Donald B. Trone, William R. Allbright, Philip Taylor, Irwin Professional Publishing, 1995. ISBN: 0786303921.

Wealth Management: The Financial Advisor's Guide to Investing and Managing Your Client Assets, Harold R. Evensky, Irwin Professional Publishing, 1996. ISBN: 0786304782.

The Wealth Management Index: The Financial Advisor's System for Assessing & Managing Your Client's Plans & Goals, Ross Levin, Irwin Professional Publishing, 1996. ISBN: 0786310200.

MAGAZINES AND NEWSLETTERS

Financial advisors keep up with the popular financial publications, among them *The Wall Street Journal, Barron's, Forbes, The Economist, Kiplinger's Personal Finance, Money, Smart Money,* and *Worth.*

Financial Planning Interactive, an online magazine. Web site: *http:// www.fponline.com*

SOFTWARE

FOR BILLING:

Centerpiece, portfolio management software, Performance Technologies, Inc., 1008 Bullard Court, Suite 100, Raleigh, NC 27615; (800) 528-9595 or (919) 876-3555. Web site: *www.centerpiece.com*

FOR FINANCIAL PLANNING:

Money Tree Software offers a suite of programs for financial planning professionals using a common data file to allow sharing data between programs. 1753 Wooded Knolls Drive, Suite 200, Philomath, OR 97370; (541) 929-2140. Web site: *www.moneytree.com*

FPLAN Professional Advisor+ is available either in modules or as an integrated program. First Financial Software, Inc., P.O. Box 770005, Orlando, FL 32877; (800) 719-8761. Web site: *www.fplan.com*

Fitness Trainer

How would you like to have all the time you want to exercise and work out and get paid for it, too? You can, because as more and more people spend their days working behind desks, at a computer, and on the telephone, fitness training of all kinds becomes ever more popular. While it would seem strange to our great-grandfathers, who spent their days in back-breaking jobs such as delivering ice or coal, the more we earn our livelihoods using our brains the more we crave using our bodies. It's not that unexpected because scientific evidence shows that being physically fit increases our alertness and energy, enables us to enjoy our leisure hours more, increases our resiliency to recover from health or other crises, helps us look more attractive, and extends our lives. Beginning with Jane Fonda's first workout video, fitness training has become a big business. And while you can't operate a gym at home, you can establish a successful business as a personal fitness trainer or coach.

Personal trainers design workout routines for individuals or small groups and guide clients through their workouts two or three times a week, either at the clients' homes or at a gym. Some trainers also teach yoga and aerobics, either in their own homes or at facilities they rent. Others specialize in fitness training for children, pregnant women, new mothers, or others with special needs. Richard Salas in Los Angeles, for example, prides himself on being the only gymnastics teacher for adults.

Although the principal users of fitness trainers are people under 35, this field is not only for the young. In fact, Laura Brooks, of Energy Unlimited in Los Angeles, believes that younger people are at a disadvantage when entering this field because they're seen as less experienced. The more background and experience you have, the more credible you will be as a trainer. But, of course, you will need to look and be physically fit because you are a role model. Being fit will help you attract clients and make it easier to talk about as well as demonstrate what you do to groups at trade shows and meetings and to the media.

You need to be able to demonstrate proper form and you may need to work out alongside your clients at times, meaning that you'll probably be exercising more hours a day than you would otherwise. Most successful personal trainers have evolved their own method of training, but whether you're teaching weight training, aerobics, or gymnastics, you'll need to watch your students closely and guide them in using safe and effective techniques. If you use a gym to work out in with your clients, you'll need to maintain a membership there.

Certification is a disputed issue in this field. There are quite a few sources of credentials, but because some companies (not all) offer them for a fee and a test instead of offering a solid training experience, the value of fitness-training credentials has become clouded. It's important to check carefully organizations that offer certification. Clients want and deserve trainers with solid know-how and experience.

Some fitness trainers specialize in working with people with particular needs, such as:

- Executives and professionals with limited time

- Older adults

- People in rehabilitation

- People with diseases, such as arthritis, cardiac problems, chronic musculo-skeletal problems, and diabetic conditions

- People with disabilities, such as being wheelchair-bound

- People seeking to lose weight

- Prenatal women

- Youth

Some fitness trainers specialize by offering specific activities such as:

- Aerobics

- Aquatic exercise

- Boxing

- Group fitness instruction

- Indoor cycling

- Martial arts

- Pilates technique

- Sports training

- Strength conditioning

- Yoga

Knowledge and Skills You Need to Have

- You must have a sound knowledge of anatomy, physiology, kinesiology, fitness principles, and exercise so you can recognize contraindications for exercise.

- You need to know how to tailor effective workout routines to the objectives of your clients that both do the job safely and keep them from getting bored with their workout routines.

- You must know how to prevent and deal with injuries and emergencies.

- You must be able to encourage, inspire, and motivate your clients to continue with you, even when they don't see immediate results. One of the most challenging aspects of this business is keeping your clients motivated to continue working out. Although it may go unstated, this is a large part of why they hire you.

- You need to be someone who can easily provide lots of personal attention and special handling.

- Because people bare their souls through their physical problems, the ability to convey trust and empathy are key.

- A solid understanding of nutrition is also helpful.

Advantages

- Most people find this work enjoyable.

- You experience the satisfaction that comes from helping people improve.

- There is a lot of contact with people. This is an extremely personal business.

- You keep fit because a demand of this field is to live a healthful lifestyle.

Disadvantages

- Like any athlete, you can overtrain and thus be hurt.

- Depending on your clientele, you may be working evenings and weekends.

- People cancel at the last minute, making it important to have a cancellation policy that protects you.

- It's normal to have a high level of client attrition. You may lose even loyal, long-term clients at any time. Therefore you need to market continually to attract a constant flow of new clients.

- You have potential liability, necessitating professional liability insurance.

Start-up Costs	Low	High
Computer fitness-training software, Web site:		
fitnesszone.com	$ 1,500	$ 3,000
Printer	$ 300	$ 800
or		
Multi-function printer/fax/scanner/copier	$ 150	$ 600

Cell phone	$	75	$ 200
Office furniture, especially an ergonomic chair	$	400	$ 1,000
Initial marketing budget and forms such as waivers	$ 1,000		$ 5,000
Proper clothing (i.e., good shoes and socks)	$	300	$ 400
Equipment and supplies such as weights, elastic tubing, and floor mats	$	100	$ 200
Professional liability insurance	$	250	$ 400
Total	$ 4,075		$ 11,600

Pricing

Depending on their reputation and locale, fitness trainers charge from $25 to $200 per session; $50 is typical.

Potential Earnings

Typical Annual Gross Revenues: $50,000 at $50 an hour, 20 hours a week (which can mean working with as few as 7 clients), 50 weeks a year. Some trainers add to their income by selling equipment to their clients.

Overhead: low (less than 20 percent).

Best Home Businesses Estimate of Market Potential

While the number of people participating in physical fitness activities goes up and down from year to year, overall participation in fitness activities grew over 20 percent from 1987 to 1997. However, the professional fitness industry is growing more dramatically. The number of people taking the ACE Personal Training Exam for example has risen from just over 3,000 in 1992 to 15,000 in 1998. The increase in the International Association of Fitness Professionals has grown from under 1,000 in 1991 to over 7,000 in 1998. The popularity of magazines such as *Fitness, Men's Health, Muscle and Fitness,* and *Shape* also indicate the growing appeal of fitness.

Best Ways to Get Business

- Encourage current clients to refer others to you.

- Make presentations in the form of workshops, seminars, and speeches in which you demonstrate what you do.

- Exhibit at health shows, and be sure to be doing things to create interest.

- "Network" with chiropractors and orthopedic surgeons and others who have patients.

- Create publicity for yourself.

- Have before-and-after photos showing the effects of your training.

- Have your own Web site. Without a Web site, you will not get as many leads from database directories maintained by organizations that consumers use to find a professional. Most online directories provide the ability to link the consumer directly to your page.

FRANCHISES

HEAD OVER HEELS, P.O. Box 530744, Birmingham, AL 35253; (800) 857-FLIP; (205) 879-6305. Offers a franchise for mobile gymnastics and motor skills.

KINDERDANCE INTERNATIONAL, 268 N. Babcock St., Melbourne, FL 32935; (800) 666-1595. Offers a franchise for teaching dance and motor-development skills to preschool-age children.

PEE WEE WORKOUT, 34976 Aspen Wood, Willoughby, OH 44094; (800) 356-6261. Offers franchises for mobile exercise instruction. Web site: *http://members.aol.com/peeweework*

First Steps

- Obtain the needed training, including attending hands-on workshops.

- Get certified. Clubs and gyms will only work with certified trainers.

- Work at a gym or other organization that allows you to take on private clients.

- Build a clientele; the best place to begin is with people you know.

Where to Turn for Information and Help

ORGANIZATIONS

AEROBIC AND FITNESS ASSOCIATION OF AMERICA, 15250 Ventura Boulevard, Suite 200, Sherman Oaks, CA 91403; (800) 446-2322, (818) 905-0040. Offers certification; publishes *American Fitness Magazine*. Web site: *www. afaa.com*

AMERICAN COUNCIL ON EXERCISE, 5820 Oberlin Drive, Suite 102, San Diego, CA 92121; (800) 825-3636, (619) 535-8227. Provides certification and has online registry for consumers to locate a personal trainer. Web site: *www.acefitness.org*

AMERICAN FITNESS ASSOCIATION, P.O. Box 401, Durango, CO 81301; (303) 247-4109.

THE AQUATIC EXERCISE ASSOCIATION, PO Box 1609, Nokomis, FL 34274-1609; (888) AEA-WAVE; (941) 486-8600. Has a certification program for instructors. Web site: *www.aeawave.com*

ACCREDIATED TRAINERS ALLIANCE. Web site lists affiliates in different parts of the U.S. that provide training leading to certification; (800) ATA-4599. Web site: *www.atafitness.com*

ASSOCIATION OF NATIONAL AEROBIC CHAMPIONSHIPS WORLDWIDE, 8033 Sunset Boulevard, #1420, Los Angeles, CA 90046; (323) 850-3777. Has a directory of sportaerobic coaches and trainers who specialize in training athletes. Web site: *www.sportaerobics-nac.com*

IDEA, 6190 Cornerstone Court, La Jolla, CA 92037; (800) 999-4332, (619) 535-8979. This large organization offers insurance but does not certify. Web site: *www.ideafit.com*

NATIONAL DANCE EXERCISE INSTRUCTOR'S TRAINING ASSOCIATION, 1503 Washington Avenue South, Minneapolis, MN 55454; (800) 237-6242; (612) 340-1306. Offers certification workshops for aerobic instructors and personal trainers as well as continuing education workshops. Web site: *www.ndeita.com*

NATIONAL FEDERATION OF PROFESSIONAL TRAINERS, P.O. Box 4579, Lafayette, IN 47903; (800) 729-6378; (765) 447-3296. Provides certification; publishes *NFPT Personal Fitness Trainer* magazine. Web site: *www.nfpt.com*

NATIONAL STRENGTH AND CONDITIONING ASSOCIATION, 1640 L Street, Suite G, Lincoln, NE 68508; (888) 746-CERT; (402) 476-6669. Offers a certification program. Web site: *www.nsca-cc.org*

BOOKS

The Business of Personal Training, Scott O. Roberts, Human Kinetics Publishing, 1996. ISBN: 0873226054. Written for club owners, it provides the owners' viewpoint on what trainers should know and do.

Essentials of Strength Training and Conditioning, National Strength and Conditioning Association, Thomas Baechle, Human Kinetics Publishing, 1994. ISBN: 0873226941.

Fitness Training for Dummies, Suzanne Schlosberg, Liz Neporent, Foster City, CA: IDG Books Worldwide, 1996. ISBN: 1568848668.

Fitness Programming and Physical Disability, Patricia D. Miller, Human Kinetics Publishing, 1995. ISBN: 0873224345.

Getting Stronger: Weight Training for Men and Women: Sports Training, General Conditioning, Bodybuilding, Bill Pearl, Gary T. Moran, Ph.D., Shelter Publications, 1990. ISBN: 0679732691.

Getting in Shape: Workout Programs for Men and Women, Bob Anderson, Bill Pearl, Ed Burke, Jean Anderson, Shelter Publications, 1994. ISBN: 0679756094.

Stretching, Bob Anderson, Jean E. Anderson, Shelter Publications, 1987. ISBN: 0394738748.

Weight Training for Dummies, Suzanne Schlosberg, Liz Neporent, IDG Books Worldwide, 1997. ISBN: 0764550365.

WEB SITES

FITNESS CONNECTION PARTNER JUMPSITE. Information about diet and exercise plus bulletin boards, a forum, and an extensive list of links to newsgroups. Web site: *http://primusweb.com/fitnesspartner*

FITNESSWORLD, sponsored by *Fitness Management* magazine, 215 South Highway 101, Suite 110, P.O. Box 1198, Solana Beach, CA 92075; (619) 481-4155. Web site: *www.fitnessworld.com*

FITNESSZONE. Fitness information, a gym locator, specifications of gym equipment and offers a *Fitnesszine* online magazine. Web site: *www. fitnesszone.com*

THE INTERNET'S FITNESS RESOURCE. Information on exercise and nutrition. Web site: *www.netsweat.com*

TURNSTEP. Offers a library of 3,000 aerobics patterns and many links. Web site: *www.turnstep.com*

Gift Basket Business

If you find yourself spending money on handicrafts and would like to find a way to earn income using your creativity and design skills, a gift basket business is something to consider. Gift baskets are part of the growing specialty-gift industry, which is expanding so rapidly because it solves a problem many people face: wanting to give that perfect stand-out-from-the crowd gift but being too pressed for time to shop for it. What can be better than giving a present that seems custom-tailored for the recipient, yet takes no time to select, wrap, and deliver? Giving gift baskets fills this need perfectly.

While the tradition of giving food in baskets has been around for centuries, the idea of giving gift baskets took off in the 80's and hasn't paused since. In fact, the industry has grown to include gift packs, individual keepsakes, imprinted specialties and decorative accessories.

While holidays, particularly those at year-end led by Christmas (plus Hannukah, Kwanzaa, Ramadan, and New Year's), account for almost half of all sales, a gift basket business can still operate year-round because many companies are using gift baskets to say *thank you* to customers, referral sources, and employees. Enterprising gift-basket designers can work with a business to integrate the companies own products into the baskets they give.

Next to the Christmas holiday season, Valentine's Day is the most significant holiday for giving gift baskets, followed by Mother's Day, Secretaries' Day, Thanksgiving, Easter, Jewish holidays, and Father's Day. Birthdays are a significant year-round source of business, too. Graduations, weddings, anniversaries, bridal and baby showers, and other special occasions provide more ways of generating income twelve months a year.

Even death and divorce have become occasions for sending thoughtful gift baskets to cherished friends and relatives.

A gift basket can be filled with traditional gourmet foods, wines, and kitchen items, or it can be a special package containing hobby items or sports gear, bath soaps and lotions, art supplies, or almost anything special. Baskets can be in many shapes and can be customized to all kinds of occupations and interests from car dealers to politicians, Realtors, children at camp, chocolate lovers, and so on. By finding out about the personalities and interests of the people you're preparing baskets for, you can add a personal touch to your baskets by including whatever items you know they would especially enjoy.

Some people create gift baskets to serve specific markets such as hospital patients. Boredom Baskets/Boxes specialize in baskets that consist of several individually wrapped packages. The baskets come with directions for recipients to open a new package each day. Each one contains both silly and useful gifts, such as decks of Old Maid cards, puzzles, and travel toothbrushes. Romance can be packaged, too, in the form of baskets filled with items like champagne splits and glasses; audio tapes and CDs with romantic music; and fragrant soaps, sponges, and bath mitts that might be used in a shared bathing experience.

With enough ingenuity and some marketing savvy you can develop a profitable part- or full-time business with a following of grateful customers who appreciate the compliments they get when their personalized gift baskets arrive.

Gift baskets can be sold through personal contact, from a Web site, or by mail. The most profitable markets are corporate buyers, followed by individual consumers. Other regular customers might include wedding planners, resort hotels, real estate agents, meeting planners, and contest operators. Selling baskets in retail locations such as coffee bars, postal receiving stores (Mail Boxes Etc.), hospital gift shops, nail salons, boutiques, and health-food stores is also done, but often such placements are on consignment, which means you only get paid if the basket is sold and you bear the risk of damage.

Mary Ann Jacobs started a part-time gift basket business, Gifts to Go, in Tucson, Arizona, while working as an accountant. Now, she's full-time and sells year-round, mainly to corporate clients. Her Southwest-style baskets shaped like coyotes, saguaro cactus, doves, and armadillos and filled with blue corn chips, Indian red popcorn, salsa, and other goodies characteristic of that region have a wide appeal and help promote the local economy.

Jacobs emphasizes the importance of having some business background. Just being an artist isn't necessarily enough to guarantee success in this field, she says. Those who do best in the business are generally those who know something about marketing, business planning, and administration. Although she has taken marketing classes, Jacobs says she does no advertising at all. Early on, she found that advertising really wasn't cost-effective for her. Instead, she gets her business through telemarketing and referrals from satisfied clients. "You have to keep in touch with the clients you already have," she advises. "Take extra-good care of them and they'll do the marketing for you" by telling other people how good you are.

Knowledge and Skills You Need to Have

- Although you do not need any particular background, you must have an artistic sense and the ability to select and design baskets that are visually appealing.

- Creativity helps. You need to be able to identify unique goods to put into your baskets to distinguish your business from run-of-the-mill baskets.

- You need to know how and where to purchase supplies at a cost-effective price to maximize your profit.

- In most states, you need a liquor license in order to sell baskets containing wine or champagne. Be sure to check in advance and comply with all pertinent laws and regulations.

- You must be able to communicate effectively with customers and have sufficient enthusiasm and personality to sell your product.

- You need to manage your time effectively so that you can make the most of peak seasons.

- Being good at organizing is essential, because an order for 100 baskets can take up a lot of space. And because a big order can result from just one telephone call, you need to be able to organize your workspace effectively so your materials won't take over your home.

Start-up Costs	Low	High
Initial inventory of baskets, alternative containers, filler (excelsior), food, and gifts	$ 500	$ 5,000
Hot- or cold-glue gun	$ 20	$ 30
Shrink-wrap machine	$ 100	$ 400
Tables for assembly, desk, chair	$ 600	$ 800
Organizational dues for networking	$ 100	$ 250
Professional portfolio of photographs of your baskets to show to prospective customers	$ 100	$ 500
Conventions, trade shows, and videos (plus travel if needed)	$ 50	$ 500
Liability insurance	$ 200	$ 400
Office furniture, especially an ergonomic chair	$ 400	$ 1,000
Initial marketing budget	$ 1,000	$ 5,000
Computer	$ 1,000	$ 1,500
Color printer	$ 150	$ 800
Total	**$ 4,220**	**$ 15,580**

Advantages

- This is an artistic business that allows you to express your creativity and your love for beautiful things.

- People delight in receiving gift baskets, so delivering your baskets is a pleasant experience. In fact, scheduling deliveries when someone is at home may result in your getting a new customer.

- You can easily start this business on a part-time basis. Start-up costs are relatively low, and it is an easy business to get into.

- You can often get free samples and other goodies from suppliers.

- When you are starting small, you have the comfort of perfecting the style of making baskets away from the customer's eyes. In a storefront you're under the gun to turn a profit quicker.

Disadvantages

- With shredded paper and inventory everywhere, this business can take over your home, creating family resentments. Plenty of storage space or a dry garage will help as will getting the help of a professional organizer to help you make efficient use of the space you have.

- You may need to work around the clock during holidays and other peak periods to market, make, and deliver your baskets. You may even be so busy at holidays that you miss out on celebrating them yourself with your family.

- You will do better at this business if you have at least one other person working with you.

- You are competing with gift-buying habits and larger mail-order companies.

- You may need to offer discounts to bigger customers like wedding planners, resorts, meeting planners, and so forth.

- You must be on an ongoing search for new and better products to keep your baskets in step with changing tastes.

Pricing

Baskets are priced anywhere from $10 to $300, with most priced between $35 and $50. Factors that enter into pricing are the products in the basket, the time the basket takes to assemble, and the uniqueness and artistic quality of the design. Most businesses give quantity discounts for corporate customers or for large orders. Corporations favor gift baskets starting at $75. Small businesses will expect to pay $25 to $30 when buying multiple baskets.

Potential Earnings

Typical Annual Gross Revenues: You can assemble about eight simply designed baskets per hour, while more complex baskets take 15 minutes or more apiece. Simple designs need not be the least expensive ones. If you sell 25 baskets a week, 50 weeks a year at an average of $40 a basket, you will produce $50,000 in gross sales. And nearly three-fourths of gift basket companies reported at least $50,000 in sales in a 1997 survey by *Gift Basket Review*. Twenty-seven percent of firms did more than $200,000! Profits averaged 22 percent of sales. However, 71 percent of the firms surveyed were located in retail stores, meaning that their overhead was higher. The most popular price point for baskets in 1997 was $46.

Immediately before holidays, a one-person business with some temporary help from family or neighbors can produce $2,000 a day. One order of 100 baskets can produce $3,000 to $5,000. Most gift-basket designers double or *keystone* their wholesale price for everything from packaging to contents. An additional 20 percent and sometimes as much as 40 percent markup is then added to cover labor. The higher markups are more customary in large urban areas. However, Shirley Frazier, author of *How to Start a Home-Based Gift Basket Business,* warns about making wild markups. Sounding a similar note, Mary Ann Jacobs counsels, "Keep prices fair."

Overhead: low (20 percent or less) but this does not include product costs.

Best Home Businesses Estimate of Market Potential

The specialty gift industry, already increasing in popularity, has gotten a shot in the arm from the Internet. Vendors are showing their wares to more people at less cost than one could with a store. People in the industry believe many potential customers still are unaware of the many benefits of gift baskets, so even more growth can be expected ahead.

Best Ways to Get Business

- Call on corporate and organizational buyers, show your portfolio, and leave sample baskets or components for decision-makers. It's a good idea to prepare how you will open your conversations, perhaps based on the kind of need a business you are calling on has. Leave something, perhaps a sample, so you will be remembered. Be sure to follow up quickly on any leads you develop.

- Sell your baskets on your Web site. It's far less expensive than having a store, yet giving you potential exposure to more people.

- Obtain publicity in local and national publications about your unique baskets.

- Network and develop personal contacts in organizations, such as trade and business associations and church groups, and periodically provide a gift basket for a door prize at their meetings.

- Talk about and display your baskets at home parties and open houses, and then take orders (as they do at Tupperware parties), and give a gift basket to the hostess.

- Give your flyers or brochures to reps exhibiting at gift shows, who can place your baskets with retailers. Be careful about placing baskets in retail stores, though, if you have items in your basket that don't stay fresh for long periods of time.

- Leave flyers or brochures with clients when you deliver their orders, and mail flyers or brochures to prospective clients.

- Exhibit at craft fairs and home shows.

- Use direct mail with your own mailing list of people who have contacted you as a result of your publicity and exhibits at shows. Sending postal cards offering tips, news or specials is particularly effective because multiple people will flip a card over and see the message. Festive mailing tubes get opened.

- Donate baskets to nonprofit organizations for their fund-raisers in exchange for an acknowledgment in their printed materials and an announcement from the podium during the event.

- Get an 800 number to use with your publicity and direct mail. Also put your Web site on every piece of literature.

First Steps

- If you have no experience in design, take a course in floral design or visual arts through a community college or a university extension program.

- Take a short course in starting a gift-basket business at an adult-education program such as the Learning Annex.

- To prepare your business, attend any of the hundreds of craft, gift, and novelty trade shows around the country, looking for product ideas and suppliers.

- Locate sources of supplies at trade shows and through wholesalers found in the Yellow Pages. Using local suppliers will reduce or eliminate shipping costs.

- Talk with people in the gift-basket business in your area.

- Obtain a MasterCard and Visa merchant account because many of your customers want to charge their purchases.

- Plan to have people available to come in and help you with assembling baskets for large orders. Assembly of less-complex baskets can be kept out of your home at a reasonable cost by using the services of sheltered workshops employing the handicapped.

- Decide on how you are going to handle food items. You need to check your own state's laws about food handling. In most states, you will not need a special permit if you use only pre-packaged foods. If you use fresh fruit, you may need a special permit. Preparing food in your own home is subject to both state and local regulations.

- Order sufficient materials and supplies for which you can get quantity discounts. Make sure the materials you use are easy to store. Do not buy merchandise that will go out of date (like a calendar), spoil, or get stale.

Where to Turn for Information and Help

ORGANIZATIONS

GIFT ASSOCIATION OF AMERICA, P.O. Box 26696, Collegeville, PA 19426; (610) 831-1841, fax (610) 861-0948. Trade association of retail stores, wholesalers, and suppliers, founded in 1952. Newsletter.

NATIONAL GIFT BASKET NETWORK, 9227 Apricot Avenue, Alta Loma, CA 91701; (909) 931-2692.

NATIONAL SPECIALTY GIFT ASSOCIATION, PO Box 843, Norman, OK 73070; (405) 329-7847. "An international trade organization with exclusive services for gift basket professionals, including: TeleGift Network wire service, bi-monthly newsletter, Preferred Vendor discounts, merchant processing and more." "The TeleGift Network" is a service for consumers similar to a floral wire service for the delivery of gifts. Web site: *www.giftprofessionals.com*

COURSES

THE GIFT BASKET MENTOR, 11861 East 33rd Ave., Unit D, Aurora, CO 80010; (800) 431-4510. Offers training programs and guides. Web site: *www.giftbasketmentor.com*

BOOKS

The Business of Gift Baskets: How to Make a Profit Working from Home, Camille Anderson and Don L. Price, 1991, P.O. Box 7000-B&B, Redondo Beach, CA 90277; (310) 316-0611.

The Complete Gift Basket Industry Reference Directory, Shirley Frazier, Sweet Survival, P.O. Box 31, River Street Station, Paterson, NJ 07544; (973) 279-2799. Lists 15 types of resources, including franchises, insurance, showrooms, and software. Annual editions.

Gift Basket Product Guide, Shirley Frazier, Sweet Survival, P.O. Box 31, River Street Station, Paterson, NJ 07544; (973) 279-2799. Web site: *www.sweetsurvival.com.* Lists manufacturers and distributors of over 300 sources of baskets, alternative containers, fillers and enhancements, foods and gifts. Indicates minimum order requirements where applicable. Annual editions.

How to Start a Home-Based Gift Basket Business, Shirley Frazier, Globe-Pequot, 1998. ISBN: 0762701447.

Great Ideas for Gift Baskets, Bags, and Boxes, Kathy Lamancusa, Tab Books, 1992. ISBN: 0830640355.

The How To's of Gift Baskets, Carol Starr, StarrGift Baskets; 1992. ISBN: 0963439200.

Start and Run a Profitable Gift Basket Business: Your Step-By-Step Business Plan, Mardi Foster Walker, Self Counsel Press, 1995. ISBN: 0889088462.

Start Your Own Gift Basket Business, Joann Padgett, Prentice-Hall Trade; 1996. ISBN: 0136032915.

MAGAZINES

By Design, P.O. Box 10384, Phoenix, AZ 85064; (602)222-1888. Web site: *www.bydesignmagazine.com*

Gift Basket Review, 815 Haines St., Jacksonville, FL 32204; (800) 729-6338; (904) 634-1902. Web site: *www.festivities-pub.com*

NEWSLETTERS

The Creative Gift Giver, 444 Whittier Avenue, Glen Ellyn, IL 60137; (630) 790-9189. E-mail: caswrite@aol.com

Gift Basket Beginner, 1906 Monongahela Avenue, Pittsburgh, PA, 15218. (412) 241-1300. Newsletter.

WEB SITES

AMERICA ONLINE has a Gift Baskets and Balloons Forum with a message area, inventory exchange section, and vendor area. Keyword: GiftBasketPro

AUTUMN WINDS attracts many Canadian basketeers. Web site: *www. autumnwinds.com*

INDUSTRY EXCHANGE has a resource directory of vendors, a message board, and a listing of trade events for business professionals in the gift and gourmet industries. Web site: *www.industryexchange.com*

WEB TREASURE DESIGN, P.O. Box 190687, Boise, ID 83719; (208) 362-3833. Web site: *www.webtreasuredesign.com*

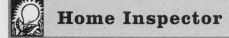

Home Inspector

If you have a background or interest in construction or a related field, you can put on a white collar and become a home inspector. Home inspection began in the 1970's and took off as real estate prices skyrocketed. Buyers became wary of paying princely prices, yet not knowing if the roof would leak or the furnace would go out the night they moved in (that happened to us in the first home we bought).

In the 1980's, lending institutions concerned about ensuring there was reasonable security for the money they were lending also began to require home inspections as a condition to making mortgage loans. Additionally, laws were passed in California, Florida, and Texas that resulted in a demand for home inspections. The California law, for example, requires that sellers disclose any known problems with their homes before sale. As a result, to protect themselves from lawsuits, some sellers started calling on inspectors, too. Now, having a home inspected is growing in popularity across the nation for both buyers and sellers. Buyers, however, account for 90 percent of home inspections.

The role of the home inspector is to take an objective look at a home and help the clients avoid costly surprises. The inspector typically spends two to three hours visually examining all aspects of a home, including the roof, foundation, attic, insulation, walkways, heating and air conditioning, plumbing, and electrical system. The inspector then tells the buyers about the condition of the home, pointing out problems, such as signs of water damage that may not be obvious to an untrained eye.

Following the inspection, the inspector prepares a written report. If defects are found, the buyer may choose either to accept the problems, obtain a larger mortgage to fix the problems, or renegotiate the offer to make the seller correct the problems.

When working for a seller, a home inspector provides information that helps the homeowners come up with a realistic price for their home based on its actual condition. After living in a home for fifteen years, owners may overlook problems to which they have become accustomed but which lower the value of the home.

Home inspectors have no vested interest in any particular work being done on the house. The professional code of ethics of the American Society of Home Inspectors (ASHI) prevents inspectors from doing the repairs they believe are needed or from offering to do them. If the inspector is still in the construction business, he or she could be seen as drumming up business as a contractor.

"This business is growing fast," Jules Falcone, a spokesman for ASHI, says. "There has been a 50 percent increase in the number of inspectors in the last five years." Falcone points out that the popularity of home inspection is spreading from urban areas, where the trend began, to small cities and even rural areas, largely because consumers everywhere are becoming aware of the value of a having a home inspected. Even so, the frequency of inspection varies widely with neighborhood and selling price. While only a small percentage of homes in rural areas are inspected, home inspections in affluent urban neighborhoods approach 100 percent. Overall, an estimated 50 to 60 percent of homes sold are inspected. Still, in some parts of the country, people have yet to hear of home inspection.

As for the future, although no laws exist that require home inspections per se, real estate disclosure laws and standards have created a climate in which buyers are more frequently opting for inspection. In addition, more careful lending practices by savings and loan associations may result in home inspections becoming as common as appraisals and termite inspections. And the federal government may soon require home inspections as a condition for obtaining FHA and VA mortgage loans. As a result, industry experts predict that home inspection will grow significantly during the new millennium when as many as 90 percent of all homes sold will be inspected.

Meanwhile, inspectors are becoming more efficient and better able to provide lengthy, customized reports thanks to advances in computer technology. More inspectors are carrying notebook computers, which allow them to generate reports on the spot. Software allows the insertion of customized stored descriptions of specific problems and remedies without extra keyboarding.

Some home inspectors are specializing, developing niches in forensic engineering or commercial buildings. Others are serving as expert witnesses or becoming expert in indoor air-quality issues or geological and weather hazards in particular geographic areas.

Membership in the American Society of Home Inspectors affords credibility to a home inspector. The association requires each candidate to pass a rigorous written test, and regular members must fulfill continuing-education requirements to maintain membership. At this writing, fewer than ten states license home inspectors, and in some states, the license requires little more than paying a fee. The task of regulating the industry is done by ASHI through its stringent membership requirements. About one-third of the approximately 18,000 home inspectors belong to ASHI.

Knowledge and Skills You Need to Have

- You need to have a background in or an understanding of construction to evaluate the structural soundness of a home including wiring, plumbing, heating, air-conditioning, roofing, and building materials. You need to be able to detect signs of failure, safety problems, wear, and age as well. Field experience and training are both essential.

- Inspectors need to have an inquisitive mind and enjoy solving puzzles. Although most work is routine, you must figure out the causes of cracks, water stains, leaks, and so forth. And you can't have a fear of heights or claustrophobia, because you will need to go up on roofs and in crawl spaces beneath homes.

- You will be working face-to-face with clients and need to have good people skills and verbal abilities to point out maintenance problems and explain how simple maintenance can prevent big problems.

- You must be able to write clear, accurate, legible reports. These reports will be vital documents in real-estate sales, so careful attention to detail and accuracy are essential to prevent lawsuits.

- You need errors-and-omissions insurance to cover your liability for oversights and mistakes. This will be difficult to obtain until you have passed the ASHI test, but once you have, you will be able to purchase it through the association.

Start-up Costs	Low	High
Training course	$ 500	$ 2,000
Desktop or notebook computer	$ 1,500	$ 3,000
Printer	$ 300	$ 800
or		
Multi-function printer/fax/scanner/copier	$ 150	$ 600
Specialized software	$ 400	$ 3,000
Cell phone	$ 75	$ 200
Office furniture, especially an ergonomic chair	$ 400	$ 1,000
Initial marketing budget including association memberships*	$ 1,000	$ 2,500
General liability and errors and omissions insurance	$ 700	$ 2,000
Tools such as screwdriver, flashlights, ladder, electrical tracer, circuit tester, volt meter, moisture meter, and gas-leak detector	$ 300	$ 800
Total	$ 5,625	$ 15,900

*Brochures and promotional materials are available from the ASHI (see below).

Advantages

- The proportion and number of homes being inspected is growing.

- The income potential is good.

- The work is varied, and much of it is done outdoors.

- With licensing in most states around the corner, you can still get in on the ground floor of a new profession. Usually when licensing is introduced, people already practicing in the field are automatically licensed or "grandfathered in." Licensing increases demand and stature and limits competition.

Disadvantages

- The buying or selling of a house is often an emotional issue, so you can be working with people whose nerves are on edge as they worry about problems and costs.

- Some Realtors regard home inspectors as a threat, fearing they'll lose the sale or reduce the commission if a problem is discovered. But with Realtors increasingly required to disclose defects, they are beginning to regard inspections as being to their benefit.

- How much business you have is tied to the ups and downs of the real estate market.

- Liability for mistakes made in inspecting a home is a risk in a litigious society.

Pricing

Fees for a home inspection range from $200 to $400, with the typical fee being $300, depending on your location. In rural areas, fees may go below $200.

Potential Earnings

Typical Annual Gross Revenues: Most home inspectors can conduct two and sometimes three inspections a day for an average of 200 to 400 inspections a year. This takes into account that home inspection is a seasonal business with December and January tending to be slow. A busy inspector can conduct 400 or more inspections per year. At an average rate of $300 per inspection, incomes range from $60,000 to over $100,000. However, expect it to take three years to get up to $50,000.

Overhead: moderate (25 percent). However, vehicle expenses can run over $10,000 a year.

Best Home Businesses Estimate of Market Potential

Home inspection will continue to grow. This requires professional home inspectors. This is a field in which people are not apt to be replaced by technology.

Best Ways to Get Business

- Get referrals from Realtors, attorneys, and mortgage lenders. Call on these professionals directly or make contacts by networking at business, trade, and professional organizations. Jules Falcone estimates that 60 to 70 percent of a new inspector's business will need to come from real estate agent referrals because the heart of this business are buyers served by agents.

- List in the Yellow Pages.

- Have your own Web page with its own domain name. The Web can be helpful if you belong to ASHI because members report getting referrals from the ASHI site.

- Give lectures and training in real estate offices on topics such as how not to let inspection kill your deal and new areas of concern. Anytime you can provide high-quality information face-to-face you will be appreciated.

- Teach courses in continuing-education programs, particularly courses for Realtors. For many courses, you can get paid.

- Join and participate in industry-related business groups, such as the Board of Realtors, Women's Councils of Realtors, as well as referral organizations with nonrealty people.

- Speak at shows, fairs, and seminars. Local ASHI chapters sometimes buy booth spaces in which members can participate, but exhibiting on your own is expensive and the return is not usually high.

- Get publicity in real estate sections of the newspaper and then use reprints in your promotional and sales materials to establish credibility. Printed advertising doesn't work unless it is targeted to the real estate community.

FRANCHISES

AMERISPEC HOME INSPECTION SERVICE, 860 Ridge Lake, 3rd floor, Memphis, TN 38119; (800) 426-2270; (901) 820-8500. Web site: *www. servicemaster. com*

THE HOME TEAM, 6355 East Kemper Road, Suite 250, Cincinnati, OH 45241; (800) 598-5297; (513) 469-2100. Web site: *www.hmteam.com*

HOUSEMASTER OF AMERICA, 421 West Union Avenue, Bound Brook, NJ 08805; (800) 526-3939. Web site: *www.housemaster.com*

WORLD INSPECTION NETWORK, (800) 967-8127. 6500 6th Ave. NW, Seattle, WA 98117; Web site: *www.wini.com*

First Steps

- If you have no background in construction or real estate, Ron Passaro, founder of the ASHI, recommends you start by reading *The Complete Book of Home Inspection,* by Norman Becker, then spend a day with an inspector to see what a day of inspecting houses is like. You may need to do this in a community where you will not be a competitor.

- If you like what you experience, you can gain the training, credentials, contacts, and experience you need by apprenticing with an established self-employed inspector. You can locate inspectors through the Yellow Pages or through ASHI local chapters. Unless you plan to be employed by the home inspector before going out on your own, expect to pay for apprenticeship.

- Join a local chapter of a national organization if a chapter is available in your area. You can learn a good deal about the field and the local market by attending local chapter meetings. "If you show initiative by attending meetings, taking seminars, people will take an interest in you," says Ron Passaro.

- Some community colleges are now offering courses in building inspections with the guidance of the association. Home-study courses are also available for $250. Such courses are advertised in the ASHI Technical Journal. You can also learn the field by purchasing one of the franchises listed above. However, don't expect to learn to be a home inspector in a one-day or one week course; it takes months, even for people with a background in construction.

- Whichever route you take, it is wise to gain experience doing inspections under someone else before you start to do them on your own. We also suggest talking with people in real estate to find out their opinions of home inspection in your community and to determine how healthy the inspection market is.

Where to Turn for Information and Help

ORGANIZATIONS

AMERICAN SOCIETY OF HOME INSPECTORS (ASHI), 85 West Algonquin Road, Suite 360, Arlington Heights, IL 60005-4423; (800) 743-2744. Certification program entitles members to use of ASHI logo. Offers training institutes and an online locator service for consumers seeking a home inspector. ASHI publishes *A Training Manual for Home Inspection* available to members at a significant discount. Web site: *www.ashi.com*

THE NATIONAL ASSOCIATION OF HOME INSPECTORS, INC. (NAHI), 4248 Park Glen Road, Minneapolis, MN 55416; (800) 448-3942; (612) 928-4641. Offers educational seminars and a referral services for consumers seeking a home inspector. Web site: *www.nahi.org*

BOOKS

The Complete Book of Home Inspection, Norman Becker, McGraw-Hill, 1993. ISBN: 0830637850.

Home Inspection Handbook, John E. Traister, Craftsman House, 1997. ISBN: 1572180463.

The Home Inspection Troubleshooter, Robert Irwin, Dearborn Publishing, 1995. ISBN: 0793110912.

How to Buy a House, Condo, or Coop, Michael Thomsett and the Editors of Consumer Reports Books, Consumer Reports Books, 1996. ISBN: 0890438331.

How to Operate a Home Inspection Business, Greg Mangiaracina, R. E. Payne, Senior Political Action Committee, PO Box 604902, Kenner, LA 70064, 1997. ISBN: 188530806X.

COURSES

Listed below are representative home-study courses. There are many more, which can be found on the Web sites of the organizations listed above.

CARSON DUNLAP AND ASSOCIATES, LTD., 120 Carlton Street, Suite 407, Toronto, Ontario M5A 4K2, Canada; (800) 268-7070; (416) 964-9415. Web site: *www.carsondunlop.com/hss*

HOMEPRO, 2841 Hartland Road, Suite 201, Falls Church, VA 22043; (800) 966-4555; (703) 560-4663. Offers both classroom and home study courses. Web site: *www.home-pro.com*

HOME-TECH, 5161 River Road, Bethesda, MD 20816; (800) 638-8292; (301) 654-8380. Web site: *www.hometechonline.com*

INSPECTION TRAINING ASSOCIATES, 1016 S. Tremont Street, Oceanside, CA 92054; (800) 323-9235; (619) 967-4184. Offers both classroom and home study courses. Web site: *www.home-inspect.com*

Image Consultant

Think of scenes from the movie *Titanic* . . . images of Napoleon posturing with one hand under his jacket . . . the regal uniforms reflecting rank in the British military. Throughout the ages, people have used clothing to communicate their place in the social order, their status. But popular awareness that how one looks and presents oneself has a direct bearing on one's career, love life, and self-esteem didn't develop until the 1970's when it grew out of the work of color analysts. Essential to this change of consciousness was the growth of personal incomes that in turn led to homes with bigger closets and apartments that could accommodate versatile and extensive wardrobes.

John Molloy, in his classic book *Dress for Success*, portrayed *wardrobing* as a science, and today more and more people subscribe to the idea that you can shape your image through your choice of clothing, hairstyle, and even gestures and speech. In addition, as the corporate world has become more competitive, businesspeople (both men and women) have come to recognize that winning the key contract or getting a job is often a question of "looking good" in the eyes of customers, increasingly demanding customers.

Thus the growing edge of image consulting lies in impression management and strategic corporate dressing. These are buzzwords for assisting all personnel with customer contact from receptionists to people answering the telephones, from sales personnel to executives, training all such employees to look and present themselves at their best. Image consultants coach and train in everything from such basics for making a positive impression as eye contact, shaking hands, grooming, body language, social graces, and etiquette to broader concerns like corporate protocol and helping with a company's visual image and its public relations.

Some consultants specialize in preparing corporate representatives for public appearances and media presentations. In industries that are adopting uniforms as working attire, image consultants get the job of recommending styles such as blazers and three-piece suits for retail personnel of both sexes. Today about 35 percent of image consulting is for corporations, according to Brenda York-McDaniel, who has been an image consultant since 1976 and whose Academy of Fashion and Image offers training for image consultants.

The bulk of the work of image consultants continues to be individual consulting, which includes working with:

- Professionals and corporate executives traveling and working internationally and in multicultural arenas on global etiquette and cross-cultural communications.

- Self-employed individuals, particularly those from high-tech industries, who must market themselves effectively and work smoothly with clients. Image consultants instruct on matters ranging from what to wear to the art of calling on people personally.

- People seeking employment or changing fields, such as those who are downsized as a result of mergers and acquisitions, who need advice on the look and behavior they will need.

- The "active" aging population concerned with maturing elegantly and updating their image. Often these people are single.

- Specialized markets, such as the health care industry, hospitality industries, and on-air television talent.

Image consultants coach clients one-on-one, taking them out to social or business events, or they may offer in-house training classes. Through videotapes, computer-aided imaging, and other audio-visual aids, image consultants help their clients use clothing, makeup, hairstyle, speech, and body stance to create a desired effect. The goal, according to Mari Lyn Henry, Association of Image Consultants International (AICI) Professional Member in New York City, is to "help people ensure that their visual image matches their personal qualities and career objectives."

Helping clients with the components of their image includes determining the kind of image the client wants to project, what their best colors are, evaluating their present wardrobe and making recommenda-tions for new clothing and accessories. Consultants advise on grooming, hygiene, fragrance choice, makeup, hair styling, skin care, as well as nu-trition, diet and exercise, components of the psychology of appearance.

Some consultants go through clients' closets, showing them how to make the most of what they have and urging them to recycle clothing that no longer works. Some consultants simply provide a plan and let the client do his or her own shopping; others go shopping with the client, and still others do their clients' shopping for them. Alternatively, clients may select items from a print catalogue, the Web or a television shopping service, but they ask the consultant for advice before actually ordering.

Today's clients are both men and women in about equal numbers, a major change from the 70's when clients were almost exclusively fe-male. Single and newly divorced men and women come to image con-sultants wanting to create a more appealing image. Neither men nor women know how to dress for casual Fridays. What is considered casual in business varies geographically and ranges from jogging suits to jeans with blue blazers.

Clients may come to the consultant having realized that they are being repeatedly passed over for promotion in favor of more attractive-looking candidates. Or they may simply be wanting to be sure they're pre-senting themselves in the best possible light. Sometimes the company pays the bill.

Sometimes the client's look simply needs updating, according to Brenda York-McDaniel. At other times, the consultant needs to help the client enhance his or her desirable features and play down or camouflage less-appealing ones through choice of color, use of accessories, or type of tailoring.

With an estimated three-quarters of all business negotiations taking place around food, a growing niche for image consultants is teaching manners and etiquette. Etiquette is taught both individually and in classes to children, newly rich high-tech executives, college juniors and seniors preparing for job interviews, MBA candidates, and retiring mili-tary personnel transitioning to civilian life. Because family meals have given way to individuals warming something up in the microwave, fewer people are learning the basics of manners at home as children, so they must learn them latter when situations arise where not having them can hamper their career and social success.

Other niches for image consulting include producing fashion shows, helping fundraisers, working with ethnic wardrobes, and assisting people who wear plus sizes and those changing gender. Image consultants also sometimes function as bridal consultants.

Knowledge and Skills You Need to Have

- You need to be an extroverted but warm and nurturing personality. An image consultant can't dictate or impose a verbal or visual persona on another person. You must provide feedback and suggestions in a tactful and caring way. This also means that you need to be a good communicator, intuitively understanding and drawing out your clients' needs and personalities in order to translate them into the components of their image.

- Creativity and a having a visual orientation are useful talents, especially if you specialize in fashion or color. Whereas image consultants in the early days of the industry were prone to follow formulas and believed there were sets of rules for how to dress for success, today the profession stresses bringing out an individual's strengths and supporting their goals within the boundaries of cultural expectations.

- The type of background you need depends on which aspects of image consulting you will be working in: wardrobe, speech, etiquette, and so forth. Typical backgrounds include experience in fashion, clothing, cosmetics, teaching, broadcasting, speech, acting, modeling, psychology and career development, home economics, and theatre.

- Image consultants need to be skillful at presenting themselves. Essentially you have to be a walking, talking, breathing example of what you teach. You need to develop or have excellent speaking and teaching skills, because this is how you get business.

- You must enjoy and be willing to learn constantly, keeping abreast of fashion and behavioral trends in business so that your skills don't become outdated.

- Because image consultants have to help clients move from field to field, they must, more than ever, stay on top of current developments in the business, fashion, and technical worlds.

Start-up Costs
Fashion/Visual Specialization

	Low	High
Training	$ 500	$ 5,000
Reference books on style, color, etc.	$ 100	$ 200
Set of color swatches	$ 200	$ 500
Computer	$ 1,500	$ 3,000
Printer	$ 300	$ 800
or		
Multi-function printer/fax/scanner/copier	$ 150	$ 600
Polaroid or digital camera	$ 80	$ 800
Personal wardrobe with two or three complete outfits	$ 1,500	$ 5,000
Office furniture, especially an ergonomic chair	$ 400	$ 1,000
Initial marketing budget including portfolio	$ 1,000	$ 5,000
Total	$ 5,730	$ 21,900

Start-up Costs
Verbal/Speaking Specialization

	Low	High
Computer	$ 1,500	$ 3,000
Printer	$ 300	$ 800
or		
Multi-function printer/fax/scanner/copier	$ 150	$ 600
Audio cassette recorder	$ 50	$ 250
Camcorder and monitor	$ 1,000	$ 1,500
Office furniture, especially an ergonomic chair	$ 400	$ 1,000
Initial marketing budget	$ 1,000	$ 5,000
Total	$ 4,400	$ 12,150

Advantages

- People are always interested in and curious about their image, making this an easy topic to talk to people about, the first step for getting business.

- There is plenty of opportunity to use your creativity.

- People appreciate what you do. Sometimes even small changes can dramatically improve the lives of your clients, and you'll learn about the sales records, promotions, and new jobs they've attained with your help.

- If you are working with wardrobes, you can often get clothing free or at a discount from retail chains.

- Image consultants are in demand as experts by the media, helping news anchors appear better on camera.

- You can add to your income by selling clothing directly to customers through appointments and with such devices as trunk shows. See the resource section for sources of clothing suppliers who distribute exclusively through personal wardrobe consultants.

Disadvantages

- Some businesspeople and companies are not familiar with the benefits of image consulting, so you must educate before you can sell your service. Some may consider image issues superficial or insignificant.

- Advertising doesn't work to sell image consulting. You usually have to demonstrate your skills and build a relationship with people before they will retain you.

- Multilevel organizations selling cosmetics have diluted the profession by casting their sales representatives as image consultants. You need to present yourself as a professional; hence, certification and training are important.

- Clients can be easily offended or resistant to your feedback and suggestions, thus good rapport and communication skills are vital.

- If your clients are people seeking employment, you may need to accept a delay before they pay you.

- To earn a sufficient full-time income, an image consultant must either do both individual and corporate work or sell clothing.

Pricing

For wardrobe consulting, according to AICI, hourly rates range from $50 to $250 with $125 being the average; for speaking coaching, rates range from $75 to $300 an hour. Full-day workshops and seminars produce fees ranging from $750 to $5,000 per day, depending on the number of participants, the company, and the nature of the workshop (speech, wardrobe, and so forth). Some consultants negotiate annual retainers from corporations for working with a specified number of executives or employees each month.

Potential Earnings

Typical Annual Gross Earnings: For a wardrobe consultant working full-time earnings are $25,000 to $100,000 per year. For a full-time speech, body language, or corporate consultant, earnings are in the $50,000 to $150,000 range. The more work with corporations, the higher an image consultant's earnings, with some reaching $250,000 a year.

Overhead: low (under 20 percent).

Best Home Businesses Estimate of Market Potential

Image consulting is a field that is subject to the ups and downs of the economy, but overall it will likely continue to grow. As the workplace and our lives become more "technofied," to the use of term of Domique Isbeque, giving many people less exposure to personal contact and making customers all the more demanding when they do interface with real people, the role of hands-on expertise from image consultants becomes increasingly more important.

Additionally, the generation following the X Generation values formality and grooming correctness more than their predecessors. This suggests they will turn more frequently to the services of image consultants. Also, we will soon be presenting our visual as well as our spoken image over the Internet so we are apt to be concerned about not only what we say but how we look when communicating with someone half a world away.

Best Ways to Get Business

- Because potential clients need to feel comfortable with an image consultant before hiring her or him, person-to-person networking is the number-one way to get business in this field. That means being involved with organizations like professional and business

associations, adult education programs, speaking circuits, and referral organizations, particularly in industries or fields in which
you have experience that can lead to prospective clients.

- Speak and offer seminars to organizations with members apt to
use your services, even if there is no fee, and use these as an opportunity to show off the dramatic results you can achieve; show
slides or videotapes of your clients before and after. (Be sure you
have obtained their written permission.)

- Because a high proportion of business comes from referrals, offer
complimentary consultations—as many as four to five a month—
with key individuals who have many contacts and are respected
for their opinion.

- Get publicity about your successes.

- Write articles with your photograph included.

- Have a Web site on which you place your photo, testimonial letters, and articles you have written.

- Offer community service programs such as assisting the homeless,
the poor, students, persons getting treatment for cancer.

First Steps

- Obtain training, including the business aspects of image consulting. Take courses to fill in gaps in your experience and to gain certification.

- Brenda York-McDaniel recommends that image consultants who
want to work with individuals begin their business as a sideline.
Often clients prefer evening and weekend sessions anyway, and by
starting part-time you can gain some experience and build a clientele before leaving your job. In your existing job, you can get
training and begin developing a clientele while maintaining contacts in your field and community. Step up involvement in activities that your corporate job enables you to have.

- If you are going to do corporate work, target a particular industry
and concentrate on marketing to that industry. Any industry in
which the appearance of the personnel plays an important role is
a good candidate, for example, hotels, entertainment facilities,

health-care industries, and retail stores. Contact the human-resource directors to discuss your doing a two- to three-hour introductory seminar for their personnel. You can identify human-resource directors through the local chapter directory of the American Society of Training and Development. Contact these individuals personally. Direct mail alone will rarely be effective.

- You might contact public-relations firms about working with their clients for media appearances.

- Expect to take two years to build a full-time business.

Related Businesses

Personal Shopper

Image consulting may involve providing your clients with a complete fashion make-over in which you actually go shopping with them and help them select a new, completely coordinated and accessorized wardrobe including shoes, hats, and coats. Both men and women use this service, usually in conjunction with looking for a new job, taking a new job, or when seeking a promotion. Another market for personal shoppers is single and divorced men and women intent on finding a mate.

Being a personal shopper can also be a business unto itself, marketed via ads seen by professionals, creating cross-referral relationships with image consultants who don't shop, hair stylists, facialists, and other providers of personal services who get to know the time pressures of their clients.

Some personal shopping services are going online, usually to market or supplement a local service. Clothing is but one of the types of merchandise someone can find online that they need help shopping for. Other items are technology, motor vehicles, toys, antiques, stamps for collectors, housing, and home-furnishing needs. Online shopping services will help customers find gifts for anniversaries, birthdays, and holidays.

Online or in person, personalized service is the key to success as a personal shopper. You must not only know fashion trends and have an eye for the aesthetic, but also be able to communicate well with your clients to understand the image they want to project and provide options for achieving it regardless of their personal physics. This may include shopping at discount stores and outlets.

Clothing Sales

Another related business is to become an independent rep or sales associate for clothing manufacturers. Some women find this a highly satisfying and lucrative way to earn a living. You bring a van-full of selected wardrobe options to your client's home for a private showing or a house party. Or you might host a trunk show in a hotel suite. Such a service caters primarily to successful professional women who don't have the time to shop, but need to look good both on the job and at career-related social events.

The following women's clothing companies have sales-associate programs:

DONCASTER COLLECTION. Tanner Company, 581 Rock Rd., Rutherfordton, NC 28139; (828) 287-4205. Web site: *www.doncaster.com*

WORTH COLLECTION, 37 West 57th Street, New York, NY 10019; (800) 967-8465; (212) 223-3757. Web site: *www.worthny.com*

CARLISLE COLLECTION LTD, 423 W 55th St., 12th Floor, New York, NY 10019 (212) 246-2555. Web site: *www.carlislecollection.com*

Where to Turn for Information and Help

ORGANIZATIONS

ASSOCIATION OF IMAGE CONSULTANTS INTERNATIONAL, 1000 Connecticut Avenue, NW, #9, Washington, DC 20036; (800) 383-8831; (301) 371-9021. Has a mentor program. Web site: *www.aici.org*

NATIONAL SPEAKERS' ASSOCIATION, 1500 South Priest Drive, Tempe, AZ 85281; (602) 968-2552. A description of NSA can be found in the Training profile.

COURSES

ACADEMY OF FASHION AND IMAGE, 19860 North 85th Avenue, Peoria, AZ 85382; (800) 450-5545; (623) 572-8719. Provides classroom and correspondences courses with certification on completion; has an alumni association with continuing education and conferences. Booklet and audio tape, *How to Start Your Own Fashion and Image Consulting Business*, available on request.

APPEARANCE DESIGN ASSOCIATES, 18951 Ansley Pl., Saratoga, CA 95070; (408) 253-0272. Classroom and correspondence colorist and stylist courses. Grants certificate.

THE IMAGEMAKER, INC., 348 Cool Springs Boulevard, Franklin, TN 37067; (615) 771-7258. Classroom and correspondence courses. Grants certificate and CEU credits. Web site: *www.imagemaker1.com*

IMAGE RESOURCE GROUP, 7804 Wincanton Court, Falls Church, VA 22043; (703) 560-3950. Certification available only for classroom course, but materials are for sale.

LONDON IMAGE INSTITUTE, 4279 Rosewell Rd., PMB 102-318, Atlanta, GA 30342; (404) 255-0009. Classroom course with certification. Web page: *www.londonimage.qpg.com*

BOOKS

Accessories, Kim Johnson Gross, Christa Worthington, Jeff Stone, New York: Knopf, 1996. ISBN: 0679445773. Other related books by Kim Johnson Gross are: *Chic Simple Women's Wardrobe; Work Clothes: Casual Dress for Serious Work; Chic Simple: Scarves.*

Attention to Detail: A Gentleman's Guide to Professional Appearance and Conduct, Clinton T. Greenleaf III, Greenleaf Enterprises, Inc., 1998. ISBN: 0966531906.

Do's and Taboos around the World, edited by Roger E. Axtell, John Wiley & Sons, 1993. ISBN: 0471595284. Other related books by Roger Axtell are: *Do's and Taboos of Hosting International Visitors; Gestures: The Do's and Taboos of Body Language Around the World; Do's and Taboos Around the World for Women in Business.*

Fabulous You! Unlock Your Perfect Personal Style, Tori Hartman, Berkley, 1995. ISBN: 0425146189.

Flatter Your Figure, Jan Larkey, Simon & Schuster, 1992. ISBN: 0671762966.

Look Like a Winner After 50, Jo Petticord, National Writers Press, Golden Aspen Publishing, 1997. ISBN: 096544340X.

Speaking Globally, Elizabeth Urech, Kogan Page, 1998. ISBN: 0749422211.

Style, Elsa Klensch, Beryl Meyer, Berkley Publishing Group; 1995. ISBN: 0399521526.

Women of Color, Darlene Mathis, Random House, 1997. ISBN: 0517175401.

Say It Right: How to Talk in Any Social or Business Situation, Lillian Glass, Perigee/Putnam, 1992. ISBN: 0399516999.

The Way We Look: Dress and Aesthetics, Marilyn R. DeLong, Fairchild Publications, 1998. ISBN: 1563670712.

NEWSPAPER

Image Networker, P.O. Box 494, Haverford, PA 19041; (610) 896-0330. Published three times a year. E-mail: image4unow@aol.com. Web site: *www.imagenetworker.com*

 Information Professional/Broker

Information is at the core of successfully producing and selling most products and services and thus it's called *the* strategic resource. But while few businesses are drowning in other strategic resources—money, materials, facilities, or personnel—most of us are drowning in information. The sheer quantity of information in the world doubles every seven years or less. Everything from backed up e-mail to piles of overflowing reading materials indicates we have too much information, yet often executives still feel they don't have the *right* information.

Thus the information professional has emerged lock step with the computer, the copy machine, the fax and the Internet. Like an investigative reporter or market researcher, practitioners of this wordy art track down and locate the specific information a business or organization needs. Originally called *information brokers,* those in this field increasingly prefer the term *information professional,* although some use such terms as *desktop online searcher* or *information retriever.*

A company, large or small, might hire an information professional to do background research about a new product concept, carry out a patent search on a product they want to introduce, to learn about companies producing related products and determine their pricing or find out as much as possible about a new market. Increasingly, companies use information professionals to track the goings-on of competitors.

Some companies have in-house research capabilities, with which information professionals may be called upon to handle overload work or do specialized research. Some information professionals subcontract with corporate or public libraries to do behind-the-scenes research for their staff.

Other professionals whose work requires them to become instant experts also hire information professionals. Lawyers, for example, may call on an information professional when preparing for a trial or to determine if a product has a history of defects in a product-liability case. Advertising agencies may seek help in developing ad campaigns. Marketing and public-relations firms may need help in preparing proposals. Private investigators or management consultants need help working on particular projects, as do corporations contemplating a merger or acquisition. Other types of information research involve science and technology, healthcare, public records, and banking, but there are no limits to the kinds of questions clients need answered.

Some information professionals do their work through interviewing and library searching, but most learn to tap into one of the 7,000 computer databases such as Dialog, LEXIS, NEXIS, and Westlaw that exist on dozens of online services and the Internet. These databases contain abstracts or the full text of articles from thousands of publications around the world, including newspapers, magazines, newsletters, professional journals, and books, thus making it possible to find just about any news item or research result within seconds rather than days or months. While some beginning information professionals seek to do all their searching on the Internet because of its obvious cost advantage, people who become established in the field find they must use the subscription databases.

Increasingly, information professionals are specializing in certain types of information. Some may focus on law, finance, or medicine, while others work in researching high technology such as bioengineering or computers. The professional who specializes can become proficient at using a small number of databases, thereby increasing his or her reputation for successful searches at a low cost. Specializing does not mean turning down all unrelated work, but it does mean presenting a coherent image and focused marketing effort.

Knowledge and Skills You Need to Have

- To do this business well, you must have a love for what Alex Kramer of Kramer Research of Washington, DC, calls "the thrill of the chase." Your clients are usually seeking details and facts that are not readily available, so you often need to skim or read volumes of data and talk with knowledgeable people to find the missing pieces.

- Creativity and persistence are required to track down information. You have to think of various possibilities for how to locate the data you need. Then you need the critical ability to distinguish what is important to your client from all the information that's available.

- Online searching can be expensive; you must, therefore, become proficient at using the specific procedures and codes required by many of the databases so that you can perform your searches in the least amount of time at a minimum cost to your client.

- Although information searching is becoming more widely used by companies, you still need to have the ability to sell an intangible service to people who may not be familiar with what you can do for them or think everything is available to them on the Internet.

Start-up Costs	Low	High
Computer	$ 1,500	$ 3,000
Printer	$ 300	$ 800
or		
Multi-function printer/fax/scanner/copier	$ 150	$ 600
Telephone headset	$ 40	$ 400
Office furniture, especially an ergonomic chair	$ 400	$ 1,000
Initial marketing budget	$ 1,000	$ 5,000
Online database access and accounts; training and documentation in their use	$ 1,000	$ 3,000
Total	$ 4,390	$ 13,800

Advantages

- Low start-up costs make this business easy to get into quickly.

- Varied work resulting in constant learning makes this business interesting.

- You are called upon to provide information of value to clients.

- You have the opportunity to be creative in discovering information and presenting what you find.

- Information continues to explode in quantity, creating a continuing need for this field.

Disadvantages

- Obtaining clients is the greatest challenge of this business, thus you can expect to spend a lot of effort and time marketing to establish a client base. That includes finding effective methods to market.

- Because it's necessary to have client contact during business hours, this is not a part-time business.

- At times, it may not be possible to fulfill client requests on time and within budget.

- Learning to use a variety of online databases can get to be expensive without proper training.

Pricing

Information professionals charge by the hour or by the job. Hourly rates range from $25 to $100, although experienced professionals may earn as much as $200 or more per hour. Pricing by the job involves estimating how many hours the job will take, allowing for unexpected difficulties in finding the information, and understanding the costs involved in online searching. Expenses such as charges for online databases and printed copies of articles you find are either billed at cost or are marked up by 15 to 20 percent.

Potential Earnings

Typical Annual Gross Revenues: $17,500 to $100,000. The low-end estimate is based on billing 500 hours per year (10 hours per week) at $35. The high end is based on billing 1,000 hours per year (20 hours per week) at $100 per hour.

Overhead: moderate (between 20 and 40 percent).

Best Home Businesses Estimate of Market Potential

This is a growing field. The Internet is a "tease," says Alex Kramer, and people realize how much information is out there and that information is expanding at an ever-quickening pace. People are realizing the value of information, which, coupled with the preference of most companies to outsource for specific expertise, will create a swelling demand for information professionals for years to come.

Best Ways to Get Business

- Network and make personal contacts in companies or organizations such as trade associations and professional organizations, particularly in industries or fields in which you have experience.

- Have your own Web page with its own domain name with testimonial letters and any articles you have written.

- Offer a toll-free number, enabling you to be more accessible and able to do work anywhere.

- Speak and offer seminars on information at meetings and trade shows.

- Write articles for magazines or newspapers or start your own newsletter.

- Collaborating with other information professionals to do specialized work and do overload work.

- Getting media publicity about you and/or information conquests you have made (with the approval of your client).

- Advertising in trade journals if you are in a specialty field.

First Steps

- Sue Rugge believes that finding a special niche is the first step in starting this business. She advises, "Specialization is necessary. I think it is essential to penetrate a market. You must have viability. Pick a market that has a trade association with local and annual meetings. Go to the meetings, speak to the group, write articles for their publications. Word of mouth is our most powerful marketing tool, but it takes a lot longer to get it going if you are trying to work in many different markets. When you can cluster your clients in a group that speaks to each other, word of mouth goes faster."

- Start marketing in a field that you know—former employers, employees, old business relationships. If you don't have enough skill to do a search yourself, you can refer it out to a specialist who can.

- Subject-area knowledge is not enough in this field; a business sense is needed, so take courses or read to learn about basic business practice.

Where to Turn for Information and Help

ORGANIZATIONS

ASSOCIATION OF INDEPENDENT INFORMATION PROFESSIONALS, 10290 Monroe, Suite 208, Dallas, TX 75229; (609) 730-8759. E-mail: hqrp@worldnet.att.net. Web site: *www.aiip.org*. Professional association for information professionals; offers a mentor program, a listserve for members, "white" papers, a newsletter, and it offers conferences and workshops. A directory of its membership listing specialties and contact information can be found on its Web site.

SOCIETY OF COMPETITIVE INTELLIGENCE PROFESSIONALS, 1700 Diagonal Road, Suite 600, Alexandria, VA 22314; (703) 739-0696. Web site: *www.scip.org*

SPECIAL LIBRARIES ASSOCIATION, 1700 Eighteenth Street, NW, Washington, DC 20009; (202) 234-4700; fax: (202) 265-9317. The Web site has an extensive listing of courses. Web site: *www.sla.org*

AMERICAN LIBRARY ASSOCIATION, 50 E. Huron St., Chicago, IL 60611; (800) 545-2433; (312) 944-6780. Web site: *www.ala.org*

COURSES

Colleges and universities, particularly those that offer graduate degrees in library science often have courses on information searching open to outside students. For example, the New School has an online course in *How to Do Research Online*; (800) 319-4321; (212) 229-5630, 66 West 12th Street, New York, NY 10011. Web site: *www.newschool.edu*

THE INFORMATION BROKERING MENTORING PROGRAM FOR BEGINNING INFORMATION BROKERS, Marketing Base; (800) 544-5924; (707) 829-9421. Web site: *www.marketingbase.com*

INFORMATION PROFESSIONALS INSTITUTE, 5619 Plumtree Drive, Dallas, TX, 75252. (972) 732-0160. Offers seminars with industry leaders. Web site: *www.burwellinc.com*

BOOKS

The Burwell World Directory of Information Brokers, Burwell Enterprises, 5619 Plumtree Dr., Dallas, TX 75252. Updated annually. Also available on CD-ROM.

Find It Fast: How to Uncover Expert Information on Any Subject, Robert Berkman, HarperCollins, 1997. ISBN: 0062734733.

Find Public Records Fast: The Complete State, County and Courthouse Locator, Facts on Demand Press, 1998. ISBN: 1889150045.

How to Avoid Liability: The Information Professional's Guide to Negligence and Warranty Risks, T. R. Halvorson, 1998. ISBN: 0938519174.

The Information Broker's Handbook, Sue Rugge and Alfred Glossbrenner, McGraw-Hill, 1997. ISBN: 0070578710.

InfoThink: Practical Strategies for Using Information in Business, Mary Woodfill Park, Scarecrow Press, 1998. ISBN: 0810834243.

Naked in Cyberspace: How to Find Personal Information Online, Carole A. Lane, Information Today, Inc., 1997. ISBN: 091096517X.

The Online Deskbook: Online Magazine's Essential Desk Reference for Online and Internet Searchers, Mary Ellen Bates, Reva Basch, Independent Publishing Group, 1996. ISBN: 0910965196.

The Reporter's Handbook: An Investigator's Guide to Documents and Techniques, Steve Weinberg, St. Martins Press, 1995. ISBN: 0312135963.

Researching Online for Dummies, Reva Basch, IDG Books Worldwide, 1998. ISBN: 0764503820.

Secrets of the Super Net Searchers: The Reflections, Revelations and Hard-Won Wisdom of 35 of the World's Top Internet Researchers,

Reva Basch, Mary Ellen Bates, Independent Publishing Group, 1996. ISBN: 0910965226.

Web Search Strategies, Bryan Pfaffenberger, MIS Press, 1996. ISBN 1558284702.

MAGAZINES, NEWSLETTERS, AND OTHER MATERIALS

Books and tapes by Sue Rugge, 46 Hiller Drive, Oakland, CA 94618; (510) 649-9743, fax: (510) 704-8646.

Database, Online, Inc, 213 Danbury Road, Wilton, CT 06897-4007; (800) 248-8466; (203) 761-1466. Web site: *www.onlineinc.com*

The Cyberskeptic's Guide to Internet Research, Bibliodata, P.O. Box 61, Needham Heights, MA 02494; (781) 444-1154. Web site: *www.bibliodata.com*

Searcher: The Magazine for Database Professionals, 143 Old Marlton Pike, Medford, NJ 08055; (609) 654-6266. Web site: *www.infotoday.com/ searcher*

 ## Mail Order/Web Merchant

The prospect of opening your mailbox to find it stuffed with checks has intrigued people for a generation, but now that we're squarely in the Cyberspace Age, does it make sense to think of mail order as a twenty-first century business? The answer is yes. Consider that the primary means of marketing America Online is by mail. As Russ Horton of Haven Software points out, "Selling on the Web is mail order. The procedures for selling online and selling via mail are almost the same—companies offering products, taking orders, fulfilling them and doing follow-up marketing. What's different is the way you capture an order, but once you have an order, it's processed just like an order taken by phone or through the mail and it's fulfilled in the same ways. The front end is different; the back end is the same."

Of course, established mail-order merchants such as L.L. Bean and Lands' End sell their goods on the Web, and some merchants like Egghead have moved lock, stock, and barrel to the Web. Many home-based mail-order companies have done the same. For these reasons and more, we agree with Russ and suggest that *Web merchant* is fast-becoming a significant aspect of the mail-order business.

Consider, too, that at the present time, twice as many people use the Internet to research products and services than use it to make purchases. Providing fax and toll-free numbers and a street address are important whether you consider yourself in the mail-order business or as a Web merchant engaged in e-commerce.

Mail order is actually part of the direct-marketing industry. Direct marketing basically means generating sales by directly communicating with consumers. In addition to selling by mail and the Web, direct marketing includes selling by telephone, newspaper and magazine direct response advertising, radio, and television (including both long-form infomercials and the short-form commercials so common on cable). While some home-based direct-marketing firms specialize in other forms of direct marketing, marketing via the mail and the Web are the most economic and viable tools for most home-based enterprises.

For a home-based business, the odds of making money are probably better using the Web than using direct mail or print advertising. It's currently estimated that one out of three Web merchants are making a profit. Although this is usually phrased negatively to indicate that two out of three aren't making money, actually this success rate contrasts favorably with the odds of making money through traditional mail order where it has been estimated that only one person in twenty-five succeeds. In addition, smaller companies are more likely to be making money on the Web at this time than large ones.

What makes the Web superior to direct mail and advertising for most home-based mail order merchants? Several things:

- Start-up costs are lower. In doing interviews for our book, *Making Money in Cyberspace*, Linda Rohrbough and we learned that on average the successful Web merchants spent $500 to $1000 to get their first Web sites up. This means they're testing their results before incurring the costs of a site with full e-commerce capabilities, which would run from $5,000 to $20,000.

- Sales costs are lower (think print catalogs, ads, toll-free calls).

- Changes and updates can be made within hours without having to throw away ten thousand inaccurate or outdated printed materials.

- While direct-mail costs are increasing, the hard costs of doing business on the Web are decreasing.

- Once a Web site is posted, it is available twenty-four hours a day, seven days a week.

- The size of your company need not be apparent on the Web. You can look better and offer more than a competitor a thousand times your size.

- Using mail-order software, one person can handle day-to-day processing of orders.

- Overall, it's easier to start up and sell over the Web than via mail.

Despite the greater ease in mounting a mail-order business, the major challenge remains the same—offering something people will buy. But if you find the right products to sell on the Web, getting people to buy is less of a puzzle.

Products that cannot be easily found elsewhere have a built-in market. By getting your Web site listed on search engines, making strategic links, and getting publicity, customers will find you. Here are some of the products with which mail-order businesses we've investigated have realized quick success on the Web: aromatherapy products, antiques (using eBay), body building supplements and oils, gas masks, ghost hunting equipment, peacocks and peacock-related products, and travel items for women. Each of these appeal to a niche market and are not products that are readily available elsewhere.

Because tastes and technology change constantly, there are always new opportunities for products and customers. Whether sold via mail, in print advertising or on the Web, the best mail-order products are ones that:

- You own and completely control, preferably manufacture, or at least can obtain from more than one supplier.

- Are not readily available in local stores.

- Are unique and attractive, lightweight, and easy to mail, requiring no special packaging, sturdy rather than fragile.

- Can be offered for a substantial markup.

- Require little inventory, because they are quickly made by you or can be handled on a drop-ship basis using reliable suppliers.

- Are consumable or part of a complete line that provides an ample base for repeat orders.

- Have no breakable mechanical parts to be returned.

Knowledge and Skills You Need to Have

- You have to be able to do research to find out what's already available. You don't want to handicap yourself by trying to sell something better that someone else has already sold cheaper.

- You will need to have or develop a number of skills for selecting, designing, or marketing your products as well as the ability to function in cyberspace.

- You must be able to wear a lot of hats and be willing to do routine, menial tasks, such as responding to requests for information and shipping orders.

Start-up Costs	Low	High
Computer	$ 1,500	$ 3,000
Printer	$ 300	$ 800
or		
Multi-function printer/fax/ scanner/copier	$ 150	$ 600
Mail order software	$ 800	$ 2,000
Web design software like *PageMill* and *Front Page*	$ 100	
Digital camera	$ 300	$ 1,000
Office furniture, especially an ergonomic chair	$ 400	$ 1,000
Initial testing	Under $500 for a do-it-yourself Web site	
	Under $1,000 for small classified ads in a niche publication	
	$8,000 for publishing a color catalogue showing products	
	$30,000 for a fully functioning e-commerce Web site	
Total	$ 4,050	$ 38,500

Note

If you ship products yourself (versus drop-shipping) you may wish to get a shrink-wrap system with a heat seal for packaging your products for $200 to $500.

If you use direct mail, you need to add the costs of renting or obtaining mailing lists, and you may wish to use a postage meter, which you can rent for $30 or more a month.

Your sales will increase by approximately 50 percent if you have the capability to take charge cards, particularly MasterCard and Visa.

Advantages

- Since there are no fixed hours, a mail-order business can be started on a part-time basis while you are still employed. Many people begin mail-order businesses by working ten or fewer hours a week.

- Because you are not limited by the overhead burden of store-based selling, you can sell products that express your passions or hobbies you love. You can specialize in products that wouldn't sell enough to support a shop.

- You can usually do a better job of providing information about your products than store salesclerks, who usually have little knowledge about what they are selling.

- You have more control over assuring that people see your products.

- A mail-order business is not dependent on weather.

- Unlike a service business that involves selling your time, with a flourishing mail-order business your income doesn't need to stop because you take time off.

- David Starkman, who with his wife, Susan Pinsky, sells 3-D photography products through their company, Reel 3-D Enterprises, finds that selling by mail is more recession-proof than selling through retail stores.

- You may not need to keep an inventory of products on hand.

Disadvantages

- To make money, you've got to locate or attract the right customers (involving a choice of medium, i.e., direct mail, Web, print advertising) for the right products with the right promotion or offer (free trials, guarantees, method of payment) for a price people will pay. This is a constantly changing puzzle.

- You are tied to the business. The business involves doing many routine tasks like filling orders and responding to customers day in and day out. This can be tiresome.

- You may have limited face-to-face contact with people, which is not a disadvantage for some people.

Pricing

While the general rule of thumb in mail order is to sell products for at least three to four times your in-the-mail cost of the products, you need to find the right pricing level for your particular type of products. If your products are unique (which is desirable) and you therefore have nothing to compare them with, try out prices on a preliminary basis with as many people as you can whom you think would be buyers of your product. (Two or three is not enough.) Such a trial will help you establish the first prices to test in your ads, direct mail, or catalogue.

Potential Earnings

Typical Annual Gross Revenues: Depends entirely on the product line, but the upside potential is greater than for most salaried jobs. Mail order can provide a part-time income or a full-time livelihood.

Overhead: low on the Web; high for advertising and mailing.

Best Home Businesses Estimate of Market Potential

Many people today are simply too busy to go shopping. While department stores struggle for survival, people have more places to shop than ever before. We believe the future of mail order for the home-based merchant is on the Web, because the Web makes it possible to reach customers economically no matter where they are located. The easy access to the goods of the world helps to propel the growing population shift of city people to rural and less populated areas. Selling via the Web is also bringing about a new era in the sale of collectibles.

Best Ways to Get Business

- Presenting an effective storefront or catalog on the Web. Structure your virtual storefront or catalog to be easy to read, professional looking, and be as interactive as possible. Respond to prospects and customers within 24 hours and update your content frequently. Make sure pictures load quickly, links are working, and no error messages are popping up.

- Getting both print and online publicity, but this usually requires that you have unique products or a unique presentation. For print, send press releases with a full-color photograph announcing your products to new-products editors of publications targeted to your customers. As your budget allows, use the services of a Web promotions expert and/or an online publicist to generate traffic to your site.

- Using meta tags on your Web pages that contain the phrases potential customers for your products will enter into search engines. Submit your site to search engines monthly.

- Establishing links from Web sites that attract your target customers. Many times you can get reciprocal links; at other times, they may involve advertising.

- Mailing a direct-mail piece to your own list; people on your list know you and/or have already done business with you.

- Advertising in publications targeted to your customers. Small print classified ads can be cost-effective.

- Renting or trading for mailing lists of people who are similar to your customers.

Related Business

Antique and Collectibles Reseller

Spurred by online auction sites such as eBay and public television's popular *Antique Road Show*, selling antique, vintage, and used merchandise is becoming one of the fastest-growing home businesses. As a reseller, you can find antiques or collectible items from china to furniture, vintage clothing to memorabilia, and can list your items online where collectors will bid on your listing. There is no charge to you for listing items you want to sell or for shopping on the site and bidding on items. Also, there is no surcharge for purchasing items. The auction site processes the sales and takes a commission, as low as 5 percent. You are responsible for fulfilling orders and sending out your merchandise.

Listings on online auction sites include a picture and description of each item, so having a digital camera with a close-up option is required. The cost of digital cameras that have sufficient quality for online use is down to only a few hundred dollars. You need to learn how to upload your photos and information to the auction site. These sites provide considerable assistance for the novice seller.

The key to success in this business is locating and recognizing items of value and knowing how to price appropriately. Resellers spend a considerable amount of their time hunting through swap meets, garage sales, antique malls, and estate and moving sales. Some resellers shop online themselves. The goal is to find items that can be sold for at least double or triple the purchase price but still be a good buy to customers. Some resellers add value to the items they resell by repairing, restoring, or enhancing them, i.e., "distressed," hand-painted or air-brushed furniture. Perusing other's online listings is one way to learn about pricing items. Other pricing resources include:

Kovels' Antiques and Collectibles Price List, Ralph M. and Terry Kovel, Crown. Published annually.

Schroeders Antiques Price Guide, edited by Bob Huxford and Sharon Huxford, Collectors Books, Schroeder Publishing Company, P.O. Box 3009, Paducah, KY 42002; (502) 898-6211. Published annually.

Many professional resellers post only select merchandise online and sell the rest at swap meets and live auctions or directly to dealers, designers, and retail outlets. The wise retailer develops a list of customers who they can contact by e-mail, fax, postcards, or telephone when they locate merchandise that would be of particular interest.

First Steps

- Do your homework. Learn about selling online and with mail order from classes, books, and by checking out what others are doing.

- Create or select your products.

- Develop a Web presence that may range from space on a mall to an information page to a full store or catalogue on your own Web site; alternatively, rent a mailing list or identify publications in which to advertise.

- Consider using a fulfillment company or a drop-shipment services call center (a newer identity for answering services). These can enable you to offer 24-hour order taking and overnight shipping. You can divide order taking from shipping, choosing to subcontract either or neither. To find fulfillment services look for ads in the trade publications.

Where to Turn for Information and Help

ORGANIZATIONS

AMERICAN MARKETING ASSOCIATION, 311 South Wacker Drive, Suite 580, Chicago, IL 60606; (800) AMA-1150; (312) 648-0536. Web site: *www.ama.org*

DIRECT MARKETING ASSOCIATION, 1120 Ave. of the Americas, New York, NY 10036; (212) 768-7277. Offers courses on direct-mail advertising and has an active program of conferences, institutes, and seminars. Web site: *www.the-dma.org*

NATIONAL MAIL ORDER ASSOCIATION, LLC, 2807 Polk St. NE, Minneapolis, MN 55418; (612) 788-1673. Founded in 1972. Targeted at small to medium-sized firms in the direct selling industry. Web site: *www.nmoa.org*

NEWSLETTERS AND TRADE PUBLICATIONS

Catalog Age, Intertec Publishing, 11 Riverbend Drive South, P.O. Box 4294, Stamford, CT 06907-0294; (800) 775-3777. Web site: *www.mediacentral.com*

Direct: The Magazine of Direct Marketing Management, Intertec Publishing, 11 Riverbend Dr. South, P.O. Box 4294, Stamford, CT 06907-0294; (800) 775-3777. Web site: *www.mediacentral.com*

Direct Marketing Magazine, Hoke Communications, 224 Seventh St., Garden City, NY 11530; (516) 746-6700. Web site: *www.hokecomm.com*

Operations and Fulfillment, Target Communications, 535 Connecticut Avenue, Norwalk, CT 06854; (203)857-5656. Web site: *www.opsandfulfillment.com*

DM News, Mill Hollow Corporation, 100 6th Ave., 6th fl., New York, NY 10013, (212) 741-2095. Daily online newsletter and weekly print publication. The online version has a directory of resources for products and services for direct marketers. Web site: *www.dmnews.com*

Mail Order Messenger, Box 358, Middleton, TN 38052. No phone; fax: (901) 376-1566. Web site: *www.momonline.com/mom*

Profit$, an online magazine, Carson Services, Box 4785, Lincoln, NE 68504; (402) 434-8480. Web site: *www.profitsonline.com*

Target Marketing Magazine, North American Publishing Company, 401 North Broad Street, Philadelphia, PA 19108; (800) 626-2689; (215) 238-5300. Web site: *www.targetonline.com*

BOOKS

101 Great Mail-Order Businesses, Tyler Gregory Hicks, Prima Publishing, 1996. ISBN: 0761503374.

Building a Mail Order Business: A Complete Manual for Success, William A. Cohen, New York: John Wiley & Sons, 1996. ISBN: 0471109460.

Building Cyberstores: Installation, Transaction Processing, and Management, Martin A. Nemzow, Computing McGraw-Hill, 1997. ISBN: 0079130909.

The Complete Small Business Internet Guide, Tom Heatherington, Lori Heatherington, Que Education & Training, 1998. ISBN: 0789718308.

Drop Shipping As a Marketing Function: A Handbook of Methods and Policies, Nicholas T. Scheel, Quorum Books, 1990. ISBN: 0899305326.

Electronic Selling, Brian Jamison, Josh Gold, Warren Jamison, Computing McGraw-Hill, 1997. ISBN: 0070329303.

How to Create Successful Catalogs, Maxwell Sroge, Anne Knudsen, NTC Publishing Group, 1995, ISBN: 0844235725. From the same publisher, also in 1995: *How to Profit Through Catalog Marketing,* Katie Muldoon, Anne Knudsen.

How to Start a Mail Order Business, Mike Powers, Stephen M. Pollan, Michael D. Powers, New York: Avon Books, 1996. ISBN: 0380784467.

How to Start a Home Based Mail Order Business, Georganne Fiumara, 1996, Globe Pequot Press. ISBN: 1564408590.

How to Start & Operate a Mail-Order Business, Julian L. Simon, New York: McGraw-Hill, 1993. ISBN: 0070575657.

Making Money in Cyberspace, Paul and Sarah Edwards and Linda Rohrbough, New York: Tarcher/Putnam, 1998. ISBN 0-87477-884-0.

Selling Online for Dummies, Leslie Lundquist, IDG Books Worldwide, 1998, ISBN: 0764503340.

SOFTWARE

Mail-order software organizes and automates order-entry, inventory-tracking, and accounting aspects of running a mail-order business. Four of these specialized programs are:

CASTLE, Haven Corporation, 1227 Dodge Ave., Evanston, IL 60202; (800) 782-8278. Web site: *www.havencorp.com*

CH-CHING!, Imacination Software, 2674 D East Main St., #122, Ventura, CA 93003, (800) 244-5332. Web site: *www.imacination.com*

EASY ORDER, The Micro Tyme Network, 1422 Pine Hill Drive, Garland, TX 75043. Web site: *www.easyorder.com*

MAIL ORDER WIZARD, Haven Corporation, 1227 Dodge Ave., Evanston, IL 60202; (800) 782-8278. Web site: *www.havencorp.com*

Mailing List Service

As much as you may hate finding your mailbox stuffed with junk mail, there is a silver lining in the growth of direct mail in this country: It means there's lots of business for mailing list services. A mailing list service is arguably one of the easiest businesses to start from home that can grow into a substantial business. The start-up costs are reasonably low, and the learning curve is short.

Home-based mailing list services help small businesses and nonprofit customers that want to use direct mail but don't have their own mailing lists, may not have them in a database, or don't have the in-house capability to make effective use of the lists they have. Mailing list services may perform a variety of tasks, but the essential nature of the business is to facilitate getting out first-, third- (bulk), and fourth-class mailings while adhering to U.S. postal regulations. The principal services offered by home-based mailing list services include:

List maintenance. Many small businesses want to use direct mail, but don't have the resources or know-how to set up and maintain their mailing lists. Therefore, a significant source of income for mailing list services involves building computerized mailing lists from data supplied by clients.

To offer this service, you begin by designing the list (which names to include, in what format, along with other facts that might be included in a database of names) and then enter the needed information. A clothing store, for example, might have the names of its clients in some sort of form, so you help create a computer database that includes all past and existing customers along with their birth dates, color preferences, and even the spouse's business address so reminders can be sent when it's time to buy birthday and other gifts. After setting up the list, you can turn it over to your client or print labels for them on a regular or on-demand basis.

Doing mailings—Letter Shop Services. Another significant source of income for many mailing list firms is actually to do the mailings for customers. Clients such as retail stores, hotels, businesses, and organizations may provide lists of names for you to put onto labels and mail out at the lowest cost. This means you do the folding, stuffing, licking, and collating. If you do much of this work, you will want to get a machine that folds, inserts, and seals envelopes at the rate of 30 or more pieces a minute. Some customers, however, in order to get their mail noticed, may want the envelopes to be hand addressed and have postage stamps applied individually.

Katie Allegato of Allegato and Associates in Kissimmee, Florida, helps many of her clients do their mailings. She obtains their mailing lists, cleans them, sorts them, and prints out labels complete with Postnet bar codes that entitles the mailing to bulk-mail discounts. She also has the labels sorted using special software so that the pieces are eligible for greater discounts if they meet the U.S. Postal Service requirements of "saturation walk sequence," or "carrier route," or "automated walk sequence/delivery point bar code."

This task is actually one of the most complex aspects of running your mailing service. As postage costs have risen and the quantity of mail delivered has skyrocketed to more than 190 billion pieces per year, the U.S. Postal Service has made major efforts to automate and computerize the delivery of all mail, bulk mail in particular. For this reason, the software that prints bar codes and sorts and categorizes mail must follow strict regulations established by the Postal Service. Doing bulk mailings thus consists of the following steps:

- Your client brings you the names of clients in some form, computerized or not.

- To achieve the lowest postal rate for a bulk mailing, you need to identify and clean the list of duplicate records and verify addresses.

- You then print out mailing labels complete with bar codes showing the delivery point codes (which is an 11-digit number that includes the zip code plus the four extra digits that were added, plus two more digits from the street address).

By following this procedure, you can generally perform a bulk mailing for a client at 5 to 10 cents less for each piece than the cost of regular first-class postage. In doing a mailing, these small amounts add up, particularly for clients who might mail 10,000 pieces every few weeks. Allegato says, for example, that one of her clients, a hotel resort in the area, might spend $10,000 to $15,000 per year in mailings, but by handling their mailings as bulk, they save $5,000 to $8,000.

List creation. While you won't be able to compete with large mail-list companies that sell thousands of names in any one of thousands of categories, you can create specialized lists tailored to your city, area, or particular client needs. Also, since large mailing houses often don't handle small requests, a home-based business is sometimes the only place a small business can go to purchase a list of 200 to 500 names. For example, some businesses only want to mail to all owner-occupied homes in a ten-square block. So you could create your own mailing list by buying print directories of your city and keying in names just for that area.

You can also create your own lists based on public records, i.e., new businesses in your city (which you get from public records of new business licenses), new homeowners in the area, sole-practitioner chiropractors, newlyweds, and so on. You can then rent your lists to marketers interested in promoting their products or services to your list. Also, you can sell monthly updates on the lists you compile. You can issue such reports every month and sell them on a six- or twelve-month subscription basis.

To increase the value of her lists and monthly reports, Allegato phones new businesses to verify phone numbers and obtains additional information that could be helpful to her clients such as: contact names, titles, whether it's a male- or female-owned business, whether it's minority owned, and whether it's a new or relocated business, as well as the size of the business based on the number of employees.

List Brokering. Some services help clients locate and select mailing lists suited to their objectives. The lists may be residential, commercial, institutional, or targeted special-interest groups. If no list exists, you may need to identify and negotiate to compile lists from associations, clubs, and other groups whose list of names can be valuable to clients. In this case, you act as a broker between list sellers and list buyers.

Teaching about mailing lists. Handling mailing lists is complex enough that many services tutor or teach small businesses that prefer to do their own mailings. This could involve such areas as teaching client's personnel to use mailing list software and how to use their lists to generate leads, obtain orders, build store traffic, and how to comply with U.S. postal regulations.

Allegato considers this is to be a great business. You can perform as many or as few of these functions as you like. You can work at your own leisure, full-time or part-time. It's also a good business to combine with desktop publishing, because many stores and businesses need help designing their flyers or brochures in addition to doing the mailings. Allegato has clients who bring her deadly ugly promotional pieces, and with her experience in direct mail, she is able to advise them herself or send them to a desktop publisher she knows.

Knowledge and Skills You Need to Have

- You need to learn about the specific U.S. postal regulations covering sorting, stuffing, traying, sacking, using bar codes, carrier route numbers, and rates so you can show clients different designs for mailing that will save them postage. You need to know about automated services offered by the postal service.

- You probably need to know how to use several database and mailing list programs.

- You need to be able to type accurately and quickly.

- You need to be responsible about meeting deadlines.

Start-up Costs	Low	High
Computer	$ 1,500	$ 3,000
Printer	$ 300	$ 800
or		
Multi-function printer/fax/scanner/copier	$ 150	$ 600
Mailing list software	$ 50	$ 1,000
Bar coding/sorting software	$ 900	$ 1,000
Permits from post office	$ 100	$ 300
Office furniture, especially an ergonomic chair	$ 400	$ 1,000
Initial marketing budget	$ 1,000	$ 5,000
Total	$ 4,400	$ 12,700

You may need to lease a postage meter machine (vendors are Pitney Bowes, Ascom Hasler, Francotyp Postalia, and Neopost) to use for clients who bring you their bulk mail already folded and stuffed in envelopes with labels and bar codes.

Advantages

- Mailing list services are relatively easy to start and sell.

- Because many businesses would like to do mailings if they knew how, your customer base can be large. This means you do not need to rely on a few important customers for most of your income.

- Your business can be operated on a part-time or full-time basis or even as an adjunct to another business.

Disadvantages

- The work is routine; many people will not find it challenging.

- The work requires exceptional attention to detail.

- Postal regulations change and are sometimes complex. You need to be sure you understand what you are doing, or your clients will find another service. The technology is also changing.

- Unless you take the necessary precautions, you risk developing repetitive-motion injuries as a result of constant keyboarding.

Pricing

For entering names into a mailing list, many services charge from 6 to 7 cents per line of input. Thus, a three-line entry consisting of name, street address, city/state/zip runs 15 to 25 cents per name. Some services charge $1 per name to maintain the list for a year.

For printing out labels, services charge from 3 to 5 cents per label (including the label stock); envelopes run 10 to 12 cents per envelope printed. Purging a list averages 1 to 2 cents per name on the list, and to use a mailer's bulk-mail permit costs an average of 4 to 5 cents per piece. Thus, a client who uses a list service to clean a list, print bar-coded labels, and get bulk-mail rates pays roughly 8 to 12 cents per name plus the actual cost of the postage, which may be as low as 14.5 cents or 19.8 cents as of this writing. A service mailing out 10,000 pieces thus earns $800 to $1,200 for the work.

Potential Earnings

Typical Annual Gross Revenues: $40,000 to $100,000 per year based on surveys of home-based mail list services.

Overhead: low (20 percent or less).

Best Home Businesses Estimate of Market Potential

The use of direct mail for marketing is projected to grow by 6 percent each year through 2003, according to a study done for the Direct Marketing Association. Linda Rohrbough, co-author of *Making Money in*

Cyberspace, who has studied the mailing list business, says, "By requiring automation, the Post Office is making it increasingly difficult for companies to do a mailing in-house. Just as IRS has created the need for tax accountants, the Post Office is good for mailing list services."

While the growth of the Internet has resulted in the number of e-mail messages surpassing first-class letters, most people's mail boxes are no less crammed with direct mail. With the expected clamp down on junk e-mail, similar to limitations on junk faxes, direct mail may appear more attractive to many firms.

One development to be aware of: the Postal Service has announced a service whereby businesses can electronically transmit documents along with their mailing lists to the Postal Service. The Postal Service will then electronically send the files to commercial printers for the documents to be printed and envelopes addressed followed by the mail pieces being deposited into the mail stream for delivery. Rohrbough believes, however, that the Postal Service will contract with mailing list companies to do the work because some companies will not want to turn over their lists to the Postal Service itself. She also projects that because these mailings will look canned, this service will not appreciably lessen the role for mailing list services.

All in all, both the Internet and Postal Service automation may stimulate the mailing list service business. Some mailing list services may wish to add managing Internet newsletter and discussion lists to what they offer, using software programs like *ListServ, ListProc, Smartlist, Post Office,* and *Majordomo,* as well as offering broadcast fax.

Best Ways to Get Business

- Directly approaching personnel of locally owned stores to ask how they handle their mailing lists. In stores that ask customers to fill out cards or to sign guest books, ask what they do with the names they get; they may need help turning these names into mailing lists.

- Calling associations, clubs, churches, and hotels in your area to see if any of them are interested in having you maintain their mailing lists or handle their mailings.

- Contacting professionals (doctors, lawyers, accountants) who may wish help in sending out newsletters to their clients.

- Spreading the word through personal contacts to reach small businesses, organizations, and churches.

- Networking in business organizations, chambers of commerce, and leads clubs. Network also with printers and desktop publishers who might be doing work for businesses about to do mailings.

- Contacting people you know or can readily meet in networking organizations who are involved in direct selling of products with companies such as Avon, Mary Kay Cosmetics, Rexall, and Watkins.

- Sending direct mail to businesses in your area.

- Having a Web site on which you list your services and provide testimonial letters.

- Advertising in the Yellow Pages.

- To get referral business, get jobs done on time and show clients how you have saved them money.

First Steps

- Learn to use mailing list software and products and services for verifying addresses and sorting.

- Attend bulk-mail workshops at your Post Office. Read their books and ask questions so that you are certain that you understand how to handle bulk mailings.

- Work on acquiring customers.

Where to Turn for Information and Help

ORGANIZATIONS

DIRECT MARKETING ASSOCIATION, 1120 Ave. of the Americas, New York, NY 10036; (212) 768-7277. Produces *Ethical Business Practices, Mailing List Practices,* and *Fair Information Practices Guidelines;* has an active program of conferences, institutes, and seminars. Web site: *www.the-dma.org*

NATIONAL POSTAL FORUM, 50 West Corporate Center, 3998 Fair Ridge Drive, Suite 300, Fairfax, VA 22033-2907; (703) 218-5015. Nonprofit educational organization that, through trade shows, assists the United States Postal Service in building relationships with mailers in using products and services offered by the United States Postal Service. Web site: *www.nationalpostalforum.org*

BOOKS

Domestic Mail Manual and International Mail Manual, Superintendent of Documents, P.O. Box 371954, Pittsburgh, PA 15250-7954; (202) 512-1800.

List Broker Manual, Timothy S. Hillebrand, Synergetics International, 857 Orchard Avenue, Moscow, ID 83843; (208) 883-1541.

Standard Rate and Data Service, 1700 Higgens Rd., Des Plaines, IL 60018; (800) 851-7737. The rate guide for mailing list rental for the entire industry. Web site: *www.srds.com*

SOFTWARE

ACCUMAIL, Datatech Enterprises, Inc., 10 Clipper Road, West Conshohocken, PA 19428; (800) 523-0320; (610) 825-6205. *ArcList,* a DOS program, preferred by some mailing list services, and *AccuZIP6,* a newer database management and postage-reduction software package are also available. Web site: *www.datatechusa.com*

MAILER'S+4, Mailer's Software, 970 Calle Negocio, San Clemente, CA 92675; (800)800-MAIL. Web site: *www.800mail.com*

MYDELUXEMAILLIST, My Software, 2197 East Bayshore Road, Palo Alto, CA 94303; (800) 325-3508; (650) 325-9383. Web site: *www.mysoftware.com.* Good for up to 30,000 names. $49.95.

AUDIO TAPES

HOW TO MAKE MONEY IN THE MAILING LIST BUSINESS, Katie Allegato and Linda Rohrbough, Brubaker Tapes, 410 Gatewood Terrace, Sierra Madre, CA 91024.

WEB SITE

The Web site of United States Postal Service (*www.usps.com*) contains information and tools for using the mail. On the site are current post office publications, business forms, mailing tips, and software tools, such as ZIP+4 Code Lookup, City State / ZIP Code Associations, and Address

Management Systems Office Locator. At *www.usps.gov/ncsc,* it is possible to clean lists online and check addresses online.

Make-Up Artist

Make-up has been a significant part of human culture from prehistoric times and applying it has been practiced as a vocation since at least the time of the Pharaohs. Just as using make-up goes back to early times, using make-up often begins early in life. Many little girls first apply it when they're playing dress-up as children. Over the centuries, a fascination for make-up has created an array of specialties for anyone who wishes to earn his or her livelihood as a make-up artist. There's something for most everyone to choose from depending upon your personality and interests. Here are the most prominent niches:

• *Body make-up* for body builders and performers called upon to expose more than their faces.

• *Broadcast grooming* makes on-air personalities and guests look natural and attractive under studio lighting. Ad agencies are also a market for this make-up specialty.

• *Ethnic make-up* serving the requirements of non-Caucasians.

• *Funeral home restoration* for open-casket wakes and burial services. This practice goes back to prehistory.

• *Glamour or basic beauty* for people having professional photographs taken; teenagers going to their proms; others wanting to look and feel great for a special occasion and those wishing to learn how to apply make-up to look their best socially and on the job.

• *Mehendi,* derived from India, for those wishing to wear make-up as decorative jewelry. This involves applying henna tattoos that are done either using stencils or freehand. Henna stains can last several weeks. Another form of temporary tattooing is done with rice paper made in New York by Temptu Studios.

• *Paramedical* for people who need to camouflage scarring from accidents, burns, and surgeries; skin disorders; the redness following cosmetic surgery; and laser resurfacing.

- *Special effects* make-up for creating disguises and unusual characters for stage, television, film and other media productions, but also for work with law enforcement agencies doing undercover work.

- *Television studio, theatre, high fashion, music videos, movie and industrial films.* Working on movie sets as a make-up artist requires admission to a union which involves passing a test that requires special training.

- *Wedding/bridal* make-up, for brides, of course, but also at times for grooms and entire wedding parties.

Doing make-up for brides and bridal parties is one of the most appealing specialties for someone who wants to work from home. A wedding make-up artist provides on-location make-up services for assuring everyone looks naturally beautiful for the ceremony, the photo sessions, and the video camera, which is used for taping the majority of today's weddings.

Make-up that might look natural and vibrant in person can look washed out on film or video. Extra make-up to make their features stand out for video, however, can make the bride and her bridal party look too made-up in person. That's where the wedding make-up artist comes in. She or he is a specialist who understands how to provide the bride and bridal party with the right balance to meet all the make-up demands of the wedding day.

The wedding make-up artist works with all kinds of clients, from young brides who are getting married for the first time to older brides who are remarrying. Two sessions are required in working with the bride. The first session, before the wedding, provides a time to find out about the plans for the wedding (the color scheme, number of people involved, and so forth) and to show the bride the various possibilities. Stephanie Belasco of Makeup Artistry in Westfield, New Jersey, calls this session the "dry run." It usually lasts an hour to an hour and a half. Then on the day of the wedding, the make-up artist arrives at the wedding site very early, before the photos are taken, does the make-up for the entire bridal party, and puts on the bride's headpiece. At this point, the make-up artist may either leave or stay on hand to touch up the make-up at various times during the festivities.

As a way to continue the relationship and build an ongoing clientele, some wedding make-up artists offer products and special make-up sessions. Stephanie Belasco builds customer loyalty for many years after the wedding by spending "a lot of time, energy, love, and care" on each client. "I offer more than just a one-day service," she explains. Some of her clients compare her to Joan Rivers because of the sense of humor she displays while she's working. Humor is just one way Belasco puts her clients at ease. "We all have the same feelings, the same insecurities," she says. "In this field you have to like people."

In contrast to the outgoing personality required for being a wedding make-up artist, funeral home restorators, for obvious reasons, can be completely introverted. Make-up artists working in the glamour settings of movie sets, high-fashion runways, television studios, and theatres, as well as those who work with photographers, need to blend into the background, which is at odds with some artists' creative spirits. Work must be done quietly and right on schedule. Sally Van Swearingen, a Los Angeles make-up artist, puts it this way, "You must sacrifice being a perfectionist in favor of being on time."

Whereas weddings and studio settings can be hectic and pressured, glamour, paramedical, and basic beauty work is often in quiet and highly personal salonlike settings, usually the artist's home, where it's desirable to interact one-on-one at a relaxed and leisurely pace.

Knowledge and Skills You Need to Have

- You need some flair for color analysis and to know which colors blend together to produce a desired effect.

- You need to have a basic knowledge of fashion and make-up trends.

- In some states in order to be a make-up artist, you need to obtain a license as a cosmetician or cosmetologist, which is a more inclusive license that includes hair. Even though licensed, make-up artists who are cosmetologists usually do not work with hair. Cosmeticians are also called aestheticians.

- Make-up artists must have good interpersonal communication skills and be sensitive to their clients' needs.

- You need to know the make-up techniques for the specialization you choose.

- Wedding make-up artists need to be empathetic and able to handle the range of emotions and ego issues that may arise for a bride under the pressure of her wedding. Expectations are high for everything to be perfect. People can become temperamental and emotional.

- Paramedical make-up artists must understand the psychological aspects of the client's problem and it's underlying physical nature. Rachel Furman, a pharmacist by training who has created MyART, a safe line of non–make-up skin-care products (800-320-4403), points out that the artist must determine if the condition is a changing one or one that is static that the client will have to deal with the remainder of her or his life. The artist must also know if there is a conflict between the make-up to be applied and the medical condition. Paramedical make-up artists must also handle the paperwork detail of patient documentation.

- Those working in studios in any media from stage to photography need to work quickly and unobtrusively, often under pressure and sometimes for long hours.

In addition to having a car or other means of transportation to get to and from locations, you will have the following expenses in starting this business:

Start-up Costs	Low	High
Make-up equipment and supplies	$ 1,000	$ 5,000
Portfolio of photographs of your work	$ 1,000	$ 2,000
Director's chair	$ 100	$ 200
Initial marketing budget	$ 250	$ 2,000
Legal fees to develop a contract for use in bookings	$ 500	$ 750
Cell phone or pager	$ 75	$ 200
Insurance for your kit	$ 200	$ 300
Total	$ 3,125	$ 10,450

Advantages

- Make-up artists are well paid for their time on an hourly basis.

- In some specialties like bridal and broadcast-studio work, you are working around happy people at exciting and positive times in their lives.

- Your work begets more work. Doing a good job for your clients can be one of your best means of marketing, because they will refer their friends and colleagues to you. If a photographer or producer likes your work, you will have long-term clients.

- In the case of wedding make-up, the work is usually on weekends, making it feasible to start on a part-time basis while you are still employed. For those who are working full-time, the main part of the week is free for family life.

Disadvantages

- Having a specialty types you because to be convincing, your portfolio has pictures of work in that specialty and not much of anything else. To do work in other specialties, it's necessary to develop a second portfolio featuring work in that specialty.

FOR WEDDING MAKE-UP:

- Wedding make-up has no built-in repeat business.

- Although weddings are positive celebrations, they can also be stressful.

- Wedding make-up work means giving up weekends, which can be hard on dating and some marriages.

- Though weddings are more concentrated during the summer, the winter holidays are slow.

FOR STUDIO WORK:

- With studio work, breaking in is a problem, but once you're in with a producer, you're apt to be used indefinitely.

- Studio work involves long hours, often twelve-hour days.

Pricing

As for most services, make-up artists can charge more in large cities than in smaller communities.

- By the hour: $25 to $100. Funeral home restoration is closer to the bottom of the range; paramedical, closer to the top.

- By the face: $25 to $150. Prom and basic beauty are closer to the bottom of the range; make-up for photographs and weddings are closer to the top. For weddings, brides are about 50 percent more than members of the wedding party; the price includes a meeting prior to the wedding. In addition, a fee can be charged for traveling to the site and for staying throughout the ceremony for touch-ups.

- By the day: $300 to $600. Industrial video is closer to the bottom of the range; studio movie work is closer to the top. In addition, artists can charge a daily "kit fee" to cover to supplies.

Potential Earnings

Typical Annual Gross Revenues:

- Faces in general—$25,000 to $50,000 based on 20 appointments a week.

- Movie work—$39,000 to $52,000 based on 65 to 87 days a year.

- Paramedical work—$50,000 to $100,000 based on 20 appointments a week.

- Wedding make-up—$21,875 to $61,250, based on doing 175 weddings a year for a bride and two members of the wedding party. Weddings are almost always on a Saturday or Sunday, and you can work a maximum of two to three weddings a day.

To increase income, make-up artists can go to manufacturers and arrange to have their individual label put on cosmetics and skin-care preparations and sell them to their clients. The products can also be sold from a Web site.

Overhead: moderate (20 to 40 percent).

Best Home Businesses Estimate of Market Potential

Paramedical make-up and ethnic make-up are growing specialties. How well wedding make-up artists do seems to depend on the ups and downs of the economy. In tough times, professionally applied wedding make-up is an expense that often gets cut. The growing numbers of older people bodes well for funeral home restorators despite the increase in cremation. In some parts of the country (principally the South), cremation rates are as low as 5 percent; in others, they are as high as 50 percent or more.

Best Ways to Get Business

- Networking in organizations and at events where people who are potential customers or referral sources for your specialty gather.

- Directly approaching photographers, funeral homes, studios, police departments, or ad agencies and letting them know you understand their needs and schedules and that they can count on you to work at their convenience.

- Putting your portfolio on your Web site.

- Getting publicity about what you do. Because this is a glamour business, it lends itself to photo displays and demonstrations, such as "before-and-after" shots, and it's ideal for print media and TV.

FOR MOVIE AND THEATRE MAKE-UP WORK

- Make a list of a dozen producers or production coordinators by name and send them your biographical information. Then call to follow up and contact them over and over.

FOR PROM WORK

- Contact high schools and colleges.

FOR WEDDING MAKE-UP

- Network in business organizations where other businesspeople involved in wedding services gather.

- Exhibit at bridal trade shows, showing your photographs and doing makeovers in your booth.

- Advertise in local bridal magazines, with coupons included for specials.

- Hold a mixer for people in the wedding business: consultants, photographers, caterers, florists, and so forth.

FOR PARAMEDICAL MAKE-UP

- Approach plastic surgeons and others who do facial surgery about work that may be at least in part in their offices.

First Steps

- Begin by finding out if your state requires that you be licensed as a cosmetician (aesthetician) or cosmetologist in order to work as a make-up artist. If so, obtain the training you need for such a license from a cosmetology or beauty school. The cost of this schooling can range from $150 to $1,000; some schools have scholarships available. The training to be a cosmetician can be completed on a full-time basis in nine weeks. Becoming a cosmetologist requires more training because you are also trained to work with hair.

- If you are considering having a studio or salon for clients in your home, check the zoning regulations for your neighborhood for any restrictions regarding offering such services in a residence and for having clients come into your home.

- Learning special techniques for camera make-up and working with different skin tones in different types of lighting requires creativity and experience. The best way to get this experience is by working with another make-up artist as an assistant.

- Practice on willing friends and relatives until you perfect your technique.

- Once you are getting good results, develop a portfolio of photos showing off your work and then start marketing yourself. Sometimes you can do make-up for photographers in exchange for getting free samples of photos for your portfolio. Sally Van Swearingen cautions that a mediocre photographer will not make your work look good. "Only work with top-notch photographers who will make your work look great," she advises.

- Choose a specialty.

- To learn movie work and to get a reel of film that shows your work that you can use as part of or instead of your portfolio, work on student films.

- Develop a contract. You may be able to borrow a contract from another artist, but it's still a good idea to have an attorney review the contract.

- In taking your cosmetics with you to jobs, Sally Van Swearingen advises, "Separate your products, taking less than full-sizes. Full bottles are heavy and if you get separated from your kit, you are out of business without back-up."

Where to Turn for Information and Help

ORGANIZATIONS

AESTHETICS' INTERNATIONAL ASSOCIATION, Sunnyvale, TX; (972) 203-8530; fax: (972) 203-8754. Umbrella association for aestheticians, massage therapists, make-up artists, cosmetologists, aromatherapists, reflexologists, holistic practitioners, nutritionists, dermatologists, and plastic surgeons, providing continuing education and conferences. Web site: *www.beautyworks.com*

NATIONAL ASSOCIATION OF AESTHETICIANS, 4447 McKinney Avenue, Dallas, TX 75205; (214) 526-0760.

NATIONAL COSMETOLOGY ASSOCIATION, 401 N. Michigan Ave., Chicago, IL 60611; (800) 527-1683. Offers certification, liability insurance, educational programs, and conferences. The Web site has a trend page showing what's hot in make-up, hair, make-up/aesthetics, nails, and business. Web site: *www.nca-now.com*

BOOKS

The Business of Beauty, Debbie Purvis, Wall & Emerson, 1994; (905) 426-4823; e-mail: odyssey7@idirect.com

The Complete Make-Up Artist: Working in Film, Television and Theatre, Penny Delamar, Northwestern University Press, 1995, ISBN: 0810112582.

A Consumer's Dictionary of Cosmetic Ingredients, Ruth Winter, Crown Publishing, 1999, ISBN: 0609803670.

Making Faces, Kevyn Aucoin, Gena Rowlands, Little Brown & Company, 1997, ISBN: 0316286869.

Milady's Standard Textbook of Cosmetology, Milady Publishing Company, 1995. ISBN: 1-56253-206-5. See the description of Milady in the resource section for *Facialist.*

Period Make-Up for the Stage: Step-By-Step, Rosemarie Swinfield, Betterway Publications, 1997. ISBN: 155870468X.

Stage Makeup Step-By-Step: The Complete Guide to Basic Makeup, Planning and Designing Makeup, Adding and Reducing Age, Ethnic Makeup, Special Effects, Rosemarie Swinfield, Betterway Publications, 1995. ISBN: 155870390X.

The Technique of the Professional Make-Up Artist, Vincent J.-R. Kohoe, Focal Press, 1995. ISBN: 0240802179.

MAGAZINES

Bride's, Condé Nast, 140 E. 45th Street, New York, NY 10017; (800) 456-6162; (212) 880-8800.

Les Nouvelles Esthetiques, 306 Alcazar Avenue, Suite 204, Coral Gables, FL 33134; (800) 471-0229.

Modern Bride, 519 Eighth Avenue, New York, NY 10018; (800) 777-5786; (212) 645-9700.

Vogue, Condé Nast, 350 Madison Avenue, New York, NY 10017; (800) 234-1520; (212) 880-8800.

VIDEO

SALLY VAN SWEARINGEN'S BRIDAL VIDEO: HOW TO BE A PHOTOGENIC BRIDE, Sally Van Swearingen and Valerie Smith, 4502 Camellia Avenue, Studio City, CA 91602; (818) 623-9309.

WEB SITE

The Beautyworks site is sponsored by *Skin, Inc.* magazine, the Aesthetics' International Association, the International Guild of Professional Electrologists, and the American Society of Esthetic Medicine, Inc. The site has resources directories, including one on make-up, which you can apply to be included in. Web site: *www.beautyworks.com*

Manufacturer's Rep—Independent Sales Representative

The effort by companies across the country to cut costs is reaching deep into the heart of how manufacturers sell their goods. Whereas in the good old days, a plastics or chemical or automotive company might have a direct factory sales force of 20 salespeople, today one in every two manufacturers use independent sales reps. Small manufacturers have always relied on independent reps, but now even large companies and service organizations seek out independent sales representative to sell their products. Some firms have hybrid arrangements employing some in-house sales personnel but contracting out some or most sales work.

Experienced salespeople tell us that being a manufacturer's representative is the graduate level of selling, offering potentially higher earnings and freedom from the company politics of being an employee. Independent reps function in virtually every industry including chemicals, adhesives, gift items, electrical components and tubing, valves, heavy machinery, and pharmaceutical products. Reps may sell:

- Products from manufacturers to other manufacturers who use raw materials or components in their finished products.

- Finished products to wholesalers or retailers, or both.

- Products to large customers like HMOs and governments.

To qualify as an independent rep, one must represent at least two companies. Reps have exclusive territories, which may encompass one or more states, counties, metropolitan areas, or zip codes in which they get credit for any sale made in their territory. Some reps handle multiple territories. How much you work at home or work from home depends on the products you choose. Some products may be sold by phone; others require local travel that can get you home each night. Others products require overnight travel. If your product requires national or international travel, you may be gone for days or weeks.

Rep agreements may also be limited to specific industries or markets. Some reps take on several kinds of products although the trend is to take on fewer and more compatible product lines in order to focus efforts and reduce costs. Some reps hire subagents to help them, creating a full-service agency.

Most reps are paid on a commission basis as is discussed under "Pricing" below. Reps must keep careful track of all their expenses, not only in order to deduct them from income for tax purposes, but also to be able to assess if a particular line is making a profit for them. A rep might have from a few thousand to over $10,000 in business expenses before a line begins to turn a profit.

Overall, however, the life of the independent rep can be gratifying and financially remunerative. Although the sad portrait of Willy Loman from *Death of a Salesman* may stay with us for years to come, the reality for independent sales is that it is one of the best rewarded vocations in capitalistic economies. Rep agencies tend to be small; the average company size is four people and 15 percent are one-person firms; 31 percent are sole proprietorships.

Knowledge and Skills You Need to Have

- You have to be able to sell. Selling is a people process, so you need charm, wit, self-confidence, and a good appearance. Much of your success depends on how you present yourself and your ability to develop relationships and to manage the relationships between the manufacturers you represent and the customers you sell to.

- It helps considerably to have a background in the products you are selling, because it's easier to understand them and explain their benefits than to sell something you know little about. More and more companies are turning to reps who have background in their technology or who have used their product and have a systemic understanding of their industry.

- Becoming successful requires developing in-depth knowledge and a solid reputation for honesty, integrity, and professionalism.

- You need to be responsive to customers' requests for information and service.

- You need to become knowledgeable about sales-commission structures so that you can cut a good deal for yourself. This means you should study the industry and know how much other salespeople in your line of work are getting (or could get) paid.

- You need to be able to multitask, as you will be handling many ideas, clients, products, schedules, and future goals all at once.

- Because import and export are increasingly important, you need to develop knowledge of import/export opportunities and requirements.

Start-up Costs	Low	High
Computer	$ 1,500	$ 3,000
Printer	$ 300	$ 800
or		
Multi-function printer/fax/scanner/copier	$ 150	$ 600
Cell phone	$ 75	$ 200
Telephone headset	$ 40	$ 400
Office furniture, especially an ergonomic chair	$ 400	$ 1,000
Initial marketing budget	$ 3,000	$ 10,000
Total	$ 5,465	$ 16,000

Advantages

- A high income comes with success in sales.

- Usually salespeople meet a lot of people and make many friends in the process.

- An independent rep has flexibility in choosing the companies they represent.

- A good income and flexible schedule enables an independent sales rep to determine his or her own lifestyle.

Disadvantages

- Perhaps the major problem with sales is payment and cash flow. It can be months before you get a check from your manufacturers because payment may not happen until goods are actually shipped or the manufacturer is paid. Also, where commissions are split, it can be difficult to keep track of what you're owed.

- Reps complain about manufacturers reducing commissions or the "house" taking over accounts as soon as they begin producing sizeable sales.

- Depending on what you sell, where you are located, and your territory, some or a great deal of travel may be required. Travel may mean higher overhead and many nights away from home.

- Sales is a competitive business; you must be aggressive in some instances and take the lumps with the sugar.

- Some large retail buyers are refusing to deal with reps, insisting on dealing directly with the supplier company. However, this battle is being fought and sometimes won in court.

- Some manufacturers eliminate reps with customer/supplier partnerships when their customers use but a single source for a product line. Some are making products available directly through the Internet, sometimes to the disadvantage of the rep.

- To retain distributors as customers, increasingly reps must perform functions that do not themselves produce sales-commission income.

Pricing

Reps are generally compensated based on commissions with rates ranging from 3 to 15 percent. The actual rate is influenced by these factors:

- Type of product line. Commissions on automotive components sold to car makers, for example, are generally lower than commissions paid on durable goods sold as consumer products.

- Number of product lines you carry for a manufacturer.

- Level of difficulty in selling a product (if you are selling against a major competitor, your commission will likely be higher than if you have little competition).

- Territory size and distance between customers, which impacts travel expenses.

- Size of the sale or customer. While most commissions are flat percentage, some commissions are paid on a sliding scale. They may be (a) lower for larger customers, higher for smaller ones; (b) lower for first orders, then higher as quantity builds up; or (c) higher up to a certain dollar amount and then decreasing.

Within the same product category, the commissions can differ widely. The most recent MANA survey in 1995, for example, found that commissions for selling industrial and maintenance chemicals ran between 7.5 and 15 percent, while paper products paid 5.5 to 12.5 percent. In addition, incentives may be offered or negotiated for such things as exceeding sales goals or growth, special promotions, introductions of new products, and developing new customers. Sometimes retainer arrangements are used either instead of a commission or in conjunction with one, i.e., when performing market research and introducing a manufacturer into a new market.

Reps may also provide services that go beyond getting an order not traditionally done by reps but by the firms that retain them, such as marketing, order entry, invoicing, and handling customer service. This is a way for companies to be "lean and mean" in an era when the stock market rewards announcements of downsizing. Reps may need to do these things to keep accounts and/or they may do them to justify higher commission rates. You need to research the field you choose and sometimes be creative.

Potential Earnings

Typical Annual Gross Revenues: Gross revenues for reps in their first to third year of sales averaged $124,000. This is gross income, however, and one must subtract considerable expenses such as office, telephone, auto insurance, gas, airfare, and so on. Still, this is higher than the average wages for salaried sales reps. The Bureau of Labor Statistics reports $47,090 for sales reps selling scientific and related products and $39,510 for sales reps selling nonscientific products.

Overhead: moderate (20 to 40 percent).

Best Home Businesses Estimate of Market Potential

Like other businesses, the selling function is subject to the sweeping changes driven by technology. The pressure to reduce costs is resulting in more firms outsourcing all or part of their sales work, thus creating opportunity for independent sales reps. On the other hand, manufacturers scrutinize their costs all the more and either expect more of independent reps or seek to eliminate them.

While some manufacturers are eliminating sales reps, can there ever be a time without a role for nose-to-nose, eyeball-to-eyeball, and face-to-face selling? Lionel Diaz, President and Chief Executive Officer of the Manufacturers' Agents National Association (MANA), points out that Diamond Jim Brady, the best known independent rep in the late nineteenth century, was intimidated by the railroads because his customers could contact suppliers directly. Similarly, the Internet enables customers to purchase products directly but it also enlarges the economy, thereby adding to the number of potential customers and providing new tools for locating and serving them.

New industries such as genetic engineering provide new markets for reps. It's very difficult for start-up firms to assemble qualified and geographically spread-out sales forces. Commissioned reps are an economical and feasible solution for them.

To survive and thrive, independent reps must adapt by fully utilizing the new tools and meeting the changing requirements of their customers. There has been a consolidation of rep firms during the 90's, but the broader use of technology and the trend toward specialization bodes well for the one-person or very small rep firm.

Best Ways to Get Business

- Using search engines, phone books, and trade-association directories on the Internet and in print to identify potential customers for your product. Visiting your local chamber of commerce to locate possible clients.

- Attending trade shows where both manufacturers and customers can be found.

- Getting listed in trade-association directories that list manufacturer reps.

- Having your own Web page describing your product lines.

- "You have to stick your head down and run," says MANA president Lionel Diaz. "Essentially, this means that hard work and lots of shoe leather are needed to be successful in this business. Getting clients involves a whole range of activities, from cold-calling to networking to making presentations to more cold-calling. Other than that, you must be driven to succeed, and you need to have a good product. No amount of fire in your belly will compensate for a bad product."

First Steps

- Determine if you have a love of selling. Diaz believes that having a dedication to sales and an entrepreneurial spirit are critical in convincing a manufacturer to take you on as an independent rep. Write down your sales goals for the next three years.

- Diaz points out that a new agent needs sufficient capital to keep going for about a year, because it takes time to build your business and, if you are compensated based on commissions only, to get paid. Some industries take a year to make payments; others, 90 days.

- Getting products to sell is a question of finding the best fit for you based on what you know, both from your education and your experience, and what you are interested in. You want to pick products you are capable of selling and in an industry in which you will be effective. You can find products by scouring online and print directories. Watch trade and local news for new companies that even online directories will not pick up for a while. The back of MANA's magazine, *Agency Sales*, contains hundreds of want ads from companies seeking reps. Before agreeing to take on a line of products, talk with sales reps who are selling to the same markets you are considering. Some ways of identifying them include getting lists of reps available at trade shows and talking with potential customers about who sells to them now.

- If you are new to the sales business, you will need to write a résumé and letter to manufacturers explaining why you want to sell their product and how you intend to do it. Diaz recommends that you ultimately have from eight to ten lines to represent because the average cost of a sales call is $300 to $400 (travel time, phone calls, gas, etc.). By having more than one product to sell to customers, you can amortize your costs over more lines. (You cannot take on, however, competing products in the same line; few manufacturers find that beneficial.) When you agree to take on a product line, be sure to sign an equitable written contract with the manufacturer.

- You need a customer base to sell to. Diaz says this is the most important part of getting started because you can easily get lines of products, but finding somebody to buy from you is much harder. He also points out that many times your customers can help you get new lines.

- Take classes in presentation skills, communication, and image to develop your polish.

- Join one or more associations of independent sales reps. The largest association of independent reps, MANA, is a horizontal organization of reps from many fields. Vertical organizations consist of reps all within the same field. See "Organizations" below for names of some of the largest vertical organizations.

- Add product lines within a reasonable timetable to achieve your maximum limit.

Also see the "Export Agent" profile.

Where to Turn for Information and Help

ORGANIZATIONS

ASSOCIATION OF INDEPENDENT MANUFACTURERS REPRESENTATIVES, 222 Merchandise Mart Plaza #1360, Chicago, IL 60654; (312) 464-0092. Serving independent sales representatives in the plumbing and heating industries. Web site: *www.aimr.net*

ELECTRONICS REPRESENTATIVES ASSOCIATION (ERA), 444 N. Michigan Avenue, Suite 1960, Chicago, IL 60611; (312) 527-3050 or (800) 776-7377. Serving sales reps in the electronics industry. Publishes *Representor* magazine. Web site: *www.era.org*

HEALTH INDUSTRY REPRESENTATIVES ASSOCIATION (HIRA), 6740 E. Hampden Ave., Suite 306, Denver, CO 80224; (800) 777-4472, (303) 756-8115. Web site: *www.hira.org*

INTERNATIONAL HOUSEWARES REPRESENTATIVES ASSOCIATION (IHRA), 175 N. Harbor Drive, Suite 1205, Chicago, IL 60601; (312) 240-0822. Web site: *www.ihra.org*

INTERNATIONAL UNION OF COMMERCIAL AGENTS AND BROKERS, P.O. Box 19352, 1000GJ, Amsterdam, Holland. Has information on contracts and the laws regulating exporting for many countries. Web site: *www.netsource.fr/acx*

MANUFACTURERS' AGENTS FOR THE FOOD SERVICE INDUSTRY (MAFSI), 2402 Mt. Vernon Road, Suite 110, Dunwoody, GA 30338; (770) 698-8994. Web site: *www.mafsi.org*

MANUFACTURERS' AGENTS NATIONAL ASSOCIATION (MANA), P.O. Box 3467, Laguna Hills, CA 92654-3467; (949) 859-4040. MANA is a horizontal organization of reps from all fields. Publishes *Agency Sales* magazine and *The Directory of Manufacturers' Sales Agencies*, an annual publication listing over 22,000 reps. Offers workshops for new agencies. Web site: Web site: *www.manaonline.org*

NORTH AMERICAN INDUSTRIAL REPRESENTATIVES ASSOCIATION (NIRA), 175 N. Harbor Drive, Suite 1205, Chicago, IL 60601, (312) 240-0820. Web site: *www.nira.org*

SAFETY EQUIPMENT MANUFACTURERS' AGENTS ASSOCIATION (SEMAA), 175 N. Harbor Drive, Suite 1205, Chicago, IL 60601; (513) 624-3535. Web site: *www.semaa.org*

SPORTING GOODS AGENTS ASSOCIATION, P.O. Box 998, Morton Grove, IL 60053, (847) 296-3670. Web site: *www.r-sports.com/SGAA*

BOOKS

Making $70,000 a Year as a Self-Employed Manufacturer's Representative, Leigh and Sureleigh Silliphant, Ten Speed Press, 1988. ISBN: 0898152410.

Selling Through Independent Reps, Harold J. Novick, AMACOM, 1994. ISBN: 0814451462. From the point of view of companies wanting to use independent sales reps.

MAGAZINES

Agency Sales. See the MANA listing above.

Representor magazine. See the ERA listing above.

SOFTWARE

MANUFACTURERS' AGENTS COMPUTER SYSTEMS (MACS), 6734 Loan Oak Blvd., Naples, FL 34109; (800) 321-1788. Web site: *www.macsworld.com*

REPS FOR WINDOWS, CBC Software, 540 N.E. Northgate Way, Suite C539, Seattle, WA 98125; (206) 448-3301. Web site: *www.repworld.com*

REP PROFIT MANAGEMENT SYSTEM (RPMS), 10610 Summit, Lenexa, KS 66215, (800) 776-7435, (913) 498-8333. Web site: *www.rpms.com*

WINREP SOFTWARE, 7701 Normandale Road, Suite 103, Minneapolis, MN 55435; (612) 897-0424. Web site: *www.winrep.com*

WEB SITES—DIRECTORIES

ELECTROBASE, COBRO PUBLISHING INC., 2100 196th St. SW, Suite 124, Lynnwood, WA 98036; (800)755-6111, (425) 778-6111. Listing and searching are both free. Web site: *www.electrobase.com*

REPLINK, listing manufacturers, sales agents, representatives, whole-salers and distributors. Listing is free but searching requires member-ship. Web site: *www.replink.com*

THOMAS REGISTER OF MANUFACTURERS, Thomas Publishing Company, 5 Penn Plaza, 9th floor, New York, NY 10119; (800) 222-7900, ext. 200. Available both in print in libraries and as an online database Pro-vides the names and addresses of manufacturers and can be used to find prospects. Web site: *www.thomasregister.com*

THE TRADE INFORMATION CENTER (TIC), operated by the International Trade Administration of the U.S. Department of Commerce, provides referrals and information on all federal government export assistance programs, general export counseling, sources of international market research and trade leads, overseas and domestic trade events and ac-tivities, sources of export financing, advice on export licenses and controls, and country-specific export counseling and assistance for Western Europe, Asia, Western Hemisphere, Africa, and the Near East. Experts from the Center provide help in accessing reports from the Na-tional Trade Data Bank and refer businesses to state and local gov-ernment offices, and private organizations that also provide export assistance. The Center's trade specialists can help you access reports from the computer, including over 200,000 government documents related to export promotion and international markets. Contact the Center by calling (800) 872-8723 or visit it on the Web at *http:// infoserv2.ita.doc.gov/tic.nsf*

Medical Billing

Medical billing services were among the most popular home businesses for the 1990's. But if there were an award for the home business with the largest contrast between people who are successful at it and those who are disappointed in it, medical billing would win hands down. A brief history of the industry explains why there's been such a wide discrepancy and why we still include it as one of the best home businesses for the new century.

Since 1990, federal law has required doctors to submit claims for Medicare reimbursements on behalf of their Medicare patients rather than having the patients file the claims themselves. Many doctors' offices have found meeting this requirement difficult, especially in conjunction with the accompanying movement toward electronic processing of claims. While some physicians set up their own billing services as stand-alone businesses, many others have turned to outside billing services to handle their billing, many of which have been home-based. The medical biller keyboards in the information necessary for billing and sends it by modem directly to Medicare, Medicaid, or intermediary clearinghouses for processing by private insurance companies.

As this trend became apparent, scores of companies began selling medical billing business opportunity packages as an easy way to make money at home, and large numbers of people entered this field after being oversold on it. While medical billing has been and remains a viable home business, it is by no means a get-rich-quick opportunity. This, we think, accounts for why considerable numbers of people have been disappointed with this business. The Federal Trade Commission has brought actions against many of these biz op vendors, although they continue to come and go.

In significant ways, the need for this service is growing, according to Gary Knox, a recognized industry authority and long-time publisher of a newsletter on medical claims. While managed health care decreases the number of claims being filed by physicians who contract with HMOs, opportunities are opening to provide services to a wide range of other health care practitioners in addition to medical doctors. These are:

- Acupuncturists
- Dentists
- Cardiac profusionists
- Chiropractors
- Occupational therapists
- Optometrists
- Osteopaths
- Physical therapists

- Commercial ambulance services
- Dentists
- Home nursing services
- Massage therapists
- Nurse practitioners
- Physician assistants
- Podiatrists
- Psychologists and other counselors
- Respiratory therapists
- Speech therapists

Doctors who have tied their practices into managed care are involved with as many as eight HMOs and PPOs as well as continuing to have fee-for-service patients for whom filing insurance claims is necessary. To keep their overhead costs down and to avoid the costs of installing, maintaining, and upgrading the hardware and software needed for electronic billing, many doctors are choosing to outsource a variety of back-office functions.

Some billing services handle other aspects of the claims process such as invoicing and collecting the 20 percent co-payment that most insurance companies require the patient to pay, keeping track of past due and uncollectible accounts, and taking phone calls from patients about their bills.

Do you have to buy a medical-billing business opportunity package to get into this field? "No," says Gary Knox, "there are other ways to get into this business." You can buy the software you need from the companies that produce it. If you want training, you can acquire that from firms and institutions that offer just that.

Knowledge and Skills You Need to Have

- Medical billing requires that you have a full understanding of the regulations for making health-insurance claims. You must keep up with billing codes and Medicare and Medicaid rules and billing procedures, which change frequently.

- Medical billers must be familiar with both of the diagnostic-and-procedure coding systems used by doctors on the claim forms to show Medicare and private insurance companies what services are being billed and why.

- You must be accurate and conscientious about getting billing done quickly. The doctor's cash flow depends on it. Inaccuracies result in delay and in the case of Medicare claims can result in fines.

- You must be able to use a computer, modem, and specialized software employed in processing claims electronically.

- Medical billers must feel comfortable marketing to and working with health-care providers and their office staff. You need to be convincing and persuasive about how you can manage their claims without errors or glitches. If you handle all of a doctor's billing and patient accounts, you must be especially organized and trustworthy, because the doctor is entrusting his financial security to you.

These requirements are fairly comfortably met by CPAs, nurses, and people with experiences as back office personnel in medical offices or hospitals and Knox reports that people with these backgrounds are coming into this field.

Start-up Costs

	Low	High
Computer with at least a 17" monitor	$ 1,500	$ 3,000
Printer, fax, copier or multi-functional machine	$ 400	$ 800
Medical billing software	$ 600	$ 6,000
Office furniture, especially an ergonomic chair	$ 400	$ 1,000
Initial marketing budget	$ 1,000	$ 3,000
Professional liability insurance	$ 1,000	$ 2,000
Total	$ 4,900	$ 15,800

Advantages

- The work can be challenging and interesting because of the complex nature of health insurance and Medicare rules.

- Once your business is established, processing claims electronically takes little time and can be done at your convenience, day or night.

- It's an at-home business for those wanting to be home to care for family members or for the homebound.

- Once you build a clientele, if you serve them well, they become an ongoing source of business, freeing you from having to market for new clients constantly.

Disadvantages

- Some communities may be saturated with medical-billing companies, so checking out your market is critical before you go into business. One way to do this is to talk with your own doctors and to call other doctors' offices.

- Selling your services can be difficult; getting past the front-office staff to the doctor or office manager takes persistence and good communication skills.

- There is a fair amount to learn if you have no experience in health insurance or medical claims.

- If you handle patient accounts, collecting money from reluctant patients can be emotionally draining.

- Unless you take the necessary precautions, you risk developing repetitive-motion injuries as a result of keyboarding thousands of claims.

Pricing

- The most common way to charge is per claim processed; the range for this is from $1.50 to $3.00 per claim, depending on competition and location. The average medical claim is for $150; the average dental claim, $155.

- Alternatively, charging a flat fee of 7 to 10 percent of claims collected is growing in popularity. This method may also be used in conjunction with one of the other methods for collecting old claims that were previously denied.

- Some medical billing services charge by the hour. Hourly fees range from $15 to $50, with the higher amounts for those services that do full-practice management for doctors.

Potential Earnings

Typical Annual Gross Revenues: $20,000 to $100,000, depending on the number of clients you are able to obtain and the number of claims processed for each client. A minimum of eight to ten doctors or practices is required to be reasonably profitable.

Overhead: low (less than 20 percent).

Best Home Businesses Estimate of Market Potential

In some communities, doctors are not yet aware of independent medical-billing services. In other areas, however, the market is saturated with billing services. Medical-claims work may shrink or grow, however, depending on the future direction of health-care coverage. However, the growing opportunities to serve other professionals keeps medical billing on our list of best home businesses.

Best Ways to Get Business

- Being referred is the best way to reach doctors and other health practitioners. Seek referrals or contacts from your own doctor and other health-care providers you know. You may be able to get help from a pharmaceutical salesperson. Pharmaceutical reps regularly see doctors in their private offices; however, expect to pay a commission for the rep mentioning you and your service.

- Spending most of your time knocking on doors or making marketing calls by phone. Your task is to get past the gatekeeper, getting an appointment for a time when you can make a twenty-minute presentation. Your appeal is to solve problems with billing, collections, and frequently changing office staff.

- Mailing brochures and letters and then following up on mailings with a personal phone call for an appointment to present your services.

- Talking with the marketing directors at local hospitals about participating in one of the monthly meetings they hold for staff doctors. After these meetings, hospitals will often have a mini-trade show so doctors can learn about new products and services.

- Hospitals earnestly market doctors, encouraging them to join their staffs. You can offer the hospital to include in its promotions a discount on your services for new doctors who affiliate with the hospital.

- Contacting the local medical society about offering a discount to its members.

- Having your own Web page with its own domain name with testimonial letters.

- Using state-of-the-art technology like a digital dictation system and offering pickup and delivery.

First Steps

- If you don't have experience in the medical field, begin by taking one of the many community-college or adult-education courses available in medical billing and coding procedures. You can also attend various Medicare-sponsored classes about electronic claims processing for Medicare claims; contact the Medicare office in your area for information about these classes.

- Before purchasing a medical-billing business opportunity or software package, be sure to shop around to compare the features and prices. The resources that follow can be helpful.

- Begin marketing. Your goal is get a base of five to seven doctors.

Where to Turn for Information and Help

ORGANIZATIONS

ELECTRONIC BILLING NETWORK OF AMERICA, INC., 293 Mountain Blvd., Watchung, NJ 07760; (908) 757-1211. Web site: *www.webcircle. com/embn*

NATIONAL ASSOCIATION OF CLAIMS PROCESSING PROFESSIONALS, 1940 E. Thunderbird Road, Suite 100, Phoenix, AZ 85022; (602) 867-9377. Web site: *www.nacpp.org*

NATIONAL ELECTRONIC BILLERS ASSOCIATION (NEBA), 2226-A Westborough Blvd., South San Francisco, CA 94080; (650) 359-4419. Offers a home-study and certification program. Web site: *wwwnebazone. com*

BOOKS

Directory of Medical Management Software, AQC Resources, 175 North Buena Vista, San Jose, CA 95126; (800) 995-8702; (408) 295-4102.

Making Money in a Health Service Business on Your Home-Based PC, Rick Benzel, McGraw-Hill, 1997. Included is a CD-ROM with demonstration versions of popular medical billing software. ISBN: 0079131395. Web site: *www.rickbenzel.com*

Also see the books listed under "Medical Claims Assistance Professional" and "Medical Coding."

NEWSLETTER

AQC Resource Newsletter: Medical Claims Processing, 175 North Buena Vista, San Jose, CA 95126; (800) 995-8702; (408) 295-4102. Newsletter for the billing industry. $59 per year. Covers marketing, hardware and software and industry trends with government and other industries that will affect medical billing.

ONLINE

Medical Billing and Transcription Section of the Working From Home Forum on CompuServe Information Service. (GO WORK on CompuServe.)

COURSES

At-Home Professions, 2001 Lowe Street, Ft. Collins, CO 80525; (800) 359 3455.

Healthcare Office Advisor, 710 East Main Street, Mesa, AZ 85203; (602) 833-2445.

SOFTWARE

Lytec Systems, 7050 Union Park Center, Suite 390, Midvale, UT 84047; (800) 735-1991; (801) 562-1568. Single user: $695; Multiuser: $995. Web site: *www.lytec.com*

Medisoft, 916 East Baseline Road, Suite 225, Mesa, AZ 85204; (800) 333-4747; (408) 892-5120. Ranges in price from $99 to $899. Web site: *www.medisoft.com*

Santiago Data Systems, 208 Legacy Plaza, West Laport, IN 46350; (800) 652-3500; (219) 362-1698. Web site: *www.sdsinteractive.com*

WEB SITES

MEDICARE. Designed by the government for seniors, it has publications available for downloading. Web site: *www.medicare.gov*

TRICARE. Information about Champus coverage for members of the Armed Forces, their dependents, and others for whom the Department of Defense is responsible. Web site: *www.ochampus.mil*

 Medical Coding

When someone sees a doctor or other health-care practitioner, notes are written, dictated, or entered directly into a computer. Afterward, two types of codes are applied: diagnostic and procedural. Though doctors themselves don't apply the codes, both are used in all doctors' offices and hospitals and are required for third-party payments from insurance companies, Medicare and Medicaid. Everything has a code, even breaking an arm in a spacecraft has its own code.

To get prompt, full reimbursement and avoid penalties, all codes must be accurate. Coding for more than the treatment actually provided or "upcoding" can result in up to $50,000 fines from Medicare or having to reimburse insurance companies. Coding for too little or "down-coding" results in losing income or causes delays in payment. In fact, one recent analysis found that due to inaccurate coding, physicians are losing five to fifteen dollars on every claim submitted to third-party payers. The codes are used by medical-billing services as the basis for billing. That's how they place a dollar amount on the treatment. The codes are also what claims-assistance professionals sometimes find missing or in error.

The codes are applied, however, by yet another specialty: the medical coder. Whereas billing is considered a back-office function, coding is a front-office function. It's done by a whole department in a hospital, a specialist on the staff of a clinic or larger medical practice, or the receptionist in a smaller office may get the job of coding. But because of the stakes involved in getting the codes right, coding is increasingly contracted out to be done off-site by medical coders or medical-coding companies.

Codes are not only vital for billing but they are also statistically analyzed to monitor performance, establish benchmarks, make improvement efforts, compare facilities, and make financial decisions. In addition to doctors' offices and hospitals being potential customers, others who use medical codes include medical researchers, government agencies, managed-care organizations, nursing homes, social service agencies, health clinics, emergency clinics, home-health agencies, ambulatory and outpatient surgical centers, and long-term care facilities.

The procedural codes are copyrighted by the American Medical Association, which earns a royalty from their publication in manuals. They are updated quarterly. Diagnostic coding was originally developed by the World Health Organization and is in the public domain.

Knowledge and Skills You Need to Have

- You must understand human anatomy, physiology, and pharmacology to do primary coding.

- You must understand medical terminology so you can use the manuals. Though memorizing the codes is neither necessary nor possible, a coder must be sufficiently familiar with the coding manuals to be able to use them efficiently.

- Coders must be able to decipher handwritten doctor and nurse notes and be willing to call with questions.

- Coders must be zealous about being accurate and attending to detail.

- To understand what companies like to see and will pay for, coders must also understand how the reimbursement process works.

Advantages

- Coders play an important role in the medical field.

- Once established with clients, coding is steady work.

- Coding is an at-home business that can be done any time, day or night.

Disadvantages

- If you have no experience in health insurance or medical claims, you have a great deal to learn.

- To break in, you must sell your skills and prove that you are capable of working dependably at home.

- It requires some convincing to get physicians to realize that a professional coder will increase their revenue, result in fewer rejected claims from insurance companies, and enable them to have better records that will help keep track of and manage their practice.

Start-up Costs	Low	High
Computer	$ 1,000	$ 3,000
Multi-function printer/fax/scanner/copier	$ 150	$ 600
Office furniture, including an ergonomic chair	$ 400	$ 1,000
Initial marketing budget	$ 1,000	$ 5,000
Manuals and dictionary	$ 200	$ 300
Software for coding	$ 500	$ 2,000
Liability insurance	$ 1,000	$ 3,000
Total	$ 4,250	$ 14,900

Pricing

Hourly rates range from $20 to $45, although piece rates apply in writing insurance company appeals, which range from $5 to $10 a case and for hospital work, which is done at a dollar per item. Certification helps coders realize higher earnings.

Potential Earnings

Typical Annual Gross Revenues: $45,000 based on working 1500 hours a year at $30 an hour.

Overhead: low (below 20 percent).

Estimate of What the Market Will Be

Medical coding is part of the health-information technology field, which, according to a 1998 U.S. Department of Labor, Bureau of Labor Statistics report, is one of the twenty fastest growing occupations in the United States.

Outsourcing is projected to grow with the increase in electronic coding. Because the codes are constantly changing and mistakes are costly, expertise is needed to apply and edit them.

Best Ways to Get Business

- Cold-calling by phone or in person to doctors' offices and other health facilities that need coding. Showing samples of what you can do and being able to take tests on the spot.

- Finding out who does the coding for hospitals and clinics in your area and if they are willing to outsource.

- Also see "Best Way to Get Business" under "Medical Billing."

First Steps

- If you don't have a medical background, you will need to get training in medical coding. As an at-home self-study course, this may take about 12 to 18 months.

- Get certified. The American Health Information Management Association offers certification as a Certified Coding Specialist in two specialty areas: hospital coding and physician-based, which focuses on coding for managed care, physician's offices, and multi-specialty clinics.

- Two years of experience is necessary for certification, so to gain experience as a coder, you can either begin working as a subcontractor or obtain your own clients to work with.

Where to Turn for Information and Help

ORGANIZATIONS

AMERICAN HEALTH INFORMATION MANAGEMENT ASSOCIATION (AHIMA), 919 N. Michigan Avenue, Suite 1400, Chicago, IL 60611, (312) 787-2672. Offers courses, certifications, and continuing-education resources. The Society for Clinical Coding is supported by AHIMA. Web site: *www.ahima.org*

COURSES AND TRAINING

AMERICAN HEALTH INFORMATION MANAGEMENT ASSOCIATION. See above.

AT-HOME PROFESSIONS, 2001 Lowe Street, Ft. Collins, CO 80525; (800) 359-3455. Provides comprehensive training in diagnostic and procedural coding, medical terminology, and medical-records handling.

More than 200 colleges and universities nationwide offer accredited programs in health information technology.

BOOKS

Cpt 98: Physicians' Current Procedural Terminology, Celeste G. Kirschner, American Medical Association, 1998. ISBN: 0899708730.

Decoding the Codes: A Comprehensive Guide to Icd, Cpt & Hcpcs Coding Systems, Alex Toth, McGraw-Hill, 1998.

Step-by-Step Medical Coding, Carol J. Buck, Karla R. Lovaasen, Margaret Biblis, W. B. Saunders Co., 1998. ISBN: 0721675360.

MAGAZINES

For The Record, Great Valley Publishing Company, P.O. Box 2224, Valley Forge, PA 19482-2224; (800) 278-4400. Web site: *www.gvpub.com*

Healthcare Informatics, 4530 West 77th Street, Suite 350, Minneapolis, MN 55435; (612) 835-3222. Web site: *www.healthcare-informatics.com*

Health Data Management, 300 South Wacker Drive, Chicago, IL 60606; (312) 913-1334. Web site: *http://hdm.fgray.com*

SOFTWARE

CodeLink and **Claims Editor Professional**, ADP Context, Inc., 241 S. Frontage Road, Suite 41, Burr Ridge, IL 60521; (800) 783-3378, (630) 654-8800. Web site: *www.contextinfo.com*

Code Breaker, Info-X Inc, 157 Veterans Drive, Northvale, NJ 07647; (800) 299-1091; (201) 767-3848. Web site: *www.info-x-inc.com*

Encoder Pro, Medicode, 5225 Wiley Post Way, Suite 500, Salt Lake City, UT 84116; (800) 765-6088. The company is also a source of printed manuals including annual editions of *Medicare Billing Guide* and *Coders' Desk Reference*. Web site: *www.medicode.com*

 Medical Claims Assistance Professional

Who hasn't heard of someone unjustifiably being turned down on a health-insurance claim? Indeed, Susan Dressler of the Alliance for Claims Assistance Professionals says that while Medicare and Medicare supplement claims are cut and dried, when it comes to reimbursements related to a retirement fund, four out of every five claims get denied. But not all turndowns are the result of restrictive insurance company policies, Dressler points out. "If a claim has to go to a mailroom to be taken apart, which frequently happens, mailroom personnel too often separate pertinent portions of the claim, which then don't reach the claims examiner."

It's foul-ups like these that help create a demand for medical claims assistance professionals. Whereas medical billing services work with health care practitioners, medical claims assistance professionals, often called CAPs, are hired by patients. CAPs file and follow-up on claims for people whose doctors don't file private insurance claims. While doctors must file Medicare claims for patients, they're not required to file private insurance company claims. Having a professional who will handle such claims is a great relief for many people who simply don't want to file their own claims as well as those who are too ill or too befuddled by the process to do it themselves.

The effective CAP knows how to spot incorrect amounts or mistakes that cost the patient money. As Dressler points out, "A lot of follow-up needs to be done after a claim is filed. Often claims don't get paid because there's little human intervention." The medical claims assistance professional goes the extra yard to reduce the chance of any foul-ups in reimbursement, and if there is one, to get it corrected.

Once a claim has been filed and processed, CAPs check the "explanation of benefits notice" to verify that the insurer or Medicare has paid the correct amount. Frequent mistakes occur with patient deductibles and stop-loss limits. Also the CAP monitors the co-payment that the patient makes to be sure that the doctor hasn't charged a larger amount than the insurer has established as the allowable fee.

Finally, if an insurance claim is denied, CAPs investigate the reason and try to get the denial overturned. Many claims are denied because of simple mistakes such as improper coding by the doctor's office, duplicated charges, or late filing. Some claims are denied based on a policy restriction, but an effective CAP can negotiate either with the insurance company to pay the claim or with the doctor to reduce the charges.

Claims assistance professionals are quickly coming into prominence. The great need for this service is the main reason for its growth. Literally millions of consumers are recognizing that they desperately need help in understanding the complexities of our Medicare and private health-insurance systems.

As one CAP put it, there are many powerful groups to protect the interests of insurance companies, hospitals, and doctors, but the average person with insurance has nobody to help him or her. Lori Donnelly, who operates a successful claims assistance business in Pennsylvania, points out that this is such a new business that many consumers don't even know about it, so there's a wide-open client base for many new businesses.

Knowledge and Skills You Need to Have

- You need an excellent knowledge of the health-insurance industry: how it works, the terminology, how claims are processed and why they may be denied, what steps a person can take to appeal a rejected claim, and how to appeal.

- You need to have a proclivity for finding mistakes in documents.

- You must be able to read and understand health-insurance policies and know what services they cover and at what rate.

- Good communication and negotiation skills are essential. You may find yourself disputing a denied claim with an insurance company on one side and, on the other, trying to get a doctor to lower a fee. You must be able to represent your clients and get them the maximum benefit possible.

- You must be patient, helpful, and empathic. Most of your clients will be seniors or families in crisis who need someone to listen thoughtfully to their medical and financial problems.

- You need superb organizational skills, because you may have as many as 300 clients, each with many insurance claims at different stages of processing.

- You also need to keep up with Medicare regulations and its changing coverages and payments.

Start-up Costs	Low	High
Computer	$ 1,500	$ 3,000
Printer	$ 300	$ 800
or		
Multi-function printer/fax/scanner/copier	$ 150	$ 600
Office furniture, especially an ergonomic chair	$ 400	$ 1,000
Initial marketing budget	$ 1,000	$ 2,500
Training, manuals	$ 250	$ 1,000
Total	$ 3,600	$ 8,900

Advantages

- This is a "feel-good" work because you are helping people maintain their health and financial well-being by maximizing their health-insurance benefits and avoiding costly mistakes made by doctors and insurance companies.

- The work is interesting, and each case is different. You can meet many kinds of people as your clients.

- Your clients appreciate and respect you. They view you as a professional and will often seek your advice on many insurance matters. CAPs are similar to tax preparers and financial consultants.

Disadvantages

- There is a good deal to learn if you have no experience in health insurance or medical claims.

- Some cases can be complicated with many doctors, clinics, labs, and hospital bills that you must unravel and put in sequence in order to negotiate with an insurance company over payments and benefits.

- You need many clients (several hundred) to build your business. If you don't come to the field with a background in the health-care or a related field that will provide you with referrals, it may take two to three years to build a practice.

- Selling your service can be difficult. Because the profession is relatively unknown, you will have to spend time and money to educate potential clients about your service and the benefits you offer before they sign on with you.

Pricing

CAPs usually charge according to one of three methods, though some use several:

- The most popular method is charging by the hour with fees ranging from $25 to $80 per hour, depending on the locale. For pure advocacy work, some charge a fixed fee. For example, Barbara Melman of Chicago charges $100 for HMO claims.

- Some charge a fixed monthly or annual fee per person or family to process and review all new medical claims they have. Typical fees range from $200 to $400 per person for a year, with a sliding discount for couples and families. This enables you to get paid in advance and makes your income more predictable.

- Some CAPs charge 10 to 15 percent of all benefits paid. This method is usually used when you work on claims that have already been denied or are old (more than two years) and have a high dollar amount.

In addition, some CAPs charge a sign-up or registration fee of $35 to $75 to cover the cost of registering a person and obtaining all his or her insurance information.

Potential Earnings

Typical Annual Gross Revenues: $54,000 based on charging $45.00 an hour and billing 1,200 hours a year; $40,000 based on having 200 clients paying an annual fee of $200 per year.

Overhead: low (20 percent or less).

Best Home Businesses Estimate of Market Potential

The shift to managed care has changed but not reduced the role for CAPs. Barbara Melman, a CAP since 1984 and columnist for the *Chicago Sun-Times*, says, "This work is more needed than ever." Pat Pane, a CAP in North Carolina, finds that "people are lost and confused." Melman goes on to say, "It was easier when people would bring in a pile of bills." In the past, people felt more comfortable having a professional handle the detailed and confusing paperwork of dealing with the system; now people need advocates to deal with the system. Moreover, managed care doesn't cover everyone. HMOs often don't serve people with Medicare. The smaller Medicare supplemental policies require the patient to file the claim in order to collect; people also have difficulty with plans that have a high out-of-pocket outlay before the plan pays.

Best Ways to Get Business

- Notifying family, friends, and others in order to secure a few initial clients. Referrals from satisfied customers and word of mouth will follow from there.

- Getting publicity about what you do. HMOs and insurance companies are unpopular and stories of David facing Goliath make good copy.

- Selected display advertising in community newspapers, local magazines for seniors, assisted-living center newsletters, and bar journals.

- Listing in Yellow Pages under Insurance Claims Processing Services.

- Giving speeches or presentations at senior centers and assisted-living facilities about how to handle claims.

- Networking in professional organizations and making personal contacts. Financial planners, bankers, lawyers, trust officers of banks, accountants, and home health-care agencies are often a source of referrals since they may have clients in need of your services. Susan Dressler tells home health-care agencies who have people going into homes that if the table is filled with bills, that's a sign they may need help with claims.

- Getting to know hospital discharge planners who may be able to refer patients to you.

- Having your own Web page with its own domain name that features testimonial letters, and perhaps some tips you've developed for how to get claims reimbursed.

Related Business

Hospital Bill Auditing

Hospital bills have become about as easy to make sense of as computer code, about as accurate as pre-beta versions of software, and large enough to buy a car, sometimes a luxury one. Several studies have shown that 75 to 90 percent of hospital bills are inaccurate—in the hospitals' favor. People are charged for services and products they never received and double and tripled charged for things they did. Some CAPs offer hospital bill auditing as a service, but some people make it a business unto itself.

A $10,000 hospital bill with a $1,500 error and a 20 percent insurance co-payment costs a consumer $300. A hospital bill auditor will typically take 50 percent of the amount recovered as a fee. Another way CAPs can save money for their customers is to check out if the co-payment was excessive, which can happen when a hospital's agreement with the insurance company gives them a discounted price below what appeared on the client's bill.

In addition to consumers, hospital bill auditors can work with self-insured health plans, insurance companies, managed-care organizations, and professionals and participate in larger recoveries. Physicians' bills and the bills of other health-care providers may also be reviewed. Software and a business opportunity are available.

Software: ProvMatch, Medco, 7011 Grand National Drive, Orlando, FL 32819; (800) 621-7557; (407) 206-8010.

Business opportunity in medical cost recovery: Healthcare Data Management, 60 Chestnut Avenue, Suite 103, Devon, PA 19333; (800) 859-5119; (610)341-8608. This company makes training available. Web site: *www.healthaudit.com*

First Steps

- Check with your state's insurance department to see if your state requires licensing of medical claims assistance professionals. Many states, including Arizona, Connecticut, Florida, New Hampshire, New Mexico, Oregon, Minnesota, and Vermont, require licensing or bonding.

- If you have little background in health insurance or medical claims, take a community-college course or purchase a manual that deals with setting up this business. Focus on learning all the basic regulations about Medicare and private insurance.

- Begin filing claims for family and friends and review the explanation of benefits they receive to learn how to spot errors and process appeals on denied claims.

- An additional path to this business is to work with an established claims professional who needs clerical assistance in exchange for learning the business.

Where to Turn for Information and Help

ORGANIZATION

ALLIANCE OF CLAIMS ASSISTANCE PROFESSIONALS, 731 South Naperville Road, Wheaton, IL 60187, (877) 275-8765; (630) 588-1260. Members are listed on a referral page on the Web site. Web site: *www.claims.org*

BOOKS

Insurance Handbook for the Medical Office, Marilyn Takahashi Fordney, W. B. Saunders Company, 1997. ISBN: 0721669875.

Making Money in a Health Service Business on Your Home-Based PC, Rick Benzel, McGraw-Hill, 1997. Included is a CD-ROM with demonstration versions of popular medical-billing software. ISBN: 0079131395. Web site: *www.rickbenzel.com*

Understanding Health Insurance: A Guide to Professional Billing, JoAnn C. Rowell, Delmar Publishing, 1997. ISBN: 0827384084.

MANUALS AND COURSES

At-Home Professions, 2001 Lowe Street, Ft. Collins, CO 80525; (800) 359-3455.

Claims Security of America, 3926 San Jose Park, P.O. Box 23863, Jacksonville, FL 32241; (800) 400-4066; (904) 733-2525.

Donnelly Benefit Consultants, 2505 Willow Park Road, Suite B, Bethlehem, PA 18020; (610) 974-8447. Web site: *www.donnellybenefits.com*

Institute of Consulting Careers, 2555 Camino del Rio South, #208, San Diego, CA 92108; (619) 295-3545. E-mail: icc98@earthlink.net

SOFTWARE

MICA, Medical Insurance Assistance, 3518 Wrightsville Ave., Wilmington, NC 28430; (910) 397-0021.

INFORMATION ON MEDICARE

Health Care Financing Administration, U.S. Department of Health and Human Services, 7500 Security Boulevard, Baltimore, MD 21444. Web site: *www.hcfa.gov*

Medical Transcription Service

Surer than a cure, notes will be an outcome anytime you and everyone else becomes a patient of a health-care professional or organization. Usually these notes are dictated, whether they're taken about physical examinations, lab tests, X-rays, operations, pathology, or psychological and psychiatric evaluations. Medical transcription is the process by which what's dictated is turned into a medical record. The growing complexity of medicine and the possibility of litigation has made medical transcription into a $50 billion industry. Virtually every institution involved in health care from doctors to imaging centers is keeping patients' records and thus needs transcriptionists.

The first priority for use of medical records is to render continuing patient care, but having a medical transcript on hand quickly is vital to a health-care provider's cash flow, because transcribed reports are being required before third-party payers will pay physicians or hospitals. Transcribed copy also supplies health-care providers with the necessary documentation for review of a patient's history and care and provides legal evidence of patient care and data for research and statistical purposes.

Hospitals and physicians in private practice are contracting out their medical transcription work. In part, this is because there is a shortage of qualified transcriptionists. According to the American Association for Medical Transcription (AAMT), this work is in demand throughout the country, and in some communities the demand is critical. Computer technology is another factor that has made medical transcription one of the best home businesses. As Pat Forbis, associate executive director for professional practices of AAMT, observes, "The technology that took us out of our homes is putting us back into our homes. Today if a transcriptionist has a modem and the proper interfaces, he or she can access hospital digital dictation equipment using the phone lines."

Independent transcriptionists tend either to take overload work from hospitals or to work with physicians in private practice. Transcriptionists doing work for hospitals must know about all specialties of medical practice, while a transcriptionist working for physicians may concentrate on a limited number of medical specialties, such as orthopedics, neurology, or surgery. Transcriptionists can also seek work from agencies, which may treat them either as subcontractors or as employees. Some of these agencies will let you work from home.

Research shows that home-based transcriptionists can be more productive than transcriptionists working in hospitals and offices. A study by the University of Wisconsin Hospital and Clinics found that statistics "consistently showed that what would take six to eight hours to produce in the office would take three to four hours to do at home."

Vicki Fite, founder of Southwest Medical Transcription, says, "Marketing this business is easy when you have a high-quality product. Physicians are quite particular, and rightly so, about the material transcribed. The one thing that can really hurt you in this field is if you put out an inferior product. If you make a bad mistake you can count on losing about five accounts from that one source."

Notes may be dictated onto a tape or directly into a computer using voice recognition software. Voice transcription, once feared as replacing transcriptionists, is proving to be a plus, because it puts a premium on the transcriptionist's editing skills instead of on their typing speed.

Knowledge and Skills You Need to Have

- You need to have the discipline to sit in front of a computer and concentrate throughout the day, with earphones linking you to transcribing equipment.

- You need superior listening skills and to be able to understand diverse accents and dialects.

- You need sufficient coordination to keyboard efficiently and accurately while listening and using a foot pedal for start-stop control of your transcription unit. The faster you transcribe, the more you earn.

- You need to understand medical diagnostic procedures and terminology and spell them accurately. You need to understand anatomy and physiology, clinical medicine, surgery, diagnostic tests, radiology, pathology, pharmacology, and whatever medical specialties you work with.

- An aptitude for language and science and a full command of the English language is necessary, because often you must become a word detective, interpreting how terms are being used. This does not preclude people who speak English as a second language; what matters is having command of English.

Start-up Costs	Low	High
Computer	$ 1,500	$ 3,000
Printer	$ 300	$ 800
or		
Multi-function printer/fax/scanner/copier	$ 150	$ 600
Transcribing unit with conversion capability to different sizes of tapes or foot petals and adapter	$ 200	$ 800
Telephone headset	$ 40	$ 400
Office furniture, especially an ergonomic chair	$ 400	$ 1,000
Reference books (medical-transcription style guide, medical dictionary, drug reference, multiple word books to address various medical specialties)	$ 300	$ 800
Specialized software (medical spelling correction, abbreviation expanders, such as PRD or Smartype, and output counters)	$ 200	$ 400

Professional liability insurance	$ 1,000	$ 3,000
Initial marketing budget	$ 1,000	$ 3,000
Total	**$ 5,090**	**$ 13,800**

Advantages

- For trained and qualified transcriptionists, this is a rapidly expanding field, growing worldwide.

- The medical field can be interesting.

- The work is steady and recession resistant.

- One can be an employee of a hospital and still be home based.

- Medical transcriptionists can transition into teaching, consulting, and doing quality assurance work.

- This is an at-home business for those for whom being at-home is important.

Disadvantages

- This is a difficult field to break into without qualifications. Thus one to two years of training and work in a hospital or clinic setting may be necessary.

- You must be highly self-disciplined and focused while you work. The work demands total concentration. Every distraction creates a slowdown in productivity and possibly quality. Also you're tethered to a pair of headphones hour after hour, day after day.

- The demand for fast turnaround creates time pressure and at least occasionally the need to work nights and weekends.

- Not everyone has an aptitude for science or language, or is temperamentally suited to do this work. One must know about anatomy, physiology, disease processes, pharmacology, medical-legal implications, security (system) and privacy issues. One must know drugs and dosages because doctors under emergency-room conditions make mistakes. If a phrase could be either "age-related" or "AIDS-related," the only clue may be the drugs being used.

- Unless you take necessary precautions, you risk developing repetitive-motion injuries as a result of keyboarding. In fact, occupational risks are high. Seventy percent of medical transcriptionists develop injuries, often to the lower back.

Pricing

Transcription charges may be calculated in several ways:

- The gross number of lines—ten to twenty cents per line (what constitutes a line varies with font size and formatting).

- The number of characters—some customers will not pay for spaces and punctuation marks.

- By the page—$5 to $6 per page—how much is on a page can vary dramatically.

- By minute of dictation—sometimes transcriptionists charge $15 to $40 an hour for physicians who are difficult to understand, particularly those with heavy accents.

- The number of kilobytes (units of 1024 bytes or characters) in an ASCII text file. Arguably this is the most objective means is billing if transcribed text is formatted as ASCII text files and the final transcribed documents are saved without line breaks. See the ASMART Web site for details.

However you charge, it is important to define what is meant by word, line, or page, because definitions vary from transcriptionist to transcriptionist and client to client. Turnaround time and technology requirements also influence pricing; you can charge more for second- and third-shift, twenty-four-hour, or weekend coverage.

Potential Earnings

Typical Annual Gross Revenues: $30,000 to $80,000 for an experienced transcriptionist, based on deriving $15 to $40 an hour. Actual earnings depend on the type of work and the equipment used.

Overhead: low (20 percent or less).

Best Home Businesses Estimate of Market Potential

There never seem to be enough medical transcriptionists. As a result, transcription work from North America is being done in places like Barbados, India, Ireland, the Philippines, and Pakistan. The reason for this is that records are being generated anyplace there is a "patient encounter" of any kind. This is necessary in a litigation-prone society. The conversion to voice technology can reduce some of the physical toll of keyboarding because it causes transcriptionists to become editors, editing what has been dictated and transmitted to a computer monitor.

Increasingly the Internet is being used to transport content, making security, storage, and destruction of records big issues. These issues need to be negotiated as part of contracts to do work for clients. The movement to electronic patient and health records has implications for how transcriptionists do their work but not for the need for edited records.

Best Ways to Get Business

- Directly soliciting work from private physicians' offices, hospital medical-records departments, emergency rooms, clinics, attorneys with medical disability and malpractice cases, pathology offices, medical examiners, coroners, radiology offices/ imaging centers, free surgery centers, urgent-care facilities, infirmaries that are part of companies, occupational-rehabilitation institutes, and government offices dealing with worker's compensation, social worker, and counseling—any place there is a patient encounter.

- Responding to classified ads for medical transcriptionists, proposing to do the work at home.

- Checking out the work with companies that contract out medical transcription work. Because of the Internet, geographical nearness is no longer the factor it was.

- Advertising in the publications of the medical societies to which physicians belong in your community.

- Taking on overload or referral business from other transcriptionists.

- Services that increase your competitiveness include: offering pickup and delivery to those using tapes; same-day service; seven-day-a-week service; a phone-in dictation system; and a twenty-four-hour or second-and-third-shift coverage.

- Using the Web to find the names of doctors in your area. There are specialized directories of physicians. For example, you can use Doctor Directory (*www.doctordirectory.com*) and MedSeek (*www.medseek.com*) to search for doctors by geographical area. The American Medical Association's Physician Search (*www.ama-assn. org/search*), which offers searches by name and specialty offers more information about the doctors you find.

First Steps

If you are making a career change to do medical transcription:

- You can do one or a combination of things to learn medical transcription, including taking a home-study course, a correspondence course, or classroom training in a vocational, technical school, community college, or hospital. Many people also take entry-level positions and obtain on-the-job training. Evaluate educational programs based on the length of the program, whether actual physician voices and dictation are included on practice tapes and how wide a variety of specialties, voices, and accents are covered.

If you already have a medical background and would like to work on your own:

- Get an indication of your current proficiency by taking some of the tests available on the Web, such as Dictated Words Test (*www.transcribeboston.com/test.htm*), Transcription Test (*www.gn-t. com*), and Comprehensive Skills Assessment (*www.meditec.com*).

- If you need a refresher course, consider purchasing practice tapes or purchasing one of the many courses available at a wide of prices and in various formats.

- When you feel ready, seek work from contacts you already have, other transcription services, or solicit clients directly. Also check out national companies that contract with transcriptionists anywhere and use the Internet for transmission of documents. Some of these companies offer online tests, such as those listed above and Web sites such as MT Daily (*www.mtdaily.com*) list them. Such companies get contracts and farm out the work, paying rates often less than those you can get if you find clients in your local area.

Where to Turn for Information and Help

ORGANIZATIONS

AMERICAN ASSOCIATION FOR MEDICAL TRANSCRIPTION (AAMT), 3460 Oakdale Road, Suite M, Modesto, CA 95355; (800) 982-2182. (209) 551-0883. The association offers certification as a Certified Medical Transcriptionist (CMT), holds conferences, and publishes the *Journal of the American Association of Medical Transcription*. It will send a career package if you send a SASE; the same information is available on the Web site. Web site: *www.aamt.org*.

ASSOCIATION FOR THE SENSIBLE METHOD OF ACQUIRING RATES FOR TRANSCRIPTION (ASMART), 7511 W. Arrowhead Avenue, Suite H, Kennewick, WA 99352. Membership is free in this organization that is advocating adopting a common method of billing. E-mail: asmart@transcribing.com.

BOOKS

How to Become a Medical Transcriptionist, Gordon Morton, Medical Language Development, 1998. ISBN: 0966347005.

Medical Keyboarding, Typing, and Transcribing: Techniques and Procedures, Marcy Otis Diehl, Marilyn Takahashi Fordney, W. B. Saunders Company, 1997. ISBN: 0721668585.

The Independent Medical Transcriptionist, Donna Avila-Weil, Mary Glaccum, Rayve Productions, 1998. ISBN: 1877810231.

Making Money in a Health Service Business on Your Home-Based PC, Rick Benzel, McGraw-Hill, 1997. ISBN: 0079131395. Web site: *www.rickbenzel.com*

Medical Transcription Guide: Do's and Don'ts, Marilyn Takahashi Fordney, Marcy Otis Diehl, W. B. Saunders Company, 1999. ISBN: 0721637981.

Saunders Manual of Medical Transcription, Sheila Sloane-Dusseau, Marilyn Fordney, W. B. Saunders Company, 1994. ISBN: 0721636756.

REFERENCE BOOKS

Transcriptionists need an English dictionary, a grammar and style guide, a medical dictionary (*Dorland's Illustrated Medical Dictionary* is highly regarded), a drug index, word books for medical abbreviations, surgery, laboratory, pharmaceuticals, pathology, and your specialty area. Well-regarded publishers of reference books are:

LIPPINCOTT WILLIAMS & WILKINS (LWW), publishers of the Stedman series, 227 East Washington Square, Philadelphia, PA 19106; (800)527-5597; (215) 238-4200. Web site: *www.lww.com*

W. B. SAUNDERS COMPANY, The Curtis Center, 625 Walnut Street, Suite 300, Philadelphia, PA 19106. Web site: *www.wbsaunders.com*

NEWSLETTERS

The Latest Word: The Bimonthly Newsletter for Medical Transcriptionists, W. B. Saunders Company, The Curtis Center, 625 Walnut Street, Suite 300, Philadelphia, PA 19106. Web site: *www.wbsaunders. com*

MT Monthly. See the listing under "home-study courses," Review of Systems School of Medical Transcription.

HOME-STUDY COURSES

There are dozens of courses to choose among. Following are some of the better known ones:

THE ANDREWS SCHOOL, 5601 NW 72nd #160, Oklahoma City, OK 73132; (405) 721-3555. Web site: *www.andrewsschool.com*

AT-HOME PROFESSIONS, 2001 Lowe Street, Ft. Collins, CO 80525; (800) 359-3455. Call for information about cost and amount of time it may take you to complete their course. This home-study course won an award for its instructional design. Web site: *www.at-homeprofessions.com*

CALIFORNIA COLLEGE FOR HEALTH SCIENCES, 222 West 24th Street, National City, CA 91950; (800) 221-7374; (619) 477-4800. Offers an interactive home-study course in medical transcription with college credit. Web site: *www.cchs.edu*

CAREER STEP, 224 South 500 West, Provo, UT 84601; (800) 246-STEP. Offers a typing speed test on its Web site: *www.careerstep.com*

HEALTH PROFESSIONS INSTITUTE, P.O. Box 801, Modesto, CA 95353; (209) 551-2112. Offers the SUM program. Also publishes the journal, *Perspectives on the Medical Transcription Profession*. Web site: *www.hpisum.com*

INSTITUTE OF CONSULTING CAREERS, INC., 2555 Camino del Rio South, #208, San Diego, CA 92108. (619) 295-3545. E-mail: icc98 @earthlink.net

REVIEW OF SYSTEMS SCHOOL OF MEDICAL TRANSCRIPTION, 809 Regency Drive, Kearney, MO 64060, (800) 951-5559, (816) 628-3013. The course features a paid apprentice program. The firm also publishes the *MT Monthly* newsletter. Web site: *www.mtmonthly.com*

WEB SITES

KAMT: George Heymont's Keeping Abreast of Medical Transcription. Articles and speeches by George Heymont, information about online forums and more. Web site: *www.wwma.com/kamt*

MEDWORD: Specializes in hyper links to other medical transcription sites and offers free clip art, and template medical reports. Web site: *www.medword.com*

MT DESK: Surgical resources, focusing on transcription of operative reports, with samples provided; a glossary of surgical terms and more. Web site: *www.mtdesk.com*

MT DAILY: Mary Morken has operated this site since 1995, and it has thousands of pages of information, message boards, and lists of companies that contract out work. Web site: *www.mtdaily.com*

 Meeting and Event Planning

When you attend meetings and events where Murphy's Law reigns supreme, do you feel the impulse to step in and get things going right? Are you the kind of person others turn to do when things need to get done? Well, that's what meeting planners do. They enable the reason people come together to be foremost at any gathering and make sure that all the mechanics of the meeting get taken care of in the background—and stay there. They keep Murphy's Law at bay by planning in advance.

If you relish arranging and designing formal events and happenings and have bang-up organizational and negotiation skills, professional meeting or event planning may be a rewarding career for you. Meeting planners usually work with corporations, associations, and nonprofit groups to plan conferences, sales meetings, conventions, trade shows, fund-raising events, special banquets, hospitality events, shareholder meetings, and other professionally oriented affairs. Because many organizations realize that they can't spare in-house personnel to handle all the details of planning a meeting or event, this work is often outsourced. Event planners focus on planning and coordinating social activities such as parties, weddings, and bar and bat mitzvahs, usually for consumers.

Meeting planners must know about many related fields, from hostelry to catering to travel. For example, planners may be asked to negotiate the best rate for a conference room at a hotel, or to buy catering services for 250 people, or to find a great deal at a golf resort where the company can have its annual retreat. Planners may also need to book speakers, buy flowers and gifts, set up special promotions, arrange for cars and limos, find entertainers, set up tours and activities for visiting guests, or any of a multitude of other things that have to do with a meeting.

The demands for a meeting planner to orchestrate many aspects of an event on schedule without a hitch can make it a high stress job, so today's planners make intelligent use of technology to accomplish their jobs without mistakes. In fact, the most effective meeting planners develop and maintain a large database of vendors and suppliers whom they can trust for flowers, food, entertainment, and other needs. They will also list hundreds of contacts they've made in the hotel and travel industries from whom they can get good rates for hotels and airlines. They may also use project-management software to keep track of the myriad arrangements behind the scenes of an event, thereby avoiding slipups and mistakes.

Ways for meeting and event planners to specialize include:

- A specific industry: such as medical, trade and professional associations (the two largest), education, university (alumni meetings, events for faculty), religious conferences.

- Incentive programs and contests for company executives and salespeople. Such programs have become a popular way for businesses to boost sales, enhance productivity, or improve safety records. In keeping with the trend for companies to downsize staff, they often contract out with specialists to provide the format and techniques for these contests. The winners of many of these contests or promotions often earn a trip or cruise to an exotic location, so the meeting planner must be able to make arrangements and book all the necessary tickets.

- Exposition management. The growth of expositions and trade shows of all kinds around the country has led to many new opportunities for people interested in either sponsoring and running expositions or managing them for other exposition companies. Trade shows run the gamut from small springtime flower and patio expositions to gigantic computer or electronic shows that bring in 150,000 people in three days. Although most exposition organizers are not home based, there are a few companies focused on smaller shows that are operated by home-based owners. In addition, many exposition companies hire floor managers to help run the shows, and these people must often work from their home. For more information on becoming involved in expositions and trade shows, contact the International Association for Exposition Management listed below.

- Party planning covers all kinds of events, such as bar and bat mitzvah celebrations, barbecues, beach parties, birthday parties, brunches and desserts, cocktail receptions, garden parties, children's parties, company parties, clambakes and lobsterfests, fiestas, housewarmings, luaus, Mardi Gras, new-age parties (with astrologers, fortune tellers, palm readers and such), parties with holiday themes, scavenger and treasure hunts, and sports-themed parties. One can also specialize in particular kinds of parties or for particular age groups, like children. Wedding planning and reunion planning are treated as separate profiles in this book. Sometimes parties can be Hollywood-scale events with professional masters of ceremonies (emcees), disk jockeys, bands, and for children, storytellers, mehendi tattoo artists, clowns, magicians, and handlers of animal menageries.

Knowledge and Skills You Need to Have

- You must have excellent organizational skills and an eye for detail.

- You also need a sound business sense, because to get some contracts, you will need to calculate a budget for the client and then stick to it. You also must have the know-how to provide clients return-on-investment reports.

- You must have excellent presentation and communication skills. You will often work with high-level executives planning a conference or convention.

- You must be good at finding high-quality goods and reliable services.

- You must be good at negotiating prices and schedules with vendors (printers, hotels, airlines, florists) and maintain the budget you were given.

- You must be responsible when it comes to handling money and paying bills, as clients often give you access to an account with which you pay printers and hotels.

- You need knowledge of the travel industry almost at the level of a travel agent if you intend to accept jobs for off-site conventions, conferences, retreats, and sales meetings. You may also need to book airline tickets, hotels, amusements, and daily events.

- You should have troubleshooter skills to solve problems, as few meetings proceed without a hitch.

- Creativity is valuable in this business. Companies are looking for new and exciting promotions and conferences beyond the realm of the ordinary. You must be able to come up with exciting and offbeat ideas that you can implement at a reasonable cost.

Start-up Costs	Low	High
Computer	$ 1,500	$ 3,000
Printer	$ 300	$ 800
or		
Multi-function printer/fax/scanner/copier	$ 150	$ 600
Contact and project management software	$ 400	$ 600
Cell phone	$ 75	$ 200
Telephone headset	$ 40	$ 400
Office furniture, especially an ergonomic chair	$ 400	$ 1,000
Reference books and dictionaries	$ 100	$ 300
Initial marketing budget	$ 1,000	$ 5,000

Professional liability insurance	$	450	$	900
Professional dues	$	300	$	800
Total	$ 4,715		$ 13,600

Advantages

- Most events and meetings are important, interesting, and upbeat occasions, and thus an enjoyable experience for a meeting planner.

- Organizing an event that comes off well, pleasing a lot of people, can be both satisfying and exciting.

- You can expect to travel a lot, often staying at exclusive resorts and great hotels for sales meetings and conventions. For some, however, the travel is a disadvantage.

- You can meet interesting people and make valuable contacts in the hotel and travel industries.

- Meeting planners often have flexibility in picking the kinds of events they work on.

Disadvantages

- Dealing with all the demands, expectations, complications, details, and deadlines a meeting planner must handle is stressful.

- You often have to put in long days and work hard when the meeting occurs. Says Pamela Freeman of Meeting Professionals International, "This mean walking in heels twelve hours a day." (Eighty percent of meeting planners are female.)

- Planning events requires near perfectionistic attention to detail. Pamela Freeman warns, "If you forget one detail, it can mess up an entire conference, and people's entire experience can be ruined by just one mistake." And, of course, that means angry clients.

- If you book entertainment, you may be considered an agent and need an agent's license, so check the regulations in your state.

- This field is subject to economic downturns; when the economy is bad, companies and people may cut back on meetings and parties or they may spend less on those they do have.

- Alcohol is available at most functions and it is a significant enough problem that Meeting Professionals International has instituted a 12-step program at its conferences.

Pricing

Meeting planners may charge either by the hour, by the day, or by the project. The average hourly fee is $40 to $60 per hour; daily fees run $400 to $500 per day. Planners handling large events such as conventions or sales conferences may try to charge 15 to 20 percent of the overall projected budget for the entire project. Rates for children's parties of several hours duration are $100 to $250.

Potential Earnings

Typical Annual Gross Revenues: $45,000 to $60,000.

Overhead: low (20 percent or less).

Best Home Businesses Estimate of Market Potential

Savvy companies know that a successful meeting can go a long way to improve customer relations or to motivate their own employees. Instead of exhibiting at trade shows, some companies are using their budgets for unique meetings and events for customers and prospects.

Many firms also use the Internet to reach out, and though the Internet is growing dramatically, the number of meetings is increasing at the same time. Opinions differ whether broader bandwidths, enabling people to simulate meetings from behind their own computers, will provide an adequate substitute for face-to-face meetings. Surveys differ on what people say they want. Our guess is that just as other means of human contact—the railroad, the automobile, the telephone, and e-mail—have resulted in more meetings, so will future advances in technology.

Human beings show no signs of eliminating meetings. Conventions, expositions, meetings, and incentive travel are now the twenty-second largest industry contributor to the Gross Domestic Product. A survey by Day-Timers found workers spend up to one-quarter of each day in meetings. At the same time, the work week is lengthening, contributing to overworked workers who expect that meetings they attend will be worth their time.

These factors, together with the reality that meeting planning is the kind of function that often gets outsourced by corporations, indicate the demand for meeting planners will grow, though Internet-based meetings may create a demand for meeting planners to plan for use of this technology.

Best Ways to Get Business

- Networking. Meeting planners are consummate networkers. They network with caterers and travel agents so they can learn about conferences and conventions that may be taking place. They network in business groups and associations with potential clients. They get business cards from every meeting and enter them into their database.

- Contacting your city's convention and visitors' bureau to learn about various meetings and events going on in your community. Then calling the appropriate organizations or companies involved to determine if they can use professional help.

- Volunteering to plan a charity or civic event as a way to demonstrate your capabilities, make key contacts, and get referrals. Volunteering to plan small parties in the community such as for Girl Scout troops and sports teams can also help make people aware of your services. But be careful about giving away too much time and free advice.

- Joining a professional association of meeting planners. Most of the members of the professional associations are employed by corporations, nonprofit, religious, and fraternal organizations that sponsor meetings and are thus potential clients. These associations also provide training and publishing directories used by people seeking meeting planners.

- Having your own Web page with its own domain name that features testimonial letters and any articles and tip sheets you have written.

First Steps

- Getting started is easier if you a have a public-relations or communications background, or if you have worked for a corporation in a meeting-planning role. If you don't have experience, you can learn about the business by working with a meeting planner in your area or by calling caterers, convention centers, and other businesses involved with meetings to see if you can help out with a few meetings on a trial basis.

- Take on one or more smaller meetings without a fee to get referral sources and testimonial letters as well as experience.

Where to Turn for Information and Help

ORGANIZATIONS

MEETING PROFESSIONALS INTERNATIONAL (MPI), 4455 LBJ Freeway, Suite 1200, Dallas, TX 75244; (972) 702-3000. Twenty-five hundred of the association's 16,000 members are home-based independent meeting planners. MPI offers certification, publishes *Meeting Professional* magazine, and has a membership kit with information for people interested in the career. Membership in the national organization enables participation in local chapters. Web site: *www.mpiweb.org*

INTERNATIONAL ASSOCIATION FOR EXPOSITION MANAGEMENT, P.O. Box 802425, Dallas, TX 75380; (972) 458-8002; fax (972) 458-8119. The association represents the interests of trade show and exposition managers; membership includes convention and visitors bureaus, convention and exhibition halls, hotels and florists—"virtually all economic interests that become involved in some aspect of the show industry." Web site: *www.iaem.org*

THE PROFESSIONAL CONVENTION MANAGEMENT ASSOCIATION, 100 Vestavia Office Park Way, Suite 220, Birmingham, AL 35216; (205) 823-7262; fax-on-demand: (877) 495-7262. A professional association for people who manage conventions and meetings. The association publishes the textbook *Professional Meeting Management* and the journal *Convene;* offers both a self-study course and an interactive online course; Certified Meeting Professional (CMP) and Certified in Exposition Management (CEM) credentials. The Web site has checklists for basic meeting contracts, timelines, pricing formulas and elements to consider when choosing a meeting site. Web site: *www.pcma.org*

BOOKS

Affairs of the Heart: How to Start and Operate a Successful Special Event Planning Service, Nancy DeProspo Gluck, Humbug Associates, Inc., 1993. ISBN: 0963808508. Mostly oriented to wedding planning but contains information on event planning.

The Art of Bartending, Mark Barrett, Berkley Publishing Group, 1997. ISBN: 0425160890.

Atomic Bodyslams to Whiskey Zippers: Cocktails for the 21st Century, Adam Rocke, Surrey Books, 1997. ISBN: 1572840102.

Birthday Parties: Best Party Tips & Ideas, Vicki Lansky (ages 1–8); The Book Peddlers, 1995. ISBN: 0916773361.

Chase's Calendar of Events, Contemporary Books, ISBN: 0809228211. Published annually. More than 12,000 entries of special days, historical events, festivals, and national and local holidays that can be used to tie into promotions and events.

Cocktail Parties for Dummies, Jaymz Bee with Jan Gregor, IDG Books Worldwide. 1997. ISBN: 0764550268.

Entertaining for Dummies, Suzanne Williamson, Linda Smith, IDG Books Worldwide, 1997. ISBN: 0764550276.

Great Games for Great Parties, Andrea Campbell, Sterling Publishing, 1992. ISBN: 0806983191.

The Party: A Guide to Adventurous Entertaining, Sally Quinn, Fireside, 1998, ISBN: 0684849607. The same Sally Quinn from the Washington social scene.

The Penny Whistle™ Party Planner, Meredith Brokaw & Annie Gilbar, Fireside, 1991, ISBN: 0671737929. Mostly for kids but has broader applicability.

Pick A Party: The Big Book of Party Themes & Occasions, Patty Sachs, Meadowbrook Press, 1997. ISBN: 0671521233.

Professional Meeting Management, The Professional Convention Management Association. See above for addresses and Web site.

MAGAZINES

Meeting News, Miller Freeman, Inc., One Penn Plaza, New York, NY 10119, (212) 714-1300. Web site: *www.meetingnews.com*

Successful Meetings, Bill Communications, Inc., 355 Park Avenue, S., New York, NY 10010; (212) 592-6263. Web site: *www.successmtgs.com*

Travel and Leisure, American Express Publishing Corporation, 1120 Avenue of the Americas, 10th Floor., New York, NY 10036-6700; (212) 382-5600. Web site: *www.travelandleisure.com*

WEB SITES

MEETINGPLANNERTIPS.COM. Semi-weekly tips are archived; new ones can be e-mailed. *www.meetingplannertips.com*

EXPOWORLD.NET is a metasite linking to over 500 of the search tools for the events industry. *www.expoworld.net*

EVENTSHOME.COM is a database of events taking place in North America and around the world listed by category and industry. *www.eventshome.com*

CONVENTIONPLANNER.COM a one-stop shopping service for meeting and event planners, convention attendees, and exhibitors throughout the U.S. *www.conventionplanner.com*

EVENTWEB NEWSLETTER is an event industry online newsletter offering Internet marketing tips to meeting, conference, and trade-show producers in North America and worldwide. *www.eventweb.com*

 ## Microfarming

Gardening ranks as one of American's top pastimes, but it can be much more than a hobby. Today you can create a full-time livelihood without owning the acres of land. A backyard, basement, or a small parcel of a few acres is all you need to grow herbs, sprouts, mushrooms, edible flowers, and specialty vegetables and fruits such as squash blossoms, white beets, blue fingerling potatoes, white asparagus, and yellow sugar baby watermelons in urban and suburban areas.

In fact, micro or vest pocket farming is becoming an important part of agriculture in America. Charles Walters, Jr., publisher of *Acres* magazine, says, "The only bright future in agriculture is to get a few acres, grow the product, and be near where the people are." Walters advises, "Find yourself a couple of hundred customers and make yourself a living."

Over the past thirty years, Americans have developed a robust appetite for exotic, healthy, and unusual foods. They are looking for colorful ingredients, new flavorings, organically grown produce, and ethnic specialties. As a result, restaurants, upscale grocery stores, health-food stores, gourmet shops, and mainstream supermarkets are increasingly offering specialty foods to their customers. Meanwhile, the public is seeking out specially grown foods, flowers, herbs, and condiments at nearly 3,000 farmers' markets, as well as at swap meets, produce stands, and country shops.

The sale of organic foods has been doubling every three and a half years since 1990, despite the fact that they are usually priced at a premium. Organics, that is those grown without chemicals, sell for 20 percent to 100 percent more than nonorganically grown foods.

The popularity of farmers' markets has been a particular boon to microfarmers. People growing the perfect lettuce or tomato often can charge more than supermarkets and have buyers standing in line. In fact, unusual items that a supermarket produce buyer won't touch may sell like wildfire at a farmers' market because they are different. Organic farmers in particular are benefiting from farmers' markets because supermarkets don't carry enough organic products to satisfy the one in ten Americans who seek them out. Other popular favorites are:

- Herbs used in cooking, teas, medicines, condiments (e.g., specialty vinegars and mustards), perfumes, and aromatherapy. Also in demand is oat grass to help the digestion of household cats.

- Fresh cut flowers sold as decoration for the home or office. Other flowers, such as carnations, bachelor's buttons, borage, calendula, pansies, and rose petals are cultivated as "edible" flowers; some bars use borage and other blooms in mixed drinks. Some flowers are sold in arrangements purchased by florists, hotels, restaurants, and offices. Dried flowers may also be sold in country shops, gift stores, and catalogues.

- Potpourris of ingredients used in gift baskets, which are also sold via mail-order catalogues and in retail outlets.

- Heirloom varieties of vegetables and fruit, whose seeds are passed down over generations.

Becoming a microfarmer often begins with a desire to get closer to nature and return to a simpler life. It's attracting green-minded people who turn their love of mushrooms or lavender into businesses. Such people seek out a lifestyle quite different from one they may have known earlier as corporate executives in major metropolitan areas. They frequently move to more tranquil places in Vermont, Oregon, Washington, Montana, Idaho, or in the warmer southern states, where they can buy a small parcel of land on which to pursue a love of nature while earning a full-time or part-time living.

Sometimes it's the desire to stay in a rural area that attracts people to specialty growing, away from traditional grain products. Robyn and Robert Rohlfing live in Plymouth, Nebraska, for example, where they are successful organic herb producers. They market most of their herbs locally and have had the same clients for nine years. Robyn calls herself an "oddball farmer" and explains that of all the herbs used in the United States for cooking and medicinal purposes, only 10 percent of them are grown in this country.

Even if you don't live in a temperate climate, you can still be in this business by growing flowers, herbs, or produce in a greenhouse. Greenhouse nurseries have become the sixth largest source of agricultural commodities in the U.S. as the interest in tropical plants, trees (for woody ornamentals), medicinal herbs, and hydroponically grown vegetables (especially tomatoes) has created a year-round demand. Greenhouse expert Ted Taylor also points to the popularity of "juicers" as another reason to be in the greenhouse business, growing organic fruits and vegetables to feed the juicer craze.

Whether your love is garlic or ginger, mushrooms or marigolds, oregano or blood oranges, there's probably a way for you to turn your love of food and flowers into a new career or just some extra cash.

Knowledge and Skills You Need to Have

- You must be willing to learn what you need to do to grow crops of sufficient quality and quantity to make a living. A love of food or for growing things is essential to keep you motivated through the entire learning process. Growing produce, herbs, or flowers is part art and part science, and mistakes are costly.

- You need to have knowledge of plants, growing patterns, plant disease, insects, fertilizers, and many other fields.

- You must be sensitive to market needs and demands, to what people want to eat, what they find appealing, who's buying what, and when they're buying.

- Good bookkeeping skills are important because you need to know what it costs you to grow and how much profit you are making.

- Tenacity and persistence are required as you contact wholesalers, supermarkets, groceries, restaurants, cataloguers, gift-basket stores, herbalists, and other potential customers to sell your goods. Selling produce or flowers is like selling any other product; you must show your customers that your product is of high quality, and you must be amenable to their needs.

Start-up Costs

"If you're already a gardener, your start-up costs will be minimal, but if you're starting from scratch, expect to spend $10,000 or more," advises Lynn Bycznski, author and publisher of the *Growing for Market* newsletter. Here's where your money will go:

• *Land.* How much land you need to earn a full-time living depends on what kind of crops you have, the time your crops need for maturity, and crop rotation. If you don't have zoning problems, or if you outgrow your backyard, find out if your city will rent low-cost land. For example, the Department of Water and Power of the city of Los Angeles rents plots of land. Or you can lease land from a friend or neighbor who has a large yard. Where crops can be in ground year-round, a quarter of an acre can be profitable. In most parts of the country with a winter season, it takes two to ten acres.

• *Supplies.* You will need seed, fertilizers, growing pots, planting boxes, hoses, and other supplies. Expect to invest from $500 to $2,000 at first. Building a small greenhouse requires $500 to $1,000 for a wood structure or $2,000 to $20,000 for a steel structure depending on size and materials used.

• *A vehicle to service your accounts.* You should be able to get a used truck for around $4,000 or a used van for $6,000 to $8,000; new delivery vans cost around $14,000 to $16,000.

• *Setting up your business.* You can set up an administrative office with computer, multifunction printer and fax, a desk, chair, and file cabinet for about $1,500. Business cards and stationery may cost between $100 to $400. While you can make labels and signs yourself by hand or with your computer and a color printer, spending one to two thousand dollars on a professional designer may produce a return many times over in increased sales.

Advantages

- There are many ways to be in this business, offering you a variety of choices if you like farming. You can specialize in flowers or produce, food items or medicines, or do bottling, pickling, drying, body-care products, aromatic pillows, or just about anything you can think of that uses herbs, flowers, or produce.

- This business provides the freedom to live an alternative lifestyle and still be close to cities.

- It provides the opportunity to experience a connectedness to the land through growing living things.

- It's a way to express an environmental consciousness while earning one's living.

- This is a business you can start part-time in your backyard or basement.

- You can meet many other people who enjoy what you enjoy through marketing your goods.

Disadvantages

- Your livelihood is vulnerable to the weather and the seasons. After all, farming is the occupation that gave rise to the saying "feast or famine." If you live in a colder clime, your profits may be too seasonal for a full-time income.

- The popularity of growing particular "in" crops may result in heavy competition. In some cases, large agribusiness is now entering niche markets, pushing out smaller growers.

- Land near cities can be expensive, and it can be difficult to make a profit. Dr. Booker T. Watley, Tuskagee University plant geneticist and agronomist, says that a farm needs to be within forty miles of an urban center with a population of 50,000 or more, reachable on a hard-surface road.

- Growing crops is hard, dirty, physically uncomfortable work.

- Within cities, if your property is not zoned to allow agricultural use, you may have problems with zoning officials.

Pricing

Here are two rules of thumb:

- Set the retail price at four times the cost of what a crop costs you to grow.

- "Price at the *harvest* rate," advises Lynn Bycznski. "That is how much you can harvest in an hour. At $50.00 an hour, you can make money."

Prices for produce, flowers, and herbs are greatly influenced by the market, meaning that you have little control over your price if your costs are higher than expected. However, you can do something to increase your earnings by implementing the advice of Richard Alan Miller, an author and leading consultant on growing herbs. He advises, "Add value before what you grow leaves the farm." For example, you can wash, cut up, and mix varieties of lettuce and charge a premium price for the resulting salad; you can process basil for pesto sauce; you can arrange flowers and sell them as bouquets; you can package fruits in gift baskets.

Potential Earnings

Typical Gross Revenues:

- $7,000 to $12,000 an acre for specialty produce sold to consumers and upscale restaurants.

- $10,000 to $12,000 an acre for herbs and spices.

- $15,000 to $30,000 an acre for cut flowers.

- Greenhouses: According to greenhouse expert Ted Taylor, a 30-by-96-foot greenhouse holding 10,000 six-inch pots can produce $2.50 profit per pot, or about $20,000 in ninety days.

- Farmers' Markets: Grower sales average $1,000 a day, according to a reader survey by *Growing for Market* newsletter. In smaller markets, sales range from $200 to $700, but in New York's Green Market, sales can reach $3,000 a day. Expect to pay between $25 and $75 a day for a space at a farmer's market, though some markets are now charging a percentage of gross receipts.

Overhead: moderate (25 to 60 percent).

Best Home Businesses Estimate of Market Potential

The desire for fresh, home-grown food, particularly organically grown food is growing and should continue to drive the demand for years to come. Helping this along is the consolidation of the supermarket industry into a handful of national chains selling things like irradiated food with a longer shelf life, prompting a percentage of the population to seek out food sources that are more personal and individualistic.

Best Ways to Get Business

- Growing a high-quality product and better yet a product that isn't available from others locally so you can have a market to yourself. As Richard Alan Miller says, "Instead of growing basil, grow Thai basil."

- Selling directly to consumers at full retail price at farmers' markets and swap meets.

- Selling directly to consumers through Subscription or Community Supported Agriculture. Sometimes eight farmers will band together to serve 350 to 700 member households. Customers pick up their food at a drop point, such as a natural food store. Stores are apt to provide this service because of the traffic it brings them.

- In a well-traveled area, you can sell products at a farm stand at full price. You need to have an attractive sign that will encourage people to stop.

- Selling directly to local restaurants, groceries, health-food stores, and exporters. Chefs may shape their menus based on unusual foods you grow. Schools, colleges, and universities are also good markets. Bring samples of your product with you when you initiate a relationship. It also helps if you make a video of your facilities and growing methods.

- If your land is located near a well-traveled roadway, charge people to harvest their own food for a 30 percent to 40 percent discount. People will come for the experience and freshness.

First Steps

1. Check your zoning to be sure your property can be used for growing food.

2. Visit farmers' markets in your area to see which products are most popular and in short supply. Talk with the market managers about what sells and what doesn't.

3. Acquire information. Here are some resources to draw upon:

   - Your state extension service. Request a meeting with a horticulturist and ask about what will grow in your area and the best ways to grow it. Ask about relevent meetings and resources in your area.

   - If you are near an agricultural university, check out what it offers for very small farms.

   - Call ATTRA, (800) 346-9140, or visit the Web site at *www.attra.org*. The Federal Information Service for small farmers offers information packets by crop.

   - Pertinent workshops listed on bulletin boards of food cooperatives.

   - Read everything you can.

   - Before deciding on what you will grow, check out federal, state, and local regulations. If you have decided to process or can what you grow, you may need special permits. Some items such as flowers may be subject to sales taxes. If you use a scale, it will need to be certified by the local agency that regulates weights and measures.

   - Begin experimenting by growing a crop in your own garden for products that will serve untapped or underserved markets.

   - Decide whether you're going to grow organically or nonorganically and whether you are going to become a commercial producer selling to food stores or a quality producer selling to upscale restaurants or directly to the public at farmers' markets.

- If you're planning to grow organically, join the organization in your state that certifies organic growers. To find out what organization does this, call the Organic Trade Association at (413) 774-7511.

- Do a feasibility study with a small crop the first year on two acres of land, if possible.

Where to Turn for Information and Help

ORGANIZATIONS

Contact the horticultural and agricultural departments of universities and the state or county agricultural extension offices in your area.

AMERICAN NURSERY AND LANDSCAPE ASSOCIATION, 1250 I Street NW #500, Washington, DC 20005; (202) 789-2900. Web site: *www.anla.org*

ASSOCIATION OF SPECIALTY CUT FLOWERS GROWERS, MPO Box 268, Oberlin, OH 44074; (440) 774-2887. For small-scale growers of flowers. Web site: *www.ascfg.org*

HERB GROWING & MARKETING NETWORK, P.O. Box 245, Silver Spring, PA 17575; (717) 393-3295. Holds conferences, publishes a journal, and offers an information packet on getting started. Web site: *www.herbworld.com*

INTERNATIONAL HERB ASSOCIATION, P.O. Box 206, Mechanicsburg, PA 17055; (717) 697-1500. Providing education and service.

NORTH AMERICAN FARMER DIRECT MARKETING ASSOCIATION, 62 White Loaf Road, Southampton, MA 01073; (413) 529-0386. E-mail: nafdma@map.com

The U.S. Department of Agriculture lists farmers' markets at *www.ams. usda.gov/farmersmarkets*

NEWSLETTERS

The growth of newsletters in this field has been tremendous over the past few years. This is a partial list, and you can learn about others by reading some of the books listed below.

Acres USA, 2617 Edenborn Ave #C, Metairie, LA 70002-7015; (504) 889-2100.

Growing for Market, Fairplain Publications, P.O. Box 3747, Lawrence, KS 66046; (800) 307-8949. An excellent monthly for small, primarily organic growers of flowers and herbs. Operates a mail-order bookstore.

Organic Gardening, Rodale Publishing, 33 East Minor Street, Emmaus, PA 18098; (800) 666-2206; (610) 967-5171.

National Wholesale Produce, Herb and Flowers Market News Report, U.S. Department of Agriculture, available from Fruit and Vegetable Market News, 230 South Dearborn St., #512, Chicago, IL 60604; (312) 353-0111. Web: *www.ams.usda.gov*

BOOKS

Flowers for Sale: Growing and Marketing Cut Flowers, Backyard to Small Acreage, Lee Sturdivant, San Juan Naturals, 1994. ISBN: 0962163511.

From Kitchen to Market, Stephen F. Hall, Upstart Press, 1996. ISBN: 1574100254.

Growing Gourmet and Medicinal Mushrooms, Paul Stamets, Ten Speed Press, 1994; (800) 841-2665. ISBN: 0898156084.

Growing Your Herb Business, Deborah Balmuth, Storey Books, 1994. ISBN: 0882666126.

Herbs for Sale, Lee Sturdivant, San Juan Naturals, 745 Larsen St. #A, Friday Harbor, WA 98250; (360)378-2648. ISBN: 096216352X.

Herbs You Can Master, Carol R. Peterson, Mt. Garden Publishing Co., 1994. ISBN: 0963962000.

Knott's Handbook for Vegetable Growers, O. A. Lorentz and D. N. Maynard, John Wiley and Sons, 1997. ISBN: 0471131512.

Native Plants of Commercial Importance, Richard Alan Miller, Oak, Inc., 493 Coutant Lane, Grants Pass, OR 97527; (541) 476-5588. Oak, Inc., also offers technical reports and farm plans.

The Flower Farmer: An Organic Growers Guide to Raising and Selling Cut Flowers, Lynn Bycznski, Chelsea Green Publishing, 1997. ISBN: 0930031946.

Marketing Your Produce, Lynn Bycznski. Available from Growing for Market, newsletter section above.

The New Organic Grower, Eliot Coleman, Chelsea Green Publishing, 1995. ISBN: 093003175X.

Secrets to a Successful Greenhouse Business, T. M. Taylor, Greenearth Pub. Co.; 1998. ISBN: 0962867802.

New Media/Multimedia Production

Probably everyone agrees we live in age of new media. But what people mean by *new media* varies. Some say it means any new type of information as well as all new ways of communicating it. Others are more specific. Ted Artz, who has done animation and special effects at Amalgamation House of Philadelphia for 15 years, says, "New media means using digital tool sets to create content. Images created for one medium may be ported to another. Even audio treatments are part of new media." Using this definition, new media right now includes digital videodiscs (DVD), CD-ROM, CD-ROM/online hybrids, Internet-based applications and products, DV video (which unlike analog video does not degrade over time), and digital video broadcasts.

In past editions of this book, we called this field "multimedia." Now we prefer "new media" not just because the term has become popular, but because we want to emphasize that newness is at the heart of this field. New tools are being developed and released continuously—without pause. Thus, this is not a field for those who want to settle into a sane and familiar pace. In this field, you'll be flying to keep your skills and your tools up with the latest technology and its applications.

The good news is that spectacular new media can easily be produced from a home office. It no longer requires large studios with hugh banks of equipment. You can work from home in new media in any combination of the following ways:

- You can produce new media for businesses, educational institutions, and other clients.

- You can develop tangible products such as games, handling your own distribution just as any other publisher does with e-commerce as a key part of your marketing. Disintermediation, that is eliminating the "middleman" and going directly to the customer, is the way of the times.

- You can develop your own product but use another publisher to market it for you, just as if you were an author and got a book publisher to publish your book in exchange for a royalty.

- You can become a new-media publisher, buying ideas from other people and outsourcing as much of the production and distribution as you want or need.

Whichever path you choose, new media is becoming a growing part of our lives. In business, it's estimated that 95 percent of content is generated digitally now; only 5 percent of things such as storyboards and illustrations are done by hand. Employee instruction and training is shifting from the classroom to the computer. Conferences, conventions, and product demonstrations now rely heavily on new media. Educators are using it in the classroom to help children learn. Families are buying new media for recreation and fun in the form of games and stories. Reference materials such as encyclopedias that used to be printed are now available in new media. New media makes cultural and geographic information available interactively to tourists in hotels and airports.

Work includes media includes animation, special effects, broadcast graphics for commercials, video and film, kiosk and Web page design, corporate logos, audio production, modeling, computer graphics, and package design.

Knowledge and Skills You Need to Have

- To do well in this business, you need to enjoy using technology to communicate in an artistic and entertaining way. Helpful backgrounds for working in new media or at least to reduce the learning curve include experience with media production, video, audio, video postproduction, camera work, or lighting.

- Creating training materials, education products, or entertainment requires artistry and a good visual and graphic-design sense combined with creativity.

- While simple presentations can be done without programming, some coding is required for animation, Web development, and interactive program content. If you cannot do this yourself, you will need to hire a programmer.

- You must be willing to stay continuously up-to-date. Ted Artz says, "You get on a wave and ride it. You must pay attention while staying immersed or someone will pass you by on the next wave. Clients hear buzzwords or learn about a new software package and you need to know about it. The waves change quickly."

- It helps not only to be sensitive to change that is occurring but also to be future-oriented enough to visualize how what you create will be used in years to come.

- Savvy about using other people's material is critical. As Dan Wodaski, who wrote *Multimedia Madness*, points out, virtually everything is owned by someone else, so you will need to obtain permissions to reuse materials in your product. Sometimes you can bargain with a photographer, for example, to use his or her photos for free if you insert a credit line. Ted Artz adds, "There's plenty of content available for low cost as shareware. But then there's ethics and there's criminality. All assets are copyrighted. Just taking is basically stealing. It starts to take food out of my mouth."

Start-up Costs	Low	High
Computer	$ 2,500	$ 3,000
Additional hardware (internal and external), such as a large monitor, high speed video and audio cards, good-quality speakers; and software from producers such as Adobe, Autodesk, Corel, and Macromedia	$ 1,000	$ 7,500
Printer	$ 300	$ 800
or		
Multi-function printer/fax/scanner/copier	$ 150	$ 600
Office furniture, especially an ergonomic chair	$ 400	$ 1,000
Initial marketing budget	$ 2,000	$ 7,500
Total	$ 6,050	$ 20,000

Advantages

- If you are someone with an appetite for change, as long as new media merits being called new, you will be continually stimulated, which for the right people means fun and excitement.

- You find new tools and ways of expressing your creativity.

- There's nothing static in this field in which there is continuing demand for services.

- As technology changes, you will continue to be in the forefront of new ideas and ways of thinking and doing things.

Disadvantages

- The learning curve is six months to a year if you don't have a background in this area.

- If you're purely technically oriented, marketing your services can be a challenge.

- Upgrading software and hardware is a continuing expense and a drag on your income.

Pricing

Hourly rates for new-media services vary tremendously. Technicians may earn from $25 to $35 per hour at first, $45 within a year, and $60 an hour within two years. High-level consultants, programmers, designers, and concept people can earn $80 to $100 per hour.

Potential Earnings

Typical Annual Gross Revenues: $25,000 to $60,000 based on billing 1,000 hours. If you create a product that sells 100,000 copies and you earn $3 to $15 royalty per copy, you can obviously do quite well.

Overhead: moderate to high (20 to 40 percent) because of ongoing need to purchase and upgrade equipment and software.

Best Home Businesses Estimate of Market Potential

Despite the emergence of the Web, changing almost every business profiled in this book in one or more significant ways, its future may not be as important as it now seems. Interactive television may take most people from behind PCs to interacting with screens on the wall. People who master and make their livelihoods in new media may be among those best positioned to benefit from such technology, making new media one of the best home businesses for the new century.

Best Ways to Get Business

- Having your own Web site as a way of introducing your work. With the coming of greater bandwidth, you will be better able to show representative samples of your work.

- Calling on ad agencies, armed with a portfolio of your work.

- Developing relationships with "gatekeepers"—individuals able to refer you business.

- Teaming up with compatible independent firms to engage a rep.

- Advertising in media and directories seen by the customers you are targeting, i.e., ad agencies or corporations for their training or presentation needs.

- Participating in trade and industry groups and volunteering to provide your skills for organizational projects that showcase your capabilities.

- Approaching and showing your work to businesses like wallpaper stores, real estate offices, and others who can use what you produce in their stores for product explanations and demos.

- If you are going to publish your own content, you need to deal with how you will get it distributed—in tangible form or electronically. This also means that you may need to associate with animators, photographers, sound experts, designers, and video producers to help you produce your idea.

First Steps

- Learn all you can by reading, on the Web, in user groups and newsgroups, attending workshops and new-media events and trade shows. Search for individuals with whom you can consult about issues you cannot find the answers for. Consider interning or temping at an ad agency or design studio.

- Tom Bunzel, author of *Digital Video on the PC*, advises that someone with an art degree or talent, learn to work "digitally" on the computer and to use a drawing tablet. He advocates studying successful new media projects, "getting under the hood to look at how it was accomplished."

- Buy software or get demo versions. Ted Artz advises, "Lock the doors and learn the software. The way software is built with all the extraneous bells and whistles, you use 90 percent of the capabilities 10 percent of the time and 10 percent of the capabilities 90 percent of the time. Experiment with individual sets of tools."

- "Master one or two skills—authoring, asset manipulation (retouching) or animation," urges Tom Bunzel. "Choose hardware to accommodate the software you use."

- Create a portfolio to show what you can do and your individual style.

Where to Turn for Information and Help

ORGANIZATION

ASSOCIATION OF INTERNET PROFESSIONALS, INC., 9200 Sunset Boulevard, Suite 710, Los Angeles, CA 90069; (800) JOIN AIP; (310) 724-6636. Chapters throughout the world. Web site: *www.association.org/start/ie40.asp*

TRAINING

Universities offer degree programs in new media, multimedia, and instructional design. Community colleges and trade schools offer relevant classroom courses in specialized areas. However, many who have entered this field have learned on their own or learned as part of a job. Some sources for learning at home are:

FIRST LIGHT VIDEO PRODUCTIONS, 2321 Abbott Kinney Blvd., Venice, CA 90291; (800) 777-1576. This company has a thirty-two-page catalogue filled with videotape-based training courses about video production and some CD-ROM-based courses. Web site: *tmwmedia.com*

MCGRAW-HILL'S NRI SCHOOLS offer a home-study course in multimedia programming. McGraw-Hill Continuing Education Center, 4401 Connecticut Avenue, N.W., Washington, DC 20008, (202) 244-1600. Web site: *www.mhcec.com*

BOOKS

Designing Interactive Digital Media, Nicholas V. Iuppa, Focal Press, 1998. ISBN: 024080287X.

Designing Multimedia: A Visual Guide to Multimedia and Online Graphic Design, Lisa Lopuck, 1996. Peachpit Press, ISBN: 0201883988.

Digital Video on the PC, Tom Bunzel, Micro Publishing Press, 1997. ISBN: 0941845214.

Electronic Publishing Construction Kit: Creating Multimedia for Disk, CD-Rom, and the Internet, Scott Johnson, Wiley, 1996. ISBN: 0471128546.

Getting Started in Multimedia Design, Gary Olsen, North Light Books, 1997. ISBN: 089134716X.

Making Money with Multimedia, Caryn Mladen and David Rosen, Addison-Wesley, 1994. ISBN: 0201822830.

Multimedia: Making It Work, Tay Vaughan, Osborne McGraw-Hill, 1998. ISBN: 0078825520.

MAGAZINES

AV Video and Multimedia Producer, Knowledge Industry Publications, Inc., 1400 Fashion Island Blvd., San Mateo, CA 94404; (650)524-1750 or 701 Westchester Ave #109W, White Plains, NY 10604; (914)328-9157. Free for qualified video, multimedia, film and television producers. Paid subscriptions also available. Current and archived issues on the Web site. Web site: *www.kipinet.com/av_mmp*

EMedia Professional, Online Inc., 213 Danbury Road, Wilton, CT 06897-4007; (800) 248-8466. Web site has selected articles from the current and past issues. Web site: *www.emediapro.net*

Inside Technology Training, Ziff-Davis Inc, 10 Presidents Landing, Medford, MA 02155; (888) 950-4302, (781) 393-3500. Web site has searchable archives of past issues. Web site: *www.ittrain.com/ittrain*

New Media, HyperMedia Corporation, 901 Marine Island Boulevard, Suite 365, San Mateo, CA 94404; (650) 573-5170. Web site: *www.newmedia.com*

Macromedia User Journal, 1503 Johnson Ferry Road, Suite 100, Marietta, GA 30062; (800) 788-1900; (770) 565-1763. Back issues are archived on the site. Links to software sites. Web site: *www. pinpub.com/muj*

Wired, Wired Ventures, Inc., 520 3rd Street, 4th Floor, San Francisco, CA 94107; (800) 769-4733; (415) 276-5000. Web site has a browser-testing service and tutorials. Web site: *www.wired.com*

NEWSLETTER

Marketing with Technology News, 370 Central Park West #210, New York, NY 10025; (212) 222-1713. E-mail: sarah@mwt.com

THE INTERNET

Web sites, newsgroups, and listservs abound on this topic and because of the rapidity of change are among the best resources. Some Web sites are organized around products, offering demos, manuals, and tutorials. For example, Macromedia supports its *Authorware, Director, Dreamweaver, Fireworks, Flash, FreeHand, Generator*, and *Shockwave* programs at *www.macromedia.com*. Autodesk supports *Kinetics* at *www.ktx.com*. The magazines listed above have Web sites with significant depth and some have message boards. You can also communicate with users in newsgroups, such as alt.multimedia, altnet.3dstudio, altnet.wavefront, comp.multimedia.multimedia., directoralt.binaries.multimedia, and misc. education.multimedia. A Web site of note to Canadians is MultiMediator (*www.multimediator.com*), which links to Canadian multimedia resources.

 Newsletter Publishing

Chances are each week you receive several newsletters in your mailbox, through e-mail or via your fax. In part, that's because it's never been easier to produce and deliver newsletters and in part, it's because newsletters are more apt to get people's attention than most forms of direct mail.

While the distinction between newsletters, magazines, and newspapers sometimes gets blurry, a newsletter is usually considered to be a publication not available on newsstands that is one to eight pages in length in a 8½ by 11 format. Outside the United States, a tabloid size is more typical.

You probably receive one or more of the 5,000 to 10,000 subscription newsletters plus your share of the hundreds of thousands of newsletters, bulletins, and similar serial publications sent to members of trade and professional associations, employees, and consumers. Employers use them for employee communication. Companies use them both to attract and retain customers. Public relations firms use them to get the word out about their clients, as do hosts of other public and private entities like health plans, homeowners' associations, and religious congregations.

Some publishers offer their readers the choice of how they'd like their newsletter delivered. Fax and e-mail newsletters offer big advantages in terms of cost and production and delivery time. Print newsletters, however, have the advantage of being something readers can carry with them and pass around. Faxed newsletters combine immediacy with portability and can be quite profitable. E-mail-only newsletters usually still fall in supposed-to-be free category, although there are some instances of print newsletter publishers converting their readers to e-mail delivery.

Some publishers are reluctant to jump to electronic delivery, realizing that once a newsletter is online, they may lose control of their copyright and may have more trouble getting paid. Thus some newsletter publishers offer only teasers or articles from past issues online.

Whatever delivery system you choose, there are three primary ways to make money publishing newsletters.

Subscription Newsletters

Earnings from a subscription newsletter come in whole or part from subscriptions paid by the readers. To boost income, some subscriptions newsletters (usually consumer-oriented ones) sell advertising, too, and increasingly also sell collateral or ancillary products and services.

The subscription newsletter publisher needs to select a potential readership that has a keen and long-term interest in a topic and is motivated and able to pay for information and analysis they can't easily obtain elsewhere. Readership needs to be narrow enough to have some special unfulfilled need yet large enough to support the publication. Discovering and satisfying the information needs of their niche is the primary mission for a subscription newsletter publisher. Nancy Mills, for example, publishes *Travelin' Woman*, a know-before-you-go newsletter for women traveling alone. Debuting in March 1994 on a $400 budget, *Travelin' Woman* attracted 500 subscribers in six months from the roughly 55 million women who travel each year. Because it was the first newsletter for these knowledge-thirsty consumers, it was written about in 80 national and international publications, generating more than 1,000 inquiries. Therefore, a rule of thumb for creating a newsletter success is to "find a niche and scratch it."

According to the Newsletter Publishers Association, the most popular and growing newsletters are related to business, communication, health, investment, international, legal, and technology topics. Niches within these broad categories might be targeted to a particular industry or a subfield within an industry, i.e., information for sufferers of a rare disease and their families; business developments in an emerging nation or group of nations; tracking an emerging field or technology such as molecular genetics; or a particular profession's use of the Internet.

Sometimes an everyday item can also be the focus of a newsletter. For example, Wendy Ballard created *Dog-Gone*, a newsletter about fun places to go and cool stuff to do with your dog. Seena Sharp of Sharp Information Research discovered several years ago there was no publication specifically about earrings and the earring market. Jewelry publications didn't provide them to any degree, yet there's an entire industry that could use the latest updates on this field.

Cheryl Woodard, author and consultant, advises, "Pick a niche whose members you already have connections with because these connections can be used in finding other subscribers. For instance, a friend started a magazine for needleworkers. It was a hobby she had been engaged in for 20 years, so she already knew all the suppliers and publishers. She also knew about a trade mailing list."

Advertising-Supported Newsletters

Whereas subscription newsletters bring in all or a substantial portion of their income from subscriber fees, advertising supported newsletters are distributed free of charge to readers the advertisers or sponsor wants to reach. Louise-Diana, for example, publishes an alternative health newsletter for women that is entirely supported through advertisers who offer holistic products and services of interest to women. This model is particularly popular for e-mail newsletters. Neighborhood newsletters are also advertiser supported and free to residents.

The goal is to line up a sufficient number of advertisers or a single sponsor to underwrite the publishing costs and the publisher's fee for writing and distributing the newsletter. This means the publisher must build up a large-enough reader list or distribution system that the publication becomes attractive to sponsors and advertisers.

Contracting to Produce Newsletters for Others

Many companies, professionals, and organizations could benefit from having a newsletter but don't have the time, resources or know how to publish their own newsletter in house, so increasingly, newsletter production is being contracted out to someone who will do it for them. Some newsletter publishers specialize in producing newsletters for a particular industry, such as banking, or a single profession, such as accounting or realty. Others focus on trade and professional associations and organizations, including churches, clubs, charities, and homeowners associations that typically need to provide newsletters to their members.

Some clients want newsletters for internal communications with employees, members, or patrons. The same or other clients want them for external communication to further marketing, customer retention or public relations objectives. The newsletter publisher may write and produce the entire newsletter for clients, including contracting with a printer and maintaining the mailing list for the distribution of the newsletter. Or they may do whatever portions of the process a client needs to supplement in-house efforts. Newsletter producers usually bill clients either a flat fee per issue or charge based on an hourly rate, but either way, each of the services performed should be priced separately. Some publishers add to their revenue by offering to provide photographs for the newsletters they publish.

Creating Newsletters Used By Multiple Clients

You can write a standard monthly newsletter usable by the same type of client, such as accountants, dentists, environmental consultants, insurance agents, or veterinarians. Because the first page is customized to have a message from the client and a photograph plus any other custom touches he or she may wish, such newsletters appear to have been produced by professionals themselves. Professionals and small companies who don't have the time, staff, or budget to produce their own newsletters are candidates for using a newsletter service.

A variation of this is to offer content for newsletters on the Internet.

For example, the Web site The Newsletter Source (*www.microsmithinc.com/main.htm*) offers thousands of articles, tips, cartoons, and quotes that it describes as newsletter stuffers for the deadline challenged. Some of these are free; others can be purchased one at a time or with an electronic subscription. Their target markets are training companies, MIS departments, corporate-training departments, and human-resource departments.

Knowledge and Skills You Need to Have

- You need to be an excellent writer, with an ability to compose succinct, informative items that meet the needs of your target audience. Newsletter subscribers don't want to wade through lengthy articles to find the information they're seeking.

- You must have a clear sense of the types of information that will interest your audience and satisfy them that they are receiving something of value. How you present information also needs a freshness that doesn't seem like it could be found anywhere.

- You need some talent for design in order to create a newsletter that is visually appealing. It helps if you are familiar with typefaces, layout, graphics, and the printing industry generally.

- Since you will be managing a business that depends on people as readers and possibly as information sources, relationship skills are necessary.

Start-up Costs	Low	High
Computer	$ 1,500	$ 3,000
Printer	$ 300	$ 800
Desktop scanner	$ 100	$ 500
Additional software, perhaps including desktop publishing, photo-imaging and mailing list, and clip art	$ 300	$ 1,000
Photocopier	$ 300	$ 800
Office furniture, especially an ergonomic chair	$ 400	$ 1,000
Initial marketing cost*	$ 1,000	$?
Total	$ 3,900	$ 7,100+

*It may be well to think of initial marketing costs as what it takes to confirm whether you have a viable newsletter concept. You can expect it to take years for a newsletter to turn a profit. While your initial marketing costs can be kept down by faxing free sample issues along with a way to respond, more typically newsletters are sold using direct mail. The mailer may be a package with a description and offer or a sample first issue along with an order form and reply envelope. If it costs you seventy-five cents per piece of delivered mail and it takes 100 pieces of mail to get one subscription (a one percent response), it costs you $75.00 to get a subscription. If you charge $45.00 a year, it will take a renewal just to pay for your cost of acquiring the subscriber (you also have the cost of fulfilling the subscription). You realize your profit in eighteen months to two years. So it becomes very important to get a high rate of renewal; otherwise, you will constantly be spending to acquire new readers from whom you will not be making a profit. This example may be optimistic, however. We used a one percent return, but responses to direct mail are declining and a one percent return is apt be higher than you get. In order to get noticed, newsletter marketers are also using different formats for their mailing, which often means higher costs per piece of delivered mail.

Advantages

- Newsletter publishers often can live anywhere.

- Once you establish a loyal following of readers, it is relatively easy to make profits through renewals.

- Newsletter publishing can lead naturally to spin-off products and services such as special reports, seminars, audio tapes, books, and even starting a mail-order catalogue company, as David Starkman and his partner, Susan Pinsky, did (see entry for Mail-Order Business).

- Because you rarely have direct contact with your subscribers (unless you're doing public-relations newsletters for local business/ professional clients), you seldom have to get dressed up to work in your home office.

Disadvantages

- Newsletters are a long-range business.

- Getting new subscribers and renewals is a constant challenge.

- You must carefully plan each article in every issue. The newsletter could fail if you don't adequately research your market to find out whether your idea is original enough, interesting enough, and if you're not capable of generating stories for years to come as well as determining whether there are enough potential subscribers to make your venture successful.

Pricing

Subscription Newsletters Newsletters sold to individuals or consumer newsletter are usually priced under $100, more often in the $25 to $45 range. While these numbers may work for large companies with significant money to invest, for a home-based newsletter publisher, it's difficult to be profitable with newsletters priced under $50 a year. Howard Penn Hudson says that "The three biggest mistakes would-be newsletterers make are: spending too much for office equipment, pricing their newsletter too low, and giving up too soon." If you need to price your newsletter above what most consumer newsletters go for, your best chance is to create a newsletter for a specialized business or professional readership. The good news is that depending on the sophistication, uniqueness, and scarcity of information you can offer, you may be able to obtain subscription prices in the hundreds of dollars a year. While there are a number of $500-a-year newsletters, one business newsletter is over $5,000 a year.

Newsletters can produce other sources of income. A 1995 Northwestern University study found that newsletter publishers reported almost half their revenue comes from selling ancillary products and services that the newsletters produce themselves or buy from others. Newsletter publishers can rent their list of subscribers as a mailing list, and develop speaking and consulting engagements by mentioning their experiences and availability in the newsletter. Sometimes newsletter publishers are hired as spokespeople by companies.

Newsletters Produced for Others Standard rates for writing in-house company newsletters range from $20 to $60 per hour, or from $200 to $500 for two to four pages and $500 to $1,000 for four to eight pages. Rates for writing for retail stores range from $175 to $300 for a four-page publication. Small associations pay from $15 to $25 per hour for writing projects; large groups pay up to $85 per hour.

Potential Earnings

Typical Annual Gross Revenues: $60,000, based on 1,000 subscribers at $60 a year. Note that getting up to 1,000 subscribers is likely to take a significant amount of marketing.

Overhead: moderate (20 to 40 percent). Overhead can be low if you are producing newsletters for others and not bearing a heavy marketing cost.

Best Home Businesses Estimate of Market Potential

The outlook for newsletter publishing is good as careers become more specialized, new industries emerge, people's interests diversify, new problems are identified, and more laws and regulations come into existence. The Internet in the words of direct response copywriter Don Hauptman is "both a threat and opportunity."

The Internet has created an expectation on the part of many people that information is a free commodity. Lots of free up-to-date information is available, but it's not always easy to find and someone needing in-depth analysis is still apt to turn to a regular newsletter from a trusted source via e-mail, fax, or land mail. So the publisher who offers something different and adds value to information through opinions and interpretations from a useful point of view will continue to be a preferred resource.

Also, publishers offering free information on the Internet find that it's one of the best ways of marketing. In revising this book, we have found publications, particularly magazines, that make their back issues downloadable and sometimes part or all of their current issue. At least some report that their marketing costs are down and their readership is up.

Cheryl Woodard says, "The Internet is not replacing other modes of communication. It makes editors' jobs much easier. You can communicate via e-mail, download government documents, get information that in the past would have required going to a library. Many newsletter publishers deliver services or products over the Web. The positive is it costs less but the negative is that subscribers expect to pay less." Another plus of the Internet is that it enables potential readers to find you. This is particularly important if your topic does not have a mailing list or some other way for you to reach out to potential readers.

While the Internet is changing newsletter publishing, it appears newsletters will be with us in the twenty-first century.

Best Ways to Get Business

- Using fax or direct mail to send sample newsletters to potential readers. Make your mailers visually arresting. Be sure to label the newsletter SAMPLE COPY in bold lettering. Include easy ways of ordering.

- Providing a sample or samples of your newsletter on your Web site with an offer. Make the editorial thrust of your Web site correspond to the subject of your newsletter.

- Uploading articles from your newsletter to relevant forum libraries with a teaser: "For more information, contact . . ." Provide contact information that will enable people to contact you online or by phone or mail. If you can, provide a link to your Web site.

- Getting your newsletter listed on Web sites that enable people to order sample newsletters.

- Collaborating with other publishers in joint marketing efforts. One way to do this is bartering mailing lists.

- Participating on message boards and in chats that attract potential readers. Position yourself as an expert and include in one of the signature lines to messages you post the name of your newsletter.

- Running small classified inquiry ads as a low-cost way of gauging interest and generating names. Then send a direct-mail package to those who respond. You save a lot by mailing only to people who have expressed interest in your topic.

- Offering a trial subscription by fax or mail. A technique some use to convert the trial subscription to a paid one is to send an invoice separately immediately after mailing the trial subscriber's second-to-last issue. The invoice instructs those who do not wish to subscribe to return the invoice marked "cancel." For those who do not pay immediately or cancel, follow-up reminder invoices are sent.

Tip: If you base a subscription price on the number of issues someone will receive rather than on a specific period of time, should you decide to increase your frequency of publication (i.e., from quarterly to monthly), you can re-bill subscribers sooner.

First Steps

- Select a subject for your newsletter, learn about your potential subscribers, and research competition as well as other efforts to serve your market. If you are not already an expert in the subject of your newsletter, read and learn everything you can to become an expert.

- Define a focus and a format for your newsletter. A key task of every newsletter publisher is to find out what information his or her readers want and need enough to pay for.

- Develop samples and test your concepts out with people who are like your prospective subscribers.

- Develop a marketing plan and begin testing it.

Where To Turn For Information And Help

ORGANIZATIONS

THE NEWSLETTER PUBLISHERS ASSOCIATION, 1501 Wilson Boulevard, Suite 509, Arlington, VA 22209; (800) 356-9302; (703) 527-2333. Web site: *www.newsletters.org*

BOOKS

Editing Your Newsletter, Mark Beach, Writers Digest Books, 1995. ISBN 0898796415.

Home Based Newsletter Publishing, William J. Bond, New York: McGraw-Hill, 1992. ISBN: 0070065578.

Newsletter Design, Edward A. Hamilton, New York: John Wiley & Sons, 1997. ISBN: 0471285927.

Marketing with Newsletters, Elaine Floyd, EF Communications, 1996. ISBN: 0963022245.

The Newsletter Editor's Handbook, Helen Ashmore, Elaine Floyd, Marvin Newsletter Arth, EF Communications, 1997. ISBN: 0963022261.

Newsletter Sourcebook, Mark Beach, Elaine Floyd, Writers Digest Books, 1998. ISBN: 0898798698.

Producing a First-Class Newsletter, Barbara A. Fanson, Self Counsel Press, 1994. ISBN: 0889082960.

Publishing Newsletters, Howard Penn Hudson, H & M Publications, 1998, ISBN: 0961764295.

Starting and Running a Successful Newsletter or Magazine, Cheryl Woodard, Nolo Press, 1998. ISBN: 0873374614.

DIRECTORIES AND NEWSLETTERS

To determine what newsletters already exist in a field, use directories available in print and to some extent on the Web. The print versions range in price from $140 to almost $500 but are available in most libraries.

Hudson's Subscription Newsletter Directory is devoted exclusively to subscription newsletters grouped into 52 subject headings. Howard Penn Hudson's firm also publishes two newsletters about newsletters, *The Newsletter on Newsletters* and *Newsletter Design,* P.O. Box 311, Rhinebeck, NY 12572; (914) 876-2081. Web site: *www.newsletter-clearinghse.com*

Newsletters in Print, Louise Gagne, editor, Gale Research Company, Annual.

Oxbridge Directory of Newsletters lists over 20,000 newsletters, of which 9,000 are indicated to be subscription newsletters. It is published annually. Oxbridge Communications, Inc., 150 Fifth Avenue, New York, NY 10011; (212) 741-0231. Oxbridge also offers the ability to do a free search by keyword in its 100,000+ publication database at *www.mediafinder.com.* Subscribers to the Oxbridge Directory can also search by publication type, subject category, target audience, circulation, advertising and list rental rates, frequency of issue, and more.

See also the "Newsletters" volume of **Standard Rate and Data Service.**

WEB SITES

4NEWSLETTERS.COM is a metasite providing links to newsletters and newsletter services. *www.4newsletters.com*

DAVID SIEGEL'S SUGGESTIONS The site offers useful ideas and includes several try-it-out-and-see-for-yourself places within the text. *www. dsiegel.com*

DESKTOP PUBLISHING FORUM on CompuServe founded by Thom Hartmann.

MEDIAFINDER. See Oxbridge Directory above.

NEWSLETTER ACCESS offers a searchable directory of over 5,000 newsletters. You can get your newsletter listed. *www.newsletteraccess.com*

THE NEWSLETTER CLEARINGHOUSE The Web site for Howard Penn Hudson's newsletters, *The Newsletter on Newsletters* and *Newsletter Design*. Hudson founded The Newsletter Publishers Association in 1976. *www.newsletter-clearinghse.com*

PUT IT IN WRITING Help in training yourself to spot the slight differences between good and bad newsletters; glossary of printing and graphic terms; newsletter design samples. *www.put-it-in-writing.com*

SHARON L. SHARP'S NEWSLETTER RESOURCES Useful links to several online newsletters that are of interest to technical communicators. *funnelweb.utcc.utk.edu/~campbell/newsletters.html*

NEIGHBORHOOD NEWSLETTERS

Neighborhood Newsletter Publishing Kit, Newsline Design, PO Box 5384, Grand Island, NE 68802. Web site: *www.kdsi.net/neighborhoodnews*

 ## Pet Sitting and Other Services for Animal Lovers

Americans are nuts about their pets. Based on the sheer numbers, pets are apparently even more popular than children. Nearly 60 percent of U.S. households have pets, compared to fewer than 40 percent with children. In fact, American homes have almost as many pets living in them as people: 31 percent of U.S. households have at least one dog, and 27 percent have one or more cats. In addition to 59 million cats and 53 million dogs, Americans own 56 million fish, 13 million birds, 11 million rabbits, ferrets, and rodents, and 3.5 million reptiles.

For many people, pets are part of the family. A 1995 survey found that 70 percent of current and former pet owners think of their pets as children. Maybe that's why seven of the ten most popular names for pets are human names and three out of four pet owners feel guilty about leaving their pets alone when they leave home.

But pet owners work and travel just like other people, so pet-sitting services are gaining in popularity. In a 1998 survey, the Iams pet food company found that 76 percent of pet owners use some type of pet care when traveling. Thirty percent use pet sitters and the nation's approximately 15,000 pet-sitting firms can't take care of all the pets that need sitting.

Usually pet-sitters care for pets, homes, and plants. They may also bring in the mail, take trash to the curb for pickup, and do other home-care things for the owner. If a pet is sick, they may take the animal to a vet or give medications. "It's a serious business no one should take lightly," says Carole Tomas of the National Association of Professional Pet Sitters. "You have to be dedicated, hardworking, and capable of dealing with many kinds of problems." Sheldon Belinkoff and his wife Janet agree. They operate a pet-sitting service with over 20 sitters and a pet transportation service. "To really make money at pet sitting," Belinkoff advises, "you need to be around seven days a week and be prepared to give up your free time. It's a seven-day-a-week business."

If taking care of critters appeals to you, here are four ways you can approach offering pet care as a service:

- You can establish a route of regular customers and make daily stops at their homes to feed, walk, and visit with pets as well as to do any other chores you negotiate.

- You can operate as an agency or referral service lining up pet sitters for your clients.

- You can actually live in the home of your clients while they are away. Such a service is either more likely to be part-time or offered through referrals from an agency with which you're listed.

- You can open your home for boarding pets. See Doggie Day Care below.

Whether you choose to do the pet-sitting yourself or develop an agency, your customers will primarily be two-career couples, working singles (single pet owners have lower blood pressure by the way than other singles), people who travel regularly or for extended periods of time like business-people or well-to-do retired people, and people recovering from surgery or illness.

Knowledge and Skills You Need to Have

- A love for pets and if you work directly with animals yourself, a hands-on, patient, caring personality.

- Knowledge of animal health and behavior.

- People skills because pet sitters must relate to owners, too.

- Enough knowledge of pet first aid to notice if a pet is having a problem.

- Discipline to make and keep a schedule and follow routines.

- The ability to profitably run a business and, if you operate as an agency, to manage employees or independent contractors.

Advantages

- Your working hours are flexible; you can be full-time or part-time.

- The unbounding affection that pets offer.

- Appreciative owners.

Disadvantages

- Rain, snow, extreme cold and heat can make your work unpleasant and part of the job can be dirty and smelly.

- Working alone. It's a seven-day-a-week business and you're especially busy on holidays. To take time off, you need to have others cover for you.

- You get attached to the pets and because of their shorter life spans, you can expect to experience your own and clients' feelings of loss when they pass on.

Start-up Costs	Low	High
Liability insurance and bonding	$ 375	$ 500
Supplies (can opener, extra leashes, flashlight)	$ 25	$ 50
Initial marketing budget	$ 1,000	$ 5,000

Cell phone	$	75	$	200
Computer with database software	$	1,000	$	3,000
Multi-function printer/fax/scanner/copier	$	150	$	600
Total	$	2,675	$	9,350

Pricing

Based on survey findings by Pet Sitters International, a full-time visiting sitter charges $12 on average per daily visit (although this price varies by area, with major cities sometimes being closer to $18 and smaller cities and suburbs only $7). Unless your travel area is very small, you will be able to cover eight to twelve visits per day (based on half-hour visits plus travel time). Eight is a comfortable number of visits to make.

If you choose to act as an agency, you may take a commission of 30 to 50 percent for each visit by an employee or independent contractor, depending on how long the sitter has been with the agency. This covers bonding and liability insurance paid for by the agency.

Potential Earnings

AS A SITTER:

Typical Annual Gross Revenues: $24,000 a year based on eight visits at $12 a day 250 days a year.

Overhead: low. Your largest expense will be your transportation cost.

Many sitters add to their income by doing other chores. Some sell pet products; some offer in-home grooming services and dog-obedience classes. See the list of other pet services below for additional possible add-ons.

AS AN AGENT:

Based on having four independent contractors making four visits at $12 a day and collecting a 40 percent commission on average, $19,200. An agent who does no sitting can work at home most of the time. Sometimes couples will have one spouse who sits and one who does agenting.

Best Home Businesses **Estimate of Market Potential**

Since we first wrote about pet sitting in 1991, the term has made it into the dictionary. Every indication is it's here to stay. Though the number of homes having pets has declined somewhat from its high in 1985, homes that have pets have more of them, and pet owners are spending more money on them. In the two years preceding 1998, spending on dogs grew by a third.

The average number of cats in a cat household is better than two and dogs aren't far behind. Since boarding pets can cost $50 a day per pet, the more pets an owner has, the more sense using a pet sitter makes. The current trend is toward smaller pet sitting agencies, according to Patti Moran, author of *Pet Sitting for Profit*, which, of course, means room for more services and favors home-based pet sitting services. In part, this is caused by the IRS wanting to treat pet sitters hired by agencies as employees rather than independent contractors, thus causing agencies with employee pet sitters to either raise their prices or make less money.

Best Ways to Get Business

- Having Yellow Pages listings under Pet Sitters, Sitting Services, Dog/Cat Exercising.

- Taking out classified ads in local newspapers.

- Establishing referral relationships with veterinarians, travel agents, cleaning services, pet groomers, pet-food stores—any service or professional a pet owner might ask about finding someone to mind their pet.

- Sending direct mail to new residents of a community, who may not yet have family or community ties.

- Posting notices on bulletin boards may produce clients, too.

- Having your own Web page with its own domain name with testimonial letters.

First Steps

- Determine if there are other pet sitters in your area by checking Yellow Page listings and talking with vets, pet stores, and other potential referral sources. Be alert to learning about unusual pets that may be in the area that existing services don't serve.

- If there are other pet sitters, ask them about the business. Their attitude as well as their words will tell you how busy they are, and you may be able to cover for one another if you establish a positive relationship.

- Fill in the knowledge you need about animal behavior, animal health, and first aid.

- Pick a descriptive and positive name for your business.

- Get insurance and bonding. This is necessary from a marketing perspective as well as for the actual protection it affords you.

- Get listed in the Yellow Pages.

Related Businesses and Up-and-Coming Niches

Animal-Assisted Therapy

The research is clear—animals will often get a better response than people from stroke survivors, the developmentally disabled, the mentally ill, isolated elders, and chronic pain sufferers. People are earning a living from bringing pets they keep in their own homes into hospitals, adult day-care centers, nursing homes, special-education schools, convalescent homes, and even individual households. For training, contact the International Wildlife Education and Conservation Foundation's "Create-A-Smile" Project, 237 Hill Street, Santa Monica, CA 90405, (310) 392-6257. Web site: *www.create-a-smile.org*

Dog Camp

Dog owners love the idea of sending their dog to camp instead of to a kennel. One camp in the Sierras is getting $1,300 a week. Also day camps are ideal near vacation spots where dogs aren't allowed at popular tourist sites. If you want to live in the kind of place people like to go camping, what a home business!

Doggie Day Care

Turning your home into a place to take in pets costs less than a kennel and may have fewer zoning problems, homeowner association restrictions and neighbor problems. Chances are the neighbors are at work during the day anyway. You can collect $15 to $30 a day per pet and offer added services like nail trimming (one company offers "pawdicures") grooming, and other pampering. Sometimes pickup and delivery is included.

Dog Teeth Cleaning

If done without anesthesia, this can be done by nonvets, though it's not the easiest of tasks. One person we know recommends having the owners give their dogs the homeopathic *Rescue Remedy* for several days in advance of the cleaning to relax the dog.

Dog Training

A well-behaved dog is necessary at the increasingly popular dog parks and for the growing number of people who take their dogs with them to the office (which more companies are allowing their employees to do). Also in addition to wanting a well-behaved dog, many owners need help with specific problems like barking, biting, and growling, i.e., some dogs suffer from separation anxiety. And, of course, some owners simply want their dog to learn some new tricks.

Mobile Grooming

You may have seen them—vans with bathing facilities inside. The pets don't even have to leave home. You do need a van, but operating a van is not apt to be as costly as renting space, and you can charge a premium for the convenience you offer.

Pet Consulting

With a consultant on almost everything else, why not consultants to help people select the right pet for their lifestyles and personalities. With some pets representing an investment of $500 to several thousands and medical care becoming vastly expensive, a $25 fee per session isn't a lot of money to get help in picking a compatible best friend. Consulting may continue after the purchase on everything from training to grooming decisions.

Pet Food and Product Delivery

An easy alternative to going to the pet or grocery store is to have whatever your pets need delivered. Pet food has a high mark-up so there's money to be made.

Pet Transportation

Pets need to be taken to and from groomers, classes, and veterinarians (vets now have 20+ specialties). Some pet taxi services come equipped with stretchers for emergencies and will arrange for shipping a pet by air.

Pet parties. Yes, pets are favored in this way, too. Singing "Happy Birthday" to barks. Lucile Gbur of Colorado Springs throws parties for pets that include invitations, party hats, gifts for the guest-of-honor, decorations, games, Polaroid photos and food for both animals and people. Lucile's parties start at $30, and for each guest in the group, she charges an additional $1 to $10, depending on the size of the dog. Senior dogs are eligible for a discount.

Pets can also be great entertainment for children's parties. Teresa Pollack brings life to children's parties with her collection of exotic reptiles including snakes, turtles, lizards, and frogs. Kathy's Critters of Los Angeles brings snakes, lizards, salamanders, newts, frogs, toads, mice, rats, Madagascar hissing cockroaches, scorpions and tarantulas to schools, parties, camps, and special events. Such events are both educational and entertaining and guaranteed to hold the interest of all.

Pooper Scooper Service

Operating like a pool or lawn service, a pooper-scooper service establishes a regular route of daily rounds, visiting each client once or twice a week. Matthew Osborn who has written a manual on pooper scooping says, "Prices around the U.S. vary from $3.50 per dog per week to $15 per week. My own fees averaged about $7.50 per client per week. Cleaning an average of 6 yards per hour earns $45 per hour." The manual is *The Professional Pooper Scooper*, P.O. Box 132308, Columbus, OH 43213; (614) 231-4101. Web site: *www.pooper-scooper.com*

Post-Surgery Recovery Care for Pets

Americans spend $3 billion on medical care for their pets on everything from CAT (no pun) scans to open heart surgery. After such serious procedures, pets often need continuing at-home care while convalescing. In addition to enabling the pet to heal in the comfort of his or her own home, the caretaker can oversee the administration of medication, change bandages and dressings, and take the pet to and from postoperative vet visits, as well as protecting the pet from hurting itself while recovering. As any pet owner knows, this can be a time consuming and nearly full-time task for several weeks, and there's no mandated leave from work for pets as yet. This service can be worth $40 a day or more.

Where to Turn for Information and Help

ORGANIZATIONS

NATIONAL ASSOCIATION OF PROFESSIONAL PET SITTERS (NAPPS), 1030 15th St. NW, Suite 870, Washington, DC 20005; (202) 393-3317. NAPPS offers certification, liability insurance and bonding, and a mentor program that matches a novice sitter with a "seasoned pro." Web site: *www.petsitters.org*

PET SITTERS INTERNATIONAL, 418 East King Street, King, NC 27021; (336) 983-9222. Offers three levels of certification, liability insurance, bonding at group rates, and background checking of personnel both in the U.S. and Canada. Web site: *www.petsit.com*

THE NATIONAL INSTITUTE OF DOG TRAINING offers Matthew Margolis' School for Dog Training as a self-study program including videos on the business of dog training, knowledge of canine behavior, skills for dog training, and specifics of marketing and managing a dog-training business. Additional two-day certification program optional. Margolis Enterprises, Inc., 11275 National Blvd., Los Angeles, CA 90064; (800) 334-3647. Web site: *www.matthewmargolis.com*

BOOKS

Pet Sitting for Profit, Patti Moran, New York: Howell Book House, 1997. ISBN: 087605596X.

The Professional Pet Sitter, Lori and Scott Mangold, Paws-itive Press, 1994; 800-PET-BOOK, ISBN: 0963544217.

WEB SITES

Canine Training Systems Home Page. Dog-training videos on obedience, protections, tracking, K-0, herding, and agility. *www.caninetraining.com/ctshome.html*

DogProblems.com. Dog-training resource center for dog owners and professional dog trainers, techniques, products, and problems-discussion group with links to other dog-training sites. *www.dogproblems.com/dog*

The Pet Groomers Page (GoTo). The AKC Electronic Zoo Cat Fanciers Pages, Pet Station, The Dog Zone, American Dog Trainers Network, *Dog World Magazine,* and much more. *www.groomers.com/links.html*

Super Dog Pet Dog Training. Hints and help with common problems includes list of dog training tools, tips and techniques. *www.superdog.com/ctshome.htm*

Photography

"If I could do anything, I'd spend my life behind the lens of a camera." If those could be your words, you can make it so. Because photos play a part in most human activities—from family life to fine art, from education to new media—you can combine a passion to take pictures with your other interests and experiences to create a fascinating career.

As a professional photographer, one decision you'll need to make, though not necessarily immediately, is whether to be a generalist or to specialize in one or several areas that are of particular interest to you. If you live in a smaller community, where versatility is a strength, you may not need to find a niche in which to distinguish yourself unless you want to. The Web allows photographers to sell photographs on many subjects from almost anywhere. But most photographers specialize they as they acquire experience and expertise and as they get a sense of the best markets for their work. Often specialties emerge from the personality and preferences of the photographer. For example, if you enjoy interacting with people, you might specialize in:

- Portraits, addressing the needs of the more than one in five American households that have professional photographs taken during the course of a year. You might further choose an even more specialized niche like taking pictures of newborns and babies.

- School photos, which includes class pictures, and may extend to sports-team photos and reunions.

- Wedding photographs, which involve lots of contact with clients.

- Publicity and portfolio photos for models, artists, actors, and actresses. Mary Ann Halpin combines her experience as a former actress with her love of photography by specializing in what's called "head shots" for actors, and actresses. Recently, however, she's developed a new specialty. She photographs pregnant mothers and has had her her first coffee table book published, *Pregnant Goddesshood, A Celebration of Life* (*www.goddesshood.com*).

- Product photos for companies that need photographs for advertisements, catalogues, and sales materials.

- Animal photos. If you love animals, you can spend your days photographing them as Vicki Holloway does, taking shots of purebred championship dogs, primarily at dog shows. George and Tia Chandler take equestrian photos; they make their photos available to owners on T-shirts. Feline Photos does the same for cat owners in southern California.

- Internet home tours. This is a new specialty we predict will spread into other fields: providing digital photos for virtual open houses that offer home buyers a 360-degree view of real estate without leaving their desk chairs. Advocates claim such "immersion images" will eventually replace the flat photos now featured on Web-based listings. (See Be Here Corp., *www.behere.com;* (888) 4-BEHERE; Interactive Picture Corp., *www.ipix.com*, (800) 336-7114; and Jutvision Corp., *www.jutvision.com*, (877) 588-8687).

You can specialize in taking photos of just about anything that fascinates you, as have the following photographers:

- Ernest Hori (*www.horizenfoto.com*), inspired by seeing a portfolio of original photographs by Ansel Adams, dedicates his career to nature photography.

- Warren Faidley, fascinated with bad weather, decided to photograph it. Every morning Faidley listens for the weather report on the Weather Channel and other sources and heads off for the worst weather around. Some days he'll drive 500 to 600 miles for the chance to get a shot. He shoots hurricanes, tornadoes, and disasters of all kinds. His photos are represented by twelve photo agents around the world and a film agent in Los Angeles who markets 35-millimeter film.

- Aaron Chang's passion is surfing. Making his living as a surfing photographer enables Chang to continue surfing virtually full-time. In addition to having a retainer from a surfing magazine, he also has a line of T-shirts and sweatshirts featuring black-and-white reproductions of his photos.

Sports offers a variety of ways to specialize, from new extreme sports to more traditional sports such as hang gliding, skydiving, and auto racing. And if you love things that move, you can work with auto or motorcycle clubs, or used-car or boat dealers who need photos for ads and the Web. If you like stationary things such as buildings, architectural photography is another specialty. If you like music, you might specialize in photographing bands and performers.

If journalism is in your blood, you can be a photojournalist taking documentary photographs, telling stories with your photos. The reader becomes a collaborator, finding meaning in your pictures. While photojournalism has declined from its peak in the period between 1930 and 1960, Bill Gates's Corbis Corporation, after acquiring a vast photo collection, is making long-term contracts with working photographers.

You can cultivate working relationships with publications as has Amy Cantrell who takes photo assignments for magazines such as *Entrepreneur* for which she recently did a cover shot of Magic Johnson. She had only 10 minutes available to do her work. While that may seem short, most photojournalists must make decisions in less than five seconds.

If you like the business world, you can work as a commercial photographer serving advertising agencies, product packagers, public-relations firms, corporations, or professionals. You can also specialize in legal, medical, scientific, or insurance work. Local, state, and federal governments also have photography needs ranging from aerial photographs to forensic photography of crime scenes and evidence.

If you wish to pursue photography as a fine art, you might capture human experience as Jeff Wall does in his giant staged transparencies created with the latest in film and computer technology and mounted on light boxes to add the glow of a cinema screen to his photos. You might travel the world, photographing the beauty of nature or foreign cultures, selling your work as salon prints through galleries, exhibits, and art fairs or published in books. Helen Garber was a graphic designer before turning to her true love of photography. She began doing portrait shots but now also travels across the country for publishers taking shots for coffee table photo books on topics from bodybuilding to circus performers.

If serving impatient and squirming people and meeting the deadlines of assignments are not to your taste, you can participate in the $800 million a year stock photography field. Stock photography is distinguished from assignment photography and other specialized fields like fashion or aerial photography in that you can take photos of virtually any topic and sell them to people who are seeking some particular photo for use in books, promotional materials, documentaries, and so forth.

A stock photographer who decides to specialize in a particular type of photo can become an important resource to buyers publications, ad agencies, corporations, and government agencies that need what you have, whether it's photos of vegetable gardening, insects, or birds. However, Rohn Engh, publisher of *Photo Daily, Photoletter, Photostock Notes Plus,* and *Photostock Notes* observes, "It's a mistake to take photos first and find a market; you should find the market first and then create your inventory." At the same time, Engh notes, "Specialist buyers expect photographers to know their subject and to speak the language of the buyer." From his surveys of his photographer clients, Engh finds that specialized photographers keep a customer an average of ten years.

Some photographers such as Aaron Chang create products from their images. Mavis Robertson uses digital imaging equipment and an inventory of retro clothing to transform the photos of loved ones into 15" Loveable Huggable Dolls. She calls her company Everlasting Photos and she sells her dolls mostly at community fairs. Other photographers sell products for taking photos, such as husband-and-wife team Susan Pinsky and David Starkman. Since childhood, both have had a passion for 3-D photography. Today, they delight the child in many a grown-up with their catalogue of paraphernalia for 3-D photography called Reel 3-D.

Knowledge and Skills You Need to Have

- You need a sensitive eye and a sense of composition to create pictures people will look at.

- You need a passion for taking pictures.

- You need the technical know-how to create professional quality images reliably.

Advantages

- You can live where you want to live. Outdoor photography is a major specialization.

- Many kinds of photography, particularly stock photography, can be done on a part-time basis.

- By making your play your business, you can turn what can be an expensive hobby into both tax deductions and a good income.

Disadvantages

- Some areas of photography don't pay well; others may require extensive travel. For stock photography, pay is much lower for individual pictures than in the commercial field.

- Overhead is among the highest for a home business.

Start-up Costs	Low	High
Equipment with good optics*	$ 1,000	$ 12,000
Computer	$ 1,500	$ 3,000
Printer	$ 300	$ 800
or		
Multi-function printer/fax/scanner/copier. Go to a service bureau for high resolution scanning.	$ 150	$ 600
Cell phone	$ 75	$ 200
Initial marketing budget	$ 1,000	$ 5,000
Total	$ 4,025	$ 21,600

*The large spread represents used equipment to top-of-the-line digital.

Pricing

In commercial photography, the photographer sets the price. The average price for professional portraits in 1998 was $54. This average covered a range of $18 for sports and team photographs to $20 for school photos and $335 for wedding or publicity photographs. For work away from home, hourly, daily and weekly location rates are used. Adding film and materials costs as separate charges helps with overhead.

The buyer sets the price for stock photographs. On a small publication, prices range from $20 for an inside photo to $50 for a cover photograph and to hundreds of dollars for covers on larger publications. National magazines will pay $1,000 to $3,000 to a photographer assigned to take a cover photo, less for feature-story photos. Rates also vary according to experience; beginners may get $25, semi-pros, $75; and professionals, $250 for the same-size photograph used for inside editorial.

Potential Earnings

Gross Income: As a weekend photographer, $7,000 to $9,000 a year; as a part-time business, $70,000 to $150,000; as a full-time business, $175,000 to $250,000.

Overhead: high; if your work is local, 50 to 60 percent; with travel 70 to 80 percent of gross.

Best Home Businesses Estimate of Market Potential

For many, the convenience of having someone else take the photos will keep photography a viable business despite the growing popularity of low-cost digital cameras. New York publishers at this date still accept conventional photographs. However, increasing numbers of businesses use digital cameras costing under $1,000 to take photos they can use on the Web but which are not of high enough quality for print. Commercial advertising, on the other hand, demands digital at a quality level that can be printed on paper. The cameras capable of taking photos for publication cost in the thousands, an investment that professional photographers are willing to make.

For stock photography, Rohn Engh says, "Now, as more and more photo buyers take advantage of searching for their specific photo needs on the Web, individual stock photographers will be able to sell directly from their files to the buyer. The Web will be a boon to the independent stock photographer."

Best Ways to Get Business

- Cold calling potential clients by telephone or in person. One Seattle photographer established his business by starting with the letter "A" in the Yellow Pages. He had plenty of business by the time he got to the letter "G." You can be more focused by seeking out manufacturers or car dealers in your local area.

- Participating in referral organizations or in trade or community associations with potential clients.

- Having a Web site on which you place examples of your work and testimonial letters.

- Buying enhanced listings on Web sites such as switchboard.com. When magazines or companies look for photographers, you can be one of the few they will find.

- Bartering your services for advertising with publications read by your target market.

- Volunteering your time to photograph events for organizations that can give your work good visibility.

- Gaining publicity from donating prints for benefits, auctions, and prizes.

- For selling stock photographs: Direct mail in the form of postcards or brochures that show your pictures or send out 8½" to 11" sell sheets. Rohn Engh recommends that you don't sell all rights to your photos. Also, stock agencies will sell your photos for you. You can find stock agencies listed on Web phone directories. An example is 911 Pictures (*www.911pictures.com*) which specializes in fire, police, and emergency photos.

First Steps

- Fill in any gaps in your technical know-how with courses, workshop, seminars, and if you can afford it, working as an assistant to a top-flight photographer.

- Assess your strengths and what you love to decide on ways to specialize. Putting your photos on the floor, into a slide projector or if they're digitized, viewing them on your computer, may help you do this.

- Determine what your competition is and, in popular specialties such as wedding photography, how well they seem to be doing.

- To sell to magazines, build a list of potential customers. Use magazine directories at the reference desk of libraries. Rohn Engh observes, "Most people send stuff to wrong markets."

- Acquire the equipment you will need.

Where to Turn for Information and Help

ORGANIZATIONS

ADVERTISING PHOTOGRAPHERS OF AMERICA, 333 South Beverly Drive, Beverly Hills, CA 90212; (800) 272-6264. Web Site: *www.apanational. com*

AMERICAN SOCIETY OF JOURNALISTS AND AUTHORS (ASJA), 1501 Broadway, Suite 302, New York, NY 10036; (212) 997-0947. Web site: *www.asja.org*

AMERICAN SOCIETY OF MEDIA PHOTOGRAPHERS, 14 Washington Road, Suite 502, Princeton Junction, NJ 08550; (609)799-8300, Web site: *www.asmp.org*

AMERICAN SOCIETY OF PICTURE PROFESSIONALS, 409 South Washington Street, Alexandria, VA 22314; (703) 299-0219. Web site: *www.aspp.com*

NATIONAL PRESS PHOTOGRAPHERS ASSOCIATION, 3200 Croasdaile Dr., Suite 306, Durham, NC 27705; (800) 289-6772; (919) 383-7246. Web site: *www.nppa.org*

NORTH AMERICAN NATURE PHOTOGRAPHERS ASSOCIATION, 10200 West 44th Avenue, Suite 304, Wheat Ridge, CO, 80033; (303) 422-8527. Web site: *www.nanpa.org*

PHOTOGRAPHIC SOCIETY OF AMERICA, 3000 United Founder Boulevard, Suite 103, Oklahoma City, OK, 73112. Web site: *www.psa-photo.org*

PHOTO MARKETING ASSOCIATION INTERNATIONAL, 3000 Picture Place, Jackson, MI 49201; (517) 788-8100. The association has a number of sections, including the Professional School Photographers Association

International and the Digital Imaging Marketing Association. Web site: *www.pmai.org*

PROFESSIONAL PHOTOGRAPHERS OF AMERICA, 229 Peachtree St., Suite 2200, International Tower, Atlanta, GA 30303; (800) 786-6277; (404) 522-8600. Web site: *www.ppa-world.org*

WEDDING & PORTRAIT PHOTOGRAPHERS INTERNATIONAL (WPPI), 1312 Lincoln Blvd., Santa Monica, CA, 90401; (310) 451-0090; fax: (310) 395-9058. Web site: *www.wppi-online.com*

COURSES

Available in virtually every community are courses from colleges to continuing education programs.

BOOKS

ASMP: Professional Business Practices in Photography, American Society of Media Photographers, Writers Digest Books, 1997. ISBN: 0927629143.

Business and Legal Forms for Photographers, Tad Crawford, Amphoto, 1997. ISBN: 188055982X.

How to Sell & ReSell Your Photos, Rohn Engh, Writers Digest Books, 1997. ISBN: 0898797748.

The Law (in Plain English) for Photographers, Leonard D. DuBoff, Allworth Press, 1995. ISBN: 1880559196.

The Multimedia Law and Business Handbook, J. Dianne Brinston, Mark F. Radcliffe, Ladera Press, 1997. ISBN: 0963917323.

Pricing Photography: The Complete Guide to Assignment and Stock Prices, Michal Heron, David MacTavish, Amphoto, 1997. ISBN: 1880559684.

RESOURCES FOR SELLING STOCK PHOTOS

Newsletters available from Rohn Engh's Photosource International, Pine Lake Farm, 1910 35th Road, Osceola WI 54020; (715) 248 3800; (800) 624 0266:

- *Photo Daily* published on a daily basis both by fax and e-mail.
- *Photoletter* published daily, weekly and semi-monthly.

- *Photostock Notes,* a monthly newsletter for communicating trends, covering copyright agencies and stock agencies that have gone digital. Sample available with SASE.

- *PhotostockNotes Plus,* a monthly newsletter for beginners.

His Web site is *www. photosource.com.* Here, photographers can describe their photos and photo buyers can find available photos in 50 subject areas. Photos can link to example photos either on the photographers' own sites or on the Photosource International site.

Professional Organizer

The professional organizer has emerged as the knight in shining armor of the information age. People today are overwhelmed with an ever-increasing flow of information. Despite electronic mail, our mailboxes are more stuffed than ever. Most people have more belongings than previous generations, as evidenced by the fact that older homes never have enough storage space. Yet most people feel they have less time than ever to manage and organize all the added stuff in their lives. The professional organizer steps into our homes and offices to help us take control and put our lives in operating order.

Professional organizers help their clients organize everything from paper files to computer files, from desktops to filing cabinets, from bookshelves to closets and kitchens. As editor turned organizer and author Harriet Schechter puts it, "As an organizer, instead of editing words, I edit other people's time and space." Stephanie Denton, a director of the National Association of Professional Organizers (NAPO) and a professional organizer in Cincinnati, believes the role of the organizer is to help turn information and data into knowledge and wisdom.

Although professional organizing is a relatively young profession, it grows at a rate of 16 percent a year. NAPO currently has almost 1,100 members. Some organizers work only in residential settings; others work exclusively in offices, serving organizations such as banks, hospitals, schools, professional practices, and other business enterprises. An internal survey in 1997, however, showed that organizing home offices—a cross between residential and office work—is the fastest-growing area. Other fast-growing specialties include small businesses, residences, and corporate executive's offices.

Time, space, and paper/information are the basic divisions in the field. Some organizers refine specialties by working with a particular type of problem or subject such as computer files and databases, collections, estate sales, filing cabinets, paper, photographs, garages, attics, basements, closets, kitchens, space designing, packing and moving, paying bills and finances, goal setting and time management, and wardrobes.

Some organizers create niches by working with specific types of clients, such as students, seniors, people with ADD, children, law offices, medical offices, and the "chronically disorganized" who need clutter control.

Harriet Schechter, whose company is called The Miracle Worker Organizing Service in San Diego, says an organizer's clients are not necessarily disorganized people. "Often they are quite the opposite," she says, "but are overwhelmed with too many projects and a reluctance to delegate." The point is, everyone who feels he or she could benefit from being more organized is a potential customer. But first, that person must decide if he or she wants the service, and then they must be willing to pay for it. At this time, only a small percentage of those who need the service are willing to pay. It's not uncommon for a potential client to wait three years before deciding to call for help.

For Schechter, this business is almost like a calling. "Good organizers have an overwhelming need to bring order to the world," she says. "They get satisfaction from helping people organize their lives." Susan Silver, Los Angeles organizer and author of *Organized to Be the Best! New Time-saving Ways to Simplify and Improve How You Work*, finds that "this is a very creative business. It provides many creative outlets to express your abilities. As an organizer, you can be an author, seminar leader, trainer, or hands-on consultant."

Silver believes that metropolitan areas provide the best opportunities for organizers because these areas have a larger market filled with people who have hectic lifestyles and are overloaded with paper and information. Oddly enough, an organizing business can actually do quite well during a recession, when companies are looking for ways to stretch every dollar. Silver explains, "In tough times we have to find better ways to do more with less." With creative marketing, this service can be positioned as a cost-saving way to trim fat and compensate for downsizing. With everyone's access to the Internet, consulting is not confined to face-to-face contact. Says Silver, "I'm doing hands-on work without even shaking their hands."

Knowledge and Skills You Need to Have

There is no specific training or background required to be an organizer. The following skills are important, however, in order to do it successfully.

- You need to be organized yourself. People expect that you have actual answers to their problems, not just intuitive ideas of how to make something work a little bit better. You should have a knowledge of various systems, products, furniture, supplies, and accessories for organizing a home or office. Dee Behrman, who specializes in working with medical, dental, and legal offices in southern California, believes that "a broad-based product knowledge is essential so you can offer your clients a range of options and customize a system for their particular needs." In working with four medical offices, for example, she found that each one wanted to use a different type of chart.

- You need to be analytical, punctual, and able to deliver on your commitments. You must be able to understand your clients' needs and develop clear plans for how to make order out of their chaos. You must feel challenged instead of stressed by disorder.

- You must be compassionate toward, not judgmental of, your clients. As Harriet Schechter says, "You must have a poker face when you see people's disorder. Some people are insane over a small pile of papers; others seem unperturbed by huge mountains of stuff." Flexibility is, therefore, an important trait. You must work with each person's individual needs and quirks; you cannot have a cookie-cutter mentality that imposes one regimen on all.

- Although many organizers are not computer mavens, a sound knowledge of computer hardware and software to streamline an office will quickly become a must for any organizer to remain competitive. For example, if you are familiar with organizer and contact-management software programs, you might be able to teach clients to adopt their software to improve their use of the computer. Alternatively, you can team up with another organizer who is strong in this area.

- You must be willing to admit you don't have all the answers and keep your mind open to new ideas and new ways of doing things.

- You need good listening skills. People want to be heard. Stephanie Denton has noticed that most people who use organizers have three or four organizing books themselves. (But do they have time to read them?)

Start-up Costs	Low	High
Computer	$ 1,500	$ 3,000
Printer	$ 300	$ 800
or		
Multi-function printer/fax/scanner/copier	$ 150	$ 600
Cell phone	$ 75	$ 200
Office furniture, especially an ergonomic chair	$ 400	$ 1,000
Initial marketing budget	$ 1,000	$ 3,000
Total	$ 3,125	$ 7,600

Advantages

- This is still a new enough field that competition may not be a significant problem.

- The need for professional organizers will grow as the amount of information we must process continues to grow and our lives keep getting more complex. Many businesses and individuals will appreciate the value of what you can do.

- Your clients can see dramatic results of your work quickly.

- It is satisfying to feel that you are helping people create order out of their chaos.

- There is ample opportunity to use your creativity.

- There are many different facets of what you can do as an organizer, so you need not get bored doing the same thing over and over again. To boost your earnings, you can diversify by writing, speaking, and offering seminars on organizing.

- This is an evolving business, so if you like to grow, working as a professional organizer matches the need.

Disadvantages

- Because this is a new field, many people don't know what an organizer is. Some confuse it with union organizer or community organizer. So you often must educate clients before you can sell your service.

- Some clients are not at all well organized (that's why they need you), so sometimes you're working with people who reschedule a lot, can't find their checkbooks, forget their appointments, and so forth.

- This work demands a lot of time and energy to get under way, and it may take as much as a year or two before you'll be able to make a full-time income.

Pricing

Organizers can charge in one of three ways:

Fixed Fee or Project Rates based on an estimate. Fixed fees are charged for specific jobs such as organizing a work space or setting up a filing system. Jeffrey Mayer of Chicago charges $1,000 to organize an executive's desk. An organizer might also charge a fixed fee to do an introductory training program, a needs assessment, a workshop, and a follow-up session. For example, Susan Silver sells such packages to corporations. Fees for such programs will vary with their length and the level of personnel with whom you are working. You can charge more to train executives than you can to train secretaries.

Hourly Rate. Fees range from $50 to $200, depending on your location, experience, and expertise. For example, someone just beginning and serving residential customers might begin by charging $35 an hour. In general, residential and garage organizers will tend to be at the lower end of the scale; corporate organizers charge more.

Retainer. Some organizers contract to work with a company for a certain period of time each month. Retainers range from several hundred to several thousand dollars a month.

Potential Earnings

Typical Annual Gross Revenues: $20,000 to $40,000, based on billing 400 to 800 hours a year (eight to sixteen hours per week) at $50 an hour. Beginners will seldom be able to bill more than a few hours a week, but people who develop a strong referral business can top the typical earnings.

Overhead: low (20 percent or less).

Best Home Businesses Estimate of Market Potential

Just as the flow of information keeps on growing, the demand for hands-on professional organizers should grow as well. A steady stream of popular books has helped organizers become accepted by businesses and institutions of all sizes.

Best Ways to Get Business

- Advertising in the Yellow Pages under Organizing Services or Personal Services.

- Getting publicity through news releases and by writing articles.

- Making personal contacts with people you meet in trade and business associations as well as with professionals who work in industries related to this field, such as business consultants, interior designers, and architects, who can refer clients to you.

- Teaching workshops and classes for community-college and adult-education programs, and speaking before community and business organizations.

- Advertising in local print publications.

- Sending direct mail to prospective clients.

- Listing in the directory of the National Association of Professional Organizers referral service. Membership also results in listing in the membership directory, which is a source of some business.

- Writing a newsletter, with organizing tips, for past and potential clients.

- Developing cross-referrals with other types of professional organizers.

- Having your own Web page with its own domain name with testimonial letters and any articles you have written.

First Steps

- Read books on organizing, time management, and efficient office systems. Develop a specialty or focus for the type of organizing you will do and which industries you want to work with.

- To practice your craft, volunteer to work for friends, charity, or non-profit organizations that will give you letters of recommendation.

- Begin speaking and offering workshops on your specialty and start networking, because these will be your primary ways to get business.

Where to Turn for Information and Help

ORGANIZATIONS

NATIONAL ASSOCIATION OF PROFESSIONAL ORGANIZERS, 1033 La Posada Drive, Suite 220, Austin, TX 78752-3880. Newsletter, conferences, local chapters, referral service, directory. Referral line: (512) 206-0151. Web site: *www.napo.net*

BOOKS

Conquering Chaos at Work, Harriet Schechter, Simon and Schuster, forthcoming in 2000.

How to Be Organized in Spite of Yourself, Sunny Schlenger and Roberta Roesch, New York: New American Library, 1996. ISBN: 0451164695.

How to Get Organized When You Don't Have the Time, Stephanie Culp, Cincinnati: Writer's Digest Books, 1986. ISBN: 0898792304. Also by Stephanie Culp: *How to Conquer Clutter;* 1989. ISBN: 0898793629. *Conquering the Paper Pile-Up,* 1990. ISBN: 0898794102.

Organized to be the Best! New Timesaving Ways to Simplify and Improve How You Work, Susan Silver, Adams-Hall Publishing, 1995. ISBN: 0944708366.

Time Management for Dummies, Jeffrey J. Mayer, IDG Books, 1995. ISBN: 1568843607. Also by Jeffrey Mayer: *If You Haven't Got the Time to Do It Right, When Will You Find the Time to Do It Over?,* Fireside, 1991. ISBN: 0671733648.

Getting Organized: The Easy Way to Put Your Life in Order, Stephanie Winston, New York: Warner Books, 1991. ISBN: 0446391735. Also by Stephanie Winston, *The Organized Executive,* Warner Books, 1994. ISBN: 0446395285.

Taming the Paper Tiger, Barbara Hemphill, Kiplinger Books, 1997. ISBN: 0812928369. Also by Barbara Hemphill: *Taming the Office Tiger,* Kiplinger Books, 1996. ISBN: 0812927125.

START-UP INFORMATION

NAPO RESOURCE REGISTRY, National Association of Professional Organizers, 1033 La Posada Dr., Suite 220, Austin, TX 78752-3880; Web site: *www.napo.net*. Send check payable to NAPO. $15.

Harriet Schechter's How to Become a Professional Organizer Resource Packet, 3368 Governor Drive, PMB 199, San Diego, CA 92122. For information, send a self-addressed, stamped, business-size (number 10) envelope.

NEWSLETTERS

The Get Organized! News, P.O. Box 144, Gotha, FL 34734; (407) 292-0911. Web site: *www.tgon.com*

Messies Anonymous Newsletter, 5025 Southwest 114th Avenue, Miami, FL 33165; (305) 271-8404. Web site: *www.messies.com*

Private-Practice Consultant

Managed care has made financial viability a constant concern for health-care professionals such as physicians, chiropractors, osteopaths, physical therapists, podiatrists, psychotherapists, and radiation therapists. Their stress and frustration levels have risen radically in response to increased competition, proliferating information, technological advances, the growing complexity of their fields and the quantity of procedures, policies, and paperwork they must contend with. The forces of change that have produced managed care are creating changes for dentists and veterinarians as well as for non–health-care professionals such as lawyers and CPAs. Even in the best of times, practicing a profession and managing a business have become two distinctly different roles, requiring distinctly different skills. To bridge this difference, professionals are turning to specialized consultants who can help them manage their practices.

Full-service private-practice consultants can handle virtually any aspect of running a professional's practice, but a great deal of the work now is providing guidance with managed care and helping professionals to make decisions that determine their financial viability. Sometimes this involves helping professionals position their practice to maximize its selling price. Forming groups through integrating practices and mergers is something in which consultants are frequently involved. Consultants may deal with payroll; hire, train, and fire personnel; handle collections; do billing; manage the facility (if the client owns a building); oversee investments and pension plans; select computer hardware and software; and provide marketing and public relations services. They may also help with patient scheduling. There are also consultants who serve as efficiency experts, providing systems development aimed at increasing their clients' productivity and profitability. Others may offer advice about taxes, government regulations, and marketing.

Some practice consultants are generalists, working with a variety of professions, although about 75 percent of the clients for this business are physicians, dentists, and professionals in the medical field. According to Charles Wold, a health-care consultant, author, and Executive Secretary of the Society of Medical-Dental Management Consultants, the more common pattern is toward specialization. Specialization can be by field (dentists or chiropractors), by practice specialty (ophthalmologists, anesthesiologists, or plastic surgeons), or by function (dealing with documentation procedures to comply with government rules and regulations or billing procedures to maximize reimbursement from third parties). Consultants can be useful to solo practitioners as well as group practices. Sometimes hospital administrators may use their services.

Although a consultant may run the entire business for a client, most are not stationed in the office but, rather, work from their own offices. They visit their clients' offices periodically to conduct business and for face-to-face meetings. The Internet is a help to one-person consultants because it makes doing research easier and provides easy access to data. Also, e-mail makes communicating with busy professional clients easier and more efficient.

Connecticut-based consultant Scott Brown, whose company is called Focus Management, works with a wide assortment of professionals, including attorneys, dentists, psychiatrists, CPAs, orthodontists, and graphic designers. His focus is to improve each practice's marketing by identifying a message the practitioner can present to patients or clients that will help bring in new referrals. After collecting data on the business, Brown helps his clients establish long-range goals to improve profitability. He then designs a marketing, training, and management plan tailored to the needs of each business, and implements the plan. Most of his consulting jobs last from six to twelve months, and clients generally see results in that time.

Brown says that the essence of his business isn't marketing, training, or management, but helping his clients reframe how they look at themselves and their practice. Much of what he encounters has to do with attitude: "For instance, they haven't set goals, are looking at the down side of the business, or haven't made enough contacts."

Success, ironically, has created some problems for Brown, who occasionally feels overwhelmed managing so many different businesses and having to switch gears between clients whose practices are so different. But he takes a philosophical view. "You have to love what you're doing, and take the ups and downs as they come," he says. "It's just a matter of trying to find the right balance."

Knowledge and Skills You Need to Have

- You must be able to "manage" a practice, which means you need to have either experience or education in office management in the medical, insurance, legal, or accounting field. Successful consultants have primarily come from two backgrounds. Some began as staff in a professional's office and learned the business from the ground up. Others are CPAs or MBAs who saw the need and decided to specialize in this field.

- In addition to being competent in handling the business side of professional practices, you must have confidence and high self-esteem in order to communicate that you know your stuff when talking with the professionals, office staff, and government agencies you will be dealing with.

- You should also have good people skills, since forming an appropriate relationship with your clients and their staffs is critical. You are a combination consultant, marketer, problem solver, motivator, and therapist.

- You need to be able to manage your time effectively in order to balance running your own business with running the businesses of multiple clients.

- You need common sense and an organized mind to deal effectively with client or patient-care issues and office systems.

Start-up Costs	Low	High
Computer (notebook preferred)	$ 2,000	$ 4,000
Printer (can be portable)	$ 300	$ 800
Fax or multi-functional machine	$ 150	$ 600
Cell phone	$ 75	$ 200
Telephone headset	$ 40	$ 200

Office furniture, especially an ergonomic chair	$ 400	$ 1,000
Initial marketing budget	$ 2,000	$ 5,000
Incorporation cost	$ 500	$ 2,000
Malpractice insurance	$ 1,000	$ 1,500
Total	$ 6,465	$ 15,300

Advantages

- This business is largely recession resistant because doctors need help running their practice as a business even more acutely in tough times.

- This is an excellent opportunity to use any management skills you may have developed during your career.

- You are working among one of the most highly educated sectors of our society, with interesting and ambitious people.

- The work involves handling a variety of problems, which means you must always learn to deal with new things. There's no boredom in this business. You can learn as much as you care to.

- Practice-management consultants may have clients throughout the country, which is a plus if you love to travel.

- The business is easy to set up from home. All you need is a phone and some office equipment. Your clients will not usually come to your office.

- Professional practice consulting offers high income potential.

Disadvantages

- It can take months to obtain your first client, creating a lag time before you make money. You might also experience peaks and valleys in your own cash flow if you do not bill consistently.

- Often you will be working on someone else's schedule because your clients will want to see you at their convenience. However, as noted earlier, if your clients use e-mail, this can be less of a problem.

- The work can be stressful because many unexpected demands arise. There is a great deal at stake in managing someone else's business. Risks are high and consequences can be significant. Your clients can see quickly if you are having an impact on their bottom line.

- As a personal service, you are limited in your earnings by how much time you can bill, unless you hire employees.

- Because of potential liability, incorporating and purchasing malpractice insurance is needed. People in the field report it's a challenge to obtain malpractice insurance with effective coverage, including attorneys fees.

Pricing

Private practice consultants charge in two ways:

By the Hour: Rates range from $75 to $300.

On Retainer: Rates range from a few hundred dollars (which purchases several hours) to thousands of dollars a month. You might give your clients a choice of an hourly rate, a monthly rate, or a six-month retainer. If they prefer a retainer, give them a discount unless you have a heavy demand for work.

Potential Earnings

Typical Annual Gross Revenues: $112,000 to $187,500 or more, based on thirty billable hours a week at $75 to $125 per hour. Income also depends on the number of practices you are managing at any given time. In 1996, surveys showed that on average dentists earned $181,000 and MDs, $215,000. A practice-management consultant's earnings can equal that of their affluent clients. Some consultants bill up to sixty hours a week.

Overhead: high (approximately 50 percent).

Best Home Businesses Estimate of Market Potential

Operating a professional practice is increasingly competitive, demanding a sophisticated management and business approach that is often unfamiliar and unappealing to professionals. As a result, the demand for professional-practice consultants has exploded in the past decade, yet only a small percentage of the 600,000 or so doctors in private practice are being served.

Though managed care has hurt consultants who focus on serving one-person and small practices, the outlook for this field remains bright for people who possess effective change strategies and can help professionals manage their changing practices. A lot of work involves helping professionals negotiate mergers or acquisitions and agreements for entering or exiting managed-care organizations. These are instances when professionals face a plethora of problems. Some private-practice consultants have made the transition from serving small practices to serving larger health organizations and this appears to be the wave of the future.

Someone with experience in the health-care field may be able to begin by consulting with larger organizations while someone without that experience can begin with smaller practices.

Best Ways to Get Business

- Having developed contacts in the medical or consulting field prior to starting the business. Networking with those contacts to get a few clients and building new contacts through professional and civic associations.

- Positioning yourself to get referrals from your first few clients. This is one of the most important and effective techniques.

- Sending targeted mailings to certain types of professionals and following through with face-to-face meetings and telephone calls. Be prepared with a high-quality, persuasive presentation that demonstrates what you can do for the client.

- Offering workshops on practice-management issues to professional medical or legal organizations in your area. You might speak on maximizing profits or on a topic that captures immediate attention.

- Writing columns with tips and guidance about practice management for business and professional journals.

- Serving on fund-raising committees in organizations that have doctors or other professionals as members.

- Having your own Web page with its own domain name with testimonial letters and any articles you have written.

Franchise

PROFESSIONAL MANAGEMENT GROUP, Box 1130, Battle Creek, MI 49016; (800) 888-1932. Provides bread-and-butter business services for professionals. They seek people who have some accounting, business, or financial background, and who are familiar with some aspects of the health-care field. They offer preceptor (observer) and mentor (apprentice) arrangements, new-consultant workshops, and continuing education. The fee is approximately $25,000, and the franchise provides geographical exclusivity.

First Steps

- Take educational programs on professional-management topics offered by institutes and professional associations.

- Work for an established firm that does professional-practice consulting. In effect, you will be apprenticing.

Where to Turn for Information and Help

ORGANIZATION

SOCIETY OF MEDICAL-DENTAL MANAGEMENT CONSULTANTS, 3646 East Ray Road #B16-45, Phoenix, AZ 85044; (800) 826-2264; fax: (480) 759-3530. Holds two meetings a year at which members share information and receive continuing education. Web site: *www.smdmc.org.* Potential clients can find a consultant from the membership directory posted on the site.

BOOKS

Encyclopedia of Practice and Financial Management, Lawrence Farber, Medical Economic Books, 1985.

How to Join, Buy or Merge a Physician's Practice, Yvonne Mart Fox, Brett A. Levine, Mosby, 1997. ISBN: 0815128789

Managing Your Medical Practice, Charles R. Wold, Ahab Press. Looseleaf, updated annually; $135; (800) 696-7090. Web site: *www.ahabpress.com*

Medical Practice Management, Horace Cotton. Medical Economic Books, 1985.

Physician Equity Groups and Other Emerging Equity: Competitive Organizational Choices for Physicians, Fred McCall-Perez, Ph.D., McGraw-Hill, 1997.

Practice Management for Physicians, Donald L. Donohugh. Orlando, FL: W. B. Saunders, 1986.

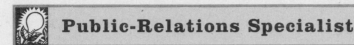

Public-Relations Specialist

To be sure, many clients hire public-relations practitioners to get publicity or "PR" or for help in managing their reputations in critical situations, but increasingly the role of the public-relations professional is to be a vital part of the brain trust of an organization. The role of the PR professional goes from sending media kits and press releases to being a two-way conduit for intelligence on and off the Information Highway.

Thus the PR specialist must be genuinely knowledgeable about the industry or industries they serve and understand what is shaping those industries. Richard George, Director of Public Relations for the Public Relations Society of America (PRSA), emphasized this point when we asked what someone in PR needs to be reading. "Five hundred futurist magazines and articles," he told us. "This is more than a tactical thing, we must have an overview of society." In other words, today's PR professional needs to be an information junkie.

Like the rest of society, the public-relations field has become specialized. PRSA identifies fifteen "elements of public relations," and these are each an arena of specialization for self-employed practitioners:

- Community Relations
- Counseling
- Employee/Member Relations
- Fund-Raising or Development
- Government Affairs, includes lobbying
- Industry Relations
- Investor or Financial Relations
- Issues Management

- Marketing Communications
- Media Relations
- Minority Relations/ Multicultural Affairs
- Public Affairs
- Publicity
- Research
- Special Events and Public Participation

PR professionals can also find niches by specializing in serving a particular type of client—business, governmental, and nonprofit. Possible specialties within the nonprofit sector include schools, colleges, foundations, hospitals, religious institutions, trade and professional associations, trade unions, and other forms of voluntary associations. Some PR professionals specialize by industry. Particularly inviting industries are high tech and health care, where some people, after leaving a salaried job, can achieve a six-figure income by working on their own. As one man told us, "I can't believe what I am making, just operating out of my home."

Some specialize in crisis communications, annual reports, internal communications consulting, copywriting, or Web publicity. Some serve only authors or actors. Others focus on environmentally conscious companies, lawyers, consultants, and doctors who seek to use PR to gain visibility in order to market their services.

PR has grown because it's proven to be a cost-effective way for businesses, nonprofit organizations, and public agencies to relate to their publics. In fact, Daniel J. Edelman, founder of Edelman Public Relations Worldwide, says PR is actually more efficient than advertising under the following circumstances:

- When introducing a revolutionary, breakthrough product for small companies with little budget for advertising.

- When the company is small, with little budget for advertising.

- When TV is not an option, as with some product that can't be advertised or does not fit well with television.

- When public opinion is negative and has to be turned around quickly.

A PR professional working independently at home can produce the quality of work once reserved for large agencies with much higher overhead. The Internet and other forms of electronic communications, coupled with the capabilities of desktop publishing and overnight and even same-day mail delivery, enables the PR specialist to communicate in multiple media and to create and send materials to and from virtually anywhere, usually instantaneously.

Judie Framan began working out of her home in southern California some eight years ago, after serving as a corporate communications manager for many years. Some of her contacts from her corporate jobs became clients, and little by little her business grew and became successful. Framan points out that companies hire freelancers in part because most have developed a special expertise and have lots of useful contacts. For instance, in the twenty-plus years she has been in the communications business, she has established relationships with a number of trade journals covering many different industries. Knowing the types of stories those editors are looking for helps her match her clients' needs with the needs of editors.

The skilled public-relations practitioner, Framan emphasizes, must be persistent and follow up on every lead. "Don't take yes for an answer," she reminds others, because even after you've gotten a commitment from an editor, you can't relax. "The amount of follow-up you have to do in public relations is unbelievable," she says. "Editors are extremely busy, and even after you've convinced someone to run your story, you need to make sure the story doesn't die." A tactful phone call can make all the difference.

Knowledge and Skills You Need to Have

- PR specialists need strong communication skills. You have to be able to write well to attract attention and interest with the materials you prepare for your clients, and you need to be able to edit, too.

- You must have good telephone skills. You need to be both diplomatic and persuasive at the same time.

- You must have a good memory for names because much of your day is spent contacting reporters, producers, and editors by phone. You need to have or be able to gain knowledge of the media that your clients want to reach and establish relationships with the editors and producers who will make publicity decisions. You need to know the deadlines they operate under; their focus or theme; types of guests they like to have on their shows and features or articles they like to run; and so forth, so you will know how to talk to them about your clients.

- You must be creative and colorful in presenting clients with a new angle that will capture the interest of their market and the media.

- You must follow trends, current events, interests, needs, and likes and dislikes by keeping up with sports, entertainment, business, technology, and world affairs. PR people read newspapers. You want to be able to shoot off a memo to a client about a negative article in *The New York Times*; you will likely impress them by being ahead of the curve; you are expected to be a sage for your clients.

- Freelance PR specialists must be able to come up with stimulating ideas on their own or collaborate with others with whom they can team up. You need to be able to organize abstract ideas or technical jargon into tangible, meaningful material for publications, speeches, newsletters, ad copy, and so forth.

- You need to master the four-step process of research, planning, execution, and evaluation, because the demand on public relations has grown. The question, says Richard George, is "Not only have you been in the newspaper, but have you changed people's minds or attitudes? Did you move the needle at all?" If you have done front-end research, was anything changed?

- A PR specialist must have a lot of energy. PR projects are referred to as campaigns. There are deadlines, and there is little down time to regroup and recharge emotionally and physically.

- You need to be able to handle rejection without taking it personally, because you need to come back another day fresh.

Start-up Costs	Low	High
Computer	$ 1,500	$ 3,000
Printer	$ 300	$ 800
or		
Multi-function printer/fax/scanner/copier	$ 150	$ 600
Cell phone	$ 75	$ 200
Telephone headset (can increase phone productivity by a third)	$ 40	$ 400
Office furniture, especially an ergonomic chair	$ 400	$ 1,000
Initial marketing budget	$ 1,000	$ 5,000
Total	$ 3,465	$ 11,000

Advantages

- This business can be exciting and vastly stimulating. It provides enjoyable and interesting experiences, and you get to meet interesting people.

- You are not limited to doing any particular thing at any given time. Throughout the day, you can move from one kind of activity to another.

- You have an opportunity to be creative, amusing, playful, and trendy.

- Public relations is perceived as prestigious.

Disadvantages

- Public relations is a competitive field. Many people who are unable to find a job in a corporation after college start doing public relations on their own, working from home. Through internships at school, they have had some experience and will work at cut-rate prices, which may bring down the price others can charge. It is also always hard to convince clients that your services are worth as much as they are, because PR results are partially intangible.

- You must prove your value over and over again with your clients. You're only as good as the PR you got on your last job. There is always the pressure of how many stories you can place and what response your news releases generate.

- The work can be stressful because of deadlines, time pressures, and the fact that often the end result for your client lies outside your control and in the hands of editors and producers who have their own priorities, whims, and preferences.

- PR is sensitive to the economy. Some businesses pull back on PR expenses if times are tough, even though such times are ideal for doing more PR.

- This business has a slow start-up. You can expect two years of taking out less than you're putting in.

- Prospecting never ends. You always need to have business lined up after your current projects come to a close. The average client relationship lasts only nine months.

Pricing

Most PR specialists operate on a monthly-fee, plus expenses, basis or on a project basis, with costs varying depending on the type and number of hours involved. Hourly rates vary widely dependent on the size of client, the industry, and the regional market, resulting in a range of $200 to $1,500 a day. An average fee for experienced public-relations professionals serving large corporations will approximate $1,000 a day while fees for those working for smaller companies average $600 per day. The highest rates for PR professionals are for those who provide counseling services; they may charge as much as $200 or more per hour.

Potential Earnings

Typical Annual Gross Revenues: $65,000 based on billing 125 days at $400 a day to $175,000 based on billing 175 days at $1,000 a day. Billing twenty hours a week (125 days) should be a minimum goal; thirty billable hours is realistic.

Overhead: low to moderate (20 to 40 percent).

Best Home Businesses Estimate of Market Potential

The Bureau of Labor Statistics projects growth for the public relations field through 2006, and the outlook for self-employed PR professionals is as good or better. When firms need a particular skill, they often don't want to hire a permanent staff person or an entire agency. The increasing complexity of public relations tasks favors specialists whose skills are needed on an on-call basis.

Also, in-house PR staff are a favorite target for downsizing by corporations and organizations. As a result, more and more companies are contracting out their public-relations work.

Best Ways to Get Business

- Networking and personal contacts in organizations, such as trade and business associations, particularly in industries or fields in which you have experience. Networking can serve two purposes: to identify clients that may want your services and to identify associations that may want you to do PR for them, too.

- Speaking before business or community groups promoting the benefits of public relations and informing audiences of the changes in public relations.

- Volunteering your skills to nonprofit organizations where you make contacts and gain visibility.

- Telemarketing, particularly if you can barter with a professional to do it for you.

- Publishing a newsletter for former and prospective clients and referral sources.

- Identifying potential PR opportunities for companies by reading the electronic news services and then contacting the companies by phone to let them know of the leads you've developed.

- Being alert to new businesses you see in upscale neighborhoods, noticing what companies are hiring in your area, contacting those that interest you and then following up.

- Having your own Web page with its own domain name with testimonial letters and any articles you have written.

First Steps

- Gain training and experience. Many colleges and universities have certificate programs in public relations that can provide you with an understanding of the field and a credential without your having to earn a four-year degree. Experience may be acquired interning with an agency or company or assisting an established freelancer, doing it for free if necessary.

- Obtain accreditation. The Public Relations Society of America offers accreditation as an APR, which stands for accredited in public relations. This credential is also being recognized by a number of smaller public-relations organizations. The International Association of Business Communicators offers the Accredited Business Communicator (ABC) credential.

Where to Turn for Information and Help

ORGANIZATIONS

INTERNATIONAL ASSOCIATION OF BUSINESS COMMUNICATORS, 1 Halladie Plaza, Suite 600, San Francisco, CA 94102; (415) 433-3400. Professional association encompassing public relations, employee and marketing communication, and public affairs. Web site: *www.iabc.com*

CANADIAN PUBLIC RELATIONS SOCIETY, 220 Laurier Avenue West, Suite 720, Ottawa, Ontario, Canada K1P 5Z9; (613) 232-1222. Web site: *www.cprs.ca*

NATIONAL INVESTORS RELATIONS INSTITUTE, 8045 Leesburg Pike, Suite 600, Vienna, Virginia 22182; (703) 506-3570. Web site: *www.niri.org/about/index.cfm*

PUBLIC RELATIONS SOCIETY OF AMERICA, 33 Irving Place, New York, NY 10003; (212) 995-2230. Sixteen special sections, 113 chapters in the U.S., publications including *Public Relations Tactics* and *Public Relations Journal*. Web site: *www.prsa.org*

BOOKS

Dartnell's Public Relations Handbook, Robert L. Dilenschneider, Dartnell Corporation, 1996. ISBN: 0850132371.

Effective Public Relations, Scott M. Cutlip, Allen H. Center, Glen M., Broom, Ph.D. Prentice-Hall, 1994. ISBN: 0132450100.

The Handbook of Strategic Public Relations and Integrated Communications, Clarke L. Caywood, McGraw-Hill, 1997. ISBN 0786311312.

How To Open and Operate A Home-Based Communications Business, Louann Nagy Werksma, Globe Pequot Press, 1995. ISBN 1564406318.

Lesly's Handbook of Public Relations and Communications, Philip Lesly, NTC Business Books, 1998. ISBN: 0844232572.

Marketing Public Relations, Rene A. Henry Jr., Iowa State University Press, 1995. ISBN: 0813822084.

Public Relations: Strategies & Tactics, Dennis L. Wilcox, Addison-Wesley Publishing Company, 1997. ISBN 0321015479.

Public Relations Writing: The Essentials of Style and Format, Thomas H. Bivins, NTC Publishing Group, 1998. ISBN: 0844203513.

Publicity and Media Relations Checklists, David R. Yale, NTC Business Books, 1995. ISBN 0844232181.

Six Steps to Free Publicity, Marcia Yudkin, New York: Plume, 1994. ISBN: 0452271924.

The Practice Of Public Relations, Fraser Seitel, Prentice-Hall, 1998. ISBN: 013613811X.

Winning with the News Media, Clarence Jones, Video Consultants, 1998. ISBN: 0961960345.

DIRECTORIES

Bacon's Information, Inc., 332 South Michigan Avenue, Suite 900, Chicago, IL 60604; (312) 922-2400. Publishes *Bacon's Radio, Bacon's TV and Cable, Bacon's Magazine, Bacon's Newspaper and Media Directory.* Complete listing of directories on Web site. Web site: *www.baconsinfo.com*

Business Periodicals Index, H. W. Wilson Company, 950 University Avenue, Bronx, NY 10452; (718) 588-8400. Annual. Web site: *www.hwwilson.com*

Gale Directory of Publications and Broadcast Media, Gale Group, PO Box 9187, Farmington Hills, MI 48333. (800) 877-GALE. Annual. Web site: *www.galegroup.com*

Gebbie Press All-in-One Directory, Gebbie Press, Box 1000, New Paltz, NY 12561, (914) 255-7560. Annual. Web site: *www.gebbieinc.com*

O'Dwyer's Directory of Public Relations Firms, J. R. O'Dwyer Company, 271 Madison Avenue, New York, NY 10016; (212) 679-2471. Also publishes *Jack O'Dwyer's PR Newsletter.* Web site: *www.odwyerpr.com*

Working Press of the Nation (5 volumes), Reed Reference Publishing, 121 Chanlon Rd., New Providence, NJ 07974; (800) 521-8110. Web site: *www.reedref.com*

MAGAZINES AND NEWSLETTERS

Inside PR, 708 3rd Ave., Suite 205, New York, NY 10017; (212) 818-0288. Weekly e-mailed newsletter. Web site: *www.prcentral.com*

PR Reporter, Box 600, 14 Front Street, Exeter, NH 03833; (603) 778-0514. Weekly newsletter of PR, public affairs, and communications. Web site: *www.prpublishing.com*

Public Relations News, Phillips Publishing, 1201 Seven Locks Road, Potomac, MD 20854, (800) 777-5006. Weekly. Web site: *www.phillips.com*

Public Relations Quarterly, P.O. Box 311, Rhinebeck, NY 12572; (914) 876-2081. Web site: *www.newsletter-clearinghse.com*

SOFTWARE

MEDIAMANAGER PR DATABASE SOFTWARE, MediaMap, 215 First Street, Cambridge, MA 01242; (617) 374-9300. Web site: *www.mediamap.com*

WEB SITES

DATABANK created by Professor contains abstracts of articles and book chapters. *www.scils.rutgers.edu/de/graphics/databank/databank.html*

PUBLICATIONS IN PR lists books and other resources. *www.prplace.com/pr_pub.htm*

PR RESOURCES ON THE INTERNET provides links. *www.publicity.org/xresource.html*

 Real Estate Appraiser

Real estate appraisers earn their living estimating the value of residential and commercial property. Real estate needs to be appraised prior to its sale, when refinancing or getting a home equity loan, when getting insurance, in the event of a loss, at the time of bankruptcy, pending a merger or acquisition, for investment decisions, during a divorce, and at many other times in the course of owning a home or building.

The real estate appraisal industry underwent a fundamental transformation in 1992 when Title XI of the Financial Institutions Reform, Recovery, and Enforcement Act (FIRREA) became effective, requiring that states establish minimum licensing and certification standards for real estate appraisal work involving many federally related transactions. FIRREA was written to counteract the inflated values that some appraisers had placed on properties in the 1980's. These inflated appraisals were significant factors in the failure of so many savings and loan institutions and the consequent bailout that cost federal taxpayers hundreds of billions of dollars.

The implications of FIRREA were clear. Because many buyers purchase homes through federally insured mortgages, now all appraisers, experienced or new, are effectively required to obtain a license or certification to practice their trade. The new law was in sharp contrast to the past, when appraisers generally learned the rules of appraisal through apprenticeship and experience. The good news, though, is that as a career, this field is thriving as old-time appraisers retire, opening the doors for new ones to come in.

According to the Appraisal Institute, the largest association of professional appraisers, the opportunities for appraisers are excellent. As they say, "With the increasing complexity of real estate investment, the need for appraisal services has grown. The increased application of environmental and other land-use regulations by local and federal governments continually provides new opportunities for appraisers."

Real estate appraisers use their knowledge of building structure, construction, finance, demographic statistics, and business trends to analyze and evaluate the value of a property. In addition to viewing the property, appraisers may also do original and secondary research, including examining public records, survey drawings, blueprints, and government regulations. Appraisers then produce a written report that documents their analyses and presents their conclusions. Banks, mortgage companies, buyers, sellers, tax collectors, lawyers—in short, all the parties to a transaction—count on the appraisal to help them close a sale or come to an agreement on a settlement price for a property. Because of FIRREA, the requirements to become an appraiser vary slightly by state but are roughly comparable. These include:

- 75 hours of course work for licensing, which allows you to appraise complex residential properties under $250,000 and noncomplex one-to-four-unit properties under $1 million.

- 105 hours of course work for residential certification for residential properties with a value in excess of $1 million.

- 165 hours of course work for general certification, which allows you to appraise residential and commercial properties at any value.

In addition, both the license and certification also require 2,000 hours of appraisal experience and the successful completion of an exam. As you can see, there is still quite a heavy reliance on experience. Appraisers must, therefore, find another appraiser to work for as an apprentice during a period of about two years before they are eligible for licensing or certification.

But appraising can be lucrative. Greg Edwards, an appraiser in Santa Monica, California, has been working in this field for thirteen years. Through his contacts and networking, he is an approved appraiser for several banks and thus finds that he is often called upon for appraisals most days of the week for at least one if not two assignments. Greg comments, however, that the appraisal business is becoming more and more computerized. In the old days, he would go to city hall to look up records on past sales of homes, whereas he now checks records using an online service so that his numbers are no more than twenty-four hours old. In addition to homes and buildings, some appraisers appraise shopping centers, industrial sites, farms, peat bogs, mines, pond bottoms, as well as collections of jewelry, art, and other valuables.

Knowledge and Skills You Need To Have

- You will need to obtain a license or certification for your state. This requires course-work time and experience, as indicated above.

- You need sound judgment, a good visual sense, and the ability to synthesize a lot of data about a piece of property.

- Appraisers must not only have knowledge of architecture, construction, and building materials, but also of finance, mortgage equity, present-value calculations, and other economic factors.

- Because appraisers write reports, you need to have a command of English and the ability to write well. You also need to know how to take photos, as most appraisals require photos of the property from outside as well as inside.

- You need to be effective at networking and getting your name around, as knowing lawyers, bankers, mortgage officers, insurance agents, and others who use appraisers can make the difference between getting business or not.

- You need to keep up your skills. Robert Snead believes appraisers need to devote one day a week to this.

Start-up Costs	Low	High
Computer	$ 1,500	$ 3,000
Printer	$ 300	$ 800
or		
Multi-function printer/fax/scanner/copier	$ 150	$ 600
Cell phone	$ 75	$ 200
Office furniture	$ 400	$ 1,000
Digital camera	$ 300	$ 1,000
Appraisal software	$ 200	$ 600
Course work for examinations	$ 1,000	$ 2,000
License or certification	$ 300	$ 1,000
Errors and omissions insurance	$ 600	$ 1,200
Initial marketing budget including organizational dues and Internet access	$ 1,000	$ 3,000
Total	$ 5,825	$ 8,800

Advantages

- This is not a desk job; you're outside much of the time instead of sitting down. An appraisal takes about four hours for a single-family home; you do need to spend about one hour, however, writing your report.

- Mobile computers and online access from almost anywhere mean you spend even less time in offices.

- Overhead and risk are low in comparison to other businesses in the real estate field.

- Your clients (banks, lawyers, etc.) become regular customers if they like your work.

Disadvantages

- Work requirements may necessitate that you attend evening meetings or do your work at the property owners' convenience at times other than 9 to 5. This can make balancing family life challenging.

- Appraisers are being sued and held legally responsible for losses of savings and loans and banks; so you need to have errors and omissions insurance.

- The new licensing/certification process is time-consuming. It may be difficult to find an appraiser to work for in your area.

- You may be stressed by tension between banks and buyers who don't want to approve a mortgage for or buy a property worth less than its selling price, and sellers and their lawyers or real estate agents who want an appraised price as high as they can get it.

Pricing

The typical appraisal fee on a residence is $150 to $550. Larger houses or commercial properties are $500 to $3000 with 1 to 2 percent at $100,000 or more. Fees are dependent on community real-estate values.

Potential Earnings

Typical Annual Gross Revenues: $75,000 for residential appraising, based on completing three appraisals per week at $500 each. Commercial appraisers, who must have more qualifications, can earn over $100,000 per year. First year, $10,000 to $20,000 and by the third or fourth year, $20,000 to 45,000.

Overhead: moderate (30 percent).

Best Home Businesses **Estimate of Market Potential**

The United States is served by 75,000 to 80,000 real-estate appraisers. Demand for appraisers is lessening as information becomes available in online computer databases, often reducing the appraiser's role to confirming data. The trend is to accomplish more appraisals in less time. While this might seem to imply there will be fewer appraisers, keep in mind that real estate is being bought and sold more frequently and fewer transfers of real estate are being done without an appraisal. In addition, people are now using appraisers as part of divorce proceedings, in valuing charitable donations for tax purposes, and filing decedent's estate tax returns.

The field remains exciting for those who keep up with change and not all do. Appraisers have been slow, for example, to use the Internet. As Robert Snead, Executive Vice President of the National Association of Independent Fee Appraisers points out, "Appraisers who think of solutions and offer consultation can do well."

Best Ways to Get Business

- Creating some samples of your work to show to prospective sources of business.

- Making personal contact with mortgage companies, savings and loans, and banks to get on their list of approved appraisers. Plan on regularly visiting prospective sources of business.

- Networking in organizations such as mortgage bankers' associations and mortgage brokers' associations.

- Joining one or more national associations for referrals.

- Having your own Web site with meta tags and links that will direct people to your site.

Related Business

Personal Property Appraiser

Appraising personal property is highly specialized based on specific expertise. The field as a whole covers both household and industrial personal property. You see such appraisers in action on the *Antiques Road-*

show on PBS. Personal property appraisers are apt to be called art appraisers or business appraisers. A personal property appraiser might be used when something of value is sold, donated to a charity, involved in a divorce proceeding, and when filing estate tax returns. Fees are based on an hourly or daily rate. It's considered unethical for an appraiser to work for a fixed percentage of the amount of value. Governments do not regulate personal property appraisers as they do real estate appraisers. The primary trade association for personal property appraisers as a whole is the American Society of Appraisers, 555 Herndon Parkway, Suite 125, Herndon, VA 20170; (800) ASA-VALU. Web site: *www.appraisers.org*. The association offers accreditation based on education, experience, and passing several written examinations.

First Steps

- Contact your state licensing division for complete details of license requirements and educational resources in your area.

- Obtain your license. Course work entails 75 to 165 hours of classroom time. You can take the course from one of the associations listed below, some of which hold their seminars around the country or at local real-estate schools.

Where to Turn for Information and Help

ORGANIZATIONS

THE APPRAISAL INSTITUTE, 875 North Michigan Avenue, Chicago, IL 60611-1980; (312) 335-4100. With 33,000 members, the largest appraisal organization composed of both residential and commercial appraisers. Offers self-study courses, seminars at various locations around the country, and exam prep materials. Web site: *www.appraisalinstitute.org*

AMERICAN SOCIETY OF FARM MANAGERS AND RURAL APPRAISERS, 950 S. Cherry St. #508, Denver, CO 80246; (303) 758-3513. Web site: *www.agri-associations.org/asfmra*

APPRAISERS ASSOCIATION OF AMERICA, 386 Park Avenue South, Suite 2000, New York, NY 10016; (212) 889-5404. This association is for appraisers of personal property other than real estate. Offers courses through New York University.

NATIONAL ASSOCIATION OF INDEPENDENT FEE APPRAISERS, 7501 Murdoch Avenue, St. Louis, MO 63119; (314) 781-6688. Lists members in an online directory, posts jobs, offers chat rooms. Members receive a free home page. Web site: *www.naifa.com*

NATIONAL ASSOCIATION OF REAL ESTATE APPRAISERS, 1224 North Nokomis NE, Alexandria, MN 56308; (320) 763-7626; fax: (320) 763-9290. Offers an apprentice program for new appraisers at no additional fee. Offers classroom courses around the nation. Web site has a member directory. Web site: *www.iami.org/narea.html*

BOOKS

Appraising Residences and Income Properties, Henry S. Harrison, New Haven, CT: H2 Company, 1989. ISBN: 0927054019.

Basic Real Estate Appraisal, Richard M. Betts, Silas J. Ely, Prentice-Hall Press, 1997. ISBN: 013742891X.

Fundamentals of Real Estate Appraisal, William L. Ventolo, Jr., and Martha R. Williams, Chicago: Dearborn, 1998. ISBN: 0793126312.

In addition, many of the associations publish their own books and notebooks. A specialty bookstore for the real estate industry is *www.realestatebookstore.com*; purchases are routed to amazon.com.

COURSES

ALLIED BUSINESS SCHOOLS offers a mail order course recommended by the National Association of Real Estate Appraisers. Also offered are courses for real-estate agents, real-estate brokers, home inspectors, and property managers. 22952 Alcalde Drive, Laguna Hills, CA 92653; (800) 542-5543; (949) 598-0875. Web site: *www.alliedschools.com*

You are apt to find courses offered locally both by real-estate schools and by the major associations that hold seminars around the country.

APPRAISAL SOFTWARE

A LA MODE, 1015 Water Wood Pkwy., Building F, Edmond, OK 73034; (800) 252-6633; (405) 359-3346; fax (405) 359-8612.

DAY ONE, 487 Devon Park Drive, Suite 210, Wayne, PA 19087; (800) 438-3291; (610) 975-9000; fax: (610) 975-9400. Offers a demo version at the Web site. Web site: *www.day1.com*

Remodeling Contractor

If you own your own home, chances are you remodeled within 18 to 36 months of buying it, and you used a professional to do the work. Two out of three Americans own their own homes and spend as much as four times the original price of the house remodeling and maintaining it. About 30 million homeowners will do some remodeling this year and, according to the Census Bureau, professionals do 78 percent of all remodeling work. In 1998, that came to $125 billion of work for remodeling contractors, up from $46 billion in 1980.

Although owners may decide to remodel at any time and some do quite frequently, houses are ripe for remodeling when they are over 15 years old. Eighty-five million homes in the United States are over 15 years old, and over 60 million are over 25 years old. So if you have the desire and know-how to help people improve their homes and office buildings, you have an enormous number of potential customers. It's estimated that seven out of ten remodelers are self-employed individuals. As Kermit Baker of the Harvard MIT Joint Center on Housing Studies reports, "This is a stealth industry."

Remodeling professionals may specialize in multiple ways. First, there's residential versus commercial remodeling. Commercial remodeling includes making tenant improvements in renter-occupied buildings; adapting buildings from one type of use to another; and rehabilitating historic structures.

Contractors can also specialize in particular types of residential remodeling, such as restoring homes damaged by fire or suffering from other insurable losses, condo/apartment remodeling, renovating historic residences, or they might specialize by architectural style. Another way to specialize is by what areas of a residence you remodel. The National Association of the Remodeling Industry keeps track of the kind of remodeling people are interested in from calls to its Remodeling Hotline. Here's what they find:

Kitchens	47%
Baths	46%
Other Interior Work	41%
Windows	39%
Room Additions	35%
Sunrooms	32%

To get ahead of the curve, consider specializing in home offices, greenhouses, additions for elder relatives, or pools, saunas and steamrooms.

Knowledge and Skills You Need to Have

- You need to have an understanding of the industry, some background knowledge in engineering, architecture, interior decoration, or the like.

- You need to have hands-on capability to do the work unless you compensate with other skills such as business management, computer operation, or interior design and contract out hands-on work.

- Even if you are not hands on, you need enough knowledge to handle scheduling and ordering and to oversee quality.

- If you broker or outsource components of the work, you need to be effective at coordinating, scheduling, and supervising other people.

Advantages

- The good feelings that come from doing work that has improved people's property and lives.

- It's a lucrative business if marketed and managed effectively.

- If you are a competent time manager, this is more of a Monday-to-Friday business than many others.

Disadvantages

- Homeowners are increasingly doing small jobs on a do-it-yourself basis.

- The labor pool of qualified and skilled people to work for you as a subcontractor or as employee is small in most areas. Thus, it's difficult to find good people.

- Being involved in so many aspects of projects can be stressful—first getting the business, then getting the project designed to satisfy the client within their budget, and dealing with suppliers, subcontractors, and employees. You need to do all of this and meet the expectations of homeowners who want their job to be perfect at a time when building materials are not as high quality or durable as they once were. John Quaregena, Chairman of the Board of NARI and president of his own company, Jay-Cue in North Bergen, New Jersey, says, "It's a difficult industry, but you can make money by being honest, giving good service, and, for longevity, being better than your competition."

Start-up Costs

	Low	High
For both hands-on contractors and brokers:		
Computer	$ 1,500	$ 3,000
Multi-function printer/fax/scanner/copier	$ 150	$ 600
Cell phone	$ 75	$ 200
Office furniture	$ 400	$ 1,000
Initial marketing budget, Yellow Page ad, job signs	$ 1,000	$ 2,000
If you do work yourself:		
Hand tools, tool pouch, handyman items	$ 800	$ 1,000
Pickup truck or van	$19,000	$ 22,500
Lettering on your truck	$ 800	$ 1,000
Equipment	$20,000	$100,000
Total	$43,725	$131,300

Pricing

Some firms do a few large jobs per year, some do many smaller jobs. Some price by the hour at rates ranging from $25 to $50 an hour or more; some by the job; others work on a contract for time and materials plus a mark-up.

Potential Earnings

Typical Annual Gross Revenues: Many specialty contractors are able to reach six-figure incomes.

Overhead: high.

Best Home Businesses Estimate of Market Potential

Two factors almost assure substantial growth for the remodeling industry. First, 3 million homes change ownership each year and second, the houses people are buying and living in are growing older. Only 15 percent of home sales are of new housing. If the economy is up, people have money to spend, and with a move often comes a remodel. If the economy is down, people remodel to make do with the home they might otherwise have sold for larger or more luxurious housing. In either case, there's work to be done by remodelers. Adding to this is a tight supply of upscale housing in some markets, often due to environmental controls, resulting in affluent owners remodeling instead of moving up.

Best Ways to Get Business

- When getting started, having a Yellow Page ad. For commercial work, listing in the "The Blue Book."

- Demonstrably thanking past customers for referrals, such as with a food gift or gift certificate to a restaurant.

- Having a Web page that shows off your work. Affluent customers turn to the Web as much or more than they turn to the Yellow Pages.

- Entering contests for awards for your work.

- Getting houses you have remodeled entered into parades of remodeled homes.

- When you work in an area, using "pardon our dust" letters and door hangers with the objective of attracting the positive attention of neighbors.

- With your customer's consent, having a "Dumpster Day" at which time neighbors can retrieve items from the remodel that would otherwise be hauled away.

- Instead of printing a brochure, putting examples of your work and other relevant information on a floppy disk or CD-ROM.

- Writing, speaking, and teaching about remodeling so you become recognized as an expert.

- Joining and participating in community and referral organizations.

- Subcontracting with lumber yards, manufacturers, distributors, and other retail suppliers for installation work.

- Surveys of remodelers indicates that nearly two-thirds of their work comes from repeat business and referrals from past customers. Keeping your business top-of-mind with past customers is a must. You can do this by remembering them with a newsletter or tip sheet such as checklists for seasonal maintenance.

First Steps

- Secure the financing to fund your start-up costs and have a way to cover your living costs for a year.

- Set up your office and obtain a vehicle.

- Start marketing.

Where to Turn for Information and Help

ORGANIZATIONS

AMERICAN SUBCONTRACTORS ASSOCIATION, 1004 Duke Street, Alexandria, VA 22314; (703) 684-3450; fax: (703) 836-3482. Web site: *www.asaonline.com*

NATIONAL ASSOCIATION OF THE REMODELING INDUSTRY (NARI), 4900 Seminary Road, Suite 320, Alexandria, Virginia 22311. The only association exclusively dedicated to remodeling whose members include full-service remodeling contractors, specialty contractors, manufacturers, designers, and suppliers. Members get leads from the NARI Web site's Find A NARI Pro database. Web site: *www.nari.org*

NATIONAL KITCHEN AND BATH ASSOCIATION, 687 Willow Grove Street, Hacketstown, NJ 07840; (800) 843-6522; (908) 852-0033; fax: (908) 852-1695. Web site: *www.nkba.org*

DIRECTORIES

Blue Book. Lists general contractors, subcontractors, architects, engineers, equipment manufacturers, material and product suppliers, and service providers. Contractors Register, Inc., P.O. Box 500, Jefferson

Valley, NY 10535; (800) 431-2584; fax: (914) 243-0287. The *Electronic Blue Book* at www.thebluebook.com contains more than 550,000 listings and 40,000 display advertisements.

Old-House Journal Restoration Directory. Annual. Ten thousand products from 1,700 manufacturers. ISBN: 999719408X.

COURSES AND TRAINING

Trade schools teach specialty trades, but there is no substitute for hands-on experience. Community colleges offer suitable business courses. Certification programs are available from many sources, including the organizations listed.

BOOKS

On Time and on Budget: A Home Renovation Survival Guide, John Rusk, Main Street Books, 1997. ISBN: 038547511X.

Professional Remodeler's Manual: Save Time, Avoid Mistakes, Increase Profits, R. Dodge Woodson, New York: McGraw-Hill Text; 1995. ISBN: 0070717974.

Profits in Buying and Renovating Homes, Lawrence Dworin, Craftsman Book Co; 1990; ISBN: 0934041571.

Renovating Old Houses, George Nash, Taunton Press, 1996. ISBN: 1561581283.

Renovation: A Complete Guide, Michael W. Litchfield, Prentice-Hall Trade, 1990. ISBN: 0131593366.

Fine Homebuilding. Web site: *www.taunton.com*

Qualified Remodeler. Cygnus Publishing, 1233 Janesville Avenue, Ft. Atkinson, WI 53538; (920) 563-6388.

Professional Remodeler. Cahners Business Information, 1350 E. Touhy Avenue, Box 5080, Des Plaines, IL 60017; (847) 390-2555. Web site: *www.proremodeler.com*

Journal of Light Construction. RR 2, 932 West Main, Richmond, VT 05477; (802) 434-4747.

Tools of the Trade. Hanley-Wood Inc., 1 Thomas Cr., NW, #600, Washington, DC 20005. Web site: *www.hanley-wood.com*

SOFTWARE

Autodesk Pro Remodeler, Autodesk, Inc., 111 McInnis Parkway, San Rafael, CA 94903; (415) 507-5000; fax: (415) 507-5100. Web site: *www.autodesk.com*

Chief Architect, Advanced Relational Technology, Inc., 301 North 3rd Street, Coeur d'Alene, ID 83814; (800) 482-4433; (208) 664-4204; Fax: (208) 664-1316. Web site: *www.chiefarch.com*

Punch List, Strata Systems; (888) 336-3652; fax: (512) 899-3427. Web site: *www.punchlist.com.*

MAGAZINES AND NEWSLETTERS

Building and Remodeling News, 600 Lake St. #C, Ramsey, NJ 07446; (201) 327-1600.

Fine Homebuilding, 63 South Main Street, Newtown, CT 06470; (203) 426-8171; fax: (203)426-3434. Web site: *http://www.taunton.com*

Journal of Light Construction, RR 2, 932 West Main, Richmond, VT 05477; (802) 434-4747; fax: (802)434-4467.

Professional Remodeler, 1350 East Touhy Avenue, Box 5080, Des Plaines, IL 60017; (847) 390-2555. Web site: *www.proremodeler.com*

Qualified Remodeler, 20 East Jackson Blvd, Chicago, Il 60604; (312) 922-5402; fax: (312) 922-0856.

Remodeling, One Thomas Circle, Suite 600, Washington, DC 20005, (888) 269-8410; (202) 452-0800.

Tools of the Trade, One Thomas Circle, Suite 600, Washington, DC 20005; (888) 269-8410; (202) 452-0800. Reports on evaluations of new tools and techniques.

WEB SITES

BUILD.COM is a search engine to enable finding building products and services. *www.build.com*

BUILDINGONLINE. A search engine for over 200,000 construction-related sites and more, including a forum. *www.buildingonline.com*

HOME BUILDING AND REMODELING NETWORK. Lots of magazinelike information from Hanley-Wood, publishers of several industry magazines. *www.hbrnet.com*

HOME IMPROVEMENT INFORMATION AND RESOURCES. Many resources relating to residential construction products and services. *www.tcmn.com/hsn/home.html*

IMPROVENET helps homeowners find contractors, designers, and products. *www.improvenet.com*

REMODELING ONLINE. Information on remodeling techniques and the business of remodeling. *http://remodeling.hw.net*

RENOVATIONS ON-LINE. An "Internet magazine devoted to renovation and remodeling." *www.homereno.com*

Résumé-Writing Service

Surveys show that Americans change jobs on the average of seven times over the course of their working lives. In a tight job market, first-time job seekers are competing toe-to-toe with a ready supply of workers who have been downsized, merged, or acquired. In times of prosperity, workers who weren't downsized have been holding on to their jobs, creating a pent-up demand to move up or on when companies swing into a hiring frenzy. Whatever the state of the economy, thousands of students and workers know it's a good idea to have a résumé handy to give them an edge in a fluid and fast-changing job market.

The result is a tremendous and constant demand for professional résumé writers who specialize in helping people develop and create a competitive résumé that will get results whether it's sent through the mail, posted on the Internet, or e-mailed to a prospective employer.

But now that anyone can log on and fill out a résumé on any number of online job sites, résumé writers can no longer simply type up someone's credentials in an attractive form. By perusing the varied quality of résumés posted on online job sites, you can see there's much more to a good résumé than filling in or laying out a string of facts. The résumé writers' greatest asset lies in their ability to interview clients to draw out what's special about their background, skills, accomplishments, strengths, and weaknesses and how and to whom they want to present themselves. Then the writer must creatively organize this information in a concise and appealing way that highlights the clients' most noteworthy accomplishments and skills so they stand out from the crowd.

Résumé services serve two primary groups of clients:

1. Job seekers who have jobs and are already part of the business and professional community. Seventy-five percent of business comes from this category, which includes those leaving the military, those seeking to advance their careers, and the growing ranks of those who have been victims of mergers, purges, or downsizings. These individuals have both the need and the money to pay for professional help.

2. To a much lesser extent, college and university students. This group includes seniors who are about to graduate, sophomores and juniors seeking internships, and older students returning to the workforce after having gone back to school. Often, however, they have access to assistance through college career centers and typically have less money to spend.

Steve Burt has operated a successful service résumé for sixteen years in Gainesville, Florida. Half or more of his clients are university students whose level of writing skills are seldom adequate to put together a competitive résumé. He says, "My clients usually come to me with nothing in hand or perhaps an old résumé. Sometimes they don't know what type of work they want to pursue, and I may find something in their background that suggests a direction for their job search. He advises that "to succeed in this business you've got to separate yourself from others and offer a high-quality service."

To distinguish their services, some résumé writers specialize in serving a particular type of clientele such as the military or those in a medical, legal, or technical field. Working with physically handicapped people referred by a local department of rehabilitation is another source of business or specialty.

Clients are customarily given a limited number of printed copies, usually 25 to 50, as part of the basic price, although additional copies or a copy on disk can be purchased for an added fee. Most résumé services offer a variety of other services for an extra fee, such as:

- Developing a salary history or reference list.

- Writing, preparing and/or sending cover letters, thank-you notes, follow-up and/or acceptance letters and reference postcards.

- Designing a letterhead so that the cover letter, résumé, and accompanying documents can be presented as a matched set.

- Mailing, faxing, e-mailing or broadcast e-mailing the letter, résumé, and other materials to prospective employers.

- Posting résumés on online job banks.

- Typing applications or forms.

- Providing additional consultations after the initial interview on such things as defining what jobs may be best to seek based on a client's background; helping clients develop a targeted job search strategy or create a Web page they can direct employers to.

- Writing telephone scripts for job seekers to use in making calls.

- Coaching clients in person, by phone, or over the Internet on how to perfect their presentation skills through mock job interviews.

- Producing a résumé on disk, CD-ROM or in HTML, providing color copies or creating a scannable or keyword résumé.

- Verifying information on résumé. This is referred to as a verified résumé.

- Critiquing, updating, rewriting, editing or redesigning an existing résumé or transferring information to a form provided by the client or online.

- Providing video résumés. Now that people can place video résumés on the Internet, it creates the need for a whole other range of services that résumé writers can provide, from coaching clients to present themselves on camera to taping, reproducing, and uploading videos.

Knowledge and Skills You Need to Have

You do not need to have a background in personnel or employment counseling to help a client develop an effective résumé. You can become an expert on résumés by reading the vast amount of material written on this subject, a representative list of which appears at the end of this section. You do need the following skills and abilities:

- The ability to access the Internet to look at listings, post résumés, and communicate often with clients.

- Extremely strong copywriting skills and the ability to organize information logically and concisely are an absolute necessity. You also need a good command of the English language, including punctuation, spelling, and grammar.

- The ability to interview people is vital. You need to be able to make them feel comfortable and draw out key information about their skills and experience.

- At the same time, you need to be able to think like the personnel directors who will read the résumés and be able to anticipate the questions they will ask so you can cover them in the résumés you prepare.

- You should have some talent for design and layout in order to put together a visually attractive résumé.

- Most important, you must enjoy this type of work. You need to be able to show a personal interest in every client's résumé and believe everyone has some valuable skills and experience that can be highlighted to get him or her a job.

Start-up Costs	Low	High
Computer	$ 1,500	$ 3,000
Laser printer	$ 500	$ 1,500
Multi-function color printer/fax/scanner/copier	$ 300	$ 600
Telephone headset	$ 40	$ 400
High-quality papers for résumés, disks	$ 100	$ 200
Office furniture, especially an ergonomic chair	$ 400	$ 1,000
Two identical comfortable chairs*	$ 600	$ 1,000
End tables or coffee table*	$ 100	$ 500
Initial marketing budget	$ 1,000	$ 5,000
Total	$ 4,540	$ 13,200

*Furniture you'll need to interview people in your home. It's best to have a separate entrance to your office.

Advantages

- You get the satisfaction of knowing you're helping others succeed. As Steve Burt says, "It's great to hear people call with a job and tell you that they got it because of the résumé you wrote."

- There is always a demand for this service, both in good economic times and bad. You're always in the mainstream of the job market and are continually learning about where employment trends are going, making you a valuable resource to your community.

- You meet people with a variety of interesting backgrounds.

- Résumé writing can be an add-on service to other businesses such as word processing, desktop publishing, career counseling, manual writing, business-plan writing, or a specialized temporary service.

Disadvantages

- People sometimes confuse résumé writing with a word-processing or desktop publishing service and expect to be charged accordingly. While some résumé services also provide word-processing, Steve Burt believes that to command fees commensurate with the level of effort and scope of work involved, résumé writers need to distinguish themselves from secretarial services, which he's done by becoming certified by the Professional Association of Résumé Writers (see "Organizations" below).

- You have to make it clear that you are a professional writer and need to charge for your knowledge and creativity.

- The work can be seasonal (particularly among the student market). This means you are often extremely busy before and after graduation times or after a large layoff or merger or following career expos.

- Because you're home-based and people often feel an urgency to get their résumé done, or can't call while they're at their office, you may get calls any time of the day or night.

- It can sometimes be disadvantageous to be home based because you may miss out on walk-in traffic. Therefore, you need to turn being home-based into an asset, emphasizing the highly personalized nature of your service.

Pricing

There is a great deal of flexibility in how a résumé service charges. Some services charge by the hour, some the job, most use a combination of the two, usually charging a flat fee for a basic package and adding on additional services either by the hour or for a fixed fee. What's included in the basic package can easily be limited or expanded to meet the demands of a particular locale, specialty, or clientele. Most services have a price sheet, identifying the services they offer and prices of each.

By the Hour: Résumé services that charge by the hour should be billing between $50 to $100 (or more) an hour, according to Frank Fox of the Professional Association of Résumé Writers (PARW).

Flat Fee: Flat fees range vary depending upon the type of résumé being prepared. Some services offer a starter or basic résumé for as low as $25 to $30, but this includes little more than laying out whatever information is provided and providing half a dozen copies on a laser-quality paper. A full-service résumé with an interview more typically runs from $85 to $150. A student's résumé might cost from $50 to $100, while an executive résumé commands $100 to $300 or more. Preparing curricula vitae will usually cost more, in the range of $200 to $500. Certified résumés are usually priced individually based upon how much information is to be verified and how difficult verification will be.

Prices for add-on services also vary greatly with cover letters available for $20 to $30, critiques or updates costing $30 to $40, and electronic posting, $15 to $75. Retyping an existing résumé or typing existing information onto a form might run $40 to $200 per page depending upon the difficulty involved, with a reduced charge for additional pages. Telecoaching or in-person or online consultations beyond the initial interview might run $50 to $75 per hour, with lower costs available for smaller time increments.

In establishing your prices, we suggest visiting a wide range of résumé services on the Web, comparing prices and determining your own based upon what you plan to offer, your level of experience, location, and what the clientele you will be targeting are expecting to pay.

Potential Earnings

Typical Annual Gross Revenues: $50,000 based on $50 an hour, 1,000 hours a year. This requires yielding $83.33 per résumé, based on preparing twelve résumés a week.

A typical entry-level or student résumé takes 1.5 to 2 hours to complete. Executive résumés will take four or more hours. This includes interviewing, writing, and meeting with the client to turn over the completed résumé and collect the fee. Keep in mind that the résumé business is seasonal, with the busiest months being January, February, March, and May and the least-busy months being July, November, and December. During busy times, Steve Burt has booked as many as twenty-three appointments a day!

Overhead: moderate (20 to 40 percent).

Best Home Businesses Estimate of Market Potential

There is every indication people will continue to need résumés whether they are to be posted, faxed on a Web service, or printed and sent in the mail. Creating a winning résumé will continue to be more than a compilation is facts. It involves a variety of skills from drawing out insights people often overlook in themselves to condensing a lot of information into clear and concise summaries and then laying it out in a visually engaging way. In a competitive job market, this combination of skills is unlikely to be replaced by electronic do-it-yourself standardized formats. In fact, the addition of electronic job searching only adds to the range of assistance the résumé writer can provide. So it appears résumé writing will continue to be a recession-resistant, evergreen home business.

Best Ways to Get Business

Living within twenty minutes of a business or industrial area, college or university so your clientele can conveniently meet with you is still helpful in marketing this business. Although with the phone, fax and e-mail, and the increased emphasis on coaching clients through the résumé process, it is now possible to develop a clientele even if you're not located near an immediate business or college district.

According to the results of the Professional Association of Résumé Writers membership study, the most successful methods for getting business are:

- Having one or more Yellow Pages advertisements, which is a must.

- Having a visually attractive Web site on which you list your services and prices, testimonial letters, and articles and tips you have written.

- Taking out classified ads under the "Employment, Professional" section in college or university newspapers and in newspapers read by businesspeople and professionals.

- Networking with professional, trade, and civic organizations and referral groups. In particular, consider joining and getting certified by the Professional Association of Résumé Writers. Besides networking opportunities, PARW now offers a rigorous certification testing process that can help establish your professional credibility.

- Sending postcards, pamphlets, or letters describing your service to graduating students, attendees at job fairs, and so forth.

- Keeping a database of your clients for one year and, prior to the end of the year, sending out a mailer (via e-mail, fax, or U.S. mail) to clients suggesting they may want to update their résumé or have you write a new cover letter for them.

- Lining up referrals from print shops, radio spots, and job fairs.

- Giving workshops, seminars, and speeches on how to write a résumé.

Other methods that can work include:

- Offering to pay a cash referral fee to existing clients who refer new clients to you.

- Developing reciprocal referral arrangements from employment agencies that don't offer a résumé-writing service. These agencies like their clients to have good-quality résumés. You may also be able to get referrals from desktop publishing or word-processing firms that set type for résumés but don't handle the professional writing of them.

- Placing notices on bulletin boards at colleges, print shops, large companies, and so forth.

First Steps

- Decide what range of services you want to begin offering and what specialty you plan to serve, keeping in mind you can always expand both services and markets as your business grows.

- If your writing skills need polishing, take a writing course. Concentrate on developing your vocabulary; it's your ammunition.

- Establish your price sheet.

- Your toughest client to get is your first one. Be prepared to answer the questions "What makes you think you could write my résumé?" and "Why your service?"

- Develop samples so people can see that you do an excellent job.

- Do several résumés for free to show sample styles for various careers.

- Obtain certification if you need to distinguish yourself in this profession.

Where to Turn for Information and Help

ORGANIZATION

PROFESSIONAL ASSOCIATION OF RÉSUMÉ WRITERS (PARW), 3637 Fourth Street North, Suite 330, St. Petersburg, FL 33704; (727) 821-2274; fax: (727) 894-1277; e-mail: parwhq@aol.com. This organization with about 700 members provides a newsletter, professional membership identification, including name and logo to use in advertising layouts, and a toll-free consultant line. It also has established professional standards and offers a Certified Professional Résumé Writer credential to individuals who pass a rigorous test. Their Web site offers a searchable database by state and is updated weekly. Web site: *www.parw.com*

BOOKS

BOOKS ON RÉSUMÉ WRITING

101 Best Résumés, Mike Betrus and Jay Block, McGraw-Hill, 1997. All of the résumés are written by professional résumé writers certified by PARW. ISBN: 0070328935.

201 Winning Cover Letters for $100,000 Jobs, Wendy Enelow, Impact Publishing, 1998. ISBN: 1570230889.

The Curriculum Vitae Handbook: How to Present and Promote Your Academic Career, Rebecca Anthony & Gerald Roe, Rudi Publishing, 1998. ISBN: 0045213263.

Electronic Resumes: A Complete Guide to Putting Your Resume On-line, James C. Gonyea & Wayne M. Gonyea, New York: McGraw-Hill, 1996. ISBN: 0079121667.

High Impact Resumes and Letters: How to Communicate Your Qualifications to Employers, Ronald L. Krannich and William J. Banis, Impact Publications, 1998. ISBN: 1570230854.

Professional Resumes for Executives, Managers and Other Administrators: A New Gallery of Best Resumes by Professional Resume Writers, David Noble, Jist Works, 1998. ISBN: 1563704838.

BOOKS ON RÉSUMÉ WRITING AS A BUSINESS

How to Start a Home-Based Resume Business, Jan Melnik, Globe Pequot Press; 1997. ISBN: 0762700688.

Straight Talk About Pricing Your Resume Services, Frank Fox, Available from PARW. 1997.

Start Your Own Resume Writing Business, Pfeiffer Staff, Pfeiffer & Co., 1994.

The Resume Pro: The Professional's Guide, Yana Parker, Ten Speed Press, 1993. ISBN: 0898154669.

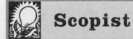 **Scopist**

Scopists operate as assistants to court reporters, so to understand what they do, you first need to understand what court reporters do and how they work. It's the role of the court reporter to record exactly what people say in the courtroom during a trial or during a legal deposition in which testimony is obtained from the litigating parties and witnesses prior to a trial. The court reporter of yesteryear worked with a stenotype machine that produced narrow paper notes, which now can only be seen in *Perry Mason* reruns. Today, modern court reporters work with computer-based writing machines that record their stenographic notes onto floppy disks. The notes are entered quickly in a raw phonetic form in which entire syllables or words are recorded using only a few keystrokes. When the court reporter goes home, however, these notes must be translated into a full transcript of the exact words and sentences for lawyers and judges to read and refer to.

The problem is that even the most sophisticated software of computer-assisted transcription (CAT) can translate a court reporter's notes only to a modest extent, leaving the transcript with punctuation errors, misspellings of proper names, untranslated text, and occasional wrong word choices such as "to" or "too" instead of "two." This means that the court reporter must spend a few hours cleaning up and formatting the transcript, a tiresome task if you've already spent five to eight hours in a courtroom or at a deposition.

Enter the scopist. The scopist reads the reporter's notes and takes responsibility for transforming them into transcripts of proper written English. The scopist rereads the CAT versions of each document, edits and punctuates the material, researches or double-checks the spelling of technical terminology, medical words, and people's names, and proofreads the document. If the scopist cannot understand a computer-translated portion of the text, he or she must also know how to read the raw steno-typed notes that are contained on the court reporter's disk.

Freelance scopists are usually hired directly by self-employed court reporters or by agencies that supply freelance court reporters. They hire scopists because the reporter only gets paid while he or she is taking notes in the courtroom or at a deposition, so it's preferable for them to utilize their time by taking notes, not transcribing and editing them. Whereas the court reporter must go to the deposition or courtroom, scopists can usually work from home unless they need to go into an agency to have access to the same software used by the court reporter they're working with.

As CAT software becomes more proficient at automatic translation of court reporters' notes, the nature of scoping may change. For the moment, however, freelance scoping can provide a good living, and thanks to the Internet, entry into this field is no longer limited to metropolitan areas. Since most work in this field is or can be transmitted electronically or via tape or disk sent by priority mail, scopists can work with clients from any part of the country.

Such access has increased the income potential for this field two or three times. "Getting work and sending files has become easy and extremely fast," says Linda Evenson, of Missoula, Montana, who has worked from home as a scopist for 20 years and serves a taskforce member of the National Association of Court Reporters.

And coming on strong is a new specialty in this field that can bring a premium price, remote real-time scoping. When reporters need to have a transcript delivered immediately, scopists can dial directly into the reporters' computers and edit the transcript, which is instantaneously viewable.

Knowledge and Skills You Need to Have

- You must be able to understand and read stenotype, because you will need to go into the raw notes of documents to check the originals when the automatic translation fails or is insufficient.

- Quick and accurate keyboarding skills are essential. The better you are, the more you earn.

- You must be good at spelling, grammar, and punctuation, and have an excellent command of vocabulary along with familiarity with medical, technical, business, and insurance terminology from a variety of fields. Many legal proceedings focus, for example, on accidents, malpractice, or lawsuits involving products or patents.

Start-up Costs	Low	High
Computer	$ 1,500	$ 3,000
Printer	$ 300	$ 800
or		
Multi-function printer/fax/scanner/copier	$ 150	$ 600
Training	$ 1,800	$ 2,500
CAT software*	$ 1,000	$ 4,000
Reference books	$ 150	$ 300
Office furniture, especially an ergonomic chair	$ 400	$ 1,000
Initial marketing budget	$ 1,000	$ 5,000
Total	$ 6,000	$ 14,200

*There are four or five main brands of computer-assisted transcription (CAT) software that aren't compatible with one another, so a scopist must either work with court reporters who use the same software or be able to use Rich Text Format (RTF) since most software is now translatable into this. With the capability to work with RTF, you can serve reporters or agencies all over the country.

Advantages

- Training to enter this field is not as rigorous as becoming a court reporter. You only have to know how to read stenotype notes, not use a stenotype machine at the high speed required of court reporters.

- The hours are flexible. You have the freedom to select your own time and work from your home.

- Scopists find being part of the legal profession interesting and report enjoying reading about cases and testimony reflecting the drama and variety of people's lives.

- This work can be done from anywhere with modem access or overnight delivery.

Disadvantages

- Scoping requires substantial preparation. Learning shorthand theory and reading stenotype can take six months or more.

- Scopists work behind the scenes. They usually do not go to depositions or trials, and so they miss out on the actual drama of legal battles.

- Scopist work can be high-pressure due to demands for short turnaround time.

- Fluctuating work load can mean feast and famine cycles.

- Getting work can be a Catch-22 situation: You need to gain a reputation and prove yourself with a court reporter before getting steady work.

- Scoping can cause eyestrain and repetitive-motion injuries from long hours of keyboarding if precautions are not taken.

Pricing

Most scopists work by the page. Although the rate varies geographically, an average fee is $.75 to $1.00 per page and more for working with tapes. On a good day, a scopist can scope 200 to 300 pages. Beginners can usually scope 100 to 150 a day. To reach 300 pages a day requires working with very proficient court reporters producing 50 to 60 pages a hour. Many scopists charge extra for expedited and one-day jobs. Some charge less for real-time reporting with the reporter doing a lot of set-up work and providing word lists.

Potential Earnings

Typical Annual Gross Revenues: Based on scoping 200 pages a day at eighty-five cents a page, five days a week, fifty weeks a year, $42,500. Scopists in the first year generally earn $10,000 to $12,000.

Overhead: low (20 percent or less).

Best Home Businesses Estimate of Market Potential

The market for scopists appears to be steadily growing as the U.S. becomes increasingly litigious. The technology court reporters use has changed, but their need for assistance has not.

Best Ways to Get Business

- Directly contacting court reporters and court reporting agencies by phone or via e-mail. You can locate court reporters through the Yellow Pages, online directories, from a list available through your state's court reporters' association, or from the membership directory of the National Court Reporters Association (see listing below).

- Participating in online forums, discussions groups, and listserve mailing lists.

- Having a Web page that attracts court reporters from other locales seeking help.

- Networking at conventions and conferences.

First Steps

- Learn the skills and information you need by taking a notereader/scopist program. Linda Everson recommends looking for programs at your community college; however, at-home study and correspondence courses are also available. Check the list of courses below or call the National Court Reporters Association for information on schools offering scopist programs.

- Call court reporters in your area to become acquainted and to find out about the market and opportunities in your area.

- Visit other scopists' sites online to check out opportunities outside your area.

Where to Turn for Information and Help

ORGANIZATIONS

NATIONAL COURT REPORTERS ASSOCIATION (NCRA), 8224 Old Courthouse Road, Vienna, VA 22182; (800) 272-6272; (703) 556-6272; fax (703) 556-6291. An association for both court reporters and scopists. Offers a monthly magazine, holds an annual conference, and sponsors continuing-education training seminars and an employment-referral service. There are also court reporter associations in most states. Contact NCRA for an association in your area for referrals to court reporter schools. Web site: *www. verbatimreporters.com*

ONLINE RESOURCES

COMPUSERVE COURT REPORTERS' FORUM. GO CRFORUM. The Forum now has a special section for scopists.

COURT REPORTERS FREE FORUM. Web site: *http://custom.forum.com/ scopists*

SCOPISTS.COM. Provides word lists, lists employment opportunities; offers a freelance directory where scopists can post their information for a fee. Web site: www.scopists.com

SCOPISTS SUPPORT GROUP. Web site: *www.delphi.com/scopists*

COURSES

Scopists may attend many of the 400 court-reporter training programs offered throughout the U.S. Although the court-reporting program takes two years or more, scopists can finish in much less time. Several schools have specific short programs for scopists. A listing of schools can be found on this Web site: *www.netins.net/showcase/crn/schools.htm*

AT-HOME PROFESSIONS, 2001 Lowe St., Ft. Collins, CO 80525; (800) 359-3455, offers a home-study course.

INTERNET SCOPING SCHOOL, Administrator, Linda Evenson, 7445 Cherokee Court, Lolo, MT 59847; (406) 273-2892. Completely online course. Web site: *www.scopeschool.com*

 # Secretarial and Office-Support Services

Successful people master knowing when to delegate but for those who don't have a secretary or an administrative assistant to delegate things to, calling upon a secretarial or office-support service can be a godsend. Office-support services go by many names—secretarial services, word-processing or typing services, office- or business-support services, and many more.

Even more varied is the range of work an office-support service may do. Services might include any of the following: word processing, transcription, editing and proofreading, business writing, preparing spreadsheets, bookkeeping, billing, database and contact management, notary services, desktop publishing, graphic design, multimedia presentations, office management and organization consultation, answering services, mailing preparation, résumé writing, Web site design, and Internet research.

Some of these services are best done as a specialty unto themselves. Someone doing bookkeeping, for example, isn't likely to be offering Web site design. Word processing is common to all office-support services, but the key factors in determining whether a given service decides to specialize or to offer a variety of office services have to do with the size of the community and the skills and preferences of the owner. In reality "the business typically grows from client requests," observes Lynette Smith, Executive Director of the Association of Business Support Services (ABSSI).

The primary markets for home-based secretarial services are:

- Brand-new businesses that have no regular support staff but can use limited support on an as-needed basis.

- Small businesses and self-employed individuals, such as consultants, real estate and insurance agents, doctors, attorneys, and private investigators where the proprietor or professional has little time or desire to do his or her own administrative work.

- Sales reps and traveling executives or "road warriors" who need office support of all kinds while they are on the road. Often the cost of secretarial services is covered on their expense accounts or is an employee business expense.

Other users of secretarial services are:

- Writers and authors who continue to handwrite their manuscripts in which case they also often want editing.

- Job seekers who need résumés done, which requires interviewing skill.

- Graduate students who need dissertations, theses, and moot court briefs. Specific knowledge of formatting and other requirements is necessary.

- Small and medium businesses that have cut back on full-time employees, cannot get them, or do not wish to invest the time or dollars in in-house systems and personnel. Some services get overflow work from insurance companies and transcription services.

Something clients increasingly are requesting of their secretarial services is to handle their e-mail traffic, both receiving and answering it, not unlike corporate managers who delegate their e-mail to assistants.

Cheryl Myers, who operates a word-processing service in suburban Chicago has had to learn skills other than word processing since she went out on her own 15 years ago. Myers advises people who want to start an office-support service to treat it as a serious business, which means, among other things, that you get a business phone line and you invest in the proper equipment, including online access.

A problem for people providing office-support on a part-time basis and who seek to serve clients who expect someone to be available during regular business hours is having their phone adequately covered. Myers remarks, "People want immediate service. They are so sick of voice mail and answering machines. The person who answers the phone personally will pick up business. When I answer the phone, they are happy just to have reached a real human being."

For the part-timer, a possible solution for this is to have your business calls forwarded to a home-bound person who can handle your calls intelligently, such as someone who is retired or disabled. Such an individual, using distinctive ringing, might work with several clients and thus answer each person's phone with a greeting in that business's name. But generally, if you are going to operate as a sideline business market, your clients will be primarily writers, students, and job seekers.

"Undercharging is another mistake novices frequently make," Myers says. "When people undercharge," says Nancy Malvin, owner of Malvin Business and Editing Services, "the business is not able to support itself." And if the business cannot support itself, it obviously cannot support you.

Competition in this field can be fierce, but tailoring your business to particular markets is a way to carve out a niche for yourself. It might be one of the markets listed above or it might be working with scriptwriters, political candidates, or local governmental bodies. Some specialties, such as transcribing legal and medical materials, pay better, but require special training or experience. Rates for academic and student work are generally less.

The key to success in this business is the quality of your work and your ability to meet your clients' deadlines. This will result in repeat business and generate referrals. To be additionally competitive, you may want to offer pickup and delivery. Some charge for additional service like this and some don't.

Knowledge and Skills You Need to Have

- According to the industry production standards established by ABSSI and the Executive Suite Association, "an average qualified operator keys in at 70 words per minute, has three to five years of office or administrative-assistant, or equivalent experience, and a good command of English grammar."

- You need to be detail-oriented, organized, and understand how businesses operate.

- This is a service business and calls for a customer-oriented service attitude. You need to have the desire and ability to pay attention to your clients' specific and sometimes unique needs.

Start-up Costs	Low	High
Computer with a backup capability such as a special drive	$ 1,500	$ 3,000
Laser printer	$ 500	$ 1,500
Multi-function color printer/fax/scanner/copier	$ 200	$ 600
Depending on how you specialize, you may need specialized software not included with your software suite, such as for desktop publishing, drawing, presentations, and contact management	$ 0	$ 750
Transcribing unit if you transcribe tapes	$ 0	$ 800
Office furniture, especially an ergonomic chair	$ 400	$ 1,000
Initial marketing budget	$ 1,000	$ 5,000
Total	$ 3,100	$ 12,650

Advantages

- It's an at-home business for those wanting to be home to care for family members or for the homebound.

- You can raise your income by providing additional services that your clients value and will pay more for, such as editing, copywriting, proofreading, mailing-list management, desktop publishing, and Web site design and research.

- Once you have a satisfied client providing basic administrative support, they will often ask for help with other things they need. It is easy to sell your other services because they have confidence in you.

- The faster you type, the more you can earn.

Disadvantages

- The field is growing increasingly competitive.

- You also have to keep up with new software and technology.

- Unless you provide services other than straight word processing, your income is limited by your keyboarding speed and the number of hours in a day.

- You may often be working under the pressure of tight deadlines. In fact, some office-support services specialize in "rush" work and derive a third of their income from premium charges.

- Unless you take necessary precautions, you risk developing repetitive-motion injuries as a result of constant keyboarding.

Pricing

For basic word processing, the rates of services that charge by the hour range from $15 to $35, with the most typical rates being $20 to $25 an hour, according to surveys by ABSSI.

Some services charge by the page, $2 to $5 for double spacing and $4 to $10 for single spacing, particularly if, because of interruptions, such as from young children, you would not be able to keep track of your time accurately. However, Nancy Malvin points out that you can use a stopwatch or software that still enables you to charge on an hourly basis.

Others services charge based on character count, such as $1 per 1,000 characters. This gets around the problems such as differences in font sizes when charging by the page but may not adequately cover the time needed for proofreading.

Another alternative that is gaining popularity and may be more palatable to clients and profitable to you is to charge by the job, using industry production standards for estimating time established by ABSSI and the Executive Suite Association. Which pricing method is best engenders heated discussions in online forums. One caution about the low ends of the ranges cited is that people who low-ball their prices have to be careful about whether they are actually making money; the low figures above reflect what some people are charging, and they are probably too low to make money.

You should charge extra for handwritten or difficult-to-read materials, highly edited originals, or materials that include statistical charts, tables, and complex documents, because it takes you longer to type them. You can also charge extra for multiple originals, copies, and other services.

Services such as consulting, copyediting, desktop publishing, graphic design, proofreading, spreadsheet design, training, and writing bear higher hourly rates, and, depending on the complexity of the task, can be as high as $75 an hour with $30 and $35 an hour being common.

Potential Earnings

Typical Annual Gross Revenues: $30,000 to $37,500, based on one operator billing thirty hours a week at $20 to $25 an hour, fifty weeks a year.

Overhead: moderate (20 to 40 percent), because Yellow Pages advertising under multiple headings can be expensive and also because you will need to upgrade your equipment and software periodically.

Best Home Businesses Estimate of Market Potential

Office technology increases, not decreases, the demand for outside services. As businesses and people increasingly have technology in their businesses and homes, success in office-support becomes more dependent on specializing in doing things that clients cannot do on their own or find it inconvenient or difficult to do.

Best Ways to Get Business

- Yellow Pages advertising under multiple categories, such as Secretarial Services, Word Processing, Desktop Publishing, and Résumés. Yellow Pages advertising stands out as the most frequent way secretarial services get business and, for some, the way they get most of their business. How frequently you get called from your Yellow Pages listings depends on what you name your business and the kind of listing you have. Some advise that you actually begin business when the Yellow Pages with your first listing or ad is distributed. Of course, that requires preparation and decisions months in advance prior to the deadline for Yellow Page ads. Since you probably have more choices than budget, an important decision is to determine what telephone books to appear in and what categories to list under. Surveying your community with questions such as "If you needed to have a letter typed, what phone book would you use to find help with this and under what classification would you look?" can help you make these decisions.

- Networking and actively participating in one or more business, professional, service, or referral organizations where you will meet prospective clients' sources of referrals.

- Direct mail to new businesses in your area and/or prospects in a specialty market you are targeting using postcards or half-sheet cards with lists of services. Follow up mailings with phone calls.

- Contacting other office-support services about overload or work in which you specialize and they do not. Responding to help-wanted ads for secretaries to induce the company to send the work out to you.

- Advertising focused within no more than a twenty-minute drive of your home. Best places to advertise are in university newspapers and church, club, chamber of commerce bulletins, especially those published by organizations of which you are a member.

- Have your own Web page with its own domain name. On the site, have copies of testimonial letters and list your services. Make sure you are linked to directories that list office-support services.

- For attracting graduate student business: notices or flyers with tear-off phone numbers on bulletin boards at colleges and universities and in facilities used by students, such as laundromats; advertising in campus papers; registering with department heads and thesis librarians; communicating with others in the same business about helping with their overflow.

- Offering discounts on future work to clients and others who refer clients to you.

- Doing business and cultivating relationships with local merchants who are in a position to refer clients, such as local office-supply stores and printers.

- Approaching hotels about offering your services to their business guests.

- Positioning yourself as a specialty service or services or as providing "office-support" services may command more respect than simply being a word-processing or secretarial service. However, people most immediately know what a secretarial service is.

First Steps

If you type less than 70 wpm, you can use a software program such as *Mavis Beacon Teaches Typing* to help you increase your keyboarding speed within just a few weeks.

Taking into account how other secretarial services are or are not specializing, considering how you might specialize serving a particular field or industry, such as screenwriters or graduate students. Consider naming your business to appeal to your market.

While you are focusing your effort at becoming a specialist, be prepared to be a generalist so you don't have to turn down work. Specialties often emerge from general work that comes in the door.

Determine if your state requires you to collect sales tax on word processing and other work you do.

Where to Turn for Information and Help

ORGANIZATIONS

ASSOCIATION OF BUSINESS SUPPORT SERVICES INTERNATIONAL, INC., 22875 Savi Ranch Parkway, Suite H, Yorba Linda, CA 92887-4619; (800) 237-1462; (714) 282-9398. Monthly magazine, unlimited free consultation time, and a free listing on ABSSI's Web site: *www.abssi.org*

INTERNATIONAL ASSOCIATION OF ADMINISTRATIVE PROFESSIONALS (formerly Professional Secretaries International), 10502 NW Ambassador Drive, P.O. Box 20404, Kansas City, MO 64195; (816) 891-6600. Monthly magazine and offers certification as a Certified Professional Secretary. Web site: *www.iaap-hq.org*

NATIONAL NOTARY ASSOCIATION, 9350 De Soto Avenue, Chatsworth, CA 91311, (800) 876-6827. Web site: *www.nationalnotary.org*

BOOKS AND MANUALS

ABSSI (contact information above) publishes the following manuals:

Pricing Manual for Business Support Services, 1997.

Industry Production Standards Guide, 1998.

Pricing Guide for Desktop Services, 1997. Also regional prices in *Desktop Services Pricing Tables,* a separate publication.

Pricing Guide for Web Services, 1998.

Starting a Successful Office Support Service, Lynette Smith, 1997.

How to Start a Home-Based Secretarial Services Business, Globe Pequot Press, 1997. ISBN: 1564409961.

Nina Feldman's Resource Package, 6407 Irwin Court, Oakland, CA 94609. E-mail: Ninafel@aol.com

See also the resources for Résumé Writing and Desktop Publishing.

NEWSLETTERS

S.O.S. Quarterly, 1431 Willow Brook Cove, St. Louis, MO 63146; (314) 567-3636. E-mail: SecSvcs@aol.com

The Word Advantage, 432 Higganum Road, P.O. Box 718, Durham, CT 06422; (860) 349-0256. E-mail: CompSPJan@aol.com

AUDIO TAPES

Making Money with a Word Processing and Secretarial Service at Home, Nancy Malvin, 109 James Drive, Troy, IL 62294; (618) 667-4666. E-mail: nmalvin@stlnet.com

ONLINE

AMERICA ONLINE has an active word processing section in its Business Know-How Forum. Keyword: officeservices.

COMPUSERVE. Word Processing Section on the Working From Home Section. Keyword: GO WORK.

Security Specialists

While most people don't assume bad things will happen to them when they leave their homes, one in three Americans have changed their shopping habits and have given up shopping after sunset due to a fear of crime. High-profile incidents like the Oklahoma City and World Trade Center bombings have accentuated the need for security because of the instantaneous attention they get on media ranging from TV to the news banners that greet us when we log online. Thus, it's not surprising that security considerations are increasingly a routine part of everything from building design to organizational policy.

One way of doing something about the forces of lawlessness is to choose a career in the security field. There are several ways you can do this while working from home: You can become a private investigator or a security consultant or specialize in something both of these occupations may do—background checking. While most people entering the private security field used to be retired law-enforcement personnel, security is now drawing more people early in their careers.

Private Investigator

While the private detectives on television and in movies have downtown offices, in reality a large percentage of private investigators (PIs) work from their homes. Also contrary to the PI's TV and movie image, being a private investigator is not necessarily a dangerous business. Most private investigators don't carry a gun, and according to Bob Taylor, an investigator from East Brunswick, New Jersey, who has been in the business for over 25 years, weapons are unnecessary.

In the past, private investigators filled their time working for attorneys on criminal and civil cases, tracking down white-collar crime for corporations, locating missing persons, and doing insurance investigations. Now, private investigators also specialize in areas like investigating corporate fraud, developing information about prospective merger partners or acquisition targets, conducting pre-employment screenings, and doing premarital background checks. Whatever their specialty, they most likely use the search capabilities of online databases to supplement or substitute for traditional means of investigation.

Most PIs are licensed. Most states require PIs to be licensed and some municipalities in nonlicensing states require them to register with the city or the police department. Also, what's defined as private investigation is quite broad in some states, encompassing doing background checks. Licensing requirements vary but usually involve one to three years' experience in some sort of investigative work, such as law enforcement or claims adjusting. Sometimes this can be met by having worked in a collection agency or having done investigative journalism. Some states will do a background check when you apply to take the tests required for a license.

Security Consultant

Security consulting involves working with clients to help them protect people, property, client lists, and proprietary technology and controlling customer and employee theft. Many people who sell security products also call themselves security consultants and while they are part of the security field, there are security consultants who don't sell product. Here are some of the various specialties in this field:

Site Consulting

Security site consultants evaluate the physical design of buildings and spaces in environments such as high-tech industrial corporations, retail franchises, distribution centers, self-storage facilities, housing developments, hotels, resorts and casinos, parking lots, transportation companies, and law firms. They determine what security problems these sites have and write reports that specify protective measures, such as guards, electronic security with cameras and electric lights, or a combination of methods and policies. To become a Certified Site Consultant by the International Association of Professional Security Consultants (IAPSC), consultants agree not to sell equipment they recommend, such as alarms or video monitoring systems. In other words, the site consultant doesn't derive any income from what he or she endorses.

Systems Design and Technical Security

The systems designer does his or her work at the design phase of security consulting, drawing up plans using software, developing specifications, and providing architectural or engineering support. A systems designer may also develop new electronic security tools to be used at a location. Technical consultants are knowledgeable about products, such as electronic security systems, their development and how to apply them. Their work may involve design and writing.

Forensic Consulting and Teaching

Steve Keller, former executive director of the International Association of Private Security Consultants, estimates that 80 percent of security consultants do some expert witness work and 20 percent do it exclusively.

They offer expert testimony in legal proceedings in which the security of a location has been broken (fires, thefts, break-ins, etc.). Many security consultants add to their income by teaching law-enforcement officials.

Steve Keller exemplifies how security consultants specialize. His focus on museums and historical sites takes him around the globe to work with many of the world's most prestigious museums. His special knowledge is of security measures to preserve artwork and sculpture from fire, theft, and vandalism.

Keller points out that specialization is a major key to success in this field. The more you specialize and develop a knowledge base in one area, the greater the chances of building your business through word of mouth and referrals, because similar security measures are needed by similar types of businesses or sites. Specialties in demand include computer security (particularly protecting e-commerce from hackers and thieves), employee background checks, and drug testing. The rise of e-commerce assures that people specializing in computer security can be kept busy.

Unlike private investigators, security consultants are not licensed. Professional recognition in the field is achieved by passing a rigorous examination given by one of the two associations listed below. However, sometimes security consulting and private investigation overlap, particularly if the security consultant conducts background investigations for clients. While some security consultants are licensed as private investigators, individuals who advertise themselves as PIs or as both PIs and consultants are not eligible for membership in the International Association of Professional Security Consultants.

Background Checking

One out of every three résumés has inaccurate information, with 10 percent of these being serious-enough misrepresentations to cause a prospective employer to pass on an applicant. About one in every twelve people lie about academic degrees they have earned, according to Edward Andler, a pioneer in this field. If getting what they're bargaining for is not enough incentive for employers to check out prospective employees thoroughly, then the courts are providing additional motivation. Courts are finding companies negligent in cases where they've failed to screen the employees they hired adequately. Former employers who fail during a reference check to disclose vital information such as a terminated employee's history of violence are also being held liable in court.

As a result, most companies today are checking into the background of prospective employees. Some companies have in-house employees who do this work, using databases such as *www.knowx.com, www.informus.com, www.advsearch.com, www.digdirt.com,* and *www.people-wise.com.* Others retain a security consultant, private investigator, or a consultant who specializes in background checking. Companies that don't do background checking are ripe candidates for a service that will do it for them.

There are three facets to this specialty:

- Background checking, which is the broadest form and may turn up criminal records, credit history, and such things as lawsuits and judgments.

- Reference checking, calling past employers and references given by applicants.

- Credentials verification of educational background.

While the databases containing such information can be used by anyone, errors can occur, and thus having a professional do this work is in the interest of companies wanting to hire personnel without making potentially costly mistakes.

While employers constitute the bulk of such clients, others who use the services of background checking specialists include people considering business dealings with another company or individual, and landlords screening tenants. Background checking can be a stand-alone business, like Edward Andler's Certified Reference Checking Company, and it's also an important aspect of both security consulting and private investigation. Some states require anyone doing background checking for others for a fee be licensed as a private investigator.

Knowledge and Skills You Need to Have

PRIVATE INVESTIGATORS

- People skills are important, including the ability to read people, develop rapport, manage conversations, and persuade people to give you information. As Bob Taylor says, "You have to be more of a communicator than a Joe Friday."

- You have to be able to write an investigative report and take a statement. One PI indicates that experience taking statements for an insurance company is similar to the kind of experience you need on this job.

- Creativity and intuition are necessary for gathering information that is sometimes difficult to find. You also need tenacity and persistence to get the information you seek. On-the-job training is critical in this area.

SECURITY CONSULTANTS

- You need the ability to analyze situations and sites. Because many of your jobs may require you to write a full security report, you should also be able to write acceptable, error-free English.

- You need to know how to draft and read blueprints. If you do design, you need to be able to use architectural drawing software.

- You must know about and understand electronic equipment such as closed-circuit TVs.

Start-up Costs	Low	High
Computer	$ 1,500	$ 3,000
Printer	$ 300	$ 800
or		
Multi-function printer/fax/scanner/copier	$ 150	$ 600
Errors and omissions insurance	$ 700	$ 2,000
Camera; PIs also need a tape recorder	$ 100	$ 1,000
Tools	$ 100	$ 300
Office furniture, especially an ergonomic chair	$ 400	$ 1,000
Initial marketing budget	$ 1,000	$ 5,000
Total	$ 3,900	$ 13,700

Advantages

PRIVATE INVESTIGATORS

- Private investigation has a mystique, cultivated by TV and movies and the industry's more colorful characters.

- Private investigators enjoy the challenge of fitting together bits of information in often varied cases.

- PIs express feeling satisfaction at capturing people who cheat others out of money and locating people being sought by loved ones.

SECURITY CONSULTANTS

- Security consulting commands professional respect, and growing concern about safety indicates this will increase.

- New technologies introduced into security work make the field challenging and interesting.

- Security consultants often describe themselves as having a passion for their field.

Disadvantages

FOR BOTH PRIVATE INVESTIGATORS AND SECURITY CONSULTANTS

- It takes at least two years to establish a clientele to operate full time.

PRIVATE INVESTIGATORS

- Hours are typically long, requiring weekend and evening work. As a result, PIs have difficulty making firm time commitments because of the unpredictable demands of some cases. If you're on a stakeout, for example, you need to stay with the person under surveillance until you get the information needed.

- As society becomes more sensitive to invasions of privacy, some channels for investigative work may be closed off.

- While marital investigations and collection work accounts for less than a quarter of what PIs do now, this kind of work has an element of risk; some people express their anger physically.

SECURITY CONSULTANTS

- As a rule, clients summon you only when they have a problem.

- Security consultants are usually not by nature "people" people and so must develop skills for relating to clients and dealing with interpersonal issues of security.

Pricing

Hourly fees for private investigators range from $25 to $125, with $40 to $70 typical in metropolitan areas.

Security consultants can command from $100 to $250 per hour. The higher fees are for forensic work and for work in larger cities.

Background checking is priced on a piece-rate basis. A background check on a prospective tenant for a landlord might cost $20; more comprehensive background checks cost around $50; and national searches of criminal records or worker compensation claims can run into the hundreds of dollars. Individual record searches such as credit reports, driving records, and education and credentials verification range from under ten dollars to almost thirty dollars each. Reference checking ranges from $15 to $50.

Potential Earnings

TYPICAL ANNUAL GROSS REVENUES

For Private Investigators: $50,000, based on billing 1,000 hours a year at $50 an hour. Private investigators also bill separately for many expenses associated with investigations, such as parking, film, tolls, and so on, as these expenses can mount up over the course of a year.

For Security Consultants: $75,000, based on billing 1,000 hours a year at $125 per hour.

OVERHEAD

For Private Investigators: moderate (20 to 40 percent).

For Security Consultants: low (20 percent or less).

Best Home Businesses Estimate of Market Potential

The growing apprehension about security and the serious measures being taken to secure it are reflected in President Clinton's closing of Pennsylvania Avenue in front of the White House. Terrorism, both domestic and international, as well as crime drives the nearly 9 percent annual growth of the security industry, which in 1995 had already reached $70 billion. Not only are companies and individuals increasingly concerned about security, but the increasing amount and complexity of security technology is driving the need for more specialized expertise.

Jim Clark, a security consultant in Cleveland, finds "security consulting as a profession is growing in quality, numbers, and as a career path." Internal security staffing is a target for corporate downsizing, with corporations preferring to get security consulting on an "as needed" basis, so home-based security consulting is expected to grow. The Bureau of Labor Statistics projects solid growth for private detectives.

Best Ways to Get Business

FOR BOTH

- Making seminar presentations and speeches.

- Getting publicity about your work.

- Having your own Web page with its own domain name with testimonial letters and any articles you have written.

- Introducing yourself to prospective clients with personal letters, followed up by phone calls.

PRIVATE INVESTIGATORS

- Directly soliciting trial lawyers and their office managers, insurance companies, and corporate personnel departments.

- Yellow Page advertising if seeking collections and marital work.

- Having a toll-free number to remove one barrier for people hesitant to call a private investigator.

SECURITY CONSULTANTS

- Joining and participating in trade associations and professional organizations for the type of clientele you are seeking (industrial, law firms, educational, historic sites, etc.)

- Getting listed in bar-association directories of expert witnesses.

- Demonstrating your expertise by writing articles and letters to the editors of newspapers and business journals. This can lead to being used as a source by journalists.

- Sending out a newsletter. Consultants specializing in computer security can customize the *Frontline End-User Awareness Newsletter* with their own company logo and message. It is available from the International Computer Security Association.

First Steps

PRIVATE INVESTIGATORS

- If you lack the experience to qualify for a license, attempt to apprentice with a private investigator.

- Obtain a license if needed. States requiring a license will usually recommend a list of books to use in studying for their exams.

SECURITY CONSULTANTS

- Obtain either an educational background and experience or experience in crime prevention. Working in a police department, military-police unit, or doing survey work for a private security service will provide the necessary knowledge and experience.

- If you lack enough experience to qualify as a security consultant, the best ways to obtain the necessary knowledge and experience is to take a job in which you conduct surveys of new-client premises for a private security service or a job in security management in which you can develop policies.

- Become certified by a professional organization.

Where to Turn for Information and Help

ORGANIZATIONS

FOR BOTH PIS AND SECURITY CONSULTANTS

AMERICAN SOCIETY FOR INDUSTRIAL SECURITY, 1625 Prince Street, Alexandria, VA 22314; (703) 519-6200. Largest international educational organization for security professionals, with over 30,000 members, including vendors; offers certification; publishes *Security Management* magazine. Web site: www.asisonline.org

FOR PRIVATE INVESTIGATORS

ASSOCIATION OF CERTIFIED FRAUD EXAMINERS, 716 West Ave., Austin, TX 78701; (800) 245-3321. Geared toward fraud and corporate security. Web site: *www.cfenet.com*

NATIONAL ASSOCIATION OF INVESTIGATIVE SPECIALISTS, Box 33244, Austin, TX 78764; (512) 420-9292. Web site: *www.pimall.com*

NATIONAL ASSOCIATION OF LEGAL INVESTIGATORS, 2801 Fleur Drive, Des Moines, IA 50321. Web site: *www.nali.com*

FOR SECURITY CONSULTANTS

COMPUTER SECURITY INSTITUTE, 600 Harrison Street, San Francisco, CA 94107. Telephone: (415) 905-2626. Publishes *The Computer Security Journal.* Web site: *www.gocsi.com*

INTERNATIONAL ASSOCIATION OF PROFESSIONAL SECURITY CONSULTANTS, 1444 I Street, Suite 700, Washington, D.C. 20005; (202) 712-9043. An association consisting exclusively of independent, nonproduct-affiliated security consultants; one year's experience required to join. Provides certification. Web site has a directory of members that is searchable by specialty and keywords. Web site: *www.iapsc.org*

INTERNATIONAL COMPUTER SECURITY ASSOCATION (ICSA), 1200 Walnut Bottom Road, Carlisle, PA 17013; (717) 258-1816. Certifies products and publishes the *Firewall Industry/Buyer's Guide.* Web site: *www.icsa.net*

COURSES AND TRAINING PROGRAMS

ION, an investigator referral service, lists private investigator schools and training sources on its Web site: *http://investigatorsanywhere.com/wo09000.html*

Community colleges and four-year colleges offer degrees in security administration.

BOOKS

PRIVATE INVESTIGATORS

Handbook on Corporate Fraud, Jack Bologna, Butterworth-Heinemann, 1992. ISBN: 075069243X.

The Investigator's Little Black Book 2, Robert Scott, Crime Time Publishing Company, 1998. ISBN: 0965236927.

Private Investigation: How to be Successful!, Bill Copeland, Absolutely Zero Loss Inc., 1997. ISBN: 0965765997.

Private Investigator's Guide to the Internet 2.0, Joseph Seanor, Thomas Investigative Publications, 1996. ISBN: 0918487943.

Requirements to Become a P.I. in the 50 States and Elsewhere, Joseph J. Culligan, FJA Inc., 1997. ISBN: 0963062115.

Undercover Operations: A Manual for the Private Investigator, Kingdon Peter Anderson, Citadel Press, 1990. ISBN: 0806511664.

SECURITY CONSULTING

The Complete Manual of Corporate and Industrial Security, Russell L. Bintliff, Prentice-Hall, 1992. ISBN: 0131596411.

Effective Security Management, Charles A. Sennewald, Butterworth-Heinemann, 1998. ISBN: 0750699078.

Encyclopedia of Security Management, John J. Fay, CPP, Ed., Butterworth-Heinemann, 1993. ISBN: 0750696605.

Introduction to Security, Robert J. Fischer, Gion Green, Butterworth-Heinemann, 1998. ISBN: 0750698608

Outsourcing Security: A Guide for Contracting Services, John D. Stees, Butterworth-Heinemann, 1998. ISBN: 0750670231.

Security Consulting, Charles A. Sennewald, Butterworth-Heinemann, 1996. The classic text in the field. ISBN: 0750696435.

The Underground Guide to Computer Security, Michael Alexander, Addison Wesley, 1996. ISBN: 020148918X.

BACKGROUND CHECKING

Check It Out!: A Top Investigator Shows You How to Find Out Practically Anything About Anybody in Your Life, Edmund J. Pankau, Contemporary Books, 1998. ISBN: 0809229005.

The Complete Reference Checking Handbook, Ed Andler, AMACOM, 1998. ISBN: 0814404057.

Public Records Online: The National Guide to Private and Government Online Sources of Public Records, Carl R. Ernst (Editor), Michael L. Sankey, Facts on Demand Press, 1997. ISBN: 1889150029.

When in Doubt, Check Him Out: A Woman's Survival Guide for the 90's, FJA, Inc., 1997. ISBN: 0963062123.

The Librarian's Guide to Public Records: The Complete State, County, and Courthouse Locator, Michael L. Sankey, Carl R. Ernst, Business Resources Bureau Publications, 1998. ISBN: 1879792427.

You, Too, Can Find Anybody: A Reference Manual, FJA, Inc., 1998. ISBN: 0963062107.

MAGAZINES

P.I. Magazine, 755 Bronx, Toledo, OH 43609. Can be found on the Web at *www.pimall.com/pimag/index.html*

Security Magazine, Box 5080, Des Plaines, IL 60018. Web site: *www.secmag.com*

Security, Technology, and Design, published by Steve Lasky, Locksmith Publishing Corp., 850 Busse Hwy, Park Ridge, IL 60068; (847) 692-5940. E-mail: slasky@worldnet.att.net

Tax Preparation Service

Despite all the passion for tax simplification, Congress has made more than 5,000 changes in the federal tax law since the last major tax reform in 1986. They passed 800 changes in 1997 alone. In 1998, changes resulted in 11 new tax forms, changes in 177 other forms, and the ballooning of the instruction booklet that comes with commonly used schedules. Form 1040 had grown to 107 pages. No wonder the tax preparation business keeps growing! Growing numbers of taxpayers are simply throwing up their hands and heading off to a tax professional.

Although most people don't realize it, the Internal Revenue Service and most states don't require someone to have a special license to prepare other people's tax returns. You don't need to be a CPA or have a degree in accounting. In fact, many CPAs know little about preparing tax returns because they specialize in other branches of accounting, such as cost accounting, property accounting, or auditing. And, of course, while the number of people who need help in filing complex tax forms and dealing with complex tax issues is growing, many of them can't afford CPA's fees.

We're not suggesting that you can just hang out a shingle and claim to be able to prepare other people's taxes. But the tax preparation field is more accessible than you may think. One way to start is to go to a school such as those operated by H&R Block. If you prove to be adept during the course, which lasts a matter of weeks, you may be offered a position with the company, enabling you to, in effect, get a paid apprenticeship. Even with this training and experience, most people won't yet know enough to be a self-employed tax preparer, although they may be capable of working for a tax preparation company with certain kinds of clients, mostly individuals,

A route to a more lucrative future as a tax preparer is to become an "enrolled agent." While the enrolled-agent (EA) designation is still not popularly known, it's been around since 1884 and is the only designation specifically granted by the federal government. It requires passing an exam and demonstrating proficiency in handling tax matters. Enrolled agents may prepare taxes for individuals, corporations, partnerships, estates, trusts, and any entities with tax-reporting requirements, and they are entitled to appear before the IRS at hearings to represent clients.

While there are no academic requirements to become an enrolled agent, the exam takes two days and is considered rigorous, with only 30 percent of the applicants passing each year. People who have worked for the IRS for five years don't need to take the test. There are about 35,000 enrolled agents in the United States compared to about 375,000 CPAs.

Another route into tax preparation is working for a state agency. That's what Gary Lundgren of Minneapolis did before going out on his own. Lundgren focuses on helping clients facing collection procedures such as losing bank accounts, homes, and businesses. He files appeals and appears before the state agency or IRS on his clients' behalf, aiming to reduce their tax liability (and often winning large concessions).

Lundgren points out that it helps to specialize in a particular area of taxes because it is hard to know it all, and specialists can charge more for their time. Enrolled agents can specialize in an area of taxation such as estate and financial planning or work with particular kinds of clients such as high tech firms or the clergy from a specific denomination and thus draw a clientele from across the nation.

Whatever your personal feelings are about taxes, they are an inescapable part of life. If you enjoy making sense of numbers, tax preparation may be just the career for you.

Knowledge and Skills You Need to Have

- You need to have a good mind for figures and a feel for the process of calculating taxes to be efficient in your work and recognize when something is not right.

- You need to be able to read quickly and understand the implications of tax cases.

- You need to have an interest in your clients' situations, being empathetic while remaining professional so as not to put yourself at risk for a client who falsifies information. You need to have high moral and ethical standards to steer clear of trouble.

- You need to be willing to spend the time it takes to keep current. Since tax law is ever-changing, you must recognize that this career requires constant learning.

Start-up Costs	Low	High
Computer	$ 1,500	$ 3,000
Printer	$ 300	$ 800
or		
Multi-function printer/fax/scanner/copier	$ 150	$ 600
Copier	$ 500	$ 1,500
Tax preparation software that prints tax forms and sends electronic filings, such as *1040 Professional Tax Consultant, Lacerte, Ortax, ProSystem, Tax Byte, TaxShop 1040, Turbotax for Professionals*, and *Ultratax/1040*	$ 100	$ 2,000
Office furniture, especially an ergonomic chair	$ 400	$ 1,000
Initial marketing budget	$ 1,000	$ 5,000
Reference materials (books, tax guides, CD-ROM publications of tax codes and interpretations updated each year)	$ 500	$ 3,000
Errors and omissions insurance	$ 200	$ 1,200
Total	$ 4,350	$ 18,100

Advantages

- Every new tax law or amendment can be thought of as "A Tax Preparer's Employment Act." The more complex the tax law, the more people are willing to turn tax preparation over to an expert, despite the availability of do-it-yourself software.

- The demand is high and ongoing. You can build a loyal clientele who will stick with you year after year. Understanding taxes can even make you popular at parties! Everyone will want to know if you can help them.

- You are a professional without having to spend years in a professional school.

- Usually you can work *at* home and, other than during the tax season, your schedule can be flexible.

Disadvantages

- Taxes are convoluted and confusing. It is nearly impossible to keep up with the entire field of taxation. You need to devote about one day per week simply to reading new tax laws and their interpretations, and as an enrolled agent, you must complete 72 hours of continuing-education courses every three years.

- Preparing tax returns can become repetitive and dull, although every company or situation is different.

- Most tax preparation is seasonal. You need to plan your cash flow well and count on doing little else but burning the midnight oil from January 1st thru April 15th every year.

- People look at using a professional as if it were insurance against an audit. There is a level of risk should you have a client who blames you for penalties even though the errors were based on their misstating facts to you. Some tax preparation firms guarantee their work, promising to pay any interest and penalties from miscalculations.

- You need lots of storage space because IRS regulations require keeping copies of your clients' tax returns for three years.

Pricing

Prices are either a flat fee per return or by the hour. For a simple 1040 return, rates range from $75 in low-cost areas of the country to $125. Complex returns are usually billed by the hour at rates ranging from $50 to $200 and can total several thousand dollars. What might otherwise be a simple return can be made complicated if your client brings in a sack full of bills for you to organize and tabulate.

Potential Earnings

Average Annual Gross Revenues: $75,000 to $140,000 based on preparing 375 to 700 returns at an average of $200 per return The average tax preparer can handle up to 700 returns per year. Actual volume, of course, depends on whether the tax preparation is done seasonally or all year-round.

Overhead: moderate (20 to 40 percent).

Best Home Businesses Estimate of Market Potential

One seemingly immutable reality of our tax system is that it grows increasingly complex and demanding. The more complex the system, the more help people and businesses need in filing their taxes despite the ready availability of tax preparation software and electronic filing of returns. Also shortages in the numbers of people entering the accounting field make tax preparation specialists all the more in demand.

Best Ways to Get Business

- Word of mouth and referrals are the two best methods for tax preparers. Taxes are a personal matter, so people tend to use someone whom a friend has recommended as trustworthy and competent. Thus, getting clients requires a lot of networking.

- Networking among CPAs, attorneys, and other tax preparers is also useful because they can refer clients to you. The culture in this field is to help one another.

- Doing seminars or teaching tax principles within organizations.

- Advertising in local publications can bring in some clientele, particularly if you have a specialty that you can advertise: partnerships, collections/audits, etc.

- Doing personalized mailings to people or new businesses that have moved into your area.

- Having your own Web site.

First Steps

- Learn how to prepare taxes for others. Classroom courses are available from H&R Block and correspondence courses are available from the sources listed below.

- To gain experience, consider working for a tax preparation company part- or full-time.

- Study for and take the enrolled agent examination.

Where to Turn for Information and Help

ORGANIZATIONS

NATIONAL ASSOCIATION OF ENROLLED AGENTS (NAEA), 200 Orchard Ridge Drive, Suite 302, Gaithersburg, MD 20878; (301) 212-9608; fax (301) 990-1611. NAEA is the principal association for enrolled agents, with 10,000 members from among the 35,000 enrolled agents in the country. NAEA has local chapters and publishes the *EA Journal*. By phoning or contacting the Web site, NAEA will provide a free copy of last year's exam, a copy of the IRS Application Forum for taking the exam (Form 2587), and a list of companies and NAEA state affiliates that offer cram courses for the exam. NAEA offers a National Tax Practice Institute that teaches enrolled agents how to specialize in representation before the IRS, which increases your ability to take on difficult audit cases. Web site: www.naea.org

NATIONAL ASSOCIATION OF TAX PRACTITIONERS, 720 Association Drive, Appleton, WI 54914; (800) 558-3402; (800) 242-3430 in Wisconsin. Members include CPAs, enrolled agents, accountants, attorneys, and financial planners. Offers training and has an online membership directory. Web site: www.natptax.com

PRIVATE FIRMS OFFERING
HOME STUDY COURSES

THOMAS TAX SEMINARS, 4833 Skycrest Way, Santa Rosa, CA 95405; (800) 638-3783. The home-study course takes between 65 and 100 hours to complete. Thomas also offers a review course for the enrolled agent examination. Web site: *www.users.ap.net/~tomtax*

SOURCES OF TAX MATERIAL IN PRINT
AND ON CD-ROM FOR TAX PREPARERS

COMMERCE CLEARING HOUSE, 2700 Lake Cook Road, Riverwoods, IL 60015; (800) TELL-CCH. Publishes the *U.S. Master™ Tax Guide* series, which includes titles such as the *The Standard Federal Tax Reports*, the annual *U.S. Master™ Tax Guide®* and the *U.S. Master™ Accounting Guide,* magazines and journals such as *Taxes—The Tax Magazine* and the *Journal Of Retirement Planning*. Web site: *www.cch.com*

RESEARCH INSTITUTE OF AMERICA, 90 Fifth Avenue, Second Floor, New York, NY 10011; (800) 431-9025; (212) 645-4800. Publications include the *Federal Tax Coordinator 2d, United States Tax Reporter,* and the *RIA Citator 2nd*. Web site: *www.riatax.com*

ONLINE SOURCES OF INFORMATION
FOR TAX PREPARERS

INTERNAL REVENUE SERVICE'S Web site has "The Tax Professional's Corner" at *www.irs.ustreas.gov/plain/bus_info/tax_pro/index.html*

THOMPSON PUBLISHING GROUP®, 1725 K Street, NW, Suite 700, Washington, DC 20006; (202) 872-4000. Web site: *www.thompson.com.* Offers the TaxLibrary Online in cooperation with tax publishers, including AccountingNet, ATX Forms, Harcourt Brace Professional Publishing, and Tax Analysts at *www.taxlibrary.com*

Links to other publications can be found at *www.taxsites.com/publishers. html*

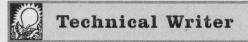 Technical Writer

When it comes to technology, being able to communicate in clear and simple English is as important as being able to write in code. Whenever any new product involving technology is introduced, there's an immediate need for an array of informative materials from brochures and manuals, to reference cards, instructional materials, reviews, and media releases. Such materials need to be written for a variety of audiences:

- The buyers of the product.

- The users (who may be different from the buyers).

- The people who install and repair the product.

- The people who sell and promote it, including the press and other media who let the world know about it.

Each of these audiences creates a need for a variety of different types of information, and it's the technical writer's job to make that information clear and easily understood by all these audiences. The technical writer can work on all different kinds of projects with all different kinds of clients, all of which can pay well. They include:

- Writing user and product manuals, hardware and software documentation, and instruction booklets on everything from toys to computers to satellites.

- Writing online help systems that go beyond or replace printed manuals.

- Writing and editing technical books.

- Writing articles for trade and popular magazines to explain concepts or products to tradespeople or consumers.

- Writing publicity materials, such as press releases and feature articles, for manufacturing and service companies that need editorial coverage in business and consumer publications.

- Writing marketing materials for technical products, i.e., brochures, sell sheets, product descriptions and so forth.

- Writing ISO 9000 documentation. ISO stands for the International Standards Organization, which sets the standard for products and processes, including documentation.

- Writing policy and procedure manuals. Nearly every company employing more than ten or fifteen people must have available standard and consistent information that spells out for employees standards for performance reviews and promotions, termination, sexual harassment, vacation and benefit terms, regulations on safety and substance abuse, dress codes, employee development, and many other issues. Some technical writers specialize in manual writing.

Harriet Serenkin, a technical writer based in New York City, primarily writes computer documentation for corporations and manuals for popular word-processing programs such as *Word* and *WordPerfect*. Having majored in math, she worked at the American Institute of Physics. From there she got on-the-job training in technical copyediting, and had experience as a science editor at a publishing house. The charm of freelancing appealed to her, though, so she eventually decided to go out on her own.

Serenkin gets most of her business through networking, particularly with colleagues in professional associations such as the Editorial Freelancers' Association, the Society for Technical Communication, and the New York PC Users Group. "I am constantly marketing," she says. "I always have business cards with me and give them out generously." She strongly believes in becoming active in trade groups—joining committees, attending meetings, getting to know others in the field. She also occasionally does some things for free, just to get publicity, such as writing a "tips and tricks" column for her PC Users Group newsletter. She has gotten paying writing jobs from readers of her column.

If you like to write and can understand and explain technical things, you can be well paid. This field is open to those who can write clearly and logically following a required format.

Knowledge and Skills You Need to Have

- Technical writers must have good writing skills and knowledge of a few specific scientific areas such as engineering, chemistry, computers, or electronics. Medical writing is a field unto itself.

- You need to have the ability to understand and translate technical information into terms that are clear and understandable to non-technical readers.

- You must be able to learn about new high-technology products in order to understand what must be communicated and at the same time have an appreciation for the needs of people who may have little knowledge, experience, or patience with technology.

- You need to know process flow charting, required by ISO, which can be done using programs such as *Flowcharter* and *Visio*.

- You must have an organized mind so that the manuals you write and edit flow logically.

- You should also be able to think visually to help determine when an illustration can help your writing.

Start-up Costs	Low	High
Computer	$ 1,500	$ 3,000
Printer	$ 300	$ 800
or		
Multi-function printer/fax/scanner/copier	$ 150	$ 600
Office furniture, especially an ergonomic chair	$ 400	$ 1,000
Initial marketing budget	$ 1,000	$ 5,000
Total	$ 2,550	$ 9,600

Advantages

- You can set your own hours and work when you want to.

- An increasingly technological world provides a growing market for technical writers.

- Making technically difficult things understandable to people can be emotionally satisfying.

- The work is varied enough so that boredom is unlikely and you're among the first to learn about new ideas and new technologies.

- This is usually an at home business and while you may have tight deadlines how you arrange your schedule for meeting them is flexible.

Disadvantages

- Technical writing is difficult work because you're dealing with information that's often hard to explain, and if you don't have a background in what you're writing about, it can take time to learn about it before writing.

- Tight deadlines are common.

- If your love is creative writing, technical writing, while certainly involving creative thinking, can feel restrictive.

- You seldom know where your next job will come from.

- Most work is to be found in metropolitan areas.

Pricing

The Society for Technical Communications conducts regular salary surveys of employed technical writers and in 1998 found the mean salary for technical writers to be $48,250 and a range of salaries from below $33,000 for the lowest 10 percent to above $68,000 for the highest 10 percent.

This translates into rates for self-employed technical writers of $25 to $80+ an hour or an average of $40 an hour. Consistent with this average, Andre Sharp, a technical writer in Los Angeles who manages the Society's job line, observes, "The bulk of work for freelancers is between $35 to $45 an hour." But many technical writers command fees of $45 to $60 an hour, points out Audrey Choden, a technical writer in Kansas City. "Even as an independent word-processing specialist, you should charge at least $30 an hour."

Potential Earnings

Typical Annual Gross Revenues: $48,000 based on billing 1,200 hours a year (24 hours per week) at $40 an hour for technical writing. Technical editing, which is slow work, ranging between three and eight pages an hour, pays about $10 less an hour than technical writing.

Overhead: low (under 20 percent).

Best Home Businesses Estimate of Market Potential

In this day and age, it's been said we need instructions for everything. As technology increases, the need to explain it grows. Safety and environmental considerations add to the complexity, necessitating the use of writers who can turn complex data into understandable instructions and information. One out of four technical writers is self-employed. The Bureau of Labor Statistics projects there will be 347,000 technical writers by 2006, up from 286,000 in 1996.

Best Ways to Get Business

- Searching online for assignments. Andre Sharp, Employment Manager for the Los Angeles chapter of the Society for Technical Communication and a technical writer himself, advises searching newsgroups using *jobs* as your search parameter. "While some work may be done in your home without seeing the company you're working for, you'll do best with companies in your geographic area." Most states and cities have online job sites where technical writing may be listed.

- Directly soliciting work from companies you want to write for, stressing the advantages of using freelance writers for peak workload situations. Companies may advertise work availability on their Web site, so you should search through sites for companies to contact.

- Posting on résumé banks to which the companies you're interested in working with subscribe.

- Participating in a visible way in trade associations and computer user groups, such as by writing for chapter publications on topics that will demonstrate your proficiency.

- Finding work through agencies that place temporary technical personnel, including technical writers.

- Responding to classified ads for technical writers online and in newspapers.

- Placing ads in the trade publications read by your prospective clients in the fields in which you work.

- Joining a writers' organization and using its job-referral service

- Becoming part of a trade publication's cadre of regular freelance contributors.

- Having a Web site on which you place testimonial letters and samples of your work.

First Steps

- To learn jargon and formatting of technical writing and layout and design skills, take a college course in technical writing. "However, you don't need to complete a full certificate program to get work," says Andre Sharp.

- Learn to use one or more high-end desktop publishing programs such as *Framemaker*, *Pagemaker*, and *Quark Express*.

- Develop a portfolio, which you may do in the class you take. Sharp says you can "take junk mail that is badly done and redo it to create a before and after picture."

- Take previous writing you've done and reformat it using the new technical writing skills you have learned.

- If your current employer has a need for technical writing, offer to take on assignments to build your portfolio and develop experience. You may make your former employer your first client when you go out on your own.

Where to Turn for Information and Help

ORGANIZATIONS

The following organizations either have people in the technical writing field or purchasers of technical writing. Also check local writer organizations.

AMERICAN MEDICAL WRITERS ASSOCIATION, 40 W. Gude, Suite 101, Rockville, MD 20850; (301) 294-5303. Web site: *www.amwa.org*

AMERICAN SOCIETY FOR TRAINING AND DEVELOPMENT, 1640 King Street, P.O. Box 1443, Alexandria, VA 22313-2043; (703) 683-8100; fax (703) 683-8103. Its special-interest groups are of interest to technical writers.

ASSOCIATION FOR EDUCATIONAL COMMUNICATIONS AND TECHNOLOGY, 1025 Vermont Avenue, NW, Washington, DC 20005. Web site: *www.aect.org*

EDITORIAL FREELANCERS' ASSOCIATION, 71 West 23rd Street, Suite 1504, New York, NY 10010; (212) 929-5400. Web site: *www.the-efa.org*

INSTITUTE FOR ELECTRICAL AND ELECTRONICS ENGINEERS' PROFESSIONAL COMMUNICATIONS SOCIETY, IEEE Operations Center, Admission and Advancement Department, 445 Hoes Lane, PO Box 459, Piscataway, NJ 08855. Web site: *www.ieee.org/society/pcs*

INTERNATIONAL ASSOCIATION OF BUSINESS COMMUNICATORS, 1 Hallidie Plaza, Suite 600, San Francisco, CA 94102; (415) 433-3400. Web site: *www.iabc.com*

INTERNATIONAL SOCIETY FOR PERFORMANCE IMPROVEMENT, 1300 L Street, NW, Suite 1250, Washington, DC 20005; (202) 408-7969. Web site: *www.ispi.org*

INTERNATIONAL SOCIETY OF TECHNICAL ILLUSTRATORS, 1075 Nalley Rd., Rock Hill, SC 29732; (803) 366-0346.

SOCIETY FOR TECHNICAL COMMUNICATION, 901 North Stuart Street, Suite 304, Arlington, VA 22203; (703) 522-4114. The Society's 22,000 members include technical writers, editors, illustrators, multimedia artists, publishers, and others whose work involves making technical information understandable. The society has local chapters in most states, some of which operate an employment referral service or résumé bank. Web sites: *www.stc.org* and *www.stc-va.org*

BOOKS

The Elements of Technical Writing, Robert W. Bly, Gary Blake, Macmillan General Reference, 1995. ISBN: 0020130856.

Handbook of Technical Writing, Charles T. Brusaw, Gerald J. Alred, Walter E. Oliu, St. Martins Press, 1997. ISBN: 0312166907.

Making Money in Technical Writing, Peter Kent, Arco Publications, 1997. ISBN: 0028618831.

Managing Your Documentation, Joann T. Hackos, John Wiley & Sons, 1994. ISBN: 0471590991.

The Microsoft Manual of Style for Technical Publications, Microsoft Press, 1995. ISBN: 1556159390.

Read Me First!: A Style Guide for the Computer Industry, Sun Technical Publications, Prentice-Hall Computer Books, 1997. ISBN: 0134553470.

COURSES

United States Department of Agriculture Graduate School offers reasonably priced courses in English and writing skills. For more information, contact the Correspondence Study Program, Graduate School USDA, Room 1112S, 14th and Independence Ave. SW, Washington, DC 20250; (888) 744-GRAD; (202) 314-3670.

See the "Training Specialist" profile for the Society of Applied Learning Technology.

Colleges and universities offer certificate and degree courses in technical writing. Sometimes offered as part of the extension program.

Training Specialist

As virtually every business and organization is undergoing the most rapid cycles of change known in human history, does anyone of us ever know enough? There's new technology to learn, new markets, new methods of selling, servicing, and interacting with customers, new management techniques, new social and cultural expectations, new government regulations to cope with, and as fewer corporate employees past their mid-forties survive downsizing and restructuring, a continual flow of young people with much to learn.

This is good news for corporate trainers. "CEOs are deciding training is an investment," says Curtis Plott, President of the American Society for Training. Today's organizations are investing in more training, and those that make the investment are seeing higher profitability, increased sales, better quality products and service, higher customer satisfaction, and better employee satisfaction. It's no surprise that the training field continues to grow, holding its own even during economic downturns.

Today most employees receive some form of training through their employer, the most prevalent programs being in job-specific skills, management and supervisory skills, computer literacy and software applications, and safety. Whatever type of training they do, companies expect a return on their investment. "The standard has gone up both in terms of what they're demanding be delivered and the skills needed to deliver it."

Organizations are turning to various sources to provide training to their personnel, in-house staff; colleges and universities; unions; trade and professional associations; government organizations; training companies such as American Management Associations, Career Track, Franklin Covey, and Fred Pryor; and, of most interest to you, specialized independent trainers. Some organizations rely on independent specialists more than others.

High-performance companies, the kind that appear on the lists of best places to work, use independent specialists at a high level—almost three our of four companies do, according to research reported in the 1998 American Society of Training and Development State of the Industry Report. Large organizations are more likely to outsource their training than smaller ones with under 500 employees. However, smaller organizations spend about half their training budgets on outside training and tuition.

Most corporate trainers specialize in one or two areas. Robert Johnson, of BJE Associates, in Campbell, California, for example, focuses on the employee development in sales skills. His clients include industrial organizations that want to increase business-to-business sales. Johnson usually works with larger companies, but on occasion he also has small-to-medium-size clients, because such companies often employ personnel who have no training in phone sales or sales presentations.

In choosing a specialty, however, keep in mind that whether a company or organization in a particular industry uses outside training, resources will vary from company to company. Some industries such as manufacturing are more apt to outsource their training while others such as health care are less apt to.

Training programs can range from a four-hour workshop to a five-day event. Trainers most often conduct their programs on the premises of their clients, although some trainers give workshops off-site usually in rented hotel conference rooms so employees can avoid the distractions of their work environment. Trainers are usually expected to provide their own visual aids and appropriate written materials. Many trainers custom-create their own workbooks or three-ring binders to give to employees as part of the package for their training, but others purchase off-the-shelf materials from any of hundreds of training suppliers and publishers.

Knowledge and Skills You Need To Have

- People skills are paramount for being a successful trainer. You must be able to communicate with groups of people and make their training a positive experience. This means being entertaining, informative, and definitely not bashful. On occasion, you must do role-playing to demonstrate a situation, so having some "ham" in you helps.

- You need to have an awareness of group dynamics and be able to interact with, respond to, and lead groups through various training activities.

- You need excellent presentation skills and/or a background in teaching so that you know how to break down information into the kind of small chunks that make learning easier.

- You need a sincere desire to help people; some people refer to this as training that comes from the heart.

- You also must know how to deal diplomatically (without losing your cool) with a difficult audience member who is demeaning the training for others. Trainers need to have resolved any personality issues they may have because someone is bound to push any hot button that's available. A trainer who inappropriately explodes or turns to putty gets in the way of the learning process and will get poor evaluations.

- Sales and marketing skills are also necessary; getting contracts for your own business takes time so you must be prepared to talk about what you do and the value of your training.

- You need to become comfortable with learning technologies, such as computer-based training, multimedia and the Internet.

- You need good writing skills for writing proposals and a statement of your work. You may also want to write some of your own training materials or customize the off-the-shelf product you buy.

Start-up Costs	Low	High
Computer	$ 1,500	$ 3,000
Laser printer	$ 400	$ 2,500
Multi-function printer/fax/scanner/copier	$ 150	$ 600

Desktop publishing and presentation software to make your own overheads, charts, graphs	$ 100	$	400
Binding machine to bind your handouts	$ 250	$	500
Reference books	$ 100	$	300
Telephone headset	$ 40	$	400
Office furniture, especially an ergonomic chair	$ 400	$	1,000
Initial marketing budget	$ 1,500	$	5,000
Total	$ 4,440	$	13,700

Advantages

- You earn your living using your wits, so training can be intellectually stimulating and rewarding.

- Trainers can derive satisfaction from helping people improve their skills and attitudes. The satisfaction of providing people with "ah hah" experiences is a special reward.

- Effective trainers, particularly those who enable people to have a good time learning, will get repeat business, sometimes year after year.

- Training is often a good step into other income-producing activities such as writing and publishing your own off-the-shelf training programs, books, tapes, manuals, and other products. These can supplement what you do or become stand-alone business activities.

- If you like to perform or work an audience, other than being a stand-up comedian, training is the venue for you.

Disadvantages

- Unless a company defines itself as having a need, training is a difficult product to sell. The selling cycle can be long. That is, it may take months or even years for a company to decide it can benefit from your training program, budget for it, and complete the process of actually bringing you in.

- Training is often perceived as being the same as buying consulting; companies may feel that they're purchasing a long-term commitment, which isn't actually true. In some industries, trainers will actively distinguish themselves as not being consultants.

- Depending on the size of the community in which you live and your specialization, you may need to travel widely to develop a large-enough client base to support yourself. This is a work *from* home business.

- You are often competing with large training companies and sometimes universities and institutions. It's a competitive field, and you need to distinguish yourself from the pack.

- Increasingly, trainers need to justify why classroom training is superior to using other learning technologies such as multimedia, computer-based learning, and interactive online courses. You have to be able to demonstrate the value of such things as personal interactions, group experiences, role-playing, live feedback, and personal coaching.

- You sometimes may need to rent space in hotels and conference centers, either for the effectiveness of the training or because the client is a small company without space for training on their premises. This means negotiating arrangements with hotels to get deals and either dragging around your own projection system, easels, flip charts, and presentation materials or shipping them and risking they won't be there when you need them.

Pricing

- Rates for independent trainers range from $600 to $2,000 a day. Discounts are sometimes offered for consecutive multi-day or multi-week training, and limits are set on maximum-class sizes.

- Sometimes a rate of $100 to $150 per hour is used with a requirement of a three- or four-hour minimum.

- Train-the-trainer sessions that involve teaching other trainers to teach command higher fees.

- When trainers work with service brokers, they may work for as little as $200 a day or give the broker a substantial percentage of their fee.

- Some trainers, particularly those training in technology areas, charge by the head, between $100 and $300 per day per trainee. Some trainers relate the per-person fee to the salary level of the employees. So training fees for a group of twelve people earning in the mid-twenties per year ($100 a day) are apt to be around $1,200.

Potential Earnings

Typical Annual Gross Revenues: Based on filling 100 days a year (two days a week) at $1,000 a day, $100,000. In the first year, expect to be able to sell $35,000 to $75,000 worth of training. With experience, some trainers make substantially more than $100,000.

Overhead: low (20 percent or less).

Best Home Businesses Estimate of Market Potential

Curtis Plott of ASTD points to three forces driving training: global competition, increased technology, and the increase of knowledge-based businesses. Professional knowledge is now spoken of in half-lives. For example, "the half-life of an engineer's knowledge is five years." The need for lifelong learning is fueling the training industry with half of all knowledge workers, including executives, professionals, and technical people, receiving training during a year.

Outsourcing of training is increasing because executives prefer to bring in trainers who have specialized knowledge and skill at the time they need them instead of assuming the ongoing costs of building an internal training staff. However, learning technologies such as multimedia and computer-based instruction are making inroads on classroom training. Trainers will need to adapt to delivering training in new ways as bandwidth increases, opening the possibilities for combining computer-based and live training.

Best Ways to Get Business

- Specializing by industry, subject, type of personnel trained, or a combination of these. Managers, supervisors, people in technical jobs, and salespeople receive the most training. Popular topics covered include team building, quality, general management skills, creativity, etiquette, change management, interpersonal skills, performance management, communication, cultural diversity, sexual harassment, the Internet, and software applications. Formal training is concentrated on employees between 25 and 44 years of age.

- Networking with and contacting human resource personnel and sales managers in your area. The more you get to know them and they know you, the better your chances of selling them your programs.

- Demonstrating what you can do by speaking before professional and trade associations in the industries in which you work.

- Having a portfolio of testimonials and recommendations from satisfied clients. Collect testimonial letters from all participants in workshops you give that you can show to prospective clients.

- Teaching as many has half a dozen workshops a year for continuing-education divisions of local colleges and universities.

- Getting your seminars listed on sites such as the Seminar Superstore, which has 60,000 training programs and is used by corporations to find training programs. Web site: *www.seminarsuperstore.com*

- Contacting past clients and checking their satisfaction; asking about others they could recommended you to.

- Writing articles and getting other publicity to expand your reputation and perception of expertise.

- Having your own Web page with its own domain name with testimonial letters and any articles you have written.

First Steps

- An academic degree or teaching experience is not always a prerequisite to becoming a trainer, particularly if you already have training experience. Because training is industry-related, you can start doing training for an industry with which you are already familiar. For example, if you used to work in banking, begin by developing seminars and workshops you can offer for banking personnel. A successful program with one client in that field can be used as a stepping stone to other clients in the field, and eventually into other fields.

- Take a presentation skills workshop that provides video feedback to build your presentation skills. Learn as much as you can about trainee behavior and what works and doesn't work by observing other people's workshops.

- Assisting an established trainer as an apprentice is another way of building training skills.

- Join professional associations, particularly ASTD. Attending ASTD's national conference can particularly valuable.

- Develop a step-by-step outline for what you intend to teach. Identify the specific skills and knowledge employees will gain. Develop the accompanying written materials you will use as handouts during your course. Test your training program by volunteering to do training for nonprofit organizations or by offering it by invitation to select contacts.

Where to Turn for Information and Help

ORGANIZATIONS

AMERICAN MANAGEMENT ASSOCIATION (AMACOM); (800) 262-9699; (212) 903-8087. Publishes hundreds of books on training and management education. Web site: *www.amanet.org/books*

AMERICAN SOCIETY FOR TRAINING AND DEVELOPMENT, 1640 King Street, Box 1443, Alexandria, VA 22313-2043; (703) 683-8100. Largest training organization with over 55,000 corporate-based professionals: managers, human-resource specialists, designers, instructors, evaluators, consultants, researchers, and educators. Offers a professional journal, local chapters, and a train-the-trainer certificate program. Publishes the respected *Training and Development Journal*. Web site: *www.astd.org*

NATIONAL SPEAKERS' ASSOCIATION, 1500 South Priest Drive, Tempe, AZ 85281; (602) 968-2552. While there are stylistic differences between speakers and trainers, many people speak professionally and train. The National Speakers' Association has a training program that it requires as a condition of membership.

BOOKS

The ASTD Technical and Skills Training Handbook, Leslie Kelly, McGraw-Hill, 1995. ISBN: 007033899X.

Basic Training for Trainers: A Handbook for New Trainers, Gary Kroehnert, McGraw-Hill; 1995. ISBN: 0074701932.

The First-Time Trainer: A Step-By-Step Quick Guide for Managers, Supervisors, and New Training Professionals, Tom W. Goad, AMACOM; 1997. ISBN: 0814479421.

ID Project Management: Tools and Techniques for Instructional Designers and Developers, Michael Greer, Educational Technology Publications, 1992. ISBN: 0877782377.

A Practical Guide to Needs Assessment, Kavita Gupta, Pfeiffer & Co; 1998. ISBN: 0787939889. This is one of many books, tapes, and videos on training produced by Jossey Bass Pfeiffer Publications, 350 Sansone Street, San Francisco, CA 94104; (800) 274-4434.

The Trainer's Tool Kit, Kathy Conway, Cy Charney, AMACOM; 1997. ISBN: 0814479448.

Training and Development Handbook: A Guide to Human Resource Development, Robert L. Craig, McGraw-Hill, 1996. ISBN: 007013359X. Considered to be the basic nuts-and-bolts how-to book for new trainers and a valued reference for experienced trainers.

Your Career in Human Resource Development: A Guide to Information and Decision, R. Stump, ASTD, Box 1443, Alexandria, VA 22313. Booklet to help readers determine whether they are suited for the human-resources field.

MAGAZINES

Inside Technology Training, Ziff-Davis Inc, 10 Presidents Landing, Medford, MA 02155; (888) 950-4302; (781) 393-3619. Web site has searchable archives of past issues. Web site: *www.ittrain.com*

Training: The Magazine of Human Resource Development, Lakewood Publications, 50 South 9th Street, Minneapolis, MN 55402; (800) 707-7749; (612) 333-0471. The Web site contains summaries of selected articles from past issues and a rating of 250 training-related sites. Web site: *www.trainingsupersite.com*

WEB SITES

TRAINERS & TRAININGFORUM ON COMPUSERVE. *http://directory. compuserve.com/Forums/DPTRAIN/Abstract.htm*

THE TRAINING REGISTRY has links to many useful training resources. *www.tregistry.com*

Also see the resources for computer training in the "Tutoring" profile.

Transcript-Digesting Service

Would you like a career in the legal field without having to be a lawyer, paralegal, or legal secretary? If you can write clearly, starting a legal transcript digesting service could be your ideal career. It requires a minimal amount of time to learn, costs little to start, and has the potential to produce a good income. As a transcript digester, also called a deposition digester, you will be summarizing statements taken under oath from parties involved in legal proceedings.

Lawyers don't like to be surprised in the courtroom when someone takes the stand. In fact, a legal maxim is to "never ask a question you don't know the answer to." Discovering what people are going to say before they appear at a trial plays an important role in the legal system. Prior to a trial, lawyers take testimony in what is called a deposition. Depositions are recorded by a court reporter, and then the entire testimony is transcribed into a document that lawyers study carefully before the trial. As you can imagine, the transcripts are quite long, so to save time for the lawyers, transcript digesters rewrite wordy, rambling, repetitive testimony using concise, well-organized, readable sentences. A good digester can condense the number of words in a transcript by 80 percent or more without cutting out relevant points.

Digesters also digest trial transcripts during the course of a trial. An attorney may need an expedited transcript of a previous day's proceedings to prepare for cross-examination. In lengthy trials, which can last for months, digests of prior testimony are essential. Digests are also used in making appeals.

Sometimes digests are prepared by trained paralegals, but digests can also be done by someone who has the ability to analyze and write succinctly. As digester Mary Barnes points out, "Good writing skills are more important in this business than legal knowledge. The writing needs to flow so the transcripts don't have to be read two or three times."

Today, more and more law firms are using outside transcript services. Since Barnes and her husband started their home-based digesting company in 1990, their business has expanded to 20 part-time employees, and Mary Barnes has developed a course to teach others how to do legal digesting.

A digester's clients range from the solo practitioner to firms with 100 or more lawyers. Each firm has its own reasons for using independent digesters. The lawyer in solo practice may be buried in motions by a large firm and need outside help. Attorneys in large law firms appreciate having their time freed up, and their clients appreciate the savings in attorney fees (many lawyers now charge up to $600 per hour).

In some regions, having transcripts digested by professionals dedicated to this function is fairly new, and some attorneys will not be familiar with outside digesting services. Mary Barnes reports that sometimes when people call to ask about her course, they sometimes say that attorneys in their area don't hire out digesting depositions. But when Mary asks how many lawyers the caller has talked with, the answer is invariably only one or two. Because not all lawyers do any or much trial work, this is too limited a sample to know if there's a market for transcript digesting in your area.

One way of determining if digesting is new to your area is to find out if others are doing it. Go to a law library and check the classified ads in bar journals and legal newspapers. Most digesters place ads in these publications, but you probably won't find them in the Yellow Pages.

Despite being new in some areas, specialized niches are developing in other locals where digesting has become popular. Medical malpractice is one example. In one area, nurses are providing a complete package of services for law firms that includes digesting transcripts and summarizing the medical evidence in a case.

Knowledge and Skills You Need to Have

- As a deposition digester, you must be familiar and comfortable with legal terminology and procedures so you can read and understand what is said in transcripts and condense it without changing the meaning.

- You must be able to read and keyboard quickly. The faster you read and type, the higher your earnings.

- You must also be able to synthesize and write concisely. The digester's role is not to decide whether testimony is relevant, but to know how to condense it skillfully.

- Prior expertise in a field can be helpful in understanding whatever terminology might be involved in a trial. For example, a construction background would be useful in cases dealing with construction defects. In other cases, a general understanding of the principles of accounting, finance, or science might come in handy.

- You must prepare your digests on a computer using word-processing software, because you will be rewriting every paragraph two or three times in order to reduce the number of words. You need an e-mail account so you can transmit your completed digests.

Start-up Costs	Low	High
Computer with large monitor	$ 1,200	$ 3,000
Printer or multi-functional	$ 400	$ 1,500
Word processing or suite software	$ 100	$ 250
Desk and ergonomic chair	$ 400	$ 1,000
Initial marketing budget	$ 500	$ 5,000
Total	$ 2,600	$ 10,750

Advantages

- Transcript digesting pays better than such similar businesses as office-support/word processing and scoping.

- You can learn what you need to know to do this business in as little as three weeks, although you will continue to hone your skills as you work.

- The work is interesting and challenging. You learn useful information that you won't come across anywhere else.

- This work is done at home.

Disadvantages

- The work is isolating. You are at your computer many hours each day.

- Because you are at the keyboard so long, you can suffer from computer-related disabilities. It's important to use an ergonomic chair, a keyboard pillow with wrist rests, and a glare screen on at least a 17" monitor. Also, you should get up frequently and walk around.

- You may have to persuade attorneys who have not used digesters that a skilled writer and nonattorney can do the work. You will have to assure them convincingly that you include everything in the transcript—not omitting facts—providing them with a rewritten transcript in concise condensed form.

- You may have to work under the pressure of fast turnaround time when attorneys need to review before proceeding with the next phase of a trial.

Pricing

Typically digesters are paid by the transcript page. You'll earn substantially less when working through an agency, but an agency is a way of getting started. Note, however, that agencies expect a digester to produce at least ten pages per hour. Novice digesters working for an agency receive $.80 cents to $1 per page. Experienced digesters working on their own get $2.50 to $4 per page. Ten to 20 pages per hour is typical for digesters to produce in an eight-hour day.

Potential Earnings

Typical Annual Gross Revenues: $38,000 to $100,000.

Overhead: low (20 percent or less).

Best Home Businesses Estimate of Market Potential

The United States has 5 percent of the world's population and 66 percent of the world's lawyers, providing lots of clients for transcriptionists. Transcript digesting is part of a trend that has been growing over the last several decades. This trend will continue.

Best Ways to Get Business

1. Associating with a court-reporting service that will subcontract digesting work to you.

2. Listing with agencies that will refer work to you.

3. Targeting attorneys who handle the type of complex litigation, such as construction defects, product liability, and toxic waste that generates dozens of depositions, especially from expert witnesses. You can find such attorneys listed in Martindale-Hubbell. Expect to use multiple methods to make attorneys aware of you and your services, such as:

   - Send mailings to attorneys who do trial work that you've targeted, following up with phone calls or personal visits and offering to do a free digest of a fifty-to-one-hundred-page deposition.

   - Making personal contacts with law firm personnel.

   - Placing classified and display ads repeatedly in legal publications that attorneys read, such as bar journals and legal newspapers, as a long-term investment to build your name recognition.

   - Directly soliciting law firms by phone and making an appointment to talk with them about your services. You can use a salesperson to set up appointments for you, but this person must know the business.

First Steps

If you have no experience, paralegal programs sometimes have courses in deposition digesting and writing skills. Or you can teach yourself digesting using the tutorials listed below. Once you've mastered the skill, you might consider working for an agency to gain experience before marketing yourself directly to law firms. You can locate transcript-digesting agencies in your community through ads in local legal publications.

Where to Turn for Information and Help

TUTORIALS/TRAINING COURSES

HILLSIDE DIGESTING SERVICES' TRANSCRIPT DIGESTING COURSE, P.O. Box 2888, Fallbrook, CA 92088; (800) 660-3376. A complete training course with exercises, samples, feedback and marketing guidance; requires a Wintel computer.

THE WORKING FROM HOME FORUM ON COMPUSERVE offers files covering the basics of digesting transcripts, a sample deposition, and sample summaries in various formats. This material is available in its Library. To find them, simply use the search words "deposition digesting."

 # Translator/Interpreter

While English is said to be the language of business, people in other countries want contracts drawn up in their local language. Of course, marketing communication is more effective in the local language, respecting the norms of the area. As we write this, the largest growth in Internet usage is by people accessing in language other than English. For those people fortunate enough to speak more languages than English, that ability can be the ticket to an interesting and rewarding home business.

Translators work with the written word; interpreters, the spoken word, but some people do both. While studying in Wisconsin, Janice Sabin de Medina, who does both translation and interpretation, found there was a market there for someone who could translate Spanish. She'd lived in Mexico and studied for a year at the University of Madrid. Her company, Fonetika, working with subcontractors, also converts English videos into other languages.

Kenneth McKethan, had always had an interest in language and got his first opportunity to work as an interpreter in high school, going to Switzerland with the Civil Air Patrol. The Swiss instructors didn't speak English. After college, he lived in Germany before returning to the U.S. to set up Techni-Lingua in Dunn, North Carolina.

Ludmilla Rusakova immigrated to the United States in 1990 to study international business. When she got to Houston, she realized she could earn a good living as a translator. Her firm, MasterWord, translates many of the languages of the former Soviet Union, and through subcontractors, Spanish.

As in so many other businesses, specialization is an asset in this field, although some specialties, such as translating literary works, prose and poetry, don't pay well. If you have a technical background of any kind, however, particularly one in a growing technology, you can earn a good living in this high-demand specialty. Another growing specialization is translating the content of Web sites into other languages so companies and organizations can attract a greater numbers of people to their sites. The world of entertainment needs translators, too, doing such things as translating scripts for dubbing, translating stage plays, and subtitling films. Interpreters can specialize in cross-cultural training for business-people, community relations, crisis intervention, or sign language. Conference translation is a possibility for people living in the cities where international organizations are located, such as New York and Washington.

Knowledge and Skills You Need to Have

- Having lived in the area of the language in which you will be working to learn the norms and culture of the area.

- Fluency in both English and the second language or languages, including colloquialisms and slang.

- Translators must be exacting and accurate because they create a permanent written record.

- For translation, an undergraduate degree in an area other than language, such as business or engineering, along with a master's degree in the primarily language you will be translating, are helpful.

- Interpreting requires concentration and focus as well as being able to comprehend meaning and be empathetic enough to anticipate what the person speaking is going to say.

- To do interpreting for courts, you need to understand court procedures. Certification is required for interpreting some languages in federal courts (currently Haitian, Creole, Navajo, and Spanish). Some state courts also require certification. Determine from the court administrator in your area what the requirements are.

Advantages

- The "field is booming," says Walter Bacak, Executive Director of the American Translators Association.

- You can work the hours of your choice in a location of your choice.

- Start-up costs and entry requirements are minimal.

Disadvantages

- Since clients may not be aware of the process of translation or appreciate the time involved, you may encounter sticker shock when you quote your prices. Therefore, in the process of selling your services, you will need to educate your clients in order to reach an equitable business agreement.

- Bacak says, "The difference between those who are successful and those who are not is business skills."

- The field is highly competitive, and competition is coming from lower-cost translators abroad, such as the former Soviet Union where English was taught extensively. However, firms wanting to protect proprietary technology often prefer American-based firms.

Start-up Costs

	Low	High
Computer with e-mail capability	$ 1,500	$ 3,000
Multi-function printer/fax/scanner/copier	$ 150	$ 600
Cell phone and/or beeper for interpreters	$ 75	$ 200
Reference books, though many glossaries can be found online	$ 300	$ 1,000
	per language	
Initial marketing budget	$ 1,000	$ 5,000
Office furniture, especially an ergonomic chair	$ 400	$ 1,000
Total	$ 3,350	$ 11,800

Pricing

Pricing may be by the word, by the hour, or by the job. Pricing by the word may be either by the source or target language, with a range as wide as $7 to $15 per 100 words. Higher fees can be commanded for working in high-demand languages and for technical, legal, and medical translation, which require a special knowledge of that field to do the work. Interpreters earn $250 a day working in the federal courts.

Potential Earnings

Typical Annual Gross Revenues: $62,500 based on yielding $50 an hour, 25 hours a week, 50 weeks a year.

Overhead: low (under 20 percent).

Best Home Businesses Estimate of Market Potential

Increases in world trade and advances in technology drive the demand for translators and interpreters. Software menus and commands need to be adapted for use in other countries. Software upgrades are coming out more rapidly. E-commerce enables even the smallest companies to have access to people all over the globe who don't speak English, provided they can transact business in the languages of these new customers. Except for the most repetitive of translation needs such as weather forecasting or technical manuals, automated translation done by computers is not expected to replace humans who can master nuance.

The demand for interpreters is growing because the United States has the highest proportion of immigrants since the turn of the last century. In cities like Los Angeles, immigrants are not reluctant to make use of the court system and require interpreters.

Best Ways to Get Business

- Directly soliciting work from law firms, public relations firms, and companies operating internationally.

- Networking with other translators for work they can refer or subcontract. Consider jointly proposing to handle the translation work for a company as a consortium.

- Participating in chambers of commerce and trade organizations that have members who participate in international trade, particularly a hyphenated organizations such as a Japanese-American Club.

- Volunteering your work in organizations that reach out to ethnic audiences.

- Having your own Web site with its own domain name, testimonial letters, and any articles you have written and other useful information that may attract hits from browsers.

- Participating in forums, newsgroups, and listserv mailing lists that correspond to your specialization.

First Steps

- Subcontract or be employed by an existing translation service or agency.

- Determine what the local sources of work are in your area. Keep in mind that in companies, the marketing department and the purchasing department may each hire translators independently of one another.

- If you are going into court translation, determine if you need to be certified and of so get required certification.

Where to Turn for Information and Help

ORGANIZATIONS AND WEB SITES

AMERICAN TRANSLATORS ASSOCIATION (ATA), 225 Reinekers Lane, Suite 590, Alexandria, VA 22314; (703)683-6100. Offers accreditation; liability insurance; publishes a journal, *The ATA Chronicle,* and a series of monographs on the translation field. On its Web site, ATA provides a model contract, links to other organizations, and reference works such as glossaries and specialized dictionaries. Web site: *www.atanet.org*

FOREIGN LANGUAGE FORUM ON COMPUSERVE. Has message sections on job and careers and business and technology. Web site: *http://go. compuserve.com/ForeignLanguage*

INTERNATIONAL ASSOCIATION OF CONFERENCE INTERPRETERS, 10 avenue de Sécheron—CH, 1202 Geneva, Switzerland. Web site: *www.aiic.net*

THE NATIONAL ASSOCIATION OF JUDICIARY INTERPRETERS AND TRANSLA-
TORS, 551 Fifth Avenue, Suite 3025, New York, NY 10176; (212) 692-
9581. Web site: *www.najit.org*

THE TRANSLATORS AND INTERPRETERS GUILD, 8611 2nd Ave., Suite 203,
Silver Spring, MD 20910; (301) 563-6450. This is the nationwide labor union for freelance and in-house translators and interpreters. Web
site: *www.trans-interp-guild.org*

COURSES AND TRAINING

A number of university continuing education programs, community colleges and proprietary institutitions offer certificate programs. The American Translators Association publishes a directory of institutions offering
translator/interpreter training in the U.S., entitled *Translator and Interpreter Training in the USA: A Survey* (2nd Edition).

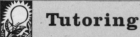 **Tutoring**

Learning to start a fire was probably one of the first things one human
being tutored another to do. Sitting around a warm fire with others
was probably the beginning of civilization. We still very much value one-
on-one instruction, and thus tutors can earn a living from their homes
helping people learn how to use computer software, understand algebra,
or pass entrance examinations. Probably because tutoring is such a fundamental human interaction, legislators have yet to require examinations
or licenses in order for one to be a tutor.

Although there are classes in almost every subject and particularly
computer-training programs, the tutor has the advantage of being able to
offer individual attention. The tutor can particularize and customize what
he or she teaches to the level and needs of each student. Many people prefer such individual instruction because it allows them to learn at their
own pace without the pressure of peers or authorities. Parents, eager for
their children to succeed, realize their children often need more personalized attention than they can get in a classroom.

There's almost no limit to specialties one can become a tutor in,
everything from assisting struggling history students pass a required
course to helping aspiring thespians master better diction or coaching an

amateur golfer on how to improve his or her swing. Generally speaking, however, there are two areas of tutoring that remain continuously in demand from coast to coast.

Computer Tutoring/Training

The line between computer tutor and computer trainer is blurred because sometimes tutors work with groups and sometimes trainers work one-on-one. But both individuals and organizations hire professionals who can teach them how to use computer technology.

Individuals who hire computer tutors for one-to-one instruction (or very small group or family instruction) include small business owners, people ready to use their first computer or upgrading to more sophisticated software or equipment, and parents eager for their children to both enjoy and master computer technology. Companies retain trainers to help entire offices or departments automate, upgrade, or switch from one software package or hardware platform to another, and to work one-on-one with managers, executives, and key personnel.

Computer trainers generally work at the client's office or home, either doing one-on-one coaching or teaching classroom style. Some computer tutors recommend hardware and software and help get it installed.

While some computer trainers learn multiple software packages in an effort to reach as wide a client base as possible, others specialize by working in particular industries, such as law, construction, or health care, or specialize in a particular software application, such as a word-processing or contact-management program. When specializing in a particular industry, trainers must have expertise in both the software involved and the ways in which the software is used in that specific business. Ann McIndoo, who has done spectacularly well as a computer tutor to the legal professional, earning over a million dollars a year in income, says "specializing enables you to get better and better at what you do" and thus be of more value to your clients.

Scholastic Tutoring

Surveys of parents of school-age children indicate that their children's education is their number one concern. Many parents want their children to get into a good school. Often the competition is tough even for preschools, but especially for private high schools and colleges. Other parents just want their kids to keep up, knowing they'll fall behind if they haven't mastered basic skills or are struggling to pass required coursework.

Large class sizes and classrooms too often turned into unsettling environments due to violence or its threat cause parents to fear that schools will not adequately prepare their children for the future. Therefore, they're turning to tutors to provide their children with the added attention they believe will make the difference.

Students in all age ranges from grade school to college are receiving scholastic or academic tutoring. Of course, if you are going to tutor in microbiology, you must be versed in it. Thus, most tutors serve grade school and high school students. The most common subject for which tutors are hired is the one students find the most difficult—math. But tutors also teach physics, science, foreign languages, writing, reading, history, and study skills. Preparing students for college entrance exams is a particularly large and growing area of tutoring. Standardized admissions tests referred to with initials such as ACT, CSEE, ERB, ISEE, PSAT, SSAT, SAT I & II, and TOEFL strike fear into the hearts of parents and students alike, driving some students to begin preparation in the summer. Coaching for exams has extended downward. For example, parents are hiring tutors to prepare fourth-graders in New York for an English exam known as "The Test." Some tutors also provide college admissions counseling or help with college admission as an adjunct to tutoring.

Most of the time students come to the tutor's home for tutoring. For a higher fee, some academic tutors will go to the homes of their students. While tutoring is usually one-to-one, some tutors will work with as many as three students at a time at a reduced fee per student. Also some tutors offer specialized instruction for students with learning disabilities.

Also a tutor may choose to operate more like a referral service, combining tutoring they do themselves with providing referrals for those they can't fit into their schedules or for students who need tutoring on subjects outside their area of expertise. They either subcontract with other tutors or arrange to receive referral fees from the tutors they refer to.

Knowledge and Skills You Need to Have

FOR BOTH COMPUTER AND SCHOLASTIC TUTORS

- You need good communication skills in order to listen to and interpret students' needs. You need to communicate directions and information in simple, clear, and concise language. As Jan Berinstein, who teaches WordPerfect, points out, computer trainers work with people who "may not know how to ask a question in a way to get the information they want. If you don't listen carefully to their questions and don't take time to give thoughtful answers, they will become frustrated."

- The patience of a saint is a must. Many people who seek tutoring aren't at all confident or adept at what you know so well. They may make repeated mistakes and ask obvious questions. They may need frequent repetition, repeated rephrasing of explanations, continual reinforcement and often lots of encouragement and reassurance.

FOR SCHOLASTIC TUTORS

- Although a degree in education is not necessary, a bachelor's degree, or, in some specialized subjects, an additional advanced degree, is needed for credibility in marketing oneself as a tutor.

FOR COMPUTER TUTORS

- You must be proficient in at least one software package and know the operating system well. You must keep pace with the cutting edge of technology and updates of the hardware or software you teach, including new versions and patches. You need to learn quickly and be open to change.

- You need to know your vertical market, whether it's law, insurance, medical, dental, auto repair, construction, or entertainment, so that when clients ask questions, you will understand what they're talking about and be able to answer in a way that makes sense to them.

- For classroom training, good presentation skills are a must. See the "Training Specialist" profile.

- You need to be able to write winning proposals, curricula, and training materials.

- Internet skills in the form of being familiar with browsers, search engines, transmitting documents and attachments "will help you get work," says Ann McIndoo.

Start-up Costs for Scholastic Tutors	Low	High
Computer	$ 1,500	$ 3,000
Printer	$ 300	$ 800
or		
Multi-function printer/fax/scanner/copier	$ 150	$ 600
If tutor in your home, a quiet room adequately furnished	$ 500	$ 5,000
Reference book and texts in subject area	$ 100	$ 300
Initial marketing budget	$ 1,000	$ 5,000
Total	$ 2,750	$ 14,700

Start-up Costs for Computer Tutors	Low	High
Notebook computer with a docking station	$ 3,000	$ 7,000
Docking station and monitor	$ 1,100	$ 1,500
Laser printer	$ 400	$ 2,500
LCD panel for making presentations	$ 700	$ 7,000
Fax or multifunction machine	$ 150	$ 600
Desktop publishing and presentation software to make your own overheads, charts, graphs	$ 100	$ 400
Binding machine to bind your handouts	$ 250	$ 500
Software necessary to serve your customers' needs (some software companies will give you free software or a special discounted consultant/trainer price)	$ 500	$ 2,000
The training costs and other costs to become certified for the software programs you teach	$ 500	$ 4,000
Office furniture, including a table for assembling training materials	$ 500	$ 1,000
Initial marketing budget	$ 1,500	$ 3,000
Insurance against loss of hardware and data	$ 900	$ 1,000
Total	$10,600	$ 31,500

Advantages

- Responding to the needs of clients provides a constant challenge and can keep the work interesting and fun.

- Helping people learn and master what you're teaching provides a rewarding sense of accomplishment.

- For computer tutors, training can be a step to other forms of computer consulting, such as customizing software or its documentation.

Disadvantages

- Tutoring is a competitive business, so you must specialize and stand out from the crowd.

- Sometimes you must work with those who don't want to be in a student role and who don't like someone else telling them what to do or knowing more than they do. Egos can be triggered whenever someone is learning something new. You must be diplomatic even when you don't feel like it.

- Computer trainers need to invest time in continual learning. Ann McIndoo attends a workshop every month. She finds reading the ads in computer magazines more important than reading the articles.

Pricing

COMPUTER TUTORS

$35 to $125 an hour; however, "hobbyists" may charge less. Setting a three-hour minimum that includes travel time avoids billing clients for travel time, which they usually resent paying. For traveling longer distances, a four-hour or greater minimum may be used. By the day, $250 to $1,200.

SCHOLASTIC TUTORS

$15 to $50 an hour. The rate varies with experience, location, and whether the tutor goes to the student's home. Students who tutor are at the low end of the range. Most tutors working in their own home charge between $20 and $30 an hour; if tutoring three students at a time, $10 to $15 each per hour.

Potential Earnings

Typical Annual Gross Revenues for Scholastic Tutors: Based on tutoring 20 hours a week, 40 weeks a year at $25 an hour: $20,000.

Overhead for Scholastic Tutors: low (less than 20 percent).

Typical Annual Gross Revenues for Computer Tutors: Based on yielding $500 a day, three days a week, forty-eight weeks a year: $72,000.

Overhead for Computer Tutors: moderate (between 20 percent and 40 percent). Primary expenses are operating your vehicle, new software and upgrades, continuing education, hardware, and books.

Best Home Businesses Estimate of Market Potential

The prospects for tutoring look good in the years to come. The ongoing concern about the quality of classroom education propels the growth of scholastic tutoring, both in subject areas and in preparing students for qualifying examinations. Although software arguably is becoming easier to use, updates are coming with increasing frequency, requiring users to learn new features and ways of doing things. Meanwhile, as software prices decline, companies are either providing less human support by putting documentation online or on CD-ROM or charging for customer support. So computer tutors should continue to do well, though tutoring will increasingly be done over the Internet as wider bandwidth enables both visual and audio communication.

Best Ways to Get Business

COMPUTER TUTORS

- Placing brochures in displays or flyers on bulletin boards at computer stores, office stores, paper supply and computer repair shops.

- Stationing yourself outside a busy computer store and letting customers who are leaving with a new computer know what you do. If possible, make appointments then and there.

- Getting certified for the software you intend to teach, which qualifies you for referrals from the manufacturer.

- Soliciting referrals from manufacturers, resellers, suppliers, and consultants who serve the same types of companies you target. You may team up with them in various ways.

- Seeking to subcontract with vendors or integrators who do the installation of computer systems for their overflow work; expect to share revenue.

- Giving speeches at business meetings and associations about the benefits of computerizing using the software you are familiar with. This is the fastest, cheapest, and easiest method to help people understand how your training can help them.

- Volunteering to speak at organizations serving your vertical market.

- Teach adult-education classes. For example, if you are targeting law firms, offer classes to legal secretaries and paralegals. Classes can both produce income as well as produce leads.

- Networking and making personal contacts through the professional, trade, or business associations of the field in which you are specializing. Sometimes, as in the legal field, you cannot join the professional association and therefore you must network through civic or other business organizations. You can also network in computer and software user groups; manufacturers can direct you to user groups in your area.

- Sending direct mail advertising to companies that have purchased particular software packages. Their names are sometimes available, listed by zip code, from software vendors. Without such a highly qualified list, direct mail is too expensive.

- Providing a quarterly newsletter highlighting information about software upgrades, user tips, and new equipment to past, present, and potential customers and everyone else you meet who could refer business to you.

- Asking satisfied clients for referrals to others who need training. Offer free or discounted advice to potential clients; for example, help solve people's software problems over the phone.

- Advertising in city business journals and computer publications or specialized trade publications for your target market.

- Listing in the Yellow Pages under Computer Training.

- Having a Web site with reciprocal links to the sites of professionals in related fields such as computer consulting as well as sites of colleagues in other parts of the country. You can increase the hits you get by using words in meta tags that people commonly use when surfing the Web. For example, describing your site with the words, "A sexy way to . . ." will attract hits you would otherwise not get.

SCHOLASTIC TUTORS

- Calling upon teachers in the subject areas in which you specialize in your area as well as with school office personnel, counselors, and principals and leaving behind an attractive brochure that features your qualifications.

- Posting flyers featuring your qualifications on bulletin boards apt to be seen by parents in your area.

- Writing articles for community publications on topics that relate to your subject with your photo and byline, including how to contact you.

- Having your own Web page with its own domain name and testimonial letters.

- Participating in community organizations.

First Steps

COMPUTER TUTORS

- Obtain certification in the software program or programs you will be teaching. You must have a solid knowledge of the software packages and equipment you will be training others to use.

- Select a vertical niche market. It should be one in which you are knowledgeable and comfortable. Survey people in the field to identify what they absolutely hate to do with their software and then be prepared to show them how to automate those things.

- If you must enter a market with which you're not familiar, volunteer to do a project for a company in the field of your choice in exchange for your learning the ins and outs and special needs of that field. Take ample time on that first project to learn as much as you can by observing and asking questions. If possible, join and become active in the professional or trade associations in the field and subscribe to publications in the field.

- Despite the informality of business dress today, Ann McIndoo advises "professional grooming" for trainers.

SCHOLASTIC TUTORS

- Considering your experience, what you are comfortable with, and the extent of competition, select a subject and age group to specialize in. Your specialty may be narrow—for example, algebra—or broader to embrace several math subjects.

- Obtain current texts and familiarize yourself with them.

- Create a brochure describing your services and begin networking with teachers, school personnel, counselors, and principals. Make the availability of your service known.

Where to Turn for Information and Help

BOOKS

COMPUTER TUTORS

The Accidental Trainer: You Know Computers, So They Want You to Teach Everyone Else, Elaine Weiss, Jossey-Bass Publishers, 1996. ISBN: 0787902934.

The Complete Computer Trainer, Paul Clothier, Computing McGraw-Hill, 1996. ISBN: 0070116393.

The Computer Training Handbook: How to Teach People to Use Computers, Elliott Masie, Rebekah Wolman, Lakewood Publications, 1998. ISBN: 0943210372.

The Computer Trainer's Personal Training Guide, Bill Brandon, Paul Clothier, Shirley Copeland, Patty Crowell, Gail Perry, Que Education & Training, 1996. ISBN: 1575762536.

See also books listed under "Training Specialist."

NEWSLETTER

The Micro Computer Trainer, Systems Literacy, Inc, P.O. Box 1032, Hopatcong, NJ 07843; (973) 770-7762. Also offers a free e-mail newsletter, Quick Training Tips. To subscribe, e-mail Loretta@panix.com and enter "subscribe tips" in the subject line.

BOOKS

SCHOLASTIC TUTORS

The Master Tutor: A Guidebook for More Effective Tutoring, Ross B. MacDonald, Cambridge Stratford Ltd, 1994. ISBN: 0935637192.

Tutoring for Pay: Earn While You Help Others Learn, Betty O. Carpenter, Charles C. Thomas Publishing Ltd, 1991. ISBN: 0398057141.

Tutoring Matters: Everything You Always Wanted to Know About How to Tutor, Jerome Rabow, Tiffani Chin, Nima Fahimian, 1999. ISBN: 1566396956.

WEB SITES

These Web sites have start-up tips and materials for sale:

CLEVER APPLE HOME BASED TUTORING PROGRAM, Clever Apple Tutoring, 132 NW Cody Drive, Lee's Summit, MO 64081. Web site: *www.cleverapple.com*

HOW TO BECOME A TUTOR, Tutor Packet, Daa Mahowald, 12866 S.E. 262nd Place, Kent, WA 98031. Web site: *http://home.vpinet.net/~mahowald/tutor.htm*

 # Web Site Designer

The Web has taken its place as a staple of communication and commerce. It will be *the* hot medium for years to come just as radio and TV were in the twentieth century. Billboards and TV commercials regularly display Web site addresses. Projections for growth of e-commerce leap by billions of dollars with each successive survey. By the time you read this entry, you're apt to be getting your daily dose of news, shopping for myriad products from computers to real estate, and looking up whatever information you need through the Web more often you do through the traditional sources of the past.

Already e-mail has surpassed the telephone as the primary means of communication by corporate managers. Some demographic groups are more likely to turn to the Web than to the Yellow Pages. To be competitive, virtually every existing business, no matter the type or size, must have a well-designed, high-impact Web site in addition to the usual brochure and Yellow Page listing.

While Web design software makes it possible for even the smallest companies to create their own Web sites relatively inexpensively, these companies know that their sites should be sophisticated yet simple to navigate and versatile. Therefore, companies are turning to professional Web designers for the expertise to create truly effective sites. In fact, it's become difficult even for a Web designer to have mastered all the tools and techniques required to produce complex Web sites. The field of Web design is becoming quite specialized.

One large division is between designers who do front-end work and those who do back-end work. Front-end design is what you see when you visit a site; back-end design comprises the behind-the-scenes elements that make the site work. Back-end designers specialize in such site functions as chat rooms, e-commerce, database integration, dynamic site elements, CGI programming, PERL scripting, Active Server Pages (ASP), Java scripts, and Java. The front-end designers specialize in designer user interfaces. In fact, a designer can master a single program such as Macromedia *Slash* or Macromedia *Shockwave* and earn a good living as a specialist in that application.

While there will always be a role for generalists who are skilled in many areas of Web design and can create a client's entire site, specialization is the best route for most designers. But, of course, clients usually expect a complete or "turnkey" solution for their Web needs, so the solo designer either needs to expand his or her skills to meet all of a client's needs or make alliances with other specialists with whom they can work jointly to serve one another's clientele.

Knowledge and Skills You Need to Have

- You need to be able to critically evaluate Internet Service Providers (ISPs) in terms of what they can support so you can match what they offer with what your clients need and what you design.

- Background in graphic design or a related field is important in creating successful Web design. Good-looking, effective sites are created from the same basic principles that govern top-flight graphic design. There are many programs that offer templates and forms for Web sites, but in the view of Todd Cranston-Cuebas of Sticky Monkey Design of San Marino, California, you will do far better with solid design talent behind you. "Anybody can fill out a template. Your skill and experience are the true assets you will have to offer potential clients."

- You need to be thoroughly familiar with how people interact with a Web site, what type of experiences they're looking for and understand the elements of an effective Web site from color and size to navigation and interactivity, including what's involved in creating activities a client may want to provide visitors such as chats to message boards, ad banners, links, click-throughs, and electronic payment systems.

- You need to be have knowledge of HTML and other programming languages such as Java. You want to be familiar with an array of basic Web tools for integrating text, graphics, animation, photographs, sound, and so forth.

- You need to have good communication skills so you can assist your clients in identifying what they want to accomplish with their Web sites, who they want to attract, and how they want their clients to use and interact with the site.

- Specialists must master their particular area of expertise.

Advantages

- Being a Web designer now is like being in on the early days of television. This medium will be expanding and evolving for years to come. It will grow and grow and grow.

- You can serve clients from anywhere.

- You can help small, specialized companies reach beyond the limitations of their local market where they may have been barely surviving. States Todd Cranston-Cuebas, "With a good site, someone with a good idea and a good product or service can reach a worldwide market because the cost for entry is the same for a small company as for a million-dollar corporation."

- Web designers are a professional community that freely shares designs and information with one another.

Disadvantages

- You need to have or develop client relations and management skills. You are both consulting and designing.

- The amount of time for client interaction for a 15-page site is the same as for a 50-page site, and it's difficult to have smaller clients bear the cost of the time required.

- The Web is always changing, which is both a problem as well as a source of excitement and challenge. You must always keep up.

- If you come from a background of designing in print or video where you can predict how something you've designed will look, you may be frustrated working in this medium. Since it wasn't designed for the use that's being made of it, knowing exactly how something is going to look is difficult to predict. Different browsers handle presentations quite differently.

Start-up Costs	Low	High
Computer with a removable storage drive such as Iomega Zip or Jaz or a Syquest drive	$ 1,500	$ 3,000
Printer	$ 300	$ 800
or		
Multi-function printer/fax/scanner/copier	$ 150	$ 600
Software such as *Freehand* or *Illustrator* to mock up a design; use Adobe *Photoshop* with add-ons, Adobe *ImageReady* or Macromedia *Fireworks* for photo manipulation. For the actual site design, on the Macintosh, Adobe PageMill, and for high-end work, *CyberStudio Pro* by Golive. For Windows, Microsoft *Front Page,* and for high-end work, Softquad's *Hot Metal.*	$ 600	$ 1,400
Office furniture, especially an ergonomic chair	$ 400	$ 1,000
Notebook computer so you can show local clients what you've designed without having to access the Web	$ 1,000	$ 5,000

If you do your primary work on a Mac, get a cheap PC and vice versa so you can view what a site will look like on the other system.	$	500	$	800
Color scanner of at least 600 dpi	$	100	$	1,000
Initial marketing budget	$	1,000	$	5,000
Access to Internet	$	250		
Books	$	200	$	400
Total	$	5,700	$	18,450

Pricing

$30 to $150 an hour. Some designers charge a flat fee that can range between less than $10,000 to over $50,000. The reported average for professionally designed sites in mid-1998 was $44,000.

Potential Earnings

Typical Annual Gross Revenues: Yearly earnings range between $25,000 to $100,000 and more.

Overhead: low if you do the work yourself; higher if you act as a contractor subcontracting out the work.

Best Home Businesses Estimate of Market Potential

The market for new or improved Web sites is still far from saturated. According to the latest U.S. Census figures, there are over 11.5 million small businesses in the United States with fewer than 100 employees (your primary market). At the time of this writing, only about half of those businesses have any online presence and only one in ten had a Web site, but another one in six expected to have one within the next year. Many businesses that have Web sites aren't satisfied with them or need to update them, providing an ongoing market for Web designers.

Best Ways to Get Business

- Having your own Web site with links to other sites you've designed is a premier way of demonstrating your capabilities.

- Identifying companies you feel you can serve particularly well and that appeal to you and directly contacting these firms about your interest in working with them.

- Getting work through artists' temp agencies so you can create a list of satisfied clients who will recommend your work and whose sites you can direct others to as examples of your work.

- Contacting local ISPs and describing your experience and skills. ISPs often offer Web site design and hosting to their customers and they often subcontract out the design work.

- Networking through local and national users' groups.

- Networking in local business organizations, particularly local chambers of commerce and referral organizations.

Related Businesses

While Web site design can be a primary business, it can also work as an add-on business to a graphic-design business. Often clients needing brochures, ads, or other printed materials will need a Web site as well.

First Steps

- Read books about Web site design. Todd Cranston-Cuebas recommends *Secrets of Successful Web Sites*.

- Learn to use Web design software.

- Visit Web sites for ideas and use the Web for information about Web design. You'll find tutorials, for example, (usually free or very low cost) from which you can learn about CGI, Perl, Java, Java Script, Active Server Pages, and HTML.

- Get on Internet mailing lists pertinent to your interests.

- Establish relationships with ISPs you can refer clients to and work with in designing and later maintaining the designs you've created.

Where to Turn for Information and Help

ORGANIZATIONS

ASSOCIATION OF INTERNET PROFESSIONALS, INC., 9200 Sunset Boulevard, Suite 710, Los Angeles, CA 90069. This association has chapters throughout the world. It offers a Certified Internet Specialist designation which can be obtained by taking an examination. (800) JOIN AIP. Web site: *www.association.org*

INTERNET PROFESSIONAL PUBLISHERS ASSOCIATION. The professional association enables its members to show their work in a portfolio section. It recognizes good design with an ongoing award program. Web site: *www.ippa.org*

COURSES AND TRAINING

CNET: THE COMPUTER NETWORK. Offers tutorials. See the Web Building page. Web site: *www.cnet.com*

ZIFF DAVIS offers many training programs in multiple ways. For an overall view of its offline and online courses, go to *www.ziffdavis.com/properties/techsupport/zdedu.htm*

LEARNITONLINE is Ziff-Davis Education's self-paced Internet-based training. For a free demo, go to *http://corp.learnitonline.com*

WEBMONKEY: A HOW-TO GUIDE FOR WEB DEVELOPERS offers daily tutorials at *www.webmonkey.com*

WEBBUILDER from PE, Inc., 601 Madison Street, Suite 200, Alexandria, VA 22314; (703) 684-3700; fax: (703) 684-3727. Web site: *www.webbuilder.com*

BOOKS

Click Here: Web Communication Design, Lynda Weinman, Raymond Pirouz, New Riders Publishing, 1997. ISBN: 1562057928.

Creating Web Pages for Dummies, Bud E. Smith, Arthur Bebak, IDG Books Worldwide, 1998. ISBN: 076450357X.

Designing Large-Scale Web Sites: A Visual Design Methodology, Darrell Sano, New York: John Wiley & Sons, 1996. ISBN: 047114276X.

Deconstructing Web Graphics.2, Lynda Weinman, Jon Warren Lentz, New Riders Publishing, 1998. ISBN: 1562058592.

Elements of Web Design: The Designer's Guide to a New Medium, Darcy Dinucci, Maria Giudice, Lynne Stiles, Peachpit Press, 1998. ISBN: 0201696983.

Information Architecture for the World Wide Web, Louis Rosenfeld, Peter Morville, O'Reilly & Associates, 1998. ISBN: 1565922824.

Secrets of Successful Web Sites: Project Management on the World Wide Web, David S. Siegel, Hayden Books, 1997. ISBN: 1568303823.

A well-regarded line of technical books and journals for back-end work is published by Tim O'Reilly, 101 Morris Street, Sebastopol, CA 95472. (800) 998-9938. Web site: *www.oreilly.com*

MAGAZINES

Boardwatch, 13949 West Colfax Avenue #250, Golden, CO 80401; (800) 933-6038. *Boardwatch* is "focused on the Internet access and Internet development communities, as well as systems professionals worldwide." Web site: *www.boardwatch.com*

C/Net e-zine. Web site: *www.cnet.com*

Internet World, Mecklermedia, 20 Ketchum Street, Westport, CT 06880; (203) 226-6967. Industry news. Web site: *www.iw.com*

Web Developer, Mecklermedia, 20 Ketchum Street, Westport, CT 06880; (203) 226-6967. Web site: *www.webdeveloper.com*

See also the Resources under the "Webmaster" profile.

NEWSGROUPS, FORUMS, AND MAILING LISTS

Newsgroups and online forums on the commercial services are helpful in getting specific questions answered quickly. (A directory of newsgroups can be found at *www.webdesignshop.com/biz.shtml.*) Mailing lists are available for virtually every software program, every major subtopic for being a developer, and for many books. They can provide a stream of ongoing professional information and conversation. They are less easy to find than newsgroups and forums but are usually associated with organizations and products and can be ascertained on their Web sites.

Webmaster

The Internet ranks alongside the telephone and the automobile in the ways it's changing how we live our lives—how we buy everything from books to automobiles, make travel reservations, get information, do our work, spend our leisure time, affiliate with other people, even connect with a doctor, or for that matter, a mate. Just as telephones require operators and automobiles need mechanics, active Web sites, particularly ones where commerce is done, need to have someone to manage, update, and oversee their operation. That's the role of the Webmaster.

Webmasters are responsible for developing and maintaining the day-to-day operations of Web sites, which includes converting editorial content into HTML, assuring that the site is working smoothly and dealing with any technical glitches. Webmasters' duties rarely, if ever, include the development of the site itself in terms of its graphic design and content. While the job description of Webmaster is evolving, we know that being one requires a combination of technical, editorial, and business know-how, requiring people to use both sides of their brains adeptly. Businesses and institutions are not just turning over the care of their Web site to someone down the hall or to the president's precocious nephew, at least not anymore.

Webmasters can work at different levels. Some do the technical work of maintaining their clients' sites; others act more like general contractors in the construction field, contracting out various aspects of site management. This means a Webmaster doesn't necessarily need to know code, but will be responsible for the quality of the code that operates the site.

Larger companies hire Webmasters as staff, though not necessarily with that title. However, Bill Cullifer of the National Association of Web-masters reports that some Fortune 500 corporations contract out for their Web management. Smaller companies and organizations are more apt to contract out for a Webmaster because they can't afford to hire someone skilled enough to carry out this role as a full-time staff person. Also their site often doesn't require a full-time investment. Thus, they outsource Web management.

Being a Webmaster is something that can be done from virtually anywhere including, of course, at home. Because of *DeskLINK* and *pcANYWHERE* software, which enables the Webmaster to access his clients' computers remotely, there is rarely any need to do work on the clients' sites.

Knowledge and Skills You Need to Have

- Good interpersonal communication skills are needed to interact with and coordinate with your client's owner and/or managers as well and with technical staff or contractors such as information architects, multimedia specialists, graphic and user-interface designers, Web programmers, editors, and Web page developers.

- You need to be able to see the big picture, which means understanding the client's objectives for sales, customer support, product information, and publicity, and how these objectives can be met online.

- Superior organizational and project management skills are required, and you should enjoy problem solving.

- A good general knowledge of the Internet and the World Wide Web in particular.

- Knowing and understanding hit/flow tracking, statistical report generation, Web quality assurance, process automation, networking fundamentals, Web server administration, and dedicated-line and dial-up communication protocols, legal issues of the web, Hypertext theory, human computer interfaces, multimedia on the Web.

- Unless you contract this to specialists, technical proficiency in HTML, CGI, Perl programming and scripting—and for some clients Java system administration in UNIX and Windows NT.

- Knowledge of the latest technology and Web management skills sets.

- Depending on the client, you may need marketing and promotional skills.

Advantages

- The work can be done anywhere, anytime.

- Being continuously challenged and stimulated. As Bill Cullifer, founder of the National Association of Webmasters, says, "You are constantly pushing the envelope."

- One of the fastest-growing fields on the planet.

- Collaborative marketing is possible.

Disadvantages

- The continual challenge of keeping up with new technology and the evolution of the Internet may be stressful.

- In such a changing field, life is never predictable.

- You will experience resistance from some potential clients in trusting an "outsider."

Start-up Costs	Low	High
Computer with 17" or larger monitor	$ 2,000	$ 3,000
Printer	$ 300	$ 800
or		
Multi-function printer/fax/scanner/copier	$ 150	$ 600
Office furniture, especially an ergonomic chair	$ 400	$ 1,000
Initial marketing budget	$ 1,000	$ 5,000
High speed access to the Internet installation	$ 300	$ 1,000
Total	$ 3,850	$ 11,400

Pricing

Rates range from $25 to $75 an hour. Some Webmasters charge a monthly management fee, generally ranging from $1,000 to $5,000.

Potential Earnings

Typical Annual Gross Revenues: $60,000 at $50 an hour, 1,200 hours a year.

Overhead: moderate (20 percent to 40 percent).

Best Home Businesses Estimate of Market Potential

A significant number of information technology jobs are going unfilled, opening the door for independent contractors. Many smaller firms and organizations' interests are better served by outside vendors. The market for independent Webmasters is just beginning.

Best Ways to Get Business

- If you are currently employed as a Webmaster or Web site developer, turning your employer into your first client.

- Searching the Web for stale sites and making proposals to the site owners.

- Getting referrals from Web designers and Internet consultants, which may involve cross-referral relationships.

- Making joint proposals with Web designers and Internet consultants so that your service is part of the package of services offered.

- Searching online job listings for Webmaster postings and convincing the listing firm to outsource the work rather than hiring someone to do it in-house.

- Writing articles and speaking about site management.

- Getting ISPs with whom you have rapport and may do business to allow you to look at their list of customers for possible leads.

First Steps

- Fill in whatever skills you lack, whether business or technical. While you can learn on your own, continuing education programs are being developed at this time. For technical matters you don't want to learn, line up colleagues you can subcontract with.

- Acquire experience in Web site management, support, and maintenance by operating your own Web site or volunteering to do so for one or more nonprofit organizations or small businesses.

- Obtain certification as a Web developer or Webmaster from one of the professional associations listed below.

Where to Turn for Information and Help

ORGANIZATIONS

INTERNATIONAL WEBMASTERS ASSOCIATION, 119 East Union, Suite E-F, Pasadena, California 91101; (626) 449-3709. Offers certifications as an IWA Certified Web Developer[SM] and IWA Certified Web Administrator[SM]. Web site has links to articles and Web resources. Web site: *www.iwanet.org*

THE WORLD ORGANIZATION OF WEBMASTERS, 9580 Oak Avenue Parkway, Folsom, CA 95630; (888) 564-6279; (916) 929-6557. Provides training, certification, support, and an annual conference. Operates Webmaster network that links customers with site developers. Web sites: *www.world-webmasters.org* and *www.webmaster-network.org*

WEBMASTER FORUM, an online forum that provides resources and a panel of experts to help you answer issues about "Webmastery." Web site: *www.cio.com/forums/career.html*

TRAINING

INTERACTIVE TRAINING, INC., 100 Cummings Center, Suite 457J, Beverly, MA 01915; (978) 921-1755. E-mail: info@trainingforum.com

BOOKS

The 21st Century Intranet, Jennifer Stone Gonzalez, Prentice-Hall Computer Books, 1998. ISBN: 0138423377.

Teach Yourself How to Become a Webmaster in 14 Days, James L. Mohler, Howard W. Sams, 1997. ISBN: 1575212285.

Webmaster in a Nutshell: Deluxe Edition, Stephen Spainhour, Valerie Quercia, O'Reilly & Associates, 1997. ISBN: 1565923057.

Webmaster Answers!: Certified Tech Support, Christopher Ditto, Osborne McGraw-Hill, 1998. ISBN: 0078824591.

MAGAZINES AND E-ZINES

CIO Web Business. Strategies for using the Web in business. Sponsored by IDG's CIO magazine. Web site: *http://webbusiness.cio.com*

Online, 110 Bridge St, Dedham, MA 02026; fax (781)461-6160. Printed version available by subscription. Web site: *www.onlineinc.com*

Techweb, CMP Media, 11111 Santa Monica Boulevard, Los Angeles, CA 90025; (310) 966-3900. The print version of the magazine is free to qualified readers. Web site: *www.techweb.com*

Web Review, Miller Freeman, Inc., 411 Borel Avenue, Suite 100, San Mateo, CA 94402; (650) 358-9500. Web site: *www.webreview.com*

Web Techniques, Miller Freeman (address above) offers free subscriptions to Internet Professionals. Web site: *www.webtechniques.com*

See also the Resources under "Web Designer."

 ## Wedding Coordinator

The one constant about weddings is that they keep getting more expensive. But that's not deterring people from getting married. If anything, current trends indicate that people are placing greater emphasis on marriage and family. Many of today's brides and grooms are children of divorce or are returning to the altar for a second or third marriage and they want these marriages to last.

Whether single or divorced, today's brides and grooms are older; and usually both have careers. They're likely to be paying for their own wedding. Families don't play the role in financing or planning weddings that they once did; family members may be dispersed across the land and beyond. Even if they are in the same community, because the bride and her mother probably both work, they seldom have the time to plan and organize the wedding. A 1997 Roper survey found brides saying that while their mothers were somewhat involved, their help was not substantial.

While couples who are paying their own bills may be cost-conscious, they want an event that's perfect. A big wedding makes a psychological statement. It says, "We're taking this marriage seriously." It's almost as if the bigger and fancier the wedding, the more of a commitment it represents and therefore the greater the chances the marriage will last.

Gerard Monaghan, who with his wife, Eileen, operates the Association of Bridal Consultants, says, "Some brides have been designing their wedding since they were two and a half years old. The informal family wedding of past decades has been replaced by the elaborate, formal wedding. Brides are opting for more formal weddings on which they can put their own personal stamp. Gaining popularity, too, are weddings as celebrations of ethnic heritage and fully costumed weddings based on medieval and Renaissance themes."

Today's typical planned wedding consists of four bridesmaids, four ushers, music, dancing, and food costing $15,000. The total cost for some weddings goes well into the millions. Collectively, people spend $34 to

$38 billion a year to create the wedding day of their dreams. Producing a large-scale, one-day event is a considerable task, and one for which most couples are not well prepared. Growing up in the more informal decades of blue jeans and beer, most couples today have little or no experience with how to create an elegant, formal occasion.

And that's where the wedding coordinator comes in. Also called *bridal consultants*, *wedding planners*, and *wedding consultants*, wedding coordinators play the role for the bride and groom that a contractor plays in building a dream home or a director plays in the making of a movie. The wedding coordinator works with the bride and groom and their families to help the couple articulate what they want, establish a wedding budget, and create their dreams within it.

The wedding coordinator coordinates the entire production of the wedding, from finding and renting the facilities (most take place in churches) to negotiating contracts and overseeing the many elements and personnel involved, such as florists, photographers, videographers, caterers, travel agents, musicians, and disc jockeys. As many as 44 different businesses may be involved (including insurance, luggage, and home furnishings for setting up the couple's first home). Gerard Monaghan says, "It's a symbiotic relationship because they blend their efforts to create a total effect."

Weddings usually involve a formal wedding gown and veil for the bride, a tuxedo for the groom, formal wear for several bridesmaids, groomsmen, and ushers, floral arrangements, invitations, special napkins, wedding cake, table decorations, beverages, music, seating for 100 to 200 people (175 is the average, with weddings in the Midwest running larger), a photographer, a videotaping service, a wedding makeup artist, a catered reception or sit-down meal, and, of course, a dream honeymoon. Some couples will want gift registries on the Internet. The wedding coordinator should be prepared to do that for them, too. "A good professional consultant will never say 'no,'" says Eileen Monaghan.

As weddings have become events that need to be planned and produced, the wedding-consulting business has become big business, growing tremendously over the past several years. One in every eight of the two and a half million weddings a year now calls upon the services of a paid coordinator.

"When Princess Diana got married, there was no list of wedding consultants," observes Gerard Monaghan. "Now there are approaching 10,000 wedding consultants listed in the Yellow Pages coast to coast." Of that number, about 50 percent are home-based. As the echo boom (the baby boomers' children) is hitting marriage age, the number of weddings is expected to rise until 2007. Thus, Monaghan predicts, the wedding-consulting business will continue to grow substantially and rapidly, which means this is a particularly good time to get into the business. Also, he believes the amount spent on each wedding will continue to rise. Because wedding coordinators typically work with weddings costing a minimum of $10,000, the upward drift of wedding spending should keep consultants busy for many years.

Knowledge and Skills You Need to Have

- Wedding coordinators need to be gregarious, enjoy pressure, and be able to keep their wits about them when all about them is in turmoil. They must be able to take the unexpected in stride and calm the nerves of those around them.

- This is a people business, so communication skills are a must. The wedding coordinator must be an expert at helping all those involved handle the tensions and emotions of situations in which feelings about every little detail run deep. For example, Gerard Monaghan points out that "one of the unspoken functions of the wedding coordinator is to serve as a buffer between brides and mothers." Sometimes extreme situations (such as the bridegroom's father who was videotaped stealing $5,000 from the bride's father) arise that test the diplomatic skills of the coordinator.

- Wedding coordinators must be creative negotiators. They must develop solutions and negotiate prices with suppliers so that a wedding costing $10,000 seems like a wedding costing thousands more, thus justifying their fee. An effective coordinator will save the price of her fee by getting discounts and avoiding mistakes.

- Wedding coordinators must be crisis consultants, handling emergencies such as heart attacks and even deaths at weddings.

- Wedding coordinators need to be effective arbitrators to help the bride and groom reach decisions harmoniously on such things as the guest list, music, and facility so that a wedding does, indeed, take place.

- Wedding coordinators must keep up with and be knowledgeable about fashion, food, music, and wedding styles.

- Wedding coordinators must have basic business and financial-management skills and organizational ability, not only to run their own business but also to oversee the wedding budget.

- A good wedding coordinator is both creative enough to talk about the nuances of wedding gowns or to make a VFW hall look like a palace, and practical enough to make sure everything gets ordered and delivered according to schedule and is in place to take place at just the right time.

- You need contacts with high-quality, reliable wedding services: photographers, printers, florists, hotels, bakeries, makeup artists, jewelers, caterers, travel agents, musicians, disc jockeys, churches, and rental halls, and the skill to coordinate them.

Start-up Costs	Low	High
Computer	$ 1,500	$ 2,500
Printer		
or	$ 300	$ 800
Multi-function printer/fax/scanner/copier	$ 150	$ 600
Wedding planning software	$ 15	$ 30
Cell phone	$ 75	$ 200
Office furniture, especially an ergonomic chair	$ 400	$ 1,000
Wardrobe*	$ 500	$ 5,000
Initial marketing budget	$ 1,000	$ 7,500
Total	$ 3,940	$ 17,630

*Wedding consulting is a glamour business, so you need to have a wardrobe, makeup, and hairstyling in accord with the image of your clientele. You need three types of outfits: (1) business suits for meetings with suppliers; (2) more casual yet attractive clothing for meeting with the bride and bridal party in the process of planning the wedding; (3) more formal attire appropriate for attending the wedding.

Advantages

- This is a glamorous, exciting, challenging business, and the work calls upon you to be creative.

- You are dealing with clients at one of the happiest times in their lives, so your work is fun most of the time.

- There is great satisfaction in creating a dream event that may live for a lifetime in a couple's memory and serve as an anchor for their marriage.

- You can branch out to plan other types of events such as corporate meetings and bar mitzvahs, particularly in smaller communities, where there may not be enough weddings for a full-time business.

Disadvantages

- The business can be very competitive and your profit margins small.

- The work is on weekends and at night, but this could be considered an advantage. Because it takes awhile to become self-supporting in this business, you can start on a part-time basis while you work at another job during the week.

- It will take three years to get fully running.

- The work is still somewhat seasonal. April through October is very busy, but the winter months are slow, and although you're planning during the slow months, you can attend only so many weddings during the busy months.

- You are coordinating many elements over which you have no control.

- Because weddings are planned six months to a year in advance, it may be at least that long before you receive a fee. Payment arrangements should be spelled out in a letter of agreement signed by the coordinator and the couple.

- If you consider all the time spent, the hourly rate in this field is generally low.

Pricing

Wedding coordinators may charge a flat fee, a per diem rate, or an hourly rate for their services. Flat fees may be from 10 to 15 percent of the wedding budget; because the average wedding involving a coordinator costs $15,000, a typical fee may run from $1,500 to about $2,000. Per diem rates range from $300 to $1,200. Hourly rates range from $50 to $150. As expected, location influences pricing. Wedding coordinators should not expect to derive commissions from referrals they make; this is frowned on professionally and discouraged legally. However, coordinators can increase their revenue by providing extra services such as renting tuxedos, printing invitations, and selling accessories.

Potential Earnings

Typical Annual Gross Revenues: $37,500 based on twenty-five weddings a year at $1,500 per wedding. A full-time coordinator working alone can service 40 weddings a year. Expect September, October, June, and August, to be your busiest months; January, your slowest. You can add to your earnings by selling invitations, accessories, and party gifts. Some coordinators rent tuxes. The Monaghans observe that most people take three years to establish their businesses and five to become profitable.

Overhead: low (20 percent or less).

Best Home Businesses Estimate of Market Potential

As the cost of weddings continues to rise, and working women (both mothers and brides) are unavailable to plan weddings, hiring an expert to manage them and help keep costs down is a winning solution for more and more people. In fact, the number of brides using wedding coordinators, though still relatively low at 10 to 15 percent, is growing faster than the rate of growth of the wedding industry. Hiring a wedding coordinator is in!

Best Ways to Get Business

- Calling on, networking with, and cross-referencing to others providing wedding services: photographers, printers, florists, hotel and banquet-hall managers, bakeries, makeup artists, jewelers, caterers, travel agents, musicians, and disc jockeys.

- Joining and participating in as many as half a dozen professional, community, and trade organizations.

- Listing in the Yellow Pages.

- Exhibiting at bridal shows, although purchasing a booth by yourself is expensive.

- Advertising in:

  - Specialty wedding publications or guides.

  - Wedding supplements to local newspapers.

  - The sports section with a guarantee of bringing the wedding in under budget.

- Having a Web site linked to many wedding-related sites. The Web is especially important for wedding coordinators located in destination locations—vacation places where people like to get married.

- Using direct mail to recipients of wedding-planning guides and sending out newsletters to prospective and past clients.

- Offering free consultations for couples, advising them of what will be involved in planning their wedding. Use this time to establish a trusting relationship and to gather information for a written proposal you can submit to them after the meeting.

- Teaching adult education courses on how to plan a wedding.

- Getting repeat business by doing parties and other events such as anniversaries for your clients, their family, and their friends.

First Steps

- To gain some experience before you begin working on your own, work for free on several weddings with an established coordinator. The Association of Bridal Consultants (listed below) offers an internship/apprenticeship program for members.

- Organize weddings for friends and relatives for free to build a portfolio of your work. Be sure to get pictures from the photographer and letters of recommendation from brides.

- Attend bridal shows to learn about the trends.

- Establish a network of suppliers on whom you can rely.

Where to Turn for Information and Help

ORGANIZATIONS

ASSOCIATION OF BRIDAL CONSULTANTS, 200 Chestnutland Road, New Milford, CT 06776; (860) 355-0464; fax (860) 354-1404. There are 1,750 members in 21 countries. Membership is composed of all types of professionals working in the wedding industry. Offers training and a professional development program, bimonthly newsletter, nationwide and regional co-op advertising, bridal and media referrals. Web site: *www.weddingchannel.com*

TRAINING COURSES

ASSOCIATION OF BRIDAL CONSULTANTS. See above.

ICS LEARNING SYSTEMS, 925 Oak Street, Scranton, PA 18515; (570) 342-7701 x 339.

THE INSTITUTE OF CONSULTING CAREERS, INC., 2555 Camino Del Rio South, Suite 210, San Diego, CA 92108; (619) 295-3545. E-mail: icc98@earthlink.net

NATIONAL BRIDAL SERVICE, 3122 West Cary Street, Richmond, Virginia 23221; (804) 355-6945. Web site: *www.nationalbridalservice.com*

BOOKS

The Complete Idiot's Guide to the Perfect Wedding, Teddy Lenderman, Macmillan General Reference, 1997. ISBN: 0028619633.

Planning a Wedding to Remember, Beverly Clark, Los Angeles: Wilshire Books, 1995. ISBN: 0934081093.

The Complete Wedding Planner: Helpful Choices for the Bride and Groom, Edith Gilbert, Allan Taber, New York: Warner Books, 1991. ISBN: 0446392162.

Weddings for Grownups: Everything You Need to Know to Plan Your Wedding Your Way, Caroll Stoner, Chronicle Books, 1997. ISBN: 0811814211.

MAGAZINES

Bride's, Condé Nast, 360 Madison Ave., 5th floor, New York, NY 10017; (800) 456-6162; (212) 880-8800.

Modern Bride, Cahners Publishing/American Baby, 200 Madison Ave., 8th floor, New York, NY 10016; (800) 777-5786; (212) 645-9700.

Vows, 522 Kimbark Street, Longmont, CO 80501; (303) 776-3103. The only trade publication in this field.

SOFTWARE

Organized Weddings, Exquisite Event Planning, Inc., 307 Donerail Avenue, Powell, OH 43065. (500) 677-1064. Web site: *www.organizedweddings. com.* Comprehensive program that enables managing client and vendor information, the ability to build permanent floor plans for reception sites, and a personal information manager.

Weddings, Innovation Multimedia, 41 Mansfield Avenue, Essex Junction, VT 05452. (800) 255-0562; (802)879-1164. Web site: *www.ad-art.com*

WEB SITES

While these sites are targeted for couples planning their own weddings, the professional will get ideas and links to useful resources and information:

www.weddingchannel.com Budget planner and a groom's corner.

www.theknot.com Extensive checklist, database, planning tools plus a message board.

www.wedserv.com Wedserv Corporation offers to couples a free downloadable wedding planner for managing a wedding in exchange for information useful to the company's associated providers.

www.weddingbells.com Sponsored by the Canadian magazine *Weddingbells,* the site is loaded with information. The magazine's wedding-planning software may be ordered from the site.

PART TWO

THE REST
OF THE
BEST

Alternative Energy Installer

If the world runs short of fossil fuels, this will be the ultimate business. In the meantime, the market for the installation of alternative energy systems is being fueled by the exodus of people from urban areas. People in increasing numbers are moving to remote locations where they do not have access to a source of power from utility companies. Or if they do, they choose not to connect to the power grid because of their values or for economic reasons.

The exodus of urban dwellers ranging from lawyers to librarians, or as they are sometimes called, "urban refugees," to the countryside is equal to the movement of a population the size of Nebraska or Nevada dispersing itself. Between 1990 and 1995, this amounted to a net gain to nonurban areas of 1.6 million people, reversing the opposite trend that existed through most of this century.

According to a Gallup survey, 56 percent of Americans prefer to live in the country or a small town. Perhaps helping this desire is the fact that people are able to save 25 to 40 percent on real estate that is not connected to the utilities lines—the "grid." They are then able to install alternative energy, usually solar, for a fraction of their real estate savings and live in beautiful remote locations without going primitive. Solar power became available in the early 80's. Before that, generators, wind, and hydro were the only sources of alternative energy. While those are still used, most people don't have access to wind and hydro. Generators depend on fossil fuels that must be transported in.

Deregulation has upset the stable world of energy and now people wanting to become "energy independent" have choices. As this is being written, 160,000 people are "off the grid," and their numbers are growing at 30 percent a year. "Some people are environmentally conscious; others don't want to use nuclear-derived power," says Richard Perez. "Some people just want to be separate from large energy companies."

Some people haven't abandoned conventionally produced energy completely. They put up a solar array to produce their own energy during the day and send any surplus they produce to the grid. At night, they draw power from the grid. At the end of the year, the small producer and the utility settle accounts based on how much energy the small producer has produced and how much this producer has consumed. Now it's cost effective to make your own energy.

While residences are the most lucrative market for installers, other customers are RV and boat owners; some commercial entities such as radio stations, bed and breakfast inns, and large resorts, particularly ones located outside the United States.

According to Richard Perez, publisher of *Home Power* magazine, about one out of five people living in remote areas have home businesses. While most of these home businesses are based on computers, others range from soap manufacturers to welding shops whose needs for power will be greater than for most residences. In places like mountainous terrain where there are predictable power outages during the winter, home-business people, even with access to the grid, want back-up energy available on a stand-by basis. To be an installer, you need to have a mechanical inclination so you can develop the technical know-how to put systems together safely. Since most installers also sell equipment, you need the willingness to educate people to the values and practicality of alternative energy.

Being an energy installer brings you into contact with interesting people often in interesting places. Energy installers report feeling good that their work is helping the planet by working with renewable energy. But there is a downside. The work can be hazardous physically when working on rooftops and high towers. The initial investment in equipment can be relatively high if you stock inventory, though it's not necessary to have an inventory to get underway. Many homeowners resist investing the $6,000 to $30,000 for a solar installation that will serve a household of four because they won't realize a payback until well into the future. But for others, alternative energy represents an immediate savings since bringing in power lines on flat land can cost $20,000 or more a mile.

Installers charge from $20 to $35 an hour with the higher rates going to installers with an electrical contractors license or an electrician certificate. Once you are underway, overhead is usually low.

The best ways to get business are to:

- Advertise locally.

- Place posters or flyers in laundromats.

- Work with real estate agents who sell "off-grid properties."

- Have your own Web site.

Learning is the first step in getting started. You can do this by taking one or more courses. Such training will cost $1,000 to $2,000. You will need tools, costing $100 to $500. Then you can begin by installing a system in your own home. You're then able to say, "I'm doing it." You can get more experience volunteering to design and install systems for neighbors. Some people get an apprenticeship with an installing dealer, usually for minimal pay. The time spent with someone who has an electrical contractor's license will count toward getting your own license. This is a field in which it's possible to work for someone else with their knowing you want to go out on your own because the more people in the field popularizing alternative energy results in more demand.

Where to Turn for Information and Help

ORGANIZATIONS

AMERICAN SOLAR ENERGY SOCIETY, 2400 Central Avenue, G-1, Boulder, CO 80301; (303) 443-3130; fax: (303) 443-3212. Publishes *Solar Today* magazine covering all solar technologies, policies, and regulations. Web site: *www.ases.org*

MIDWEST RENEWABLE ENERGY ASSOCIATION holds a large annual fair with dozens of workshops. 7558 Deer Rd., Custer, WI 54423; (715) 592-6595; fax: (715) 592-6596. Web site: *www.the-mrea.org*

SOLAR ENERGY INTERNATIONAL teaches people how to design, maintain, and install alternative energy systems. While most of the workshops are offered in Colorado, others are offered in other locations. They also offer a seminar, "Successful Solar Businesses," taught by Richard and Karen Perez. P.O. 715, 76 South 2nd Street, Carbondale, CO 81623; (970) 963-8855. Web site: *www.solarenergy.org*

DIRECTORIES AND CATALOGUES

Backwoods Solar Electric Systems, 1395 Rolling Thunder Ridge, Sandpoint, ID 83864; (208) 263-4290. A well-done and comprehensive catalogue that includes the personal commentary of the owners, Steve and Elizabeth Willey. Web site: *www.backwoodssolar.com*

BOOKS

In Earth's Company: Business, Environment, and the Challenge of Sustainability, Carl Frankel, New Haven, CT: New Society Publications, 1998. ISBN: 0865713804.

Cannibals With Forks: The Triple Bottom Line of 21st Century Business, John Elkington, New Haven, CT: New Society Publications, 1998. ISBN: 0865713928.

The Natural Step for Business: Wealth, Ecology and the Evolutionary Corporation, Brian Nattrass and Mary Altomare, New York: Random House, 1995. ISBN: 0679763996.

MAGAZINES AND NEWSLETTERS

Home Power, P.O. Box 520, Ashland, OR 97520; (530) 475-3179; or (530) 475-0830; (800) 707-6585. Karen and Richard Perez. The magazine is fully available on the Internet. Web site: *www.homepower.com*

Windpower Monthly, The International Journal of Wind Energy Development, PO Box 4258, Grand Junction, CO 81502. Phone and fax: (970) 245-9431. Web site: *www.wpm.co.nz*

WEB

THE SUSTAINABLE BUSINESS NETWORK provides a focal point on the Web for a wide range of environmental business sectors, from recycling to green building, from renewable energy to organic products, from social investing to certified forestry; (800) 567-6772. Web site: *www.envirolink.org/sbn*

 Aromatherapist

Aside from perfumes and air freshners or truly noxious substances, the effect of odor on our health and well-being has been greatly overlooked in this country until recently. Research has been accumulating, however, that fragrances can have a significant effect on our homes, workplaces, and overall health and well-being, affecting alertness, performance, stress levels, general health and even heart rate, mood, muscle tension, and blood pressure.

The Japanese commonly use scents to increase productivity in the workplace, and in one experiment, worker errors dropped 21 percent when the air was scented with lavender, 33 percent when jasmine was added to the air, and 54 percent when a lemon aroma was used. Other research confirms improved performance by adding the following scents to the air:

- Improved work efficiency: lavender, jasmine, and lemon.

- Learning aids: basil, rose, bergamot, and cardamon.

- Reduced anxiety: basil, bergamot, cedarwood, and hyssop.

- Reduced stress: rose and tangerine.

- Relaxing: lavender, chamomile, apple, and spice.

- Stimulating and invigorating: lemon, jasmine, pine, eucalyptus, and rosemary.

Results like these are fueling the rapidly growing field of aromatherapy. Today's aromatherapist works with over 300 essential oils and hydosols (colodials suspended in water) to effect changes in the health and well-being of their clients. Both of these tools are distillations from plants in quantities that are considered to be therapeutic and have not been adulterated with synthetic substances. They are inhaled, spritzed, or dispersed throughout the room by a diffuser, some of which are heat driven by candles or light bulbs, others by electronically powered air pumps and a glass vessel.

Aromatherapy can be used for medicinal and first-aid purposes for everything from helping a child who's sick with the flu, to reducing symptoms of menopause, helping with weight loss, or reducing stress. Some preparations have antibacterial, anti-inflammatory, and antibiotic properties. Others simply improve emotional, sensual, and psychic well-being. Still others can be used to decrease harmful bacteria in cleaning supplies or to rid a dog's coat of fleas.

Aromatherapists are often trained in other health-related fields—as massage therapists, aestheticians, chiropractors, or psychotherapists. However, knowing and applying aromatherapy is a science and art in and of its own, requiring a combination of knowledge of the human body and good communication and listening skills.

According to Jeanne Rose, past president of the National Association

of Holistic Aromatherapy, "Aromatherapy is now a $300 million a year busi-
ness estimated to quadruple in the next five years." She reports that most
aromatherapists are small businesses owned predominately by women selling essential oils and other aromatherapy products. There are over 2000
such businesses that earn over $100,000 a year in North America.

Where to Turn for Information and Help

ASSOCIATIONS

INTERNATIONAL FEDERATION OF AROMATHERAPISTS, Department of
Continuing Education, Room 8, Ravens Court Park, London 26 OTN,
UK; Phone: 081 864-8066.

NATIONAL ASSOCIATION FOR HOLISTIC AROMATHERAPY, P.O. Box 17622,
Boulder, CO 80308; (888) ASK-NAHA. Publishes the *Scentsitivity
Quarterly Journal* and holds an annual international conference and
trade show. On the Web, you can find directories of aromatherapy
schools, home study courses ($5.00), practitioners, and recommended
reading. Web site: *www.naha.org*

BOOKS

The Complete Book of Essential Oils & Aromatherapy, Valerie Ann
Worwood. San Rafael, CA: New World Library, 1991.

The World of Aromatherapy, Jeanne Rose and Susan Earle. National Association of Holistic Aromatherapy, 836 Hanley Industrial Ct., Suite 4,
St. Louis, MO 63144; (888) ASK-NAHA; (314) 963-2071.

SCHOOLS

PACIFIC INSTITUTE OF AROMATHERAPY, PO Box 606, San Rafael, CA
94915; (415) 479-9121.

THE MICHAEL SCHOLES SCHOOL FOR AROMATIC STUDIES, 117 N.
Robertson Blvd., Los Angeles, CA 90048; (310) 276-1191, offers a
home-study course, aromatherapy classes throughout the world, and a
teacher-training program. E-mail: mhscholes@aol.com

PRODUCTS

ORIGINS stores sell a line of essential oils aromas called Sensory Therapy
along with diffusers for subtly filling the air with positive fragrances;
(800) 723-7310.

WHITE ROSE OF PROVENCE offers a line of essential oils and diffusers in room or whole house models; (800) 677-2368.

JOANN BASSETT'S BASSETT AROMATHERAPY offers a line of fragrances and diffusers via mail; (800) 738-8678 or on the Web. Web site: *www. aromaworld.com*

Astrologer

Whether viewed as entertainment, science or the occult, astrology is rapidly becoming a popular tool in many people's lives. Astrologers, also called astrologists, are in demand in person, by phone, in magazine, newsletters, via e-mail, and on the Web. In fact, 37 percent of Americans say they believe in astrology, according to a Lou Harris poll. Karen Mc-Cawley, who teaches astrology in southern California, believes the reason for such growing popularity is simple. "Astrology is helpful for understanding and making decisions in many areas of your life."

Business people are consulting astrologers on business prospects. One French business school reports that 10 percent of French businesses use astrologers, usually for a second opinion about job applicants. Here in the U.S., while companies may be hesitant to broadcast their use of astrology, a wide range of financial and consumer product companies keep consultants like Barrie Dolnick busy using astrological charting to assist them in long-term strategic planning, new-product evaluations, team-building and one-on-one management counseling.

Investors are consulting astrologers on the stock market. Several multimillion-dollar investors publicly acknowledge their use of astrologers. Leading financial investment astrologers are now interviewed routinely along with other market forecasters. Arch Crawford, for example, specializes in market timing—the art of calling when it's time to move money in and out of the stock market. He calculates his market timing based on planetary cycles and technical analysis and shares the results through his newsletter *Crawford Perspectives*, subscriptions $250 a year. Crawford's wife, Carolyn Snedden, prepares personalized horoscopes for investors for $150 each.

Parents of newborns are having charts done to help them understand their child's basic personality and nature to guide them in rearing their children most successfully. Magazine editors are seeking out astrologers.

Specialized magazines from the *Sports Traveler* to *Elle Decore, Latina Style, Fortune,* and *Forbes* are providing readers with niche horoscopes related to finance, home decorating, style, parenting, sports, health, and more.

Individuals from corporate executives to New Age devotees and politicians are calling for private astrological readings and eagerly refer friends and associates to their favorite practitioners. There are a wealth of specialties in this field from financial astrology, to medical, psychological, relationship, predictive, sun sign, and karmic astrology. Some astrologers have even more specialized niches such as horse racing or what Greg Howe of Astro Neumeric Systems calls asrto*carto*graphy. For $20, Howe will provide charts to help people analyze where to move; Box 336 K, Ashland OR 97520; (800) 627-7464.

Historically, astrology has been a home business. Private practitioners have been creating complex hand-calculated, customized charts based on mathematical formulas for their clients for decades, meeting personally to interpret the results in private consultations.

The computer has dramatically changed this field, however. Whereas it once took years of study and hours of labor to create and interpret a detailed astrological chart, with professional astrological software such as *Solar Fire* and *Kepler,* an astrological devotee can create in ten minutes what it would have taken hours to do. And with a color printer, you can print out beautiful four-color custom charts and reports instantly with attractive graphics and designs. Professional astrology software begins at around $150 to $350 and costs up to $1,000 and more.

Astrological forecasting software requires only the customer's date, place, and time of birth. The more experience you have in this field, of course, the more helpful you can be in interpreting the meaning and significance of computer-generated charts and reports or customers.

Often it's the personal approach and interpretation of the astrologer that will bring people back again and again and lead them excitedly to refer their friends and family. Rates for an astrological chart and analysis range from $25 to $500. The average is around $200 for a natal reading of 2 to 3 hours.

Where to Turn for Information and Help

ASSOCIATIONS

AMERICAN FEDERATION OF ASTROLOGERS (AFA), P.O. Box 22040, Tempe, AZ 85285; (480) 838-1751. Offers study courses. Web site: *www.astrologers.com*

NATIONAL COUNCIL OF GEOCOSMIC RESEARCH (NCGR), 260 North Haverhill Road, Kensington, NH 03833; (603) 778-9862. Has many local chapters. Web site: *www.geocosmic.org*

INTERNATIONAL SOCIETY OF ASTROLOGICAL RESEARCH (ISAR), P.O. Box 38613, Los Angeles, CA 90038; (805) 525-0461 Web site: *www.isarastrology.com*

ASSOCIATION FOR ASTROLOGICAL NETWORK (AFAN), 8306 Wilshire Blvd., Suite 537, Beverly Hills, CA 90211; (800) 578-AFAN. Web site: *www.afan.org*

BOOKS

The Astrologer's Handbook, Louis Acker and Frances Sakoian, New York: HarperCollins, 1995.

The Only Way to Learn Astrology, Marion D. March and Joan McEvers, ACS Publications, Astro Communications, 5521 Russin, San Diego, CA 92123. (800) 888-9983. Has catalogue of many other books as well. Web site: *www.astrocom.com*

HOMESTUDY COURSES

NOEL TYL, 17005 Player Court, Fountain Hill, AZ 85268; (602) 816-0000.

JOANNE WICKENBURG, 3010 Russet Road, Brier, WA 98036; (425) 672-8548.

SOPHIA MASON, 7780 Jill Drive, Parma, OH 44134; (440) 888-4746.

ONLINE COLLEGE OF ASTROLOGY, Ena Stanley; (713) 665-5230. Web site: *www.astrocollege.com*

SOFTWARE

MicroCycles Software, owned by Steve Hines, P.O. 3175, Culver City, CA 90231; (800) 829-2537; (310) 202-8337. This company provides information and consultation on over 300 astrological software packages. Call for a catalogue, 10 to 5 PST. Or for the latest software updates and advice on which package would be best suited to you, visit them on the Web. Web site: *www.microcycles.com*

MAGAZINES

The Mountain Astrologer, P.O. Box 970, Cedar Ridge CA 95924; (800) 287-4828.

TRAINING PROGRAMS

There are professional training programs in most cities such as Aquarius Workshops in southern California, PO Box 260556, Encino, CA 91426; (818) 782-5573. Web site: *www.members.tripod.com/~aspects*

WEB SITES

www.astronet.com

www.altastrology.com

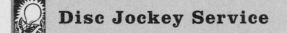 **Disc Jockey Service**

If you love music and have a personality that inspires people to have a good time and party, you can earn your living as one of 21,555 freelance or mobile disc jockeys (DJs). Mobile DJs provide professional sound at conferences, parties, weddings, and special events in homes, clubs, churches, hotels, public halls, schools, and companies for far less than the cost of live musicians. They occasionally work for nightclubs, too, although their mainstay is freelancing for people at private occasions.

As a DJ, you select and supply the music and the equipment to play it on. You usually also need to provide some patter to entertain the audience and encourage everyone to dance. Essential equipment includes two high-quality compact-disc players, a cassette deck (to play tapes handed to you by people in the audience and as a backup for the CD players), and if you intend to use records, a professional turntable. You will also need a mixing console, a power amplifier, speakers with clear output, and a cordless microphone for your banter with the audience. You can also add strobe lights and other special effects to enhance your presentation. (With all the equipment, you will also need a van or station wagon to transport it safely, plus a dolly or rolling cart.) The setup for basic equipment runs about $3,500 to $5,000, but you can also find it used for under $1,000.

The most crucial part of your equipment is your disc collection. If you already own a sizable collection of dancing CDs, you can often start out by purchasing a few hundred more new releases to complement what you have. With the cost of CDs, many DJs now scout used CD stores for good values in dance music. In all, you will need to spend $1,000 to $2,000. More useful than buying one popular disc at a time, though, is to sub- scribe to one of the companies that produces CDs specifically for DJs; each month, you are mailed a number of discs that contain a mix of pop- ular dance songs in whichever style you need: country/western, rap, rock and roll, heavy metal, or whatever. Call Promo Only at (407) 331-3600 or RPM at (800) 521-2537. Such companies produce discs especially for mobile DJs, preselecting the most popularly chosen numbers by audi- ences so that you don't waste your money buying an entire CD to get one or two hot songs.

In addition, there are several new techniques of running a DJ party that are changing the nature of the business that you need to take into ac- count. First, over the past five years, karaoke has become a popular fad among many kinds of crowds.

In karaoke, a guest comes onstage and sings the lyrics to a song while the exact music plays in the background. Lest the words be forgotten, the crooner watches them appear on a computer screen so that he or she can pretend to be the original singer. This new art form has not meant much in the way of new equipment, because the CD player is already built into your system. All you need are the special CDG discs (compact disc with graphics) that contain the lyrics with the music background and a monitor connected to the CD player to show the lyrics. Karaoke is a crowd pleaser, says Jeff Greene, owner of Party Time DJs, because "it serves the function of allowing the guests to become the entertain- ment and be the center of attention. Instead of having a DJ be the enter- tainment, the audience is the show. Guests themselves become stars." Greene admits that many people are shy and too reluctant to participate, but he adds wryly that "once you get the crowd singing, you can't stop 'em."

He also points out that owning the karaoke equipment is a good side- line business for a DJ because many nightclubs don't own the equipment themselves, so they hire a mobile DJ for the one or two nights of the week when they feature karaoke.

A second technique for running your DJ business is to offer many more choices than straight DJ work. Greene says that his company offers clients a full range of options: there's your basic spin man at the bottom; then it moves on up to a style of DJ who plays full host to the party, complete with games and prizes such as Blues Brothers sunglasses, maracas, and inflatable instruments. His company has also expanded into doing videos of the event for an extra charge.

As you can see, being a simple DJ is not what it used to be in the old days of plastic platters. These days, DJs can charge from $50 on up to $150 per hour. Greene is even able to charge as much as $300 per hour for his top-level DJs. (He now has a dozen employees and three regional offices, all of which grew from his home-based business within five years.) Many DJs also accept jobs at nightclubs that don't pay as well, but if you get your name in their advertising, it's good exposure for your business. Be sure that they let you hand out business cards or flyers, too.

Referrals are the best way to get business says Jim Tremayne, editor of the *DJ Times*. There are two caveats. First, the work is often seasonal, with especially heavy bookings during the Christmas holidays, spring prom season, May and June (weddings), and early fall (parties). There are lots of events in between, but you will have to develop your reputation in order to get the word-of-mouth referrals you will need. Second, you must be sure that the music you play appeals to your clientele. That means in some areas of the country you may need to have country-and-western or Caribbean or mariachi or polkas.

Also, beware of trendy music, Greene warns—the kind that appeals to the 14-to-18 age group—lest you invest in a few popular CDs and, the next week, they are dead.

Where to Turn for Information and Help

MAGAZINE

DJ Times, a magazine for learning the DJ business; (800) 937-7678; (516) 767-2500. Web site: *www.djtimes.com*

ORGANIZATION

THE AMERICAN DISC JOCKEY ASSOCIATION posts job leads for all ADJA members on the ADJA Web site, where you can also check how to join.

The association is located at 10882 Demarr Rd., White Plains, MD 20695; (301) 705-5150. Web site: *www.adja.org*

TRADE SHOW

DJ TRADE SHOW INTERNATIONAL, the DJ expo held every year in August in Atlantic City, has over 150 exhibits and 30 seminars and is a great place to find out about the mobile disc jockey business. For more information visit the *DJ Times* Web site: *www.djtimes.com*

Doula Service

In the past, relatives and friends usually helped women prepare for the birth of a new baby. After the delivery, they helped out with cooking, cleaning, and child-care advice. But in today's mobile society, friends and loved ones are often miles away when a child is born. That's why doula services are a small, but booming phenomenon.

Doulas don't deliver babies. Nor are they nannies. The word, pronounced DOO-la, is of Greek origin meaning handmaiden or mother's helper. They are educated to assist mothers by providing emotional and physical support during childbirth and personal advice and assistance during the early days after the baby comes home. Doulas either choose to assist in labor or with postpartum care and rarely do both, according to Chris Morley, who operated a private doula service for 10 years, employing 25 to 30 postpartum doulas. In 1996, she began consulting for hospitals throughout the United States and now focuses on hospital programs. As founder and president of her firm, Tender Care, she educates hospitals about implementing doula programs to enable them to offer the most comprehensive maternity benefits possible.

Whereas doctors and midwives are often only present during the delivery itself and only minimally afterward, doulas remain with the mother throughout the entire delivery and beyond. They might suggest different positions or breathing techniques to ease labor pain or to comfort the mother in moments of panic, fear, or distress. After delivery, the doula may provide advice on breastfeeding and help the new mother through the first one to four weeks at home with the baby.

Research shows childbirth goes more smoothly with the help of a doula. Labor is 25 percent shorter. The need for pain relief is 60 percent less. Cesarean sections are reduced by 15 to 50 percent and forceps deliveries go down by 40 percent. There's also a 60 percent reduction in epidural requests, a 40 percent reduction in oxytocin use, and a 30 percent reduction in analgesia use. In addition, two months after birth, women who have been assisted during labor are assessed to be more sensitive, loving, and responsive to their infants.

Insurance rarely pays for doula services except through a hospital. This is in part the result of new state laws that require medical insurers to provide 48-hour care after childbirth. One way to get started, Morley says, is to work through a hospital that trains and contracts with doulas. Growing numbers of hospitals such as the University Hospital and Medical Center at Stony Brook on Long Island are planning to have doulas on-call 24 hours a day. Others like Santa Monica-UCLA Medical Center are providing eight free hours of postpartum doula care.

Training to become a doula normally consists of a three-day to one-week course, says Kathie Lindstron, president of Doulas of North America, (DONA) an international organization that trains and certifies doulas. The course will include such things as the basics of anatomy and the labor process as well as techniques for providing emotional and physical comfort during labor. Training also includes attendance at three deliveries.

Charges for doula services, according to Morley, range from $16 to $25 an hour plus a $25 consultation fee. Fifteen hours of care over five days averages $300 for hospital-based and independent doulas. Other ways for independent doulas to get business include advertising in local newspapers and the *Wet Set Gazette*, which is published locally through Dydee Diaper Service, listed in the Yellow Pages.

Where to Turn for Information and Help

ASSOCIATIONS

DOULAS OF NORTH AMERICA (DONA); (500) 448-3662. Offers certification for labor doula work, conferences and workshops, and a quarterly newsletter. Their Web site provides a way for the public to locate member doulas in their area. Web site: http://www.dona.com

BOOKS

A Good Birth, A Safe Birth, Diana Korte, Roberta Scaer, Leslie Baker, Harvard Common Press, 1992. ISBN: 1558320415.

The Birth Partner: Everything You Need to Know to Help a Woman Through Childbirth, Penny Simkin, Harvard Common Press, 1989. ISBN: 1558320105.

The Complete Book of Pregnancy and Childbirth, Sheila Kitzinger, Knopf, 1996. ISBN: 067940289.

Pregnancy, Childbirth & the Newborn, The Complete Guide, Penny Simkin, Janet Whalley, Ann Keppler, Meadowbrook Press; 1991; ISBN: 0671741829.

Mothering the Mother, How a Doula Can Help You Have a Shorter, Easier and Healthier Birth, Marshall Klaus, Phyllis Klaus, John Kennell. Perseus Books, 1993. ISBN: 0201632721.

Special Women: The Role of the Professional Labor Assistant, Paulina Perez, Cheryl Snedeker, Pennypress, 1994. ISBN: 0964115999.

WEB SITES

http://childbirth.org/doula123.html

Drafter/Computer-Aided Design

From architecture to printed circuit-board design and from fashion design to product engineering, the expanding field of computer-aided design (CAD) has completely changed the way inventors, builders, electricians, plumbers, and creators of all kinds visualize new ideas. Similarly, an interior designer can construct an office or conference room, paint colors or scan in wallpaper for the walls, and reconfigure the placement of furniture until the most attractive combination is achieved. And a civil engineer can produce a layout of every street in a city and show the effect on traffic of installing a new set of lights at a busy intersection.

As a result of this technology, there will be tremendous growth over time in the need for specialists who can work with people in many fields integrating the hardware and software of CAD with the needs of the profession. Depending on your background and interest, you might therefore explore establishing a CAD-based company specializing in any of many design fields: architecture, civil engineering, electrical or plumbing layout, fashion, interior design, landscaping, mechanical engineering, and many others.

Hal Rozema of Phoenix breaks the work available for drafters into five categories:

1. Working for architectural and engineering firms by the project or by the hour, either in-house using the firms' equipment or in your own studio. An Autodesk survey found that one in every four architects don't have computers in their offices, and fewer than 10 percent use 3-D as a design tool.

2. Doing overflow work from architectural and engineering firms in your studio.

3. Working with your own clients on tasks such as small restaurants, homes, and smaller shopping centers.

4. Obtaining work through agencies, such as headhunters and job shops.

5. Participating as part of a virtual office with other professionals.

To do well in this field, you need to be able to visualize things in your mind. This capacity is thought to be developed in infancy. You'll also need to be trained in CAD, but this training can be acquired in community colleges and trade schools, as well as in correspondence courses. You'll also need to have a basic knowledge of construction that is best obtained from experience on construction sites.

To be in this business, you will also need to invest heavily in high-quality hardware, including a minimum of a Pentium or Power Mac computer with at least 32 megabytes of RAM and a Zip and other high-density disk drive and a 32-bit bandwidth modem. You will be most efficient using your CAD software if you also have a 3.2 GB or larger hard drive, a mouse, a light pen or graphics tablet with a puck, and a high-resolution graphics video card. You will need a flatbed scanner and for plotting drawings or designs, you should have a laser or inkjet printer with as much memory as you can afford.

This is challenging work that provides ample contact with people involved in building things. The opportunities for success are enormous if you can offer special expertise in a particular field and if you know your way around the hardware and software. CAD designers can be paid $50 and more per hour for developing computer models of a design, blueprints, and even three-dimensional animated sequences that simulate the item, be it a building, a room, or a product being used.

On the other hand, as we've mentioned, this business requires a significant initial investment in hardware and software. This means the start-up costs for this business will be higher than most home businesses, running from $6,500 to $20,000. In addition, you will need to spend a few months completing specialized training programs. But as we mentioned, the training is widely available in technical schools and community colleges.

Also, because the technology in this is a field is rapidly changing, you'll need to stay abreast of changes and continually invest in needed upgrades in your equipment and software. Such upgrades will mean higher overhead costs than less technology-intensive businesses. Also, because of the cost of their services, CAD designers are vulnerable to economic downturns.

The very things that make this business challenging can also make it lucrative. CAD designers can charge from $15 to $50 an hour depending on experience and location. And when business is good, working 50 hours a week is not uncommon. Thus, incomes can go over $100,000 for sought-after designers, especially in circuit-board design. When working in home design, rates run from $.90 to $1 a square foot.

The best ways to get business include having a Yellow Page listing, creating a Web site that shows examples of your work, developing relationships with architectural and engineering firms, working through agencies and contractors if seeking residential work, having a brochure that illustrates your work, and making teachers at Home Depot and other hardware-store seminars aware of your work.

Where to Turn for Information and Help

ASSOCIATIONS

AMERICAN DESIGN DRAFTING ASSOCIATION, P.O. Box 11937, Columbia, SC 29211; (803) 771-0008. Publishes *Design Drafting News*; certifies school curriculums; certifies drafters with a test of general knowledge of drafting and does not cover computer-aided drafting. It's the only membership organization dedicated exclusively to the professional designer drafter in all disciplines including manufacturing, utilities, construction, engineering, government, and education. Web site: *www.adda.org*

BOOKS

Autocad 14 Bible, Ellen Finkelstein. Foster City, CA: IDG Books World-wide, 1997. ISBN: 0764530925.

Autocad 14 Fundamentals, Michael E. Beall, Howard M. Fulmer, Indi-anapolis: New Riders Publishing, 1997. ISBN: 1562057677.

Mastering Autocad: Release 11, George Omura. San Francisco, CA: Sybex; 1997. ISBN: 0782121098,

Inside Autocad, Michael E. Beall (Editor), Indianapolis: New Riders Publishing, 1997. ISBN: 1562057553.

MAGAZINES AND NEWSLETTERS

Cadence, 525 Market, Suite 500, San Francisco, CA 94105; (415)278-5246. Web site: *www.cadence-mag.com*

WEB SITE

www.autodesk.com

AUTOCAD FORUM ON COMPUSERVE provides support as well as demos of applications for AutoCAD, a widely used CAD program.

TRAINING

MCGRAW-HILL'S NRI SCHOOLS offer a home-study course in computer-aided drafting. McGraw-Hill Continuing Education Center, 4401 Con-necticut Avenue, NW, Washington, DC 20008; (202) 244-1600. Web site: *www.mhcec.com*

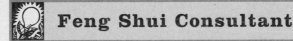 **Feng Shui Consultant**

The desire to escape a sense of unrelenting stress has led to the grow-ing interest in the art of feng shui, the art of understanding how the physical environment affects physical, mental, and emotional well-being. Although it is rooted in ancient Chinese traditions, in the Western world it incorporates the considerable body of scientific research referred to as environmental psychology. Many studies now show that as Winston Churchill said, "First we shape our buildings, thereafter they shape us."

Clearly, our designed environments do shape our behavior and how we feel in them. Psychologist Roger Barker conducted a series of classic studies that demonstrate how surroundings play a critical role in molding our behavior, thoughts, and feelings. While contemporary society may challenge us with stress, depression, and insomnia, our living environments can affect us in positive ways. Selective use of space, light, color, sound, and placement of objects can elevate our emotions, change our moods, boost our health, and encourage mental alertness.

This is evident at even the most primitive level. It was once thought that the nucleus of the atom directed the functions of the cell. Now, cell biologist Bruce Lipton at the University of Wisconsin has discovered that if the nucleus of an atom is removed, the cell goes on functioning for some time before it dies. Thus, he's found that it's the membrane of the cell that actually directs the nucleus. The membrane takes in information from the environment that it provides to the cell, proving that the same plants placed in different environments will adapt into distinctly different plants.

This helps us understand the subtle work of the feng shui consultant. Feng shui consultants create environments where we can think and behave more in keeping with our desires. They learn how people process visual, auditory, and olfactory information and how the mind interprets these environmental stimuli. For example, an important aspect of feng shui is how color affects our physiology and emotions.

Many consultants work with an octagonal compass called the ba gua. Its eight sections correspond to the different aspects of life—health, family, money, career and fame, as well as the various elements of nature and the birth date of the inhabitants. Using this tool, consultants of the Compass School can recommend improvements to enhance any environment from an entire community to a corporate office building, a home, individual office, or desktop. Consultants of the Black Hat School use the front door or the main entrance to a room instead of a compass to analyze a room in terms of its feng shui.

Nancilee Wydra, a leading feng shui author and founder of the Feng Shui Institute of America, points out that this is the only field in which perception is used as the primary focus for space planning. Consultants learn how color, shape, sound, placement and content of paintings and art objects affect human contentment, vitality, interpersonal relationships, health, stamina, and success.

Realtors are particularly avid users of feng shui consultants because homes and buildings that have been "feng shui-ed" sell faster. New home owners, newlyweds who have just moved into a home together, as well as road warriors who spend countless nights in hotel rooms are among those using this service.

Other clients include companies seeking better morale and higher profits, hospitals, hospices, clinics, extended-care facilities, and those suffering from chronic illnesses, especially those with environmental sensitivities. Users of feng shui consultants also include schools, universities, city planning departments, developers, landscape firms, park services, museums and other cultural facilities, and small businesses. All have contributed to the rapid rise of this field.

In fact, in the U.S. there are more feng shui consultants today than there are architects. Many architects, interior designers, and decorators are incorporating this practice into their work. Background in these or the following fields are helpful in becoming a feng shui consultant: fine arts, health care, environmental studies, city or regional planning, landscape design, psychology, social work, psychobiology, and baubiology (which focuses on the effects of toxic substances in the environment).

Feng shui consulting is an exciting field for someone with good problem-solving and interviewing skills who is at home with the subtleties of human communication. Fees for a feng shui consultation vary depending on locale from around $75 an hour up to several hundred dollars an hour. To calculate the charges in a particular area, Nancilee Wydra finds that the feng shui consultant can charge midway between the going hourly rate for a massage therapist and a lawyer. If, for example, massage therapists in a community generally charge $60 an hour and lawyers in that same area charge $175 an hour, the feng shui consultant would most likely be able to charge $125 per hour.

Referrals from excited and satisfied clients are the best source of business, so networking is an important way for feng shui consultants to get business. Working through real estate agents, holistic medical practitioners, and designers is another means of getting business as is writing and speaking on the benefits and nature of feng shui.

Neat Niches

Energetic Cleansing

Referred to as "psychic housecleaning" by *Elle* magazine, energetic cleansing is based on the scientific principle that objects are made of energy and spaces hold energy. We've all experienced going into a room, office, or home that seemed to have "bad vibes." Energetic cleansers clear out negative energetic fields in a location. They're hired mostly by real estate agents who are having trouble selling what seem like perfectly "saleable" homes.

Enough slow properties sell immediately after Eleni Santoro's cleansings that she's busy, working mainly in New York, but taking an occasional client in other parts of the country. A listing that had been on the market for 8 months without a single offer sold in less than 10 days after Santoro's cleansing. She charges realtors $300 to $2,500 per cleansing. Other clients include decorators and new commercial tenants.

Color Therapy

This exciting new field was developed in England only 10 years ago. Already there are over a million people using it worldwide, and it's catching on quickly in the United States. After training in England, Ayn Cates was among the first to bring color therapy, or auro-soma as it is also called, to the U.S. only 8 years ago. Already it has been approved by the FDA and the National Board of Certified Counselors. Cates is busily training people as auro-soma therapists through three six-day intensive programs or six three-day intensives. Most consultants practice from their homes.

Where to Turn for Information and Help

TRAINING

FENG SHUI INSTITUTE OF AMERICA (FSIA), P.O. Box 488, Wabasso, FL 32970; (888) 488-3742. Their home study course and week-long on-site professional certification program is the oldest in the country and is accepted by the American Society of Interior Designers, state professional regulatory boards, and facility managers for continuing education training. FSIA has regional chapters, an advanced feng shui teacher-training program, a professional referral system, and lists of publications and books in ancillary fields, as well as publishing a newsletter, *Windwater*. Web site: *www.windwater.com*

BOOKS

Designing Your Happiness: A Contemporary Look at Feng Shui, Nancilee Wydra, Heian, 1995. ISBN: 0893468118.

Feng Shui, The Ancient Wisdom of Harmonious Living for Modern Times, Eva Wong, Shambhala Publications, 1996. ISBN: 1570621004.

The Power of Color, Faber Birren, Citadel Press, 1997. ISBN: 080651857X

The Power of Place: How Our Surroundings Shape Our Thoughts, Emotions, and Actions, Winifred Gallagher. New York: Harper Perennial Library, 1994. ISBN: 0060976020.

Fund-Raiser

Nonprofit organizations, schools, research and educational institutions, arts and cultural organizations, like museums, symphony orchestras and theatres, churches and religious organizations, and political campaigns and ballot initiatives are among the many organizations and special-interest groups that need to raise money. But they're competing for shrinking levels of contributions.

The current edition of *Giving and Volunteering in the United States* reports per household charitable contributions are dropping slightly each year.

Convincing people to give is increasingly time consuming, requiring far more than a simple direct-mailing request. Thus the professional fund-raiser is always in demand. More than 3,500 fund-raising professionals have been certified by the National Society of Fund Raising Executives.

Fund-raisers develop, coordinate, implement, and evaluate fund-raising campaigns. Campaigns may include a combination of special events, board relations, mailings, telephone-solicitation banks, proposals, public relations, and presentations. Fund-raisers also conduct market surveys and feasibility and planning studies.

Interpersonal skills, a comfort-level with asking for money, and the ability to fit in and communicate with people who have money are some of the skills of a good fund-raiser.

But fund-raising is increasingly high tech, too. Fund-raisers must manage databases of donors, track their giving patterns and develop customized direct-mail campaigns. Recruiting, training, motivating, and managing volunteers and professional staff may also be part of the fund-raiser's responsibilities.

A primary way fund-raisers find clients is through referrals from board members and colleagues, so personal networking is important. Other marketing strategies include listings in directories and placing ads in trade periodicals and the Yellow Pages. Writing articles and speaking on fund-raising topics can also lead to business.

How fund-raisers charge for their services separates the ethical fund-raisers from the boiler-room operations that interrupt dinner hours. Fund-raisers bill for their services on an hourly or project basis. Even when billing is on a project basis, the number of hours are used as the basis for costing. Hourly rates range from $50 to $300, approximating that of attorneys. Fees based on the financial goal for a campaign or on the amount of money raised are considered unethical by the professional associations and most consultants.

Most states require fund-raising professionals and the charities they work for to register and follow certain procedures before beginning a fund-raising campaign.

Where to Turn for Information and Help

ASSOCIATIONS

AMERICAN ASSOCIATION OF FUNDRAISING COUNSEL, 37 E. 28th St., New York, NY 10016; (212) 481-6705. An association of fund-raising firms. Web site: *www.aafrc.org*

NATIONAL SOCIETY OF FUND RAISING EXECUTIVES, 1101 King Street, Suite 700, Alexandria, VA 22314; (800) 666-FUND; (703) 684-0410. There are 17,000 members in 149 chapters. An association for individuals that provides a credentialing training program for fund-raising executives. Maintains a collection of over 3,000 reference works and publishes a quarterly journal, *Advancing Philanthropy.* Web site: *www.nsfre.org*

NEWSLETTERS

Non-Profit Nuts and Bolts, a monthly subscription newsletter for non-profit professionals; 4623 Tiffany Woods Circle, Oviedo, FL 32765; (407) 677-6564. Web site: *www.nutsbolts.com*

WEB SITES

THE NON-PROFIT TIMES. Web site: *www.nptimes.com*

PHILANTHROPY NEWS DIGEST. Web site: *http://philanthropy-journal.org*

www.clark.net/pub/pwalker/fundraising_and_giving

Graphology

Graphology is the science of assessing an individual's personality or identity by a careful, systematic evaluation of the motor patterns, graphic habits, and movements reflected in his or her handwriting. Long accepted in European scientific circles, it has only more recently begun to be used with more popularity in the United States. Handwriting analysis has developed over more than three and a half centuries. It's based on the fact that handwriting is a highly complex process involving the brain, nervous system, motor muscles and reflexes, coordination, memory, and eyesight.

Writing is such a unique performance that it's similar to fingerprinting or DNA analysis. The chance of someone writing exactly like another person is one in 68 trillion. One's signature is so unique that it is recognized by the court system for its authenticity and originality. The graphologist is trained to determine personality characteristics by studying the space, form and movement of handwriting. The analysis identifies core personality traits or potential, not necessarily who a person is now or who they will become.

While many people study graphology as a personal interest, professional graphologists assist businesses with personnel screening, work with therapists, teachers, social workers, and psychologists to assist their clients and do personal and compatibility analysis. Some do vocational appraisals as well as compatibility and personal analysis for private clients. Others work with the legal system (including prisons, police departments, and lawyers) doing jury screening and forensic analysis, offering court testimony and examining documents for forgeries and employee theft.

Personnel profiling is one of the more popular specialties. Many graphologists work with *Fortune* 500 companies. Others work with schools helping teachers find the best learning mode for struggling students. Some specialize in what's called graphotherapy, helping clients make personality changes by making voluntary changes in their handwriting. The graphotherapist identities both negative and positive personality attributes reflected in a client's handwriting and provides written exercises to be done consistently twice daily over a period of weeks to help minimize the weaknesses and enhance strengths.

Most graphologists are self-employed, according to Kate Wright, office administrator for the American Association of Handwriting Analysis and head of her own company, HandWRIGHTing Resources. Graphologists have a great deal of flexibility in their schedules. It can be an excellent source of supplemental income, as you can take on as few clients as you wish, she points out, but it also can produce an excellent full-time income, up to six figures in some cases. Depending on the specialty, one large company, agency, or institution can keep a graphologist busy full-time with repeat business. Additionally, graphology is essentially an at-home business. You may spend some time meeting with clients on their premises, but you will spend the majority of your time analyzing handwriting samples and preparing reports at home. This makes it a family friendly business. Also, because many analysts never meet their clients in person, it's a business you can do from anywhere.

To succeed in this field you need to enjoy working closely with people and doing detailed work. You need good writing and grammar skills and must know how to say what you see in forthright yet diplomatic, tactful ways. This field requires a lot of learning. While self-study programs are available, to learn the field involves more than simply reading about it. You must do it, so usually it takes two to three years to feel fully competent. Then, because the field is a dynamic, evolving one, it requires life-long learning. Most graphologists participate regularly in study groups and periodic seminars.

You may need to work on deadlines to finish analyses for clients. Confidentiality is essential. Sometimes helping people accept what they may not want to hear can be challenging. As in many other fields, marketing and getting business is a common challenge, because practitioners often prefer doing analysis to promoting and selling. Since there are marketing methods for all personality styles, however, successful graphologists find ways to market themselves that are in keeping with their personalities. Some do cold calls to companies. Others get referrals through networking. Many lecture and give speeches on graphology. Some use direct mail. Fees range from $75 or $100 to $300 for an analysis.

Other than the basic costs of starting a business, like marketing, getting your business license, and setting up a business telephone line, start-up costs and overhead are quite low after the graphologist has obtained the training needed to work competently. Equipment is limited to a simple measuring device such as a protractor or a grip especially made for handwriting analysis and a magnifying glass. A well-lighted work area is another requirement, along with plastic page protectors to cover original writing samples. Having unlined paper and a variety of writing tools for clients to chose from in providing writing samples is important.

Kate Wright emphasizes, "Graphology is seldom an end in itself; it's a tool for understanding more about ourselves and one another."

Where to Turn for Information and Help

ASSOCIATIONS

AMERICAN ASSOCIATION OF HANDWRITING ANALYSTS (AAHA), PO Box 95, Southfield, MI 48037; (248) 443-8312. AAHA publishes the bimonthly newsletter *Dialogue*, has an extensive library, and offers seminars and conventions and an accreditation program for advancement and certification. Web site: *www.handwriting.org/aaha*

THE ASSOCIATION FOR GRAPHOLOGICAL STUDIES (AFGS), formed in 1984 for the purpose of instructing students in the science of handwriting analysis and graphotherapy. AFGS also offers course materials. 13771 Conner Kroll Pkwy., Fisher, IN 46038; (317) 578-4778. Web site: *www.ivic.net/~afgs*

BOOKS

GRAPHOLOGY

The following books are recommended by the Association of Handwriting Analysis for beginning the study of graphology.

Personality in Handwriting: A Handbook of American Graphology, Alfred O. Mendel, Rudolph Arnheim, Newcastle Publishing Co, 1990. ISBN: 0878771530.

GRAPHOTHERAPY

The following books are recommended by the Association for Graphological Studies for those interested in studying graphotherapy.

Grapho-Therapeutics, Paul de Sainte Colombe.

Health Clues in Handwriting, Rose LaJoie Toomey.

Writing, a 72-page workbook with 10 lessons and over 300 samples.

COURSES

HANDWRITING ANALYSIS: A FUNDAMENTAL COURSE. A 12-month self-study course offered by the American Association of Handwriting Analysis from HandWRIGHTing Resources, P.O. Box 3087, Southfield MI 48037; (248) 443-8315. E-mail: hwateacher@aol.com

HEALTH CLUES IN HANDWRITING COURSE, The Association for Graphological Studies, 665 San Rodolfo Drive, Suite 124, Solana Beach, CA 92075; (760) 722-7711.

THE ASSOCIATION FOR GRAPHOLOGICAL STUDIES offers introductory- and intermediate-level courses, as well as a course entitled "Health Clues in Handwriting." 13771 Conner Knoll Pkwy., Fisher, IN 46038, (317) 578-4778.

WEB SITE

THE GRAPHOLOGY BOOK STORE. Web site: *www.graphology-l.com/bookstore/0.html*

Hauling Service

Getting rid of things is not a new problem, but it can be a major one. Every time you move, you discover things that don't work, don't fit, or that you simply don't want. This happens even when you don't move. What do you do with the old refrigerator or range when you buy a new one? Or that ratty-looking sofa that your mother insisted you take? Or the debris from the last remodeling project you finally got finished? Or the broken chair? Or the rusted fender in the garage? Or the old fence, the garden debris, the old shed that finally fell down? Unless you have a truck, you have to call someone to haul this stuff away, because most garbage services won't touch it.

That leaves a wide-open opportunity for a hauling service. And what you get paid by the hour or the load is not all the income you can earn.

One person's junk is another person's treasure. People get rid of old things such as oil paintings, antiques, rare books, presents they don't want, left-over construction materials, and reusable things of all sorts. You can keep, donate to charities, or sell items of value. The possibilities for selling things is almost limitless through the classified ads, at flea markets or garage sales, or to anyone who can use what you've got. And because you've got a truck, you can deliver, too.

All you need is a pickup truck or van, preferably one that's equipped with a hydraulic lift gate, along with tarps, blankets, rope, and a hand truck or four-wheel dolly. Of course, you can have more than one truck or van, but if you do, your zoning laws may require you to keep the vehicles in a commercial area, so check with your city. Some hauling services may also arrange for roll-off dumpsters to leave at a site, but storing these may also be subject to your zoning laws.

Your other primary need is to identify places to which to take dispos-able materials that you haul away. You must make preliminary inquiries with companies that accept these materials. Scrap-metal companies may or may not take old appliances. Dumps may not accept certain types of furniture. Secondhand shops may not want old mattresses or appliances that don't work. You will find that most of these places will pay you for the materials they accept. If you also charge the consumer or business for hauling away the waste, you will be able to keep your rates competitive enough to make it worth your while on both ends.

Some states require a special license to move other people's stuff, so check this out as well as dumping regulations in your area. Unless you are close to a state line and your business will take you across that line, you will not be bound by Interstate Commerce Commission regulations. In addition, if you are hauling debris, be sure that no hazardous materials such as paint are included. Dumps will not accept hazardous materials, and if they see you dumping them, you will face either a warning or the termination of your account or both. If you discover hazardous materials in the load, remove them and have a specially licensed firm cart away the material for you.

To promote your business, leave stacks of business cards and well-done flyers or simple brochures with realtors, contractors, apartment-rental services, condominium-management offices, appliance stores, furniture stores, garden-supply stores and nurseries, and senior-citizen clubs. Because consumers usually start out by calling scrap-metal compa-nies, secondhand stores, and interstate movers (for whom their job may be too small), you should be sure these businesses are aware of you. Keep in touch with them regularly so they will refer clients to you. Going to auctions can also be a good source of business. Let the auction personnel know you're there, and by having a sign painted on your truck or using a removable magnetic sign, people will notice you. Often other moving jobs or other kinds of handy work will develop from a satisfied customer.

Classified or small display ads in your local paper and Yellow Pages ads are important ways of getting business. We met someone once who claimed he got all the business he needed from the Yellow Pages because of the name of his company Grunt N' Dump.

Where to Turn for Information and Help

For further information, refer to *How to Earn $15 to $50 an Hour and More with a Pickup Truck or Van*, by Don Lilly, Ballwin, MO: Darian Books, 1994; (314) 391-1434; $16.95. Also available from Don Lilly is a plan to build an inexpensive liner for your pickup truck, *Pick Up Truck Dump Box Plan*, $10.00, and *The Flea Market Handbook*, $9.95, by Robert Miner, which explains how to sell the items you are paid to haul away.

Related Businesses

Tree Service, Furniture Renovation, Moving Service, Lawn Aeration (contact Don Lilly at above address for a copy of *Lawn Aeration: Turn Hard Soil into Cold Cash*, by Robin Pedrotti, $19.95).

 Indoor Environmental Tester

In the 1980's and early 1990's, the environmental movement and the health movement converged and turned indoors with the realization that our homes and offices are assaulting us with a variety of pollutants that are making us ill. Indoor environmental experts tell us that everyone is environmentally at risk today. Most people are so conditioned to feeling less than optimal that we don't even recognize it.

Even a common product such as shoe polish contains benzene, a carcinogen, but most people are unaware of the potentially dangerous pollutants like these throughout our lives. To help raise awareness, CHEC, the Children's Health and Environmental Coalition, is uniting hundreds of grassroots groups across the country that are working to counter the harmful impact of environmental contaminants, particularly those that research finds account for recent increases of cancer in children.

Increased awareness of the danger of indoor pollution is giving rise to a variety of new businesses through which people can turn their personal commitment to improving the environment into concrete services from which they can earn a living. The most promising of these is testing the indoor environment for unhealthy conditions and working with home-owners, businesses, office-building supervisors, architects, real estate agents, and many others to increase awareness of environmental dangers and to test these environments and fix any problems discovered.

Over the past five years, testing services have gathered so much mo-mentum, that while it used to be upscale homeowners who previously formed the clientele, now major corporations and industries are spending money to make sure their environments are safe. This trend will increase, too, as various government agencies, particularly the Office of Safety and Health Review Commission (OSHA), and Congress prepare new guidelines to regulate office-building air-quality standards, smoke-free en-vironments, and other hazards. Typically, specialists who work in larger industrial settings are called industrial hygienists while those specializing in the residential market are referred to as indoor environmental testers.

Environmental testers test for a variety of things:

• **Indoor air pollution** caused by mold spores, dust, bacteria, formalde-hyde, and toxic gases, such as carbon monoxide and sulfur dioxide. Such pollution can come from appliances, furnaces, stoves, air-conditioning vents, copy and fax machines, furniture, rugs, paper products, and many other building materials or office-supply materials.

• **Electromagnetic radiation** from high-voltage transmission lines, home electrical wiring, meters, appliances, electric blankets, water beds, video display terminals (VDTs), and other office equipment.

• **Lead found in paint, dishware, lead solder, and crystal**. Lead can also be tracked in on shoes from the ground (which got there as airborne residue from car exhaust) and deposited onto rugs.

• **Geomagnetic influences** such as magnetic grid crossings and under-ground water under a room.

- *Toxic substances* of all kinds in carpet fibers, dyed fabrics, cosmetics, foods, pesticides, and many common cleaning supplies.

- *Asbestos used in insulation.*

In short, indoor environmental testers may get involved in testing in many areas, and the field is already giving rise to a number of new subcategories of professions.

Certified Bau-biologist

A bau-biologist is a "building biologist" (bau is German for building), someone who is trained to look at many aspects of the indoor environment of a building and determine if there are toxic elements present in the building materials, air quality, and furniture.

EMF Testers

EMF testers, short for electromagnetic field testers, examine bedrooms, offices, and particularly computer areas for low-frequency emissions from the video terminals. Although science has yet clearly to define just what, if any, are the effects of low-frequency electromagnetic fields emitted from VDTs and other electronic equipment, studies from Finland, Sweden, and elsewhere have raised concern by linking such emissions with brain tumors, childhood leukemia, cancer, and miscarriages.

Air Quality Testers

These experts focus on measuring dust and toxic particulates in the air that might irritate people with asthma, sinus conditions, cancer, leukemia, and other illnesses that are severely aggravated by poor air quality.

Radon Testers

Radon testers must now be licensed in many states to perform radon tests on houses and buildings. (The EPA will soon require that nearly all houses be tested for radon upon sale.)

Lead-Abatement Specialists

Lead-abatement specialist must be licensed to supervise the removal of lead from homes and buildings.

Mary Cordaro is a certified bau-biologist and environmental consultant in Los Angeles whose company, A Room of One's Own, diagnoses problems associated with sick-building syndrome. As Mary says, the corollary to this industry is that one must not only diagnose the problem, but also be prepared with ideas for how to solve or abate it. This means that you must become familiar with alternative building materials, furniture suppliers, and other ways of building and solving problems. In the past few years, however, Mary's business has expanded enormously, and she now finds herself working with many architects, real estate agents, and designers who seek her assistance at earlier and earlier stages of home design.

Joe Riley's business, Healthwaves, specializes in testing for electromagnetic problems. Together with his wife, a Ph.D. in neurophysiology, he checks for electrical problems, and although they do not fix the problems themselves, they began earning $1,000 a week right away. Referrals keep his business going week after week.

Audrey Hoodkiss came into the field because of her own environmental illness. She had been an interior designer when she developed a chemical sensitivity. She now works with medical patients who need to redecorate to create a healthier environment.

Jim Nagra worked as a taxi driver to support himself while he started what has become a successful business as an environmental-equipment broker. He sells everything over the phone, from environmentally safe shoe polish to pollution-busting vacuum cleaners.

These are just a few of the examples of this emerging environmental business, ripe for creative development. They and other businesses in various stages of being defined could develop into some of the fastest-growing opportunities of the 90's.

Environmental testing requires the ability to synthesize vast amounts of information, because new research on environmental and health issues is surfacing weekly. New problems, remedies, and resources, new non-toxic and low-toxic materials, and new shielding mechanisms are becoming known, requiring some understanding of chemistry and toxicology. You have an ongoing obligation to clients to stay educated; constant reading, networking, and periodic attendance at professional workshops are called for.

This work demands an intense interest in health and a willingness to be self-taught, because there are few courses in this area. You need to maintain your own constant research to keep abreast of changes in both abatement and remediation solutions. You also need to know a lot about products that are on the market and specialize in one area of inspection.

Interpersonal skills are required to advise people who are living with extreme difficulty because of serious sensitivities or illnesses. You also need to be able to recognize the emotional needs of hypochondriacs and psychosomatics and not let them become dependent on you. Intuition and the ability to be highly sensitive to your own bodily reactions is helpful (however, you don't want to use your own body to sense for problems; use meters).

Start-up costs in this field can run from around $8,000 to $30,000 depending upon the type of testing one is doing. Most of these costs involve purchasing professional-quality testing equipment.

Few insurance companies will cover environmental testers for liability because there is no category as yet for this business. To get a business liability insurance policy, you may need to call yourself an interior designer and you must also write waivers into your contracts that say that you are not responsible for any abatement work that is performed by other contractors after you.

This is a challenging and stimulating field that will certainly grow. It provides the environmentally conscious with the opportunity to do meaningful work. Helping people feel better and get well can be highly rewarding and fulfilling.

However, when you work in sick buildings, you will expose yourself to hazardous pollution. Most of your clients will be cancer patients and people who are environmentally ill, so this work can be emotionally draining. You will need to guard against absorbing the emotional pain of the people you serve. Also, this work is still viewed by many as controversial, particularly the electromagnetic aspects. You may feel that you have to justify what you're doing to some people. Of course, you need to acquire a lot of technical knowledge.

Environmental testers charge either by the hour or by the job. The latter is especially common when working with people on fixed incomes. Hourly rates range from $60 to $150, with $75 the most typical. Representative on-the-job rates are $125 to $150 for an electromagnetic check for mildew for senior citizens, $300 to $600 for a 2,500-square-foot home. Rates for evaluating a commercial building can go as high as $5,000.

Typical annual gross revenues are around $75,000 based on billing 20 hours per week, 50 weeks a year, at $75 an hour. An experienced tester can complete electromagnetic checks in two to three hours. Full-home checks may take three to ten hours. Overhead in this business is moderate to high, running from 20 to 40 percent depending on many pieces of testing equipment you need to purchase and maintain.

While all business owners must be able to promote their businesses, the ability to promote one's business is particularly important in this field according to Helmut Ziehe of the Institute for Bau-Biology and Ecology, because many people are unaware of it and its benefits. Here are some suggestions for promotion:

- Developing relationships with doctors and dentists who will refer patients with possible environmentally caused complaints. Some doctors will subcontract with a tester and include the testing service as part of a patient's total health-care program, in which case the tester's findings are reported directly to the doctor, who will relate them to the patient. Doctors practicing alternative medicine are more likely to be willing to make referrals than traditional MDs and dentists.

- Local chapters of the Human Ecology Action League (HEAL), P.O. Box 41926, Atlanta, GA 30359; (770)248-1898. Organizations of chemically sensitive or electro-sensitive people.

- Getting listed in health- and environmental-resource guides.

- Getting referrals from environmental-resource groups and city planning departments.

- Listing in the Yellow Pages under Environment and Ecological Services and listings related to hazardous-waste disposal.

- Making contacts at environmental conferences, symposiums, and trade shows.

- Speaking and conducting seminars on indoor pollution.

- Writing articles for magazines and newspapers.

- Obtaining publicity about your work.

- Have your own Web site.

This is a fast-changing field. You need to develop a broad and eclectic understanding of what's going on in building biology (a term popular in Europe), indoor ecology, and suspected health problems. Contact recognized organizations and authorities in the field. Start conducting environmental audits for family and friends, and encourage them to refer clients to you.

Increasing understanding of the relationship between harmful substances in our indoor environments and our health will drive the growth of this business as more people seek to rid their homes and offices of toxicity. Although large metropolitan populations are more open to this field than people in smaller Midwestern areas, interest in indoor environmental testing is definitely growing as evidenced by the growing number of people who are entering the field.

Where to Turn for Information and Help

BOOKS

Dampness in Buildings, Alan Oliver, James Douglas, J. Stewart Stirling, Blackwell Science Inc, 1997. ISBN: 0632040858. Covers mildew.

The Green PC: Making Choices That Make a Difference, Steve Anzovin, Blue Ridge Summit, PA: Windcrest/McGraw-Hill, 1994. ISBN: 0830643117.

Home Safe Home, Debra Lynn Dodd. New York, NY: Tarcher/Putnam, 1997. ISBN: 087477859X.

Living Downstream, Sandra Steingraber. Reading, MA: Addison-Wesley Publishing, 1997. ISBN: 0375700994. Covers pesticides.

Water, Electricity and Health, Alan Hall. Hawthorn Press, 1997. ISBN: 1869890949.

MAGAZINES AND NEWSLETTERS

Delicate Balance, 1100 Rural Avenue, Voorhees, NJ, 08043; (609) 429-5358.

Environ: A Magazine for Ecologic Living and Health, Wary Canary Press, Box 2204, Fort Collins, CO 80522; (303) 224-0083.

Indoor Air Review, IAQ Publications; (301) 913-0115. Monthly.

VDT News, P.O. Box 1799, Grand Central Station, New York, NY.

TRAINING

INSTITUTE FOR BAU-BIOLOGY AND ECOLOGY, Box 387, Clearwater, FL 33757; (727) 461-4371. The Institute advises starting with its home-study correspondence course, covering construction materials, architecture, and related topics. Three six-day classes are offered on location (in Florida), and you can obtain certification within a year. Once certified, the Institute lists graduates on its Web site by location. Web site: *www.bau-biologieusa.com*

SAFE ENVIRONMENTS, Berkeley, CA; (510) 549-9693; contact David Bierman.

WORKSHOPS

A ROOM OF ONE'S OWN. Mary Cordaro gives workshops in consulting and bau-biology; (310) 838-2892.

FRANCHISES

ADVANTAGE RADON CONTROL CENTERS, 804 Second Street Pike, Southampton, PA 18966; (800) 535-TEST; (215) 953-9200.

ENVIRONMENTAL AIR SERVICES, The Dwyer Group, 1010 North University Parks Drive, Waco, TX 76707; (800) 583-9100; (254) 745-2400.

PROFESSIONAL HOUSE DOCTORS, 1406 E. 14th Street, Des Moines, IA 50316; (515) 265-6667; (800) 288-7437. Web site: *www.prohousedr.com*

In-Home Health Care

The Labor Department predicts home health care will have the largest job growth of any industry through 2005. The swelling numbers of aging, of course, are the population most in need of home health care, but other vulnerable groups are also being cared for in a home environment. The government has provided funding for emotionally disturbed children and adolescents and individuals with developmental disabilities to receive home care.

Driving the 12 percent annual growth of home care are three major facts:

- People don't want to be institutionalized.

- Institutionalizing people is expensive, thus governments are, as they have been for decades, emptying institutions.

- Patients are being quickly released from hospitals after surgery and illness.

Most home health care dollars go to governmental programs and large corporate contractors. But there are opportunities for people to carve out home-based businesses in the $42 billion that was spent in 1997. Almost one-fourth or about $10 billion of this spending comes out-of-pocket from individuals seeking care for their relatives and friends. Also, some corporations that get large government contracts contract with individuals to take patients into their own homes.

The economics of in-home care make sense. At-home care may cost less than even the overhead at a hospital or any other institution, and most daily-care (unskilled) attending can be provided by any reasonably trained person or family member.

As a business, the term "in-home care" means two types of arrangements:

- You take people in your home and take care of their daily needs and minor medical treatment.

- You go to someone's home or arrange for other people to go to someone's home (like a referral service) to take care of people.

Here's an overview of each:

In Your Home.   Corporations such as Mentor, a Boston-based human services company, engage you as an independent contractor, to take patients into your home. The types of problems such patients have include emotional problems, developmental disabilities, head injuries, and substance-abuse problems.

You take only one person into your home at a time. The care provider helps prepare the person for a successful transition back to their own homes as soon as possible. In the case of an emotionally disturbed patient, the mentor provides praise and other rewards for positive behavior and controls, as necessary, out-of-control behaviors by the patient.

No particular background is needed to do home health care, although a criminal record will be a problem. You need to be a compassionate and caring person and have good communication skills. Being established in a community helps, though people in all stages of life may do this work—single, empty nesting, parents with children. You do need a spare bedroom, because that's where your charge lives, and a vehicle for taking the person to outside appointments.

Compensation as an independent contractor is about $50 to $60 for each day a patient is in your home. If the services needed are more demanding because of medical needs, the compensation will be higher.

In the Person's Home.   Another alternative is to find reliable, qualified people to send as aides to homebound patients. The aides perform any number of services for the client, from cleaning and cooking, to running errands or taking the person to doctor's appointments. In some cases, the aide simply provides companionship for the patient, making sure that the person doesn't fall or forget to take a medication.

To avoid being an employment agency or nursing registry, which require licensing, this business is like a specialized referral service dealing with homemakers and companions for people who need home-care assistance. The patient pays you a referral fee only and then pays the aide directly. There are two requirements to making this business successful: You must find reliable, honest, and diligent aides, and you must find clients who need them. Like an executive search service or even a nanny agency, this kind of referral service can be hectic to operate, because you're a middleperson, working with both the caregivers and with those needing care.

Typical fees for an in-home care referral service are two- to four-weeks' salary for the aide, about $400 to $800. To show good faith, many services promise that if the aide does not work out for any reason within the first month, they will replace the person with a new candidate at no charge.

Where to Turn for Information and Help

MANUAL AND AUDIO TAPE

INSTITUTE OF CONSULTING CAREERS, INC., 2555 Camino Del Rio South, Suite 208, San Diego, CA 92108; (619) 295-3545. E-mail: icc98@earthlink.net

VIDEO

BELSON/HANWRIGHT VIDEO, 4635 San Andreas Avenue, Los Angeles, CA 90065; (800) 222-5244.

IN YOUR HOME CARE AGENCY

MENTOR, 313 Congress Street, Boston, MA 02210; (617) 790-4800. Web site: *www.mentormpn.com*

Interior Designer/Decorator

Never in recent history have we expected so much from our homes or tried to squeeze so much into them. We want our homes to have everything from gourmet kitchens and children's play rooms, to in-home entertainment and workout centers, spas, and fully functional home offices.

The result is that Americans are redecorating and enhancing their homes at an unprecedented rate. A survey for *Home* magazine indicated that 46 percent of Americans planned to redecorate or remodel in the next five years, compared with 35 percent who did so in the previous five years.

The high price of buying a home motivates many to improve on their existing home instead of moving up the housing ladder, while others are purchasing increasingly more elaborate homes and then tailoring them to their personal lifestyles. Last year 30 million homeowners spent $121.1 billion in home improvements. This year, the figure is expected to leap to $126.7 billion.

These trends mean lots of work for interior designers. According to a Lou Harris survey, almost one out of every seven Americans gets help from a professional home decorator. These numbers translate into five million clients for professional designers in the residential market alone. And, according to Joe Pryweller, senior editor at the American Society of Interior Designers, about half of all designers work primarily with business and industrial clients (contract work), in addition to those who work with residential clients.

Interior *decorators* can and often do practice without formal credentials, but interior *designers* must have a bachelor's degree, and be certified by the respected American Society of Interior Design. They also must be able to read blueprints, develop estimates for commercial as well as residential remodeling projects, know whether it's possible to knock down a wall without damaging the structure of building, know building and fire safety codes and space planning. Both decorators and designers need to have a sense of color and balance or proportion, a positive attitude toward change so they can both keep up with fashion trends and at the same time be responsive to what the client desires, and the ability to communicate through graphic presentations.

Designers are now able to use computers in working with clients. With computer-aided design software, such as *Autocad* or *Archicad*, it's possible to devise and present design solutions to clients with three-dimensional realism.

Decorators and designers charge for their services in several ways. Some charge a flat fee for design work. Others charge by the hour, at rates ranging from $35 to $125. Still others add a service charge of approximately 20 percent to items they buy for clients, such as furniture, fabric, and floor coverings. Still others charge their clients the retail price of items they are able to purchase wholesale, keeping the difference as their fee. Thus, the client gets the designer's service at a price no greater than he or she would have paid for the products at retail. To avoid misunderstandings, it's important to formalize a client relationship with a contract or a letter of agreement.

Decorating Den Interiors is one franchise available in the decorating field. It's a shop-at-home interior decorating service. The franchisee drives to a client's home or office in a van that's loaded with samples of wall coverings, fabric, furniture, accessories and flooring. This service allows busy customers to preview and order decorating options from large samples they can see in the lighting and color of their existing furnishing. The profit of the Decorating Den franchisees comes from selling items at retail that they purchase at wholesale. Being affiliated with 700 franchisees provides the purchasing power to offer clients special promotions and discounts.

Neat Niche

Staging Consultant. Decorators in large metropolitan areas are pioneering this new specialty. Staging involves decorating homes that are about to be offered for sale in a way that accentuates its value. Usually working through referrals from real estate agents, a staging consultant can be helpful to any homeowner intent upon selling their home for or near to their asking price. The consultant might suggest putting away personal items that could be offensive to some buyers such as alcohol, nude paintings, gun collections or mounted wild game heads. They might suggest more subtle changes such as a different color of bedspread or recovering ragged upholstery. Sometimes their advice involves making more substantial changes like repainting a room, removing stained or outdated wallpaper or replacing unattractive furniture with rented furnishings.

Basically the staging consultant will suggest removing or concealing anything that draws potential buyers' attention to the decor and furnishing of the home instead of to the value, beauty and/or functionality of the actual space of the house. The service is generally offered in upper middle class and wealthy neighborhoods where homes sell for at least $400,000. It is especially valuable when decorating a home that is vacant. Or as a consultant work with developers to decorate model homes.

Suggestions from staging consultants often violate traditional interior design rules, so in addition to a good eye for the aesthetic, they need to have excellent communication skills to prevent owners from taking their suggestions as criticism. Fees run from $200 for a walk-through, making a range of suggestions to the owner, to over $50,000 for overseeing mini-remodeling and/or being given carte blanche to redecorate.

Where to Turn for Information and Help

ASSOCIATIONS

AMERICAN SOCIETY OF INTERIOR DESIGNERS, 608 Massachusetts Avenue, N.E., Washington, DC 20002; (202) 546-3480. This is the largest professional association in this field. Members include interior designers who have completed a degree program or have many years of experience, as well as designers who are working toward their degree.

The society has several classes of members, including professionals who have obtained a four-year college degree in interior design and/or have acquired sufficient years of experience to pass a three-day examination to become certified as interior designers. Sixteen states, plus the District of Columbia and Puerto Rico, now require licensing of interior designers. Web site: *www.asid.org*

BOOK

How to Start a Home-Based Interior Design Business, Suzanne Dewalt, Globe Pequot Press, 1997. ISBN: 1564408604.

MAGAZINES

Interior Design, 345 Hudson, 4th floor, New York, NY 10014; (212) 519-7200. Web site: *www.cahners.com/mainmag/id.htm*

Interiors, 1515 Broadway, New York, NY 10036; (212) 764-7300.

Interiors and Sources, Clark Publishers, 840 U.S. Highway 1, Suite 330, North Palm Beach, FL 33408; (561) 627-3393. Web site: *www. isdesignet.com*

Contract Design, 1 Penn Plaza, New York, NY 10119; (212) 714-1300. Specializes in office design.

FRANCHISE

DECORATING DEN INTERIORS, 19100 Montgomery Village Avenue, Suite 200, Montgomery, MD 20886; (800) 332-3367; (301) 272-1500. Web site: *www.decoratingden.com*

WEB SITES

This site provides links to the trade associations serving the home furnishings industry. *www.homefurnish.com/tradeorg.htm*

 ## Leak-Detection Service

Imagine being able to offer a service that can save a building owner from replacing a $100,000 roof by fixing a $50 piece of pipe or that can save a gas station $250,000 with a $4,000 repair! That is exactly what the field of leak detection can do.

Leak detectors locate leaks in just about any kind of system that uses pipes and distribution transition lines: from plumbing and sewer pipes in homes, to piping lines at gas stations and fire sprinkler systems in skyscrapers, to swimming pools and public water reservoirs. Leak detectors are even hired to find leaks in pneumatic tubes at bank drive-in tellers.

To detect leaks, inspectors may use inert gases, radio signals, ultrasonic listening devices, thermographs to detect moisture, and nuclear instruments. Few leak-detection companies have all types of equipment needed to detect all varieties of leaks, so most specialize in one area or another. For example, Elsie and Ted McConnel have built a thriving home-based business detecting roof leaks using a nuclear instrument called a Datamax, which they saw exhibited at a trade show they attended because they were managing an apartment building. These leak-detection devices are nondestructive and use special instrumentation to detect hydrogen contained in moisture. The reading from the instrument is then put into a computer, which produces a roof graph showing the condition of the roof. Clients then use the graph in a process that leads to a precise repair.

Leak detection has become a significant industry for a variety of reasons. First, there is always an array of sophisticated new equipment that can be used to find leaks of all kinds. American Lead Detection, Inc., for example, has developed the ALD 300 pipe, cable, and sewer locator that can successfully locate concealed pipes to avoid damage when digging for construction, remodeling, or repair. Their most advanced equipment utilizes computer technology to determine the exact position of a leak based on a series of trial correlations and a thorough examination by the technician. Under development is a device that will detect leaks in large bodies of water such as reservoirs, dams, tanks, and concrete and vinyl-lined pools.

Second, the cost of construction and new building-code requirements in many parts of the country have made inspections for leaks a necessary step prior to any roof repair. In fact, in areas where buildings are susceptible to moisture damage, inspections are often part of a regular building maintenance program on an annual or biannual basis. Third, with the price of water skyrocketing in many parts of the country, home developers and local governments take immediate action when they believe they may be losing thousands of gallons of costly water from swimming pools, fountains, or water-storage facilities. Finally, leak detection has benefited from the variety of natural disasters that have hit the country, such as earthquakes and hurricanes. For all these reasons, many leak detectors can keep busy sixty to seventy hours per week.

No specific experience is required to go into this business, but good hearing and a mechanical aptitude are helpful when it comes to using the necessary equipment. You also should enjoy marketing yourself, as the best methods for getting business are contacting those people who install piping systems: plumbers, pool experts, water purveyors, and service people who work with concealed piping.

In addition to landlords and commercial-property owners, construction contractors, insurance companies, home inspectors and building-protection services are also big users of leak-detection services. Since leaks are often covered under homeowners insurance policies, when claims are made, the insurance companies need someone to detect and repair the leaks. Leaks are a big concern to both homebuyers and sellers. Existing leaks must be repaired to pass inspection, and claims made after purchase through building-protection insurance often involve addressing unanticipated leaks.

Prices for residential leak inspections range from $200 to $300 and usually take only a few hours to accomplish. The price for leak detection at industrial sites can run into the thousands. Leak detectors may also handle the repair work or subcontract it out, adding substantially to their profit. Total income from leak detection can therefore be quite good, with businesses typically showing earnings of over $75,000 a year; earnings of more than $250,000 are not unusual.

Where to Turn for Information and Help

A franchise is available in this field from American Leak Detection. This company provides an eight-week training course and a vast assortment of equipment begining at $49,500 and going up to $95,000. (This company is listed on the SBA Registry, however, so their franchise agreement has been reviewed and approved for bank loans, although, of course, the franchisee must also be approved.) Nearly all of their 290 franchise units operate from their homes. For further information, contact American Leak Detection, at 888 Research Drive, Suite 100, Palm Springs, CA 92262; or call (800) 755-6697 or (619) 320-9991. Web site: *www.leakbusters.com*. Franchisees get business referrals from their listing on the Web site, and interested visitors can link directly to a franchisee's own site if they have one.

Mediator

In recent years, mediation and arbitration, two forms of Alternative Dispute Resolution, or ADR, have achieved broad acceptance as methods of settling conflicts. According to the American Arbitration Association, growth of this field has been explosive since the 1980's for several reasons:

- **Speed.** Due to the burdens of criminal cases, tight budgets, and other factors, the court system is increasingly clogged despite efforts to expedite due process.

- **Cost.** Attorney's fees and other legal costs continue to rise.

- **Informality and flexibility.** Mediation occurs in a more businesslike manner than litigation that is highly structured, formal, and adversarial.

- **Privacy.** Mediation, unlike disputes settled in court, is not open to public scrutiny. Hearings and rewards are kept private and confidential.

- **Finality.** Mediation is final, binding, and legally enforceable, subject only to limited review by the courts.

Many states now require most civil cases to go first to mediation or arbitration, and only if the parties can't reach an agreement does the matter go on to the courts. For instance, the Minnesota Supreme Court has adopted rules requiring ADR in virtually all kinds of civil litigation (divorce and child custody disputes are exempted, as they are in most parts of the country). At least forty-six of the fifty states now have some type of official ADR program.

Unlike an arbitrator, a mediator does not decide the merits of a particular case or rule in favor of one of the parties. Rather, the mediator helps people on opposite sides find common ground, make compromises, and settle their claims. The mediator's role is advisory. They may offer suggestions, but resolution of the dispute rests with the parties involved. Arbitrators and mediators are sometimes referred to as neutrals.

Certain types of disputes lend themselves to mediation, whereas in other types of disputes mediation would not be appropriate. Mediation works best where the parties have roughly equal bargaining power. Where power is unequal, traditional litigation may be more suitable, because litigation offers added protection to the weaker party. Mediation is commonly used in business, insurance, labor relations, environment, public policy, family, securities, technology, employment, construction, international trade, homeowners', real estate, and transportation cases, among others. Millions of commercial contracts now contain clauses that provide for Alternative Dispute Resolution.

Mediation is a business you conduct from home. Even if you use your home office for business calls or administrative work, you certainly would not want the mediation to take place in your home. Rather, you must conduct mediations in a formal, neutral, and controlled setting such as a conference room.

Mediators must receive some training, but at present there are no uniform nationwide standards for training or credentialing mediators. Only about a dozen states actually require mediators to be licensed; but in only one of those states, Florida, are mediators required to be attorneys. However, in order to become impaneled as an American Arbitration Association mediator, you must meet certain specific requirements. The AAA and other groups will probably hammer out some national standards by the end of the decade.

Retired judges and lawyers constitute the majority of mediators, but a legal background isn't necessary. The AAA's national roster of arbitrators and mediators lists more than 20,000 individuals from diverse fields and professions. One mediator we spoke with emphasized that having "a background as a human being" was the most important criteria. If you have significant experience or expertise in a particular field or industry, such as construction, human resources, real estate, or labor relations, you may want to specialize in that area. Mediators should also be good consensus builders, have calm and soothing personalities, be creative at solving problems, and act in a professional and dignified manner. And, of course, mediators also must be completely unbiased and come to the process free of conflicts of interest.

Mediators usually charge by the hour or by the day. The fees normally are split by the disputing parties. Hourly rates vary from about $50 to $250, depending on the person's educational and occupational background (retired judges and lawyers tend to be at the higher end of the scale), his or her mediation training, and his or her area(s) of specialization. Another factor in what a mediator can charge is supply and demand. In some parts of the country, the abundance of mediators has depressed rates.

One disadvantage of this type of work is that you are frequently dealing with people who are angry, and you have to be very careful not to get caught in the crossfire. On the other hand, it feels good to help people reach a constructive solution to their problems.

Jim Stott of Stott, Monsma & Associates in Westlake Village, California, says it's possible to make a living as a mediator, but not by sitting and waiting for the phone to ring. Financially successful mediators probably spend 80 percent of their time doing marketing and only 20 percent conducting mediations.

Stott stresses the importance of networking with people we call gatekeepers as well as attorneys, accountants, and mental-health professionals who are involved in mediation and doing other kinds of marketing. When he started doing mediation, Stott says, he worked the "rubber chicken circuit, the Rotary, Kiwanis, and so on," giving speeches about conflict resolution. To generate business, he does conflict-prevention training, writes articles on the subject, and does pro bono work, particularly for churches.

People who want to go into this field should find a particular niche.

Resources

For further information, contact a community mediation center in your area and ask about volunteering. Or call The American Arbitration Association, 335 Madison Ave., New York, NY 10017; (212) 484-4000. The AAA provides training and certification for mediators, sponsors conferences, and publishes *Dispute Resolution Times*, a quarterly newsletter, and *Dispute Resolution Journal*, also quarterly ($55 annual subscription). Extensive bibliographies on this field appear on the AAA Web site. One such list is entitled the Fundamentals of Mediation and is available to nonmembers for $20. One book that provides an overview of the ADR process is *ADR in America*, by Robert Coulson, New York: American Arbitration Association, 1993 ($19.95). It may be ordered directly from the Publications Department of the American Arbitration Association, (212) 716-5800; fax (212) 541-4841. Web site: *www.adr.org*

Mystery Shopping

The business of mystery shopping has really taken off since the first edition of this book. Although mystery shoppers have been around in some industries for years, management gurus like Tom Peters breathed new life into this service when they began preaching the customer service gospel. Businesses can get customer input from feedback cards and toll-free telephone numbers, but these techniques don't reveal many problems that turn off customers. Research shows that nine out of ten dissatisfied customers will stop patronizing a firm without registering a complaint. They will, however, speak negatively to between nine and twelve other people about their dissatisfactions.

Today growing numbers of retail stores, financial institutions and even government agencies wouldn't think of operating without the feedback from mystery shoppers. The mystery shopper can save a client from losing business and their reputation by posing as a regular customer and then reporting to the client about how he or she was treated and about other matters of business concern to the client.

The mystery in mystery shopping is what makes it effective because the identity of the evaluator is not known to the establishment's employees. Some market research firms and private investigators do this work, but it has become an established niche of its own with over 500 mystery shopping services in the nationwide, double the number just five years ago! Mark Michelson, head of Michelson & Associates, a shopping service in Atlanta, is spearheading the first national conference of mystery shopping services and estimates that mystery shopping is a $500 million industry.

When Elaine Locksley worked in banking, she relied heavily on the evaluations of mystery shoppers so when she decided to go out on her own she started her own mystery shopping service. She launched The Locksley Group in Pacific Palisades, California, from her home with her two daughters as partners. They did all the work themselves from signing on the clients, to shopping and preparing reports for them. At first they worked primarily with banks, then expanded into working retail stores as well. Now Locksley has fifteen to twenty thousand shoppers in her database who work with her as independent contractors. One client alone requires 3300 individual associates per month to shop their stores.

Today, mystery shopping services work in almost every sector from museums and airports to amusement parks, fast food restaurants, gas stations, hotels, real estate brokerages, bowling alleys, doctor's offices, re-tirement homes, and movie theaters. Using mystery shoppers is appealing because it generally costs less than buying electronic surveillance systems or keeping constant watch on employees. There's room for growth because there are still many companies needing the service who are not yet using it.

One limitation, however, is that some states may define mystery shopping as undercover surveillance, which means that if the state also requires private detectives to be licensed, mystery shopping without a PI license may be illegal in those states. For example, Michigan is known for the stringent enforcement of its private investigator licensing law and there mystery shoppers are required by the state to be licensed private detectives.

Mystery shoppers are used to gather the following kinds of information for clients:

• *Check the quality of customer service.* Besides department stores, car dealers, and shopping malls, some of the other clients using mystery shoppers include charitable organizations and governmental organizations such as airport authorities who lease to restaurants, car-rental agencies, and gift shops. The hospitality industry is a big user of mystery shoppers: Hotels want to know how guests are treated. Restaurants want to know if their facilities are kept clean, how quickly customers are served, and about the quality of the food served.

• *Discover if employees are taking money from the till, stealing merchandise and supplies, or short-changing customers.* Employees account for two of every three dollars of loss from shoplifting and other theft. So businesses where the owners are not physically on the premises want to make sure they are not being victimized by their own employees. This aspect of mystery shopping is called integrity or honesty shopping. In some states it can only be done by private investigators. Bartenders, for example, are watched to see if they give free drinks to friends. Mystery shoppers go to the movies and count the number of ticket buyers to match the total against those reported by the theater manager.

• *Monitor the effect of employee-training programs.* Mystery shoppers are sent in, for example, before and after customer service, safety, and security training. Bank employees once played a more passive role, now they are expected to actively suggest other services to customers based on the situation presented or hints dropped about their needs. Shopper reports can let the bank know if the training to help tellers and officers assume this new role is working.

• **Learn if mutual fund sales representatives are telling the truth to their investor customers.** The Federal Deposit Insurance Corporation uses mystery shoppers to monitor companies it regulates. If serious regulation of the life insurance industry ever occurs, mystery shopping will most likely be widely used.

• **Determine how billing is done by cellular phone companies.** Mystery shoppers let cellular phone companies know if their billing practices are accurate.

• **Find out how collection departments and agencies are treating people who don't pay their bills.** Companies want to know if those collecting money for them are effective without violating laws regulating collection practices.

• **Check out the performance of competitors.** Clients want to know how the service rendered by their competitors stacks up with their own.

• **Check security measures.** For example, a mystery shopper may sneak into a movie theater without buying a ticket to determine if the theater staff notices and how they react. A mystery shopper whose looks can pass for those of a juvenile might try to buy an alcoholic beverage drink or sneak into an R-rated movie theater.

Work as an Independent Contractor

You have two choices in considering a home-based mystery shopping service. You can work as an independent contractor with one or more of the 500 mystery shopping companies in the country in which case you earn about $7 to $10 to shop and prepare your reports. Most independent contractors do mystery shopping as sideline or part-time venture. Some even take their payment in products or services of the client—not bad if you're evaluating a cruiseline experience! And you can set your own hours and decide when you'll take on assignments. But, of course, the more willing you are to take assignments when they're needed, the more likely services are to contact you.

If this appeals to you, the best way to get listed in the database files of mystery shopping services is to look in the Yellow Pages, scour help-wanted sections, or contact stores where you'd like to shop and ask them for the name of the mystery shopping service they use. Shop'n Clek Inc., in Atlanta, for example, has 50,000 freelance shoppers in their national and international databases.

Each mystery shopping service has its own shopping and reporting guidelines and they will train you. In general, however, a professional mystery shopper needs be a good observer without being noticed and have a keen memory to later recall details. A shopper needs to look like anyone. His or her appearance and personality should not stand out or be memorable. They need to be good enough actors that they appear to be nothing more than ordinary customers so they can return to stores without being spotted as shoppers. Opportunities also exist for people with expertise in particular industries such as food, banking, and real estate, who can recognize theft, unsafe operations, and other activities particular to that industry.

Finally, if you want to be called with any regularity, you will need to be reliable. The service will need to be able to count on you to get into the field promptly and complete your evaluations accurately and on time.

Start Your Own Shopping Service

Alternatively, you can start your own mystery shopping company. Many companies work in various industries, but some specialize, focusing, for example, on tourism, real estate, or home building. One company works only with amusement parks, another only with restaurants.

To start your own mystery shopping service, you will need good selling skills to line up clients and the ability to recruit subcontractors and manage their activities. You will also be responsible for preparing final reports for your clients. You should have experience in budgeting and finance as you may be dispatching many shoppers to many locations for a variety of clients simultaneously and have to pay shoppers for their work before you get paid by your clients for an entire project.

Usually mystery shopping services negotiate fees for each project separately depending on how many stores there are to be shopped in a chain, how frequently an establishment is to be shopped, how long the shopping experience will take, what services will be provided and the type of report desired. Charges might run from $75 to $150 per establishment. Mike Bare who specializes in restaurants and hotels has shoppers who tape record the evening and transcribe the play-by-play experience. Joseph

Woskow, president of Mystery Shoppers Inc. in Houston, shows his clients a videotape record of shopping experiences. The package for such high tech visits can cost as much as $1,000.

BOOK

Get Paid to Shop: Opportunities in the Mystery Shopping Business, Judith G. Rappold, Business Resources Publications, 1999, ISBN: 0966758013.

Personal Historian

Perhaps it's the result of Baby Boomers hitting middle age. Or possibly our increasingly mobile society is leaving us with a yearning to reconnect with our roots. Whatever the motivation, growing numbers of people want to preserve their family histories. At least 74 million American have written a family history or created a family tree, *American Demographics* magazine reports.

Gradually, over the past half dozen years, we've become aware of a growing number of personal historians whose business is to help families, individuals, or organizations articulate their history in a written, video, or audio format or CD-ROM.

Kitty Axelson-Berry, founder and president of the Association of Personal Historians (APH), thinks that we're genetically tribal and that preserving our community history is part of what makes us human. "Immigrant generations are so anxious to get away from a difficult past," she points out, "that often they intentionally don't pass along the stories from the old times." The result is what she calls a widespread "cultural amnesia," or story-loss, that leaves new generations with the sense of rootlessness, alienation, and hunger for a knowledge of the past that so many people are experiencing at this time in our country.

For some personal historians such as Ellie Kahn, whose company is Living Legacies, their business has grown out of an interest in documentary film. Having complied nearly 80 histories in book, video, or audio format over the past ten years, Kahn has been a pioneer in this emerging field. Many of her clients are churches, synagogues, and other institutions that want to provide others with a glimpse of their organizational history. Others are individuals telling multi-generational sagas.

Other times, as is the case of videobiographer J. Bruce Long of Reel Life Stories, the business arises from a long-standing interest in folklore and personal stories. Usually hired by children wanting their parents' or grandparents' lives turned into a video heirloom, Long helps ordinary people tell their life stories.

Since the telling of family stories can be a emotionally charged and cathartic experience, it's natural that Sarah Ghitis of Decatur, Georgia, came into the field from a background in psychological counseling, teaching, and television. She teamed up with broadcast journalist and storyteller Audrey Galex to form Roots & Wings Life Stories. Over the past six years they've created more than 100 videos of family and organizational biographies and conducted dozens of Recording Your Roots workshops.

"Our business is about helping clients distinguish between nostalgia and reflection and to take up their responsibility to history," says Axelson-Berry of the APH. "About 50 percent of personal historians work in print," she reports. Twenty five percent conduct do-it-yourself workshops, and the remaining 25 percent are split between those who do personal or organization histories in audio, video, and CD-ROM.

Neat Niches

Personal Histories on CD-ROM. On the high-tech front, Peter Farquhar, whose company is TomboMedia, teams up with oral historians like Elisabeth Wright and produces personal family and organizational histories on CD-ROM. While the oral history remains the backbone of the production, with CD-ROM, Farquhar can digitize hundreds of family photos and home-movie clips and integrate them into the memoir.

Always interested in history and multimedia, Farquhar began combining his passions six years ago when doing his own mother's oral history became his pilot project. "It's become economical now to do all this at home on your desktop," he says.

A CD writer runs less $500. The entire system scanner, computer, video camera and writer for scanning and digitizing for archival purposes currently runs from $6,000 at the low end to $10,000 in the mid-range to $15,000 for a high-end system. Once the CD master has been made, it's then sent out to a CD replicator.

For an average CD oral history with approximately 200 pictures, a couple hours of audio and home movies and a variety of family documents, Farquhar charges about $23,000. This may sound like a lot, but he points out that's not any more than the average kitchen remodel. So, it's all a matter of what matters to a family. For the price of a new kitchen, they can have 100 or 200 CD's through which they can pass on the equivalent of boxes of family history in perpetuity.

Farquhar also teaches workshops for oral historians on taking their business high tech. You can visit his Web site at *http://members.aol.com/ Tombomedia/history.html* to take a peek at this new medium or contact him regarding upcoming workshops at (415) 346-5205.

Toby Young of Orange, California, recently started her business, TDY Life Stories, doing personal and family histories. She'd always wanted to be her own boss, and having been a legal secretary and an English teacher, she had originally thought she'd start a word-processing service, but nearly a year ago she decided to do oral histories instead. After reading and studying the field, she found she could get the business underway through networking and referrals from the Oral History Program at Cal State Fullerton.

Young interviews her clients using a prepared questionnaire. The interview, which she tapes, takes a couple of hours. She then transcribes the interview, edits the transcript using word processing and then the client edits the transcript. Using her laser printer, she prints out the final document, has it bound, and provides ten copies to her client. Usually she charges $500, which covers the entire process, although she does extra for more complex interviews or to add photographs.

She says of her new business, "I adore it. I'm in seventh heaven doing personal histories because I love people and I love to write. I'm very good at editing and I feel I'm really providing a service. Everybody enjoys telling their life story and I make a good listener. The family is delighted to have their loved one's life preserved."

Her only problem, she finds, is getting the word out. But as she does, many people tell her they wish they'd known about her services before their relatives died.

Fees for personal histories run from $500 for smaller-scale projects that involve only a couple of hours of interviewing to $35,000 for projects that involve 20 hours or more of interviewing or the incorporation of multiple media. This service is best marketed as an investment on par with other significant or once-in-a-lifetime purchases: buying a luxury car, adding a deck or patio to your home, having a wedding reception, or taking an exotic cruise.

Since personal histories are an investment in future generations, how long they will last is an important consideration in deciding which medium to work in and what to charge. According to the Council on Library and Information Resources in Washington, DC, acid-free or buffered paper lasts up to 500 years. Video and audio tapes last fewer than 20 years under ideal storage conditions, which mean running them at least once annually; CD-ROMs last for 10 years, but the hardware and software involved in using them becomes obsolete in 5 years.

Since people over the age of 85 are the fastest growing segment of the population, this field has a promising future, and with today's technology it can be provided to people anywhere. Distance is not a barrier any more. Axelson-Berry predicts, "Within the next 20 years, every family who can will document their family history before it's lost."

Related Field

Scrapbooking

An off-shoot of this field is the booming business of scrapbooking—the making of "memory books," vibrant collages of enhanced photographs done with state-of-the-art noncorrosive materials and designed to last a lifetime—or more. This trend has spawned a booming crafts industry of products, magazines, books, and classes. Wendy Elliot, for example, is an oral historian who has authored several books on how people can research and create their own family memoirs.

Lisa Bearnson edits *Creating Keepsakes* magazine, a bimonthly that covers everything from how to take better pictures to journaling and writing background notes about photos. Marielen Christensen of Spanish Fork, Utah, has a business called Keeping Memories Alive, selling all the materials you'd ever need to create your own family scrapbook.

A St. Cloud, Minnesota, company, Creative Memories, has built an army of independent home-based consultants selling scrapbooking products through in-home classes and workshops for people wishing to create their own memory albums. The company was founded in 1987 by Minnesota businesswoman Cheryl Lightle and Montana homemaker Rhonda Anderson. With only six consultants in 1987, they now have 36,000 consultants worldwide.

Consultants receive 30 percent commissions on all products right from the beginning as well as customer fees for classes, recruiting commissions, and special incentives. For more information, they are at 2815 Clearwater Rd., St. Cloud, MN 56301 (320) 251-7524. Web site: *www.creative-memories.com*

Here's Another Unique Twist

Architectural Historians. James Sazevich is a house historian. Instead of constructing family or personal histories, he records histories on historical buildings and family homes. Tim Gregory is referred to as a house history detective. He calls himself a building biographer. One of his clients wanted to know why his house had a large foyer and two front doors. Searching through archives, Gregory found that it all made sense since the original owner was a doctor who saw clients in his home.

Where to Turn for Information and Help

As you can see, there are many routes into this field from simply having an interest or background in personal history, to a background in writing, videography, photography, crafts and oral history. To learn more, you'll find oral history programs available through some colleges and universities. Also there's a growing wealth of information on oral history on the Web.

ASSOCIATIONS AND INSTITUTIONS

THE ASSOCIATION OF PERSONAL HISTORIANS (APH), founded by Kitty Axelson-Berry of Modern Memoirs at 34 Main Street #6, Amherst, MA 01002; (413) 253-2353. Web site: *www.personalhistorians.org*. APH also hosts the APH listserve. For a subscription contact gwings@vnet.net. They also offfer a membership directory and resource guide.

CALIFORNIA STATE UNIVERSITY AT FULLERTON ORAL HISTORY PROGRAM offers referrals and transcription services to oral historians and provides a brochure and other materials on how to set up oral history interviews. You can contact them at P.O. 34080, Fullerton, CA 92634-9480.

THE ORAL HISTORY ASSOCIATION, Box 97234, Baylor University, Waco, TX 76798, operates a listserve on the Internet through which you can communicate with oral historians. E-mail: oha-l@ukcc.uky.edu

ORAL HISTORIES FOR PROFIT by Audrey Galex is a set of collected notes and handouts from a presentation for the Oral History Association. It's available from Roots & Wings, 28402 Plantation Drive, Atlanta, GA 30324; (404) 816-6331.

BOOKS

Your Life as Story, Tristine Rainer. Tarcher/Putnam, 1997. ISBN: 0874778611.

The New Diary, Tristine Rainer. Tarcher/Putnam, 1978. ISBN: 0874770610.

The Healing Art of Storytelling, A Sacred Journey of Personal Discovery, Richard Stone, Hyperion Press, 1996. ISBN: 0786881070.

For All Time, A Complete Guide to Writing Your Family History, Charley Kempthorne. Boynton/Cook Publishers, 1996. ISBN: 086709381. A variety of other valuable books about this field are listed on the AHA Web site: *www.personalhistorians.org*

SOFTWARE

Software is also available for creating personal histories. There's *Echo Lake,* by Delrina, and *Family Tree Maker,* from Banner Blue Software, as well as photo-editing software such as Adobe's PhotoDeluxe, Canon's *PhotoOrg,* and Corel's *PhotoHouse.*

 # Plant Caregiver

If you love plants and flowers and feel you have an affinity for making them prosper and grow, becoming a plant caregiver might be the career for you. Plant caregivers do a wide range of tasks for residential and commercial clients. They water and fertilize plants on a weekly basis, weed and prune as needed, design and lay out plant arrangements, diagnose diseases and care for sick plants, and perform many other tasks to ensure that a client's plant environment is healthy and colorful.

Getting into this business requires a love of plants and knowledge of how they thrive. You'll need to have familiarity with many kinds of indoor plants so that you can recommend and select arrangements for your clients, varying the plant colors and textures to create a harmonious, pleasing environment.

Plant Parenthood in southern California is an example of a successful venture in this field. The company began when its owner, Jeanne Jones, who had a background in botany, realized that taking care of plants was an appealing way for her to make a living. Her first contract originated from friends who owned a company located in an office building, and they arranged for her to come in and care for the plants in several offices. Jeanne then expanded her business using ads in the Yellow Pages, but now word of mouth and referrals mostly drive the growth of her business. Jeanne also has a few affiliations with nurseries, which recommend her to customers who ask the nursery if they know anyone who can help take care of their plants. Jeanne's clients include residential and commercial facilities. Although Jeanne does not do this, other avenues to get business include teaming up with architects, interior designers, indoor environmental testers, and even maintenance and cleaning services.

To get started, begin with customizing and equipping your van. It will serve as your mobile workshop. You should have ample shelving and areas for your toolboxes and a hand cart. Have your company name, logo, and phone number painted on the rear door of your van, so it can serve as a tasteful moving billboard. Select a memorable name and phone number. Selecting a uniform for you and any staff you will have is also advised.

Other ways to get business include having a Yellow Pages listing, sending out brochures, visiting professional and retail offices personally to introduce yourself and your service, networking, and of course, word of mouth from satisfied customers.

Plant caregivers charge between $15 to $25 per hour, although the best way to charge is to get a retainer contract for several months at a time based on weekly visits. Jeanne goes into a new client's location to assess the needs and bases her rate on how many hours she feels she needs to spend there. She agrees that if you have three to four large clients per day at an average of $75 per visit, you can easily earn $225 to $300 a day. Of course, one advantage of the business is that you can work as many days as you like. Income potential averages from $30,000 to $90,000 annually.

Plant-caregiving services thrive best in warmer areas where people tend to have plants blooming year-round, but the business can work well in any locale. It also helps to focus your clientele in one area to reduce the amount of time you spend driving from customer to customer. The one problem with the business is that taking care of plants is viewed as a luxury, so some clients cancel their contracts in a recessionary climate or if their own business can't afford to keep you.

Where to Turn for Information and Help

BOOKS

Plant Care, The Best of Fine Gardening, Gardening Magazine Fine, 1994. ISBN: 1561580864.

The Plant Care Manual: The Essential Guide to Caring for and Rejuvenating over 300 Garden Plants, Stefan T. Buczaci, Crown Publishers, 1993. ISBN: 0517592835.

Rodale's No-Fail Flower Garden: How to Plan, Plant and Grow a Beautiful, Easy-Care Garden. Joan Benjamin & Barbara Ellis, Rodale Press, 1997. ISBN: 0875969542.

Water Plants: An Illustrated Guide to Varieties—A Step-by-Step Handbook for Cultivation and Care, Andrew Mikolajski & Peter McHoy. The New Plant Library, Westminister, MD: Lorenz Books, 1997. ISBN: 1859673902.

The Guide to the Plant Health Care Management System, M.A. Smith, International Society of Arboriculture, 1995, ISBN: 1881956091.

 Proposal and Grant Writer

There are literally thousands of "requests for proposals" (RFPs) put out each year by various governmental agencies. The federal government, state governments, cities, counties, and special districts in every field of endeavor request proposals for everything from developing or building military equipment, to installing high-technology equipment in offices here and overseas or furnishing desks and chairs in a government office building. In fact, just about any company that wants to do business with the government (at the federal, state, and city level) must write a lengthy, detailed bid or proposal to get the contract. These proposals often must be highly technical, laying out the exact method of accomplishing the goal, with schematics, timetables, management methods, budgets, and company profiles.

The problem with this process of RFPs is that many companies that could do a very good job of providing whatever service is needed don't have the skill to write proposals that would give them a chance to do the work. Thus there is a large market for specialized technical writers and proposal writers who can help firms prepare and submit high-quality documents that will win bids. Such writing professionals know the rules and regulations governing the creation and formatting of formal proposals and they can produce them much more quickly, intelligently, and knowledgeably than the company wanting to make the bid. In some cases, the proposal writers will learn about the RFPs before the companies do, and so they can also bring prospective business to a company by notifying them of the release of the bid request.

Sometimes proposal writers are generalists with a broad knowledge of diverse fields, but many are specialists in a single area with a background in agriculture, communications, engineering, business, medicine, or another advanced industry. Some writers have enough specific experience in a field that they even advise their clients on how to improve upon the original idea or product that is the subject of the proposal.

Nevertheless, as Steve Wilson, a proposal writer in Lansing, Michigan, says, "Any writer with good skills can do this work, whatever your background. Like lawyers, it doesn't matter who your client is; if you can write logically and can understand the technology enough to explain it, you can do it."

Other than their writing ability and specific experience in a field, proposal and grant writers must also have excellent communication and presentation skills because they are frequently interacting with high-level managers and executives of companies. They must also be willing to travel (a nice perk, according to Wilson), because some proposals require the writer to go on location to view the site or equipment. Wilson has been to Kuwait and Southeast Asia several times.

Proposal writers should also be well versed in using spreadsheet, database, and desktop-publishing software, because their job often includes producing the final documents along with financial projections, budgets, bidding information, graphs, charts, and tables, all of which must be handsomely laid out and printed. Even if they don't do the actual desktop publishing, they must know how to get the documents published and printed.

The best way to get business in this field is to be proactive. Wilson reads the *Commerce Business Daily* almost every day, searching for proposals that he has an interest in. When he sees a proposal he might develop, he does some preliminary research and calls a few companies that might be interested in bidding on it. In this way, he helps companies become aware of RFPs and is, therefore, more likely to get the work. Other than such research, nearly all proposal writers agree that word of mouth is the next-best marketing method, if you have a successful track record. Some writers will also do advertising or direct mail to companies that might be interested in government or foundation funding.

Making a living as a proposal and grant writer may require a few years of experience as you learn the ropes and develop contacts. Some proposals take one or two days to write, but many can take months to research and create. A successful writer in a specialty area such as energy or business can charge from $2,000 to $10,000 per proposal, depending on length, and may have annual earnings from $50,000 to $150,000.

Other jobs for proposal writers include writing grant proposals for the thousands of grants available each year from over 35,000 private foundations and corporations that provide money to individuals and nonprofit associations for myriad civic, educational, and social-welfare programs. Writers may also work on proposals for companies seeking seed money from the Small Business Administration through their Innovative Research (SBIR) program.

Once a company has gotten a contract, another service a grant writer can offer is to assist them with federal contract compliance. Smaller companies are not staffed to meet the onerous paperwork requirements of holding a government contract, particularly a federal contract. From this need has emerged a cadre of consultants who provide this service on a contractual basis. To do this requires significant experience in administering federal contracts.

Where to Turn for Information and Help

Catalogue of Federal Domestic Assistance, available in print form from the Government Printing Office but free if you retrieve it online from the Federal Assistance Program Retrieval System. Web site: *www.gsa.gov/fdac/*

Commerce Business Daily, lists all federal RFPs; it's available in libraries and online. Web site: *http://cbdnet.access.gpo.gov*

Government Assistance Almanac, by J. Robert Dumouchel, Omnigraphics, Inc., is a better-indexed version of the Catalogue of Federal Domestic Assistance. Annual. ISBN: 0780803698.

Lesko's Info-Power II, Matthew Lesko, Visible Ink Press, 1996, ISBN: 0787608807.

H. SILVER AND ASSOCIATES, 1875 Century Park East, Suite 1030, Los Angeles, CA 90067; (310) 785-0518. Offers seminars and videos on propsal writing. Web site: *www.hsilver.com*

THE GRANTSMANSHIP CENTER, PO Box 17220, Los Angeles, CA 90017; (213) 482-9860. Web site: *www.tgci.com*

You also will need copies of the *U.S. Government Style Manual* and *The Chicago Manual of Style.*

Red Tape Expediter/ Complaint Service

You're waiting for a variance approval from city hall and no one will return your call. Your credit report is wrong and you don't know what to do. The airline just lost your luggage—again.

If you're seething from all too familiar complaints like these, Complain to Us of Somerville, Massachusetts, will take your complaint, make phone calls, and write the letters to help get your problem solved. They're among the nation's growing number of complaint services.

Life, it seems, is growing more complex, business and government more impersonal and bureaucratic. Our days are packed to the brim and overflowing. Then along comes a complication we just don't have the time or energy to untangle. Where do we turn? Increasingly, people can turn to professional red tape expediters and complaint services to help handle life's complexities be they botched bills, wrecked credit, defective products, or difficult bureaucrats.

David Kalp stumbled into this brand-new field when spending cutbacks eliminated his job with the state of California. Since government jobs were tight at the time, he wasn't sure at first what he'd do. Then he had an idea. He knew the kind of red tape a business faces in walking all types of development projects through state government departments for needed approvals. But he knew that bureaucracy like the palm of his hand. Thus his Red Tape Expediter Service was born.

Sandy Rattigan, cofounder of Complain to Us with her husband Gary, learned the ropes of handling grievances as a billing and collections manager for a hospital. After many years on the job, she decided she wanted to be the good guy for a change. Since 1997, the Rattigans have been dealing with complaints ranging from getting a refund on a defective carpet, to resolving a dispute with a bank, and arranging for reimbursement of medical costs for a man who was injured on a travel adventure

Complain to Us has griped for more than 250 clients at car makers, airlines, insurance companies, credit agencies, department stores, and hospitals, and they boast a 65 percent success rate! Not bad when you consider that by the time most of their customers call, they've already tried just about everything.

While the Rattigans spend most of their time writing letters, sending e-mail, and working the phones, Kalp often hand-carries clients' applications and documentation through government channels.

Neat Niches

There are many neat niches in this field. While the Rattigans handle mainly consumer complaints, and Kalp handles the intricacies of government agencies, you may be able to specialize in a field related to your background and experience. Here are two niches others have found.

Tax Defender

Richard Schonfeld specializes in handling tax complaints. He has dedicated his life to rescuing people from problems with the IRS. He knows how to do it because he began his career working for them. "I was young and inexperienced," he remembers, "but I didn't like being the bad guy and felt the IRS was often unfair. They placed liens on houses, they garnished wages. Lives were being ruined, and I couldn't be part of that."

Years after leaving the IRS, he was laid off from the aerospace industry where he had worked as a senior executive, so he took a few years off to do some soul-searching. "I was fed up with corporate accounting. I wanted to do something meaningful."

The result was a decision to dedicate his practice to the underdog, protecting the average guy who was being hounded by the IRS. "When people come to me they're often paralyzed with fear. Some have considered suicide, or their marriages are breaking up. What I do brings a sense of calm to their lives," Schonfeld states. And when it comes to defending his clients against the IRS, Schonfeld won't take no for an answer. "I make it my business to interpret for the IRS, and my clients almost always end up winning."

Investment Fraud Arbitrator

Working as a compliance and corporate officer for brokerage firms, Paul Young saw firsthand the daily conflicts played out between the duty of security investment brokers to do what's right for their clients versus their desire to make a higher commission. Too often, he says, the latter wins out. Hence he left his job to take on a mission.

He created Securities Arbitration Group, a company that represents "burned" investors. Young helps people recover money they've lost due to fraud and abuse perpetrated by licensed stockbrokers and firms. And he does so with a missionary zeal, eagerly carrying his message to radio and television and operating a Securities Fraud Hotline as a clearinghouse for information on investment fraud.

"I represent the victimized individual investor in binding arbitration," he says. "And the cases are pathetic. One client lost a $31,000 inheritance. Another lost a $50,000 investment he was making for his children's education. Still another lost his life savings of $100,000 and was living on Social Security." But Young asserts, "I recover these losses. I have an 85 percent victory rate!"

Whatever red tape niche you choose, of course, you've got to know, or learn, the ins and outs of handling the complexities of the kinds of complaints you choose to handle. But what else do you need? "Patience," for one thing, say the Rattigans. And you've got to be a superb communicator. You need tact and nerves of steel. You can't get angry. No shouting, no swearing, no threats. But you must also have bull-dogged persistence. "Most companies try to wear you down, so you'll just go away. They make you jump through the hoops So you've got to keep your cool no matter what."

Fees in this field depend on the financial stakes for those you serve. If you're walking environmental-impact statements through state and local governments, you can charge in the thousands. In dealing with individual consumer complaints, however, the Rattigans charge $50 per hour and find that most complaints take an hour or two. If the case involves a refund or reimbursement, they charge a 30 percent commission instead of an hourly fee.

Referral Service

Have you ever had something break and not known whom to call to fix it? Sure, the Yellow Pages have listings, but how can you know who's good and who's a rip-off? Most city people don't know, and who has time to do research? That's where a referral service can help. You've probably seen ads on television for services offering referrals to doctors or dentists. This idea can be applied to almost any area of need and interest: appliance repair, art events, auto repair, baby-sitters, caterers, child care, contractors and tradespeople, hairdressers, house sitters, landlords, musicians, nannies, party locations, pet sitters, plumbers, printers, real estate agents, restaurants, roommates, shopping information, special events, therapists, travel and tourist information, tutors, wedding services, even friendship or a mate.

Referral services may be set up to receive their income in one of several ways. Probably the most common is for the service to charge the business or professional a fee, with the service free to the consumers. The business might pay the fee monthly or annually, or pay a commission on each referral. Services that offer roommate matching, friendship matching, matchmaking or house/pet/baby-sitting often charge both parties equally. Matchmaker Janis Spindel finds dates for busy Wall Street professionals. She charges her male clients $10,000 for a dozen dates over the year. Female clients pay $5,000 (they don't need as much help, she claims). Her company, Serious Matchmaking, has a track record that lives up to its name and its fees: 294 monogamous relationships and 70 marriages over the six years since she started her service.

An online referral service is another option, with users paying on a per-use basis or buying an annual subscription good for a certain amount of research time. Some referral service owners make close to $100,000 per year, but don't expect that to come quickly. You may make only $3,000 or $4,000 the first year.

The key to a successful referral service is the quality of the research you do in order to screen the businesses and professionals you send people to. Your credibility depends on people being able to trust the accuracy or your information and the reliability of those to whom you refer them. Therefore, you must gather enough information so that either you can refer with confidence or the consumer can make an informed decision.

Teddi Kessie, owner of The End Result, a referral service specializing in the building trades in Sherman Oaks, California, personally interviews each tradesperson and checks references, licensing, bonding, and insurance. She advises caution and reliance on personal judgment and intuition. Some referral services specializing in professional services, such as dentistry or therapy, use a review board to approve professionals to be served. You'll also need to drop vendors from your referral list who don't meet your standards or about whom you get complaints that are not solved to the customer's satisfaction.

All you need to start a referral service is a business telephone line and well-organized information. It's basically a database service that requires a computer and database software that allows vendors to be listed by the criteria the consumer requests. (Or you can run the business manually if you prefer, but using a computer is far easier.) You'll also need business cards and brochures or flyers suited to the type of vendor you specialize in making referrals to.

For example, let's suppose you are starting a home-repair referral service. Leave flyers with hardware stores and post them on grocery-store bulletin boards, on church bulletin boards, on car windshields, and in mall or boutique parking lots. If you can afford to do so, advertise on the radio and television (it can be cheaper than you think!), in a *Pennysaver*-type newspaper, and/or in the local newspaper. Such advertising will not only attract calls but also make it easier to sell your services to vendors, because they see you making an investment to reach people who want to use them. You can also write articles for local publications on choosing the right repair person.

Kessie considers herself a combination personal counselor and go-between when problems arise. She adds value to her service by advising homeowners what to expect from various types of repair and remodeling projects. "When you put in a new kitchen floor, it will be higher than the old one; your refrigerator may not fit where it used to, and you won't be able to remove your dishwasher without cutting up the floor." These kinds of tips will save clients unforeseen hassles and keep them coming back to you. On occasion, Kessie has also mediated between tradesperson and homeowner when a dispute arose, and once or twice she's covered the (modest) cost of the repair herself when she was unable to effect an agreement.

Where to Turn for Information and Help

FRANCHISES

HOMEWATCH, 2865 South Colorado Boulevard, Suite 203, Denver, CO 80222; (303) 758-7290.

NATIONAL TENANT NETWORK, Box 1664, Lake Grove, OR 97035; (800) 228-0989. This firm offers computerized tenant-screening services for landlords.

PUBLICATIONS

How to Make a Success Out of a Referral Service, Teddi Kessie, 13061 Hartsook Street, Sherman Oaks, CA 91423. $49.95, plus $5 shipping and handling. Write for brochure.

How to Make Money by Turning Away Customers: An Information Package on Running a Successful [computer and office-support] Referral Service, 6407 Irwin Court, Oakland, CA 94609; (510) 655-4296. $75.

The Complete Guide to Owning and Operating a Successful Homeowner Referral Network, Debra M. Cohen. 1539 Hewlett Avenue, Hewlett, NY 11557; (516) 374-8504. Web site: *www.homeownersreferral.com*

Relocation Expert

About 16 percent of Americans relocate every year. Of course, many of these moves are employment related; others are by choice. The relocation expert assist companies who are transferring employees to new locations or others wanting to relocate. According to the Employee Relocation Council (ERC), in a tight labor market, companies are increasingly using relocation programs as recruitment tools. An ERC poll shows that 15 percent of companies experience major difficulties in recruiting new hires in their industry and an additional 49 percent have moderate difficulty attracting new employees to specific industries.

As a result, about 80 percent of companies are using relocation assistance as a recruiting tool. Forty-three percent have increased their relocation assistance in an effort to help recruitment. ERC statistics show that companies relocate an average of 225 current and 74 new hires annually at a cost of from $45,373 per transferees who are homeowners to $9,280 for new hires who are renters. ERC membership alone includes over 12,000 individuals and companies specializing in some form of relocation assistance.

In the past, relocation experts concentrated almost solely on house hunting for transferees. But changing economics and social trends have expanded their roles considerably. More women in the workforce means spouses must find jobs when their mates are transferred. Today's increased emphasis on the family means the concerns of children, especially teenagers, who don't want to move, must be addressed. Families caring for elderly relatives also have special needs when taking jobs in a new location. The opening of international markets means more people are relocating in foreign countries.

Therefore, the relocation expert today must maintain a network of referral sources for everything from mortgage bankers to home inspectors, school counselors to doctors and dentists, eldercare providers to pet sitters. In fact, ERC members now represent over 80 specialties. There are consultants who help companies develop relocation programs. There are personal counselors who assist employees manage and coordinate their relocation. There are those who specialize in auto and motor vehicle transportation, household-goods transportation, and pet transportation. There are personal counselors who help employees and their family members with relocation decisions, electronic home marketing services, international relocations, spousal career counseling and job search services, cross-cultural training for those moving to foreign countries, expatriate administration, financial services, and real-estate management.

Whether assisting an entire company to relocate or working with specific individuals being transferred, the relocation expert must have a wealth of local knowledge, know the pros and cons of a community from climate to Internet access and housing prices. They must know the real-estate market and understand finances. They must be willing to work evenings, weekends, and holidays and enjoy handling details, researching options, and problem solving. They must be caring individuals with immense patience and good communication skills.

Relocation experts can market directly to work with their own corporate or individual clients or, as many do, they can work with clients by affiliating with and/or obtaining referrals through local real-estate companies.

Neat Niches

While by far the majority of relocation experts work with corporations transferring employees, there are a growing number of individuals like Bill Seavey whose Greener Pastures Institute outside San Luis Obispo, California, specializes in pre-move counseling for individuals who want to move to remote rural locations. Seavey also has a newsletter, *Greener Pastures,* and has authored the book *Mover to Small Town America.*

Marilyn and Tom Ross, authors of the book *Country Bound,* began offering similar services after trading an office suite in southern California for a remote 320-acre horse ranch in the Rocky Mountains. Ruth Holcomb of Santa Fe, New Mexico, has created her own unique niche. She operates the Network for Living Abroad and helps individuals who want to move to foreign countries.

If this business appeals to you, but you'd like to do something a little different, here's a possible up and coming new niche to explore. Forty-five percent of baby boomers believe they will move into another home once they retire, and nearly half of the potential movers think that home will be in another state. Florida and North Carolina are the top intended destinations.

Where to Turn for Information and Help

ORGANIZATIONS

EMPLOYEE RELOCATION COUNCIL (ERC), 1720 N St. N.W., Washington DC 20036; (202) 857-0857. Web site: *www.erc.org.* They offer publi cations, special reports, and industry updates. A certified relocation professional program encourages members working in specific aspects of employee relocation to gain extensive and useful knowledge of all areas of employee relocation. A major purpose of this program is the achievement of a common and universal understanding of the entire employee relocation field and to recognize those professionals mastering this body of knowledge.

REGIONAL RELOCATION GROUPS. The ERC is also affiliated with an independent network of relocation expert groups across the country. For a complete list of these groups, check the ERC Web site. For information on how to start a group in your area contact the ERC by phone.

COLDWELL BANKER has a relocation expert training program. Graduates receive a Certified Residential Relocation Certificate. To locate the branch nearest, you visit their Web site at *www.coldwellbanker.com*

Repair Services

Despite the fact that America is said to be a disposable society, most of us prefer to hold on to what we have if we can keep it working long enough. We don't want to dispose of a vacuum cleaner that falters just after the warranty expires. We don't want to take the riding lawn mower to the dump just because the engine stops. We don't want to throw out our favorite chair just because it has a rip in the upholstery. But we simply don't know how, nor do we usually have the time, to fix things that break down, rip, or tear. That's why there are literally dozens of business possibilities for profitable repair services.

Repair services run the gamut from the jack-of-all-trades handyman who does small home repairs and remodeling to specialists who repair everything from small engines and screens to vinyl seat covers and fine china. There are specialized repair services for furniture, woodwork, windshields, telephones, clocks, watches, home appliances, and electrical items such as vacuum cleaners and VCRs. (See the entry on "Computer Repair and Maintenance" for this related specialization.) One man who called in to a radio show on which we were appearing in Chicago told us he was making $60,000 a year gluing things that are broken. He'd begun his business in the garage ten years earlier charging only $3 an item. Now he charges $75 an hour and specializes in serving antique dealers and collectors.

A repair business can be started on a full-time or part-time basis. To get started, you might focus, for example, on repairing old watches and clocks, by contacting antique shops and their customers. Or the vinyl-repair service might approach sports facilities, restaurants, hospitals, offices, used-car dealerships, hotels, government agencies, movie theaters, home and apartment owners or real estate agencies about mending rips, tears, and color damage in such things as dinette seats, auto seats, waiting-room seating, theater or auditorium seats.

Specialized equipment is needed for many types of services, but other than the cost of the necessary equipment, the start-up costs for a repair business are modest: business cards, well-done flyers or simple brochures stating what you do, and multipart forms for quotes or proposals and invoicing. Rates vary greatly, ranging from $15 to $125 per hour, depending on what you repair and your location. You can also increase your income by stocking replacement parts, which you buy wholesale from suppliers, and charging a markup.

Consider what you have a knack for repairing and, if necessary, what training you'll need and where that's available through community colleges, trade schools, home-study courses. If you're concentrating on small jobs, which is what clients usually have the most difficulty finding people to do, keep your travel area as localized as possible to reduce the amount of nonbillable time you spend driving.

Repair work can come in through either the front door or the back door. Front door repairs are those from customers who contact you. This work may be done on the customers' premises or on your premises. Back door repairs refer to work that's brought into a retailer's repair shop or establishment; which the retailer then subcontracts out to an outside repair person who does the work on their own premises.

To get front-door work, you can do any of the following:

- Distribute well-done flyers or simple brochures in your neighborhood. If what you repair is also used in offices (e.g., furniture, leather, vinyl, and so forth), leave brochures in office buildings, schools, and businesses.

- Post flyers with tear-off phone numbers at bus stops and on kiosks and bulletin boards.

- Run classified and small display ads in neighborhood publications and local business journals, which reach potential customers at a reasonable cost.

- Advertise in the Yellow Pages.

Directly contacting retail shops who might need to contract work is usually the best sources of getting back-door work, although networking, direct mail, and a Yellow Page listing can also be worthwhile to create visibility for your business.

If you plan to do work on your premises, be sure to check your zoning laws regarding what type of work can be done from a home in your neighborhood. Noisy equipment and frequent customer visits are excluded in many communities. Also check restrictions about signage if you're intending to hang out a sign in front of your home. Many communities do not allow commercial signs in residential areas.

Once you have clients, the best marketing method is word of mouth. One handyman we know in Los Angeles is able to do all his work within a five-mile-square area because word of mouth from satisfied customers generates plenty of new clients on a regular basis.

Where to Turn for Information and Help

SMALL ENGINES

MCGRAW-HILL'S NRI SCHOOLS, 4401 Connecticut Avenue, N.W., Washington, DC 20008. Offers a course in small-engine repair that includes a small engine and generator.

FURNITURE

THE FURNITURE MEDIC, 860 Ridge Lake Blvd. Memphis, TN 38120; (901) 820-8600; (800) 877-9933. Offers an on-site furniture restoration and repair service that can be done from home.

UPHOLSTERY

THE FOLEY-BELSHAW INSTITUTE, 6301 Esplanade, Redondo Beach, CA 95926. Publishes a book that teaches the art of upholstery.

VINYL

VINYLMAN, 9561 Imperial Highway, Downey, CA 90242; (562) 401-3305. Provides materials to set up a vinyl-repair inventory.

DR. VINYL & ASSOCIATES, 9501 East 350 Highway, Raytown, MO 64133; (800) 531-6600. A vinyl and leather repair and dyeing franchise.

WINDSHIELDS

GLASWELD, P.O. Box 5755, Bend, OR 97708; (800) 321-2597. Offers start-up kits in a range of prices.

HOME REPAIRS

HOUSE DOCTORS HANDYMAN SERVICE, 6355 East Kemper Road, Suite 250, Cincinnati, OH 45241; (800) 319-3359. Performs the kind of home repairs that appear on a "honey do" list that can be done in a day or less.

BOOKS

How to Start and Manage a Farm Equipment Repair Service Business, Lewis & Renn Associates; 1996. ISBN: 1887005269.

Opportunities in Installation and Repair Careers, Mark Rowh, Vgm Career Horizons, 1994. ISBN: 0844241369.

How to Start Your Own Appliance Repair Business from Home Without Capital or Experience: For Major Appliances, Longhurst Rey D., Repair Master, 1988. ISBN: 1563021102.

Restoration Services

Consumers no longer simply cover stained hardwood floors with linoleum. They want their floors sanded, stained, and finished to bring out the old luster, sometimes with modern protections. They don't throw out old rugs and carpets; they want them repaired and restored. They prefer the old enameled iron or porcelain plumbing fixtures to the new plastic variety, and they want someone to refurbish the old finishes. They don't take the old dining table to the dump; they want it carefully hand stripped, and they want the damage repaired and the wood and carvings restored to their original beauty. They sometimes even want to have the furniture stripped and then do the rest themselves. They don't want to rip out and replace old tile work. They want to see cracks and glazing repaired and refinished. They don't tear down old houses; they want to match the detailing that remains and restore old homes to their original appearance.

Both appreciation for what's old and the cost of what's new or too expensive to maintain are making restoring architectural features, plumbing fixtures, floors, and antiques into lucrative businesses that can be started on the side and built into full-time businesses. Each specialty provides a natural market for the skilled craftsperson or someone wishing to develop a skill. Restoration services are also needed after natural disasters such as floods and earthquakes, as well as after fires. For instance, after the Los Angeles earthquake, many people wanted to have their furniture, tile, and rugs repaired.

In addition to working with residential clients, you can also work with commercial ones, such as antique shops and interior designers. A business or an apartment or hotel owner can save thousands of dollars by restoring floors, bathrooms, tile, or even quantities of damaged furniture rather than replacing them. While serving commercial clients is more costly, it is also more profitable, especially when your services are paid by your client's insurance company. Insurance companies often prefer paying for restoration because usually it doesn't cost as much as replacement.

Historical restoration of homes, churches, and boats is an interesting niche, as is the restoring of marble, slate, resilient and wood floors. Restoring these expensive surfaces is a growth area in this field because they require maintenance. Thus you can charge more. And, after all, every building has a floor and everything in the air lands on it. They all take a beating.

Start-up costs for a restoration business depend entirely on the particular type of restoration service you wish to perform. Your costs can range from just a few hundred dollars to purchase supplies (strippers, rags, steel wool, sandpaper, and so on) if you set yourself up in business or you can spend as much as $17,500 to buy one of the many restoration franchises in bathroom and kitchen tile refinishing, carpets, or fixtures. In fact, there are a number of franchises that provide training, tools, and materials for a turnkey business. A few are listed below, but it is wise to read through several business magazines and identify as many franchises as you can, call them to investigate their fees, royalties (if any), and training, and make your decision based on what is best for you financially.

Fees usually involve getting a deposit from the customer to cover parts and materials with the balance due upon completion or delivery of the work. Like many repair businesses, it's important to provide the customer with a written estimate of costs and time involved and to get a signed contract before beginning the work so both you and the customer know precisely what work will be done and for what price.

Also, because people can be sensitive to smells and are more aware than ever of chemical sensitivities, having business liability insurance is a necessity. Because there are risks and liabilities involved in using restoration materials, you need to know about the nature and properties of the products you're using. Fortunately, information and education is widely available. As in the cleaning business, of which restoration is considered to be a part, knowing about the sensitivities to what's being added to the environment while you work is part of what separates the professional from the fly-by-night company. As Bill Griffin of Cleaning Consultant Services, Inc., which publishes *Cleaning Business Magazine*, says, "Anybody can do it, but doing it right is another story."

In addition to technical expertise, running a restoration service also requires an understanding of marketing and management. You can reach residential customers through Yellow Pages ads; flyers posted on bulletin boards and kiosks, and in antique shops, hardware stores, and lumber yards; radio advertising; and tear-off pads. Reaching commercial clients is far easier, though. You can contact them with letters, brochures, and personal selling. Sometimes a single commercial client can become an ongoing source of business, keeping you busy part of each week.

In either case, in addition to having a Yellow Pages ad, you will want to get as much publicity about your service as possible. Publicity will give you credibility with both consumers and businesses. Your publicity campaign might involve writing articles on restoration for local newspapers or regional magazines or giving seminars and speeches. Topics might include how to decide if something is worth restoring, the various types of restoration methods available (including the pros and cons of each), how to find a qualified contractor or the ways to prolong the life of wood, tile, enamel, floors, or whatever your specialty might be.

To attract publicity, you can also send out news releases that focus on a particularly unusual item or location that you've restored to the home-improvement or antiques editor of your local newspaper. Having a local twist to the story helps. And, of course, so do pictures. Always take before and after shots or videos of your work. Having certification or special training can also give your promotional activities greater impact.

Although restoration work may be physically demanding, the restoration business is not just for men. Successful bath and kitchen refinishing businesses are owned by women who excel at networking and aggressively market their knowledge and skill. And there's no shortage of customers in sight. There are over 100 million homes and 14 million businesses in this country. It is likely that the older ones need work done on them and the newer ones aren't made of lasting quality. Cleaning, maintenance, and restoration become critical. The restoration business can not only be profitable but also can provide you the enjoyment of seeing your labor help create a nice-looking, clean, and completely refurbished room or piece of furniture.

Where to Turn for Information and Help

ASSOCIATIONS

Association of Specialists in Cleaning and Restoration (ASCR), 8229 Cloverleaf Dr., Suite 460, Millersville, MD 21108; (410) 729-9900. Web site: *www.ascr.org*

TILE, BATH, AND KITCHEN REFINISHING

Bathcrest, 2425 South Progress Drive, Salt Lake City, UT 84119; (800) 826-6790.

PERMA-GLAZE, 1638 South Research Loop Road, #160, Tucson, AZ 85710; (800) 332-7397.

WORLDWIDE REFINISHING SYSTEMS, 500 Lake Air Drive, Waco, TX 76710; (903) 892-3117.

FIXTURES

WORLDWIDE REFINISHING SYSTEMS, 500 Lake Air Drive, Waco, TX 76710; (903) 892-3117.

CARPETS

INSTITUTE OF INSPECTION, CLEANING AND RESTORATION CERTIFICATION (IICRC), 2715 E. Mill Plain Blvd., Vancouver, WA 98661; (360) 693-5675. Offers nine categories of certification and approved classes. Organization has certified 14,000 carpet cleaners. Web site: *www.iirc.org*

LANGENWALTER CARPET DYE CONCEPT, 1111 South Richfield Rd., Placentia, CA 92670; (800) 422-4370.

BOOKS AND MAGAZINES

Cleaning Consultant Services, Inc., publishes *Cleaning Business Magazine* and many books on topics related to cleaning and restoration such as *Oriental Rug Repair, Formica Restoration and Repair, Technical Guide to Water Restoration Damage, Fire Restoration and Insurance Work, Wood Furniture Touch-Up, Tile and Grout Repair* (a book and video combination), *Know-How* (which covers minor carpentry, electrical and plumbing), *Comprehensive Deodorization*, and *Restorative Drying*, among many others. For a catalog, contact them at 3693 East Marginal Way South, Seattle, WA 98134; (206) 682-9748. Web site: *www.cleaningconsultants.com*

 ## Reunion Planner

The new millenium will occasion lots of events that are the stock in trade for reunion planners who can be thought of as combination party planners and private investigators. Reunions provide the basis for an uplifting kind of service business. "People like to return to their age of innocence," says reunion planner Sunny McGinnis. This perhaps explains why high school reunions account for 99 percent of professionally planned reunions.

In the past, reunions were arranged by women who had more time than today's working women, but today reunion committees turn to professionals. What primarily differentiates reunion planners from professional party or event planners is their ability to locate long-lost class members. The tasks of a reunion planner involve searching for missing class members, mailing invitations, receiving reservations, hiring the band or disc jockey, arranging for food and the photographers, producing name tags with yearbook pictures on them, and otherwise coordinating and staffing all aspects of the actual reunion. Unlike other event planners, reunion planners typically take on financial responsibility for the event.

The focus of the reunion party is the people, not the event. It is a highly specialized undertaking, and even the criteria for selecting locations, food, and decorations are different from those associated with other kinds of parties. Still a relatively new field, there are believed to be fewer than a hundred reunion planners in the country as of this edition.

Locating classmates primarily involves searching computer databases of telephone directories, birth and marriage records, voter registration lists, credit report headers, and Department of Motor Vehicles records in the few states that still allow this. This is supplemented with phone calls to friends, neighbors, associates, college record keepers, alumni associations, and previous employers. The size of this research task is one of the reasons reunion planners start their work a year or more in advance of a reunion.

The biggest change in this business since its beginnings in the 70's is the shift in emphasis from telephoning to database searching. As a result, reunion planners do not need employees to spend long hours on the phone and are able to do this work at home themselves. But the work is not entirely home-based because reunion planners don't meet with their clients (the reunion-planning committees) at home; ordinarily, they meet at the hotel or other facility where the event is going to take place.

Judy and Shell Norris, founders of the National Association of Reunion Managers and who were among the first reunion planners, find this work to be seasonal. The season runs from April through Thanksgiving. Geography influences when people hold their reunions. In the Northeast, 80 percent of the reunions take place on Thanksgiving weekends and are one-night events. In Florida and other areas with beaches, reunions take place in the summer and are multi-day happenings.

A particularly desirable kind of reunion are those for people who as children attended American schools in various countries. For the most part, their parents were career military personnel. These reunions are desirable because they last over multiple days and planners can earn a commission on hotel-room bookings since virtually everyone attending travels to get to the reunion. Population density is important; the more successful reunion planners are in larger metropolitan areas.

Another reason reunion-planning committees use professionals is because a committee is not likely to have the same success as a professional planner in locating class members. The key is access to databases that charge a fee for use. It's not feasible for a committee to purchase access for one event, whereas a professional reunion planner can spread the costs among many clients.

Reunion planners take their fee from the money paid by each attendee. The more people who show up, the higher the income per reunion. Thus reunion committees do not risk any money, and reunion planners are rewarded for their success in generating large turnouts.

To get started, begin with fewer reunions so you can take the time to go through the learning curve. To realize a return on your time, reunion planners advise setting a minimum, such as a class having at least 300 members. Focus on high schools because experience has taught professional reunion planners college reunions don't produce enough income to justify a professional's time.

Similarly, family reunions are usually too small to be profitable. But the baby boom generation is valuing family ties like no other in recent years, thus family reunions are growing in popularity. Additionally, reunions for Vietnam veterans will be a source of business for reunion planners.

To get an idea of how many reunions are being held in your area, just count the number of high schools. Each year there are likely to be as many as eight reunions per high school: five-year, ten-year, fifteen-year, twenty-year, twenty-five-year, thirty-year, forty-year, and fifty-year. On average, 137 people will attend a reunion, paying $60 to $100 each with $60 being typical for a one-evening event. Planners should expect to realize a ten percent profit after all costs are deducted. For classes with fewer numbers, the planner might negotiate a flat fee.

A recent survey by the National Association of Reunion Managers found that 40 percent of reunion planners plan fewer than 25 events a year; 40 percent plan 25 to 75 events, and 20 percent plan more than 75 reunions a year. Annual income from reunion planning can range from a modest sum based on part-time work to six figures, with $45,000 being an average net income.

To get started, you need business cards, stationery, a brochure, and a computer with a database and desktop-publishing software. Much of your business will depend on networking and your ability to make contact with reunion committees. Start with your own high school or your spouse's or your children's. Make contact with hotels, printers, display companies (for decorations), florists, caterers, public-address system providers, booking agents, photographers, name-badge suppliers, restaurants, and any other service that might be useful in planning a reunion.

Sunny McGinnis, who also trains reunion planners, says that repeat business is common. "Once people have a reunion professionally planned, they never want to do it themselves again. Our best customers are ones who planned a reunion themselves and then had the next reunion professionally planned." Referrals are another important source of business. When a reunion is a smashing success, participants and planning committee members not only are eager to repeat that success themselves the next time, they're happy to refer others who want to enjoy their reunions without the headaches and hassle of doing it themselves.

Where to Turn for Information and Help

TRAINING

REUNION BUSINESS CONSULTANTS, P.O. Box 21127, Tampa, FL 33622; (800) 586-2586; (813)978-1515; fax: (813)971-5030. Provides self-study training to become a reunion planner. Web site: *www. reunioncelebrations.com*

TRADE ASSOCIATION

NATIONAL ASSOCIATION OF REUNION MANAGERS, P.O. 23211, Tampa, FL 33623; (800) 654-2776. The Web site contains a directory of firms so that people seeking out professional help can locate a reunion planner in their area. Web site: *www.reunions.com*

SOFTWARE

Fleming Software, 21434 South Richard Court, Oregon City, OR 97045; (503) 631-7892. Produces software for reunion planning.

Family Reunion Handbook: A Guide for Reunion Planners, Barbara E. Brown, Thomas Ninkovich, Reunion Research, 1998. ISBN: 0961047062.

Fun & Games for Family Gatherings: With a Focus on Reunions, Adrienne E. Anderson, Reunion Research, 1996. ISBN: 0961047054.

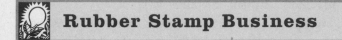

Rubber Stamp Business

This business surprised us because we usually associate rubber stamps with the knob-handle commercial ones with messages such as "Paid in Full" and "Handle with Care." These kinds of stamps are usually obtained at stores. Beyond this, there's another aspect to rubber stamps, and this is the world of *art* rubber stamps.

The making and selling of art rubber stamps is primarily done by home-based businesses, though some of these grow into full-fledged stores. A significant number of people love art stamps and buy them through mail order, at arts-and-crafts shows, and in specialty stores. People selling the art rubber stamps are known to sell as much as $2,000 to $5,000 worth of them a day at arts-and-crafts shows.

People adorn envelopes and stationery with rubber-stamp impressions of animals, moons, stars, clouds, people, rockets, spaceships, and an endless variety of designs. Using an embossing powder, raised impressions can be created. Metallic and glow-in-the-dark inks humble the customary red and blue stamp pads available in office-supply stores. Special inks enable stamps to be used on fabrics, glossy wrapping papers, foil, and mylar. You can also use rubber-stamping techniques to make badges, buttons, and magnets to be sold as gift items by using a Badge-a-Minit system (Badge-a-Minit, 348 North 30th Road, Lasalle, IL 61301; 800-223-4103; about $50).

It is not difficult to make your own rubber stamps, and you can use free public-domain clip art, which offers an almost unending supply of subjects. If you like to create your own designs, rubber stamps can be the vehicle for you to be a commercially successful artist, with thousands of people enjoying your creations.

In addition, new technology has made making stamps easier. Instead of using hot-metal type, matrix boards, and a vulcanizer to melt rubber, nowadays you can produce stamps quickly and easily with a personal computer and laser printer used in conjunction with a photo-polymer system ($2,800). If you are making art stamps in bulk, however, you will still need to make them from rubber, although you can make the pattern plate with the photo-polymer system. If you don't want to invest in the system right away, you can have someone else make the pattern plates for you until you have a good idea what your average volume will be. A washout unit ($3,500) to wash the liquid resin out of the plate is a big advantage, although you can wash by hand with soap and water.

If you make your own stamps, you can sell them at about six times the cost of your materials at retail or three times cost at wholesale; if you re-sell other people's stamps, you can expect to double your money. Bobby Boschan, who is a partner in Stamps, Stamps, Stamps, in Los Angeles, told us that many manufacturers sell both retail and wholesale.

Linda Bjorge, owner of L & W Stamps, a home-based manufacturer of business stamps in Onalaska, Wisconsin, says that you need to be an accurate speller with artistic ability and attention to detail. You don't really need technical skills, because the suppliers provide excellent technical support.

Where to Turn for Information and Help

MAGAZINES

Marking Industry Magazine, Marking Devices Publishing, 113 Adell Place, Elmhurst, IL 60126; (630) 832-5200.

Rubber Stampin' Retailer, Marking Devices Publishing, 113 Adell Place, Elmhurst, IL 60126; (630) 832-5200. For sellers of art stamps.

Rubberstampmadness, 408 SW Monroe Avenue #210, Corvallis OR 97330; (541) 752-0075.

SUPPLIERS

JACKSON MARKING PRODUCTS, 9105 N. Rainbow Lane, Mt. Vernon, IL 62864; (800) STAMP-CALL; (618) 242-1334; fax: (800) STAMP-FAX. Web site: *www.rubber-stamp.com*

STEWART-SUPERIOR CORP., 352 Fail Road, Laporte, IN 46350; (800) 621-1205; (219) 362-9921; fax: (219) 362-1678. Web site: *www. stewartsuperior.com*

LOUIS MELIND CO., 7631 N. Austin Ave., P.O. Box 1112, Skokie, IL 60076; (847) 581-2500.

MOUNTS AND HANDLES

M & R MARKING, 100 Springfield Ave., Piscataway, NJ 08855-6969; (732) 562-9500; fax (732) 562-9515. Web site: *www.mrmarking.com*

WEB SITES WITH LOTS OF LINKS

www.cyberhighway.net/~istation/crafts/rslinks.htm

www.wearpages.com/joanwear/links.htm

 **Sign Maker**

Can you imagine a city or town without signs? Probably not, because signs are everywhere, not just street signs and "House-for-Sale" signs, but signs on trucks, storefronts, buildings, short and tall posts, in front of homes and farms, scattered through all parks and zoos, in other words, generally in most places where we work or play. These signs tell us more than the name of the business or individual occupying a building; they give us more than a direction or an instruction. A good sign not only conveys basic information about who or what is located there but also communicates something about the occupants and what they do.

Ken Berry got the idea for a sign-making business when visiting a friend who published a magazine for people selling their own homes. Ken's friend was overwhelmed with work, so when Ken answered the phone for him and discovered people were asking where they could get a good real-estate sign, he went home and started making "For Sale by Owner" signs that he now sells through retail outlets such as hardware stores. Ken's company, Sign Power, also makes customized signs for Realtors, lumber companies, contractors, architects, roofing companies, boat shops, boat owners, and even for other sign makers.

To make good signs, you need to have an eye for design, although sign making now is simpler than it was in the past, thanks to computer-design programs, scanners, clip art, and special plotters that hold a knife that cuts pressure sensitive films and vinyls. The same process can be used for signs on trucks, cars, awnings, banners, and T-shirts.

To sell your sign-making services, you need a good collection of samples to show clients. This is so important that when he first started, Berry even made signs for new clients at near cost in order to have them for his portfolio. Another idea is to create custom signs for worthy causes or for highly trafficked locations that will get people talking about your work.

A natural source of customers is people who have signs that need replacing; it just takes observation and shoe leather to find them. Berry says, "The trick is being willing to make sales calls. People will procrastinate about making a sign, so you need to go to them. Then you need to show them enough samples that they become involved in making a choice, not deciding yes or no."

Real-estate brokers are a good source of referrals as well as of information on what people are paying for signs and whether they're happy with the quality of the signs they have. Another source of customers is new businesses, which you can find in the listings of new businesses in your city's daily or weekly business journal.

Yellow Page advertising can be expected to more than pay for itself. Research shows that businesses frequently turn to the Yellow Pages when needing signage.

Start-up costs for a sign business run about $6,000 to $12,000, including a computer, plotter that cuts vinyl, scanner, CD-ROM drive, and supplies. You should also count on periodic investments in new technology to remain competitive, because new processes and equipment are regularly being invented. This equipment allows you to do small runs of signs, but if you have to fulfill a large order of say fifty signs, you'll need to use a printing press to save time and cut costs. A used press will cost $6,000 to $7,000, and you'll need enough space both for the press and for drying racks for the signs. If you don't have a printing press, you can either subcontract the printing to another sign maker or find a printer in your area. Printing on plastic is almost as economical as printing on cardboard, and your customers will be happier.

Small runs of signs made by the 42,827 sign-making firms in the United States sell for $30 to $50 for a one-sided 18-by-24-inch sign and $60 to $100 for a two-sided version. To be sure your prices for custom signs are profitable you can calculate them by starting with the cost of your time, adding the cost of your materials, plus 40 percent. Assume your material costs $100. Your hourly rate is $60, and you estimate the job from start to finish will take 2 hours, your labor would be $120. Add $140 (materials plus 40 percent) to this, and your price for the sign would be $260, plus any applicable taxes.

The market for signs is endless. An increasing number of customers want unusual and creative designs.

Where to Turn for Information and Help

ASSOCIATIONS

INTERNATIONAL SIGN ASSOCIATION, 707 N. St. Asaph Street, Alexandria, VA 22314; (703) 836-4012. Web site: *www.signs.org*

MAGAZINES

Sign Business magazine is the leading publication in this field and contains many articles of interest and ads for equipment and franchises. 2800 W. Midway, Broomfield, CO 80020; (303) 469-0424, ext. 126. The Web site includes a bulletin board. Web site: *www.nbm.com/signbusinesss*

SignCraft magazine, PO Box 60031, Fort Myers, FL 33906; (800) 204-0204; fax (941) 939-0607. Web site: *www.signcraft.com*

WEB SITES

INTERNATIONAL SIGNS ONLINE is a Web site with lots of links. Web site: *www.signshop.com/ussc/index.html*

 Tour Operator

Travel is the world's largest industry, employing one out of nine workers, and it continues to grow, reaching over four trillion dollars annually as the new century dawns. People spend more of their leisure time traveling than they do reading, watching sports, pursuing hobbies, or even attending church and cultural events. Leisure accounts for four out of five trips people take. So if you love travel or helping other people to travel, there are several ways you can earn your living working from home in this industry.

We'll describe three such ways in this and the two following profiles, but other businesses in this book, such as newsletter publishing and mail order, can also be based on a love of travel. There are many travel-related newsletters on topics that range from traveling with grandchildren or pets to traveling in particular countries. Mail-order catalogues and commercial Web sites on travel gear, travel destinations, and travel tales also abound.

A travel business we don't profile because so little of it is done at home is delivering new recreational and specialty vehicles such as ambulances, school busses, and other kinds of vehicles that aren't transported by trucks. (There's actually a book about this, *How to Get Paid $30,000 a Year to Travel,* by Craig Chilton, (800) 247-6553 or e-mail: xanadu6@ibm.net.)

Becoming a tour operator, however, is one way to do some traveling but still work for the most part at home. Tour operators organize and conduct the tours for their clients, charging the participants a fee sufficient to cover their costs and make a profit. Home-based tour operators specialize by creating tours based on personal interests or hobbies or by serving specific kinds of travelers. For example, Patricia and Ronald Douglas operate Northstar Tours specializing in tours for senior citizens, who are a rapidly growing part of the travel market. Some tour operators serve people with special problems, such as people facing a terminal illness but wanting a last grand trip.

Today, many of the most popular tours involve sports and adventure, such as rock-climbing tours, kayaking tours, bicycle tours, walking tours, river-rafting tours, cave exploring tours, and cross-country or downhill ski tours. In fact, between 1992 and 1998, 31 million Americans took what's called "hard-adventure" vacations.

For example, one popular type of tour to package is wilderness adventures for women over the age of thirty who are inexperienced with the outdoors. Other tour operators specialize in tours for families with children or side trips for business executives attending trade and professional conventions. One tour operator we know, an artist with a French wife, makes a nice part-time income taking students to the mountains in France each summer where they study watercolor and paint to their heart's content, living in houses belonging to his wife's family.

Some tour operators specialize in unusual, informative, or entertaining local day, weekend, or evening tours, such as Dinner After Dark or the Chocoholics' Shopping Spree. Tours can be organized around any interest. In fact, one place to begin is to think about your own interests and experience. People have done just that in organizing tours based on their love for fitness, bird watching, spirituality, English gardens, and great vineyards.

To succeed as a tour operator, you must have knowledge of uniquely pleasurable locations and experiences you can share with others. For example, if you lead or plan tours to Europe, you need to be fluent in one or more European languages and know the countryside and sites where you will be traveling and/or sending your clients. If you lead rock-climbing expeditions, you must be an expert climber and be familiar with the particular routes you will be covering.

As a tour operator, you orchestrate the entire trip for all those who participate. You plan the tour, make the travel arrangements, recruit the participants and sometimes lead the tour yourself or hire others to do so. Recruiting participants means selling your tours, filling all the openings. The Internet makes finding people with highly specific interests easier and less expensive. In fact, by having a Web site devoted to your subject, you can attract the specific kind of people you need to help fill your tours.

Nevertheless, there are considerable up-front costs involved in undertaking a tour like attractive brochures, direct mailings, tour buses, and insurance, which is apt to run into the high four figures. So you need to get nonrefundable partial or full deposits to help cover costs. You must estimate those costs accurately in advance, and then keep within your budget. You can set your fees at 40 percent above your costs. So if you package five tours a year for twenty people each and charge $2,000 for the tour, your gross profits will be $80,000.

Your success as a tour operator depends on getting the people, getting the money and planning and providing appealing, rewarding tours because much of your future business will come from repeat customers.

Resources

ORGANIZATIONS

ADVENTURE TRAVEL SOCIETY, 6551 S. Revere Pkwy., Englewood, CO 80111, (303) 649-9016. Web site: *www.adventuretravel.com*

THE NATIONAL TOUR ASSOCIATION, Box 3071, Lexington, KY 40596; (800) 682-8886; (606) 226-4252. Web site: *www.ntaonline.com*

BOOKS

The Intrepid Travelers Complete Desk Reference, Sally Scanlon, Kelly Monaghan, Intrepid Traveler, 1997. ISBN: 1887140069.

Start and Run a Profitable Tour Guiding Business, Barbara Braidwood, Susan M. Boyce, Richard Cropp, Self-Counsel Business, 1996. ISBN: 1551800578.

See also the Resources in "Travel Agent/Outside Salesperson."

Travel Agent/Outside Salesperson

Travel agents are heading home, according to Joan Ogg, coauthor with her husband, Tom, of *How to Start a Home Based Travel Agency*. "Due to automation, the Internet, the costs of storefront agencies, and caps on commissions placed by airlines, being home-based makes sense for a travel agency. Established travel agents with a clientele can take their work home, lower their costs, and keep their earnings up." And why not? A large travel agency with multiple offices found that ninety percent of its clients never came to one of its offices.

Although restrictions on airline ticketing make it difficult, though not impossible, for a newcomer to open a full-service travel agency at home, you can enter the travel field by associating as an outside salesperson with one or more established travel agencies willing to work with you, and most agencies will. Your affiliation can run the gamut from simply referring business to the agency, for which you can negotiate a commission, to actually making travel plans and arrangements for your own clients. People who only make referrals are called referral agents.

In working with your own clients, you research their options, get prices, advise them on their choices, make the bookings with suppliers, and enter the information into your computer, so the travel agency can simply transfer what you've provided into a computerized reservation system (CRS), and if there are paper tickets, print them out. When you provide this level of service, you can negotiate as much as sixty to eighty percent of the commission.

If you're going to operate as an outside salesperson, most experts recommend working with a travel agency in your own community. You don't need to pay an agency thousands of dollars to allow you to become an outside sales representative who will be bringing them business! The Federal Trade Commission has cracked down on a number of such agencies, called "card mills" that have been charging individuals for the privilege of independently working through them.

Bill Landgrover of Dallas, Texas, exemplifies a successful home-based travel agent. Landgrover was an avid traveler who made his living as a computer programmer when an unfavorable legislative change in the independent contractor status made him rethink his career. Coincidentally, a friend asked for help in planning a skiing trip to Europe. Landgrover did this and enjoyed planning that trip and thus began D&B Tours International in 1988.

Having made this decision, Landgrover found himself going head-to-head with the big agencies that dominate the travel business. He realized he could not achieve the volume of business that would allow him to compete on price, so instead he concentrated on providing things he could compete on—value and service.

Landgrover gives personal attention to his clients, spending the time to pull together the details of complex and highly personalized itineraries. While large travel agencies have the edge when it comes to getting people from point A to point B for the cheapest fare, those same agencies won't spend the time Landgrover did to put together an itinerary for a client who had a particular three weeks to take a complex and very specific trip.

His client wanted to go from Dallas to Bangkok, Adelaide, Melbourne, Tasmania, and Dunk Island plus take an Australian Outback tour. Landgrover set up the itinerary even though all outback tours during the three weeks she was available were sold out from his U.S. suppliers. Working into the wee hours of the night, he called a supplier in Australia and was able to arrange her Outback tour. He also arranged for the documents she would be needing for her other stops to be waiting for her at the hotel in the middle of the Outback.

Landgrover's experience illustrates how a person willing to go the extra mile with clients can save them money. A couple was planning a week-long vacation in Maui. They wanted to travel first-class, stay in a luxury hotel on the beach with an ocean-view room, and have access to a four-wheel drive vehicle for three days. The best price they could find on first-class airline tickets was $3490 each but their budget for the entire trip was just $7,000 for the two of them. Landgrover was able to put together a package with first class round-trip tickets on the same airline, seven nights in a five-star hotel with the ocean view (and breakfast daily), plus their 4-wheel drive vehicle for the entire trip . . . all for $7,100.

The key to Landgrover's success is not only personal attention and time. He knows the travel business. He belongs to and takes an active role in travel associations. He's an Accredited Cruise Counselor through

Cruise Lines International Association's Management Institute at University of Miami and is certified by the Institute of Certified Travel Agents. He attends supplier seminars and other presentations. "Often I'll ask my colleagues if they'll be going to a breakfast seminar and they'll tell me, 'Oh, that's too early for me!'" he says. "But I go because I need to know as much as I can about all the options available for my clients."

Landgrover isn't particularly philosophical about his success. "Any travel agent can do what I do," he says, "if they want to take the time and the trouble."

Where to Turn for Information and Help

BOOKS

Home-Based Travel Agent: How to Cash In On the Exciting New World of Travel Marketing, Kelly Monaghan, The Intrepid Traveler, P.O. Box 438, New York, NY 10034, (212) 569-1081, 1999, ISBN: 1887140107.

How to Start a Home Based Travel Agency, Tom and Joanie Ogg, Tom Ogg and Associates, P.O. Box 2398, Valley Center, CA 92082; (760) 751-1007; 1997, ISBN: 1888290005.

Selling Cruises: Don't Miss the Boat, Tom and Joanie Ogg, Tom Ogg and Associates, 1998, ISBN: 188829003X.

ORGANIZATIONS

THE AMERICAN SOCIETY OF TRAVEL AGENTS, 1101 King Street, Suite 200, Alexandria, VA 22314; (800) 275-2782; (703) 739-2782. Web site: *www.astanet.com*

INSTITUTE OF CERTIFIED TRAVEL AGENTS (ICTA), 148 Linden St., PO Box 812059, Wellesley, MA, 02482-0012 (781) 237-0280, ext. 152. ICTA offers a home-study course, "Travel Career Development," and offers a certification program. Web site: *www.icta.com*

NATIONAL ASSOCIATION OF COMMISSIONED TRAVEL AGENTS (NACTA), P.O. Box 2398, Valley Center, CA 92082; (760) 751-1197. Web site: *www.nacta.com*

Travel Consultant

People's appetites for leisure travel has turned to more unique and customized experiences. Vacationers, particularly younger and more affluent ones, are choosing what the travel industry calls "hard adventure vacations," such as retracing the route of an historic exploration or heading off into challenging remote locations or uncharted territories. Others are seeking to explore the location of their ancestral origins or the intricacies of special interests such as the birthplaces of rural French Impressionist artists, Middle Eastern antiquities, or sacred Celtic ceremonial sites. Such unique experiences require highly personalized service, something most travel agents usually can't provide. It's not only just a matter of the time involved, they simply don't have the in-depth knowledge it takes to plan the kind of rarified travel experiences discerning and affluent travelers are desiring.

But someone who has such expertise or is willing to acquire it can become a travel consultant, charging their clients, usually between $50 and $100 per hour, to research and plan once-in-a-lifetime experiences. Consultants use their intimate knowledge of a country, region, or interest area to plan customized tours for clients who are willing to pay for special advice. Depending on how much detail the client wishes, the consultant may provide a detailed hour-by-hour itinerary, complete with personalized recommendations for romantic or native restaurants, secluded spots, specialized museums and galleries, or exciting nightlife or festivals. Some travel consultants furnish 80-page custom-written books about the itinerary, supplemented with maps and other helpful information.

Consultants sometimes also arrange the bookings, faxing, or phoning of hoteliers and innkeepers, and then have a local agency cut the tickets. In short, the consultant's services complement rather than substitute for those of travel agents. They may or may not receive a referral fee or commission.

Being a travel consultant is extremely personal, so you have to interview your clients in-depth and with enough skill that you can understand their needs. You need to be able to pick up on likes and dislikes the client has about traveling. This ability to go right to the heart of the client's needs and make appealing suggestions will also help you get their business in the first place. You have to know the destination like the back of your hand as well, or have reliable access to essential information, including facilities for special dietary and transportation needs, cultural interests, shopping, and a host of other details. This means you have to visit the destinations often, so part of your income must go to cover your own travel expenses, even if they are deductible as business travel.

Marjorie Shaw, who operates Insider's Italy in Brooklyn, New York, and Kajsa Agostini, owner of Point of View in Tarzana, California, agree: this is not a business you can delegate. It requires your personal knowledge, attention, and skill. You must be bilingual if your destination is a non-English-speaking one, and you must understand both cultures—ours and that of the destination—so you'll know what will appeal to your clients as well as where to find it. Both Ms. Shaw and Ms. Agostini were born in the country they now specialize in; Italy and France respectively. It's so important to travel to your destination often that Ms. Shaw estimates your travel expenses will be 20 percent of your gross revenues. For those who love this business, however, that's a coveted perk they cherish.

Where to Turn for Information and Help

See the Resources for the other travel-related businesses.

APPENDIX

Lists of Top-10 Best Businesses

Best All Around

Bodywork/massage therapy
Coaching
Computer consulting
Computer repair
Elder services
Financial advice
Pet sitting
Technical writing
Tutoring
Webmaster

Fastest-Growing Fields

Coaching
Computer consulting
Computer programming
Elder services
Financial advisor
New media
Public relations
Security specialists
Technical writing
Webmaster

Highest Demand—Easiest to Sell

Cleaning services
Computer repair
Home inspection
Medical transcription
Résumé service
Tax preparation
Technical writing
Tutoring
Web design
Webmaster

Most Recession Resistant

Business brokering
Bookkeeping
Computer consulting
Computer repair
Medical claims assistance
Medical transcriptionist
Repair services
Résumé writer
Secretarial services
Tax preparation

Lowest Start-Up Costs

Cleaning service
Coaching
Executive search
Family child care provider
Make-up artist
Pet sitting
Professional organizer
Secretarial and office support
    services
Technical writer
Transcript digesting service

Lowest Stress

Aromatherapy
Bodywork and massage therapy
Facialist
Feng shui
Fitness trainer
Mailing list service
Microfarming
Pet sitting
Photography
Tutoring

Evergreen Businesses

Astrology
Bookkeeping service
Caterer
Computer consultant
Computer programmer
Computer repair
Hauling service
Mailing list service
Medical transcriptionist
Tax preparation

Up-and-Coming Home Businesses

Bodywork and massage therapy
Coaching
Doula
Elder care
Feng shui
Financial planner
Home inspector
New media
Personal chef
Web merchant

Easiest to Enter

Cleaning services
Elder care
Errand service
Gift basket
Mail order
Mailing list service
Manufacturers agent
Microfarming
Pet sitting
Tutoring

Highest Income Potential

Business Broker
Coaching
Computer consulting
Elder services
Executive search
Financial planning
Manufacturers agent
Professional practice consulting
Technical writing
Web design

Best-Kept Secrets

Alternative energy installation
Doula service
Expert referral service/broker
Feng shui consulting
Image consultant

Indoor health care
Medical claims assistant
Medical coding
Private practice consultant
Red tape expediter

Do You Have Questions or Feedback?

Paul and Sarah want to answer your questions. They can usually respond to you if you leave a message for them. Web site: *www.paulandsarah.com*

If you wish to write, you can write to Paul and Sarah in care of "Start Up," *Entrepreneur Magazine,* 2392 Morse Avenue, Irvine, CA 92614. Your question may be selected to be answered in their column; however, they cannot respond to every letter.

About the Authors

Paul and Sarah Edwards, authors of eight books that have sold over a million copies, are often described as the nation's self-employment experts. They have worked from home for over twenty years. Their weekly column is syndicated by the Los Angeles Times News Syndicate and they write monthly columns for *Entrepreneur's HomeOffice* and Price Costco's *Connection.* Since 1988, they have produced and broadcasted their hour-long show *Working from Home* on the Business News Network.

Since 1990, their mission—which they express through print, via electronic media, and as speakers—has been to help people make the transition from the job economy of lifetime employment to the faster changing but potentially more satisfying world of self-employment. They live in California.

Other Books by Paul and Sarah Edwards

Use the table below to locate other books that contain the information you need for your business interests.

Subject	Finding Your Perfect Work	Getting Business to Come to You	Home Businesses You Can Buy	Making Money in Cyberspace	Secrets of Self-Employment	Teaming Up	Working from home
Advertising	Yes			Yes			Yes
Business opportunities			Yes	Yes			Yes
Business planning							Yes
Children and child care							Yes
Closing sales	Yes				Yes		
Credit							Yes
Employees							Yes
Ergonomics							Yes
Failure					Yes		Yes
Family and marriage issues						Yes	Yes
Financing your business					Yes		Yes
Franchise							Yes
Getting referrals	Yes	Yes					Yes
Handling emotional/ psychological issues					Yes		
Housecleaning							Yes
Insurance							Yes
Legal issues						Yes	Yes
Loneliness, isolation							Yes
Managing information							Yes
Marketing		Yes Focus of book			Yes Attitude	Yes	Yes
Marketing materials		Yes		Yes			
Money				Yes	Yes	Yes	Yes
Naming your business		Yes					
Negotiating						Yes	Yes
Networking		Yes				Yes	
Office space, furniture, equipment							Yes
Outgrowing your home							Yes
Overcoming setbacks					Yes	Yes	
Partnerships							Yes
Pricing				Yes			Yes Principles
Profiles of specific businesses				Yes	Yes		
Public relations and publicity			Yes	Yes			Yes
Resource directory			Yes	Yes	Yes		
Selecting a business/ career/business opportunity	Yes Focus of book		Yes				Yes
Software							Yes
Speaking		Yes					
Start-up costs							
Subcontracting						Yes	
Success issues					Yes	Yes	
Taxes						Yes	Yes
Time management					Yes	Yes	Yes
Zoning							Yes

Complete Your Library of the Working from Home Series by Paul and Sarah Edwards

These books are available at your local bookstore or wherever books are sold. Ordering is also easy and convenient. To order, call 1-800-788-6262, prompt #1, or send your order to:

Jeremy P. Tarcher
Mail Order Department
P.O. Box 12289
Newark, NJ 07101-5289

For Canadian orders:
P.O. Box 25000
Postal Station 'A'
Toronto, Ontario MSW 2X8

		Price
_____ Finding Your Perfect Work	0-87477-795-X	$16.95
_____ Getting Business to Come to You,		
2nd Revised Edition	0-87477-845-X	$18.95
_____ Home Businesses You Can Buy	0-87477-858-1	$13.95
_____ Making Money in Cyberspace	0-87477-884-0	$15.95
_____ Making Money with Your		
Computer at Home, Expanded	0-87477-898-0	$15.95
_____ Secrets of Self-Employment, Revised	0-87477-837-9	$15.95
_____ Teaming Up	0-87477-842-5	$13.95
_____ Working from Home, Fifth Edition,		
Revised and Expanded	0-87477-976-6	$18.95
	Subtotal	_____
	Shipping and handling*	_____
	Sales tax (CA, NJ, NY, PA)	_____
	Total amount due	_____

Payable in U.S. funds (no cash orders accepted). $15.00 minimum for credit card orders.

*Shipping and handling: $3.50 for one book, $1.00 for each additional book. Not to exceed $8.50.

Payment method:
Visa   MasterCard   American Express
Money order

Card # _____ Expiration date _____

Signature as on charge card _____

Daytime phone number_____

Name _____

Address _____

City _____ State _____ Zip _____

Please allow six weeks for delivery. Prices subject to change without notice. Source key WORK